MW00748592

Belgian Waffles

and other treats

Enjoy the book

Max.

TEXT: JAN GHEYSENS - PHOTOGRAPHY: TOM SWALENS - STYLING: DEBBY DE MANGELAERE

Belgian Waffles
and other treats

lannoo

foreword

At MAX's you can feel perfectly at home and at a party at the same time. I discovered the place six years ago and have been a regular customer ever since. Just as regularly you will meet pleasant people there, and many artists and colleagues from the world of entertainment have long ago found their way to the Etablissement MAX.

What is there here that is so special? Waffles. In all their glory, dressed in golden coats, with a scent that makes your mouth water, and a taste to delight the palate. And then there is Yves, who with unabated enthusiasm, with a twinkle in his eyes and a broad smile, looks on at his customers' enjoyment of the delicacies he dishes up for them. And then there is the ambiance: a splendid setting that tells of a history of more than a hundred and fifty years, of clouds of lace and sophisticated scent.

At MAX's you are served with class, with style, and above all with friendliness. I feel particularly at home there, because I have my own table, just by the kitchen. And time and again I revel in the treats I am offered there. I hope for a long, long time to come.

Koen Crucke

MAX, for the love of the Belgian waffle

Thanks to the stories told by Yves, direct descendant of Maximilien Consael, of the history and origin of the Belgian waffle, we can take a stroll back in time.

Anecdotes about fairs, placed in a setting that has evolved from 1800 to today, and stories such as that of the honey cake as the predecessor of the waffle, result in a fascinating review that makes easy reading.

Both the recipes for Belgian waffles and fritters and their history have been passed down from generation to generation, becoming enriched with anecdotes on the way. Hence we get a striking and unique picture, coloured by the aroma and taste of almost two centuries of delicious confectionery. Add to this the special atmosphere of the 'kermis' and the evolution of a simple waffle stall into a prestigious hall of mirrors, and you end up with a gripping tale that you won't want to put down.

If the history is fascinating and significant, then the recipes are even more so. Throughout the narrative you gradually begin to feel you want to taste all these delicacies for yourself. And you can do that in today's Etablissement MAX in Ghent. But you can also treat yourself at home, since fortunately the recipes of all the specialities which have come down to us through two centuries, have been written down and preserved. We would like to offer you a selection of these recipes to round off the story. Does that mean that the secret recipe of the Belgian waffle is revealed? To know the answer to that, you will have to read the book from beginning to end.

What is in any case certain is that Yves shows you, among other things, how to make perfect crêpes. He also explains how from a special mixture you can bake all kinds of waffles.

And then there is the archive. A treasure trove of furniture and décor has been preserved. Yves also possesses boxes full of newspaper clippings, photos and letters about more than 150 years attendance at fairs. Golden books in which crowned heads, princes and members of the aristocracy have penned their appreciation of the delicacies offered them. And stories about often adventurous journeys to fairs in other countries to sell Belgian waffles there. In short: this story should have been written long ago.

Jan Gheysens

introduction

contents

history

Etablissement MAX, fair stand, 1900

Etablissement MAX, 2006

Etablissement MAX, the staff in 1936

Etablissement MAX, Yves and his staff, 2006

Pierre-Max Consael, 1937

The Consael family

How it all began

The first time we find a mention of the Consael family is at a fair in 1808. They had a stall on the Poeljemarkt, the poultry market in Ghent. There they offered the predecessors of waffles – spice cake and honey cake. These are already described in reports from neighbouring countries from around 1712 – so almost a century earlier. But it was 1808 before they turned up in Flanders.

The founder of the Consael dynasty, as we now know it from its waffles and other delicacies, was Maximilien Consael. He was the one who around the middle of the nineteenth century thought up the idea of mobile stands, from which pastry baked from fresh dough could be served at carnivals and fairs.

Fair stand, 1920

After consultation with a painter-decorator, he had the first stand built around 1845. The luxurious interiors, with painted wood panels, mirrors and red plush, were the product of his imagination. The façade of the stand was decorated with the name 'MAX' and the subtitle 'Beignets aux pommes' (apple fritters).

The great success of this formula was achieved not in Flanders, but in the Netherlands. There were two very large fairs there every year, one in Amsterdam and the other in Rotterdam. Maximilien sold mainly fritters there, and to a lesser extent *smoutebollen*, doughnut balls, which in his luxurious stall were cooked under the eyes of his customers. Records of the time tell how you could find the MAX stall by the smell of the fresh pastry.

These Dutch fairs were in fact literally a small gold mine. The Consael family came back to Flanders at the end of the season with all their possessions, and among their baggage were several suitcases full of gold coins. The wealth of the Consael family of those days was without doubt due to the success of their sales in the Netherlands.

During the winter the showmen and stallholders who were based in Ghent all assembled on the Riedijk, a large open space. For the duration of the winter they parked their caravans next to each other in circles. This created a very dangerous situation, because if a fire started anywhere, all the adjacent caravans were liable to catch fire. So Maximilien soon decided to leave the open space and spend the winter in a house.

The fortune earned in the Netherlands was used in Flanders to lay down a firm foundation for the future. Maximilien and his wife bought a hundred and one houses in streets next to each other. They rented these out, and with the proceeds from the last of them they paid the taxes on all their other property. All their houses were on the Blandijnberg and were later subject to a compulsory purchase order and sold to build Ghent University on the same site.

In the winter the Consael family themselves also lived in a town house on the Blandijnberg. This was next to a large, covered shed, which served as a depot, a building where repairs and maintenance work were carried out on their stoves and the interior of their luxurious stand.

From Belgium to the Netherlands

When the season came round again, the heavy wagons in which the sections of the stalls were stacked, together with the caravans in which the family lived, were driven to Ghent Sint-Pieters Station. At first the wagons were drawn by horses. At the station the wagons were transferred via loading platforms to open goods wagons to be taken to the Netherlands. The family caravans travelled with them too, and the family lived in them en route.

Such a journey was not without its hazards: the wagons were firmly anchored on the open flats of the train, but the speed of the train made it impossible to leave the caravan during the journey.

Price lists of the MAX stand, 1864 and 1868

The cost of the journey was calculated on the basis of the weight of the wagons, each of which had to be weighed beforehand on the loading platform. Because Maximilien hated having to pay out so much money, he once got the men who travelled with him to sabotage the weighbridge. That meant that the weight had to be estimated. This came to much less than it really was, so that the journey became affordable.

The train travelled to Amsterdam, where the wagons were taken off the train. Then Maximilien hired some strong Brabant draught horses to pull the heavy weight to the market place, where the stand was erected for the fair. The residential caravans were sited behind the stand, so that the Consael family could actually live at the fair.

At the end of the nineteenth century the horses were replaced by tractors, which went with them wherever they went.
The men, more specifically the fritter cooks and later the waffle bakers, helped with the loading, off-loading, and setting up of the stall. They lived in the storage wagons, which had space for four bunk beds.

From the first, Maximilien made it a habit to take a nucleus of permanent staff with him to the carnivals and fairs at home and abroad. These men, cooks and helpers, were paid a fixed wage. On top of that their travelling expenses, accommodation and food were taken care of. They were paid all the year round, because during the winter they were available for maintenance work on the stoves and smartening up the painted panels, which always suffered to some extent from the travelling.

The waiters received no wages. Their reward came from the tips. The fact that they could afford to live in hotels illustrates how much they earned working for MAX.

A job as a waiter at MAX was highly sought after, so during the winter, when the Consael family was in Ghent, they had plenty of applications.

A well-kept family secret

It was Maximilien – and later his successors – who each morning was the first in the stand, long before it opened. It was – and still is today – the privilege of the eldest son of the house to make the dough.
Its composition is one handed down from generation to generation and it is only the men of the family who make the dough.

MAX stand, 1891

Between the kitchen and the public area, where the cooking was done and the products served, was a small room where the dough was made, kept closed so that none of the staff could see in what quantities the ingredients were mixed.

There was an obvious reason for this secretiveness. There were many interested parties who would like to equal the success of the MAX stalls. They started from the supposition that once you knew the secret of the mixture, it would be easy to do your own baking during the fair and in that way get rich quickly.

Various publications in the 19th century tell of the illnesses and harmful results of bad food items sold at carnivals and fairs. Many stallholders tried to sell waffles, doughnuts or pancakes made from a cheap and badly constituted dough or batter. This resulted in complaints about indigestion or diarrhoea.

The waffle and the iron

The secret of the kind of Brussels waffle you find at Etablissement MAX is, of course, not only concealed in the constituents of the dough. The irons used to bake the waffles are also of crucial importance.

Maximilien Consael had his first irons cast in accordance with one particular concept. The iron is polished inside, but not treated. This makes it porous and susceptible to the smallest variations in temperature. Originally the waffle irons were heated in charcoal embers. Irons with very long handles were used for this. Because they got red hot, the waffle baker wore leather gloves for his work.

When a switch was made to gas as a source of heat, it was necessary to cast new irons.
Because Maximilien was afraid that other people would use his old irons, he threw them all away, with the exception of one for his personal use.

He designed a new set of irons which he had cast by a smith. The principle of the old irons was used here, too. In the constituents of the alloy care was taken that the iron was porous enough so that the dough heats and bakes in the right way.

*The original waffle irons,
still in use by Yves
in his Etablissement MAX*

The irons in which Yves bakes waffles in today's Etablissement MAX, are still the original ones.
They are now almost 150 years old.
Casting a waffle iron is not an easy job. First a wooden model is made. The waffle baker examines this model and has it shaped until it has the right proportions. Then this wooden model is reproduced in iron, so that several specimens of it can be cast.

From the Netherlands to Belgium

Around 1900 the Netherlands started to issue various decrees affecting the production and sales of food-stuffs at fairs. Strict regulations were laid down forcing many owners to adapt the arrangement of their stalls, or even to get entirely new ones.

Moreover, there was at this time also a period of great urban redevelopment. Many public open spaces were newly laid out, and paved with expensive tiles. The disadvantage of these tiles was, however, that they broke up if you put too much weight on them. So the burgomaster of Amsterdam published a

decree which included a ban on bringing heavy transport wagons onto the fairground. They had to be parked nearly a kilometre away and all the necessary equipment, such as stoves, decorative panels, counters and such like, had to be dragged by hand from the wagons to the site.

This made the Consael family decide not to travel to the Netherlands any more. They shifted the area of their operations to Belgium, where they became well-known in Wallonia and Brussels as well as in Flanders at the many carnivals and fairs.

The name Consael is in fact still a familiar one today among their northern neighbours. To understand this we must go back to the regulations that applied within the family itself. The eldest son was automatically the lawful successor of the proprietor of the stand. If there were more children, they were given their share when they came of age, so that they could make a good start in life. In return for this they had to sign an agreement saying they would never use the name 'MAX' on any stalls where they sold waffles at carnivals or fairs.

Various male members of the Consael clan opened bakeries after leaving the parental home, but then under their family name. This explains why you can still find a celebrated waffle and 'poffertjes' bakery in Rotterdam, belonging to the descendants of Victor Consael, one of the younger sons.

When around 1900 the family decided no longer to travel to the Netherlands with the MAX stand, they worked the largest fairs in Belgium instead, those of Liège, Brussels, Antwerp and Ghent.

Because the MAX stands needed an enormous amount of space, and moreover had to be close to connections for gas, they were allotted a permanent site at the various carnivals and fairs. That was only to their advantage: the Consael family knew the precise spot where they had to set up their stand, and the public knew year after year just where they had to go to eat a good waffle or fritter. These rulings also excused the Consael family from the annual meetings at which the various stand sites were sold by auction.

*The MAX stand
at the time of the world exhibition
in 1913*

A story of success

The MAX stand in fact continued to expand. Originally it had consisted of a space for baking, with in front of it a counter and some duckboards on which the public waited for their turn. Later a kind of terrace was built in front of the stand, on which chairs and small tables could be set out where customers could eat on the site. The next expansion was internal. The space was enlarged, separate alcoves were built in, and some tables set near the stoves.

An interesting detail: the benches in the alcoves, covered with red plush, were so narrow that it was impossible to sit on them for long. So the customers never stayed long after they had eaten their waffles or doughnuts, and the alcoves quickly became available for the next customers.
During the period of greatest expansion, around 1925, the Etablissement MAX stand could accommodate about 150 customers. They were served by a staff of about thirty-five, made up of cooks, general assistants who cleared and washed up, and the waiters.

The erection of this enormous stand was done with great precision. First the wooden floor was laid. Usually the ground on which they had to build was not paved, so that a great many supports and loose planks had to be put under the floor to make it level. On the floor came the side panels; which served to support the whole structure. Then the posts were put in place, the screens between the boxes or alcoves, and finally the roof. That was made up of very heavy corrugated iron sheets.

Once the roof was on, the pace became a little more relaxed, because they were – as they said at the time – 'protected from all weathers'. Then the false ceilings and the decorative elements were added. The furniture was set out and the heaters and cooking equipment put in their place. If necessary, an extra coat of paint was applied on top of existing paint. When the big stall was disassembled for the last time, one of the panels was subjected to a test and found to have twenty-five layers of paint superimposed on each other.

Staff problems

Everyone in regular employment was paid for the whole year, including the seasons when there were no fairs. For a long time the Consael family recruited their staff in Merksem, near Antwerp, where there was a special institution for disadvantaged people. Many of them were physically disabled, so that it was almost impossible for them to find employment.

The Consael family was always very compassionate and socially committed, so that it is not surprising that they gave these people, of whom many were at a loose end, an opportunity. The Consael family trained them to cook, to help in the kitchen, or to do general odd jobs. These people were often so grateful that they stayed with the family for years, and did their work with an extraordinary sense of responsibility.

The social commitment of the Consael family was very soon widely known. They were therefore often approached by people who were in difficulties, who had been ruined by their children or were at a low ebb through adversity. The Consael family usually tried to help them by giving them temporary employment or setting them to work in the waffle stall.

Yves' grandmother, Simonna Consael, often took on the most difficult cases. She always started by providing them with a blue apron and putting them in the kitchen to wash up. If they proved to be doing it well, worked diligently, or seemed capable, they were switched to baking. They were paid more for that. Grandmother often told stories about the gratitude she had been shown, and by which her social commitment was richly rewarded.

Of course, this was occasionally also abused. It was the custom for all the staff to eat together before the stall was opened to the public. A meal was cooked for about thirty-five members of staff, who at twelve o'clock precisely, an hour before the opening, were served with a free meal. It sometimes happened that an employee would eat his or her fill and then disappear for the rest of the day. Such misdemeanours were not tolerated because the Consael family felt that this would deprive others in need of help, who were prepared to work after a meal, of their chance of a better social life. So anyone who abused the system was immediately dismissed.

Grandmother Simonna Consael at the age of 2, with her mama

During the first half of the twentieth century the legislation on employment, pay and dismissal was completely changed. Social statutes were introduced which particularly imposed many obligations on employers, with financial implications. The Consael family, too, with their travelling stand, had to comply with the new requirements. To keep thirty-five men and women in employment for the whole year became financially impossible. So for the first time there was a departure from the tradition that laid down that brothers and sisters who were not expected to manage the stand had to be paid off. From then on every member of the family was more or less obliged to help with erecting and dismantling the MAX stand, and with serving at carnivals and fairs.

Grandmother Simonna Consael

In those days Simonna Consael, Yves' grandmother, married a son of the De Vliegher family, owners of a roundabout and a dodgem car stand. Such a marriage was not unusual. Owners of fair stalls usually had close social links with each other, because for three-quarters of the year they were running their attractions next to each other at the same fairs. Simonna went to live with her in-laws and helped with the running of the dodgem cars.

A few years before the celebration of the MAX firm's 100th anniversary, her father, ('Pierre Max', as he was popularly known), who was then the head of the family, died. His widow did not survive him for long, so that there was no clear successor to run the Etablissement MAX. An additional problem was that both Simonna and her three brothers, Maximilien, Albert and François, made claim to the inheritance.

The name 'MAX' was worth a great deal of money, and the family possessions, which included the stand, the large house on the Melkerijstraat, and the adjoining storage sheds, had to be divided among the heirs.

This could not have happened at a worse moment. World War II had just ended; Europe was licking its wounds and making a slow start on its redevelopment. Most people were trying to pick up the pieces of their lives again and to build up their social status. So there was little call for carnivals and fairs.

In addition, in the De Vliegher family into which Simonna had been accepted, things did not seem to be going too well either. Her husband, Alfred, only received a small percentage of the profits, while he actually did all the hard work of the erection, maintenance and dismantling of the roundabout and dodgem

Grandmother Simonna Consael, aged 6

cars. This led first to tensions, and then to violent quarrels, until the De Vliegher-Consael couple left the De Vliegher parental home for Etablissement MAX.

This was against the family tradition, because until that moment no one with a name other than Consael had shared in the running of the stand. However, Alfred De Vliegher turned out to have a strong gift for public relations. He had good contacts with the burgomasters and councillors of the towns where fairs were held, was well-read, and moreover, was very much on top of what was then called 'modern' accountancy. Because of this he was very quickly accepted by the direct descendants of the Max family and he actually became part of its central core. The down side of this collaboration was that four families had to live from the profits of one – albeit an enormous one – waffle stand. The strict social legislation meant that the staff also cost a great deal of money. In the long run this made the situation untenable.

Maximilien, Simonna's eldest brother, began to look for a solution. This he found in Liège during the annual carnival there. Not far from the square where the fair was held, there was a splendid restaurant, 'Le Pré Normand', looking for someone to take it over. The restaurant was owned by Baroness Lamby, at that time famous for her jam factory in Wallonia, which had gone bankrupt. The restaurant was on offer at a low price.

Maximilien suggested to his sister Simonna that she should run the restaurant with her husband, while the rest of the family went on travelling round the fairs all summer. During the winter the brothers and their families would help in the restaurant in Liège. And so it was done. The restaurant with Simonna and her husband must have had an incredible success, because a few years after taking it over they were working with a staff of seventy to keep the business turning over. The restaurant consisted of two parts: a bakery where fresh waffles were baked, and a dining room where you could lunch or dine in the most luxurious surroundings. 'Le Pré Normand' very quickly became well known among rich and poor, and was just 'the place to be' in Liège in the 1950s.

It was at that time that the tradition started which Yves still continues today. Etablissement MAX opened in the late morning with aperitifs, after which you could lunch. From 2 till 6 the kitchens were closed to give way to the sale of waffles, fritters and *oliebollen* (deep-fried doughnuts). Then the kitchen opened again for dinner. The place usually closed around midnight. The restaurant worked with no fewer than three house orchestras, taking turns with each other, and was open for seven days in the week. Although there were about three hundred places for customers, it was usually fully booked. Anyone still having lunch by about 2.30 was politely asked to leave, because all the seats were reserved for customers who came to eat waffles and fritters. These customers in their turn had to go at about 6 o'clock, because of the reservations for dinner that evening.

Above the restaurant there were four flats: one for each of the brothers and for the De Vliegher-Consael husband and wife team and their family. However, the brothers only lived there in the winter, outside the carnival season.

1890, 'La Friture Hollandaise',
one of the first stalls (still without seating)

It stays in the family

A rather strange story from that time is undoubtedly that of the marriage of Maximilien with Eulalie Consael, his own aunt. She brought the 'Friture Hollandaise' (Dutch fries) in her dowry, a smaller, less luxurious stall which worked nearly all the fairs.

Although this stall was the property of a direct descendant of the Consael family, it could not bear the name 'MAX' because at that time the first-born son was travelling round with the original 'mother stall'. Eulalie, daughter of the owners of 'Friture Hollandaise', fell in love with her nephew Maximilien Consael and captured him. After their marriage there was no longer any objection to the use of the name, since Maximilien was the first-born. So Eulalie added the name 'MAX' to the stall.

With Friture Hollandaise MAX, Maximilien and Eulalie built up a good, wide base of regular customers in the towns they worked. Their stall sold all kinds of freshly made confections which were deep-fried in oil – hence the name friture. So it wasn't just a 'chippie' of the kind we are familiar with today.

1921, the bakery boys

Meanwhile the original Etablissement MAX stand continued to travel round fairs and carnivals. The 'Friture' became its direct competitor, since at the big fairs you could buy exactly the same fried products at either of the two different stands.

To avoid an escalation of the arguments starting within the family, Maximilien and Eulalie decided to go to different fairs, in towns and districts which the large stand did not visit. So they travelled to Ostend, Louvain, Bruges and Courtrai, while the large stand went to Liège, Brussels, Antwerp and Ghent. Later, when peace had been restored in the family, they decided to join forces. The smaller stall, the Friture Hollandaise MAX was sited next to the mother stand, so that the two had a total frontage of 90 metres, and the family had the largest waffle stand at the fair.

However, this situation could not last. Joining the two stands meant that there was only one lot of takings to be divided among four families. They had to be shared among the families of the three brothers and their sister Simonna Consael, who was still running her restaurant in Liège.

With the object of getting their hands on more profit than the rest of the clan, each family quietly started to cheat with cash receipts. Fewer receipts were recorded than there really were. And some orders 'slipped

MAX stand in 1946

past' the till without a receipt, with the money just going into someone's pocket. No wonder that when accounts were drawn up at the end of the fair, the turnover of the business appeared to have dropped spectacularly!

However, the costs of staff went on rising, so that a financial debacle threatened. The Liège restaurant also started to do badly. Social legislation became so strict that the seventy employed staff went off with the lion's share of the takings.

Simonna Consael refused to work round the clock for the sole benefit of her employees, and decided to close the business. Her husband, the son of the De Vliegher family, wanted to prevent this. He went to visit his father and asked him to invest in the restaurant. Father De Vliegher was only willing to put money into the business on condition that Simonna's brothers should be removed from it. His reasoning was simple: he was quite prepared to help his own son, but not the rest of the Consael family. So Simonna asked her brothers to withdraw from the business. In this way the restaurant could continue to exist.

One of the last fair stands, 1969

Meanwhile Friture Hollandaise MAX had become a thriving business. The 'smaller' fairs were gradually developing into leading events, while those in the large cities tended to attract fewer people. Moreover, the large cities increasingly demanded higher rents for the stalls, so that stallholders were obliged to pass on these increases to their customers, because otherwise they would be trading at a loss. As a result the price of a ticket to the attractions increased.

In the small towns site rents remained relatively cheap. This benefited the customers, who could obtain the same quality, but at a cheaper price. Large numbers of people at the fair also meant more hungry people. The stalls with foodstuffs enjoyed successful days and had a larger turnover than their colleagues with prestigious offerings in the large cities.

Losses

After a few years it became clear that the boom in the restaurant industry was over.
The public, who quickly became accustomed to innovations, soon started to by-pass Le Prix Normand, to the advantage of a few trendy businesses in the centre of Liège. Simonna Consael watched the decline with sadness, and determined to get rid of the restaurant before it was too late. She pulled a good takeover price out of the fire, and went back to Ghent with her husband, who by training was in fact a motor mechanic.

He had learnt that trade so that he could personally maintain the motor transport with which his parents travelled from fair to fair. Now, so many years later, he determined to turn this knowledge to advantage. It was the 1960s and the car was slowly but surely beginning its unstoppable advance in society and on the urban street scene. Alfred De Vliegher razed the properties on the Brugse Steenweg, which he had inherited, to the ground, and there built what was for that time a super-modern garage with three flats above it.

Meanwhile Simonna's mother had died. This meant that she and her three brothers had to share out the property of Etablissement MAX among each other. This led to one of the unhappiest periods in the family history. Alfred de Vliegher demanded that he and his wife Simonna should have a quarter of the family heritage. Because there was no liquid cash from which to pay this out, he sent a bailiff to seize the original stand of Etablissement MAX.

This meant the end for a monument in the history of fairs and carnivals of more than a century old. The stand was brought into the MAX workshops in Ghent. The façade was thrown on a heap in the warehouse, the interior was sold for a hundred thousand francs to a firm in the Antwerp area who hired out party decorations, and the gas stoves, pots, pans, dishes, plates and other usable material transferred to Friture Hollandaise MAX.

Simonna Consael always kept the surviving decorative elements of the large stand, in the hope that one of the grandchildren might be able to do something with them.

Just when the garage on the Brugse Steenweg was flourishing, Alfred De Vliegher fell ill. Cancer was diagnosed. That disease felled him within a year. Simonna Consael became a widow and the owner of a large garage.

Later the Friture Hollandaise MAX also disappeared from the Consael family heritage. When Maximilien was 74 and neither of his two daughters wanted – or was capable of – working the stall, he sold it. In the sales contract he stipulated that the name 'MAX' should only be used at fairs and in the context of the original stand.
Both the name 'MAX' and the patent for its use remained the property of the Consael family, so only direct descendants of the family have the right to open a business under the name 'MAX' in a house in the city.

That family links are very important among the Consaels is proved by the fact that Simonna, after the death of her husband, got in touch with her brothers again and continued to maintain very good relations with them.

Those close links are in fact not only an aspect of the Consael family, but are a very common phenomenon among fair stallholders. The social context of the fairs displays a steadily recurrent pattern. It is mostly the same stallholders who appear with their attractions at carnivals and fairs. There they meet each other again and in this way a tight social link is built up between families. For that reason, too, there is much inter-marriage in the fairground world. The children of the different families grow up together and grow up within the only world they know: that of the fairground. It was also a tradition that children of stallholders had free entry to all the attractions of the other families.

Yves: The sixth direct descendant

The young Yves considered his grandmother Simonna an absolute darling. He had a boundless admiration for her dedication, her unselfishness and, above all, for her iron will in forging the bonds of the family tightly together. Yves had, of course, grown up with her, because his parents – as was usual among showmen – lived with her.

At a young age Yves acquired an appreciation for the taste and smell of waffles. One of his cousins, the son of one of his grandmother's brothers, made waffles and *oliebollen*, deep-fried doughnuts, at trade fairs. Because he was extremely busy, he often called on Simonna Consael to help him. There was nothing she liked to do better, because in that way she could again serve customers with the traditional waffles and fritters for which her family was so famous.

Little Yves found it strange that his grandmother was away so much. And every time she came home in the evening, you could smell the scent of waffles on her clothes. Yves asked if he might accompany her to a trade fair some time. In this way he made his first direct acquaintance with a waffle stall. When he was nine years old his grandmother made him a white waistcoat. A white apron and a cap completed the picture, and Yves could help in the stall. He immediately fell in love with the atmosphere. He plainly had the Consael family gene in him and from then on he had only one end in view: to bake his own waffles and develop the 'MAX' name further.

Each year Yves could also be found in the Friture Hollandaise MAX when it occupied its site at the Ghent Mid-Lent fair. He enjoyed being in the company of his great-uncle Maximilien and aunt Eulalie.

However, during one of the fairs he experienced the shock of his life. Maximilien wanted to give him their dog as a present. When Yves asked why he didn't want to keep the animal any longer, his great-uncle told him that he had sold the stall. He was seventy years old and was retiring with his wife, to live in a flat. This was a real tragedy for the young waffle baker. How in God's name could anyone sell such a splendid stall?

Being curious, Yves went exploring in his grandmother's enormous cellars when he was about ten. There was everything that had survived from the MAX family stand, such as the crockery, silver coffee filters, the original waffle irons, and much more. Yves was fascinated by the waffle irons. He unpacked them one by one, and took them into the garden. There he cleaned them until they were as good as new. When his grandmother asked what he was doing, Yves simply answered that he wanted to bake waffles. His grandmother tried to change his mind, but soon realized that she would not succeed in doing so.

Then, with Yves, she collected a gas stove from the cellar. That in its turn was polished. Grandmother taught Yves how to make the dough, and after a little while he was baking waffles as if he had never done anything else. He appropriated some of the workspace, cleaned it up and decorated the walls with photos of carnivals and fairs, where his grandparents had created a sensation.

When he had learnt all he could about waffle baking, his grandmother taught him to make deep-fried doughnuts, and then fritters.
Then, when every boy from twelve to fourteen years old was chasing after a football, Yves turned himself into an expert cook for the parties, birthdays and get-togethers of the family.

Meanwhile he went to a hotel school, because he wanted to gather sufficient knowledge to cook. He also wanted to get a diploma, because in that way he could carry out his trade in conformity with the legal requirements. It will be no surprise to learn that Yves was a brilliant student at the hotel school. Whereas at primary school he had shown no interest, in the kitchen of the hotel school he stood out as an extremely hard-working and inquisitive young man. His marks were brilliant and he came top throughout his course, because this was what he was interested in; the kitchen was his favourite environment.

At the end of his studies he had to do a placement. He looked for one and found the ideal place to complete his studies in Oostakker, close to the basilica of Our Lady, in the celebrated Hotel de Lourdes, at that time run by Willy de Mey. One of the specialities of their kitchen was baking waffles. So Yves took a job there as a waiter. This gave him the chance to work in a waffle-baking environment and at the same time learn how to be a waiter. He learnt how to treat customers, sharpened up his commercial understanding, and gained an insight into the organization of a business where dozens of people had to be served at the same time.

Yves worked for several years in the hotel. Then he was called up for his military service. Because he wanted to go on working during that period, he convinced his superiors by all kinds of tall stories to post him to Ghent. This made it possible for him to spend all his available free time as a waiter, or helping in the kitchen, where grateful use was made of his talents.

With all this Yves had, of course, only one ambition. He wanted to save as much money as possible to build up his own business. He also worked as the chief assistant to the barracks chef, who regularly arranged parties for first or special communions, wedding anniversaries, and other such occasions, and gladly called on Yves, because he knew the tricks of the trade. He was, of course, paid for his services, and so managed to build up a nice nest egg.

Meanwhile Yves also worked as a chef for the officers' mess. There was plenty of work in the kitchen and there were not many skilled assistants available. This meant that Yves regularly did several shifts every day, resulting in a great deal of overtime. In the end, the head chef allowed Yves

to go home a month before the end of his military service, to compensate for his overtime. Yves immediately started arranging the interior of a building on the Beverenplein in Ghent. A month later, the day after he was officially released, he opened his first business. Where he could, he worked the decorative elements of the original stand, preserved by his grandmother Simonna, into the interior.

When he moved a few years later, and developed his Etablissement MAX on the Gouden Leeuwplein, in the centre of Ghent, he had his interior decorator reproduce the whole atmosphere of the original fairground stand. Most of the decorative elements still available were integrated into the decoration and are still there to be admired today.

Grandmother Consael's death

One of the most emotionally charged moments of Yves' life was undoubtedly the death of his beloved grandmother. She used to come to the Gouden Leeuwplein almost daily.

She carried out little domestic tasks, such as sewing the gilt buttons onto the waiters' waistcoats. She also very regularly inspected the many photographs of the history of the Consael family, which can be admired everywhere on the walls of the business.

The Ghent Floralies of 2005 was a particularly busy period for Yves and his staff. Customers were often queuing, waiting for a table to come free, and the kitchen was working flat out. On Sunday afternoon, Eddy, Yves' friend, received a telephone call with the message that grandmother Simonna's health had taken a dramatic turn for the worse. She had been taken to the University Hospital, and would probably not last out the night.

Yves was at that moment busily at work; the restaurant was packed, and the kitchen could hardly cope with the stream of orders for waffles, fritters and pancakes. So Eddy decided to wait before telling Yves the bad news. In the late afternoon, when Yves was just preparing a new batch of dough, there was another phone call. Only then did Eddy tell Yves that he must go immediately to the hospital if he wanted to see his grandmother still alive. Together they rushed in all haste to the hospital.

When Yves reached his grandmother's bed, she was no longer moving. Everyone in the room told him that she was quietly dying. Yves took her hand and said: 'Bomma, I'm here, it's Yves.' She opened her eyes and saw that he was wearing his white waistcoat and his apron. She drew him a little closer, took a deep breath, and said: 'Yves, you were my littlest one, but the one I loved most.' Then she shut her eyes again. Then her daughter, Yves' mother, said: 'She was born ninety years ago to the smell of waffles, and now you are here, standing so close to her. The smell of fresh waffles in your clothes fills this whole room. The circle is closed, she can die in peace.'

Yves kept watch the whole night by her bed, supported by his friend Eddy. When dawn broke he had to leave the room, because the nurses wanted to wash her. When he was allowed back a little later, he held his grandmother tight. She opened her eyes and Yves said: 'This is the last time we can look in each other's eyes. You have striven enough. You have accomplished all you wanted to do. Now rest, you have deserved it.' Simonna gently nodded her head and went to sleep with the image of her best-loved grandchild imprinted on her retina.

What will the future bring?

Etablissement MAX went on working the carnivals and fairs right up to 1974.

That is when Eulalie and Maximilien, who were then running it, retired. There was, alas, no immediate successor.

Yves only took up the torch in 1980. However, he no longer travelled to fairs and carnivals, because the tradition of the wonderful, great stand, with its mirrors, red plush and decorated walls, where it was such fun to sit and eat a waffle, had been forgotten by the general public.

That is why Yves started his first business on the Van Beverenplein in Ghent. There he offered lunch at midday, waffles, fritters and pancakes in the afternoon, and a light dinner in the evening. In 1999 he moved to the Gouden Leeuwplein where his business still is. In this context the important fact is that Yves still always bakes waffles with the original family waffle irons, now more than a hundred years old, which are still heated in the flames of the gas stoves.

What of the future? What will happen when Yves decides to give up baking?

He thinks and hopes that one of his sister's sons has caught the bug. He can see himself in his nephew, who is inquisitive about the make-up of the dough, and likes to help make waffles and pancakes when he comes to visit his uncle. Yves hopes that he will continue with the business, so that the name MAX and the Consael clan will carry on.

Moreover, that would also be the ideal solution. If Yves should be fortunate enough to live to the ripe old age his forebears enjoyed, then he would still be able to come every day to enjoy the smell of the fresh waffles and fritters. Yves is a Consael in heart and mind, and dreams only of one thing: to spend the rest of his life baking waffles and all that involves. It is in fact his ambition and his ideal to die like his grandmother with the scent of waffles in his nose.

Waffles, pancakes, fritters and their history

The ancestor of the waffle iron is recorded from around the year 1200. A blacksmith had made a plate with shallow pits in it. When dough was pressed onto the plate, the pattern of the pits would show up in the dough. In the course of subsequent centuries, people tried to improve on the shape and the pits.

The first descriptions of waffles date from the eighteenth century; the first illustrations can be seen in Pieter Breughel's painting of the *Battle between Carnival and Lent* in the sixteenth century, while the earliest forms of waffle irons can be traced back to the fifteenth century.
These irons give a good picture of what waffles must then have looked like. They are round in shape with little squares or blocks, which give the waffle its name. The Old-French *wâfla* actually means honeycomb and this lies at the origin of the later waffle, because its pattern of small regular squares is exactly the same.

The earliest known waffle irons from the fifteenth century bear the arms of Jean sans Peur and Philip the Good. At that time a waffle iron was an expensive item. On the birth of a girl it was often given as a present. The name of the child and its date of birth might be engraved on the iron, and she would take the iron with her when later she married and left home.

And there is also documentation referring to waffles being made round the cradle of a new-born infant. The midwife baked waffles beside the childbed to offer them as bringers of luck to all those present.

For the recipe of the dough we must go back a very long way in history. The ancient Greeks used to make a kind of pancake which they baked between two hot iron plates. The Romans, too, used irons like this. Their pancakes were prepared without yeast and were called *oblata,* meaning 'offering' or 'oblation'. Today these flat wafers are still used as the host in Christian communion services.

During the Middle Ages flat pancakes were still baked, though they were made in different shapes. For instance, they might, immediately after baking, be rolled round a finger into a horn shape, and filled with syrup or fruit jelly. These were, in fact, the earliest ancestors of the ice-cream cornets we use so often today.

In Paris a waffle was called le plaisir, because the bakers offered them
to rich ladies with the remark: *'Madame veut-elle goûter au plaisir?'*

In the nineteenth century in Antwerp people baked *'krokantjes',* 'crisps'.
These waffles were mainly baked in winter. They were very crisp and
were dipped into hot spiced wine before being eaten.

Dutch waffles were originally quite a bit smaller than Belgian ones.
The Dutch used to put nutmeg into the dough and, after baking,
scattered sugar and cinnamon over the waffles, giving them a spicier taste.

For the Liège waffles egg white was used instead of yeast to make the dough rise. The dough was made of expensive, nutritious kinds of flour,
a lot of egg white, and milk. There was also a cheaper variant, made out of low-grade flour, water and barley. This inferior waffle was sold to
the poor, who only paid a few cents for it.

Fritters were first mentioned by the Roman historian Cato, who lived between 234 and 149 BC. He talks of small balls of sourdough that were
fried brown in oil, in which they took on all kinds of fantastic shapes. They were dipped in melted sugar before they were eaten.

It is in 1399 that we find the first documents mentioning apple fritters. During the banquet to celebrate the marriage of Henry IV of England,
a delicacy was served which was described as follows: 'A slice of sour apple is coated with a batter of egg yolks, flour, beer and yeast, before
being deep-fried in frying fat.' These fritters were served very hot and richly strewn with sugar.

In the Dutch cookery book *Grond-beginzelen der keuken-kunde* (Basic principles of kitchen skills) of 1758, there is a remarkable recipe for fritters. There is no mention of apples here, but of a dough consisting of flour and eggs. Small balls of this were fried in melted butter, lard, or
burnt rape oil. For the better classes a variant was given consisting of a mixture of wheat meal, cream cheese, eggs, sugar, wine and the zest of
lemons.

Nowadays no one would dream of making their own fat for deep-frying. But at the start of the twentieth century this was quite different. In
the *Nieuwe Kookboek* (New Cookery Book) of 1915 we find the following recipe: 'Use beef fat or fat from a calf's kidney or lard for melting
down. Wash the fat in lukewarm water and cut it into small pieces which you put through the mincer. Put it in a cast-iron pan without a lid
and melt it on a moderate heat. Take care that the colour does not change, and that no taste of frying comes from the fat. Pour it all through a
sieve, press the dripping out, and keep the fat in an earthenware pot, which should be covered with a cloth to keep the dust out.'

recipes

Mini Waffles today,
as they are served with coffee
in Yves' Etablissement MAX

Preamble

It is amusing to browse through cookery books of the past and to read the inventive recipes for pastries and confectionery. It is almost unthinkable that you would be using these original ingredients today. Most of them you would not even be able to find, or at least not in their authentic form.

Even in the days of the Greeks and Romans, around the beginning of the Christian era, people were looking for a variety of ways to prepare sweet cakes and pastries. And it was no different in the course of past centuries.

It is not possible to discover precisely when the first real waffles and pancakes were baked. There are so many conflicting stories, that it is impossible to pinpoint a date which is historically correct. But we do know when the first pancake and waffle stalls appeared at carnivals, fairs and kermises in the Low Countries and surrounding areas. They are mentioned in chronicles from the beginning of the nineteenth century.

It is not our intention to give a historical reconstruction of the evolution of waffle baking here, but simply to dig up a few very old recipes from the mists of time. These recipes are all special, on the one hand because they are all part of history, on the other, because they are all among the favourite delicacies used by Yves, owner of Etablissement MAX and direct descendant of the Consael family.

As mentioned earlier in this book, it was Maximilien Consael who at the Brussels fair of 1856 baked the very first Brussels waffle. This we know for certain, because both family chronicles and contemporary publications mentioned it.

In his cookery book of 1560 Voselman only gave 'guidelines' for the preparation of the waffle mixture and for baking waffles. This needs to be mentioned, because at the time recipes were written down in a completely different way. No exact quantities were ever given for the ingredients. This is because the composition of every recipe contained a personal touch which was usually passed on from mother to daughter. On the left: some examples.

EXAMPLES OF OLD RECIPES

'To make good waffles':
Take grated old white bread. Add an egg yolk to it and a spoonful of powdered sugar. Mix half water and half wine together with ginger and cinnamon. Add this to the bread crumbs and bake in a cast-iron frying pan in a little oil or some melted butter.

'To make small waffles with eggs':
Grate dried white bread. Add as many eggs as it takes to make a liquid batter. For each dozen eggs add one glass of wine, in which sugar has been dissolved to make it quite sweet. Add some melted butter and stir well. Bake in a frying pan with melted butter. You can also make this batter with wheat flour, but the waffles are nicer if they are made with bread crumbs.

Syrup waffles

In a recipe book dating from 1784 we find this preparation for syrup waffles, which were famous in the Netherlands, where they are extremely popular even now:

Ingredients

For the waffles:
300 g cane sugar
450 g butter
3 eggs
3 tablespoons milk
600 g flour
1 level teaspoon cinnamon
1 pinch of salt

For the syrup:
600 g cane sugar
300 g butter

Preparation of the syrup

⊙ Heat the butter in a pan and stir in the cane sugar until it has melted completely.

⊙ Keep the mixture lukewarm and stir it regularly until it is used for the filling.
In this way you avoid it congealing.

Preparation of the waffles

⊙ Mix the cane sugar with the eggs and the milk. While stirring, add the flour, cinnamon
and cut-up pieces of butter. Scatter a little salt in and mix everything well.
Shape the dough into twelve little balls.

⊙ Heat the waffle iron until it is quite hot. Push the ball of dough into the iron and bake the waffle
for 1/2 minute.

⊙ Cut the waffle through the middle into two thin waffles and spread them first with butter
and then with syrup.

⊙ Join the two parts together again, or keep them separate. You can eat these waffles hot or cold.

We return to the present day to describe a few recipes (and often also their history or origin). In each case we will give the number of people (or of the product) for which the recipe is intended and we have searched as far as possible for the original – and sometimes centuries old – methods of preparation. Enjoy!

The Brussels waffles

The history of the Brussels waffle as we know it starts with Maximilien Consael, who in 1856 was the first to appear at fairs with a luxurious stand, decorated with mirrors, inscriptions in gold, and red plush. Together with his wife he worked out a recipe for a light dough, which he baked in irons which were specially designed for the purpose, with twenty 'holes'. At first the waffles were baked on the hot embers of burning coal, but because this was very cumbersome, they soon changed to gas.

The authentic Brussels waffle was first presented at the Brussels fair of 1856. The waffles you can enjoy at Etablissement MAX today are still made to the original 1856 recipe. They are baked in the authentic irons, which are still heated on gas burners.

Nowadays you will find many imitations which are baked in an electric waffle iron, but the pure taste of the Brussels waffle will only come into its own if it is baked as it is in Etablissement MAX.

The MAX secret is not only in the dough – Yves mixes the ingredients as prescribed in his ancestors' secret recipe – but just as much in the waffle irons which were specially made in 1839 to Maximilien Consael's specifications.

We give two recipes: one with yeast and one without. The second one is obviously lighter, but both are equally delicious.

Brussels waffles with yeast

Ingredients

RECIPE FOR ABOUT 20 WAFFLES

2.**¼ ~~½~~ cups** 500 g flour
3/4 cup 200 g butter
1.8 tbsp 25 g fresh yeast
4 eggs
1/2 litre water
1/2 litre milk
1.8 tbsp 25 g caster sugar
1 tsp 5 g salt
powdered sugar for dusting
vanilla

Method of preparation

⊚ Heat the water until it is lukewarm and beat the eggs into it. **+1 tsp vanilla**
Sift the flour into it and mix everything with a whisk. Beat the salt and sugar into the batter.

⊚ Heat the milk until it is lukewarm. Dissolve the yeast in it and add the mixture to the batter.
Beat well until you have a light mixture.

⊚ Melt the butter in a saucepan, but don't allow it to go brown.
As soon as the butter is a golden colour you can mix it into the batter. Stir well.
Blend the batter with a mixer, put it in a warm, draught-free place and leave it to rest
for half an hour.

⊚ Heat the waffle iron until it is quite hot. Use a small jug to pour some batter onto the middle
of the waffle iron. Close the iron and turn it over at once. Let it bake for 3 to 4 minutes.
Turn the iron over again and take the waffle out of the mould with a small knife.

⊚ Put it on a plate and dust it with powdered sugar.

Do you want to eat your waffle in the traditional way?
In that case you should just use a knife to cut this delicacy into strips, which you can eat in fingers.
Obviously you can serve this waffle with all kinds of accompaniments, such as whipped cream,
fresh fruit or jam.

In 1839 Maximilien Consael designed large cast-iron waffle irons with
uniform squares. He had his name engraved on the lids and experimen-
ted with a special dough that was light and airy.
Using this dough, he eventually produced a rectangular waffle which
he introduced to the public in 1856 at the Brussels Kermis. He chris-
tened this delicacy the 'Brussels Waffle'.

Brussels waffles without yeast

Ingredients

RECIPE FOR ABOUT 12 WAFFLES
10 egg yolks
1/2 litre milk
1 sachet vanilla sugar
16 egg whites
250 g flour
200 g butter
1 pinch of salt

Method of preparation

⊙ Heat the milk until it is lukewarm and take it off the heat.
Mix in the egg yolks and beat them with an whisk. Sift the flour into it and mix it with the milk.

⊙ Melt the butter in a saucepan and take it off the heat as soon as it is a golden colour (so don't allow it to become brown). Add the vanilla sugar and the melted butter to the batter and stir it well.

⊙ Beat the egg white to a stiff consistency in a separate mixing bowl.
Fold it through the batter a little at the time and then stir it in well until you have a very light mixture.

⊙ Heat the waffle iron until it is quite hot. Pour some batter from a jug onto the middle of the waffle iron.
Close the iron and turn it over at once. Let it bake for 3 to 4 minutes.
Turn the iron over again and take the waffle out of the mould with a small knife.

⊙ Put the waffle onto a plate and dust it with powdered sugar.

Do you want to eat your waffle in the traditional way?
In that case you should just use a knife to cut this delicacy into strips, which you can eat in fingers.
Obviously you can serve this waffle with all kinds of accompaniments, such as whipped cream,
fresh fruit or jam.

The original accompaniment for fresh waffles was sugar and melted butter. Modern consumers leave out the butter, because it seems to make the waffle too rich.
These days it is trendy to order a waffle filled with four or five kinds of fruit.

The Liège waffle

The difference between the Brussels waffle – a speciality of Etablissement MAX – and the Liège waffle is first and foremost in the shape. The Brussels waffle is large and rectangular, the Liège waffle is smaller and rounded. Because the mixture for the Brussels waffle is light, it can be baked crisp. The batter for the Liège waffle is rather rich. It contains more sugar, cinnamon and butter and is very rich in calories as a result. There is also a notable difference between the small squares (or 'holes') in the waffle. The Brussels waffle has twenty, while the Liège one has twenty-four.

Ingredients

RECIPE FOR ABOUT 20 WAFFLES
500 g flour
14 g dried yeast
2 tablespoons soft brown sugar
1 egg
1,2 dl warm milk
1,2 dl water
1 tablespoon clear honey
250 g butter
1 teaspoon salt
200 g 'suikerbrood' (sugared brioche)
1 pinch cinnamon

How to prepare the batter

⊙ In a large bowl mix the yeast with 350 g flour. Add the sugar and stir well. Pour the milk and water into the mixture while stirring. Mix everything to a creamy mass. Cover the bowl with a clean tea towel and leave the mixture to rest for about quarter of an hour in a draught-free place.

⊙ Stir the remainder of the flour, the honey, the cinnamon, the butter and the pieces of sugared brioche through the mixture. Stir well.

⊙ As soon as the mixture is firm enough, you can knead it into a ball with your hands (which you have obviously scrubbed very clean in clear water beforehand). Put this ball in a mixing bowl, cover, and leave to rest for 10 minutes. Next divide the dough into small balls of about 100 g each.

⊙ Heat an iron for Liège waffles. When it is quite hot, put a small ball of dough in the middle of the open iron. Close the iron and allow the waffle to bake for about 10 minutes. Take the waffle out of the iron and serve it steaming hot.

In medieval cookery books remarkably few recipes are to be found for sweet waffles. In these days sugar was after all a very expensive product which could only be bought from apothecaries. There were, of course, a few pastry cooks who put this sweetener into tarts, waffles and pancakes, but these delicacies were only designed for the rich, who had to put down a substantial sum of money for them.

Heavenly egg dessert

Ingredients

RECIPE FOR ABOUT 10 DESSERTS
120 g caster sugar
1 dl water
8 egg yolks
grated rind of an unsprayed lemon
almond oil

Method of preparation

⊙ Bring the water and sugar to the boil, and stir continuously until it has formed a thick syrup.

⊙ In a separate bowl beat the egg yolks.
Pour the syrup in a thin stream into the egg yolks while stirring continuously.
Pour the mixture through a fine sieve and stir in the grated lemon rind.

⊙ Grease four small baking tins (each with a content of about 1 decilitre) with almond oil.
This is best done by using a pastry brush.

⊙ Pour the batter into the greased moulds and leave it to rest for a moment.

⊙ Meanwhile fill a roasting tin in the oven three-quarters full with boiling water.
Put the small cake tins with the batter in the water and leave them to set for about 10 minutes in the oven at 180 °C.
If the surface of the mixture gives slightly when it is pressed, the egg cakes are ready.
If necessary, wait a few minutes more to achieve this result.

⊙ Take the moulds out of the water and leave them to cool.
Next turn them over, each one on a separate small plate, as you do with a pudding mould.
Cover the dishes with plastic film and leave them to cool in the refrigerator for at least half an hour.

⊙ Serve this dessert very cold.

The cornet from which we eat ice cream was originally also a waffle. Immediately after baking, these were curved round a finger and rolled into the shape of a little horn. When it was cool, it was a crisp cookie, perfect for holding ice cream. The idea of shaping these cornets originated with some American bakers around 1896.

Quark balls

Ingredients

RECIPE FOR ABOUT 20 BALLS
4 rounded tablespoons flour
70 g clear honey
500 g low-fat curds
4 eggs
1 rounded teaspoon cinnamon
grated rind of an unsprayed lemon
olive oil (for deep-frying)

Method of preparation

⊙ Leave the curds to drain in a sieve and press out all excess liquid with a fork.

⊙ In a small bowl beat the eggs till light and airy.
Add the curd, cinnamon and grated lemon and stir until you have a firm mixture.
Mix half of the flour into this batter.

⊙ Cover with a clean tea towel and leave to rest for about 10 minutes in a draught-free place.

⊙ Wash your hands thoroughly. Dry them well and dust them with flour. Pick off pieces of dough about the size of a ping pong ball, roll them into a ball shape and put them next to each other on a shallow dish.

⊙ Heat the olive oil in a frying pan with a high brim.
When the oil is sufficiently hot, fry the balls (about six at a time) golden brown in the oil.
Leave them to drain on a few sheets of kitchen tissue which can absorb the excess oil.

⊙ Once the quark balls have all been fried and drained, you can arrange them on a preheated dish.
Put them close together and drip some honey over them.

⊙ Serve while they are still slightly warm.

The recipe for waffles is passed down from generation to generation. It varies regionally and is strictly determined by the ingredients and their individual proportions. The special ingredient in the mixture that makes the Etablissement MAX waffles special, is a well kept family secret.

Sponge cake fritters

Ingredients

RECIPE FOR ABOUT 16 CAKE FRITTERS
1/4 litre milk
140 g butter
120 g fine caster sugar
250 g flour
stick of cinnamon, about 5 cm long
small piece of unsprayed and
well-washed lemon rind
small piece of unsprayed and
well-washed orange rind
4 eggs
100 g finely ground breadcrumbs
1 cup walnut oil
8 tablespoons olive oil
powdered sugar
ground cinnamon

Method of preparation

⊚ Melt the butter in a deep saucepan. Take care not to let it turn brown.

⊚ Stir 200 g flour into the melted butter.
Bring this to the boil, stir in the sugar and wait until it has dissolved completely.
Pour the milk into a separate pan. Add the lemon and orange rinds and bring to the boil while stirring. Pour the milk slowly and while stirring continuously into the mixture in the other pan.

⊚ Separate the eggs. Keep the egg white in the refrigerator.

⊚ Take the pan from the heat and remove the rinds.
Blend the egg yolks into the mixture, using a mixer.

⊚ Grease a rectangular baking tin of about 15 x 28 cm with walnut oil. The easiest way to do this is with a pastry brush, because you can grease the tin very evenly in this way.

⊚ Pour the mixture into the mould in a layer about 3 cm thick.
Leave to cool for at least 4 hours in a draught-free place. It would be best if you could leave the mixture to cool in the refrigerator overnight. In that case you should cover the baking tin with a piece of aluminium foil which you prick in several places so that the heat can escape.

⊚ When the mixture is completely cold, turn the baking tin over onto a large dish.
Divide the mixture into squares of about 5 cm.
Cut the pieces in half and then from corner to corner, so that they form triangles.

⊚ Beat the egg whites with a mixer to a stiff consistency. Dip the pieces of batter into the remaining flour, then in the egg white and finally into the breadcrumbs.

⊚ Heat the olive oil in a deep fryingpan. Deep-fry the triangles to a golden yellow.
Let them drain briefly on kitchen tissue and arrange them on a serving dish.
Dust with powdered sugar and a little ground cinnamon.
You can eat these sponge cake fritters either hot or cold or with various kinds of jam.
They are delicious with a strawberry, red-currant or apricot jam.

Fritters with orange blossom

Ingredients

RECIPE FOR ABOUT 30 FRITTERS
500 g flour
2 egg yolks
1 pinch of salt
20 g fresh yeast
1 tablespoon soft butter
1/4 litre mineral water (still!)
10 drops of orange-blossom water
1 litre olive oil for deep-frying
powdered sugar

Method of preparation

⊙ Sift the flour into a mixing bowl. Pour in the water in a thin trickle while you stir well.

⊙ Melt the yeast in a little lukewarm water and stir it into the batter.
Stir well and cover the bowl with a clean tea towel.
Leave the batter to rest for 15 minutes in a draught-free place.

⊙ Beat the egg yolks in a small bowl and add them to the batter.
Next stir in the butter and a pinch of salt.
Finally stir the orange-blossom water into the mixture and give it all a good final stir.

⊙ Heat the oil in a deep-frying pan. With a tablespoon take small pieces of the mixture out of the bowl.
Shape them into small balls (you can do this with two spoons which you repeatedly rinse in cold water).
Let the balls of dough slide into the hot oil and fry them until they are golden yellow.
Scoop them out of the oil with a metal skimmer and leave them to drain for a moment on some kitchen tissue.

⊙ Arrange the balls on a serving dish or in a basket and dust them with powdered sugar.
Serve these fritters at once, because they are nicest when they are still hot.

For a festive variant you can replace the orange-blossom water with a teaspoon of rum, Grand Marnier, or Amaretto.

The first fair stalls selling waffles and doughnuts in the Low Countries date from the mid-fifteenth century. At that time annual fairs were held based primarily on the sale of horses. These events soon attracted more people than just horse-copers and horse lovers. So acrobats and conjurers came to entertain the public. The success of these annual horse fairs grew visibly. Consequently there was a need for food and drink. At first beer and wine were available, but it was sweetmeats in particular which met the public taste. Then waffles (in their most primitive form) and doughnuts (in those days made of semolina) established a firm base at horse fairs and later at the 'kermis'.

Potato fritters

This, too, is a very old recipe. It originates from Bergerac, a region in the French Périgord, where it is now no longer as common as it used to be. For its preparation we searched for the original recipe of a century and a half ago.

Ingredients

RECIPE FOR ABOUT 6 PERSONS
500 g small potatoes
500 g flour
1 1/2 tablespoons powdered sugar
1 pinch of salt
1 sachet vanilla sugar
oil for deep-frying

Method of preparation

⊛ Wash the potatoes clean under cold running water. Boil them for about 20 minutes and then pull the peel off. Crush them very fine while they are still warm, and scatter the powdered sugar and salt over them. Sift the flour in small quantities into the potatoes, while you knead them well.

⊛ When all the flour has been used up, make a ball of the dough. Wrap it in a clean tea towel and leave it to rest for 4 hours in a cool, draught-free place (not in the refrigerator!).

⊛ Heat the oil in a deep frying pan until it is quite hot.
Dust the work surface with a little flour, roll out the dough to a thickness of about 1 centimetre, and cut out round or triangular shapes from it. Fry these one by one in the hot oil. Scoop them out of the oil as soon as they are brown, and allow them to drain on kitchen tissue.

⊛ Arrange the fritters on a serving dish and dust them with the vanilla sugar.

> The first Mid-Lent fair in Ghent dates from 1563. The Mid-Lent fair marked the opening of the fair season in Flanders.
> The original fairs grew round the horse fairs. There were stalls where visitors to the market could buy all kinds of foodstuffs. Later stalls with games came, too. Often a farce or one-act drama was performed, where strange individuals such as giants, dwarves, bearded ladies and similar characters made an appearance. Later these phenomena moved into separate tents, where they performed as a kind of freak show.

Venetian fritters

These fritters, of which a description can be found as early as the chronicles of the Roman Empire, are a typical dessert served during the famous Venetian Carnival. Nowadays these chiacchere sfrappole *are prepared throughout Italy during the carnival period.*
There are obviously many variations to the recipe, but we have tried to reproduce the original one.

Ingredients

FOR 4 PERSONS
275 g flour
65 g fine caster sugar
50 g butter
5 cl milk
1 teaspoon grappa (Italian spirit)
1 teaspoon orange-blossom water
1 egg
1 sachet vanilla sugar
1 pinch of salt
oil for deep-frying
powdered sugar to dust

Method of preparation

⊙ Beat the egg in a deep mixing bowl and add the caster sugar to it. Beat the sugar into the egg and then add the grappa, the orange blossom water, the salt and the vanilla sugar.

⊙ Melt the butter and pour it into the mixture as soon as it is liquid.

⊙ Sift the flour a little at a time into the bowl and mix it through the batter. Stir well so that there are no lumps, and continue sifting the flour into the bowl until it has all been used up.

⊙ As soon as the mixture is firm enough, you can knead it with your fingers until it is a firm dough. Continue to knead until the dough no longer sticks to your hands (this usually takes 10 to 15 minutes).

⊙ Divide the dough into two balls and put them in turn on a work surface which has been dusted with a little flour. Roll out a ball of dough until you have a sheet about 3 mm thick.

⊙ Cut the flat sheet of dough into fluted rectangles. You can do this with a pastry cutter as used for cutting pastry or pizza. The rectangles should be no more than 2 cm wide and 3 cm long.

⊙ Heat the oil for frying and put about five fritters in it.
Leave them in till they are a beautiful golden brown colour, scoop them out of the oil and leave them to drain on kitchen tissue. Keep on frying until all the fritters are ready.

⊙ Arrange them on a serving dish and dust them generously with powdered sugar.

⊙ These Venetian fritters can be served with a sweet orange marmalade.

Deep-fried churros

This recipe, which is Spanish by origin and is there known as churros, *became popular in South-America. According to tradition, the churros were first made around the year 1000 by shepherds who sometimes roamed around with their flocks for months and were looking for a surrogate for bread. They kneaded some flour with water and fried it in oil. Because it was too bitter to their taste, they added sugar. From this the churro was born, as we know it today.*
In 1511 Diego Velázquez sailed for Hispaniola. On board his ship were some young shepherds with a number of sheep. The shepherds continued to prepare their deep-fried twists on their distant journey, which caused the Cubans to call their flock 'the churro sheep from Spain'. This breed is still known in South-America.
The churros are prepared with or without sugar, so that they are suitable for eating as a dessert, a snack, or as a replacement for bread during a meal. In South-America they are even filled with cheese, meat and vegetables.

Ingredients

RECIPE FOR ABOUT 30 CHURROS
2-3 PERSONS
300 g flour
1 pinch of salt
1/2 litre water
olive oil for deep-frying
powdered sugar

Method of preparation

⊚ Bring the water to the boil with the salt. Take the pan from the heat and sift the flour into it.
Beat to a firm batter, preferably with a mixer with dough hooks.
The dough is ready when it comes away easily from the pan.

⊚ Cover with a clean tea towel and leave to rest in a draught-free place for 10 minutes.

⊚ Meanwhile heat the olive oil in a pan.

⊚ Spoon the batter into a piping bag with a fairly wide, toothed nozzle.
Next spout knobs of dough of about 5 cm into the hot oil and fry them till golden brown. Remove them from the oil with a metal skimmer and leave them to drain on kitchen tissue for a moment.

⊚ Put about ten deep-fried churros on a small plate and dust them with powdered sugar.

You can also serve these churros in a paper cone, in the same way doughnuts are sometimes served. Churros are a treat for young and old!

Pancakes or crêpes: what is the difference?

Crêpes are a very thin and light variant of pancakes. The big difference between the two is in the ingredients for the batter. Crêpes contain only about 2/3 of the quantity of flour used for pancakes. You can also experiment endlessly with crêpes, whereas pancakes are preferably consumed without too many additions..
We start with a recipe for pancakes and their variants.
After that we will turn our attention to crêpes.

There are numerous variants of this tasty dish. The ancient Greeks were already making pancakes. They prepared a dough which they flattened and baked between two hot iron sheets.
The Romans adopted the recipe when they conquered Greece, but because they found the dough too heavy, they left out the yeast. This made the Roman version very thin and almost transparent. This pancake lies at the basis of the consecrated wafer of the Christian communion service.

Pancakes (basic recipe)

Because there are so many variants of pancakes, we give the basic recipe and a few suggestions for enriching it.
This recipe is for eight to ten pancakes, provided they are cooked fairly thinly. If you make them thicker, this recipe will be enough for six to eight pancakes.

Ingredients

FOR ABOUT 8-12 PANCAKES (THIN)
OR 6-8 (THICK)
200 g flour or self-raising flour
2 eggs
1/2 litre milk
1 pinch of salt
70 g butter for frying

Suggestion

You can vary the way you bake the pancakes by putting smaller quantities of batter in the pan. For instance, with a tablespoon, pour three small quantities of batter into the same frying pan.

Cook them until the top begins to dry, turn the little pancakes over and allow the other side to become pale brown as well. You can serve several of these small pancakes on one plate. In this case dust the whole plate with soft white sugar.

Method of preparation

- Sift the flour into a large mixing bowl and scatter the salt into it.
  Make a well in the middle and break the eggs into it. Stir everything together with a whisk.

- Slowly add half of the milk. Mix it with the flour and eggs, and stir until you have a smooth mixture. Next beat the rest of the milk through it so that the batter becomes lighter.

- Cover with a clean tea towel and leave to rest for about 1/2 hour in a draught-free place.
  During this rest period the starch will absorb the milk, so that the batter thickens.

- Heat a knob of butter in a frying pan which should be large enough but not deep.
  As soon as the butter starts foaming the pan should be removed from the heat.

- Pour a little batter from a small jug into the bottom of the pan and with a twisting movement make sure that the whole bottom is covered. Put the pan on a moderately high heat and leave the batter to cook until the top of it begins to dry.

- Turn the pancake over with a long, flat, narrow kitchen spatula and allow the other side to bake for about 1/2 minute until it is pale brown. Take care the pancake is still supple when you take it out of the pan. Use the spatula to put the pancake on a plate, folded over double.

- If you put the plate in a roasting tin with warm water while you continue baking, the cooked pancakes will stay warm longer. Finish off the pancakes by dusting them with soft white sugar (scattering it very thinly). Serve them with butter, syrup, honey or jam. You can also put a bowl of soft brown sugar on the table, because that goes particularly well with this delicacy.

If you order pancakes in Etablissement MAX, you will always be served two, which have been cooked at the same time. Yves always has a number of identical frying pans standing ready so that the pancakes ordered can be ready at the same time.

Pancakes with raisins

Ingredients

see basic recipe
+ 100 g raisins

Method of preparation

Rinse the raisins under a stream of cold water and then leave them to swell for about an hour in a small bowl of water. Pour the water away, allow the raisins to drain on a kitchen tissue, and stir them into the batter before resting it.

Apple pancakes

see basic recipe
+ 4 apples

⊙ Peel the apples and slice them into wafer-thin slices using the slicer on a grater (don't use the grater itself, but the side with the slicer on it). Obviously you throw away the cores.

⊙ Heat the butter in the frying pan. Remove the pan from the heat as soon as the foam fades away, and cover the bottom with the slices of apple. Dust them with a little ground cinnamon.

⊙ Allow this to cook for about 1 1/2 minutes on a moderate heat. Next add the batter (see basic recipe). Follow the cooking instructions as described above. Before serving, sprinkle ground coffee sugar or demerara sugar over the pancakes, instead of powdered sugar.

Cheese pancakes

see basic recipe
+ slices of semi-mature cheese
(as thin as possible)

⊙ Fry the pancake on one side as described in the basic recipe. As soon as it starts to dry on top, remove the pan from the heat and turn the pancake over with a spatula.

⊙ Put the slices of cheese across the whole surface of the pancake.
Cover the pan and put it on a very low heat to allow the cheese to melt.

⊙ As soon as this has happened you can turn the heat up to moderate again.
Cook for another 1/2 minute and slide the cheese pancake onto a plate.

⊙ This pancake is not, of course, sprinkled with sugar. If you like, you can sprinkle a little kirsch over it.

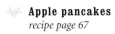
Apple pancakes
recipe page 67

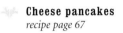
Cheese pancakes
recipe page 67

Crêpes

Ingredients

RECIPE FOR ABOUT 16 CRÊPES

120 g flour
3 eggs
4 to 5 dl milk
1 pinch of salt
70 g butter for frying

Method of preparation

- Sift the flour into a large mixing bowl. Add the salt.
  Make a well in the middle of the mixture and break the eggs into it. Stir with a whisk.

- Slowly pour in 1/3 of the milk and mix it with the flour and the eggs.
  Continue to stir until you have a smooth mixture.
  Next beat in the rest of the milk so that the batter becomes lighter.

- Cover with a clean tea towel and leave to rest for about 1/2 hour in a draught-free place.
  During the resting time the starch will absorb the milk, so that the batter thickens a little more.

- Heat a knob of butter in a frying pan which is large enough but not deep.
  Take the pan off the heat when the foam on the butter begins to recede.

- Pour a little batter onto the bottom of the pan and make a twisting movement to make sure that it covers the whole of the bottom. Put the pan on a moderate heat and allow the batter to cook until it starts to dry at the top. Crêpes need less time to cook than pancakes, because the batter is much thinner.

- Turn the crêpe over with a long, flat, narrow spatula or palette knife and quickly allow the other side to cook to a golden brown. Make sure that the crêpe is still supple when you take it out of the pan.

- Put it on a plate with the aid of the spatula and dust it with a thin layer of powdered sugar. Fold it over, and then again, so that you get a triangle with a round base. Put four of these folded crêpes on a plate.

- If you put the plate in a roasting tin of hot water while you continue to cook, the finished crêpes will keep warm longer.

- Serve the crêpes with butter, syrup, honey or jam.
  Powdered coffee sugar goes particularly well with these crêpes.

Crêpes Suzette

There are two theories about the origin of these crêpes, flamed in brandy. According to the first, the genuine Crêpe Suzette is a waffle spread with butter and with a flavour of Curaçao and mandarin juice. However, the following theory is generally accepted to be the correct one.

Around 1896 a sixteen-year-old pupil of the famous Auguste Escoffier was working in the Café de Paris in Monte-Carlo. Edward VII, while still Prince of Wales, was a regular customer, accompanied by a very beautiful young lady, who one day fancied pancakes.

The young chef cooked these fresh in the dining room. When they were finished, he sprinkled a dash of brandy over them. But he was a little careless when he took the pan from the heat, and the brandy caught fire. While he looked for something to douse the flames, they went out by themselves.

The prince wanted to taste the pancakes. He declared them to be particularly good. When the young chef asked him if he could name this delicacy after the prince, the chivalrous answer was that he would prefer it to be given the name of his lady: Suzette.

Ingredients

see basic recipe
+
100 g soft butter
100 g powdered sugar
1 orange
2 tablespoons liqueur (preferably Mandarine Napoléon or Grand Marnier)
4 tablespoons liqueur for the flambé
grated peel of an orange

Suggestion

Sometimes flaked almonds are added. If you wish to do this, they should be added to the grated peel in cooking.

Method of preparation

- Make eight very thin crêpes as described in the basic recipe. Dust with a thin layer of powdered sugar and fold them up. Allow them to rest while the juice is being prepared.

- Press an orange and pour the juice into a small jug. Add to this two tablespoons of an orange liqueur, such as Grand Marnier or Mandarine Napoléon.

- Grate the peel of an unsprayed and previously well-washed orange. Stir 100 g powdered sugar into approximately 100 g soft butter until the mixture forms a creamy substance.

- Spread the bottom of the frying pan with about half the butter mixture, using a pastry brush. Spread the remainder of the mixture on the top and bottom of the crêpes. Sprinkle the grated peel into the butter in the pan and allow it to warm slowly. Put the crêpes next to each other in the frying pan and pour the orange juice over them.

- Leave the crêpes to warm through well, while the juice evaporates. Turn them over once, so that they are warmed through on all sides.

- Pour about four tablespoons of liqueur into a small saucepan. It is best to take the crêpes and the saucepan with the liqueur to the table. Use a match to light the liqueur. Pour the burning liquid over the crêpes and serve them at once.

Crêpes with compote

Ingredients

see basic recipe
+
compote

Method of preparation

⊚ When the crêpe is cooked, slide it onto a plate. Spread a line of fruit compote down the middle of the crêpe and roll it up. Put it on a plate which is kept warm over hot water and make the next one.

⊚ Provide three to four crêpes for each portion.

⊚ If you vary the fruits you use for your compote, you constantly provide a pleasant surprise for your guests.

⊚ Before serving, dust the whole plate with a thin layer of powdered sugar.

Maximilien Consael was famous for his gruff approach. He disliked beating about the bush and often shocked friends or enemies with his blunt interjections.

During one of the early trips to the Netherlands the family stand was put up in Amsterdam. A wealthy party came in, installed themselves in one of the alcoves and pulled the curtains shut, so that they could laugh and flirt as they liked. Maximilien hurried to the alcove and threw the curtains open with a thunderous: 'You are not in a brothel or a whorehouse, here, Sir!' One of the company stood up and asked Maximilien if he knew who he was. He answered in the negative and his guest then made himself known: 'I am Prince William of Orange, Sir.'

Maximilien blushed and quickly closed the curtain again with his own hand…

Crêpes au gratin

Crêpes can be served very successfully as a starter by giving them a savoury filling. This is not a new idea: the well-known Chinese spring rolls are in fact nothing but thin sheets of dough filled with vegetables, herbs and spices, and meat. The difference is that the crêpes are not deep-fried but cooked in a frying pan. You can give your inspiration free rein for the filling. Below we will describe one delicacy which can serve as an example.

Ingredients

see basic recipe
+
150 g finely chopped pieces of white chicken meat
1 tablespoon finely chopped parsley
2 tablespoons finely chopped mushrooms
2 tablespoons finely chopped grated carrot
low-fat butter
grated Emmental cheese
1 dl white sauce

Method of preparation

⊙ Make about eight crêpes as described in the basic recipe. Allow them to rest while you make a ragout of the chopped white chicken meat, mushrooms, grated carrot and chopped parsley. Make sure that the ragout is fairly dry and and can easily be scooped up without spilling over the edges of a serving spoon.

⊙ Spread a portion of ragout across the middle of each crêpe.
Roll up the crêpe and fold over the ends, so that it is partly closed up.

⊙ Grease an ovenproof dish with low-fat butter suitable for baking. The best way to do this is with a pastry brush and semi-soft butter, which will spread easily.

⊙ Put the crêpes side by side in the dish. Sprinkle a layer of grated Emmental cheese over it.
Put the dish in the middle of a preheated oven (225 °C) and heat it well until all the cheese has melted.

⊙ Next put the grill at the hottest setting and allow the cheese to become golden brown under it.

These crêpes can be served as a starter.
With the addition of a few extra vegetables it becomes a delicious lunch.

The Consael family followed the customs of the middle classes. Among themselves they spoke only French, but to their employees they spoke in the Ghent dialect.
This sometimes led to hilarious scenes, such as when their great-grandmother issued orders in the local dialect, while at the same time trying to stop the dog barking in French.

Breton crêpes

Crêpes have been eaten in Brittany since the Middle Ages, so it is no wonder that for generations they have been part of the everyday cuisine there. Just as in Belgium you can find establishments specializing in genuine Brussels waffles – such as Etablissement MAX – there are a number of places in Brittany specializing in authentic crêpes where you can taste crêpes prepared in a thousand and one different ways.
You will find two basic kinds of crêpes: savoury ones, filled or served with substantial ingredients, which form a meal in themselves, and sweet ones which are, of course meant to be eaten as a dessert, or with coffee or tea. True Bretons drink a cup of mild cider with their crêpes.
The griddle or frying pan for Breton crêpes is always greased with a piece of fresh bacon rind.
Ask your butcher to give you a piece with skin: it makes greasing easier.

Ingredients

250 g buckwheat flour
2 dl water
2 dl milk
2 eggs
2 teaspoons butter or 1 fresh piece of bacon rind
1 pinch of salt

Method of preparation

⊙ Beat the eggs in a small bowl. Sift the buckwheat flour into a large mixing bowl, make a well in the middle and pour the beaten eggs into it.

⊙ Stir the eggs into the flour. At the same time add the water little by little.
Next add the milk too, and stir everything until you have a smooth and nicely liquid batter.

⊙ Cover the mixing bowl and put it in the refrigerator for 2 hours.

⊙ After resting, heat a large round griddle to cook the crêpes, or a large, shallow, cast-iron frying pan. Rub the griddle or the pan with the bacon rind. If you don't want to use bacon, you can use a little butter, but that means departing from the original Breton recipe.

⊙ Spoon a generous tablespoonful of batter into the pan and turn it round at once, so that the batter is spread around well. If you use a griddle, then use a spatula or other wide blade to spread the batter as soon as it goes in. In this way you will get a thin crêpe.

⊙ As soon as the batter has set, the crêpe should be turned. Leave it to cook until it is golden brown.

⊙ Remove it from the pan or the griddle, and put it on a plate which is keeping warm on a pan of hot water, so that the crêpes are kept hot. Continue cooking in this way until all the batter has been used up.

⊙ Serve the Breton crêpes with butter and unsweetened whipped cream and serve a glass of mild cider with it.

Suggestions

Breton crêpes can be filled with whatever you fancy. You may like to use wheat flour instead of buckwheat flour (for sweet crêpes) or half buckwheat and half wheat flour. If you stir a little melted butter into your batter, the crêpes will be crisper. A little caster sugar mixed into the batter will make them sweeter. The savoury variety can be filled with all kinds of ragout, provided it is not too liquid.

Poffertjes without yeast

The history of 'poffertjes' – tiny, puffed-up pancakes – is very like that of waffles. In the fifteenth century irons were for the first time made with small recesses (the predecessors of the 'squares' in waffles) and experiments made with small cakes baked on iron griddles.
The batter for 'poffertjes' can be made with or without yeast. Without yeast the poffertjes can be made more or less at once; a batter with yeast will have to rise for about an hour.
You will need a special griddle or pan for poffertjes, known as a poffertjes pan. You should be able to buy them in Belgium or the Netherlands in shops where they sell cooking utensils.

Ingredients

RECIPE FOR ABOUT 50 POFFERTJES
1 egg
300 g selfraising flour
1/8 litre unsweetened cream
1 1/2 teaspoons salt
2 teaspoons cooking oil
3 teaspoons very fine crushed sugar
3 dl milk
corn oil for frying
powdered sugar

Method of preparation

- Sift the selfraising flour into a large mixing bowl. Add the salt and stir it in.

- Beat the egg with the unsweetened cream.
  Add about 1 dl milk and mix in the sugar as well.

- Pour this mixture into the selfraising flour, beating it continuously with a whisk.
  By adding the liquid slowly, you avoid getting lumps in your batter.

- Make the batter thinner by adding the cooking oil and the remainder of the milk
  while still beating continuously.

- Use a pastry brush to grease the recesses in the 'poffertjes' pan or griddle with corn oil.
  Allow the pan to become quite hot and fill the recesses 2/3 with batter.

- Cook them on a moderate heat until the top of the poffertjes is nearly dry.
  Turn them over, turn the heat up as much as possible, and cook the other side to a golden brown.

- Arrange the poffertjes on a plate, dust them generously with powdered sugar, and serve them hot.

- Remember to grease the recesses every time before you fill them again, otherwise the poffertjes
  will get stuck in the holes.

Poffertjes with yeast

Ingredients

RECIPE FOR ABOUT 50 POFFERTJES
1 egg
300 g flour
4 teaspoons baking powder
15 g fresh yeast
1 1/2 teaspoons salt
3 teaspoons very fine crushed sugar
4 dl milk
corn oil for frying
powdered sugar

Suggestion 1

You can serve the poffertjes with small pots of jam. Choose a whole range of different tastes, and put small spoons in the pots so that people can vary their choice while they eat.

Method of preparation

⊙ Sieve the flour into a large mixing bowl. Add the salt and stir it in. Heat the milk in a saucepan until it is lukewarm.

⊙ Scoop a cup of milk from the saucepan and dissolve the yeast in it. Pour the dissolved yeast into 1 1/2 dl of lukewarm milk. Add the sugar and beat the mixture until it is smooth.

⊙ Make a well in the middle of the flour and slowly pour in the milk while you stir well. Break the egg into it and beat it through the mixture with a whisk. Now add the rest of the milk while continuing to beat well, until you have a smooth batter.

⊙ Cover the bowl with a clean tea towel and leave the batter to rest for 1 hour in a warm and draught-free place.

⊙ Grease the recesses in the poffertjes pan or griddle with corn oil. The best way to do this is with a pastry brush. Allow the pan or griddle to become really hot and fill the recesses 2/3 with batter.

⊙ Cook on a moderate heat until the top of the poffertjes is almost dry. Turn them over, turn the heat up to high, and cook the other side until golden brown. Arrange the poffertjes on a plate, dust them generously with powdered sugar, and serve them hot.

⊙ Remember to grease the recesses with corn oil every time before your refill them, because otherwise they will get stuck in the holes.

Suggestion 2

To vary the taste of the poffertjes you can mix all kinds of ingredients into the batter before you allow it to rest. Some examples:
⊙ Stir a sachet of vanilla sugar into the batter.
⊙ Add about three teaspoons of grated rind of an unsprayed and previously well washed lemon to the batter.
⊙ Mix two teaspoons of cinnamon into the batter.
⊙ Enrich the batter with an aroma. You will find an almost endless choice of small bottles of aromas in the baking section of your store. Read the directions on the label and add the correct number of drops.
⊙ Pour a tablespoonful of liqueur into the batter. You can choose between a fruit liqueur, amaretto, rum or even a sweet liqueur.

Buttermilk rounds

This very old recipe is something very special. It has been handed down from generation to generation, while various chefs have – as is so often the case – made small alterations to it.
We have researched the original recipe.

Ingredients

RECIPE FOR ABOUT 16 ROUNDS
250 g flour
4 teaspoons baking powder
1 pinch of salt
50 g soft butter
1 tablespoon lukewarm water
3 teaspoons dried yeast
2 eggs
1/2 dl buttermilk
flour for rolling out dough
baking paper
jam, whipped cream and butter

Method of preparation

◉ Preheat the oven to 200 °C while you prepare the dough.

◉ Sift the baking powder, the flour and the salt into a large mixing bowl and knead the soft butter through the mixture until it is crumbly.

◉ Dissolve the yeast in a tablespoon of lukewarm water.
Beat the eggs in a separate bowl and mix the dissolved yeast and the buttermilk into them.

◉ Pour this mixture into the flour mixture while stirring continuously.
Make sure you end up with a soft, elastic dough.

◉ Dust the working surface with a little flour and roll out the dough until you have a slab about 1 cm thick.

◉ With a mould or a glass (no more than 5 cm in diameter) cut out round pieces of dough. Shape the remaining dough into a ball, dust it with flour, roll it out again and cut more circles out of it. Repeat this until all the dough has been used up.

◉ Put the circles of dough on a baking tray which has been covered with baking paper. Put the baking tray in the middle of the preheated oven and bake the rounds golden brown in about 15 minutes.

◉ Arrange the hot buttermilk rounds on a plate and serve them hot or cold with whipped cream, jam and butter. They are a delicious treat with coffee or tea, and a unique dessert after lunch.

As they are quite rich, it is better not to serve them in the evening, but keep them firmly shut away in a biscuit tin.

Apple omelette

Ingredients

FOR 4 PERSONS
100 g butter
3 cooking apples
3 cl calvados
5 tablespoons calvados for the marinade
6 eggs
1 pinch of salt
1 tablespoon powdered sugar

In the trade jargon the take-away counter was called the 'flatbed', since it consisted of just one level surface, without decoration or shelving. There was no need to display anything, and no stock to show off, so this counter had a flat top. The waffles and fritters were packed and sold from it.

Method of preparation

⊚ Peel the apples, cut them lengthwise and remove the core. Cut them into very thin slices. Put the slices in a deep plate and pour calvados over them as a marinade.

⊚ Leave to rest for at least 1 hour.

⊚ Melt a tablespoon of butter in a high-rimmed frying pan. Put the apple slices neatly next to each other in the pan and sprinkle them with a few drops of calvados. Braise the apple on a moderate heat until done.

⊚ Take the pan from the heat as soon as the apple is done and let it rest for a moment.

⊚ Meanwhile preheat the oven to 250 °C.

⊚ Beat the eggs in a small bowl. Add a pinch of salt and a teaspoon of powdered sugar.

⊚ Heat the rest of the butter in a pan which is not too large, but has a high rim. Heat the butter well and then add the eggs.

⊚ When the eggs begin to set spoon the braised apples on top. Leave it all to set for a moment.

⊚ Cook the omelette on the other side by turning it. Do this by putting a plate, which is larger than the rim of the pan, on top of the pan. Take the pan from the heat and turn it over, so that the omelette rests on the plate. Next slide the omelette back into the pan and return it to the heat.

⊚ When the omelette is ready, slide it onto an ovenproof dish. Roll up the omelette, put it in the middle of the dish and scatter the remainder of the powdered sugar over it. Leave the omelette in the middle of the oven for about 3 minutes to warm it through.

⊚ Meanwhile heat the remainder of the calvados in a metal kitchen spoon. Take the omelette out of the oven, light the calvados and pour it over the omelette.

⊚ Serve immediately.

Apple dumplings

This centuries-old French recipe reached us by a very roundabout route. Although these days apple dumplings are made in quite a different way, it is nice to follow the original recipe for a change.

Ingredients

RECIPE FOR 4 PERSONS
4 apples
4 slices of frozen flaky pastry
5 teaspoons fine caster sugar
1 pinch of ground cinnamon
1 egg yolk
4 cl calvados
100 g unsweetened cream

There is a lot of uncertainty about the origin of the *oliekoek* (literally 'oil cake', a kind of turnover). At the first stalls to serve them they were called fritures; all kinds of food fried in oil were sold there. At some point doughnuts were added to the assortment, but exactly where or when this occurred is not recorded.
The earliest accounts in the Low Countries that mention these delicacies date from 1877, where there is a reference to Dutch *oliekoeken*.

Method of preparation

⦿ Allow the slices of flaky pastry to defrost for about a quarter of an hour and briefly roll them with a rolling pin to make them supple and pliable. Cut each slice into triangle, as large as possible, which should later cover the whole apple.

⦿ Preheat the oven to 200 °C.

⦿ Peel the apples. Remove the cores with an apple corer or a sharp, pointed knife, but be sure to leave the stalk in place! Cut off the rounded part of the apple at the base so that it will stand upright.

⦿ Mix the caster sugar with the ground cinnamon. Turn the apples upside down and fill the opening from which you have taken the core with this mixture.
Close it with a small lump of leftover flaky pastry.

⦿ Put each apple on a little triangle of pastry with the stalk pointing upwards.
From the top of the apple gather the points of the pastry together, dampen the seams with a little water and stick them neatly together.

⦿ Add a few drops of water to the egg yolk and beat it in a small bowl.
Spread the pastry round the apples with egg yolk. The easiest way to do this is with a pastry brush.

⦿ Dampen a baking tray very lightly with a mist of water. Put the apples in their pastry coat on the baking tray and put this in the middle of the oven. Leave it to cook for about 45 minutes at about 200 °C. The egg yolk will colour the pastry a wonderful gold.

⦿ Leave the apple dumplings to cool for some 5 minutes, and then sprinkle them with the calvados.

⦿ Serve at once with whipped, unsweetened cream.

Tarte Tatin

The cradle of this now world-famous tart is the village of Lamotte-Beuvron in the French department of Loir-et-Cher, where at the end of the nineteenth century Stéphanie and Caroline Tatin ran a small hotel with a celebrated restaurant.

Stéphanie ruled over the kitchen. Chronicles of that time label her as a very inventive chef. The high point for the Tatin sisters' business was the annually recurring hunting season, when both the hotel and the restaurant were always fully booked.

Because one day her kitchen help had not turned up, Stéphanie was left completely on her own one afternoon to prepare the whole dinner. She had to rush to be able to serve all the customers in time and was very nervous. While she was preparing the last dishes for the main course, she realized that she had forgotten to make a dessert. She called on her sister for help.

Caroline began like lightning to peel cooking apples, which she then sprinkled with sugar and put in the oven to cook. Half an hour later Stéphanie opened the oven to see what her sister had prepared. She realized that Caroline had wanted to bake a fruit tart but had forgotten the pastry, so Stéphanie rapidly kneaded a ball of dough, rolled it out and spread it over the apples in the oven.

When the pastry had cooked to a lovely golden colour, Stéphanie took the baking tin out of the oven. She turned it over onto a serving dish, pushed the slices of apple back into the pastry and without batting an eyelid presented the tart as a speciality of the house. The guests pronounced it delicious. The recipe was written down and has since then conquered the world.

In the course of the years changes and additions to the original recipe have, of course, been made. That is a pity, because the original recipe for Tarte Tatin still wins hands down.

Ideally you need a thick-walled pan to make this tart. The pan, made of stainless steel or from non-stick coated material, has to fit in the oven. If you are planning to bake a tart occasionally, you will do better to buy a suitable baking dish that fits perfectly in your oven and can be used for various different recipes.

Our method of preparation follows the original recipe and is intended for 4 to 5 people.

During the most successful period for the MAX waffle stand two bakers made thirty-six waffles every two minutes. When Maximilien Corsael judged that the waffle irons were hot enough and that the dough had rested for long enough, he gave the signal for the bakers to start, after which they went on baking without stopping into the early evening.
On an average afternoon a couple of thousand waffles were consumed; some of them were eaten in the dining room, while some customers queued at the counter to take waffles home, or just to eat them as they went along.

Tarte Tatin (recipe)

Ingredients

RECIPE FOR 4-5 PERSONS

For the pastry:
250 g flour
flour for dusting the work surface
125 g soft butter
1 egg
1 pinch of salt
1 tablespoon caster sugar

For the filling:
12 tablespoons caster sugar
1 kg firm cooking apples
120 g butter

Method of preparation

⊚ Sift the flour into a large mixing bowl and add the salt. Make a well in the middle of the flour, break the egg into it and add the butter. Sprinkle the flour with two tablespoons water. Add the sugar and mix everything carefully with the tips of your fingers.

⊚ Make sure that the mixture gradually becomes firmer. When the dough comes away from the bottom of the bowl, you can take it out. Dust the work surface with flour and put the dough on it. Knead it for about 5 minutes until you have a firm ball.

⊚ Wrap this ball in a clean tea towel and leave it to rest in a cool place (but not the refrigerator or in a draught) for 1 hour and 15 minutes. Sprinkle the bottom of a pan with 10 tablespoons of caster sugar. The layer has to be about 1 cm thick. Sprinkle the sugar, which should be spread out equally, with about 1 dl water.

⊚ Preheat the oven to 200 °C while you prepare the apples. Peel the apples and divide them into quarters. Remove the core from all of them and put the pieces of apple on the sugar in the pan. Melt 100 g butter in a saucepan and pour it over the apples.

⊚ Put the pan with the apples and the sugar on a low to moderate heat. Turn the apples frequently, so that they can absorb the caramelized mass forming at the bottom of the pan. When they are half done, remove the pan from the heat.

⊚ Lift each piece of apple with a spatula and push a little butter under it. Distribute the apples equally again across the bottom of the pan and scatter the remainder of the powdered sugar over it.

⊚ On a work surface dusted with flour, roll out the dough to a thin sheet. Put it on top of the apples and put the pan in the middle of the oven. Bake it at 200 °C for about 1/2 hour, until the pastry is a golden yellow.

⊚ Take the pan out of the oven, put a large serving dish upside down on top of it, and turn the pan, so that the tart is on the dish with the pastry side down. Press the apple pieces down into the pastry with a spatula or wide-bladed knife.

⊚ This delicious tart can be served hot, lukewarm, or even cold.

Choux de Paris

An item from the Consael family's secret book of recipes. Yves' great-grandfather was the first to make the so-called Choux de Paris. They were an immediate hit with the public.
Whereas the well-known éclair has a custard filling, cream puffs are filled with whipped cream. However, these 'Parisian profiteroles' have a delicious filling of crème pâtissière.
This recipe will produce about ten Choux de Paris.

Ingredients

FOR ABOUT 10 CHOUX

For the profiteroles:
100 g butter
125 g flour
5 eggs
1/4 litre water
2 tablespoons chopped almonds
1 pinch of salt
1 tablespoon fine caster sugar
soft butter for the baking tray
powdered sugar for dusting

For the crème pâtissière:
75 g very fine caster sugar
40 g flour
3 egg yolks
1/4 of a vanilla pod
2/3 litre milk

Method of preparation

⊚ Preheat the oven to 220 °C.
Bring the water, the butter, the salt and the sugar to the boil in a large saucepan.

⊚ Sift the flour and add it all at once to the mixture in the pan.
Stir with a wooden spoon until the mixture comes away from the bottom of the pan.

⊚ Remove the pan from the heat and leave it to cool a little. Next stir the four eggs one by one into the mixture. Stir it all very well until you have a pliable batter. If it is too firm, stir in an extra egg.

⊚ Grease a baking tray with a little soft butter.
This is best done by spreading the butter evenly over the tray with a pastry brush.
Put the mixture into a piping bag. Pipe little balls of about 3 cm diameter onto the baking tray.

⊚ Beat the remaining egg in a small bowl. Spread the egg over the éclairs with a pastry brush and sprinkle the chopped almonds over them.

⊚ Put the baking tray with the profiteroles in the oven and bake them golden brown at 220 °C in about 12 minutes. Keep a careful eye on the baking time and remove the profiteroles from the oven as soon as they are golden brown.

⊚ Leave them to cool and meanwhile make the crème pâtissière. Beat the egg yolks together with the sugar in a mixing bowl until the sugar has been completely mixed in with the egg yolk.

⊚ Pour the milk into a sauce pan. Cut the vanilla pod lengthwise in half and put both halves in the milk. Heat it all up together.

Choux de Paris

- When the milk reaches boiling point, pour it all at once into the mixture of egg yolks while you continue to beat it firmly with a whisk. As soon as it has all been very thoroughly mixed, pour the mixture back into the milk pan.

- Leave it on moderate heat while you carry on beating steadily with a whisk. Make sure nothing sticks to the bottom of the saucepan, because otherwise the crème pâtissière will burn.

- After about 5 minutes the mixture will have thickened considerably. Remove the saucepan from the heat and put a piece of aluminium foil on the crème (on the crème, not on the pan!). Leave it to cool like that in a cool but draught-free place.

- Put the cooled crème in a piping bag. Make a small hole at the bottom of the éclairs and fill them with this delicious crème.

- Serve the Choux de Paris on dessert plates and dust them with powdered sugar before serving.

Every time the waffle irons have been thoroughly cleaned, Yves treats them as if they were brand new ones. Before they can be put to work, they must first be heated up and then treated with a special protective coating he has composed for them.
It demands great skill and much experience to keep a waffle iron at the right temperature while you are baking. The gas flame has to be regularly adjusted and the irons must never be allowed to get too hot or too cold. To achieve this you have to move them continually from one place on the gas stove to another.
It usually takes about two hours to get the stock of waffle irons in Yves' kitchens to a suitable temperature to start baking. From all this you can conclude that the secret of the perfectly baked Brussels waffles does not lie only in the composition of the dough, but first and foremost in the make-up of the iron and the art of heating it. So it goes without saying that a waffle baked in an electrically heated iron will never be a true Brussels waffle, as it is when it has been baked on a gas flame.

Pão de Lo

(Portuguese sponge cake)

You may wonder why this recipe is one of Yves' favourites. This is partly because he enjoys experimenting with tastes, and partly because he often talks to people of various nationalities about their favourite desserts. Years ago an elderly Portuguese lady persuaded him to try this recipe. He has been very fond of it ever since .

Pão de Lo dates from the fourteenth century and originated in the generally very sweet Arabian cuisine, which was introduced during the Moorish conquest of Southern Europe. This is why Spain and Portugal today have many desserts which are of Arabic origin.

This spongy cake, which is not as sweet as some other Arabian honey preparations (such as the familiar baklava), owes its name to the fact that after baking it is not firm, but light and soft.

Ingredients

RECIPE FOR 6 PERSONS
10 tablespoons flour
13 tablespoons fine caster sugar
6 eggs
2 tablespoons butter

Method of preparation

⊚ Preheat the oven to 250 °C. Allow the butter to soften and use it to grease a cake tin.
   Use a cake ring, so that you end up with a circular cake without a middle.

⊚ Separate the eggs and put the egg yolks and the egg whites in separate large mixing bowls.
   Beat the egg whites until stiff. Beat the egg yolks until they begin to foam.
   Next beat the egg yolk little by little into the white.

⊚ Add the sugar while beating continuously.
   Then sift the flour into it, while continuing to beat steadily.

⊚ Pour the mixture into the cake tin and bake it in the oven for 45 minutes at 250 °C.
   Prick the cake with a cocktail stick to check if it is cooked.
   If no uncooked cake mixture or cake clings to the cocktail stick, the cake is done.

⊚ Remove the cake from the oven and leave it to cool in the cake tin for 10 minutes.
   Take it out of the tin and leave it to cool down completely on a grid.

In some regions the cake is given a special aroma by adding a little zest from an unsprayed lemon; in other regions a little cinnamon is added to give this cake a specific taste.

Langues de chat

This is a very old Egyptian recipe. Many years ago, when Yves read in a tourist guide book about biscuits shaped like cats' tongues, he consulted an Egyptian chef he knew, who told him that descriptions of Langues de chat *are found in hieroglyphics from the days of the pharaohs. In Egyptian tradition the cat was a sacred animal, and people believed that eating biscuits shaped like a cat's tongue would bring happiness and prosperity.*

Ingredients

FOR ABOUT 20 LANGUES DE CHAT
4 egg whites
10 tablespoons fine flour
5 tablespoons powdered sugar
4 tablespoons whipping cream
3 tablespoons butter
1 pinch of salt

Method of preparation

⊙ Add the salt to the egg whites and beat them to firm peaks.
Sift first the sugar and then the flour while beating them firmly through the egg whites.

⊙ Whip the cream until stiff and mix it through the mixture.
Add a large tablespoon of soft butter and mix everything well.

⊙ Preheat the oven to 220 °C.

⊙ Cover a baking tray with baking paper. Pour narrow, oblong strips of the mixture, about 3 cm in length, on it. Put the baking tray in the oven and leave it to bake for half an hour at 200 °C.

⊙ Take the tray out of the oven and allow the biscuits to cool completely.

If desired, you can pour a little melted chocolate over both ends of each biscuit, which you then leave to set. However, according to the original recipe the langues de chat are served without any garnish with tea (or in our regions with coffee).

A perfectly baked waffle must satisfy two requirements: it must still be a little soft inside, but crisp on the outside.
The proper way to eat a waffle is to scatter icing sugar over it and spread it with fresh butter. Then you cut the waffle into strips. You eat these strips in your fingers, so that you can enjoy the full taste of a fresh waffle.

Violet preserve

This recipe dates from the days of the rule of Charles V, who was born in Ghent on 24 February 1500.
The emperor took great pleasure in richly laden tables and banquets.
He brought the best chefs in the continent of Europe to Ghent to prepare their specialities for him.
Among these rich offerings Yves discovered this special preserve of violets.
You can also use exactly the same recipe for rose petals (and actually we prefer that).

Ingredients

460 g violet petals
1350 g coarse granulated sugar

How to make the preserve

⊙ Pick the petals off the most beautiful violets you can find. Put them in a stone bowl and add the sugar. Crush them with a mortar until everything is well mixed.

⊙ Put the mixture in a cooking pot and heat it on moderate heat. Allow the sugar to melt slowly, and stir occasionally so that nothing sticks to the bottom.

⊙ Leave the preserve to simmer for about another ten minutes after all the sugar has melted. Stir occasionally.

⊙ Remove the pot from the heat and leave it to cool. When cool, spoon the preserve into jars.

You can keep this preserve for a maximum of three weeks in a dark, cool place, or in the vegetable drawer of the refrigerator.

Suggestion

The recipe for rose petals is exactly the same as for violets. The proportions of flowers and sugar is the same too. In southern countries even carnations are picked bare these days to make this kind of preserve. This is not recommended here because carnations tend to be sprayed with insecticide. But you can grow you own small bush carnations to make it.

Whatever kind of flowers you use, take care only to use the flower petals and none of the foliage, pistils or stamens.

At every fair a large alcove or box in the dining room of the big stand was reserved for the fair authorities and for the local dignitaries. In this way they kept on good terms with the authorities, who in their turn made grateful use of the free offerings, which were put in front of them as occupants of these privileged seats.

Egg balls with orange

A recipe from the early Middle Ages, which was tried out for the first time by Juan de la Mata, a famous chef who worked for extremely rich, aristocratic families. This delicacy was served as a snack between meals, and was at the time particularly popular with children.

Ingredients

FOR ABOUT 12 BALLS
4 egg yolks
115 g fine caster sugar
1 teaspoon orange aroma
8 teaspoons of sweet orange preserve
powdered sugar

Method of preparation

⊙ Pour the orange preserve and the orange aroma into a sauce pan and put it on a moderate heat.
Add the sugar and whip it with a whisk into the syrup.

⊙ Push the egg yolks through a sieve into the mixture and stir it well.
Remove the pan from the heat as soon as the mixture has become compact.

⊙ Transfer everything into a small bowl and leave to cool.

⊙ With a teaspoon scoop small lumps out of the cold mixture.
Put them in a bowl of powdered sugar and briefly roll them into small balls.

⊙ Put the balls on a small dish and dust them with a little powdered sugar before serving.

Unlike Belgium today, when the attractions and stalls in kermises and fairs may stay open to the public for as long as they like, in past times a closing hour was laid down. The local constable or responsible authority would go round the whole fair ordering the stallholders to close down.
Because there were still always dignitaries, councillors, the burgomaster or other important people in the last alcove, reserved for important people by the Consael family, the big Etablissement MAX stand often managed to escape this rule. Those responsible for maintaining order did not dare turn out such important personages, and consequently the MAX stand stayed open until they left. As that meant the public, too, could enter to consume their waffles, the big stand usually stayed open until three of four in the morning.
In the long run it obviously became known that you could visit MAX as late as that, and customers would wander in until long after midnight.

Fig tart with rose petals

This recipe is first recorded among the classical Romans.
It is still prepared in Italy in rural districts.

Ingredients

1 kg ripe, sweet figs
a large bowl with fresh petals from red roses
fine caster sugar

Method of preparation

⊙ Carefully cut away the heart (the base of the stalk) of each fig.

⊙ Cover the bottom of a large, rectangular, glass dish with straight sides with a thick layer of rose petals.
Scatter some fine caster sugar over them.

⊙ Put half the figs (without cutting them through) on top of the petals, with the round side uppermost.

⊙ Cover all this generously with a new layer of rose petals, sprinkle more sugar over them and finish off with a second layer of figs.

⊙ Spread a sheet of aluminium foil over the whole surface of the dish.
Gently push it down so that the figs press closely together.
Wrap the entire dish in aluminium foil and put it in the vegetable drawer of the refrigerator.

⊙ Leave to rest for two days.

⊙ Serve a portion on a dessert plate. If desired, finish off with a dot of whipped cream, but this is not really necessary, because this dessert is particularly sweet.

Diabetics sometimes wonder if they should eat waffles. The Brussels waffle made by Etablissement MAX contains no sugar, so diabetics can eat them. If you want a sweeter one, you can dust them with sugar substitutes, which are these days available in powder form.
However, we would definitely advise diabetic patients against eating the Liège waffle, because the waffle mixture is based on more than 50 per cent sugar.

Pears in broth

This rather strange delicacy is particularly popular in Spain and Portugal.
The recipe was written down around 1811 by Francisco Montiño, a chef famous for his desserts
based on fruit, and sweetened meat broths.
On hot summer days these pears in broth taste delicious.

Ingredients

6 fine large pears
1/2 litre meat broth
100 g superfine caster sugar
1/2 tablespoon rice flour
1/2 teaspoon ground cinnamon
200 g ground almonds
1 pinch of salt

Method of preparation

◉ Make 1/2 litre meat stock from a stock cube and strain it through a fine sieve into a medium-sized cooking pot. Add sugar and cinnamon and stir well.

◉ Peel the pears, cut them into quarters and remove the cores. Put the pieces of pear in the stock, bring to the boil and leave to simmer gently for 15 minutes.

◉ Scoop the pears out of the pot and put them next to each other on a serving dish.

◉ Stir the rice flour and the ground almonds into the stock with a whisk. Add a pinch of salt and give everything another good stir.

◉ Pour the resulting sauce generously over the pears, dust with a little powdered sugar and serve at once.

Waffles became popular in Central and Southern Europe at about the same time. In French chronicles of 1270 giving a description of protected trades, we can read that patents were issued to bakers who on Sundays heated up their irons in front of the church, so that they could offer their waffles for sale there.
These waffles were not desserts or confectionery, but savoury snacks. The dough was based on meat, game, fish and poultry. And sometimes you also came across a dough which included crushed pears. The waffle irons were decorated with all kinds of religious symbols which were printed on the waffle in the baking, so that the clergy would be persuaded to give permission for the sale of waffles on Sundays in front of the church.

Fresh fruit wine

The aristocracy of the mid-sixteenth century were very fond of this excellent, cool fruit wine.
This alcoholic drink, combining white wine, fruit and sugar, was served lavishly at banquets.
On a sultry summer evening it is an excellent digestif after a good dinner.

Ingredients

2 litres dry white wine
30 g ground cinnamon
1/4 teaspoon ground nutmeg
1 tablespoon ground ginger
450 g superfine caster sugar
1 lemon
4 purple plums
4 white peaches
4 fresh apricots
a handful of sweet, white grapes

Method of preparation

⊛ Pour the wine into a not too large, tall bowl. Add the cinnamon, nutmeg, ginger and sugar. Stir well.

⊛ Peel the lemon and remove the stones from the plums, peaches and apricots.
Cut the fruit into small pieces.

⊛ Add all the fruit to the wine, stir well and cover with cling film to protect the contents from the open air.
Put the bowl into the refrigerator for a minimum of 1 1/2 hours.

⊛ Pour the cool mixture through a sieve into a jug and serve the fruit wine in cold glasses.

It would be nice if present-day customers could reflect for a moment on the rituals of the past, which were associated with the consumption of waffles. Because Yves prepares everything in the original, traditional way, you can only order waffles during a limited period of time. The irons must be at an ideal temperature, and can only be kept at this temperature for a few hours. When a waffle iron has cooled down, it often takes as long as an hour to bring it back to the right temperature. Because it literally becomes a case of 'heating up' in that event, you also risk having a less tasty waffle. This is why in Etablissement MAX you can only order fresh waffles between 2 and 6 o'clock in the afternoon, the time when they make sure to keep the waffle irons at the right temperature.

www.lannoo.com

Lannoo Publishers
Kasteelstraat 97 – B-8700 Tielt
lannoo@lannoo.be
De Wetstraat 1 – NL-6814 AN Arnhem
info@terralannoo.nl

TEXTS
Jan Gheysens

FOREWORD
Koen Crucke

PHOTOGRAPHY
Tom Swalens, except pp. 10 to 25: Archive Yves Van Maldeghem, MAX

STYLING
Debby De Mangelaere

WITH THANKS TO
Koffies De Draak, Carlsberg

TRANSLATION
Alastair and Cora Weir

LAYOUT
quod. voor de vorm. – www.quod.be

© Lannoo Publishers, Tielt, 2006
D/2006/45/261 – NUR 441
ISBN 10: 90 209 6661 8
ISBN 13: 978 90 209 6661 9

Printed and bound by Lannoo Printers, Tielt, 2006

All rights reserved. No part of this book may be reproduced, stored in a retrieval system, or transmitted in any form or by any means, electronic, electrostatic, magnetic tape, mechanical, photocopying, recording or otherwise, without the prior permission in writing of the publisher.

THOMSON
—————
RSE TECHNOLOGY

ssional ■ Trade ■ Reference

GW00647351

CUBASE SX/SL 2
P O W E R !

By Robert Guérin

DOWNLOADS
AVAILABLE

INCLUDES CD-ROM

REE CSi Limited Edition CD

RMAN

Cubase SX/SL 2 Power!

Copyright ©2004 Muska & Lipman Publishing, a division of Course Technology.
All rights reserved. No part of this book may be reproduced by any means without written permission from the publisher, except for brief passages for review purposes. Address all permission requests to the publisher.

All copyrights and trademarks used as examples or references in this book are retained by their individual owners.

Credits: Senior Marketing Manager, Sarah O'Donnell; Marketing Manager, Heather Hurley; Manager of Editorial Services, Heather Talbot; Acquisitions Editor, Todd Jensen; Senior Editor, Mark Garvey; Associate Marketing Manager, Kristin Eisenzopf; Retail Market Coordinator, Sarah Dubois; Production and Copy Editor, Marta Justak; Technical Editor, Greg Ondo; Proofreader, Deana Casamento; Cover Designer, Nancy Goulet; Interior Design and Layout, Jill Flores; Indexer, Kelly Talbot.

Publisher: Stacy L. Hiquet

Technology and the Internet are constantly changing, and by necessity of the lapse of time between the writing and distribution of this book, some aspects might be out of date. Accordingly, the author and publisher assume no responsibility for actions taken by readers based upon the contents of this book.

Library of Congress Catalog Number: 2003115713

ISBN: 1-59200-235-8

5 4 3 2

Educational facilities, companies, and organizations interested in multiple copies or licensing of this book should contact the publisher for quantity discount information. Training manuals, CD-ROMs, and portions of this book are also available individually or can be tailored for specific needs.

MUSKA&LIPMAN

Muska & Lipman Publishing,
a Division of Course Technology
25 Thomson Place
Boston, MA 02210
www.courseptr.com
publisher@muskalipman.com

About the Author

Robert Guérin has been a composer for the past 15 years and a music enthusiast since 1976, Robert has worked on different personal and commercial projects such as feature and short films, television themes, as well as educational and corporate videos. Composing, arranging, playing, recording, and mixing most of his material, he has developed work habits that allow him to be creative without losing a sense of efficiency.

As a professor, Robert has put together five courses covering a wide range of topics, such as computer software for musicians, digital audio technologies, sound on the Web, sound in multimedia productions, how to get job interviews when you're a musician, hard disk recording, and many more topics. He has been a program coordinator at Trebas Institute in Montreal and a part-time professor at Vanier College, also in Montreal. Robert has developed online courses on sound integration in Web pages and has written numerous articles for audio- and music-related online magazines.

As an entrepreneur, he has developed many skills necessary in today's cultural world. Robert has expanded his knowledge and expertise to ensure his business survival by adopting new multimedia and Web related technologies.

Robert is also the author of three other books with Muska & Lipman: *Cubase VST Power!, Cubase SX Power!,* and *MIDI Power!* He is currently working on a new book called *Inside the Recording Studio*, which should be released in 2004.

Acknowledgments

I would like to give thanks to everyone who helped and supported me throughout the writing process, which includes all the staff at Course Technology (Mark, Todd, and Marta) and the staff at Steinberg Germany (Lars Baumann, Helge Vogt, Arnd Kaiser, and, of course, Karl Steinberg).

Merci à tous!

Contents

7—MIDI and Audio Recording 161

8—MIDI Editing Windows 189

12—Mixer and Channel Settings 299

13—Working with Automation 325

xii

Introduction

Cubase has been around for a while now. I remember using its ancestor, the Pro 24 software on my Atari ST in 1987 to create musical arrangements for composition assignments during my university training years. Since then, many things have changed, and Cubase has made the transition from a MIDI sequencer to a Virtual Studio Technology (VST) software. This updated version of Cubase SX and SL grows on the knowledge that Steinberg has acquired from years of user comments like yours and the stable audio engine it developed for its Nuendo application. It also reintroduced some features previous VST users loved, but that had been removed in the first SX/SL version, like Warp tool, which is similar to the Cuepoints/Hitpoints in the Mastertrack of VST 5.1. If you are new to Cubase, you can expect this software to help you through your entire musical creation process. If you are a veteran Cubase user, you will find many of the things you loved and a few new features that are worth the upgrade. The Freeze function, which allows you to render VST instrument tracks temporarily to save CPU power, is definitely one of those features that make it worth upgrading. Hopefully, in both cases, this book will help you to get the most out of this great tool.

Like any software, as it allows you to do more things and do them in a more intuitive way, the learning curve becomes more and more abrupt. You will find very extensive documentation on all available features found in Cubase on the CD-ROM provided with the software (or installed in the Documentation folder in the Cubase program folder), but you will have to sift through over 1400 pages of electronic format documentation. For most users, this might seem like an overwhelming task. This book will provide you with the most important features, as well as some lesser-known features, in step-by-step examples that include online tutorial files to practice what you have learned in many of the chapters.

Beyond describing the features of the program and how they work, I address the "why" to use certain features and "when" they can become useful to you. All of the Cubase SL features are included in Cubase SX, so for those of you who have this version of the software, the book should address your questions as well. Since Cubase is also available in both Macintosh and PC versions in quite similar environments, it doesn't really matter which platform you are using—the way to use the features and functions will be the same.

I offer you my 15 years of experience working with the software, as well as my insight into some tips and tricks that have been very useful in getting the job done throughout these years. As a professor and program coordinator in sound design vocational schools in Canada, I have answered questions from many students who have wanted to work with this tool to create music. I have drawn from their most frequently asked question list and answered them in a way that I hope you will find enlightening.

Enjoy.

About Online Exercises

At the end of Chapters 4 through 13 and Chapter 16, you will find a section called "Now You Try It." These sections refer to online exercises that you will find at the following address:

▶ http://www.wavedesigners.com

At this address, you will find a link for Cubase Exercises. Follow this link and then read the instructions from there. These exercises will give you a chance to practice what you have learned during the chapter. Most of the steps needed to perform the tasks in the exercises are described in this book, so you may want to keep your book close by if you are not familiar with these procedures at the beginning. Each chapter available contains a series of steps that you can follow while online or that you can print to work offline. Along with these steps, you will find a content file to download. This content file contains a saved Cubase Project and, in some cases, media content required for the exercises. It is therefore important that you download the files first, save them on your hard drive, and load them up in Cubase before you start working on the exercises themselves. You may also download all the content files needed for all the exercises at once. You will find a link to this file on the same site.

You will need to use a file decompression utility to access the content found inside some of the downloadable documents; specifically, the content with zip (for PC users) or sit (for Mac users). These files contain not only a Cubase Project file, but also additional content files, such as audio or MIDI files that are used in the exercises. PC users working under XP can use the built-in Zip decompression utility to decompress these files, while OS X users can also use the built-in StuffIt utility. You can also download these applications at one of the following addresses:

▶ Download a copy of WinZip at www.winzip.com.
▶ Download StuffIt at www.stuffit.com.

Make sure the media files (such as audio files) are located inside an audio folder under your project's folder. If for some reason Cubase can't find the audio files, use the Find Missing Files option in the Pool menu to locate these files on your hard disk.

How This Book Is Organized

Let's take a look at what you will find in these pages through a short description of each chapter. At the end of this book, you will also find six appendices that will surely come in handy once you understood what MIDI is all about.

▶ **Chapter 1, Introducing Cubase:** This chapter contains an overview of MIDI and digital audio to make sure you understand the underlying concepts related to Cubase as a digital audio multitrack recorder and MIDI sequencer.

▶ **Chapter 2, A Guided Tour of Cubase SX/SL:** This chapter shows you most of the panels, windows, and dialog boxes you will encounter in your Cubase projects. We will look at how to access each one of these windows and give a short description of their purpose in Cubase.

▶ **Chapter 3, Getting Started:** Here we will look at how your computer needs to be configured in order to ensure the best possible results when using Cubase.

▶ **Chapter 4, Navigating the Project Window:** Finding your way around a project means that you can get to a part of your project easily, without having to rely on scrollbars all the time. We will look at how you can achieve this through the use of markers and Transport panel functions. You'll get an overview of the different context menus available in most of the Cubase windows and panels.

▶ **Chapter 5, Working with Tracks:** When working on a project, you will be using the Project window, which is your main workspace. It is important to define each area of this window and understand why, when, and how to use it. We will also discuss the use of VST instruments and external MIDI device configurations so that Cubase can understand which tools you use outside the computer. Once your external devices are configured in Cubase, you will be able to control them directly from Cubase.

▶ **Chapter 6, Track Classes:** Unlike an audio multitrack recorder, Cubase records not only digital audio, but also MIDI events and automation. It does so through several Track classes. Each class of track allows you to perform different tasks. This chapter discusses each one of these Track classes so that you will know when to use them in your project. This chapter will also include information on effects available in each Track class.

▶ **Chapter 7, MIDI and Audio Recording:** This chapter will look at the process of getting content into Cubase: recording MIDI and audio events, as well as the Import feature. We will also look at the quantizing concept.

▶ **Chapter 8, MIDI Editing Windows:** This chapter focuses on the different MIDI editing environments found inside Cubase.

▶ **Chapter 9, Audio Editing:** This is the audio version of Chapter 8, where all the audio editing windows are discussed.

▶ **Chapter 10, Browsing and Processing Options:** In this chapter, we look at a few new editing environments, such as the Project Browser and the Offline Process History panel. We will also explain how and why you should use offline audio processes, rather than adding audio effects that are processed in real time as you play the project.

▶ **Chapter 11, Project Editing:** This chapter offers information on the audio editing principles (nondestructive editing vs. destructive editing) used in Cubase. It also discusses the variety of ways you can zoom in and out of your work by using shortcuts and menu options. Furthermore, the chapter looks at the functions and options found under the MIDI and Edit menus, as well as editing events directly in the Project window. The Project window is where your arrangement takes place.

▶ **Chapter 12, Mixer and Channel Settings:** Once you have recorded and edited audio and MIDI events, the next most important task is to start thinking about mixing them. Here you will find information on how to use the mixer and most importantly, what you can expect the mixer to do for you. This implies a look at the different channel types represented in the mixer, as well as different mixer routings available when using groups and effects.

► **Chapter 13, Working with Automation:** Cubase not only offers you a recording and editing environment for your musical projects, but it also allows you to automate a mix. It does so by creating automation subtracks to tracks containing audio or MIDI events. We will look at how to use these automation subtracks and how to create and edit automation to make sure your musical mix sounds as good as you hear it.

► **Chapter 14, Working in Sync:** Synchronization today implies many things. Here we will try to define how it relates to Cubase and how you can get Cubase to work in sync with other devices, both inside the computer and outside of it. We will also discuss how to use the VST System Link to get different computers running a compatible application to work together as one big studio system that stays in perfect synchronization without using network connections.

► **Chapter 15, Mixdown and Mastering:** Once all is done, you need to print your final mix to a format that you can distribute to people who don't have Cubase. Getting your music out there is almost as important as making it. With this in mind, this chapter looks at how you can create a mixdown of your project so that it can be mastered, converted, and distributed on a CD or on the Web.

► **Chapter 16, Score Editing:** Creating musical scores with MIDI tracks in your project can produce high quality results. We will take a look at how the score functions work inside Cubase and what you need to do to convert your music into printable notes on a piece of paper.

► **Appendix A, The How To Do It Reference Guide:** This appendix gives you a quick reference to all the "How To" sections discussed inside the book, organizing them into simple to use and musician-oriented categories so that you can quickly find what you are looking for.

► **Appendix B, Using MIDI Effects:** Here you will find a description of the MIDI effects and how they can be used on MIDI tracks for both technical and creative purposes.

► **Appendix C, Logical Editing:** For the logical musician that lies inside of you, here is the Logical Editor found in Cubase. This appendix describes how you can use this tool to edit MIDI events in a way that may take much longer in other editing windows.

► **Appendix D, Optimizing Through Customizing:** Sometimes, it's easier when you can configure Cubase to respond the way you want it to. This appendix offers you a few solutions on how you can customize certain parameters so that they do exactly that.

► **Appendix E, Surround Mixing in SX:** SX users will come across surround sound capabilities. This appendix describes how you can use these features to create surround sound mixes and output your mixes to a suitable multichannel format.

► **Appendix F, Cubase Resources on the Web:** For those of you who would like to find out more on Cubase or have practical questions, you will find additional resources related to Cubase here.

So there you have it. I hope you will enjoy this book as much as I think you will.

Keeping the Book's Content Current

Everyone involved with this book has worked hard to make it complete and accurate. But as we all know, technology changes rapidly, and a small number of errors may have crept in. If you find any errors, have suggestions for future editions, have questions about the book or other topics, or simply would like to find out more about Cubase or audio-related subjects, please visit the support Web site at the following address:

▶ **www.wavedesigners.com**

1

Introducing Cubase

Before starting your work in Cubase, it is important to understand what Cubase is all about, what it can do, and how different MIDI and digital audio really are. So, in this chapter, you will learn about these and gain a better understanding of some basic MIDI and digital audio principals.

Here's a summary of what you will learn in this chapter:

▶ How Cubase evolved through the years.

▶ An overview of Cubase's basic concepts.

▶ A brief introduction to MIDI fundamentals.

▶ A brief introduction to digital audio fundamentals.

▶ How sound is digitized and what the parameters are that affect the quality of your digital audio recording.

▶ How MIDI and digital audio are handled inside Cubase.

▶ Understanding MIDI tracks, ports, channels, inputs, and outputs.

▶ What are audio tracks, channels, inputs, and outputs?

▶ What is the basic concept behind 32-bit floating-point digital audio recording?

▶ Why the sound card you use affects the quality of your digital audio recording.

What Is Cubase?

Cubase is a toolbox for musicians. In that toolbox, you will find tools to record, edit, mix, and publish MIDI and audio information, as well as tools to convert MIDI into printable sheet music.

In 1984, Steinberg created its first MIDI sequencer, which became known in 1989 as *Cubase*. This tool was designed to help musicians capture their performances in a MIDI sequencer. With the advent of MIDI, the computer could talk to musical instruments and vice versa. At that time, the processing power of computers was insufficient to properly record digital audio, so, musicians had to wait another 10 years before they could record audio digitally by using a computer. Steinberg was one of the first companies to develop an integrated system that could record to both MIDI and digital audio.

In 1996, Cubase became not only a MIDI sequencer but also a full audio production tool, contributing in many ways to the development and democratization of the creative process that lies inside every musician. Cubase VST (Virtual Studio Technology), the predecessor to Cubase SX, made this possible by providing the necessary software tools, replacing many hardware components with its software equivalent. Cubase SX/SL 1.0 integrated features that were developed in earlier versions, added new features, and streamlined them in a new, easier-than-ever interface. With the release of Cubase SX/SL 2, the earlier advancements have been refined even further, allowing you to work with a more mature piece of software. For example, you can now render temporary versions of your MIDI tracks passing through VST instruments to free up resources. You can also use the Time Warp tool to match tempo-based events with visual cues when working with video content. Another cool editing feature new to SX/SL 2.0 is the ability to repeat parts or events in a track by using the Pencil tool. These are just a few of the new features that you will find in this new version. Here is an overview of these tools:

▶ **MIDI recording environment**. Cubase records and plays back MIDI information. This is the backbone of the music creation process since MIDI still is the most flexible way available to record musical ideas and edit them later.

▶ **MIDI editing environment**. Once your MIDI information is recorded, you can edit it using one of many editing windows available in Cubase.

▶ **Virtual Instruments**. If you don't own external sound modules, Cubase provides you with a way to generate sounds using a format called *VST instruments*, which is a virtual instrument (a software emulation of a synthesizer). This synthesizer resides inside your computer and uses your sound card to generate its sounds. You no longer need to purchase expensive synthesizer modules, since they are part of your "Virtual Studio" environment.

▶ **Audio recording environment**. Cubase is a very powerful yet straightforward multitrack recorder that uses your computer's components as a digital audio workstation.

▶ **Audio editing environment**. After your sound is captured on disk, Cubase provides all the tools necessary to cut, copy, paste, punch in, punch out, enhance, and manipulate your audio signals in an intuitive working environment.

▶ **Mixing environment**. Once you have recorded, edited, and manipulated your MIDI and audio information, you can mix every track by using a virtual mixing console not unlike its hardware counterpart. This virtual mixer can accommodate multiple buses, multiple effects, MIDI tracks, virtual instrument tracks, groups, and audio tracks. Finally, you can automate your mix easily and create complex mixes without leaving your computer. And, if mixing with your mouse is not your cup of tea, you can connect one of several compatible hardware controllers to get a more interesting tactile experience during your mixing process.

▶ **Effects galore**. Using the built-in audio and MIDI effects, adding third-party effects, or using effects already present on your system (like the DirectX effects available in Windows), you can color your sound in a wide variety of ways. The Macintosh version supports only VST effects. Your imagination is your only barrier here.

▶ **Multimedia production environment**. Along with audio production, Cubase offers many synchronization tools useful in multimedia productions and video productions, making it a great postproduction environment for today's producers. Cubase now supports more import and export formats than ever, making it a great tool to prepare content for the Web, as well as for high quality surround (SX only) productions.

A Brief Overview of MIDI

MIDI stands for "Musical Instrument Digital Interface." It represents two things: First, MIDI is a communication system used to transmit information from one MIDI-compatible device to another. These devices include musical instruments (samplers, synthesizers, sound modules, drum machines) and computers (or other hardware devices, such as synchronizers). Second, it represents the hardware. the ports and jacks found on all MIDI instruments and the MIDI cables connecting them to allow the transmission of musical data. Each time a key is pressed or a wheel is moved, one or more bytes are sent out from a device's MIDI out port. Other devices connected to that sending device are looking for those bytes to come over the wire, which are then translated back into commands for the device to obey.

MIDI sends information at a rate of 31,250 bps (or bits per second). This is called MIDI's *baud rate*. Since MIDI is transferred through a serial port, it sends information one bit at a time. Every MIDI message uses 10 bits of data (eight for the information and two for error correction), which means that MIDI sends about 3,906 bytes of data every second (31,250 bps divided by 8 bits to convert into bytes). If you compare this with the 176,400 bytes (or 172.3 kilobytes) transfer rate that digital audio requires when recording or playing back CD-quality sound without compression, MIDI may seem very slow. But, in reality, it's fast enough for what it needs to transfer. At this speed, you could play approximately 500 MIDI notes per second.

What Does MIDI Transmit?

MIDI sends or receives the following information:

▶ Events related to your performance, such as a note played or released.

▶ Parameters for these actions, such as the channel setting. Each MIDI cable or port can support up to sixteen channels of information, much like having up to sixteen separate instruments playing at once.

▶ Wheels and pedal controls (pitch bend wheels, modulation wheels, sustain pedals, and switch pedals).

▶ Key pressures of pressed keys, also known as *Aftertouch* information, sent by the controller keyboard or by the sequencer to a sound module. Note that not all keyboards support this function, but when they do, the information is sent as MIDI data.

▶ Program changes (or patch changes), as well as sound bank selections.

▶ Synchronization for MIDI devices that have built-in timing clocks. These timing clocks may determine the desired tempo of a drum machine, for example. Through synchronization, MIDI devices can also follow or trigger other devices or applications such as sequencers or drum machines, making sure each one stays in sync with the "master" MIDI clock.

▶ Special information, also called *System Exclusive messages*, used to alter synthesizer parameters and control the transport of System Exclusive-compatible multitrack recorders.

▶ MIDI Time Code or MTC, which is a way for MIDI-compatible devices to lock to a SMPTE device. a translation of SMPTE into something MIDI devices can understand.

MIDI transmits performance *data*, not sound. You can think of MIDI as an old player piano using a paper roll. The holes in the paper roll marked the moments at which the musician played the notes, but the holes themselves were not the sounds. MIDI information is transmitted in much the same way, capturing the performance of the musician but not the sound of the instrument on which he or she played. In order to hear the notes that MIDI data signifies, you will always need some kind of sound module that can reproduce the musical events recorded in MIDI. This sound module could be an external synthesizer module, a sampler, a virtual synthesizer inside your SX software, or even the synthesizer chip on your sound card. This is precisely one of the types of information Cubase allows you to work with—recording a musical performance through your computer, using a keyboard to trigger the events, and Cubase as the recording device and the sound generator, thus creating a virtual paper roll inside the application.

MIDI Connectors

MIDI devices typically have either two or three MIDI-connector plugs: In and Out, or In, Out, and Thru. Usually, two-port configurations are reserved for computer-related hardware (see left side of Figure 1.1), as well as software-based synthesizers. This is due to the fact that the output connector can be switched within a software application, usually to act as a MIDI output or as a MIDI thru connection. Hardware devices, on the other hand, will typically host the three-connector configuration, as seen on the right side of Figure 1.1.

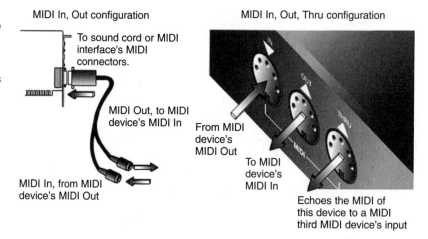

Figure 1.1
On the left is an example of a two-connector configuration typical of computer MIDI interfaces. On the right is a three-connector configuration typical of keyboards and sound modules.

MIDI In, Out configuration

To sound cord or MIDI interface's MIDI connectors.

MIDI Out, to MIDI device's MIDI In

MIDI In, from MIDI device's MIDI Out

MIDI In, Out, Thru configuration

From MIDI device's MIDI Out

To MIDI device's MIDI In

Echoes the MIDI of this device to a MIDI third MIDI device's input

MIDI Out

MIDI does not transmit sound over wires the way audio components in a sound system do. Instead, MIDI sends a message capsule that contains an identifier portion and its associated parameters. For example, when you play a note, the identifier would be that this is a "note on" event, and the parameters would represent the note number corresponding to the key you pressed, along with a velocity parameter indicating how hard you hit that note.

As you play on a MIDI keyboard, the computer in the instrument examines your performance. The instrument's computer then converts the performance into a stream of MIDI code that translates your actions. That information is sent out over an instrument's MIDI output to other synthesizers that reproduce the performance using their own sounds.

A MIDI output will not echo (retransmit) any MIDI events your device receives from its MIDI input. If you wish to do so, you will need to use the MIDI Thru connector, which is described below.

MIDI In

MIDI keyboards can be viewed as two machines in one (see Figure 1.2):

▶ A MIDI interface: The computer processor that monitors the keyboard, program memory and front panel displays, and MIDI ports.

▶ A sound module: The part under the control of the onboard computer, the electronics that actually make the sounds.

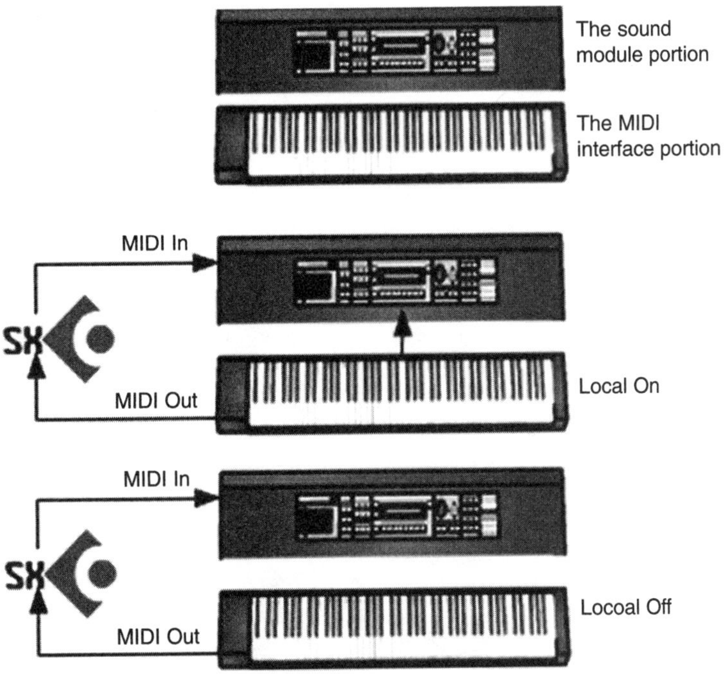

Figure 1.2
Configuring your
keyboard's MIDI input.

The sound module portion

The MIDI interface portion

MIDI In

MIDI Out

Local On

MIDI In

MIDI Out

Locoal Off

The MIDI input receives incoming MIDI information and sends it to the instrument's computer. The computer analyzes and acts upon the information in much the same way as a performance on the original instrument, such as pressing a key to play notes. It makes no difference to the sound-making parts of a synthesizer whether the command to play notes comes from a key press on the instrument itself or as a command from other MIDI devices.

When you are working with a sequencer such as Cubase, it is recommended that you set your keyboard's Local properties to *off* since both Cubase and the keyboard would be sending MIDI information to the sound module portion of your keyboard if your keyboard was connected to Cubase through MIDI. The local setting on a keyboard tells this keyboard to play the sounds directly when you press the keys when it is set to on and does not play the sounds when it is set to *off*. In other words, setting it to *off* will disconnect the bridge that exists inside your keyboard between the actual MIDI input (the keyboard) and the sound module part that allows you to hear the keyboard's sounds as you play the keys.

When using Cubase, you will use your keyboard to send MIDI to it through this keyboard's MIDI Out. Cubase will then record the information you play and send it back to your keyboard through its MIDI In connector. If your keyboard's MIDI setting is not set to local off, the sound module portion of your keyboard will play the sounds twice: once when you play the notes on your keyboard and once when Cubase sends the MIDI information back to it.

On the other hand, if you have a sound module without a keyboard, you will not need to take this precaution, since there is no MIDI being sent to the device's MIDI input besides what is connected to this input.

MIDI Thru

MIDI Thru retransmits the MIDI data that came through the MIDI input of a device so that it can be received by another device in a chain. An important concept to understand when putting together a MIDI-based music system is that anything played on a keyboard goes only to the MIDI Out and not to the MIDI Thru. This third port is very useful when you want to avoid MIDI loops when hooking your MIDI devices together.

A MIDI loop occurs when MIDI information is sent from one instrument to another and then back to the initial instrument. This will cause the instrument to play each note twice and, in some cases, will cause a feedback of MIDI data that could potentially cause your sequencer to crash.

If you have a MIDI patch bay or a multiport MIDI interface—MIDI devices with multiple MIDI inputs and outputs called MIDI ports—you are better off using a separate MIDI output for each connected device, thus reducing the amount of information flowing in a single MIDI cable. Each MIDI port in a MIDI setup sends or receives up to sixteen MIDI channels. For example, if you are using a MIDI interface with four MIDI ports, you will have four MIDI inputs and four MIDI outputs and will have control over 64 MIDI channels. If you do not own a multiport or MIDI patch bay, daisy-chaining MIDI devices using the MIDI Thru socket is your best bet (see Figure 1.3).

Figure 1.3
Using the MIDI Thru
connector to hook
multiple MIDI devices
together.

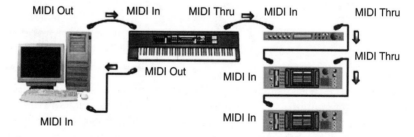

A Brief Overview of Digital Audio

If analog recording helped bring the industry to where it is today, digital recording will help carry it until the next technological milestone. With computers and processing chips becoming more and more efficient in transforming information, audio developers saw the potential this new technology could offer. Fifty years later, digital audio has proven itself to be a great tool helping us with recording, restoration, creation, and editing.

If the quality of digital components in the late eighties and early nineties was not up to par with the high end analog technology, the new digital standards are promising much greater fidelity than even the best analog recorders. At this point, the advantage of digital audio is clear. And for those who miss the "analog feel," it is possible to marry the two technologies to achieve the best possible results.

Understanding how sound is transformed into digital audio will help your recording, editing, and mixing sessions. If you understand the process, you will be in a better position to predict and control the result. This will save you time and most likely produce better results.

Digital audio recordings, like analog audio recordings, are not all created equal. Recording with higher digital resolutions and superior equipment (analog-to-digital converters) in conjunction with the technology available in Cubase SX/SL will allow you to create better-sounding results. Let's look at how this works and how digital recordings are different from analog recordings.

What Is Analog Sound?

When a musical instrument is played, it vibrates. Examples of this include the string of a violin, the skin of a drum, and even the cone of a loudspeaker. This vibration is transferred to the molecules of the air, which carry the sound to our ears. Receiving the sound, our eardrums vibrate, moving back and forth anywhere between 20 and 20,000 times every second. A sound's rate of vibration is called its frequency and is measured in hertz. (The human range of hearing is typically from 20 Hz to 20 kHz (kilohertz).) If the frequency of the vibration is slow, we hear a low note; if the frequency is fast, we hear a high note. If the vibration is gentle, making the air move back and forth only a little, we hear a soft sound. This movement is known as amplitude. If the amplitude is high, making the windows rattle, we hear a loud sound!

If you were to graph air movement against time, you could draw a picture of the sound. This is called a *waveform*. You can see a very simple waveform at low amplitude at left in Figure 1.4. The middle waveform is the same sound, but much louder (higher amplitude). Finally, the waveform on the right is a musical instrument, which contains harmonics—a wider range of simultaneous frequencies. In all of these waveforms, there is one constant: The horizontal axis always represents time and the vertical axis always represents amplitude.

Figure 1.4
The vertical axis represents the amplitude of a waveform and the horizontal axis represents time.

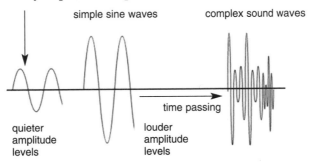

Real life sounds don't consist of just one frequency but of many frequencies mixed together at different levels of amplitude (loudness). This is what makes a musical sound interesting. Despite its complexity, a waveform can be represented by a graph. At any given time, the waveform has a measurable amplitude. If we can capture this "picture" and then reproduce it, we've succeeded in our goal of recording sound.

A gramophone record does this in an easily visible way. Set up a mechanism that transfers air vibration (sound) into the mechanical vibration of a steel needle. Let the needle draw the waveform onto a groove in tinfoil or wax. "Read" the wiggles in this groove with a similar needle. Amplify the vibration as best you can. Well done, Mr. Edison!

Instead of wiggles in a groove, you might decide to store the waveform as patterns of magnetism on recording tape. But either way, you're trying to draw an exact picture of the waveform. You're making an analog recording by using a continuous stream of information. This is different from digital audio recordings, as you will see later in this chapter.

The second dimension of sound is amplitude, or the intensity of molecule displacement. When many molecules are moved, the sound will be louder. Inversely, if few molecules are moved in space, the sound is softer. Amplitude is measured in volts, because this displacement of molecules creates energy. When the energy is positive, it pushes molecules forward, making the line in Figure 1.4 move upward. When the energy is negative, it pushes the molecules backwards, making the line go downward. When the line is near the center, it means that fewer molecules are being moved around. That's why the sound appears to be quieter.

Space is a third dimension to sound. This dimension does not have its own axis because it is usually the result of amplitude variations through time, but the space will affect the waveform itself. In other words, the space will affect the amplitude of a sound through time. This will be important when we talk about effects and microphone placement when recording or mixing digital audio. But suffice it to say now that the environment in which sound occurs has a great influence on how we will perceive the sound.

What Is Digital Audio?

Where analog sound is a continuous variation of the molecules of air traveling through space creating a sound's energy, the digital sound consists in a discrete—noncontinuous—sampling of this variation. In digital audio, there is no such thing as continuous—only the illusion of continuum.

In 1928, mathematician Harry Nyquist developed a theory based on his finding that he could reproduce a waveform if he could sample the variation of sound at least twice in every period of that waveform. A period is a full cycle of the sound (see Figure 1.5) measured in hertz (this name was given in honor of Heinrich hertz, who developed another theory regarding the relation between sound cycles and their frequency in 1888). So, if you have a sound that has 20 Hz, you need at least 40 samples to reproduce it. The value captured by the sample is the voltage of that sound at a specific point in time. Obviously, in the 1920s, computers were not around to keep the large number of values needed to reproduce this theory adequately, but as you probably guessed, we do have this technology available now.

How Sampling Works

In the analog world, the amplitude is measured as a voltage value. In the digital world, this value is quantified and stored as a number. In the computer world, numbers are stored as binary memory units called bits. The more bits you have, the longer this number will be. Longer numbers are also synonymous with more precise representations of the original voltage values the digital audio was meant to store. In other words, every bit keeps the value of the amplitude (or voltage) as

Figure 1.5
The bits in a digital recording will store a discrete amplitude value, and the frequency at which these amplitude values are stored in memory as they fluctuate through time is called the sampling frequency.

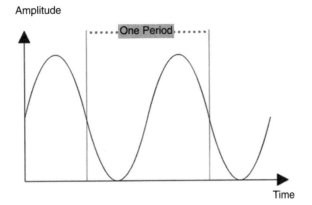

a binary number. The more bits you have, the more values you have. You may compare this with color depth in digital pictures. When you have eight bits of color, you have a 256-color palette, a 16-bit resolution yields over 65,000 colors, a 24-bit resolution offers over 16.7 million colors, and so on. In sound, colors are replaced by voltage values. The higher the resolution in bit depth, the smaller the increments are between these voltage values. If you were to calculate the distance between New York and Paris using the same accuracy as the one provided by a 24-bit digital recording system, you would be accurate within a foot (13.29 inches or 0.34 meter to be precise). That's an accuracy of 0.0000005%! It would be fair to assume that most high resolution digital audio systems are fairly accurate at reproducing amplitude variations of an audio signal.

This also means that the more increments you have, the less noise your amplifier will create as it moves from one value to another.

Because the computer cannot make the in-between values, it jumps from one value to the next, creating noise-like artifacts, also called *digital distortion*. This is not something you want in your sound. So, the more values you have to represent different amplitudes, the more closely your sound will resemble the original analog signal in terms of amplitude variation. Time (measured in hertz) is the frequency at which you capture and store these voltage values, or bits. Like amplitude (bits), the frequency greatly affects the quality of your sound. As mentioned earlier, Nyquist said that you needed two samples per period of the waveform to be able to reproduce it, which means that if you want to reproduce a sound of 100 Hz, or 100 vibrations per second, you need 200 samples. Recording the amplitude of a sound through time is called your sampling, and since it is done at a specific interval, it is referred to as a sampling frequency. Like the frequency of your sound, it is also measured in hertz. In reality, complex sounds and high frequencies require much higher sampling frequencies than the one mentioned above. Because most audio components, such as amplifiers and speakers, can reproduce sounds ranging from 20 Hz to 20 kHz, the sampling frequency standard for compact disc digital audio was fixed at 44.1 kHz—a little bit more than twice the highest frequency produced by your monitoring system.

The first thing you notice when you change the sampling rate of a sound is that with higher sampling rates (more samples) you get a sharper, crisper sound with better definition and fewer artifacts. With lower sampling rates (fewer samples) you get a duller, mushier, and less defined sound. Why is this? Well, since you need twice as many samples as there are frequencies in your sound, the higher the sampling frequency, the higher the harmonics will be; and that's where the sound qualities mentioned above are found. When you reduce the sampling rate, you also reduce the bandwidth captured by the digital audio recording system. If your sampling rate is too low, you not only lose harmonics but fundamentals as well. And this will change the tonal quality of the sound altogether.

Figure 1.6 shows two sampling formats. The one on the left uses less memory because it samples the sound less often than the one on the right and has fewer bits representing amplitude values. As a result, there will be fewer samples to store, and each sample will take up less space in memory. But, consequently, it will not represent the original file very well and will probably create artifacts that will render it unrecognizable. In the first set of two images on the top, you can see the analog sound displayed as a single line.

Figure 1.6
Low resolution/low sampling rate vs. high resolution/high sampling rate.

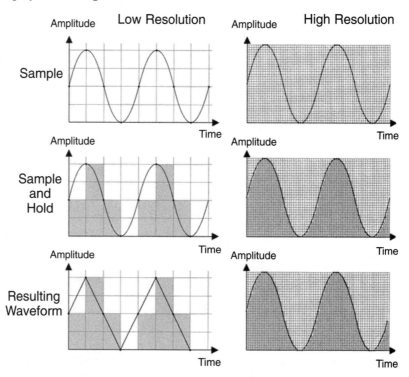

The center set of images demonstrates how the amplitude value of the sample is kept and held until the next sampled amplitude value is taken. As you can see in the right column, a more frequent sampling of amplitude values renders a much more accurate reproduction of the original waveform. If you look at the resulting waveform in the lower set of images, this becomes even more obvious when you look at the dark line representing the outline of the resulting waveform. The waveform on the right is closer to the original analog signal than the one on the left.

Sampling is simply the process of taking a snapshot of your sound through time. Every snapshot of your sound is kept and held until the next snapshot is taken. This process is called "*Sample and Hold.*" As mentioned earlier, the snapshot keeps the voltage value of the sound at a particular point in time. When playing back digital audio, an amplifier keeps the level of the recorded voltage value until the next sample. Before the sound is finally sent to the output, a certain amount of low-level noise is sometimes added to the process to hide the large gaps that may occur between voltage values, especially if you are using a low bit rate and low sampling rate for digital recording. This process is called dithering. Usually, this makes your sound smoother, but in low-resolution recordings (such as an 8-bit recording), it will add a certain amount of audible noise to your sound. If this dithering wasn't there, you might not hear noise, but your sound would contain more digital distortion.

So how does this tie into Cubase? Well, Cubase is, in many ways, a gigantic multitrack sampler, as it samples digital audio at various sampling rates and bit depths (or resolutions). Whenever you are recording an audio signal in a digital format, you are sampling this sound. Cubase will allow you to sample sound at rates of up to 96 kHz per second and at bit depths of up to 32 bits. How high you can go will, of course, depend on your audio hardware.

How Does Cubase Handle MIDI and Audio?

Unlike a tape recorder, Cubase records not only audio information but MIDI as well. Cubase SX/SL handles MIDI through MIDI ports, MIDI channels, and MIDI tracks and handles audio through audio inputs, audio tracks, mixer channels, and audio outputs (see Figure 1.7).

Figure 1.7
How the MIDI and audio data flows from inputs to outputs in Cubase.

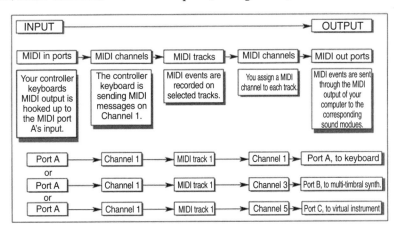

MIDI Port

A MIDI port is a hardware (physical) or software (virtual) point of entry or point of exit for your MIDI data. The number of physical MIDI ports is determined by your computer's MIDI interface. This can be a stand-alone MIDI interface or MIDI connectors found on your sound card. If you have a sound card that has four MIDI inputs and four MIDI outputs, you will have four MIDI ports available for this interface in Cubase. On the other hand, if you are using Cubase to send or receive MIDI information to and from another application inside your computer, you will also be using virtual MIDI ports.

Why virtual? Because they do not require additional hardware. This is the case when you are using a VST virtual instrument (this will be discussed in Chapter 5) or when working with third-party software such as Propellerhead's Reason, Tascam's GigaStudio, Ableton's Live, or others. Whenever you load virtual instruments, they create virtual ports that are available in Cubase for you to use as if they were plugged in to your computer through an actual MIDI port. The virtual ports will, in other words, allow you to receive MIDI from these applications or send MIDI to them.

The MIDI port determines which physical or virtual MIDI socket information is coming from and going to (see Figure 1.8). Each MIDI port can carry up to 16 MIDI channels.

Figure 1.8
Example of a MIDI input
port selection menu.

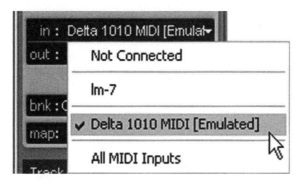

How To

To view a track's MIDI input and output port setting:

▶ Click on the Show Inspector button in the project window's toolbar (Figure 1.9).

Figure 1.9
The Show/Hide Inspector
button found in the
project window's toolbar.

Each MIDI track has its own MIDI input port setting and output port setting. This way, you can choose to record MIDI from different MIDI sources directly in your project, just as long as you have a MIDI input device, such as a keyboard, connected to these input ports.

Which MIDI input port appears in your track input port selection field depends on the ports that were set as active in Cubase's MIDI device setup window. This will be discussed later in this chapter.

MIDI Channel

Each MIDI port will support up to 16 simultaneous MIDI channels. In Cubase, the channel used by the MIDI device connected to the MIDI input has little effect over the result. It is the MIDI output channel of a track that determines how the incoming MIDI data is interpreted. For example, if your MIDI keyboard is connected to the MIDI input of your computer's MIDI interface, you need to tell Cubase where the MIDI is coming from through the MIDI input port selection mentioned above. Let's suppose you have connected a multitimbral instrument to the MIDI output port of this track. A multitimbral instrument can play one sound per MIDI channel. So you might have a piano on channel 1, a guitar on channel 2, and a bass on channel 3. If you change the channel on the track, you actually change which instrument will play the MIDI data that was recorded on it, or the MIDI data going through it as it is being played.

You have to select a MIDI channel in order to send information to a particular patch or preset in your MIDI instrument. Once your MIDI channel is selected, you can assign a patch to it, like a bass, for example. A MIDI channel can play only the assigned patch for the instrument you wish to play or record MIDI with. You can change the patch or preset along the way, but you can have only one patch or preset assigned to that channel at a time. In other words, you can have up to 16 sounds/patches/MIDI devices playing simultaneously on one MIDI port.

If you run out of MIDI channels for one MIDI port, you will need to use another MIDI port to play the MIDI events. Each virtual instrument loaded into Cubase's memory will create its own virtual MIDI port, so running out of MIDI channels is unlikely inside Cubase.

In Figure 1.10, you can see that the MIDI in port is set to All MIDI Inputs, which implies that any device sending MIDI to Cubase will be recorded. However, the MIDI out port is set to a1 MIDI out, which also implies that whatever comes in or whatever is already present on this MIDI track will be sent out to this MIDI port. Selecting the MIDI channel will cause all MIDI events on this track to be sent to this MIDI channel. In this case, the pointer displays channel 4 as the new selected MIDI channel. Letting go of the mouse while this channel is selected will cause the check mark appearing next to the number 1 in this list to move to number 4. When you play or record events from this point on, all events will be heard through this MIDI port (the a1 virtual instrument) and MIDI channel 4.

Figure 1.10
Selecting a MIDI channel
for a MIDI track.

MIDI Track

A MIDI track usually contains MIDI information for one channel at a time. When you play on a keyboard, it sends out MIDI events on a MIDI channel that is recorded on a MIDI track. You then assign a MIDI channel to that track to get the appropriate sound at the output as mentioned previously.

Cubase doesn't replace the original MIDI channel information that you record. It simply puts a filter at the output of the track in order to hear the MIDI events played on the MIDI port and channel you decide. This makes the MIDI recording process much simpler because, otherwise, you would have to change the MIDI channel of your MIDI input device and inside Cubase.

Each track has its own MIDI input and output port setting as well as its channel setting. You can also record from multiple input sources and multiple channels simultaneously on a single track by selecting the appropriate settings for this track; however, it is recommended that you keep each musical part on a separate track for easier editing later. Since you can create as many MIDI tracks as you need in Cubase, you don't really need to worry about running out of them.

Audio Connections

New to Cubase SX/SL 2.0 is the concept of audio connections. An audio connection is a way to create a link between your sound card's audio connectors and an audio track. The link provides you with a way to configure these physical inputs and outputs into mono, stereo, or surround connections (with SX only). That way, when you decide to record an audio track in mono, all you need to do is use your mono connection, which is configured appropriately. These links or connections are called buses, and there are two types of buses: input buses and output buses.

So why this additional layer? By doing so, you can use the same physical connection in different configurations; for example, if you have an ADAT connection on your sound card, you can configure the same inputs in different bus configurations. If you look at Figure 1.11, you can notice that the ADAT 1 is configured as a mono bus as well as part of a stereo bus. Similarly, the ADAT 5 is used both as a mono bus and as part of a surround bus.

You can save the bus configurations as a template or with your project file. If you intend to always use the same connection setup throughout your projects, then using a template file will most likely suit your needs. If you find yourself using different configurations each time you begin a new project, then you can simply set the connections once at the beginning of a project. Cubase will save these connection configurations along with the project file so that you don't need to repeat the configuration every time.

After the bus configurations are created, you don't really need to worry about them since whenever you want to select an audio input or output in Cubase, you will see and choose from the bus configurations you made earlier.

Input Buses

An input bus is a bridge between the physical inputs of your sound card and the source for the audio that you want to record onto an audio track. By selecting an input bus, you simultaneously decide if the audio track will record mono, stereo, or surround content, depending on how you configured this input bus in the first place.

Figure 1.11
How audio inputs become input buses through the audio connections in Cubase.

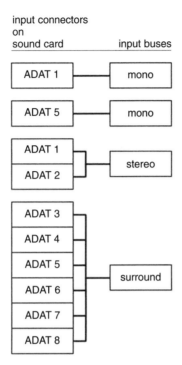

Each physical connection on your sound card can be routed to one or more input buses. However, if you choose to record on several tracks simultaneously using different input buses that share one of the sound card's input, you will end up recording the same material on all the tracks that share this input. For example, let's say you create two audio tracks, hook up a pair of microphones to record a stereo guitar feed and another mike to record vocals. In this case, you probably want the guitar track to be stereo and the vocal track mono. If you've configured a stereo input bus to use the physical inputs 1 and 2 and a mono input bus to use the physical input 1, then you'll be recording a stereo guitar on one track and a mono guitar on the other track. But if you've hooked up your vocal mike in input 3 and configured an additional mono input bus to use that connector, you'll be able to record all three audio inputs simultaneously.

If you are using Cubase SL, you won't have control over the level of a signal coming into an input bus, but Cubase SX will allow you to adjust this level in order to prevent clipping or undermodulation (low input level). Cubase SL users will need to adjust the input level of a signal by using the controls available on their sound card's control panel or on the output level of the device being recorded in order to make changes to the input level of their sound card.

In Figure 1.12 you can see how Cubase associates input buses with your ASIO device physical inputs (known as ports). In this case, there are three stereo input buses and three mono input buses that can be used whenever you want to record digital audio. You may also create new ones. The Bus Name column displays the names of the inputs as they will appear when you need to select which input bus to use in a recording situation.

Figure 1.12
The VST Connections
panel— looking at the
input buses.

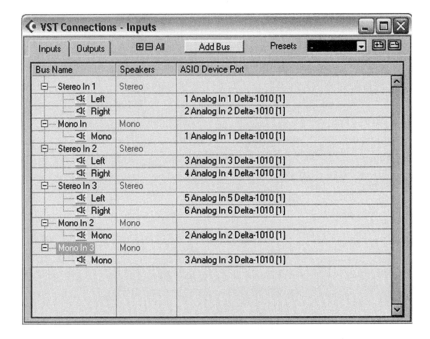

Output Buses

Output buses enable you to monitor the content of an audio track through a set of audio outputs on your sound card. As with input buses, you can create several output bus connections, depending on your needs. Essentially, you will need to have at least one mono output bus if you have mono content, a stereo output bus if you have stereo content on an audio track, and a surround output bus if you need it as well.

You may also decide to record a signal using a pair of inputs—let's say 1-2—and monitor through another pair of outputs, like 3-4, for example.

Figure 1.13 is similar to Figure 1.12, with the exception that this figure represents the output buses with their respective ASIO device port settings.

Audio Track

An audio track in Cubase is similar to an audio track in an audio multitrack recorder. It has, however, the advantage of being either mono, stereo, or multichanneled to support surround sound (Cubase SX version only), depending on the audio bus configuration you choose. You can create as many audio tracks as you need in Cubase. This said, you will probably be limited by your computer's speed, disk access, or memory capacity at one point, so working within these limits will be your only concern.

Your project's settings will determine the audio bit depth and sample rate recorded in an audio track; however, the bus selection and the number of audio channels it supports are determined at the time you create an audio track. When you create an audio track, Cubase will ask you which configuration you wish to use: mono, stereo, or one of many multichannel configurations. This will ultimately influence your choice in input and output buses later on. For example, if you want

Figure 1.13
The VST Connections panel—looking at the output buses.

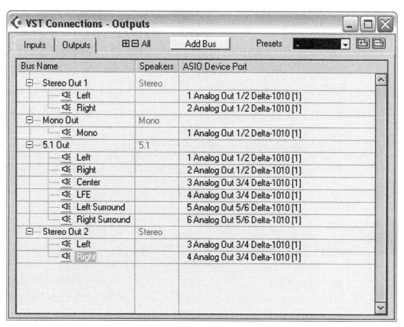

to create a vocal track, you could create a mono track and then select a mono input bus. But you can also use one of the channels in a stereo bus or one of the channels in a surround bus as its input source as well.

As logic would have it, however, to monitor or record stereo content, you will need to have a stereo or multichannel track. Placing a stereo audio event on a mono audio track will still allow you to hear the content, but, as you would imagine, in mono only. As for surround or multichannel events, you will need an equivalent or higher number of channels in the bus assigned to this track. For example, you could record an LCRS (Left, Center, Right, Surround) mix in a 5.1 surround audio track. Playing a multichannel audio source through a mono or stereo track will not allow you to monitor the audio as it was intended. For example, monitoring a 5.1 audio event in a stereo track using a surround output bus will cause all the information to play over the center channel, thus creating distortion on this track.

As a rule of thumb, you should:

▶ Record mono signals on mono tracks using a mono input bus or one of the channels on a stereo or multichannel bus and monitor through a mono bus.

▶ Record stereo signals on stereo tracks using a stereo input bus and monitor through a stereo bus.

▶ (Cubase SX only) Record multichannel signals on equivalent multichannel audio tracks using the same type of input bus and monitor through the same type of multichannel output bus.

Mixer Channel

Whenever you create a track in Cubase, you create a Channel. Channels appear in the Mixer panel as shown in Figure 1.14, as well as in the Inspector area of a selected track (project window) under the Channel section as shown in Figure 1.15.

A channel in Cubase is similar to a mixer channel on a hardware mixer with some exceptions:

► If you set a track to record or play stereo or multichannel events, the mixer channel will display information for all channels. On hardware mixers, stereo channels would take two channel strips.

► If you use a virtual instrument such as a software synthesizer, it will create a MIDI channel that will allow you to control the MIDI automation for this virtual instrument and a special type of audio channel to add audio effects or equalizer parameters. If your virtual instrument supports multiple channels, there will be as many channels created in the channel mixer as there are output channels for this instrument. For example, loading the LM4-Mark II drum machine will create a set of three stereo channels and six mono channels in your mixer.

► When you want to add an effect, a reverb for example, you create an effect (FX) track, which in return creates a special channel in the mixer.

► Because this is a virtual mixer environment, it is a dynamic mixer too. In other words, you can create group channels when you need them and add audio channels as well as MIDI channels as you create audio or MIDI tracks in your project.

Figure 1.14
The Mixer panel mirrors all the channels (and their settings) found in your project.

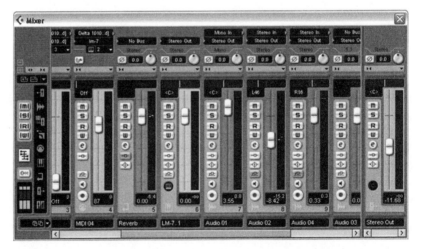

Figure 1.15
The channel section displays the channel settings for a selected track in the Inspector area of the project window. Making a change in the mixer will be reflected here and vice versa.

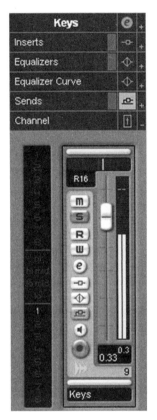

About 32-bit Recording

Most audio hardware available today supports 16-bit resolution. Some better quality sound cards also support 20- and 24-bit resolutions. With the 16-bit resolution (see Figure 1.16), the vertical steps corresponding to voltage values are few and far apart. In the 24-bit resolution, there are many more steps (also called *Quantum*) than in 16-bit recordings. In the 32-bit, the binary word is twice as long, but as you will see in the Table 1.1, instead of having 65,535 steps, you have more than four billion steps. Finally, in 32-bit floating-point resolution, you still have more than four billion steps; however, they are not fixed but variable points that adjust themselves according to the needs of the audio waveform. This dramatically increases the dynamic range (range between the loudest sound before digital clipping and softest audible sound) of a digital audio recording. On the minus side, it also increases the hard disk space needed to record digital audio as well as processing time when applying changes, such as adding an effect to a sound. Ultimately, to record using precisions higher than 24-bit resolutions, you'll need a fast computer, fast hard drive, and lots of memory, both in disk space and in RAM.

Figure 1.16
Understanding the importance of bit resolution in digital audio recording.

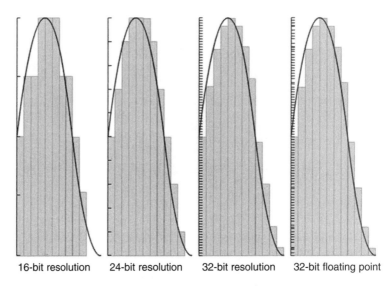

16-bit resolution   24-bit resolution   32-bit resolution   32-bit floating point

Table 1.1 illustrates the different values that can be stored in their respective resolutions:

Table 1.1
Minimum and Maximum values for 16-, 24- and 32-bit resolution audio signal

Resolution	Minimum Value	Maximum Value	Dynamic Range	Hard Disk Space (min/mono)
16-bit	-32,768	32,767	96 dBFS	5,168 KB
24-bit	-8,388,608	8,388,607	144 dBFS	7,752 KB
32-bit	-2,147,483,648	2,147,483,647	193 dBFS	10,336 KB

Recording audio up until now was limited to fixed integer values, as mentioned previously. With floating point, the computer adds a decimal value and can move that decimal point wherever it needs it in order to get greater precision. Here's an example: Let's say you have an analog signal coming in at 1.2245 volts. If you have a system that provides only two decimal points, your resulting value would be 1.23 or 1.22. In both cases, this would not be very precise, but it's as precise as the recording system could be. Floating point technology simply adds a decimal value (up to seven) as needed, making the recorded value exactly 1.2245. This kind of technology yields a dynamic range of almost 200 dB! This dynamic range means that you can drive your guitar without ever worrying about digital clipping. You should still be careful, though, because while there might not be digital clipping in your signal, you might still have digital distortion, which sounds like analog distortion. And, any way you look at it, unwanted distortion/noise is never a good thing.

Remember that the bit depth (resolution) of the mixdown does not have to be the same as the recorded tracks. Cubase allows you to select a different format to mix down your tracks when you are finished working on them. This process happens because Cubase records in a format that is superior to the quality available on regular CD players. So, a good rule of thumb to follow is always work with the best quality your entire system supports (all devices involved in the recording process especially), saving the downgrading for the last step before burning to CD. If your hardware and software can handle it, go for it. But remember this: Audio CD format supports only 44.1 kHz, 16-bit stereo files. So, if you don't convert your audio beforehand, you won't be able to write it in audio CD format.

Do I Have the Right Hardware?

To use 24-bit or 32-bit recording, you need to have a 24-bit compatible sound card to actually have better quality sound. Recording in 24-bit or 32-bit with a 16-bit sound card will only make your file larger; it will not give you better results. Not to mention that your 16-bit sound card might not even be able to play back the audio recorded at 24-bit. This said, you have to understand that 24-bit recordings take up 1.5 times as much space as a 16-bit recording, and that 32-bit recordings take up twice the space of a 16-bit recording and make more demands on the CPU and hard disk performance of your computer. The kind of hard disk and RAM you have in your computer will greatly influence the performance of your system when using 24- or 32-bit recording.

2

A Guided Tour of Cubase SX/SL

This chapter provides an overview of Cubase SX/SL's many workspaces. Veteran Cubase users will find this chapter useful in providing information about new features, windows, panels, and workspaces. For all you Cubase "newbies," welcome to the Cubase family of users. You will get acquainted with the different windows and tools in this chapter and find out how to access these windows. It's always good to go through a quick overview to get a first impression, then stop reading, look at the software, and find where things are located to get a sense of the working environment. Look at this chapter as your guided tour to a world of possibilities.

Here's a summary of what you will learn in this chapter:

▶ The name and purpose of each window, dialog box, and panel most commonly used in Cubase SX/SL.

▶ How to access these windows, dialog boxes, and panels.

▶ What the different editing environments are and how you can use them in your project.

▶ How Cubase is organized.

To make sure you understand the terminology, here's how some of these elements are defined:

▶ A **window** contains a toolbar at the top and sometimes on one side. It may also have a menu bar at the top of the window. You can edit information inside a window (as with other elements). You don't need to press any buttons to accept or apply changes made to windows. When you make changes to information within a window, they are automatically updated.

▶ A **dialog box** appears when you want to apply a process or transformation that requires you to accept or apply this process. It is usually associated with a function, such as the Save function or a setting of some sort, such as the Metronome Setup or the Project Setup dialog box. When a dialog box is open, you most likely have to close this dialog box by accepting or denying the changes in order to do something else in your project.

▶ A **panel** is similar in nature to a front panel of a device. Panels have controls or fields in which you can make selections. Panels do not have any menus or toolbars and do not have any confirmation or cancel buttons. An example of this is the Mixer panel, which allows you to mix channels, route signals, assign effect to channels, and modify their parameters, as well as other mix-related tasks.

The Project Window

The project window (see Figure 2.1) is your main working area. In Cubase SX/SL, you can load different projects. When you make a project window active (bring it on top of others by clicking in it), all other project-related windows also update their content to display the settings of this active project window. The project window is divided into seven areas:

▶ **Toolbar.** Accesses the most common tools and functions used in this window, as most toolbars do. It appears on the top of the project window, covering the width of the window.

▶ **Event information line.** Displays information on selected events. You can use it to rename these selected events or edit the event's start, end, length, and so on.

▶ **Overview.** Displays the whole project and frames the current portion of the project currently viewed. You can quickly zoom to a specific point or move your point of view by using this area.

▶ **Inspector.** Gives you detailed information on a selected track. Each track has different information represented in this area, depending on the track's type.

▶ **Track list.** Displays vertically stacked tracks available in your project. Each track also displays information related to its track type (audio, MIDI, marker, video, and so on).

▶ **Event display.** Displays events in time as well as automation lanes associated with events on tracks.

▶ **Zoom.** Enables you to view your project in different ways, focusing on a particular section, track, or event, or simply to get an overall view of your project.

Figure 2.1
The Cubase SX/SL project window.

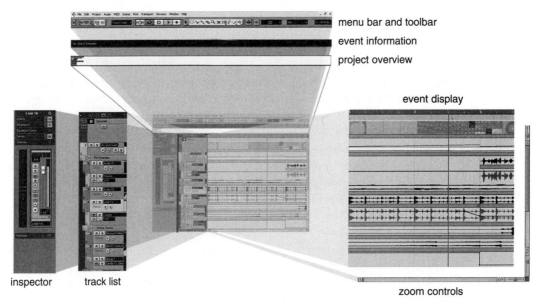

menu bar and toolbar
event information
project overview

event display

inspector   track list

zoom controls

Channels

The concept of channels is fairly important in modern digital audio production. Whenever events are recorded in a project, they go into a channel. So, in order to record anything, you need to create a track for it, which in turn, creates a channel that separates its settings from the track (channel) next door.

The VST Channel Settings panel offers the best look at all the parameters assigned to any types of channels inside a project. Since it's so important, you can access it by pressing the Edit button from the following places:

How To

To view the VST Channel panel:

▶ Project window > Inspector area > Channel section.

▶ Mixer Panel (F3) > individual channel.

▶ Project window > Track List area > individual channel.

In Figure 2.2, the example shows an audio output channel in surround format and its associated effects routing in the surround output bus.

Figure 2.2
The VST Channel
Settings panel.

Mixers

The Mixer panel (see Figure 2.3) is your virtual mixing console. It monitors inputs and outputs, adjusts levels, assigns effects or inserts, adjusts the equalization, changes the routing of a signal, records and plays back mixing automation, as well as finalizing your project's mix. Each channel in this mixer can be edited in a separate channel setting window for greater control over this channel; however, the Mixer panel allows you to see what you normally need to see when mixing

How To

To view the Mixer window:

▶ Press the F3 key on your keyboard.

▶ Or click the Track Mixer button in the Devices panel.

▶ Or select Devices > Track Mixer from the menu bar.

Cubase SX Mixer panel (extended) with inputs, putputs and project channels

Cubase SL Mixer panel doesn't offer the extended panel or the input channels

Figure 2.3
The Cubase SX Mixer panel (extended on top and similar to SL on the bottom) with inputs, ouputs, and project channels.

Surround Pan

A feature only available on the SX version, the Surround Pan (see Figure 2.4) panel controls the positioning of a sound inside a surround audio channel configuration when you are working with surround sound.

How To

To view the Surround Pan panel:

▶ Double-click in the surround channel's pan area of the Mixer panel.

▶ Click on the Show Surround Pan button in the extended portion of the Mixer panel (this extension is also only available in the SX version).

Figure 2.4
The Surround Pan panel
(Cubase SX only).

The Transport Panel

The Transport panel (shown in Figure 2.5) controls different aspects of your project, such as the position of your left and right locators, Punch-in and -out modes, Cycle modes, playback and recording functions, as well as tempo, click, and sync functions. Also, new to this version is the possibility of monitoring your system's performance as well as the main stereo output levels.

How To

To view the Transport panel:

▶ Press the F2 key on your keyboard.

▶ Or select Transport > Transport Panel from the menu bar.

Figure 2.5
The Transport panel.

Metronome Setup Dialog Box

The Metronome Setup dialog box (see Figure 2.6) configures your metronome's click. A metronome click is useful mostly when recording events, but you can also use the metronome during playback to make sure the timing of your recorded performance is accurate.

How To

To view the Metronome Setup dialog box:

▶ From the Transport panel, Ctrl(PC)/⌘(Mac)-click the Click button.

▶ Or select Transport > Metronome Setup from the menu bar.

Figure 2.6
The Metronome Setup dialog box.

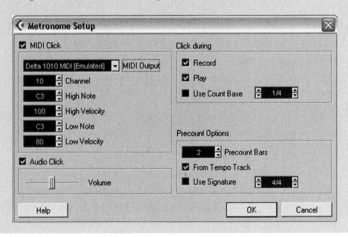

Synchronization Setup Dialog Box

If you are working with video or need to synchronize Cubase with another MIDI device, you can use the Synchronization Setup dialog box (see Figure 2.7) to properly configure Cubase. This dialog box sets Cubase as the master or the slave and also enables you to echo synchronization information to various outputs and in different formats.

How To

To view the Synchronization Setup dialog box:

▶ From the Transport panel, Ctrl(PC)/⌘(Mac)-click the Sync button.

▶ Or select Transport > Sync Setup from the menu bar.

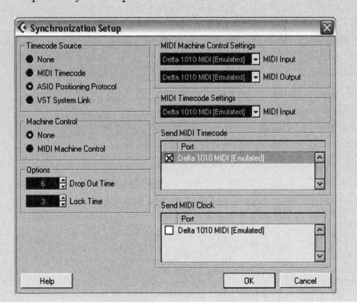

Figure 2.7
The Synchronization
Setup dialog box.

CHAPTER 2

The Devices Panel

You can access many of the different windows and panels allowing you to configure devices in Cubase SX/SL through the Devices panel (see Figure 2.8). When this panel is visible, you can click on any button in the panel to access its content. The content of each panel is described in this section. This panel also displays any Rewire-compatible applications installed on your computer (Rewire will be discussed in Chapter 12). If you don't have any Rewire-compatible applications or USB/MIDI controller surface, such as the Steinberg Houston in this example, you won't see any in this panel.

How To

To view the Devices panel:

▶ Select Devices > Show Panel from the menu bar.

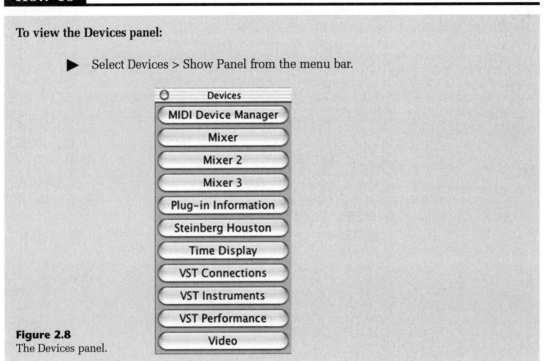

Figure 2.8
The Devices panel.

Plug-in Information Panel

Cubase supports two (Mac version) or three (Windows version) types of plug-ins: VST, DirectX (only on the PC version), and MIDI plug-ins. You can use the Plug-in Information panel (see Figure 2.9) to manage which plug-ins appear in your menu when selecting plug-ins for destructive processing or as a nondestructive process, such as FX channels. This panel displays information about each plug-in installed on your system and also allows you to specify the folders containing your shared VST plug-ins.

How To

To view the Plug-in Information panel:

▶ Click the Plug-in Information button in the Devices panel.

▶ Or select Devices > Plug-in Information from the menu bar.

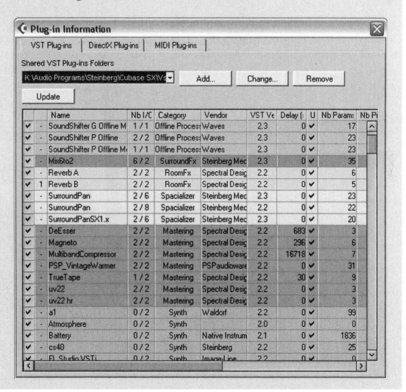

Figure 2.9
The Plug-in Information panel.

Time Display

Cubase users working with video know that sometimes seeing the time displayed in different formats simultaneously onscreen is very helpful. New to this version is the time display panel (see Figure 2.10) which does exactly that. You can still see the time displayed in the transport bar and through the play line position, but this time display can be scaled to the size you need it to be so that when you're spotting a commercial, writing down SMPTE cues, you don't need to squint in front of the computer to see where the cue should go.

Figure 2.10
The Time Display panel.

VST Connections

The VST Connections (see Figure 2.11) manages (creates, deletes, renames) audio buses that will be available within your project. It also allows you to associate ASIO-compatible sound card devices to these buses. The number of actual buses you create in a project is up to you, but the number of simultaneous audio ports is determined by your sound card's physical connections.

How To

To view the VST Connections:

▶ Press the F4 key on your keyboard.

▶ Or click the VST Connections button in the Devices panel.

▶ Or select Devices > VST Connections from the menu bar.

Figure 2.11
The VST Connections panel—Inputs tab.

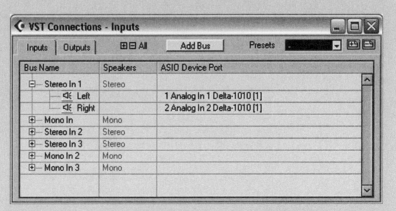

VST Instruments Panel

VST instruments or VSTi are VST-compatible software instruments that you can load inside Cubase SX/SL. To load, edit, and manage these virtual instruments, you can use the VST Instruments panel (see Figure 2.12). After an instrument is loaded into memory, you can send MIDI events to it by using a MIDI track to generate sounds. New to this version of Cubase is the possibility of freezing the MIDI events played through the VST instrument. This creates a temporary audio rendering of the MIDI events passing through the assigned VST instrument and unloads this instrument from memory, thus freeing up some computer resources. You'll find more about this in Chapter 5. Note that you can load up to 64 VST instruments in the SX version and up to 16 in the SL version.

How To

To view the VST Instruments panel:

▶ Press the F11 key on your keyboard.

▶ Or click the VST Instruments button in the Devices panel.

▶ Or select Devices > VST Instruments from the menu bar.

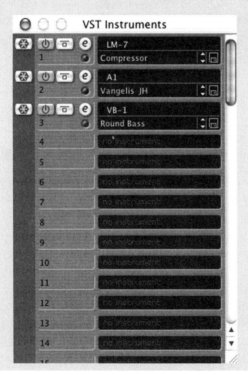

Figure 2.12
The VST Instruments
panel.

VST Performance Panel

Cubase SX/SL monitors the performance of both your CPU and your hard disk. This capability can be useful to measure when it's time to start creating audio tracks, which contain effects, or create submixes to reduce the load on your computer, especially when your performance indicator shows a high level of activity on a constant basis. If you hear your audio stuttering while playing back your project, take a look at the VST Performance panel (see Figure 2.13). This panel will show you if the CPU is overloaded (top bar); if it is, you should unload some of the real-time processes. On the other hand, if the hard disk is overloaded (lower bar), mix down some tracks. If that doesn't work, try increasing the buffer sizes in the ASIO control panel.

To view the VST Performance panel:

▶ Press the F12 key on your keyboard.

▶ Or click the VST Performance button in the Devices panel.

▶ Or select Devices > VST Performance from the menu bar.

Figure 2.13
The VST Performance panel.

Video Display Window

You can load video files into a Cubase project when working on multimedia projects or film projects. Cubase will support a number of formats: QuickTime, AVI, or MPEG on both Mac and PC versions, Windows Media Video on the PC version only and DV format on the Mac version only. Cubase SX (not SL) for PC will also support Windows Media Video Pro format. When you import a video file into a project, you will need to create a video track in order to place the video file on this track. That will allow you to view the video information while working on the audio.

How To

To view the Video Display window (see Figure 2.14):

▶ Press the F8 key on your keyboard.
▶ Or click the Video button in the Devices panel.
▶ Or select Devices > Video from the menu bar.

Figure 2.14
The Video Display
window.

The Project Tools

The project tools are special windows and dialog boxes in which you will find information about settings that affect your entire project, such as sampling format, project tempo, time signature, and Markers, as well as events found in an active project.

Marker Panel

Markers and cycle markers (also commonly known as *regions*) allow you to identify certain points and easily navigate throughout these points in your project. For example, you can create cycle markers (regions) for your chorus, verse, and bridge, and create markers at other places in your project, such as at the start of a specific cue. Each time you create a marker, it is added to your marker window, allowing you to go directly to that location using keyboard shortcuts, by selecting it in the marker track or through the Transport panel. You can also use cycle markers to quickly zoom in to this area of your project.

How To

To view the Marker panel (see Figure 2.15):

▶ Press Ctrl(PC)/⌘(Mac)+M on your keyboard.

▶ Click on the Show Marker button in the Transport panel.

▶ Or select Project > Markers from the menu bar.

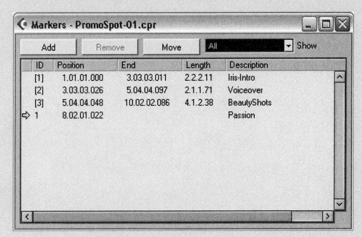

Figure 2.15
The Marker panel.

Tempo Track

During the course of your project, you might want to create tempo changes or add meter changes. These changes are stored in a special Tempo track (shown in Figure 2.16), which is not visible in your main project window. To access this information, make changes to it, or add values, you need to open the Tempo Track window. After you add information to this window, you need to make sure that the Master button found on the Transport panel is active or you won't hear the tempo changes made in this track. Cubase will, on the other hand, change meter values (time signature) as this information is necessary to properly divide the project into the correct number of bars and beats.

How To

To view the Tempo Track window:

▶ Press Ctrl(PC)/⌘(Mac)+T on your keyboard.

▶ Or Ctrl(PC)/⌘(Mac)-click the Master button found on the Transport panel.

▶ Or select Project > Tempo Track from the menu bar.

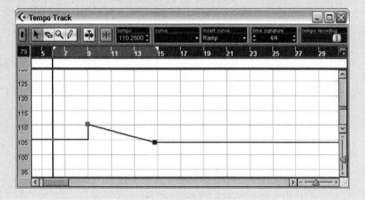

Figure 2.16
The Tempo Track
window.

Browser Window

If you want to look at all the events found in your project, organized by type of events, the best way to do this is through the Browse window (shown in Figure 2.17). Unlike the Pool or the List Editor, this window views all the events, including MIDI and automation events, markers, tempo, and time signature changes.

How To

To view the Browse Project window:

▶ Press Ctrl(PC)/⌘(Mac)+B on your keyboard.

▶ Or select Project > Browser from the menu bar.

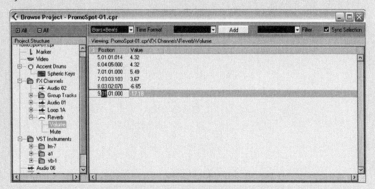

Figure 2.17
The Browse window.

Beat Calculator Panel

Sometimes, you might have a song in mind with a specific tempo, but aren't quite sure what that tempo is. That's when the Beat Calculator (see Figure 2.18) comes in handy. It allows you to tap in a tempo, turning the tempo you had in mind into your project's tempo or simply add a tempo change in your project at the current location.

The Beat Calculator is also useful when you want to find out the BPM of a drum loop. For example, you can play the drum loop from the pool and tap along with the beat. The tempo you see in the Beat Calculator after a few constant bars will be that of the audio loop you are trying to find.

How To

To view the Beat Calculator panel:

▶ Select Project > Beat Calculator from the menu bar.

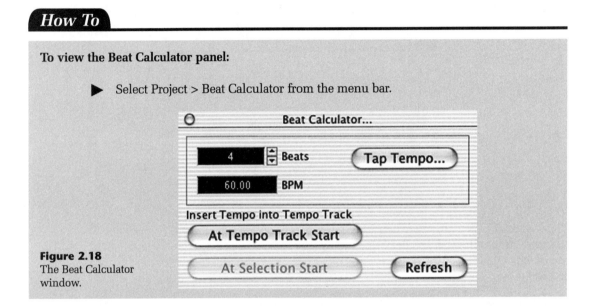

Figure 2.18
The Beat Calculator
window.

Project Setup Dialog Box

When you begin a new project, you should use the Project Setup dialog box (shown in Figure 2.19) to set the digital audio properties (sampling rate, bit depth, format of audio recording files) for this project. The Project Setup dialog box also selects the preferred display format and frame rate (if necessary) for the project.

How To

To view the Project Setup dialog box:

▶ Press Shift+S on your keyboard.

▶ Or select Project > Project Setup from the menu bar.

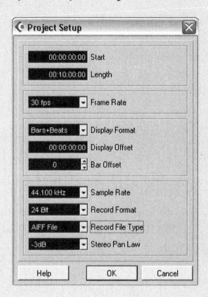

Figure 2.19
The Project Setup dialog
box.

MIDI Windows

Cubase offers different editing environments for MIDI events, depending on the type of MIDI events you want to edit. For example, if a track contains melodic or harmonic content, you can use the MIDI editor known as the *Key Editor*. On the other hand, if the events you want to edit are percussion or drum based, you can use the Drum Editor, which makes it easier for you to associate pitch values to actual instrument names, such as kick, snare, timbales, conga, and so on.

MIDI Device Manager

The MIDI Device Manager (see Figure 2.20) installs or removes an external MIDI device in your setup and attaches it to a specific MIDI port so that it becomes available in a MIDI track when selecting MIDI ports. You can configure all your external MIDI devices using this device manager. It also configures the patch names for these devices so that you can change the programs on this device directly from Cubase's inspector or track list area.

How To

To view the MIDI Device Manager window:

▶ Click the MIDI Device Manager button in the Devices panel.

▶ Select Devices > MIDI Device Manager from the menu bar.

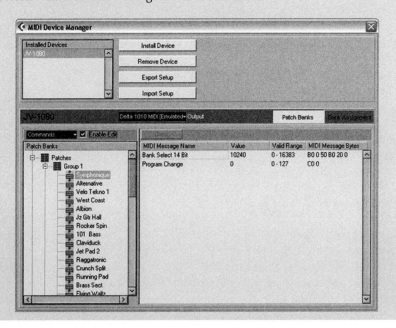

Figure 2.20
The MIDI Device Manager window.

Key Editor

The Key Editor (see Figure 2.21) is probably the best-known editing environment for MIDI events, allowing you to modify not only note events, but also MIDI channel messages, such as velocity, aftertouch, pitch bend, or control change messages. To use the Key Editor, you need to select one or several MIDI parts, or a MIDI track in the project window; otherwise, the Key Editor is not available.

How To

To view the Key Editor window:

▶ Select a MIDI part in the project window and press Ctrl(PC)/⌘(Mac)+E.

▶ Or double-click on a MIDI part in the project window.

▶ Or select a part in the project window and then select MIDI > Open Key Editor from the menu bar.

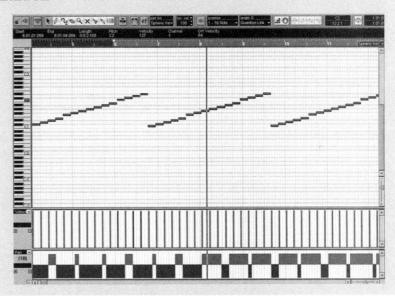

Figure 2.21
The Key Editor window.

Quantize Setup Panel

Quantizing enables you to match recorded MIDI events to a predefined grid in order to add rhythmic precision to these events. You can also use quantizing creatively, adding a swing feeling to straight MIDI note events, for example. The Quantize Setup panel (see Figure 2.22) configures how quantizing will be applied to the selected MIDI events or parts. You can later save quantization settings to use them in other projects or even use groove templates that have been extracted from an audio drum loop's rhythmic information.

How To

To view the Quantize Setup panel:

▶ Select MIDI > Quantize Setup from the menu bar.

▶ Or, from within any MIDI editing window, including the project window, select the Setup option at the bottom of the Quantize drop-down menu.

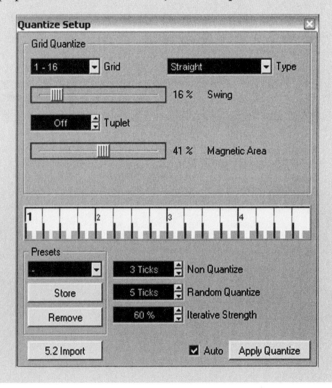

Figure 2.22
The Quantize Setup panel.

Drum Editor

The Drum Editor, as with the Key Editor, edits MIDI events; in this case, the editor is designed to handle percussion and drum maps. Most drum sounds are short by nature and usually drum patches are laid across a keyboard range, each key playing a different instrument. Drum maps are used to identify each note value (see Figure 2.23). In the Drum Editor, lengths of events are not displayed as they are not relevant to editing; instrument names, on the other hand, are associated with each pitch value to make editing a specific instrument easier.

How To

To view the Drum Editor window:

▶ Select a part associated with a drum map in the project window and press Ctrl(PC)/⌘(Mac)+E.

▶ Or double-click on a MIDI part associated with a drum map in the project window.

▶ Or select a part in the project window and then select MIDI > Open Drum Editor from the menu bar.

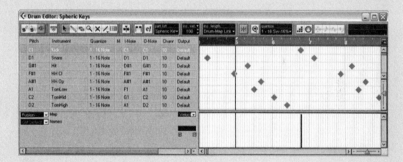

Figure 2.23
The Drum Editor window.

Drum Map Setup Dialog Box

A drum map is a list of percussive instruments associated with pitch values in a MIDI-based rhythmic part or track. You can choose from a list of ready-made drum maps or create your own custom drum maps. The Drum Map Setup dialog box (see Figure 2.24) allows you to manage these maps.

How To

To view the Drum Map Setup dialog box:

▶ From the Inspector panel of a MIDI track, select Drum Map Setup from the Drum Map field's drop-down menu.

▶ Or, inside the drum editor, select Drum Map Setup from the Drum Map field's drop-down menu found in the lower-left portion of the window.

▶ Or select MIDI > Open Drum Map Setup from the menu bar.

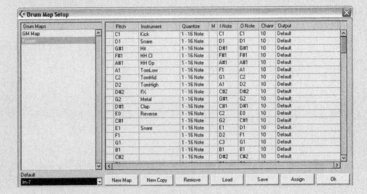

Figure 2.24
The Drum Map Setup
dialog box.

List Editor

The List Editor (see Figure 2.25) is another MIDI environment that displays MIDI events in a table (list) format for numerical editing. Contrary to the Browser panel which also displays a table listing of events, the List Editor is limited to editing only MIDI events.

How To

To view the List Editor window:

▶ Select a MIDI part in the project window and press Ctrl(PC)/⌘(Mac)+G.

▶ Or select a part in the project window and then select MIDI > Open List Editor from the menu bar.

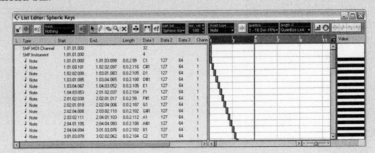

Figure 2.25
The List Editor window.

Score Editor

The Score Editor (see Figure 2.26) is for musicians who want to convert MIDI events into musical notation and then print the final result on paper for safekeeping or to use in a studio session with live musicians. With the scoring functions, you can create complete scores and individual music sheets for individual musicians. Note that score editing only works with MIDI events, not audio events.

How To

To view the Score Editor window:

> ▶ Select a MIDI part (or parts) in the project window and press Ctrl(PC)/⌘(Mac)+R.

> ▶ Or select a part (or parts) in the project window and then select MIDI > Open Score Editor from the menu bar.

Figure 2.26
The Score Editor window.

Audio Editing Windows

Because audio and MIDI are two very different types of events, it is normal that they get their own editing tools and windows to manipulate, transform, and process these events. The Media Pool is where you will find all the audio events associated with your project. The Sample Editor is where you will edit them, and the Audio Part Editor is where you will organize when they play inside an audio part.

Media Pool Window

The Media Pool (see Figure 2.27) allows you to see the audio and video files and their associated regions used in your current project. This window enables you to manage your files, import or export media files, monitor file use, and display file and region information, as well as a graphic representation of these files and regions.

How To

To view the Media Pool window:

▶ Press Ctrl(PC)/⌘(Mac)+P.

▶ Or select Project > Pool from the menu bar.

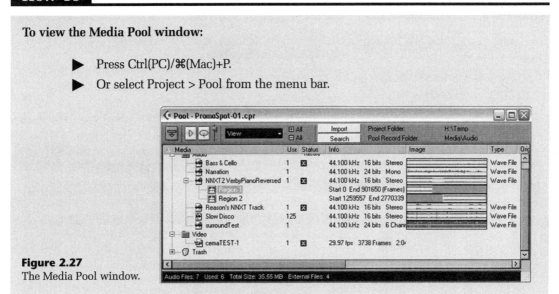

Figure 2.27
The Media Pool window.

Audio Part Editor

On an audio track, you can have audio parts and audio events. An audio event is a single instance or reference to a file that is self-contained on this track. However, an audio part is a container that can hold several audio events or regions. By default, editing these audio parts is done in the Audio Part Editor window (see Figure 2.28). Here, you can move the audio events in time inside the part itself, create fades or crossfades between events, adjust event-related volume envelopes, and quantize audio events to a quantize grid setting. You can also modify audio events and create new regions in the Audio Part Editor.

How To

To view the Audio Part Editor window:

▶ Select an audio part (or parts) in the project window and press Ctrl(PC)/⌘(Mac)+E.

▶ Or double-click on an audio part in the project window.

Figure 2.28
The Audio Part Editor window.

Fade Editor

When working on audio events in the project window or in the Audio Part Editor, you can use fade envelopes at the beginning or at the end of this event to create a fade-in or a fade-out. You can also create fade-ins and fade-outs using offline processes. In the former method, fades are rendered in real time through processing, while in the latter, audio segments containing the actual fade portion of the audio are created on your hard disk, making it less processing intensive for your computer. By creating an additional audio segment, it allows you to safely create volume changes to the audio file without modifying the original content. The Fade Editor (see Figure 2.29) chooses the type of curve you want to apply to the fade itself.

Figure 2.29
The Fade In dialog box.

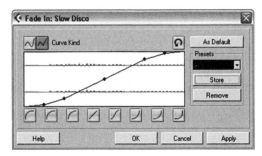

Crossfade Editor

The Crossfade Editor (see Figure 2.30) is similar to the Fade Editor, with the exception that it controls the fade curves for two overlapping audio events, thus creating a crossfade between these two events. As with the Fade Editor, you can't create crossfades in the Sample Editor, nor can you create crossfades between two audio parts that contain several audio events embedded in them.

CHAPTER 2

Figure 2.30
The Crossfade dialog box.

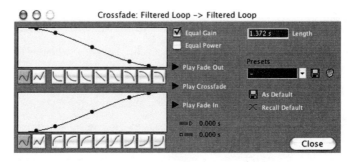

You need to access the events from within the Audio Part Editor or the project Window and open the Crossfade Editor from there. Using the Crossfade Editor is explained in Chapter 9.

Auto Fades

Sometimes, the beginning of an audio event doesn't start with its waveform at the zero crossing (silence on the amplitude axis). This may cause a little clip or glitch at the start of the audio event. To prevent this from occurring, you can use the Auto Fades dialog box (see Figure 2.31). When this function is enabled, it will create a short (up to 500 milliseconds) fade at the beginning and end of the audio event to smooth out any amplitude jumps that could be audible and unwanted. The Auto Fades dialog box adjusts the parameters associated with this function. Note that this can be applied globally—affecting all audio tracks in the same way—or individually for each track. You'll learn more about this in Chapter 9.

Figure 2.31
The Crossfade tab in the Auto Fade's dialog box.

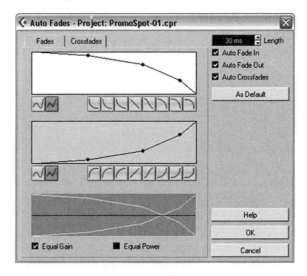

Sample Editor

The Sample Editor (see Figure 2.32) enables you to edit audio clips (the representation inside the pool of an audio file on your hard disk) or an audio event (when an audio clip is used in a project, an audio event is created), process it, and create regions or hitpoints. Hitpoint is a term invented by Steinberg to represent a special audio marker—a marker that divides your audio clip or event into slices corresponding to specific audio elements, such as a kick, a snare, or a crash in a drum loop. You can later quantize these audio slices without affecting the pitch or quality of the audio file.

You can also use the Sample Editor to apply offline processing to your file. Offline processing implies that the processing is not calculated every time you play the audio file, but rather processed once using the parameters inside an effect. Cubase will then create an additional audio segment in a special "Edit" folder (under your project's folder) where it will read the processed portion of the file (more on this in Chapter 10).

How To

To view the Sample Editor window:

▶ Select an audio clip (file) or audio event in the Audio Part Editor and press Ctrl(PC)/⌘(Mac)+E.

▶ Or double-click on an audio clip (file) or audio event in the Audio Part Editor.

▶ Select an audio clip (file) or audio region in the Media Pool and press Ctrl(PC)/⌘(Mac)+E.

▶ Or double-click on an audio clip (file) or audio region in the Media Pool.

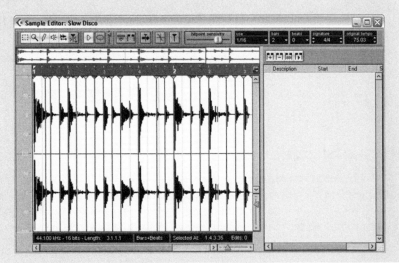

Figure 2.32
The Sample Editor window.

Spectrum Analyzer

The Spectrum Analyzer (SX version only) provides information about a selected audio event's average amplitude level over a frequency range. This can be useful for pinpointing frequencies that need to be equalized, for example. The Spectrum Analyzer (see Figure 2.33) displays this information in an X/Y, two-dimensional graphic, where the X axis represents frequencies and the Y axis represents amplitude values.

How To

To view the Spectrum Analyzer dialog box:

1. Select an audio clip (file) or audio event in the Audio Part Editor or in the Media Pool.
2. Select Audio > Spectrum Analyzer from the menu bar.
3. Adjust the settings or leave as is and click Process.

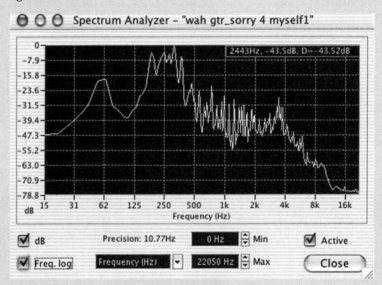

Figure 2.33
Cubase SX's Spectrum Analyzer dialog box.

History Box

Steinberg introduced the offline processing concept with SX/SL 1.0 as a way of offering multiple undo levels. This comes in especially handy when working with audio processing, since sometimes you have to process an audio file in order to free up some memory. But what happens if you change your mind about the effect you applied 15 steps down the road? Read on to find out.

Edit History

The Edit History dialog box (see Figure 2.34) views, selects, and undoes steps you have performed, giving you some piece of mind when you want to experiment a bit with your current project.

How To

To view the Edit History dialog box:

▶ Select Edit > History from the menu bar.

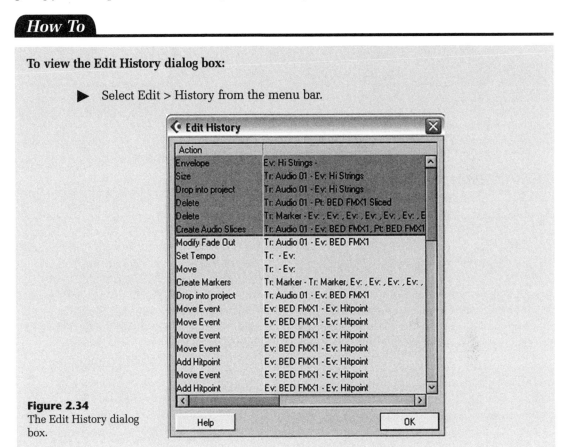

Figure 2.34
The Edit History dialog box.

Offline Process History

If undoing every step you made is not what you had in mind, maybe the Offline Process History dialog box will help you with going back in time. The history, in this case, corresponds to the processing steps applied on a digital audio event. Furthermore, every digital audio event in your pool that has been, at one point or another, edited through offline processing will keep track of what has been done to it. So for example, in Figure 2.35, we can see that three processes have been applied to an audio file. If you wanted to restore the file as it was before you applied any process in that list, you could simply select it and remove it from this list to go back to where you were.

How To

To view the Offline Process History dialog box:

▶   Select Edit > History from the menu bar.

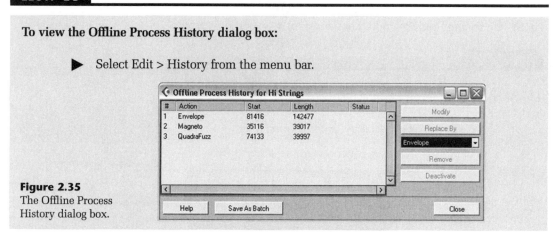

Figure 2.35
The Offline Process
History dialog box.

VST Effects and Instruments

Steinberg introduced the VST (Virtual Studio Technology) system in 1996, allowing Cubase users to include virtual effect processing to audio tracks in their projects, such as equalizers, compressors, and so on. Since 1999, VST instruments allow Cubase users to insert software synthesizers as sound modules inside the Cubase environment. Cubase SX/SL comes with built-in VST effects and instruments, but also plays host to third-party applications that have been developed to run under this system. As a result, Cubase not only offers tremendous flexibility in music creation, but it also offers an open platform for future expansion.

For example, the new Q (see Figure 2.36) VST effect (SX version only) offers a high-quality stereo four-band parametric EQ. The Multiband Compressor (SX version only) seen in Figure 2.37 compresses the dynamic of an audio signal by using up to five user-defined bands. This is very useful when you want to compress certain areas of a frequency bandwidth more than others or to enhance a range of frequency while applying heavy compression on others.

Figure 2.36
The Q VST effect
processor.

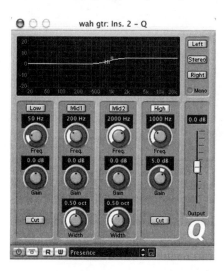

Figure 2.37
The Multiband
Compressor VST effect
processor.

Steinberg also redesigned and renamed the TrueTape tape saturation simulator plug-in introduced in an earlier version, which now comes under the name Magneto (see Figure 2.38).

Figure 2.38
The Magneto VST effect
processor.

CHAPTER 2

3

Getting Started

Preparing your computer for Cubase means that your operating system, sound card, and MIDI interface are installed properly and configured for optimal audio operations. Running an application such as Cubase requires a stable computer environment and lots of available computer resources, especially when using effects and software instruments. Making these resources available to Cubase will help you get the most out of your working session. Operation systems are designed to look good and do many things. In most cases, you will need to change your computer's configuration to emphasize performance rather than looks.

Here's a summary of what you will learn in this chapter:

▶ How to choose the right driver for your sound card when working in Cubase.

▶ The difference between dedicated, DirectX, and multimedia ASIO drivers.

▶ How to set up your sound card driver and default MIDI ports in Cubase.

▶ How and when to use Direct Monitoring.

▶ What you should consider when running audio applications simultaneously with Cubase.

▶ Different connection scenarios between Cubase and your studio equipment.

▶ How to create a new project and configure it for your needs.

Setting Up Your Peripherals

Before you can do anything in Cubase, you must make sure that your software is properly installed on your system, that you have a stable operating system, and that the latest drivers for all your peripherals are installed, including peripherals you think are not related, like video card and network card drivers. If you find that your operating system crashes often for no apparent reason, reinstalling it might be a good idea. This may save you from experiencing problems later on. In a perfect world, this would be done automatically. But because there are probably as many systems out there as there are Cubase users, you will need to run some little tests to allow the software to establish what is the best configuration for its optimal performance. You must then tweak this a bit further before you can establish what is the best configuration for your optimal performance.

The first thing you will want to set up is how Cubase communicates with the operating system, the MIDI device, and the sound card's driver. Because Cubase uses both MIDI and digital audio, you will need to set up both drivers properly.

Sound Cards and Drivers

Cubase handles both MIDI and audio recording, which makes it important to configure these peripherals appropriately. One of the most important steps in configuring sound cards and MIDI interfaces is to make sure you have the proper drivers installed on your computer. Properly installed sound cards and MIDI interfaces will make working with Cubase a great experience, while working with a doubtful configuration will make working with the same software a nightmare.

Mac users have no choice but to use ASIO drivers provided by their sound card manufacturer, or if you are OSX, the Core Audio subsystem provided by Apple. PC users can choose from three types of drivers supported by Cubase: card specific ASIO drivers, generic ASIO multimedia drivers, and DirectX ASIO drivers. Always use a card that has ASIO drivers written specifically for this card if you want to have a good experience with Cubase or other Steinberg products.

ASIO Drivers

ASIO drivers are also *strongly recommended* by all Steinberg products. ASIO is the acronym for *Audio Stream Input/Output*, a technology developed by Steinberg that allows a sound card to efficiently process and synchronize inputs and introduces the least amount of latency, or delay, between the inputs and the outputs of the sound card. The smaller the latency, the shorter the time between what you record and what you hear recorded once the signal has been processed by the computer. High latencies are often troublesome when recording live material because there is always a delay when monitoring the audio. The greater the latency time, the more noticeable the delay will be. ASIO drivers have a short latency because they do not send the signal into the operating system before sending it to its outputs. Therefore, you can record music while playing back tracks without any noticeable differences. A typical latency for a sound card using a dedicated ASIO driver should be below 10 milliseconds. Note also that latency affects the response time of VST instruments, the output and input monitoring in a channel, and the response time of faders and knobs inside Cubase.

It goes without saying that this type of driver is highly recommended. In fact, if you went through the trouble of buying this book and Cubase SX, chances are that you are serious about making the most of your audio investment. You should therefore use a sound card that has an ASIO driver written especially for it. Most professional sound cards today support this format, but if in doubt, consult both Steinberg's Web site and the sound card manufacturer's Web site for information about ASIO compatibility.

DirectX Drivers

If your sound card doesn't offer an ASIO driver written for it, you will need to use Microsoft's DirectSound technology, which is part of DirectX. On the other hand, if it does, you can skip this section as you should not use this driver anyway. The DirectX driver should be included with your sound card. When using a DirectX driver you will also have to use the ASIO DirectX Full Duplex driver, which is provided by Steinberg on your Cubase installation CD. In the absence of a sound card-specific ASIO driver, the ASIO DirectX driver provides the next best (but by far not the most desirable) solution. This driver will allow Cubase to communicate with DirectX and allow full duplex on your sound card. Full duplex implies that you can record and play back at the same time using your sound card (in contrast, half duplex allows only one operation at a time, play or record). Since Cubase has to communicate with DirectX through the ASIO DirectX driver and then DirectX communicates with the sound card, expect higher latencies when using this type of driver setup.

To set this driver up, you will need to use the ASIO Direct Sound Full Duplex Setup window to configure your sound card properly (see Figure 3.1). This window lists all DirectSound compatible input and output ports on your system. Devices that are checked will be available inside Cubase. You can find the ASIO DirectX Full Duplex setup utility in a special ASIO folder under the Cubase program folder. To launch it, simply locate its icon or alias and launch it from there.

How To

To configure your DirectSound drivers:

▶ To activate a port, check the box found on the left of the device's name. To deactivate it, uncheck it.

▶ The buffer size is used when audio data is transferred between Cubase and the audio card. Larger buffer sizes will ensure that playback will occur without glitches, while smaller buffer sizes will reduce the latency. The default buffer size appearing in this column should be fine in most cases; however, if you want to solve crackling sounds in your audio when using this driver, you may increase the buffer size by double-clicking in this column and entering a new value. Try to keep these values within increments of 512 samples.

▶ If you hear a constant offset (delay) during playback of audio and MIDI recordings, you can adjust the output or input latency time by using offset value. In most cases, you should leave this at its default zero value. If you are noticing a delay at the output, increase the output offset and if you are noticing a delay at the input, increase the input offset.

▶ The Sync Reference option lets you determine how MIDI will be synchronized with the audio. You can choose to synchronize MIDI to the audio input or audio output. This will also determine which offset value you should adjust as mentioned above.

▶ The Card Options should be left with the Full Duplex option selected; however, if you are noticing problems while this is selected, you can check the Start Input First option.

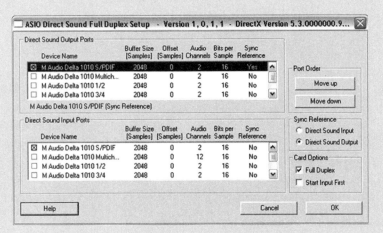

Figure 3.1
The ASIO Direct Sound
Setup dialog box.

Multimedia Drivers

If your sound card does not have dedicated ASIO drivers and your computer (PC) does not have DirectX drivers either, you will need to use the ASIO Multimedia driver. As with the DirectX configuration, Cubase will communicate with your sound card by passing through the ASIO multimedia driver, which communicates to your Windows driver, which communicates with your sound card. That's a long way to go and as you might have guessed, longer delays (latency) are to be expected.

The ASIO multimedia driver is a standard (generic) ASIO driver provided by Steinberg, allowing you to record and play audio through your sound card when using Cubase. You should use this driver only if you don't have a dedicated ASIO driver or DirectX installed on your computer (again, this applies only to PC users). Before running Cubase for the first time, you will be asked to profile your ASIO Multimedia driver. If you've never done this, now is a good time to do so. If you have a dedicated ASIO driver, you can skip this step since the settings will not influence your work inside Cubase because you won't be using the driver anyway.

You can find the ASIO multimedia setup utility in the same special ASIO folder as the ASIO DirectX mentioned earlier, under the Cubase program folder. To launch it, simply locate its icon or alias and launch it from there.

How To

To configure your Windows multimedia drivers:

▶ In the ASIO Multimedia Setup dialog box (see Figure 3.2), you will find a preset field. If your card is listed there, select it. If it isn't, run the setup in Advanced mode by clicking on the Advanced Options button.

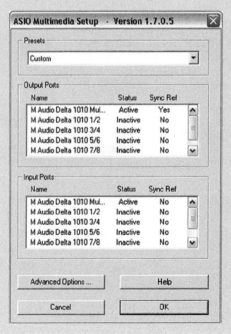

Figure 3.2
The ASIO Multimedia
Setup dialog box.

▶ As with the DirectX dialog box, you will find all input and output ports for your sound card listed (see Figure 3.3). A check mark next to the device's name indicates that a device will be available in Cubase. If you wish to use your sound card with a different sampling rate than the one indicated in the corresponding field, select the new sampling rate and run a simulation to make sure the buffer size for this device at the selected sampling rate will be appropriate.

▶ Use the Global Settings area to change the Sync Reference and Card options for your sound card. You should leave these options at their default values unless you run into some problems when checking the buffer size and sync. Avoid using DMA block with any PCI sound card.

▶ In the Card Options field, uncheck Use 16-bit only if you are sure your sound card does not support more than 16-bit resolution. If this option is checked, you need to make sure not to select 24-bit mode recording once inside Cubase.

▶ If you want to test the proper buffer size for each active input and output port, select the port and click on the Detect Buffer Size button. It is recommended that you wait for the detection process to be completed before doing anything else on your computer. This will provide a more accurate detection of the appropriate buffer size for your device.

▶ Once completed, verify your buffer size and sync reference by clicking on the Check Buffers and Sync button. If the device passes the test, then run a simulation as explained in the next paragraph. If the test fails, a dialog box will appear offering possible solutions to improve your settings.

▶ The Run Simulation button tests the current settings for your sound card when using the ASIO multimedia driver in Cubase. It is important that you test your settings whenever you make changes to them.

▶ If you are satisfied with your settings, you can store the changes as a preset by clicking on the Store button.

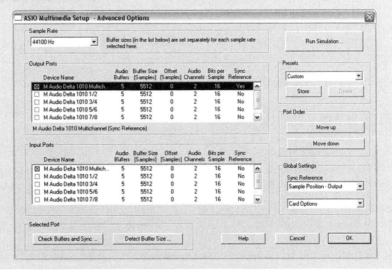

Figure 3.3
The ASIO Multimedia
Advanced Options Setup
dialog box.

MIDI Interfaces and Drivers

Installing a MIDI card requires you to use the driver that comes with the hardware. This is usually quite simple and is explained in your hardware documentation. Hardware specifics will not be discussed here, because there are too many MIDI and audio interfaces out there to cover them thoroughly. But to make sure everything is set up properly, one good starting point is to verify that your MIDI port appears in your system configuration.

How To

To make sure your MIDI port is installed properly on a PC running Windows XP:

1. Click on Start > Settings > Control Panel.
2. In the Control Panel, double-click on the System icon.
3. Click on the Hardware tab to make it active and then click on the Device Manager button.
4. Locate the Sound, video and game controller entry and expand the list to view the items under this entry.
5. Double-click on your MIDI interface or sound card if you have a MIDI port on it to view its properties.
6. The device's Properties dialog box will appear. Click on the Properties tab inside the dialog box to view if your port is installed properly.
7. In this dialog box, you will also find a Properties button. Select your installed MIDI port and click on this button to see if there are any messages warning you that the device is not installed properly or if this device is in conflict with another peripheral.

At this point, if you have not seen any question marks or exclamation marks next to your device and if there is no indication that it is not installed properly, you should be able to use this port in Cubase. If, on the other hand, you have found a problem, you should try reinstalling the driver for this peripheral and follow the installation procedure provided by your device's manufacturer.

Looking at Figure 3.4, if your device were not installed properly, you would see a red X or a question mark on the device's icon in the list. If the device were installed but not working properly, an exclamation mark would appear over your device's icon in this same list.

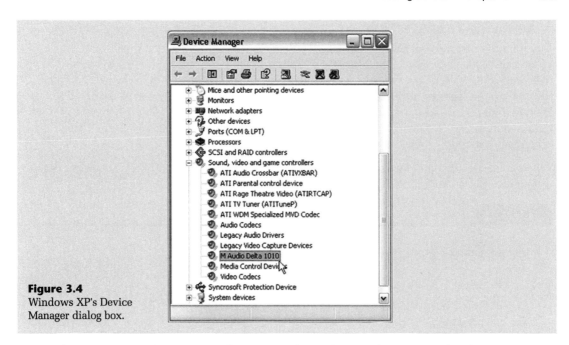

Figure 3.4
Windows XP's Device
Manager dialog box.

You might want to consult your manufacturer's Web site for specific settings related to your MIDI or audio device. This Web site will probably provide you with a driver update and tips on configuring your device with Cubase and other software.

Monitoring Audio

Monitoring audio here refers to the possibility of listening to an audio signal as it enters the computer hosting Cubase. There are three basic audio monitoring methods when working with Cubase (see Figure 3.5): monitoring through Cubase, monitoring through an external mixer, and direct monitoring, which is a combination of the two previous methods.

Figure 3.5
Different methods of
monitoring audio.

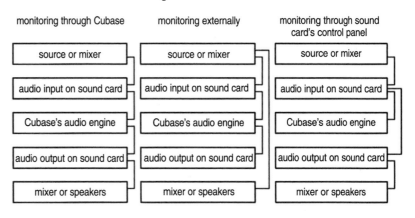

Monitoring Through Cubase

When monitoring through Cubase, the signal enters the VST audio system, is routed and processed inside Cubase, and then sent to the sound card's output port. For this to work well, you need a sound card with a low latency; otherwise, the signal coming out of Cubase, once it has been processed, panned, leveled, and equalized, will be delayed by the amount of this card's latency. With lower latencies, this delay will not be noticeable, but with higher latencies, it will definitely throw off someone trying to record a new track while listening to what has been previously recorded.

When you monitor sound through Cubase, there are four different monitoring preferences that influence when an audio track starts monitoring an incoming signal.

How To

To set up auto monitoring preferences:

1. Select Preferences in the File (PC) or Apple (Mac) menu.

2. Scroll down the list on the left and select VST at the bottom of this list (see Figure 3.6).

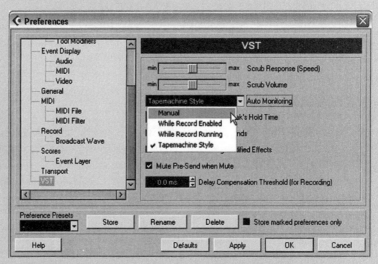

Figure 3.6
Changing the Auto Monitoring options in the VST Preferences.

3. In the right section, select one of the four auto monitoring options: Manual, While Record Enabled, While Record Running, and Tape Machine Style.

▶ **Manual** monitoring allows you to switch to input monitoring by pressing on the Monitor button in the track's channel mixer or the mixer panel (see Figure 3.7).

Figure 3.7
The Monitor button in the channel mixer.

▶ **While Record Enabled** will switch the channel into input monitoring as soon as you enable the Record Enable button for this channel (this is the red button below the monitor button in Figure 3.7).

▶ **While Record Running** will switch all the record enabled channels into input monitoring when you hit the Record button on the Transport panel.

▶ **Tape Machine Style** will switch a selected audio track into input monitoring automatically when recording or when the project is stopped, but will revert to output monitoring when you press play. This mode is similar to traditional analog tape recorder behavior.

4. Click Apply and then OK.

Monitoring Externally

When you monitor through an external mixer, what you are monitoring is routed and processed through an external mixer or a sound card mixer application, not inside Cubase. Think of external monitoring as a direct output on a mixer: a point going back out right after coming into Cubase, but before any type of control or processing can occur. When monitoring through an external mixer, you should avoid also monitoring through Cubase simultaneously, as you will be hearing two different signals with a delay between them. You can monitor an audio signal that has been previously recorded without any problem, but make sure to mute the track being recorded inside Cubase to avoid this double-monitoring problem when using an external mixer.

CHAPTER 3

Direct Monitoring

Direct monitoring mode (with ASIO 2.0-compatible sound cards): Direct monitoring controls the monitoring from the sound card's control panel. The options available to you will therefore be sound card dependent. Cubase SX users can also use the input bus faders to adjust the input levels, but since the signal is sent back out right away, you won't be able to monitor (visually) the signal inside the track's audio channel. You can't apply processing, such as EQ or insert effects, and monitor these effects while recording when direct monitoring is active. The sound is sent directly to Cubase, but you are monitoring the input, not what's coming from Cubase. Because this monitoring is done through the sound card's mixer utility, it bypasses the VST audio engine that sends the signal into the Cubase mixer for processing. This gives you the opportunity to monitor what is coming into Cubase directly through your sound card's outputs without adding any delay between the input and the output. Direct monitoring is the best way to get a signal sent out to a pair of headphones during recording, without adding latency. However, if your sound card's latency is not noticeable and you wish to add a reverb into the headphone mix, for example, you will be better off not using the Direct Monitoring option, as processing inside Cubase is bypassed altogether.

How To

To enable direct monitoring mode:

1. Select the Device Setup option from the Devices menu.
2. Click on VST Multitrack in the list to view its panel on the right side.
3. Check the Direct Monitoring option and then click on the Apply button followed by the OK button.

Selecting Devices in Cubase

Now that you have made sure your MIDI and audio drivers are installed properly, let's take a look at how you can activate them in Cubase. The Devices Setup dialog box activates/deactivates MIDI ports, selects the appropriate ASIO driver for your sound card, and configures other aspects of Cubase. Among these other settings, you will find the VST System Link settings, which allow you to network different computers through any digital audio connection. You can also select the video player driver used to display video files that you may load in a project and remote control devices that will control certain aspects of your mixing. However, in this chapter, we will discuss only the MIDI and audio settings and leave the other settings for later, as they become relevant.

First, you must select which MIDI port you want to use as your default MIDI port. In most cases, this will be the MIDI port connected to your MIDI keyboard.

How To

To set your default MIDI device:

1. Select the Device Setup option from the Devices menu.
2. Click on Default MIDI Ports in the list to view its panel on the right side. Notice that there are two tabs in the right side of this dialog box: Setup and Add/Remove. The Add/Remove tab will be used only to add remote control devices to your Device Setup dialog box.
3. From the MIDI Input drop-down menu, select the appropriate MIDI input.
4. From the MIDI Output drop-down menu, select the appropriate MIDI output.
5. Click the Apply button.

How To

To configure your sound card in Cubase:

1. Select the Device Setup option from the Devices menu (if you are not already there).
2. Click on VST Multitrack in the list to view its panel on the right side.
3. In the ASIO Driver field, select the appropriate driver for your sound card. If you have a dedicated ASIO driver for your sound card, it is strongly recommended you use it.
4. If you are using a dedicated ASIO driver, you can set the clock source by clicking on the Control Panel button. You can choose if you want your sound card to follow an incoming digital clock source or use its own clock source for digital timing. The clock source dictates the sampling frequency. If you don't have any other digital audio devices connected to your sound card, this should always be set to internal. Since each sound card offering a dedicated ASIO driver is different, the options you will find in this panel will also be different Figure 3.8.

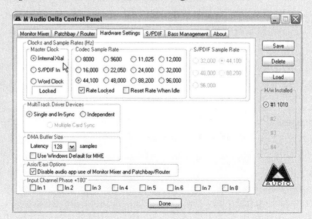

Figure 3.8
The Control panel for the Delta-1010 from M-Audio.

CHAPTER 3

If you run into audio dropouts or if your hard disk performance indicator often peaks, causing audio dropouts, you may adjust the number of disk buffers and their sizes in the Device Setup dialog box. Increasing the number of buffers and their size will reduce the load on your hard disk, helping it by loading a portion of the audio in a memory buffer to prevent stuttering in your audio when the hard disk is not quick enough. The negative effect of this, however, is that higher buffer sizes and additional buffers will increase latency. If you don't notice any changes in your audio after increasing these values and you notice that your hard disk performance meter still indicates that your hard disk access peaks, you might need to get a faster hard disk or mix down some of the tracks to reduce the disk access. To view the VST Performance meter panel, press the F12 keyboard shortcut or select Devices > VST Performance. You can also see the performance of your computer on the default transport panel.

How To

To modify the number of disk buffers and their size:

1. Select the Device Setup option from the Devices menu.
2. Click on VST Multitrack in the list to view its panel on the right side.
3. Use the arrows to the right of the values next to the Number of Disk Buffers or double-click on the value and enter the desired value.
4. Use the drop-down menu next to the Disk Buffer Size to select a different buffer size value.
5. Click Apply when done.

Running Other Audio Applications Simultaneously

There is not much to say about running other nonaudio-related applications simultaneously, besides the fact that if you are running applications that require memory and CPU power, these resources won't be available to you in Cubase. Some background applications might start doing a hard disk scan in the middle of a recording. A good example of this would be Find Fast, an applet that comes with Microsoft Office, or Norton Antivirus system scan.

Any background memory or hard disk-intensive applications should be disabled when using Cubase. A good rule of thumb to follow is to not run other nonessential applications when running Cubase to improve your performance. If you want to find out what is running inside your Windows system, press Ctrl+Alt+Del. This will bring up the Windows task manager window that shows you which applications are currently running. For example, you can click on the Processes tab to view how much memory Cubase uses (see Figure 3.9).

You can end a process or an application (depending on whether the Applications or Processes tab is active) by selecting the item in the list, right-clicking on it, and selecting the appropriate option. Nothing you do in this dialog box can harm your system in any way. Note that once you reboot your system, the applications that were running before you ended them will be back in business. So, changing the settings for these applications is a good idea. The more icons you have in the bottom right corner of your taskbar, the more applications are running in the background, using

Figure 3.9
The Windows task
manager window.

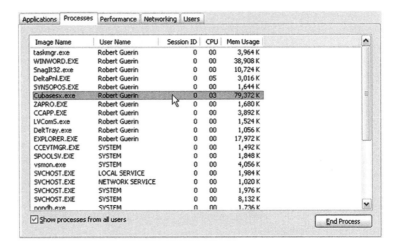

valuable resources. Make sure you keep those to a minimum. If you can, try to use a separate computer for your Internet activities. Antivirus utilities can use up to 30 percent of your system's resources.

If you are running OS X on a Macintosh computer, you can also view the active processes by accessing the Process Viewer. You can access the Process Viewer window by selecting the Finder's menu; then choose Go > Applications > Utilities Folder > Process Viewer (see Figure 3.10).

Figure 3.10
The Process Viewer
window on OS X.

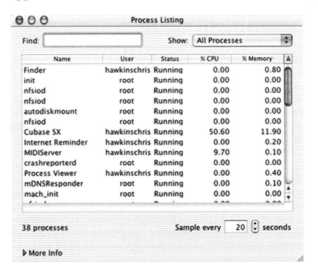

There is a way to deactivate certain applications that are not necessary while running Cubase to free up resources. The most effective way to do this is to choose any program that is loaded on the Dock and then choose the File > Quit option. You can do this is in the Process Viewer; however, you need to be sure you know what you are turning off.

The situation is different if you try to run another audio-related application. To run audio-related applications simultaneously with Cubase, you will need a sound card that provides a multiclient driver. What is a multiclient driver? Basically, it is a driver that allows different applications shared access to the sound card. Think of it this way: A single-client access is like going to the grocery store and having only one cash register open. Everybody has to line up and wait their turn to pay for their groceries. A multiclient driver is like having two or three cash registers opened where people can go to a second or even a third cash register if the first is busy.

When Cubase is loaded, it generally takes over the controls of the sound card, leaving it unusable for other applications that would need it as well to run simultaneously, such as a third-party virtual sampler. If you don't have a multiclient driver, there are ways around it, but with some limitations.

Steinberg provides an engine called *Rewire* that lets you share audio resources between Steinberg products and other Rewire compatible products, like Live from Ableton and Reason from Propellerheads or Sonar 3 from Cakewalk. This is discussed in Chapter 11.

For other types of software, such as Tascam's GigaStudio or GigaSampler, you will have to load this software first and set Cubase as your default sequencer from within the GigaStudio or GigaSampler environment. After this is done, you can launch Cubase from the Sequencer button within GigaStudio or GigaSampler. If you have problems doing this, try disabling audio outputs in GigaStudio that you want to use in Cubase (for good measure, keep outputs 1 and 2 available for Cubase) and disabling audio inputs and outputs that you want to use in GigaStudio. By doing this, you are effectively assigning certain outputs of your sound card to Cubase and others to GigaStudio. You should also check the Release ASIO Driver in Background option found in the Device Setup dialog box (see Figure 3.11).

How To

To release the ASIO driver when Cubase is in the background:

1. In the Device menu, select the Device Setup option.
2. In the Device Setup window, click to highlight the VST Multitrack option.
3. In the Setup section, check the Release ASIO Driver in Background option.
4. Click OK to complete.

Figure 3.11
Activating the Release ASIO Driver in Background option in the Device Setup dialog box, under the VST Multitrack section.

When running such a setup, you are imposing a huge load on your computer resources and are also testing many compatibility issues between the different manufacturers of software and hardware. If you are experiencing difficulties, here are a couple of places to look for information:

▶ Visit Steinberg's site to see if there is any additional information on the issue you are having.

▶ Visit your other software manufacturer's Web site as well; it also might have some answers for you.

▶ Check on your sound card manufacturer's Web site to see if you have the latest drivers for your sound card, and take a look at the support, troubleshooting, or FAQ section to find additional help.

▶ Use discussion forums to share your problems with others; chances are, someone else had the same problem you have and might have a workaround for you.

Hooking Up Your Equipment

There are many ways to hook up your equipment to your computer, and it all depends on what you want to do and what type of equipment you want to hook up. On this topic, there are two major problems you want to avoid:

1. Having too much sound—what is normally called a feedback loop.

2. Having no sound at all.

The following figures represent simple, yet effective ways to connect your equipment. Obviously, there are many more combinations, and you should try drawing out one for your own studio to help you organize your wiring effectively.

Figure 3.12 shows a very modest MIDI setup, using the audio outputs of the keyboard to feed the self-amplified studio monitors. An alternative to this, especially if you want to record the MIDI coming out of your keyboard into a digital format, is to hook up the audio outputs of your keyboard to the inputs of your sound card and the outputs of your sound card to the inputs of your speakers. The way the diagram is shown, this allows you to use the sound card's input for an acoustic instrument or a microphone. Remember that microphones have a low impedance output (microphone inputs) and that, normally, your sound card's inputs are high impedance (line inputs). You will probably need a microphone preamplifier if you want to use it in this way and avoid using the microphone inputs on a sound card.

The MIDI input of the keyboard would go in the MIDI output of the computer, and the MIDI output of the keyboard would go in the MIDI input of the computer.

The way you connect your audio outputs depends on the audio system at hand. If you have powered monitors, you can hook up the audio outputs of your computer or keyboard directly to them, sending the left signal to the left speaker and the right signal to the right speaker. If you are using an amplifier, you can do basically the same thing, but you should send the signal to the amplifier first and then distribute the audio signal from the amplifier to the speakers.

Figure 3.12
Simple setup without any
mixer for a single source
monitoring.

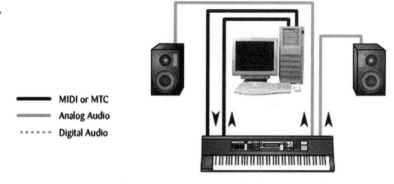

In Figure 3.13, a small desktop mixer has been added. This will be necessary if you are using more than one audio source (in this case, the keyboard and sound module). This way, you can have as many audio sources as your mixer has inputs. You then feed the output of your mixer into your computer. This can be a bit tricky if you have only one set of outputs on your desktop mixer. Most desktop mixers have a different volume control for monitoring and master outputs. You should take the audio outputs of the computer and feed them into a separate pair of inputs that can be routed to a signal path that doesn't go back into itself (in this case, the computer), like a tape return, for example. If you have direct outputs or buses on your mixer, use those to send the signal to your computer rather than using the main outputs. This way, you can monitor independently the sound going to the computer and the sound coming from the computer without having the computer go back into the mix.

Notice that the MIDI Thru of the keyboard is used to echo the output of the computer into the sound module.

Figure 3.13
Simple setup with a
desktop mixer for
multiple-source
monitoring.

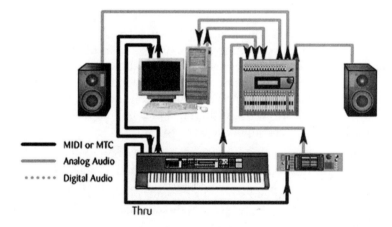

Figure 3.14 shows a setup using a multiple input/output sound card without the use of a mixer, which will allow you to use the Cubase mixer as a mixing table. While this is not the most flexible way to work, if you are on a budget and can't afford a mixer, it's a good compromise.

You need to send all the audio outputs to separate audio inputs on the sound card and a pair of outputs from the sound card to speakers for monitoring. A MIDI patch bay has been added to help with the MIDI patching, but this is not necessary. If you don't have a MIDI patch bay, you will need to send the MIDI Thru of your keyboard to the MIDI In of the sound module and the MIDI Thru of the sound module to the MIDI In of the drum machine (or other sound module), making the keyboard and computer front and center in your MIDI routing (keyboard's MIDI out to computer's MIDI in and vice versa).

Figure 3.14
Setup for a MIDI studio
using a MIDI patch bay
and multiple input sound
card without any mixer.

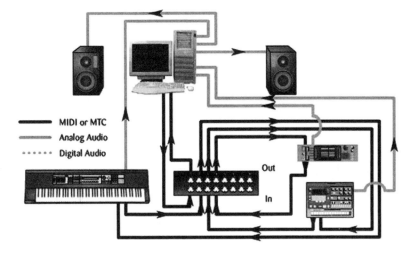

Figure 3.15 shows a setup using a simple digital in/out sound card that feeds and receives information through digital transfer from the digital mixer. As in Figure 3.13, you might want to use an extra pair of audio outputs to monitor the output of your computer without sending it back into the signal of the mixer, once again creating a feedback loop.

Figure 3.15
Setup for a MIDI or audio
studio using a digital
mixer and a sound card
providing digital inputs
and outputs.

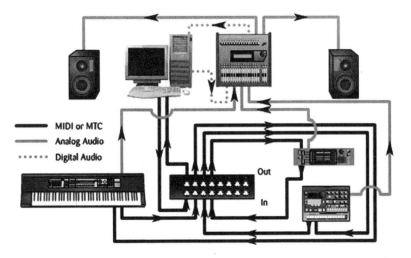

Creating a New Project

Projects in Cubase SX/SL are the equivalent of documents in Word, an image file in Adobe's Photoshop, or any other software-specific file format. A project holds all the information needed to recreate the work, with the exception of media files, which are saved as separate entities on your hard disk and referred to by the project file when editing it.

Cubase VST users will notice that this is a bit different, since there are no longer any distinctions between arrangement files and song files. In theory, you can have as many projects opened inside Cubase as you wish; however, in practice your system's resources will most likely dictate how many projects you can load into memory simultaneously. When you have more than one project window opened inside Cubase, you can drag events from one project to another.

When you launch Cubase, it will prompt you to select a new project template (see Figure 3.16) if this is your first time, or it will ask you if you want to open an existing project (see Figure 3.17). Templates are simply project files that were saved as templates inside the Cubase SX program folder. To learn more about how to create templates, see Appendix D.

Figure 3.16
The New Project
Template Selection dialog
box.

Figure 3.17
The Open Project dialog
box.

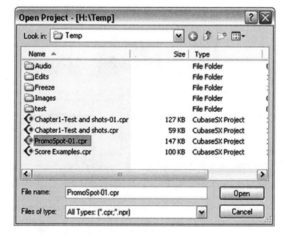

Let's start by creating a new project.

How To

To create a new project:

1. If Cubase prompts you to open an existing document (Figure 3.17), click on the New Project button. Otherwise, you will see the New Project dialog box.

2. In the New Project dialog box, select an Empty project.

3. Click OK. Cubase will then prompt you to select a folder. This should be the location where you want to save your project file. Cubase will automatically create subfolders to store audio, image, and fade files inside this folder.

4. Select the drive and folder inside that drive (if necessary). You may also choose to create a new folder by clicking on the Create button (Figure 3.18). After you've entered a name for your new folder, click on the OK button.

5. Click OK once again with the newly created folder selected to close the Select Directory dialog box.

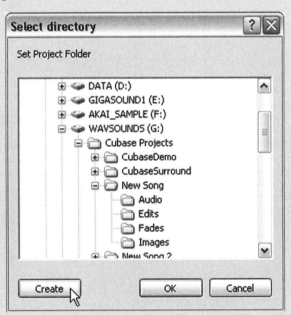

Figure 3.18
The Select Directory dialog box allows you to choose an existing folder or create a new one for your new project.

Cubase creates an empty project, or it will automatically create a project with tracks corresponding to the template file you decided to open. For example, if you selected the Stereo Mastering Setup template, you'll get a single stereo audio track with the highest resolution (32-bit) supported by Cubase, as well as a marker track to navigate within the mastering project. One thing you should keep in mind is that each project file should be saved in its own folder and setting up your project should take place *before* you start working in it rather than after. So let's set up our project.

CHAPTER 3

Setting Up Your Project

Each project is saved as a CPR file, which is short for Cubase PRoject file. Inside this project file you can have a number of MIDI, audio, or video event references, as well as automation, effect, and VST instrument settings. Note that audio or video events are not saved with the project file. References to these media files are kept inside the project file, so when you load the project file later, it will find the media files where you left them, or if you have moved them since the last time you saved the project file, it will ask you to find them in order to load them properly inside the project. Furthermore, if you delete the folder containing the audio files used in a project file without backing them up beforehand, you will no longer be able to use this audio in your project, and Cubase will warn you that it could not load certain audio (or video) files.

As for the project settings, they refer to four groups of settings: the duration of the project, the frame rate when working with video, the display format and its display offset value, and finally its digital audio recording settings.

How To

To set up your project:

1. Press Shift-S (or Project > Project Setup) to open the Project Setup dialog box.

2. Leave the Start field at its default setting. If you want your project to start at a different time than zero hour, zero minute, zero second, and zero frame, you can enter the proper value in this field. This will simply add the value you enter to the time displayed in your project. For example, adding 01:00:00:00 will cause the beginning of your project to correspond to this time instead of the usual 00:00:00:00.

3. In the Length field, click on the minute value and enter 01 or if you have a mouse with a scroll wheel, you can scroll forward to increase the value (see Figure 3.19). This will cause the project to have a length of one minute. In other words, if you plan on creating a project with a specific length, this is where you determine the time at the right edge of a project. Setting up the length will also influence the proportion of time displayed in the overview area of the current project.

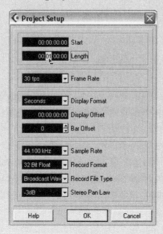

Figure 3.19
Increasing the values in a field by using a mouse with a scroll wheel.

4. If you are working with video file or synchronizing to an external time code provided by a video tape you can set the Frame Rate field to the corresponding value of the frame rate of the video or time code format of the external sync signal. This will ensure that the time displayed in Cubase in time code format corresponds to the time code format with which it is synchronizing.

5. In the Display Format, select Bars+Beats from the drop-down menu to determine how time is displayed in your project. You can change this later while working in your project.

6. The Display Offset value can be left at its default value, in most cases, but if you are synchronizing your project to an external video that starts at a frame other than zero—for example, if your tape starts at 01:59:45:00—you might still want your project to start at the position 00:00:00:00. Then you would set the Display Offset value at 01:59:45:00 for your start position (00:00:00:00) to correspond to this time.

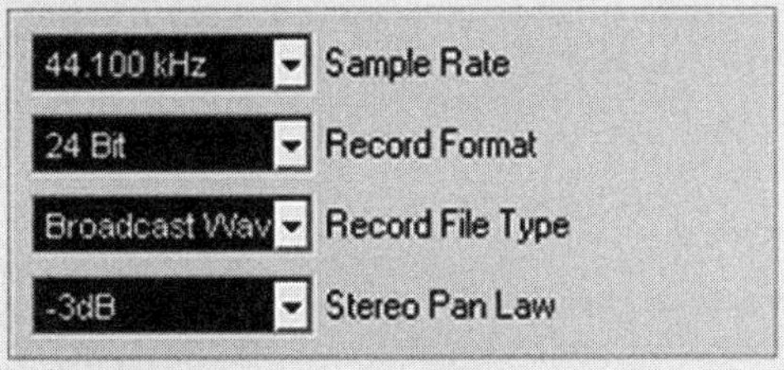

Figure 3.20
The digital audio project recording preference settings.

7. Set the Sample Rate field to the desired rate (see Figure 3.20). Once you set a sample rate for your project, you will not be able to change it later since all the sounds in your project will have to be at this sample rate. If you want to import audio files that use a different sample rate, you will need to resample them at the current project's sample rate in order for these files to play correctly in your project.

8. In the Record Format field, select the desired format from the drop-down menu. You may select any format supported by your sound card. Unlike the sample rate, you can import or record audio files with different bit depths in a single project. However, the record format selected here will determine the number of bits each sample will use when recording digital audio information in this project.

9. From the Record File Type, select the desired file type. The Broadcast Wave File format is identical to the Wave format with one exception: it enters text strings that will be embedded in your audio files. These text strings can contain information about you, your project, and time stamping information about the audio file itself. By using this file type, you don't have to enter this information later since it will be done automatically. You'll learn how you can enter this information shortly. The Wave 64 (SX only), on the other hand, is a Sonic Foundry proprietary format that supports files larger than 2GB. Wave 64 files are similar in their audio content to other wave or aiff files, but they are simply better suited for live concert recordings in surround format, where file size can reach the limit of regular wave file capacity fairly easily.

continued

10. In the Stereo Pan Law field, select the default –3dB from the drop-down field. When panning a channel, you want the left, center, and right pan position to sound equally loud. Selecting a –3dB setting or –6dB setting will ensure this. Otherwise, selecting the 0dB setting will cause the center pan position of a channel to sound louder. If this is what you want to achieve, then you can select this setting for a subsequent project. This is due to the fact that when two similar signals are panned to the center, they double-up, causing the perceived loudness to be 3 dB higher than a single audio signal. For example, two trumpet players will be 3 dB louder than one trumpet player, unless you pan both tracks hard left and hard right.

11. Click OK when done.

4

Navigating the Project Window

Now that you have Cubase installed and running correctly, it's time to delve into *using* it. The heart of Cubase is the project window, which is the main window that appears when you create a new file or launch Cubase, depending on the start-up preferences. Understanding how the project window works and what you can do in it is crucial to your work in Cubase—that's why we are going to spend an entire chapter making sure you understand all the nuances associated with it. Anything you do outside this window (but inside Cubase) will always be reflected in some way in the project window. These changes might not appear at first glance, but they will certainly affect the project's behavior. For example, if you delete a clip in another window, such as the media pool, it will show up in the project window if the audio clip you deleted in the pool is used in the project. If you change a MIDI channel, that change will be reflected in the project window. It is your main working area.

Here's a summary of what you will learn in this chapter:

▶ How to use the toolbar buttons.
▶ The different areas in the project window and how to use them.
▶ What markers are and how to use them.
▶ How to use the Transport panel.
▶ What the Tempo track is.
▶ Troubleshooting tips when you have problems with MIDI.
▶ An overview of the project window's context menus.

Project Window Options

Now that you have created a new project and set its properties, let's take a closer look at the project window in front of you. In Figure 4.1, you can find a quick reference to all the components included in this project window.

The rectangular button found in the upper left corner of the project window is the active project indicator. Since you can have more than one project open at the same time, the project that contains a blue button with a small rectangle inside indicates the active project. A project that is

Figure 4.1
The project window's
multiple areas, tools,
buttons, and shortcuts.

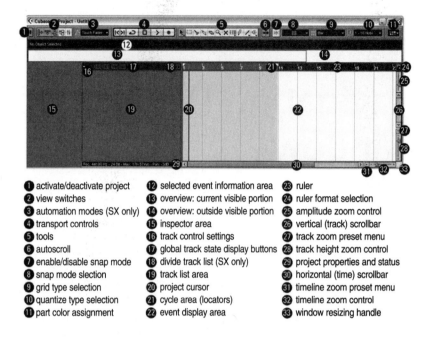

● activate/deactivate project
● view switches
● automation modes (SX only)
● transport controls
● tools
● autoscroll
● enable/disable snap mode
● snap mode slection
● grid type selection
● quantize type selection
● part color assignment

⑫ selected event information area
⑬ overview: current visible portion
⑭ overview: outside visible portion
⑮ inspector area
⑯ track control settings
⑰ global track state display buttons
⑱ divide track list (SX only)
⑲ track list area
⑳ project cursor
㉑ cycle area (locators)
㉒ event display area

㉓ ruler
㉔ ruler format selection
㉕ amplitude zoom control
㉖ vertical (track) scrollbar
㉗ track zoom preset menu
㉘ track height zoom control
㉙ project properties and status
㉚ horizontal (time) scrollbar
㉛ timeline zoom proset menu
㉜ timeline zoom control
㉝ window resizing handle

open but not currently active will display a circle inside a grayish button. In Figure 4.2, the active
project is currently displayed behind the inactive project. You can have many projects open
simultaneously, but only one active project at a time.

Figure 4.2
Active and inactive
project windows inside
Cubase.

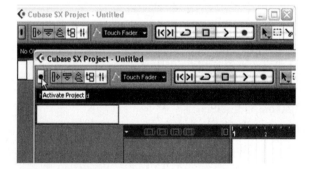

Project Window Display Buttons

The display buttons found in the upper-left corner of the project window (see Figure 4.3) quickly
display or hide certain areas of the project window or open different windows easily from the
project window.

▶ **Show/Hide Inspector.** Shows the inspector area of a selected track. The inspector
area displays information on the track's settings. Each type of track will display
information relating to its particular type.

▶ **Show/Hide Event Information bar.** Shows information for a selected part in the
upper portion of the project window. You can use this area to modify this
information.

Figure 4.3
The project window
Display Option buttons.

> **Show/Hide Overview.** Displays your entire project, spanning from the left to the right of your project window. The current visible portion of your project is displayed by a blue outline in the overview bar. You can use the overview to jump to another section of your project or to zoom to a region in this project. The total time displayed in the overview depends on the Length field value in the project's preferences (Shift-S).

> **Open Media Pool.** Opens the project's Media Pool window.

> **Open Mixer Panel.** Opens the project's Default Mixer panel.

Project Cursor Selection Buttons

In the middle of the project window, you will find a series of tool buttons (see Figure 4.4) that you can also find by right-clicking anywhere inside the project window. Most of these buttons are not new to Cubase SX/SL; however, there have been a few changes made in this toolbar since previous versions. Let's take a look at what each tool does.

Figure 4.4
The project window
Cursor Tool Selection
buttons.

> **Object Selection and Sizing tool** (see Figure 4.5): Selects events or parts by clicking on these events or by dragging a box over several events or parts when using the tool in normal sizing mode. (This is the default tool in Cubase.) The small arrow on the bottom-right corner of the button indicates that there are different modes to this tool. In fact, there are three sizing modes available. Normal Sizing resizes a part's start or end position. The second mode, Sizing Moves Contents, resizes the start or end position, but moves the content inside the part in the direction of your resize. The third selection/sizing mode is the Sizing Applies Time Stretch mode, which time-stretches the events inside a part to correspond to the new size of the part. These modes will be further discussed in Chapter 9.

Figure 4.5
The Object Selection
drop-down menu.

▶ **Range Selection tool.** Allows you to click and drag over multiple tracks and multiple parts and then you can apply different range-specific editing processes, such as delete, cut, insert, or crop to the selected range. These editing functions will also be discussed in Chapter 9.

▶ **Split tool.** Splits a selected part or parts anywhere, depending on the grid selection setup.

▶ **Glue Tube tool.** Joins an event or a part to the next event or part in the same track, creating either a continuous event (if you use the glue tube after splitting an event in two) or a continuous part containing two events if you either glue two nonconsecutive events or two parts together.

▶ **Eraser tool.** Erases one or several events/parts from a track. For example, if one event is selected, it will only erase one event.

▶ **Magnifying Glass tool.** Zooms in to your project by dragging a box around the area you want to view more closely or simply you can click to zoom in one step closer. You can also zoom out by using the Alt(PC)/Option(Mac) key and clicking or by double-clicking to move back a step.

▶ **Mute tool.** Mutes an event or a part on a track, or multiple parts or events, if more than one is selected. This is an alternative to erasing a part or an event. Muted events are not heard during playback; however, they can be unmuted later. If you need to mute all the parts or events on a track, you would be better off using the Track Mute button, which will be discussed later in this chapter.

▶ **Time Warp tool.** Provides a way to insert tempo changes for musical events to match up with video sequences. You can also use time warp when you need to figure the tempo of something you just recorded without knowing what the tempo was originally. As its name suggests, it warps or transforms linear time, the time of sound cues and digital audio recording, into musical time, the time of MIDI files and tempo-based events. And vice versa (see Figure 4.6). More on this in Chapter 9.

Figure 4.6
The Time Warp Tool modes.

▶ **Draw tool:** Draws in a part on a track or a series of automation points.

▶ **Line tool:** As with the selection and sizing tool, the line tool offers different operation modes (see Figure 4.7). Adds automation by creating a line between two points. The parabola, sine, triangle, and square modes allow you to create different types of automations, creating automation points that recreate the shape of the selected mode. For example, using the line tool in sine mode to add automation on a pan would create a panning automation shaped like a sine wave. These editing modes will also be discussed in Chapter 11.

Figure 4.7
The Line modes drop-down menu.

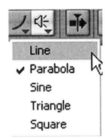

▶ **Play/Scrub tool:** Offers two modes to choose from. The play mode allows you to listen to an audio event or part from the point where you click until the moment you release the mouse. The scrub mode allows you to drag your cursor back and forth over an audio event or part to monitor the audio in the direction and speed your mouse is moving (see Figure 4.8).

Figure 4.8
The Play and Scrub drop-down menu.

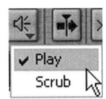

Project Transport Control Buttons

In Cubase SX/SL, there are two sets of transport controls. The project window itself holds the same controls as the transport panel, with the exception of the fast forward and rewind buttons: Go to Previous Marker, Go to Next Marker, Cycle Mode Toggle button, Stop, Play, and Record. The transport panel is a floating panel (you can move it around inside Cubase) and for space ergonomics purposes, it is possible to hide the transport panel and use the project window's transport controls if you want to do so. New to this version is the possibility to customize all the tools that appear in the toolbar, so if you don't want to see the Transport Control buttons there, you can hide them from view in the project window. To find out how to do so, go to Appendix D.

Figure 4.9
The project window's Transport Control buttons: Stop, Play, Record, and Cycle mode selection.

Another button related to transport is the Auto-scroll button found to the right of the Scrub button (see Figure 4.10). This button when active (blue state) will follow the position of the project cursor in time as the project moves forward, refreshing your display every time the project cursor moves past the right edge of the window. If you do not want for this to occur, you can deactivate the auto-scroll function.

Figure 4.10
The Auto-scroll or Follow
Song button in its active
state.

Project Editing Setup Buttons

When working on a project, you will be recording and editing events and parts in tracks. Moving events around is a task that you will probably do quite often. Determining exactly where you want to move it is your decision, but helping you in determining the accuracy of this movement is Cubase's task. This is done through a magnetic grid. How this grid works depends on how you want it to.

On the project window's toolbar, to the right of the Follow Song or Auto-scroll button (by default) is the Snap to Grid Toggle button. This button will restrict the movement of parts and events in your event display area to the settings found in the fields to the right of the Snap button. In other words, in its active state (blue) it uses the snap mode in the next field (to the right) to determine what becomes magnetic. Cubase offers seven modes from which to choose.

Figure 4.11
Grid and quantize
controls.

> **Grid.** A grid is defined by the grid setting found in the field to the right of the grid mode. In Figure 4.11, this is set to Use Quantize, which is the field to the right of the grid setting. In the same figure, this is set to 1/8 Note. In other words, an 1/8 magnetic grid will be available when the grid mode is selected. If, on the other hand, your project displays time values rather than bars and beats, increments of milliseconds would be displayed rather than note subdivision values. In the case of time code display, a frame count will be displayed instead. This makes it easy to snap events to any kind of grid, depending on the project at hand. The snap to grid mode is the default snap mode in Cubase.

> **Events.** The start and end of parts or events, as well as markers on marker tracks, become magnetized. So when you move a part, it will snap to the previous or next event as you move closer to it. This makes sense when you need to make sure there are no spaces between events or parts on a track, rather than aligning events to a grid as described previously.

> **Shuffle.** Moves events or parts that are adjacent to other parts by switching places with them. In Figure 4.12, tracks 1 and 2 are before-and-after shuffle examples with two consecutive parts. Tracks 3 and 4 are before-and-after shuffle examples with four consecutive parts. As you can see, the Part 01 is the part being shuffled around in both examples.

Figure 4.12
Using the grid in Shuffle
mode.

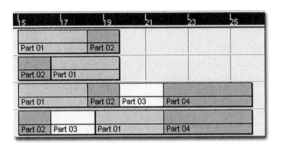

▶ **Magnetic cursor.** When this snap mode is active, the project cursor (play line)
becomes magnetic. Moving an event or a part close to it will cause the part to snap
to the cursor's position.

The other grid modes are combinations of these four previous modes.

▶ **Grid + Cursor.** The grid and cursor become magnetized when moving events or
parts.

▶ **Events + Cursor.** Events and parts edges, as well as the cursor, become magnetized
when moving events or parts.

▶ **Events + Grid + Cursor.** The events (or parts), the grid, and the cursor become
magnetized when moving events or parts.

The grid setting field to the right of the snap mode field enables you to set a value that will
determine how far apart each vertical time line in the grid will be magnetized. For example,
having a grid set at 1/1 implies that there will be one vertical timeline with every bar, to which
events, parts, and automation will stick when you move or create something in this window. A
1/16 grid implies that there will be such a line 16 times in each bar. Note that this value will only
become active if the grid is part of the snap mode you selected. For example, choosing the
magnetic cursor as the only snapping element will make changing the grid value useless. Also, the
values in this field will vary depending on the project's ruler display.

▶ If the time is displayed in bars and beats, the grid will display a choice of bars,
beats, or quantize value.

▶ If the time is displayed in seconds, the grid will display a choice of millisecond
increments.

▶ If the time is displayed in frames, the grid will display a choice of subframe, frame,
or second increments.

▶ If the time is displayed in samples, the grid will display a choice of sample
increments.

When using a bars and beats display in the ruler along with a grid snap mode that uses the
quantize value as its setting to determine which values are magnetized, you can select the quantize
value in the field to the right of the grid settings field. In other words, the quantize value field—as
with the grid setting field—becomes active and relevant when the snap mode selected makes use
of a grid.

CHAPTER 4

Quantize Values

Quantize values divide each bar in fractions equivalent to a note value. Typically, a 1/4 quantize value indicates that there will be a grid line at every quarter note. There are three groups of quantize value fractions: normal, tuplet and dotted. The normal fractions (1/2, 1/4, 1/8, 1/16 and so on) represent note values that can be divided by two. For example there can be four quarter notes in each 4/4 bar, eight eighth notes per 4/4 bar and sixteen sixteenth notes per 4/4 bar. Tuplet notes can usually be divided by three. For example, a 4/4 T value means that you can have up to six quarter note tuplets per 4/4 bar, twelve eighth notes per 4/4 bar, and so on. In other words, for every two notes in normal quantize value you have three notes in tuplet quantize value. A dotted quantize value represents one and a half normal quantize value. For example, three quarter notes are equal to two dotted quarter notes.

In Cubase, these quantize value differences are indicated with a T for tuplets, following the quantize value and a D for dotted, also following the quantize value. In Figure 4.13, a piano roll example of different quantizing values shows the different lengths and proportions each note (and silence) takes when changing the quantize value's grid.

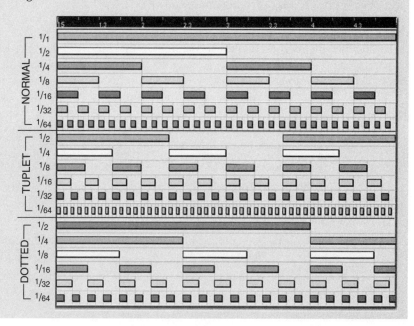

Figure 4.13
Example of quantize value lengths and grid size in a 4/4 bar.

Figure 4.14 shows you a simple little option that lets you define colors for each part in the Arrange window's Track View section by clicking on the Part Colors option. If this item is checked, the files and segments will be displayed with the colors of their respective parts. You can click on a part or select a track and then use one of the colors in the Part Colors option to apply it to your selection. Although adding colors to parts might help you in organizing your events on tracks, they will not add anything to the events because they are merely visual references.

CHAPTER 4

Figure 4.14
The Part Color drop-
down menu.

This option can be very useful when working with many tracks. You can group tracks by color or assign a name to each color so that you know what is what later on. For example, your rhythm section can be different shades of green, your wind section different shades of blue, and so on.

How To

To create your own custom colors and associated color names:

1. Click on the Select Colors option at the bottom of the Part Colors option drop-down menu. The Event Colors Setup dialog box will appear as shown in Figure 4.15.

2. Select a color to edit in the Part Colors area.

3. Type in a new name for that color by clicking inside the field next to a color swatch.

4. If you want to change the default color, change the color by using the Color Picker option.

5. Repeat the previous steps for another color if you want to create more custom colors and associated names. The buttons found below the Event Colors allow you to insert/remove color swatches and associated names, increase/decrease the color palette's intensity, increase/decrease the color palette's brightness, or load/save color presets.

6. Click OK when you are done.

Now that you have created custom colors and names associated with these colors, you can apply these colors to events and parts in your project.

Figure 4.15
You can customize colors
and add names to reflect
what each color should
represent in the Event
Colors Setup dialog box.

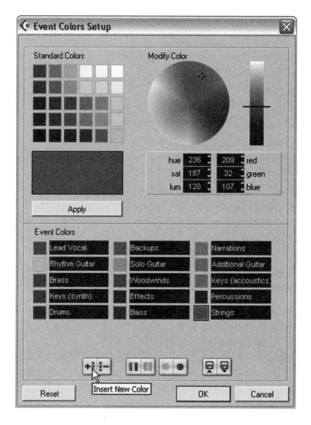

How To

To assign a color to parts and events:

1. In the project window, select the part(s) or event(s) for which you want to assign a color.

2. Select from the Events Colors drop-down menu one of the colors.

Setting Up a Quantize Grid

We've discussed how quantize grids work and looked at how you can magnetize different elements in the project window using the snap mode. Some snap modes don't take the grid into consideration, and therefore won't be affected by the quantize setup; however, the quantize grid serves not only for moving events but also influencing how parts are created and where markers will be placed. In other words, setting up an appropriate grid before you start working will help you get the result you want more effectively. For example, if you enable the snap, assign the grid to the snap mode and the bars as your grid type, when you create a new part using the pencil tool or when you record an event, the newly created part or recorded event will start at the closest bar from its beginning and will end at the closest bar after you stop recording or let go of the pencil tool. In such an example, you would only be able to create parts or events that increase in length by one bar at a time. Here's another example: if you're working with a video file and only want to create events that begin or end on a frame change, you simply need to change your ruler to display timecode and select the appropriate value in the grid type (in this case 1 frame). By doing so, whenever you record a new event or draw in a part to hold events (MIDI or audio), it will begin and end only at the same moment a frame ends and another one begins.

How To

To enable and configure a snap to grid setting:

1. Enable the Snap button.
2. Select the appropriate snap mode setting. For example, select Grid.
3. Select the appropriate grid mode setting. For example, if you chose Grid, you could select Bar, Beats or Use Quantize. If you chose Use Quantize, you will need to set the quantize value you want to use as your magnetic grid, otherwise, your grid setting is complete.
4. If you chose the Use Quantize option in the quantize setting field, select an appropriate quantize value for your grid.

If you choose to snap to events, shuffle, or magnetic cursor rather than grid, the quantize value will have no effect when you resize or move events.

Working with Markers

Markers are used to define different sections or locations in your project and make it easy to go back to that section or location later in your work. There are two types of markers in Cubase, and then there are the locators. The left and right locators are special cycle markers in a project. These locators are used to identify the current start and end locations when playing in cycle mode. They also play a role in identifying the punch-in and punch-out location during recording. You can quickly move your project cursor to the position of the left or right locators by using the numbers 1 and 2 respectively on your numeric keypad. Here's a look at the two types of markers:

▶ Cycle markers are similar to the left and right locators as they identify the beginning and ending of a range or section in your song. After you create cycle markers, you can move your left and right locators to the position of a cycle marker by double-clicking on it. Cycle markers are identified by numbers within brackets ([1]) in the marker track's inspector area or in the marker window.

▶ Markers identify a single position in your project, and they are identified by numbers without brackets in the track's inspector area or in the marker window. You can quickly move your project cursor to the position of the first six markers using the numbers 3 to 9 on your numeric keypad or by clicking on the numbers 1 through 15 to access the first 15 markers in the markers section inside the transport panel.

The locators are always present in your project; however, it is easier when a marker track is present in your project if you want to use markers and cycle markers. This said, you don't have to create a marker track but if you want to see where your markers are besides consulting the marker window, you will need to create this marker track.

How To

To create a marker track:

1. Right-click (or control-click on a one-button mouse) in the track list area.
2a. From the drop-down context menu, select Add Marker Track.
2b. Or select Add Track > Marker from the Project menu.

A marker track will appear in your project. If you wish to bring this marker track above the other tracks to quickly find your markers, you may click in the marker track's list area and drag to the desired position in the same track list area (above or below the current location). Note that you can only have one marker track per project.

To manage and view your markers, you can use either the inspector area of the marker track or bring up the marker window (Ctrl-M on PC or ⌘-M on Mac), as shown in Figure 4.16. These two windows will display the same information: the marker's ID number and its position, along with the end and length information for cycle markers. You can also add a description field to give a name to both types of markers.

Figure 4.16
The inspector area of the Marker track and the Markers window displaying your project's marker information.

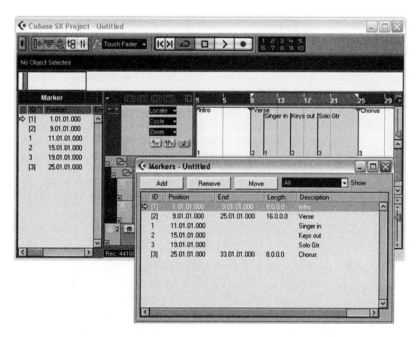

Adding Markers

Before we look at how to use markers to navigate in a project, let's take a look at how you can create markers. There are many ways of creating markers in Cubase, which are described in details in the operation manual of the software, so we will look at the easiest way to create both types of markers. This method implies that you have created a marker track in your project. So if you haven't done so already, create a marker track in your project.

How To

To add cycle markers in a project:

1. Make sure your snap mode is active and the grid setting is set appropriately (see section above for instructions). For this example, you can leave it at Snap to grid and have your grid set to bars.

2. Above the numbers in the ruler, when the pencil appears, click and drag over the timeline to create a lighter blue cycle line over the area you want to define as a cycle marker. In Figure 4.17, a line is drawn between bar 49 and 61.

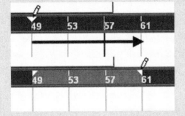

Figure 4.17
Dragging a cycle region to define the cycle marker's boundaries.

3. In the marker track's list area, click on the Add Cycle Marker button, as shown in Figure 4.18.

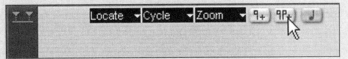

Figure 4.18
The Add Cycle Marker button.

4. Make your newly created cycle marker active by clicking anywhere inside this marker in the marker track. The cycle marker's boundaries should become red and two handles should appear at the boundaries of this cycle marker.

5. In the event information line (if you can't see it, click on the Show Event Info button in the project's toolbar), click under the field Name and enter a descriptive name for your cycle marker. Figure 4.19 shows that the cycle marker has been named "New Region."

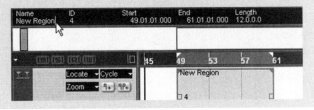

Figure 4.19
Entering a descriptive name for your cycle marker.

How To

To add markers in a project:

1. Make sure your grid setting is set appropriately. For this example, you can leave it at snap to grid and have your grid set to bars.

2. In the ruler bar, click at the location (bar number) where you want to insert a marker. This should move your play cursor to this location.

3. In the marker track's list area, click on the Add Marker button, as shown in Figure 4.20.

Figure 4.20
The Add Marker button.

4. Make your newly created marker active by clicking on this marker's line in the marker track. The marker should become red.

5a. In the event information line, click under the field Name and enter a descriptive name for your marker.

5b. Or, to insert a marker at the current project cursor location, press the Insert key.

Navigating Using Markers

The whole purpose of creating markers or cycle markers is to give you a tool that will allow you to move quickly from one spot to another in your project. Another advantage of using cycle markers is that it also allows you to zoom into a region of your project. More specifically, focus your work on the events found within a cycle marker's range.

How To

To move your play cursor to the position of a marker:

▶ For markers with ID numbers between 3 and 9, press the corresponding number on your numeric keypad.

▶ For any markers using the inspector area of the marker track or the marker window, click in the column to the left of the marker's ID number.

▶ Make the Markers option visible in the project window's toolbar and select the desired marker number (1 through 10).

▶ Make the Marker option visible in the transport panel (right-click inside the transport panel and check the Marker option) and select the desired marker number (1 through 15).

How To

To move the left and right locators to the position of a cycle marker:

▶ In the inspector area of the marker track, click in the column to the left of the cycle marker's ID number.

▶ Or, in the marker window, click in the column to the left of the cycle marker's ID number.

▶ Or use the default key commands Shift+B and Shift+M to go back or move to the next marker respectively.

How To

To zoom into the location of a cycle marker:

▶ In the bottom right corner of your project window, to the left of the time magnification bar, click on the arrow pointing down and select the desired cycle marker name you wish to zoom to, as shown in Figure 4.21. The names of your cycle markers should appear in this drop-down menu.

Figure 4.21
Using cycle markers to zoom into a region of your project.

Editing Markers

Once you've created markers, you can edit their position, names, and ID numbers, as well as removing unneeded markers. Changing the ID number of a marker, for example, allows you to optimize your markers by assigning the ID numbers 3 to 9. This will allow you to access these locations quickly through the numerical keypad on your computer.

How To

To rename a marker (or cycle marker):

▶ From the marker window, click on the name in the description column and type a new name.

▶ Or, from the marker track's inspector area, click on the name in the description column and type a new name.

▶ Or, from the event info line, select the appropriate marker and change the name field to what you want.

How To

To change the ID number of a marker (or cycle marker):

▶ From the marker window, click on the ID number in the ID column and type a new number (note that this will have little effect on numbers higher than 9 or on cycle markers).

▶ Or, from the marker track's inspector area, click on the ID number in the ID column and type a new number.

▶ Or, from the event info line, select the appropriate marker and change the ID field to what you want.

You can edit the position of markers, move cycle markers, or change their range in many ways. However, the easiest way to move cycle markers or markers around is probably still through the marker track. You can also edit the position or length in either the marker window or the marker track inspector area if you prefer. Here's how to edit the position or range of markers and cycle markers by using the marker track.

How To

To move a marker or cycle marker:

1. Enable the Snap to grid option if you wish and set the grid property appropriately if you want your markers to move only to specific bars, beats, or time values.

2. Click and drag the marker you want to move and drop it in the marker track at the desired location as shown in Figure 4.22.

As you see in this figure, a pop-up balloon tells you how far (in bars here) the region has moved. Notice that the object selection tool shows a square box outline below the pointer to indicate that you are moving an object, as is also the case when moving an event on a track.

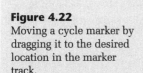
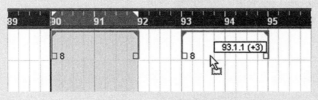

Figure 4.22
Moving a cycle marker by dragging it to the desired location in the marker track.

CHAPTER 4

How To

To resize a cycle marker:

1. Enable the Snap to grid option if you wish and set the grid property appropriately if you want your cycle markers to move only to specific bars, beats or time values.

2. Click and drag the square handle found at the cycle marker's edges to the desired location as shown in Figure 4.23.

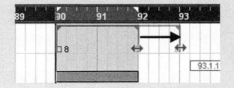

Figure 4.23
Resizing the end (or start) of a cycle marker.

Removing Markers

When a marker doesn't serve its purpose anymore, you can remove it from your project.

How To

To remove a marker (or cycle marker):

▶ From the marker window, click the marker you want to remove and press the Remove button.

▶ From the marker track, click on the appropriate marker to select it and hit the delete key.

▶ From the project's browser window, select the marker you want to remove and press delete, or use the Eraser tool by clicking on the marker you wish to remove.

The Transport Panel

The Transport panel is a multitask floating panel. There are 10 areas on the Transport panel, each of which allows you to control an aspect of your session in progress. By default, Cubase will display the Transport panel; however, you can use the F2 key on your keyboard to display or hide this panel. This section steps you through the different areas and their available options on the Transport panel. Now let's look at each item found on the multifunctional Transport panel.

Performance

The performance item offers the same information as the VST Performance panel (F12 to quickly access this panel). Here, the information is nicely displayed in a smaller format and moves wherever you move the Transport panel (Figure 4.24), making it much easier to monitor your computer's performance while working on a project. The performances monitored here are the CPU load (on the left) and hard disk load (on the right). When one of the two performance bars reaches the top and stays there, causing the red LED to light up in the display, you should think of reducing the load specific to that performance. For example, VST effects and instruments can use up a lot of CPU power. Try freezing a track played by a VST instrument to free up some processing power (see Chapter 5 for more on this). If you have extensive disk access, try disabling audio tracks that are not currently in use. Muting them doesn't mean they are not read by Cubase, simply that they are muted (see Chapter 9 for more on this).

Figure 4.24
The performance indicator in the Transport panel.

Record Modes

The Record mode section allows you to set the Linear Record mode (top) and the Cycle mode (bottom) as shown in Figure 4.25. The Linear Record mode offers three options: Normal, Merge (which are the same for audio, but act differently with MIDI), and Replace. All three options will determine how Cubase will handle overlapping recorded events.

Figure 4.25
The Record mode and Cycle mode options on the Transport panel.

▶ Normal Record mode means that when you record MIDI events over existing MIDI parts, Cubase will create a new part, which will overlap the existing MIDI part without changing the previous content or location of these parts. As for audio recording, it implies that a new event is created over the existing audio event.

▶ Merge Record mode means that when you record MIDI events over existing MIDI parts, Cubase will merge the new content and the existing content into a new merged part.

▶ Replace Record mode will remove any existing event or part over the period overlapping with a new recording on a specific track. This would have the equivalent result of a typical punch-in/punch-out operation on a standard analog multitrack recorder.

How To

To change the linear record mode on the Transport panel:

1. Click on the drop-down menu next to the current visible option in this portion of the Transport panel (by default, this should be set to Normal).
2. Select the desired mode from the drop-down menu.

The Cycle record mode (see bulleted list) offers four options, which determine how MIDI and audio will be recorded during a cycle recording. A cycle recording occurs when the Cycle button is active on the Transport panel. When you are in Cycle mode, Cubase will continuously play the content found between the left and right locators. Each time Cubase starts again at the left locator, it is called a *lap*. How the events are handled during a recording lap depends on the cycle record mode. For audio cycle recordings, the way the events are recorded will also depend on the cycle recording preferences found in Preferences > Record > Audio Cycle Record Mode options under the File menu (PC) or Apple menu (Mac). The following two modes apply only to MIDI recording.

▶ **Mix.** Each time a lap is completed, the events recorded in the next lap are mixed with the events from the previously recorded lap. This is the perfect mode to build up a rhythm track, adding each musical part over the previously recorded one. All events are recorded inside a single part.

▶ **Overwrite.** Each time a lap is completed, the events recorded in the next lap will overwrite (replace) the events that were previously recorded. Use this when you are trying to get the perfect take in one shot—just make sure to stop recording before the next lap begins, or your last take will be overwritten. If you stop playing at the end of a lap and stop recording in the middle of the next lap, without having played a note in that lap, you'll be OK. Overwrite will only "overwrite" when there are new events recorded during the current lap.

The following two modes apply to audio recordings as well, but are also found under the same cycle record mode selection drop-down menu.

▶ **Keep Last.** This mode will keep whatever was recorded in the last completed lap. So if you start playing a lap but stop before it's done, it will not keep that lap. However, if you complete a lap and stop halfway during the next lap, as with the overwrite, the last completed lap will be the one kept. This is a good mode to use when you'd like to record different takes until you get the perfect one. The main difference with overwriting is that in the case of audio recordings, each lap you recorded is still available in your project. Depending on your audio cycle recording preferences, this can mean that Cubase has created regions each time a lap is completed, keeping the last region as the active and visible one onscreen.

▶ **Stacked.** This is a great way to use cycle recording when you are not as proficient as you would like to be with your playing skills. Every time you complete a lap, an event is created and Cubase continues recording, creating a new event on the same track, lap after lap, stacking up events. Once events are stacked, you will only hear the last one recorded, but you can use the best moments of each take to compile an edited version of the part you were trying to record.

Figure 4.26
Comparing the Keep Last
and Stacked cycle
recording modes.

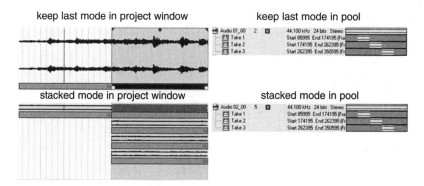

How To

To change the Cycle recording mode on the Transport panel:

1. Click on the drop-down menu next to the current visible option in this portion of the Transport panel (by default, this should be set to Mix MIDI).

2. Select the desired mode from the drop-down menu.

Below the Linear and Cycle Record modes you will find the Auto-quantize Toggle button (AUTO Q). When this option is enabled (button is lit and the text next to the button reads "ON"), MIDI recordings will snap to the current grid and quantize values without additional steps. For example, use this option when you want to make sure that what you record through MIDI is tight with the current groove of a song.

Locators

This section of the Transport panel allows you to numerically edit and monitor your left and right locators, move your project cursor to the locator's position, as well as set Punch-in/Punch-out and Pre-/Post-roll options (see Figure 4.27).

Figure 4.27
The Locators' options on
the Transport panel.

How To

To position your project cursor at the locator's position:

▶ Click on the L or R found on the left of the locator's address in the Transport panel. Note that you can achieve the same thing by pressing the key 1 (for left) or 2 (for right) on the numeric keypad.

How To

To change your locator's position in the Transport panel:

▶ Above and below each digit found on the Transport panel, there is a sensitive area. Clicking on this sensitive area will cause your cursor to change to an arrow with a plus or minus sign. If you click above, the value will increase; if you click below, the value will decrease. Once a series of values is selected, you can also use the scroll wheel on your mouse to increase or decrease these values.

▶ Or you can click on a value and enter a new position for this value by using your keyboard.

NOTE
Most numeric value fields such as the left and right locator position in the Transport panel can be adjusted in the same way. For example, you can change the value of a selected MIDI event in the Key editor by using the scroll wheel of your mouse. Similarly, in most instances where you will see time or bar/beat values, each digit can be edited separately or as a whole. For example, if you click in the beat value of a bar/beat location, and then change a 2 to a 1, only the position of the beat will be affected. Moving the scroll wheel of the mouse will have the same effect. Experiment with these behaviors because they will help you get a better feel for the software's flexibility.

You can also change the left and right locators' position by using the position of the project cursor as a new left or right locator position.

How To

To change your locator's position to the current project cursor position:

1. To set the left locator, hold the Ctrl(PC)/⌘(Mac) key and click in the ruler at the desired location where you want to position your locator.

2. To set the right locator, hold the Alt(PC)/Option (Mac) key and click in the ruler at the desired location where you want to position your locator.

Below the L and R in this portion of the Transport panel are the Punch-in and Punch-out buttons, which transform the left locator into a punch-in point (where a recording will begin) and the right locator into a punch-out point (where a recording will stop). For example, you could start your recording at bar one of your project, but the actual recording process will only begin at bar three and stop recording at bar four if your left locator is set at 3.01.01.000 and your right locator is set at 4.01.01.000 while the Punch-in and Punch-out buttons are active. This can be useful to replace events between these two locations (left and right locators) while making sure what is before or after doesn't get edited. Perhaps the most effective way to use the punch-in and -out is along with the preroll and postroll fields.

The preroll and postroll functions found to the right of the punch-in and punch-out functions respectively, allow users to determine a time value before Cubase goes into record mode at the punch-in location (preroll), and the time it continues playing after it goes out of record mode at the punch-out location (postroll). This allows you to configure an automatic punch-in and punch-out on a selected track, while having Cubase play back the project before it starts recording, giving you time to prepare yourself to record the line you want to replace.

This said, you don't need to use the preroll or postroll functions in the context of punch-in/-out, but it is probably the most common use for it. In essence, use the preroll or postroll functions when you want Cubase to start its playback slightly before the left locator and finish slightly after the right locator.

How To

To set up automatic punch-in and -out with a preroll and postroll:

1. Set your left locator to the appropriate time location where you want to punch into your existing events.

2. Set your right locator to the appropriate time location where you want to punch out of the record mode.

3. Enable the Punch-in and Punch-out buttons on the Transport panel. If you want Cubase to replace all existing events from a specific location, leave the Punch-out button disabled.

4. Set a value for the preroll. This is the amount of time, bars or beats depending on the ruler format displayed, that Cubase will play before the left locator. If the amount of time exceeds the amount of time that it normally takes for Cubase to reach the left locator's position from the beginning of the project, it will simply pause for that equivalent amount of time. For example, if you enter a value of 10 bars and you want to punch in at bar 5, then Cubase will count five bars before bar one and will then start to play until it reaches bar 5, at which point it will go into record mode.

5. If needed, set the postroll time as well (found below the preroll time).

6. Disable the Click button in the Transport panel; otherwise, Cubase will use the metronome's precount setting rather than the preroll setting.

7. Enable the Preroll/Postroll options on the Transport panel (see Figure 4.28).

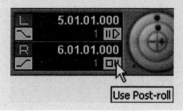

Figure 4.28
The Preroll and Postroll functions enabled on the Transport panel.

8. If you want Cubase to stop automatically after the punch-out time, select File > Preferences from the menu bar. Then select the Transport option and check the Stop after Automatic Punch-out option.

9. Press play or record. Cubase will go into Play mode until it reaches the punch-in time and then switch to Record mode. If you have enabled the Punch-out button, it will revert to play mode at that location. If you have checked the Stop after Automatic Punch-out option, it will also stop playing after the postroll time value entered.

Shuttle, Jog, and Nudge

The nudge, jog, and shuttle wheels (SX only) are useful editing tools that allow you to move quickly within a project while listening to the audio/MIDI. Here's an overview of these functions:

▶ **Shuttle wheel (outside ring):** By moving the ring to the right or the left, you cause the project cursor to move forward or backward in time. The farther away from the center position you move the wheel, the faster the playback will be. The maximum shuttle speed is indicated by the small markings on the lower half of the shuttle, on each side of the ring itself. To stop or slow down the shuttle, bring the ring back toward the center or press the Stop button (or press the spacebar). You can move the wheel by clicking on the ring itself and moving your mouse to the left or right.

▶ **Jog wheel (middle ring):** By holding down the mouse button over the jog wheel and moving it toward the right or left in a circular motion, the project cursor will move forward or back in time. Contrary to the shuttle wheel, you can turn the jog wheel as much as you want. This is a great tool to look for specific cues in a project. The speed at which you move is determined by the speed at which you move your mouse, so typically, you would use a jog wheel when you are looking for something, going slowly over events. When you stop moving the mouse, the jog stops.

▶ **Nudge frame buttons (inside the jog wheel):** These two buttons will move your project one frame ahead (plus sign) or one frame behind (minus sign), no matter what your time display may be. The frame format, however, is determined by your project's frame rate preferences. Obviously, if you don't work with video, nudging the project cursor a frame won't necessarily be useful to you if you're used to work with bars and beats.

Figure 4.29
The shuttle, jog and nudge functions on the Transport panel.

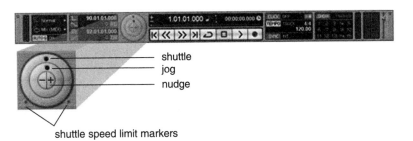

Main Transport

The main Transport buttons allow you to navigate through your project as a regular transport control panel would. In the upper portion, it displays the current location of the project cursor in two customizable formats. When you change the time format on the left, it will also change the time format in the project's ruler. The time format on the right does not have the same effect; it is there only to provide better information about time and position in a different format. Between the two formats is a toggle button, which allows you to switch the position of the two current displayed formats. In Figure 4.30, the time is displayed in bars and beats (left) and in time code (right). The small plus and minus sign on the left of the time display allows you to nudge the position of the project cursor one unit at a time. Below the time display is a project cursor overview display (blue line), which enables you to monitor the location of the project cursor as your project moves along. You can click on the line to grab your project cursor and move it to any location you desire in the project, or click anywhere in that area to make your project cursor jump to that location immediately.

How To

To change the time format displayed in a project by using the Transport panel:

1. Click on the drop-down menu to the format icon of the left time display in the Transport panel.
2. Select the desired time display format.

The Transport Control buttons allow you to do the following (from left to right):

▶ Go to the previous marker or beginning of the project in the absence of markers.

▶ Rewind:. You can adjust the winding speed factor in Preferences > Transport > Wind Speed Factors area of the File menu (PC) or Apple menu (Mac).

▶ Fast Forward: See note above.

▶ Go to the next marker or the end of the project in the absence of markers.

▶ Enable/Disable Cycle mode: When this button is enabled, Cubase will play continuously the events found between the left and right locators. You can quickly enable or disable this by either clicking on the button to toggle its position or by using the forward slash (or divide sign) on the numeric keypad on your keyboard.

▶ Stop: When you press stop after playing the project, the cursor stops and stays at this location. If you press stop a second time, it will go to the previous stopping point.

▶ Play.

▶ Record: In most cases, pressing record will also engage the Play button and start recording from the current project cursor location until you press stop, unless you have enabled the punch-in/punch-out functions or preroll/postroll functions. Cubase will only record on tracks that have been armed (made record-ready) for recording.

Figure 4.30
The Main Transport
buttons and the project
cursor location indicator.

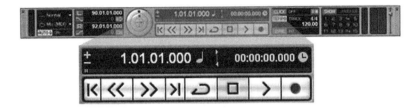

Click, Tempo, and Sync Controls

In this portion of the Transport panel, you have control over three aspects of your project (see Figure 4.31):

▶ **Click.** This button enables or disables the metronome click. Ctrl(PC)/⌘(Mac)-click will bring up the metronome setup dialog box. When the metronome click is enabled, the word click is lit, and the field next to the button displays the word ON. You can also enable or disable the Precount option by clicking on the button to the right of the Click button in the same area of the Transport panel. The Precount option will count a certain number of beats before it actually starts playing or recording. The exact number of beats it will count before the starting point is user-defined and will be discussed in Chapter 7.

▶ **Tempo.** This button allows you to enable or disable the Tempo track. This is the equivalent of the Master track, familiar to Cubase VST users. Ctrl(PC)/⌘(Mac)-click will bring up the tempo map window, which will also be explained further in Chapter 5. When the tempo map is disabled, you can change the tempo setting of the project by clicking on the tempo and using your mouse's scroll wheel to increase or decrease the tempo. Enabling the tempo map also allows you to change the tempo of a project in time. Otherwise (when master is disabled), the tempo will remain fixed at the BPM speed displayed in this area. To the right of the Tempo button, you will find the current project's tempo and time signature.

Figure 4.31
The Click, Tempo, and
Sync options on the
transport panel.

▶ **Sync:** This button allows you to enable or disable the synchronization functions. Ctrl(PC)/⌘(Mac)-click will bring up the synchronization setup dialog box, which will be explained in Chapter 12. When this button is enabled, the type and status of sync Cubase receives is displayed on the right of the button. If you don't need to sync with other devices, this area will most likely display INT, telling you that the sync is provided internally.

ABOUT THE TEMPO TRACK

The tempo track (formerly known as the Master track) is a special hidden track that holds your tempo changes and key signatures. All the tempo changes that you make in the tempo track window or the project's browser editing window will play back when you activate the Tempo button on the Transport panel. However, the time signature will be heard even if the button is not activated. This is logical, since your time signature needs to be activated in order for MIDI elements to lock with bars and beats throughout the project.

Marker

We discussed markers earlier in this chapter. The Transport panel displays (by default) a series of shortcuts that allow you to:

▶ Open the Marker window by pressing on the Show button (see Figure 4.32).

▶ Jump to a specific marker by clicking on the corresponding number in the Transport panel's marker area.

▶ Set the current project cursor location as a marker by Alt(PC)/Option(Mac)-click on the desired marker number.

Figure 4.32
The Marker options in the Transport panel.

MIDI and Audio Activity

The MIDI and audio activity displays (see Figure 4.33) enable you to see if MIDI is coming in (red activity color), or going out (green activity color), or if the audio is coming in or out (green for both input and output) of Cubase from and to external devices. If you're not hearing anything (MIDI or audio), try taking a look at these activity meters first. If you see activity here, then the problem might be outside Cubase. If you don't see activity here when you should, it's possible that Cubase is not receiving or transmitting MIDI or audio properly. Note that MIDI or audio metronome activity will not be displayed in these activity output meters.

Figure 4.33
The MIDI activity input and output monitors on the Transport panel.

If you are not seeing any MIDI activity when sending messages from an external controller, make sure the selected MIDI track's MIDI out and in ports are configured properly.

MIDI events recorded and sent to a VST instrument will not show up in the MIDI activity monitors. However, if you are not seeing any MIDI activity when playing recorded MIDI events that are supposed to go to an external device, chances are this is caused by one of two reasons:

▶ There is no MIDI present in your project.

▶ You have not set the track(s) containing MIDI events to play on a physical MIDI port such as your MIDI interface.

For example, if your external instruments are not receiving MIDI data, try loading a Virtual instrument (VST instrument) and route your MIDI track to that VSTi's MIDI port. If you hear the MIDI going into the VST instrument, then try reassigning the previous MIDI output port to this track. If you still don't hear MIDI coming from your external instrument, your problem is probably somewhere else.

▶ Make sure your MIDI connectors and cables are connected properly. If they are, try switching them around to see if one of them is faulty.

▶ Are the MIDI ports you're trying to use properly configured in the device setup dialog box?

▶ Is your MIDI interface installed properly?

▶ Is the MIDI thru active in Cubase? To check this out, select File > Preferences > MIDI in the menu bar.

Audio Level Control

To the extreme right of the Transport panel is a small fader, which mirrors the stereo output bus fader. Adjusting the level of this fader will affect the audio level the same way as if you were to open the mixer panel and adjust the stereo output bus fader. You should also see this control move if you have recorded any automation on this particular bus. When you click on this audio level control, a larger fader will pop up to help you control the level (see Figure 4.34).

Figure 4.34
Audio level control fader
on the Transport panel.

Context Menus in the Project Window

In the project window, as in many other windows in Cubase, you will find that right-clicking (Ctrl-click for Mac users) in different regions will reveal a number of options related to the area in which you click, as displayed in Figure 4.35. In many cases, these context menus allow you to choose options that are also available in the menu or tool bar of the project window. However, having these options readily available in your workspace makes it easy to stay focused in that area and apply changes to events without having to move your mouse across the screen all the time.

You will learn more about these context menus as we learn how to edit events and work with a project.

Figure 4.35
The different context menus in the project window.

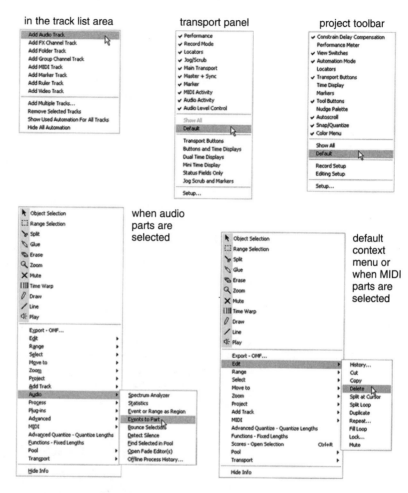

As you can see in Figure 4.35, the default context menu, selected MIDI, or selected audio context menus display three parts separated by a line. The first one on top allows you to change your cursor to a different tool. The second part offers different functions and subfunctions that you can apply in this context. For example, when an audio event is selected, you can select the Audio > Event as Region option to create a region in the media pool from the visible portion of the event in your project's event list area. If you are a veteran Cubase VST user and are longing for the simple toolbox through the right-click (Ctrl-click on Mac), you can now customize this preference:

How To

To display only the toolbox when right-clicking in the project window:

1. Select Preferences > Editing option from the File (PC) or Apple (Mac) menu.
2. At the bottom of the Editing pane, add a check next to the "Popup toolbox on right-click" option.

From this point on, a traditional toolbox will appear when you right-click (see Figure 4.36). This said, if you want to access the default context menu once again, simply hold the Ctrl(PC)/⌘(Mac) key as you right-click (or Ctrl-click on Mac).

Figure 4.36
The traditional right-click
(Ctrl-click on Mac)
toolbox.

Now You Try It

For information about using the instructions found in this section and to find out where you can get the working files, please consult the section called *About the Exercise Files* in the Introduction section.

CHAPTER 4

5

Working with Tracks

In a project, you work with different types of musical or sonic events. These events take place on tracks and occur at the appropriate time in these tracks. Different tracks hold different events or event types. For example, audio tracks hold audio events, marker tracks hold Marker information, and MIDI tracks hold MIDI events. These types of tracks are called *track classes*, and Cubase uses these different track classes to store the different types of events supported within a Cubase project. If you compare this with a multitrack recorder, which records only one type of information—audio—you can quickly realize how versatile and powerful Cubase really is because all this information is handled by a single software.

Before you can add anything in a Project window, you need to create tracks corresponding to the type of content you want to record and then configure the tracks properly to achieve the result you want. Because Cubase is more versatile than a multitrack tape recorder, it's also a bit more demanding. But as you will quickly realize, it's also quite easy to get up and running, creating the music you wanted to do but couldn't with a simple tape recorder.

Here's a summary of what you will learn in this chapter:

- ▶ How to recognize and work with the different areas in the Project window.
- ▶ Discover the different tools available in the Inspector and Track List areas.
- ▶ Find out what a VST instrument is and how you can use it in a project.
- ▶ Install and manage external MIDI sound modules through the MIDI Device Manager.
- ▶ How to use the Tempo track to add tempo changes and time signature changes to a project.

Project Window Areas

When you work with tracks in the Project window, most of your time is spent between the Inspector, the Track List, and the Event Display areas. The Inspector area displays information about a selected track and may be divided into several sections, depending on the track class or track type you have selected (explained later in this chapter). The Track List area displays all the tracks that are part of your project, stacked one on top of the other. Again, the content of the Track List area for a given track varies depending on its track class. Finally, the Event Display area displays recorded events—the actual audio and MIDI content of the project itself—and its associated automation.

CHAPTER 5

The Inspector

As mentioned previously, you will want to use the Inspector area whenever you want to view or edit certain details pertaining to a selected track in your Project window. What you find in the Inspector area also varies depending on the track's class. For example, when a MIDI track is selected, the Inspector area is divided into six sections: the MIDI Track Setup, Parameters, Inserts, Sends, Channel, and Notepad. Each one of these sections allows you to modify a certain amount of information that affects how the events on the track behave or play back. So, in the same example of a MIDI Inspector's area, you can use the (Track) Parameters section to transpose all the events on the track. Other track classes, such as Folder Tracks (this is also explained later in Chapter 6), do not display as many sections in the Inspector area.

Nevertheless, you will find elements (such as buttons and fields) that are common to different Inspector areas of different track classes and also with other areas within the Project window. For example, this is the case with the Read/Write Automation buttons, which are found in both the Inspector and the Track List, as well as in the Mixer panel.

When the Inspector area holds more than one section, the title bar and a Control button for that section are always visible. The Control button is found on the right of the section's title bar. This button allows you to reveal or hide the content of the selected section. In Figure 5.1, you can see this button, which looks like a little arrow pointing down. This indicates that the section can be expanded or maximized. If the arrow points up, it indicates that you can minimize the panel. In addition, when a track supports an insert or send effect *and* an effect has been assigned to this track, the control button is colored (turquoise), indicating that there is an effect assigned in the section for that track. The same coloring applies to control buttons on tracks that support EQs, except in this case, an active EQ is displayed as green. Finally, when a yellow rectangle appears next to this Control button, it indicates that there might be some effects assigned in the section, but that they have been bypassed. Bypassing an effect or an EQ setting is a great way to compare before and after without having to reset all the parameters involved or to listen to a signal without any processing.

Figure 5.1

The upper-right corner of this image shows the Control button for this Inspector's area section.

folded   unfolded

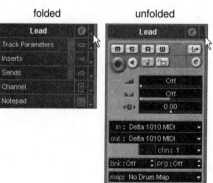

By default, when you click on one section to expand it, any other expanded section automatically minimizes itself. When a section is minimized, all the settings you have made in that section remain intact.

CONTROLLING MULTIPLE SECTIONS SIMULTANEOUSLY

If you want to maximize more than one section of the Inspector area at once, hold the Ctrl(PC)/⌘(Mac) key down as you click the section's Control button. You can also minimize all opened panels at once by holding the Alt(PC)/Option(Mac) key down while clicking on any one of the section's Control buttons. Inversely, you can maximize all the sections at once by using the same key combination.

The Track List

The Track List area allows you to view all of your tracks at once, which makes it easy to enable multiple tracks for recording or to organize your material by type of content. Whenever you move or change a setting in the track list, the changes are reflected in both the Inspector area of this track and in the Mixer panel. If you move the position of a track—placing it above or below its current position, for example—all the events in the event display area will follow this move. The content of each track in the Track List area also depends on the track's class. You can also use the Track List area to reveal any automation information available in a subtrack. When you want to record or edit automation for a track, the automation data is kept along with the track itself in a subtrack found below the track (hence the name "subtrack"). Usually, there is one subtrack for each type of automation your track contains. For example, you could have two subtracks to your track; one could contain volume automation and another, pan automation. Finally, you can also resize each track individually to fit its content on your screen from the Track List area.

How To

To change the order of a track in the Track List area (see Figure 5.2):

1. Click the track you want to move in the Track List area.

   A red line appears to indicate that Cubase knows you want to move this track (as shown in the first image on the left side of Figure 5.2). To select multiple consecutive tracks, click the first track, hold down the Shift key, and then click the last track you want to move. To select multiple nonconsecutive tracks, click the first track, hold down the Ctrl(PC)/⌘(Mac) key, and then click on any other track you want to move (note that after the tracks are moved, all the nonconsecutive tracks appear consecutive).

2. Drag the track to the desired location.

   In the middle section of Figure 5.2, you can see the (green) line indicating where the track would appear if you released the mouse.

3. Release the mouse button when you are satisfied with the new location.

   As you can see on the right side of Figure 5.2, the track appears where the (green) line was; in this case, between Audio 02 and 03.

Figure 5.2
Changing the order of a track in the Track List area.

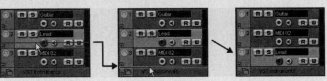

How To

To reveal or hide a track's automation subtracks:

1. Right-click on the track for which you want to see the used automation in the Track List area.

2. Select the Show Used Automation option from the context menu. If you want the used automation visible for all tracks, select the Show Used Automation for All Tracks option instead.

Or:

1. Click the plus sign in the bottom-left corner of the desired track in the Track List area to reveal its automation subtrack. In Figure 5.3, when you click the plus sign, two subtracks are revealed (lower portion of the figure). When you want to view more automation subtracks, you can click the plus sign found in the lower automation subtrack. In other words, clicking the plus sign of the track reveals the last state your subtracks were in, and if you click the track's minus sign, it hides all subtracks. Clicking the plus sign of an automation subtrack reveals the next automation subtrack, whereas clicking the minus sign of the automation subtrack hides only that subtrack from the Track List area.

2. Click the minus sign when the track shows its subtrack(s) to hide the subtrack(s). Hiding the subtrack(s) does not remove the automation recorded on this track. It only hides it from view.

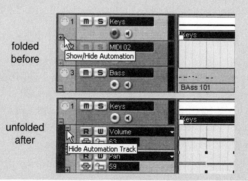

folded before

Figure 5.3
Clicking the plus sign of a track in the Track List area reveals automation subtracks.

unfolded after

In each automation subtrack, you will find two fields. The first displays the automation parameter's name used by the subtrack. In Figure 5.3 these were Volume and Pan. The second field represents the value of the automation parameter at the location from the project cursor's position. In Figure 5.3, the volume is at 43 and the pan is at 58. You can also change the automation parameter displayed in the subtrack if you wish.

How To

To change the automation parameter displayed in a subtrack:

1. Expand your track to reveal its subtracks.

2. From the Automation Parameter drop-down menu, select the appropriate automation parameter that you want to view or edit in that subtrack. Note that parameters containing information appear with an asterisk at the end of their names in this menu.

If the parameter you want to view is not in the drop-down menu, select the More option at the bottom of the menu and then choose the appropriate automation parameter from the dialog box that appears.

How To

To resize an individual track's height:

1. Bring your cursor over the lower edge of the track you want to resize.

2. When your cursor changes into a double-headed arrow (see Figure 5.4), drag your mouse up to reduce the track's size or down to increase its size.

You can also resize the entire Track List's width and height by dragging the right edge of the Track List area when your cursor changes into a double-headed arrow or by dragging the lower edge of a track using the same method (see Figure 5.4). Moving the border to the left reduces the size, whereas moving it to the right increases the Track List's width. Note that you cannot resize the left edge of the Track List to increase the space used by the Inspector.

Figure 5.4
Resizing an individual
track's height.

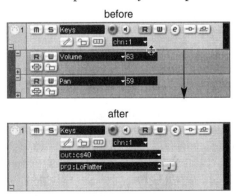

The Event Display

The Event Display area allows you to edit and view parts, events, and automation information found in your project. Because most of the work you will do in this area is related to editing, we discuss the functions and operations for the Event Display area in Chapter 9.

Nevertheless, for the time being, it is important to understand that you will find the content of each track (events, parts, and automation data) in this area. Whenever you record audio, MIDI, or automation, this is where it will appear.

VST Instruments (VSTi)

VST instruments—VSTi, for short—are software-based synthesizers that use the ASIO 2 protocol developed by Steinberg to generate or output their sound through the computer's sound card. They are, in essence, special audio plug-in effects working within Cubase. These audio plug-in effects generate the sounds triggered by MIDI events recorded in a project. This is done by assigning the MIDI output of a track into the audio VSTi plug-in effect.

This opens up a whole world of exciting possibilities for any music enthusiast, as well as for hard core music veterans. VST instruments are activated through the VST instrument panel found in the Devices menu (or by pressing F11 on your computer keyboard). The VST Instrument panel is like an empty rack of instruments in which you load instruments as you need them. You can load up to 64 VSTi per project in SX 2.0 (16 in SL). Each number found on the left of the panel corresponds to an individual instrument slot. The controls for each instrument are identical. By default, these slots are empty. You can click on the instrument list in the VST Instrument panel to access installed VST instruments on your computer (see Figure 5.5); you can select the VSTi that you want to activate. To install a VSTi, follow the instructions provided by the plug-in manufacturer.

Figure 5.5
The VST Instruments panel.

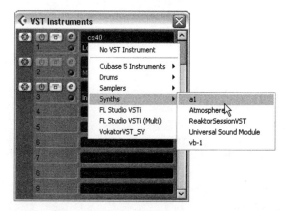

When selected, the VSTi is also activated by default. You can always deactivate a VSTi without unloading it by pressing the Active/Bypass button next to the number for the VSTi in the VST Instruments panel. When a VSTi is loaded and activated, an additional MIDI port appears when you click on a MIDI track output setting. In Figure 5.6, the Groove Agent VSTi has been loaded, so it is now available as an output device. This means that you can use one of 16 additional MIDI channels, not to mention that you can also load more than one instance of a VSTi in memory. When you activate a second instance of the same instrument, in this example the a1, a new virtual port will be created with a different name to differentiate each VSTi currently loaded into memory. VSTi MIDI outputs are handled in the same way as regular MIDI output devices.

Figure 5.6
All VST instruments that
are loaded appear as an
additional MIDI output.

Because VST instruments are MIDI controlled, yet use your sound card to generate their sounds, Cubase creates two separate, but linked channels in the Mixer panel: one MIDI channel to control MIDI-related events and another audio channel to control the audio output. This means that you can add MIDI effects and automate MIDI control changes through the MIDI track in which you find the VSTi, and you can add audio effects, automation, and EQ to the audio channel created in the Mixer panel. If you look at the track list area, you will also notice that a VST instruments folder track is created as soon as you activate a VSTi. Inside this special folder track, you will find an additional folder subtrack for all the currently active VSTi loaded into memory. These special folder tracks, however, will not contain any MIDI or audio events but will contain automation you record (see Chapter 13 for more on automation).

Setting Up a VSTi

Using a VSTi is quite simple. The hardest part is usually choosing the sounds for the new project.

To set up a VSTi in your project:

1. Make the VST Instruments panel visible (you can press F11 on your keyboard).

2. From the VST Instruments panel, select the first available slot in the rack and click anywhere on the drop-down menu where it currently says "No VST Instrument." This reveals the installed VSTi on your computer.

3. Choose a VST from this menu to activate it. The blue active button next to the selected instrument reveals that this instrument is ready to be assigned to a MIDI track.

4. Create a new MIDI track or select an empty one.

5. In the MIDI track's setup section of the Inspector area or in the Track List area, select the VSTi you just activated from the MIDI Output Port drop-down menu.

6. If you haven't already configured your MIDI input, you might want to do this before continuing. Click the MIDI input port and choose the MIDI port from which the incoming MIDI events will be sent to the VSTi. In most cases, this will be the port that connects your controller keyboard to Cubase.

continued

7. You can select a program for the VSTi through the Program field in the Setup section of the MIDI track if the VSTi supports this option. If your VSTi doesn't load presets into memory by default, you can click on the Edit VST Instrument button (see Figure 5.7) to load them from the instrument's interface. Clicking the Edit VSTi button opens up the VSTi's interface panel. When presets do load automatically, use the small arrows in the field to change your selection among the currently loaded presets.

LOADING PRESETS INTO A VSTI

You can also use the drop-down menu below the VSTi's name in the VST Instruments panel to select a preset program or the program (preset) selection menu on the VSTi interface panel itself. Exactly how you select preset patches may depend on the VSTi itself. Read the documentation accompanying the application to find out more about this.

Figure 5.7
The Edit VST instrument button in the MIDI track's setup section of the Inspector.

WANT TO USE YOUR EXTERNAL KEYBOARD CONTROLLER?

Make sure that the MIDI Thru Active check box is checked in Cubase's preferences [Preferences > MIDI under the File menu (PC)/Cubase menu (Mac)]. Otherwise, you won't be able to use your external keyboard controller to send MIDI events to your VSTi. This should be selected by default, but if for some reason MIDI didn't make it to your VSTi even after checking the input and output port correctly, try looking at this option to make sure it's active.

With most VST instruments, you can also create your own preset programs and save them for later use. There are two types of files you can save: instruments and banks. Instruments usually hold settings for a single sound, whereas banks hold a set of sounds, presets, programs, or instruments (depending on the name you or the manufacturer call it). You can also load multiple instruments, but you can only load one bank at a time.

How To

To load a bank or instruments in a VSTi:

1. Bring up the VST Instruments panel and its editing interface panel (see Figure 5.8).
2. To the right of both panels, you will find a File menu. Click it to reveal its options.
3. Select the Load Bank or Load Instrument option, depending on what you want to load into the instrument's memory. Remember that if you are using a VSTi sampler, this might require the VSTi to load some samples into memory as well, so it might take a little while. If the loaded VSTi does not need to load samples, then it should be fairly quick because this file only contains parameter setup information.
4. Browse the folder on your hard disk in which banks or instruments are stored.
5. Choose the desired program from the corresponding menu in the VST Instruments panel (as mentioned earlier in Step 7 in the previous section).

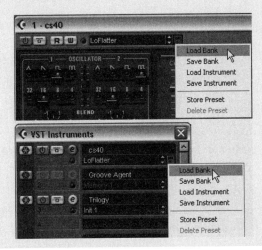

Figure 5.8
The top portion represents the File menu in the VSTi's editing interface panel and the botton represents the VST Instruments panel.

If you make changes to a VSTi's parameter in order to create the sound you need from the current preset, you might want to save these changes for later use. Remember that most customized settings on a VSTi's interface panel will not stay in memory once you change the preset number or quit Cubase. Preset settings are not saved unless you specifically save them as described in the following "How To" section.

How To

To save a bank or an instrument for a VSTi:

1. After making changes to a program or a series of programs in a bank, repeat Steps 1–2 from the previous exercise on how to load a bank or instruments.

2. From the File menu, simply select Save Bank or Save Instrument.

3. Select an appropriate folder in which to save your file. It is a good idea to keep your bank and instrument files in the same folder to avoid searching all over your hard disk for these files in the future. If you use a sampler VSTi, you might already have a folder in which samples are stored. You can either save the bank or instrument files in that folder or in a folder above, depending on your folder structure organization.

VSTi Included with Cubase

Steinberg provides you with three VST instruments when you purchase Cubase.

▶ **a1.** A powerful dual oscillator synthesizer, with up to a sixteen-voice polyphony

▶ **VB1.** A four-voice polyphonic virtual bass simulator using physical modeling parameters

▶ **LM-7.** A twelve-voice/part polyphonic drum machine

Obviously, Steinberg is not the only manufacturer developing VST instruments. You can find additional resources and links to some manufacturer's Web sites in Appendix F.

VSTi and Latency

Because VSTi play through your sound card, latency plays a great role in how effective the instruments really are. Because latency introduces a delay between the time a key is played and the time a sound is heard, the shorter that delay is, the more realistic the experience will be. Make sure your system is configured properly, as outlined in Chapter 3, and always use the ASIO driver provided by your sound card manufacturer. If your latency is equal to or greater than 25 milliseconds, you might find it disconcerting to play a VSTi, especially when playing parts with high rhythmic content, because there will always be a delay between the moment you press the keys on your keyboard and the moment you hear the sound. The smallest theoretical latency is 0 milliseconds, but in reality, you can expect at least a 1.5- to 3-millisecond latency, which is pretty good. So, to get a good experience with VSTi, try setting your sound card driver preferences (if you have a dedicated ASIO driver for your sound card) and Cubase to have latency below 10 milliseconds.

If your sound card doesn't provide an ASIO driver with low latency, you can always use a non-VST instrument to input MIDI events, changing the MIDI output of a track after the events are recorded back to the VSTi output. This way, you don't get the latency delay during recording and because latency does not affect timing, the events are played in sync with other events once recorded.

The Device Manager

As you have seen earlier, it is possible to create program changes or tell a MIDI track to play a specific program and bank from the MIDI Settings section in the Inspector area and the Track List area. When working with a VSTi, this is quite easy to deal with because when you select this VSTi as the MIDI output port for the track, the track's settings adjust themselves to the parameters found for that instrument. So, for example, if you load the a1 VSTi, the Bank Selection field disappears because you can only have one bank at a time. Also, the Program field displays the VSTi's loaded sounds so that you can pick the sound you want to hear by name directly in the track itself.

Working with external MIDI devices is a bit trickier because all the manufacturers do not necessarily offer the same sound architecture or sound name. To access these sounds directly from the MIDI track's setting section in the Inspector, you need to tell Cubase which external device is hooked up to your MIDI output, what MIDI output it uses, and load which MIDI instructions should be sent to this device in order to get the name of the patch from this device's LCD display to match with the list inside Cubase's Inspector area. Fortunately, most of these devices already have scripts that you can load from the Cubase CD. However, you do have to install these devices through the Device Manager to let Cubase know what is in your studio and address it properly.

When you open up your MIDI Device Manager for the first time, it will be empty because you have not defined any devices in your setup yet. You can access your Device Manager in a couple of ways:

▶ Select the MIDI Device Manager option in the Devices menu.

▶ Or click the MIDI Device Manager button found on the Devices panel if it is visible (Devices > Show Panel).

Adding a MIDI Device

After you have identified your external MIDI devices, you can proceed with their installation inside the MIDI Device Manager.

How To

To add a MIDI device:

1. Open the MIDI Device Manager panel.
2. Click the Install Device button. The Add MIDI Device dialog box appears, displaying a list of existing device definitions (see Figure 5.9).
3. Scroll this list, select the device you want to install, and then click OK. Your selected device now appears in the MIDI Device Manager panel.

continued

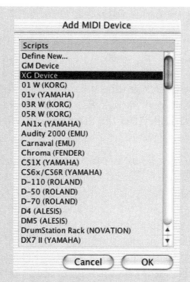

Figure 5.9
The Add MIDI Device
dialog box.

4. Click the device's name in the Installed Devices section to select it. You should see a listing appear in the Patch Banks section (see Figure 5.10).

5. Click the MIDI output to the right of your device in the center of the window and select the MIDI interface to which this device is hooked up. When you select this instrument from the track's MIDI output port, the device's name appears along with the associated MIDI port used to connect Cubase to this device, as shown in Figure 5.11.

6. Repeat this operation for each MIDI based external sound module in your studio.

7. Close the panel when you are done by clicking the X in the upper-right corner of the window. The changes remain even when the window is not visible.

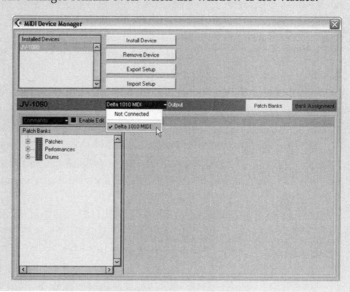

Figure 5.10
The MIDI Device
Manager panel.

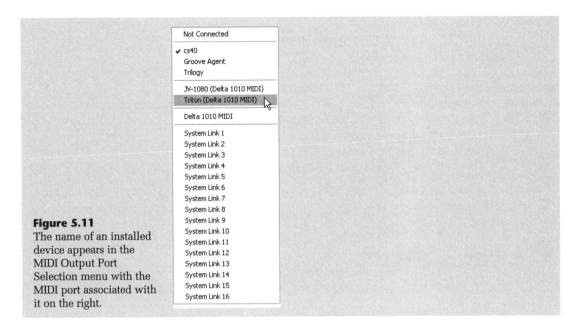

Figure 5.11
The name of an installed device appears in the MIDI Output Port Selection menu with the MIDI port associated with it on the right.

If your MIDI device is not included in this list, you might have to create it yourself. Remember, however, that if you are using a MIDI sampler, creating such a device definition in the MIDI Device Manager is pointless because a sampler generally does not have a fixed set of programs it loads by default when you turn the sampler on. In fact, that might be why your device is not listed in Cubase's list of devices!

This said, if you do have a MIDI device with programs and banks that are not defined already in Cubase, you can create your own MIDI device in the Device Manager. Because creating a device from scratch is intricately linked to the device in your setup, you need to refer to your owner's manual and the online documentation (under the MIDI Devices and Patches section) provided with Cubase to find out how to create your own custom device with patch names, banks, and specific MIDI messages associated with it.

Managing a MIDI Device

After a device is installed, you can reorganize its Patch Bank list, export or import other devices, and rename items in the patch banks. For example, the Roland's JV-1080 patch list is organized in patches, performances, and drums. Inside the Patches folder, there are some 20 groups in which all the actual preset names of this MIDI device are found (see Figure 5.12). However, if you've ever used or seen the JV-1080, programs can be grouped by type of sounds rather than taking programs 0 to 31 and putting them in a group. So, you can start from the original instrument definition and create your own structure to better suit your needs; this makes it easier for you when you want to find the right sound for your track.

Figure 5.12
On the left, you can see the original Patch Bank list provided by Cubase; on the right, you can see the modified list that corresponds to the user's preferences.

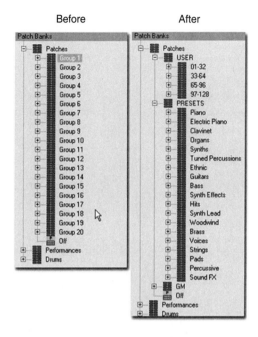

How To

To add a bank to your device's setup:

1. In the MIDI Device Manager panel, select the device for which you want to add the content in the Installed Devices section of the MIDI Device Manager.

2. Check the Enable Edit check box.

3. Select the Create Banks option from the Commands menu if this is what you want to do.

4. A new bank is created called New Bank. Double-click this new entry and type a new name for this bank.

5. If you have more than one bank in your device's Patch Bank list, you will see a Bank Assignment tab appear to the right of your Patch Bank tab. When you click on this tab, Cubase allows you to associate MIDI channels with specific banks. For example, if you have a drums bank, you might want to assign this to Channel 10. This way, when you assign this device to a MIDI output port and select Channel 10, the programs listed in the Inspector correspond to associated drum banks. Simply select the banks from the drop-down menu next to each channel to associate a bank with a channel.

If you want to add a bit more order in your presets, making it easier to find them when the time comes, you can create folders for different types of presets, like putting all your piano related sounds under a "piano" group.

How To

To add a preset or a folder to your device's setup:

1. In the MIDI Device Manager panel, select the device for which you want to add the content in the Installed Devices section of the MIDI Device Manager.

2. Check the Enable Edit check box.

3. Select the bank or folder in which you want to add the preset or (sub)folder.

4. Select the New Preset or New Folder option from the Commands menu.

5. Double-click the new entry to rename it.

6. If you have added a preset, you need to add the relevant MIDI message information associated with your device in the right portion of this window.

If you would like to add more than one preset at a time when creating your device presets in the device manager, you can use the Add Multiple Presets option to do so.

How To

To add multiple presets to your device's setup:

1. In the MIDI Device Manager panel, select the device for which you want to add the content in the Installed Devices section of the MIDI Device Manager.

2. Check the Enable Edit check box.

3. Select the bank or folder in which you want to add the multiple presets.

4. Select the Add Multiple Presets option from the Commands menu. The Add Multiple Presets dialog box appears (see Figure 5.13). In this dialog box, you need to insert the appropriate information relating to the MIDI messages that need to be sent to your MIDI device in order to change the program correctly when a preset is selected. The following steps describe a simple MIDI message containing a list of eight banks and eight presets, for a total of 64 possible program changes. This might not be how your device is set up, but you can use these steps to figure out how to get your device to work correctly.

5. By default, the first line shows Program Change. Click this name and select from the pop-up menu the appropriate bank select message for your MIDI device (because this is an example, you might not need to assign a bank message at all).

6. In the Range column, enter "0-7" to create eight banks.

7. Now click under the bank select message to add a program change message associated with each bank.

8. In the Range column of the program change row, enter "0-7." This creates eight programs in each bank, ranging from number 0 to number 7.

continued

9. In the Default Name field, enter the default name you want to give to the newly created presets. In Figure 5.13, the default name is "Preset." Cubase automatically numbers all the presets created.

10. Click OK when done.

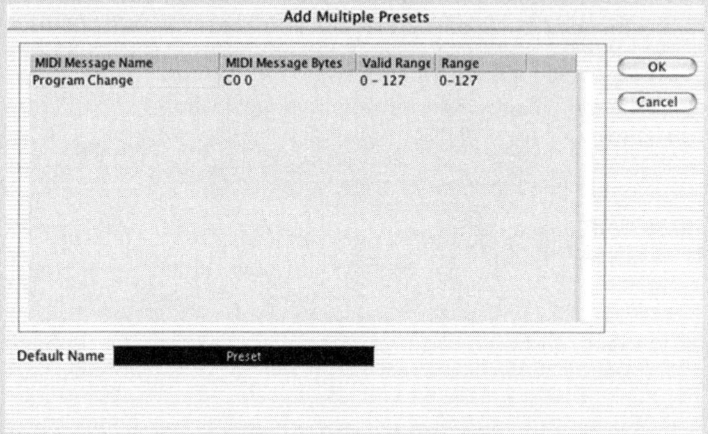

MIDI Message Name	MIDI Message Bytes	Valid Range	Range
Program Change	C0 0	0 – 127	0–127

Add Multiple Presets

Default Name   Preset

Figure 5.13
The Add Multiple Presets
dialog box.

When you select the bank or folder in which you have created these multiple presets, you will find a list of preset names. In our example, there are 64 presets numbered from Patch 0-0 to Patch 0-7 for the first bank, then Patch 1-0 to Patch 1-7 for the second bank, and so on. Selecting one of these presets reveals (in the right side of the MIDI Device Manager panel) the actual MIDI message sent to the device.

If you've made some adjustments to your MIDI device listings in the MIDI Device Manager panel, you may want to export these changes to a file so that you can retrieve them later if you ever have to reinstall your software or simply use your device with Cubase in another studio. To do so, use the Export Device function. This allows you to export all the patch bank settings to a file that you can later copy on a floppy disk and carry with you. When you get to the other studio or reinstall Cubase on your computer, you can import your file into the MIDI Device Manager to access your customized settings once again.

How To

To export a MIDI device setup file:

1. In the MIDI Device Manager panel, select the device setups that you want to export to a file.

2. Click the Export Setup button.

3. Choose an appropriate folder and name for your file.

4. Click the Save button. This creates an XML file.

How To

To import a MIDI device setup file:

1. Open your MIDI Device Manager panel.
2. Click the Import Setup button.
3. Browse to the location of the file you want to import.
4. Select the file and click the Open button. This adds the device to your MIDI Device Manager panel.

Adding a new device to a setup does not change or influence how the existing devices are handled, so you don't have to worry about messing things up by installing another device, even temporarily. You can always remove a device you no longer use or need.

How To

To remove a MIDI device from the MIDI Device Manager:

1. Select the device in the MIDI Device Manager's Installed Device section.
2. Click the Remove Device button.

If you made a mistake or are not satisfied with an entry in the patch banks, you can simply click the entry and press the Delete key to remove it from the list. You can also change the order in which items appear and rearrange the list to better suit your needs.

How To

To move an item in the list:

▶ Simply click and drag the desired entry to its new location. You can also move more than one item at a time by using the usual methods: Click the first entry and shift-click the last item to select consecutive entries, or Ctrl(PC)/⌘ (Mac)-click the different entries you want to select.

Using Installed Devices in the Inspector

After you've installed these devices in your MIDI Device Manager, you can use the Program field in the Inspector or the Track List area of a MIDI track to select a program by name. When selecting an entry in this field, Cubase sends the appropriate MIDI message to your external MIDI device in order for you to hear the selected sound.

How To

To assign a program to a MIDI track:

1. Start by setting your MIDI track's output to a device defined in the MIDI Device Manager.

2. In the MIDI setting of the Inspector area or in the Track List area, click the Program field (prg) to reveal its content (see Figure 5.14).

3. This field reveals the patch bank structure as defined in the MIDI Device Manager. Use the Filter field if you are looking for a specific name. In Figure 5.14, the name "West" was entered, which reveals all the programs that contain this word in their name.

4. Select the program by clicking on its name. By doing so, Cubase sends a MIDI message to your device causing it to change its program. You can listen to the sound if you want or select another entry if you want to hear another sound.

5. Clicking once again on the selected sound or clicking outside this drop-down menu selects the sound and hides the menu once again.

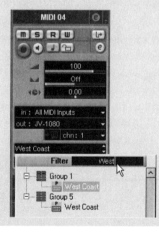

Figure 5.14
Using the Program field along with the Filter option to pinpoint the sounds you want.

About the Tempo Track

The Tempo track in Cubase essentially allows you to insert tempo and key signature changes to your project. You can access the Tempo track by Ctrl(PC)/⌘(Mac)-clicking on the Tempo button found in the Transport panel, by selecting the Tempo track option in the Project menu, or by pressing the default key command Ctrl-T(PC)/⌘-T(Mac).

The top toolbar in this window (Figure 5.15) offers the following tools:

▶ The Activate/Disable button allows you to toggle the Tempo track on or off. This button is lit when it is active. When the Tempo track is off, you can set a different tempo in the Transport panel's tempo field. This provides a way to set a slower tempo for hard-to-play passages when recording in MIDI. Any tempo changes found in the Tempo track will not be reproduced during playback when the Tempo track is disabled. You will notice that when the Tempo track is disabled, the word "Fixed" appears next to the Tempo toggle button in the Transport panel, indicating that the tempo changes will not take place. Furthermore, the tempo will be the one visible in the Transport panel at that time (by default, this is set at 120 BPM). The time signature changes will still take place as usual even if the Tempo track is disabled, as you will still need it to record events in the proper bars and beats.

▶ The next four buttons are the Object Selection, Eraser, Zoom and Draw tools. These tools perform the same functions as they do in other editing environments.

▶ The Auto Scroll and Snap buttons offer the same functionality as their project window counterparts.

▶ The Tempo field displays the tempo value of a selected tempo point from the tempo display area below. When a tempo is selected (this only works when a single tempo value is selected, unlike the example found in Figure 5.15), you can use this field to change the tempo value through the up and down arrows to the right of the field, or you can type in a new tempo value.

▶ The Curve field allows you to select how the tempo changes between two selected tempo values. You will not be able to use this field if you don't have at least two tempo points selected. You can choose either Ramp or Jump. When a ramp is created, the tempo will move gradually from one point to another, as displayed between bars 9 and 13 in Figure 5.15. When a jump is created, the tempo will stay the same until the next tempo change, at which point it jumps to the next tempo value in the line, as displayed between bars 13 and 22.

▶ The Insert Curve field allows you to determine how the following tempo changes will relate to previous tempo change values along the tempo line. As with the Curve field, you can choose either Ramp (gradual change of tempo from one point to the next) or Jump (sudden change at the location of the new tempo change). Note that if the Snap mode is on, the position where the tempo changes can be entered will be determined by the snap mode's grid and quantize settings, which are set in the project window.

▶ The Signature field allows you to change the value for the selected signature in the Signature bar found below the Ruler bar.

▶ The Tempo Recording slider allows you to record tempo changes in real time by moving the slider to the right to go faster or to the left to go slower.

Below the Toolbar you will find the Ruler bar. This bar offers similar functions as Ruler bars in other windows. However, at the left of this bar, you will find a display that shows the current location of your cursor in the tempo display area below. You can use this to pinpoint the desired tempo value when inserting these values in the Tempo track.

The Time Signature bar displays the time signatures in your project. When you start a new project, by default you will find a single 4/4 time signature entry at the beginning of this bar. But as you can see in Figure 5.15, you can add several other time signatures along the project's timeline. This will also change the spacing between each bar to reflect the time signature's value.

The main area of the Tempo track is, of course, the Tempo Display area. This consists of a tempo ruler displayed vertically along the left side of the window and an area where tempo changes appear along the tempo line. Each tempo change is represented by a square handle along this line. When you insert a new tempo change, the line before and after this new tempo will join the tempo using the current Curve and Insert Curve settings.

In the lower right corner you will find the horizontal and vertical zoom bars, which allow you to adjust the zoom level for the timeline displayed in the Tempo track, as well as the tempo precision displayed in the tempo ruler, respectively.

Figure 5.15
The Tempo track window.

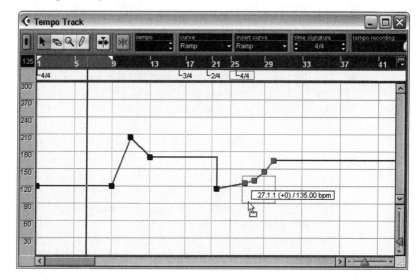

How To

To add a tempo change:

1. In the Tempo track, click on the Draw tool in the toolbar.
2. Select the desired option in the Insert Curve field.
3. Activate the Snap button if you want to position your tempo at the Snap mode's current Grid setting. It is recommended that this be on if you want your tempo changes to occur at bar changes.
4. Position your cursor in the time and at the tempo height you want to insert the tempo change. You can use the cursor location field to the left of the ruler to guide you along the tempo value.

How To

To add a time signature change:

1. In the Tempo track, click on the Draw tool in the toolbar.
2. Click inside the Time Signature bar at the location where you want to insert a time signature change. This will add a time signature using the current value displayed in the Signature field.
3. With the new time signature still selected (a red square appears around the selected time signature), change the values in the Signature field to represent the appropriate time signature you want to add.

If, for some reason, you change your mind about a tempo change value, you can move one or several tempo changes to a new tempo and time.

How To

To move a tempo change or time signature change:

1. Select the Object Selection tool from the toolbar.
2. Click on the tempo or time signature you want to move and drag it to the desired location.

You can also move more than one tempo change at a time by dragging a box to select a range of tempo changes. Selected tempo change handles will appear red, as will the lines between these tempo changes.

If you wish to change the curve type between two or more tempo changes, you can select the desired tempo change points and then select the desired value in the Curve field. For example, if you have selected three tempo changes, with a jump curve between the first and second tempo and a ramp between the second and third tempo, selecting a ramp will create a ramp between the first and second, leaving the curve between the second and third intact. Note that jump curves are displayed by blue line segments between two tempo changes, and ramp curves are displayed by a dark green line segment between two tempo changes.

CHAPTER 5

How To

To erase tempo or time signature changes:

▶ With the Object selection tool selected, click on the tempo or time signature you wish to erase to select it and press Delete or Backspace. To erase several events, simply drag a box over the desired tempo or time signature changes and use the Delete or Backspace keys.

▶ Or select the Eraser tool and click on the events in the Tempo track.

Now You Try It

For information about using the instructions found in this section and to find out where you can get the working files, please consult the section called *About the Exercise Files* in the Introduction section.

6

Track Classes

When you create a new empty project, as you did in Chapter 4, a blank project appears with no tracks. No matter what you decide to do from this point forward, you need to add tracks to your project. In Cubase, tracks are just like containers. Without tracks, you won't have containers into which you can record events.

Here's a summary of what you will learn in this chapter:

▶ Explore the different tools available in the track Inspector and Track List areas.

▶ What track classes are and what purpose they serve.

▶ What are the differences between MIDI and audio effects?

▶ What are the differences between track insert and send effects?

▶ Define the Cubase audio hierarchy in terminology and learn how it applies to your project.

▶ Organize your project by using folder tracks.

▶ Learn when and why you would use group tracks.

There are eight types, or classes, of tracks:

▶ Audio tracks for audio events and automation.

▶ MIDI tracks for MIDI events and automation.

▶ Effects (FX) tracks for audio plug-ins that are being used in the current project by several audio tracks. Previous Cubase users will notice that this replaces the VST Send effect and VST Master effect panels.

▶ Folder tracks to group other tracks into, such as different takes of a solo, VST instruments that are used in a project, and automation of the master bus outputs.

▶ Group channel tracks, which group different track outputs into a single output bus channel or simply group them under a single group channel in the mixer panel. This provides a common set of controls for all the channels assigned to this group. For example, you can have all the backup singers grouped to the same group fader. When you want the background vocals to go down, you only need to reduce the level of this group fader, rather than reducing the level of all the backup singers' tracks.

▶ Marker tracks, as you saw in Chapter 4, easily manage your Markers.

▶ Ruler tracks (SX only) allow you to view the time displayed in more than one format simultaneously. For example, if you're working with a time-coded video project, you might need to see this timecode while you're working on cues, but also need to see where bars and beats fall to add musical events at the proper times.

▶ Video tracks synchronize your music to a digital video file.

Adding Tracks

How To

To add a track to your project:

1. Click Project > Add Track from the menu bar.
2a. From the Add Track's submenu, select the appropriate type of track you want to add.
2b. Or right-click(PC)/Ctrl-click(Mac) in the Track List and select the type of track you want to add.

Notice that with both methods, the Multiple option is also available, which enables you to add more than one track of the same class simultaneously. You can't, however, add several tracks of a different class (or type) at once.

Let's take a closer look at these track classes and their specifics.

MIDI Track

This class of track is for MIDI events. You can use MIDI tracks for any type of MIDI events. MIDI tracks contain MIDI note events, controllers such as velocity, modulation wheel, pitch bend, and so on. They also contain any type of MIDI automation information generated by the Channel Settings panel, such as automation for MIDI effects that might be assigned to a track. MIDI tracks can also contain MIDI filters and effects, such as MIDI compression, which is also discussed in the next sections. Recorded MIDI events are saved with the project file itself. When you associate a drum map to a MIDI track (this is explained later in the chapter), events in that track will become associated with the Drum Editor window rather than the Key Editor window.

When you record MIDI events, such as a musical performance, through your MIDI controller, these events are stored in a part, which appears on the MIDI track's Event Display area in the project window. You can have many parts containing MIDI events on your track, and parts can overlap each other on the track. Parts that are underneath other parts on the same track will still be active, and events inside them will still be heard when you play the track. You can compare a part to a container of MIDI events. In the case of MIDI, these containers can be stacked one on top of the other, playing either different drum instruments, different channels (if the MIDI track is set to play any MIDI channels), or simply as part of your working process.

In the example in Figure 6.1, there are three different parts playing at the same time on the same track, creating a rhythmic pattern. These three parts could be playing over different channels or not. However, you should know that when parts are stacked one on top of the other in a MIDI track, the only visible part is the one on top of the others. If all the parts are of equal length, this might lead to confusion because you will hear the parts playing, but you won't see them unless you select all the parts by dragging your Selection tool over the visible part and opening your selection in the MIDI (Key or Drum) editor.

Figure 6.1
Overlapping MIDI parts
on a MIDI track.

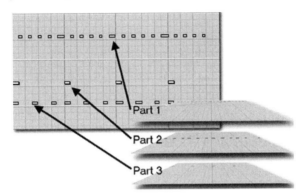

Setting Up a MIDI Track

To use a MIDI track, you must choose a MIDI input port and a MIDI output port. The MIDI input port records incoming MIDI events on the track. For example, if a controller keyboard is hooked up to your MIDI input port A, you can set your MIDI track to either All MIDI Inputs if you want any incoming MIDI ports to be recorded onto the selected track or set the track to MIDI input port A to record events only from your controller keyboard. This can be set as follows:

How To

To set your MIDI input port:

1. Make sure the MIDI Thru is active [File(PC)/Cubase(Mac) > Preferences > MIDI].
2. Select the MIDI track you want to set up for input.
3. Make the Inspector area visible.
4. Make the first panel in the Inspector area visible, as shown in Figure 6.2.
5. Click the arrow to the left of the MIDI Input Port field to reveal the available MIDI input ports.
6. Select the appropriate port.

Notice in Figure 6.2 that a MIDI port is already present because you can set a default MIDI port for your MIDI tracks. Whenever you create a MIDI track, it uses this default setting.

CHAPTER 6

Figure 6.2
The basic track settings
for a MIDI track in the
Inspector area.

How To

To set a default MIDI port device for all projects:

1. Select Devices > Device Setup from the menu bar.
2. Make the Default MIDI Ports entry active by selecting it.
3. Click the MIDI Input drop-down menu (the field to the right of "MIDI Input") to select the appropriate default MIDI input port, as shown in Figure 6.3.
4. Repeat this last step for the MIDI output port.
5. Click the Apply button and then click OK.

Figure 6.3
The Device Setup dialog
box sets a default MIDI
port.

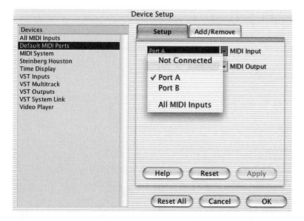

Let's take a look at each element found in both the Inspector's Track Setting area and the Track List area. Each number in Figure 6.4 corresponds to a number in the following numbered list. On the left you can see the inspector area when a physical MIDI port is selected, and on the right, the same area when a VSTi is assigned as a MIDI port output.

Figure 6.4

The MIDI track Inspector and the track list area for a MIDI track.

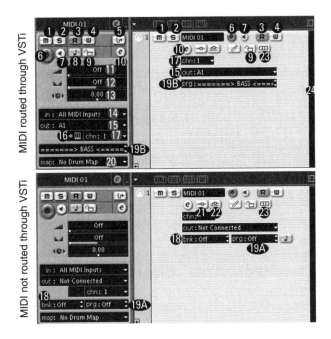

1. **Mute:** Mutes the track during playback.

2. **Solo:** Solos the track (mutes all other tracks).

3. **Read Automation:** Reads recorded automation on this track.

4. **Write Automation:** Writes automation on this track.

5. **Input Transformer:** Transforms MIDI messages between the MIDI input and output of this track. For example, you can use this to filter the MIDI input port's channels, allowing only the desired input channels to play through the MIDI output for this track.

6. **Record Ready:** Arms this track for recording. When you press the record button on the transport panel, incoming MIDI events will be recorded on this track.

7. **Monitor button:** Uses the MIDI Thru to hear MIDI messages coming in without recording these messages when in Record mode.

8. **Timebase Format:** Switches the track between linear time and musical tempo. When a track is displayed in musical tempo, changing the tempo of the song adjusts the events in the part according to the tempo setting. When a track is displayed in linear time, changing the tempo of the song does not affect the start position of the parts.

9. **Lock button:** Locks your track from editing.

10. **Edit MIDI Channel Settings:** Opens the Channel Settings panel to edit these settings.

11. **Track Volume:** Sets and monitors volume for the MIDI track. This uses the MIDI control change message number 7 and displays any volume automation for your track.

12. **Track Pan:** Sets and monitors pan for the MIDI track. This uses the MIDI control change message number 10 and displays any pan automation for your track. Any MIDI pan automation recorded will show up here.

13. **Track Delay:** Adds a positive or negative delay in milliseconds to your track. Events with a negative delay play earlier, whereas positive values change the timing of events to occur later in time. Track delays are great to offset a copy of a track that contains MIDI events. By assigning the copied track to another instrument and adding a slight delay, you can quickly get a thicker sounding part. Try it with strings parts or other parts that are not timing-sensitive.

14. **MIDI Input Port:** Sets the input port for the track. MIDI events coming through the input port can be recorded onto the track or monitored through the MIDI output port setting. Note that you can't select which MIDI input channel passes through a MIDI track, but usually, this is not a problem. If you do need to select which channel comes in, try the presets available for the Input Transformer (version 2.01 or better).

15. **MIDI Output Port:** Sets the output port for the track. MIDI events recorded on this track play through the device or software connected to this output port. You can also use the output port to monitor incoming MIDI events through a different port.

16. **Edit VST Instrument:** Brings up the VST Instrument panel, which allows you to edit the instrument's parameters and settings. Note that this button is only visible when a VSTi is assigned to this track. MIDI tracks assigned to a physical MIDI output, a non-VSTi compatible MIDI port, or Rewire MIDI output will not display this button.

17. **MIDI Output Channel:** Sets the MIDI channel used by the MIDI output port to play MIDI events on this track.

18. **Bank:** Sets a bank value associated with your MIDI device's preset structure. Typically, programs are grouped in banks of 128 sounds each (this is the maximum number of sounds MIDI can support). To access sounds above this value, banks are created. You can access up to 128 banks of 128 programs using this setting.

19a. **Program:** Specifies a program number to the MIDI device or software instrument associated with this track.

19b. **Preset Selection:** With some VSTi or MIDI devices that have been configured through the MIDI Device Manager panel, you can select the presets the instrument should play by using this drop-down menu. When this is possible, the preset selection menu will replace the bank and program settings field and the names for the instrument's presets will appear here.

20. **Drum Map:** Associates a drum map with the MIDI events on this track. This is useful when you record a drum part on this track. You can also use the Drum Map setting in the Track List area.

21. **Insert State:** Monitors the state of MIDI insert effects assigned to this track. The button is turquoise when an insert effect is assigned to the track, and a yellow rectangle will appear in the Sends title bar in the Inspector area. Pressing this

button will cause the MIDI to bypass the inserts. When an insert is bypassed, the MIDI events do not go through the current inserts, but the insert settings remain untouched.

22. **Sends State:** Monitors the state of MIDI send effects assigned to this track. The button is turquoise when a send effect is assigned to the track, and a yellow rectangle will appear in the Sends title bar in the Inspector area. Pressing this button will prevent the MIDI on this track from going through the MIDI send effects, but the sends settings remain untouched.

23. **Lane Display Type:** Displays overlapping parts on several lanes inside the MIDI track. Clicking on this button will reveal a menu with different lane display options. When the lane display is set to Off, overlapping parts will go back to the usual display (for previous Cubase owners). Fixed and Auto lane display will spread overlapping parts over the corresponding number of lanes.

24. **Output Activity:** Monitors event activity for the track. In MIDI tracks, this may be any MIDI messages (note, controllers, and sysEx if it is not filtered by Cubase). With audio tracks, this activity represents the playback level or the input level, depending on the track's Monitor state.

MIDI Track Parameters

MIDI track parameters allow you to change how the MIDI in a track is played in real time. In other words, it does not affect the recorded MIDI events, but rather transforms them on their way out to the MIDI output port. It's kind of like looking at yourself in a distorted mirror at the county fair. You do not actually have a big head, small neck, big belly, and small legs, as seen in the reflection. You simply appear like that in the mirror. MIDI track parameters are similar. They transform the data going out. Since they don't affect the MIDI data, the track parameters do not appear in the MIDI editors. Also, MIDI track parameters will affect all the parts on a track.

These parameters provide a convenient way to try things out without changing the original MIDI messages because you can bypass these parameters at any time by activating the Bypass button next to the track parameter name in the Inspector area (see Figure 6.5). When a track parameter is assigned, the upper-right corner of the Track Parameter section is purple. When you click the track parameter's Bypass button, a yellow rectangle appears next to the track parameter's activity settings indicator. Whenever you bypass the track parameter settings, the track will play the MIDI events on the track as if there were no track parameters applied to the track. This is very useful when you want to do a comparison listening of your events.

Figure 6.5
The Track Parameters section found in the Inspector area of a selected MIDI track.

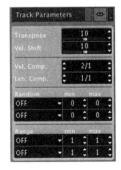

The Transpose field enables you to set a value between -127 to +127. Each value corresponds to a semitone below or above the current note. Positive values transpose notes higher; negative values transpose notes lower. This affects all the notes found on this track. If you want to try changing the pitch of a song to find out if you can sing it better in another key, this is a great tool to use.

The Velocity Shift field sets a value between -127 to +127 as well; however, in this case these values add or remove the value from the MIDI event's velocity for the selected track. For example, adding a value of "10" causes all MIDI events to play at their recorded velocity plus 10. When most of what you recorded is great, with the exception that the MIDI events were recorded slightly too soft (low velocity) or too loud (high velocity), use this to alter the overall velocity of your recorded events.

The Velocity Compression field uses a multiplication factor, which compresses or expands the velocity of MIDI events on a track by its corresponding multiplication factor. This factor is defined by a numerator (left value) and denominator (right value). The resulting fraction is applied to the track's velocity level. You can see an example of this in Table 6.1.

Table 6.1
How track parameters affect MIDI events

Track Parameter	Note 1	Note 2	Note 3	Note 4	Comment
Before Filters					
Velocity Value	50	70	35	100	Recorded velocities
Vel. Comp. (1/2)	25	35	17	50	Velocities heard after compression
Vel. Shift (+50)	50	50	50	50	Added to the previous velocities when heard
After Filter	75	85	67	100	Resulting velocity that can be heard

The Length Compression field also uses a multiplication factor, which compresses or expands the length of MIDI events on a track by its corresponding multiplication factor. This factor is defined by a numerator (left value) and denominator (right value). For example, a factor of 2:1 means that all notes will be of double length and a factor of 1:3 means that all notes will be one-third their original lengths. Note that this does not affect when the events play in time, only their length.

Below the Length Compression field, you will find two Random generators with their corresponding fields. These two fields act independently from one another and serve to introduce random values to the position, pitch, velocity, or length of MIDI events on this track. This can be useful with clear rhythmic or melodic parts rather than with tracks containing long sustained notes. In other words, the randomness is more obvious when events occur more often. Under each Random generator is a field that lets you choose what type of randomly generated value you want to add (position, pitch, velocity, or length). You can then set a minimum and maximum value for these random values. A wider range between the minimum and maximum value creates a more pronounced effect, whereas a smaller range creates a more subtle effect. With the position and length selections, you can set the minimum and maximum values from -500 ticks to +500 ticks, respectively. For the pitch and velocity, you can set these values between -120 and +120 (this corresponds to semitones when used with pitch). Note that you can't set your minimum value to a higher value than the maximum value.

At the bottom of the Track Parameters section are two Range fields with associated minimum and maximum values that work just like the random minimum and maximum fields. However, in this case, the Range fields, as the name suggests, are used to set a range for which events are included or excluded from processing. There are four Range modes:

▶ **Velocity Limit.** Use this mode when you want all notes to play within a certain velocity range. Any note that plays at a velocity outside the range is either brought to the minimum value in the range if it is below this value or brought to the maximum value in the range if it is above this value. Any other velocity values (which are found within the defined range) play unchanged.

▶ **Velocity Filter.** Use this mode when you want to isolate notes that play within a certain velocity range. Notes outside the range, either above or below, are simply not played back.

▶ **Note Limit.** Use this mode when you want all notes to play within a range of notes. Note values that are below or above this range are transposed an octave up or down, respectively, in order to play within the range. If your range is too narrow and notes still don't reach the range after transposing an octave up or down, they are transposed to the center note value found within your range. For example, in a range between C4 and G4, A4 is transposed to an E4.

▶ **Note Filter.** Use this mode when you want to isolate certain note pitches within a certain range. Notes with pitches outside the range are not played back.

About MIDI Effects

Before we discuss MIDI track inserts and sends, it is important that you understand the difference between a MIDI effect and an audio effect.

You may already know about audio effects and how you can use them to make your audio tracks sound better or different. In this respect, MIDI effects are similar to audio effects. However, the process is quite different with MIDI than it is for audio. When you apply a MIDI effect to a MIDI track, you are not processing the sound generated by the MIDI device (VST instrument or hardware sound module). In fact, you are using a process that adds or changes the MIDI events that are recorded on your track in real time. For example, when you are adding a MIDI delay to your MIDI track, Cubase generates additional MIDI messages to simulate an echo effect by using MIDI notes. Because these effects are playing in real time, just as audio effects, you can rest assured that your MIDI events on your track are not modified in any way, except at the output, where the MIDI effect actually takes place.

If you are using a VSTi, you can combine both types of effects: audio and MIDI. This gives you even more flexibility in your creative process. However, you cannot use audio effects on external MIDI devices because the audio of this device is not processed by Cubase until you record the audio from this external MIDI device onto an audio track inside your project. We'll get to this subject later, but for now, understand that a MIDI effect can be applied to any MIDI track in two ways: through a MIDI track insert and through a MIDI track send. Both methods instruct your MIDI sound module how to play the MIDI events according to the settings found in the MIDI effect.

You will find more information on what each MIDI effect does and how to use them in Appendix B.

MIDI Track Inserts

Below the Track Parameters section in the Inspector area, you will find the MIDI Track Inserts section, which adds a MIDI effect to your MIDI track (see Figure 6.6). When you are using an effect as an insert, you are sending the MIDI events recorded on this track into a selected effect. This effect then generates the necessary MIDI events through the MIDI output port of the track containing the effect. It is the device's (sound module) job to actually play the resulting MIDI effect along with the original recorded MIDI material. As you can see in Figure 6.6, you can have up to four MIDI insert effects assigned to each MIDI track. When a MIDI insert effect is selected from its drop-down menu, a panel opens up to reveal its settings. Once closed, you can access the insert's settings panel by clicking on the "e" button above the appropriate insert. You can also force Cubase to open the parameters of a MIDI effect in its own window if, by default, they open in the Track Inserts section. You can do so by Alt(PC)/Option(Mac)-clicking on the Edit MIDI Effect button. Here are some of the things you can do with MIDI inserts:

How To

To add a MIDI insert effect:

▶   Select a MIDI effect from one of the four drop-down menus.

How To

To edit a MIDI insert effect's parameters:

▶   Click the Edit MIDI Effect button (see Figure 6.6).

To bypass one or all MIDI inserts from playback:

▶   If you want to bypass all effects, click the Insert Bypass button at the top of the MIDI Track Inserts section. The MIDI Track Insert section's top-left corner turns yellow, indicating that the effects are bypassed. Because you can always see the top part of the Track Inserts section, you can easily change the status (active or bypassed) of your inserts by using this bar.

▶   If you want to bypass only one effect, click the Activate/Deactivate button above the effect you want to bypass. By default, an effect is activated as soon as you select it from the drop-down menu. By deactivating it, you can do a comparison listening without having to reset your effect each time.

Figure 6.6
The MIDI Track Insert
section in the Inspector
area.

As you can see in Figure 6.7, when you assign a MIDI insert to a track, it only affects the events on this track, and you can only use the track's MIDI output port to generate these effects. This said, if you want to use one device to play the original content and another to play the processed information, you can use a MIDI track send. If you want to maximize or minimize this section in the Inspector area, click the button found in the upper-right corner of the insert's title bar.

Figure 6.7
The signal path of a MIDI
track insert.

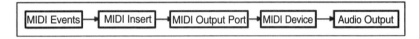

MIDI Track Sends

When you want to send the result of a MIDI effect played through a different MIDI device, you can use the MIDI track sends instead of the MIDI track inserts because the track sends offer an additional setting for MIDI output ports and MIDI channels. As you can see in Figure 6.8, the signal can be routed to two different outputs. In other words, if you don't need the effect to play through the same MIDI port and channel, use the track insert. However, if you want your effect to play through another port and channel, or you want to send the MIDI events before or after the volume control setting of the MIDI track, use the track sends.

Figure 6.8
The signal path of a MIDI
track send.

The options for the MIDI track sends are fairly similar to the ones found in the Track Inserts section (see Figure 6.9). In addition to the options explained earlier, below the MIDI Effect Selection, you will find a field that lets you choose the appropriate MIDI port for the MIDI events generated by the MIDI effect along with a MIDI channel setting. Found between the Activate/Deactivate MIDI Send FX button and the Edit MIDI Effect button is the Pre-/Post-fader toggle button. In its default Post-fader mode, the volume level of the channel will affect how the MIDI events are treated by the MIDI send effect. In the toggled Pre-fader mode (the button becomes yellow), the volume control level of your track has no effect on the MIDI events sent to the effect.

CHAPTER 6

Figure 6.9

The MIDI Track Sends section in the Inspector area.

effect in pre-fader mode

effect in post-fader mode

on/off effect button

MIDI output port for the effect

open MIDI effect edit panel

MIDI effect selection

MIDI channel for the effect

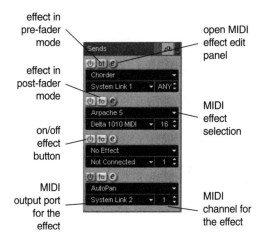

How To

To assign a MIDI track send:

1. Unfold the Sends section for the selected MIDI track (upper-right corner of the section).

2. From the MIDI Effect selection drop-down menu, choose an appropriate effect.

3. Under the selected MIDI Effect field, choose an appropriate MIDI port for the output of the MIDI effect. This affects where the MIDI events generated by the effect will be sent.

4. Next to the output port, select an appropriate MIDI channel for playback.

5. Select Pre- or Post-fader mode, according to your preference. Remember that in the default Post-fader mode, volume automation on your track may affect how the MIDI events are treated by the MIDI effect.

MIDI Channel

The MIDI Channel section (see Figure 6.10), found at the bottom of the Inspector area, offers many of the same options as you find in the MIDI Setting section of the Inspector area, as well as the Track List area for a MIDI track. It also mirrors the information you find in the Mixer panel for this specific track class, as well as most of the buttons that we have seen earlier in the Track List and Track Setting section of the Inspector area. You can use this section to set the pan and volume levels of the device associated with this track. You can also use this section to change or monitor which insert or send effects are active. Finally, below the volume fader is the track's name field, which you can use to rename the selected track.

Figure 6.10
The MIDI Track Channel
section in the Inspector
area.

Notepad

You can now add little bits of information with each track by using the Notepad section. Use it if you need to exit quickly and just want to keep some notes on the current state of your project, describe which device was used for this track, if it was changed from its original setup and so on—anything you feel is worth writing down. If you save your file, only to reopen it in a few months, you might not remember what is what. The Notepad allows you to refresh your memory.

Simply type in the text field area. Any changes you make will be saved with the project file.

Audio Track

The audio track class is used to hold audio events, audio parts, and automation information. When you record audio on a track, an audio event is created in your project. Each audio track can play one audio event at a time. This implies that if you overlap audio events, you only hear the event on top of the others. You can change the order of these events to hear a different part.

How To

To change the order of overlapping parts or events:

1. With the Selection tool, click the event (or part) you want to send to back or bring to front.
2. While the event is selected, right-click and choose the appropriate option under Move To from the context menu.

Remember that you can also do this with a MIDI part. However with MIDI parts, you will still hear the overlapping parts no matter what the order might be.

In order to record audio information in a project, you will need to start by creating audio tracks, just as you need to create MIDI tracks if you want to record MIDI events. When you create audio tracks, you need to make a choice about how you want your track configured. In Cubase SL, this choice allows you to pick between mono or stereo tracks (one or two channels). Events recorded on a mono track will be recorded in mono format and events recorded on a stereo track will be recorded in stereo interleave format. Stereo interleave means that both channels (left and right) are recorded into the same file. With Cubase SX, the choice widens to include surround sound formats such as LCRS (left, center, right, and surround), 5.0, 5.1 or one of many other multichannel format.

Once an audio track is created, you can record and import or move audio from the pool into this track. By assigning the track to an output bus, it will allow you to monitor its content through that output bus. For best and predictable results, you should always import audio files into a track that corresponds to the same configuration. For example, you should always drag stereo files onto stereo tracks and mono files onto mono tracks.

How To

To add an audio track to a project:

1. Right-click(PC)/Control-click(Mac) in the Track List area of the project window. You can also select Add Track > Audio from the Project menu.
2. From the context menu, select Add Audio Track.
3. In the Add Audio Track dialog box, select a track configuration from the drop-down menu.
4. Click OK.

QUICKLY ADDING MORE TRACKS
After you have added an audio (or MIDI) track, double-clicking under that track in the track list area will create another track of the same class.

About Audio Terminology

To work with audio inside a Cubase project, it is important to understand the audio terminology associated with your project. In Cubase, audio is referred to as audio clips, events, parts, regions, and slices. This section describes how, when, and why these terms are used.

Audio Clips and Audio Events

In the project window, recorded audio is referred to as an *audio event*. Audio events are the representation of the audio clip, which is the file recorded onto your hard disk. In essence, when you edit an audio event, you edit the graphic representation of an audio file, named *audio clip*, inside Cubase without changing the original content found on your hard disk. When an audio clip is placed on a track in a project, it becomes an audio event. So the difference between an audio clip and an audio event is that the event plays at a specific time in a project and is also used in a project, whereas clips don't have a playback time associated with them, and they are found only in the pool window.

Audio Regions

Audio clips in the media pool can also contain regions. Regions can be created automatically when recording in Cycle mode, or you can create regions manually inside the sample editor. Typically, regions represent a portion of an audio clip or audio event.

When placing an audio event that contains several regions in an audio track, it is possible to change which region will play without changing the event's location. You simply need to tell Cubase to play another region instead. For example, if you have recorded three takes of a solo performance in Cycle Recording mode, each time the recording started a new lap, a region might have been created (this depends on the recording preferences found under File (PC)/Cubase(Mac) > Preferences > Record > Audio Cycle Record Mode options). You can later decide which lap you wish to listen to by selecting which region is active (on top).

Audio Slices

Another type of Event/Region combination found in Cubase is called an *audio slice*. Slices are used with rhythmic parts, such as drum loops. You can create slices only inside the Sample Editor window. Using the Hitpoints tool allows you to define where important beats or slices occur in rhythmic or percussive musical content. For example, you can cut a drum loop in individual hits. Each hit is what Cubase then calls a *slice*. These slices do not appear in the Pool like the regions will; however, when you place a drum loop sample containing slices on an audio track, Cubase creates a part that holds this drum loop, and each event in the part corresponds to a slice of the audio clip. By dividing rhythmic audio events using slices, you can later quantize these events the same way you would quantize MIDI events. Furthermore, you can change the tempo of a project, and each slice's start point will keep its relation in the beat. If an audio file containing a rhythmic part is not sliced, changing the tempo will not affect this loop's start point, but the rhythmic accuracy will shift since the tempo of the audio loop and the project do not match anymore. If you take a look at Figure 6.11, you will see a part as it appears when an audio drum loop has been sliced and placed on an audio track. The same content is represented in both portions of Figure 6.11; however, the top portion represents the slices when the project plays at a tempo of 148 BPM, whereas the bottom portion represents the same slices played at a tempo of 79 BPM. As you can see, the beats occur at the same location in the bar/beat grid, but there is space added between each slice when the loop is played at a slower tempo.

Figure 6.11
Example of a drum loop sliced using hitpoints.

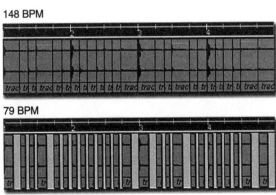

Finally, you can have audio parts in your project. Audio parts are containers of audio events, regions, or slices. An audio part does not represent a recorded or imported audio event, but you can place audio events inside of a part. You can also convert an event into a part, and you can place additional audio events inside an existing part. In other words, audio parts are similar to MIDI parts in that they hold information that can be moved across other audio tracks or in time. Audio parts are useful when you want to move multiple events together, such as the ones found when using slices, for example.

Figure 6.12 is divided into three parts. On the left, you can see where to find the different types of audio terms mentioned in this section. In the center, you can see the hierarchy between the different terms, and on the right, a diagram displaying how this hierarchy works in your project. By default, when you double-click in the project window on a part, it launches the Audio Part Editor. Once inside the Audio Part Editor, you can drag other regions, events, or sliced events into a part. When you double-click on an event or a region inside the audio editor or in the project window, it launches the Sample Editor. You can't drag anything in the Sample Editor.

This hierarchy allows for nondestructive editing because what you normally edit is the audio clip, its associated event, regions, and slices, not the audio file itself. When a portion of the audio event is processed, Cubase creates an additional audio clip on the hard disk containing the newly processed section of your audio. The audio parts containing references to processed audio material update themselves to correspond to this new link.

Figure 6.12
The audio terminology's hierarchy.

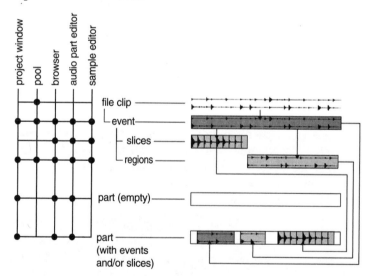

Setting Up an Audio Track

The following numbered list describes the different buttons and control elements found in both the Inspector area and the Track List area for an audio track (see Figure 6.13). It is important to understand what these buttons do as they will be used throughout your work on a project when audio tracks are involved.

Figure 6.13
The Track Parameters section found in the Inspector area of a selected audio track.

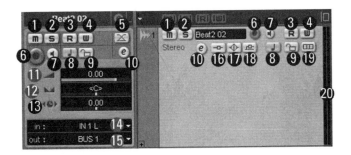

1. **Mute:** Mutes the track during playback.

2. **Solo:** Solos the track (mutes all other tracks).

3. **Read Automation:** Reads recorded automation on this track.

4. **Write Automation:** Writes automation on this track.

5. **Auto Fade:** Brings up the Auto Fade dialog box, which lets you set how fades and crossfades are handled on this track.

6. **Record Ready:** Arms this track for recording. When you press the record button on the Transport panel, incoming audio signals will be recorded on this track.

7. **Monitor button:** Uses the channel's level meters as an audio input monitor. You can't adjust the input level using the channel fader, but you can use this to monitor the level coming in and adjust it by using an external level adjustment or the audio input bus (SX only). You can also use this to monitor incoming signal without recording it when pressing the Record button on the Transport panel.

8. **Timebase Format:** Switches the track between linear time and musical tempo. When a track is displayed in musical tempo, changing the tempo of the song adjusts the events in the part according to the tempo setting. When a track is displayed in linear time, changing the tempo of the song does not affect the start position of the parts.

9. **Lock button:** Locks your track from editing.

10. **Edit Audio Channel:** Opens the Channel Settings panel to edit the settings associated with this type of channel.

11. **Track Volume:** Sets and monitors the volume level for this track. Automation or volume changes made in the track's channel and project's mixer are displayed here as well.

12. **Track Pan:** Sets and monitors the pan position for this track. Automation or pan changes made in the track's Channel Settings panel and project's Mixer panel are displayed here as well.

13. **Track Delay:** Adds a positive or negative delay (in milliseconds) to your track. Events with a negative delay play earlier, whereas positive values change the timing of events to occur later in time.

14. **Audio Input Bus:** Sets the input bus for the track. An audio signal coming through the input bus can be recorded onto the track or monitored through the audio output bus if the Monitor button is enabled (see above).

CHAPTER 6

15. **Audio Output Bus:** Sets the output port for the track. To hear audio events recorded on this track, you need to select the output bus that is associated with a physical output on the computer's sound card.

16. **Insert State:** Monitors the state of the insert effects. The button is blue when an insert effect is assigned to the track, and a yellow rectangle will appear next to it when the Bypass button is active. Clicking on this button will bypass any audio inserts you have assigned to this track.

17. **EQ State:** Monitors the state of the EQ. The button is green when one or more of the four bands are in use by the track, and a yellow rectangle will appear next to it when the Bypass button is active. Clicking on this button will bypass any equalization settings you have assigned to this track.

18. **Sends State:** Monitors the state of the send effects. The button is blue when an insert effect is assigned to the track, and a yellow rectangle will appear next to it when the Bypass button is active. Clicking on this button will stop any audio from being sent to an FX channel in this track.

19. **Lane Display Type:** Displays overlapping parts or events on several lanes inside the audio track. Clicking on this button will reveal a menu with different lane display options. When the lane display is set to Off, overlapping parts will go back to the usual display (for previous Cubase owners). Fixed lane display will spread overlapping parts or events over the corresponding number of lanes. Note that events that would appear on top of overlapping events will appear in lower lanes. Since each audio track can only play one audio event at a time, audio events on lower lanes will prevent audio events on higher lanes from playing.

20. **Output Activity:** Monitors event activity for the track. In audio tracks, the number of actual activity meters will depend on the track's configuration. Mono tracks will display a single output meter while a surround track configuration will display as many output meters as the track contains. With the audio track in input monitoring mode (the monitor button is active), the activity represents the input level instead.

Audio Track Inserts

In Cubase SX, you can have up to eight insert effects per channel and up to five in Cubase SL. The signal from an audio track is routed through each active insert effect one after another. In other words, the output of one insert effect feeds the next one, and so on, from top to bottom (see Figure 6.14).

REDUCING PROCESSING POWER NEEDED BY USING SENDS INSTEAD OF INSERTS

Because each instance of an effect that is loaded into an insert effect slot uses as much processing power and memory as it does in send effects, it is strongly recommended that you use track send effects when you use the same effect with the same settings on more than one track. This reduces the amount of processing power needed to process the audio and also reduces the amount of memory needed to load each instance.

To monitor how your computer is doing in terms of system resources, you can take a look at the VST Performance panel or on the Default Transport panel. The default key command to open the VST Performance panel is F12. You can also open it by selecting its option in the Devices menu. This way, you can make changes to your project before your computer starts to become overloaded.

Figure 6.14
The Track Inserts section from the Inspector area of the audio track.

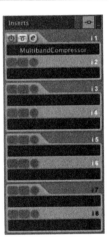

Each insert effect slot has four controls: the Active/Deactivate, Bypass, and Edit effect setting buttons. Below these buttons you will find a field where you can select which effect should be added to the track. These controls are similar to the ones explained earlier in the MIDI Track Inserts section. You will also find two buttons in the title bar of this section:

▶ The Bypass Inserts button bypasses all insert effects found on this track. As with the Active/Bypass button found on each insert, this can be useful to monitor your track with or without effects without having to make changes to these effects. When the inserts are bypassed, a yellow rectangle appears at the location of the Bypass Insert button.

▶ The Track Insert section's Control button in the upper-right corner maximizes or minimizes this section in the Inspector area. As with all other Control buttons in the MIDI track's Inspector, the Control button has two states: the default project color means that there are no inserts on this track and turquoise means that there are inserts on this track

Adding an insert effect, bypassing an insert, or all inserts is done exactly the same way as with MIDI track inserts. Please refer to that section in this chapter if you are unsure about the procedure.

CHAPTER 6

USING INSERTS 7-8 FOR POST-FADER PROCESSING

Normally, when using inserts, the signal passes through the effect before the volume control (prefader) and before any EQ is applied to the track. However, with inserts 7 and 8 (SX Only), the signal is sent to the insert after the volume control (postfader) and after the EQ for this track.

This type of insert is best suited for effects that need to be inserted regardless of the volume and EQ settings, such as final dynamic processing using limiters or dithering processes. For that reason, you should use the inserts 7-8 on output buses during the mastering process. This will be discussed further in Chapter 15.

Audio Track Equalizer

Below the Track Inserts section, you will find the track's Equalizer section (EQ). Each audio track you create has a four-band parametric equalizer (see Figure 6.15). An equalizer allows you to control the gain of a specific band of frequencies. The frequency found at the center of this band is displayed in the EQ. The width of each band depends on a setting called Q. These four bands are called (from top to bottom in the Equalizer section): Hi, Hi Mid, Lo Mid, and Lo.

Figure 6.15
The Equalizer Section from the Inspector area of the audio track.

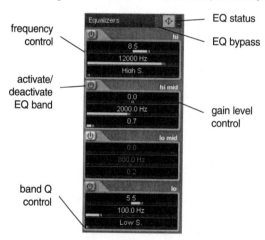

frequency control

activate/ deactivate EQ band

band Q control

EQ status

EQ bypass

gain level control

Most of the features for each EQ band are similar with the exception of the Hi and Lo bands. In the Hi band, setting the Q completely to the left creates a high shelf, which means that any frequency above the center frequency for this band is affected by the gain control. Inversely, if the Q is set completely to the right, it creates a low-pass filter, where every frequency above the band's center frequency is reduced. For the Lo band, setting the Q completely to the left produces a low shelf and setting the Q completely to the right creates a high pass, as shown in Figure 6.16.

Figure 6.16
The different types of shelves and pass filters found in the Hi and Lo band EQ.

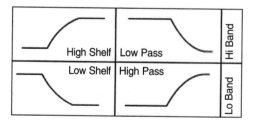

To adjust an EQ band from the audio track Equalizer section:

1. Make the Equalizer section visible for the track you want to adjust.

2. Find the center frequency you want to adjust by dragging the slider bar under the numeric display of the frequency, by clicking on the frequency value and using your scroll bar to increase or decrease the value, or by double-clicking on the value and entering a new value between 20 and 20,000 (which corresponds to the range of each band).

3. Adjust the amount of gain or reduction you want to apply by using the gain control values. You can adjust these values the same way you can adjust the frequency (as seen in Step 2). However, the minimum and maximum values for this field are -24 to +24 (which correspond to dB values).

4. Adjust the width of your band by changing the Q value for the appropriate band. Smaller values result in wider bands, whereas higher values result in narrower bands.

5. Repeat these steps for each band in your EQ.

You can bring back each value to its default position in the EQ by Ctrl(PC)/⌘(Mac)-clicking on the appropriate field. You can also do a before/after comparison listening by deactivating the band. This acts as a band bypass. When you are bypassing the EQ bands, the settings remain unchanged.

Note that you can also adjust the EQ settings (as well as inserts and sends) through the Mixer panel and the Channel Settings panel. Finally, you can also bypass all bands in the EQ by clicking on the Bypass button in the Equalizer section's title bar.

Equalizer Curve

The Equalizer Curve section of the Inspector area (see Figure 6.17) offers a graphical display, representing the current EQ settings for the selected audio track. Each band is represented by a point along a centered horizontal line. This center line represents an EQ in its default state, which implies that no changes have been made to the audio's frequencies. Frequencies are displayed from low on the left, to high on the right of the display. The space above the centered line represents a gain in the frequency while the space under the centered line represents a cut in a band's frequencies.

Any changes you make in the Equalizer section will be visible here, so you can use this area to quickly glance at the EQ settings for this track, but the EQ curve also draws your EQ settings for the track. Here's how:

How To

To adjust the EQ settings using the Equalizer Curve:

▶ To add an EQ band: Click where you want to add it on the EQ's curve. The band numbers correspond to their respective frequency range. This implies that the area where you click in the display will influence which band number appears. Remember that if you want to use a low shelf, low pass, high shelf, or high pass filter, you will need to click near the left or right extremities of the display, depending on the band you want to activate.

▶ To change the gain without changing the frequency: Hold the Ctrl(PC)/⌘(Mac) key down while you drag the band's handle in the graphical display.

▶ To change the frequency without changing the gain: Hold the Alt(PC)/Option(Mac) key down while you drag the band's handle in the graphical display.

▶ To change the band's Q: Hold the Shift key down and move your mouse up to increase the width of the Q (the Q value will actually go down) and move your mouse down to decrease the width of the Q (the Q value will actually go up).

Figure 6.17
The Equalizer Curve display in the Inspector area.

Audio Track Sends

As with track inserts, the track sends for audio tracks are similar to MIDI track sends, with a few differences to point out. First, let's start with the title bar. In the MIDI Track Sends section (and in the audio Track Sends section), you have a State button that views if there are currently any sends assigned to the selected track. The button is colored when this is the case. To the left of the Sends state button is a Bypass button. You can click on this area to bypass all the sends at once without changing any settings in this section. When all the sends are bypassed, you will see a yellow rectangle next to the sends turquoise State button (see Figure 6.18). You may also stop sending a signal from this track to an effect by deactivating it (the first button on the left over each sends).

For each audio track send, you have three buttons above the effect's name that resemble the MIDI track sends: the Activate/Deactivate (or Bypass) button, the Pre-/Post-fader toggle button, and the Edit Effect Parameter button. Below these three buttons, you will find the name of the send effect. The effect name displayed here represents the effect associated with an FX track. In other words, to assign an audio track to a send effect, you need to create an FX track and load an audio plug-in effect into that track's insert effect. You can only have a total of eight send effects per audio track (five in SL), but you can create as many FX tracks as you want. This means that you don't need to share the same send effects for all the audio tracks in your project. For example, you might have 10 FX tracks where the audio track 1 uses sends 1 through 4, audio track 2 uses sends 1 through 4 as well, but in both cases, the signal might be sent to different FX tracks altogether, with track 1 going to FX tracks 1, 2, 3, and 4 while track 2 might be sending its signal to FX tracks 3, 5, 7, and 9.

Figure 6.18
The Track Sends section
from the Inspector area of
the audio track.

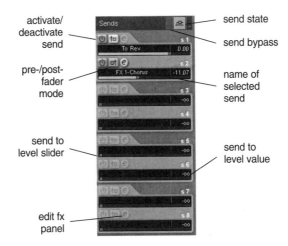

Below the effect's name is the Send to Effect Level setting. This setting controls how much signal from this track you want to send to the selected FX track. Audio sent to an FX track (which then routes the signal into an audio plug-in effect) is processed at the level at which it is sent. The more signal you send to the effect, the more you hear the processed sound for this audio signal. The idea is to give you control over how much effect you want over each individual track without having to load multiple instances of plug-in effects.

SENDING A SIGNAL TO AN FX TRACK

In order to send a signal to an FX track, you will need to create an FX track and assign a plug-in effect to that track beforehand. To find out how to do this, go to the FX Track section later in this chapter.

SENDING A SIGNAL OUTSIDE CUBASE

You can also use sends to route your signal to an additional set of output buses on your sound card. This might come in handy when you want to send a signal to a headphone amplifier outside of your computer during a recording session or if you want to process the signal with a hardware device rather than a plug-in.

In order to send your signal outside Cubase using sends, you will simply need to select the appropriate output bus where you want to send the signal instead of an FX track.

This works better if you have a spare set of outputs (more than two) that can be dedicated as a send to effect bus. You should create a separate output and input bus and label them respectively FX Sends Bus and FX Return Bus. Labeling your input and output buses as such will make it easy to recognize them when assigning a track's send effect to a sound card's physical connectors.

How To

To send an audio track to an FX track:

1. Unfold the Sends section in the Inspector area of the audio track.

2. Select the desired send effect from one of the Send Effects plug-in selection fields. You can also send an audio signal to a group channel (if one exists) or an output bus.

3. By default, selecting an effect in the first two send effect slots will activate this effect automatically, but you will need to activate the effect if you are selecting any other send effect slot (3-8 with SX or 3-5 with SL).

4. In the Send Effect section for the audio track, select Pre- or Post-fader, as desired. You can see how the signal is routed in Figure 6.19. In Post-fader mode, the signal sent to the effect is taken after the audio track's channel volume level and volume settings.

5. In the Sends section of the audio track, raise the level sent to the effect until the desired effect is reached.

ADJUSTING THE OVERALL LEVEL OF AN FX

To adjust the overall level of the effect in the mix, you will need to adjust the FX channel's volume level. Changing this level will influence all audio tracks that are being routed through that FX channel.

After completing these steps, you need to fine-tune both the level being sent to the FX channel as well as the level returning to the mix from the FX channel until the appropriate blend is found.

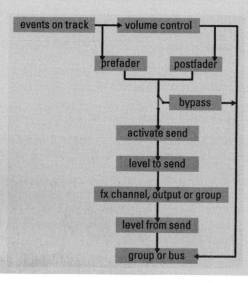

Figure 6.19
The audio send signal
path diagram.

To send the signal of one track to more than one send effect, repeat the same steps as mentioned earlier in this section for another effect. Unlike insert effects, each send effect is processed in parallel, not in series. This implies that the order in which the signal is sent to the send effect does not influence the end result.

As you can see in Figure 6.19, there are many places you can bypass the effect. The following list describes the differences between each one and how you can use them.

How To
_____

To bypass/activate the signal sent to all send effects in a track:

▶ Use the Bypass button found in the Sends section's title bar (in the Inspector area of the audio track).

How To
_____

To bypass/activate the signal sent to one send effect in a track:

▶ Use the Bypass/Activate button found above the effect's name in the Track Sends section in the audio track's Inspector area.

How To
_____

To bypass all the tracks sent to the same effect:

▶ Use the Bypass button found on the FX channel track list or in the FX channel's settings.

Audio Track Channel

The Track Channel section (see Figure 6.20) in the Inspector area offers control over the track's audio channel. Most of these controls are also present in the Inspector's Setup section or in the Track List area. You will find a description of each button found in the Track Channel section in the "Setting Up an Audio Track" section found earlier in this chapter. This said, because these controls are the same as the ones found in the Setup section, the Track List area, the Channel Settings panel, and the Mixer panel, any changes you make in any of these windows is updated automatically in every one of them. For example, if you change the volume level in the Channel section, this is reflected in the Channel Setup section as well as in the Channel Settings and the Mixer panels.

CHAPTER 6

Figure 6.20
The Track Channel
section from the
Inspector area of the
audio track.

FX Track

FX tracks are special Cubase channels to which an audio signal can be sent. What makes them different from other audio tracks is the fact that they play host to VST plug-in and DirectX plug-in (PC only) effects. An FX track is a host for audio effects that are assigned through inserts. In other words, just as you assign an insert to an audio channel, you assign an insert in an FX Track. With Cubase SX, you can create a chain of up to eight plug-in effects (five with Cubase SL). Each FX track has its own channel in the Mixer panel and offers most of the settings found in an audio track/channel.

You can't choose the input bus for an FX track because all FX tracks will receive their signal from the sends of audio channels (including VSTi channels, but not its MIDI counterpart). This also means that you can't record any audio into an FX track, but you can certainly record the output of an FX track. Because the main purpose of an FX track is to provide a way to add effects to a project, you can't send an effect to a send effect either.

How To

To add an FX channel track to a project:

1. Right-click(PC)/Control-click(Mac) in the Track List area of the project window. You can also select Add Track > FX Channel from the Project menu.

2. From the context menu, select Add FX Channel Track.

3. In the Add FX Channel Track dialog box (see Figure 6.21), select a track configuration from the drop-down menu. This will determine how the effect will process the signal going through the effect. Keep in mind that most current plug-ins are configured for stereo audio processing.

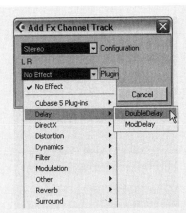

Figure 6.21
The Add FX Channel
Track dialog box.

4. Select the desired plug-in from the drop-down menu. If you are not sure which plug-in you want to use at this point, you can leave the plug-in field to "No Effect" and change it later on. This will simply create an empty FX channel, which can also serve to send an audio signal to an external source.

5. Click OK.

The controls found in the FX channel's Inspector area (see Figure 6.22) that can also be found in audio tracks will play the same role in both cases, so you should refer to the section above to find out more about them.

Figure 6.22
The Inspector area of an
FX channel.

Folder Track

Folder tracks, as you might have guessed, are used as folders in which you can put any class of tracks, including other folder tracks. You can use folder tracks as you would use folders in your computer, putting different tracks that relate to a specific kind of track inside a folder, identify them, and mute or hide the folder track to give you more working space on your screen. For example, if you have several percussion tracks, you could create a folder, name it "Percussions," and move all the percussion tracks inside this folder track. When you're not working on your percussions, you can fold the folder track to minimize the space all the percussion tracks would otherwise use on your desktop. When the time comes to edit these tracks, all you need to do is unfold the track to reveal all the tracks and controls inside.

When tracks are moved inside a folder track, a folder part is created in the Event Display area, which lets you see the contents of the folder track even when this track is minimized.

The Inspector area of the folder track only contains one section. This section contains the name of the tracks you moved inside the folder track. Whenever you click on the name of a track in this section, the track's Inspector area is displayed below the folder section (also in the Inspector area as shown in Figure 6.23).

Figure 6.23
The Inspector area of a folder track; when a track name in the folder track is selected, Cubase displays that track's Inspector area below.

Notice in Figure 6.23 that at the top of the folder track's Inspector area, there are buttons found in other track classes (and explained previously). These buttons affect all the tracks inside the folder track. For example, clicking the Mute button in the Inspector area of a folder track or in its Track List area mutes all the tracks inside the folder track. Similarly, clicking the Lock button locks all these tracks from editing. As you would guess, this makes recording, monitoring, muting, soloing, or locking multiple tracks simultaneously very easy.

HINT
Remember that to add a track of any class to your project, you can right-click(PC)/Ctrl-click(Mac) in the Track List area and choose Add track (of the desired class) from the context menu. You can also choose the desired track class from the Project > Add Track submenu.

How To

To move tracks into a folder track:

1. Click and drag the track you want to move to a folder track as shown in the top part of Figure 6.24.

2. When a green line appears near your folder track, drop your track into the folder track by releasing the mouse button (as shown in the center image of Figure 6.24).

3. Repeat this process to add additional tracks. You can drag multiple consecutive tracks simultaneously into a folder track by clicking the first track in the Track List area and then shift-clicking the last track you want to move into the folder track. To move nonconsecutive tracks, use the Ctrl(PC)/⌘(Mac) key to select your tracks before moving them.

Figure 6.24
Moving tracks into a folder track.

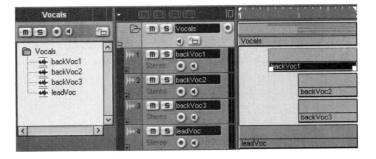

To remove tracks from a folder track, simply move them outside of the folder track, just as you moved them inside of it.

When tracks are added to a folder track, a folder part is created, as shown in Figure 6.25. As you can see in the same figure, the folder part displays the position and colors used by the parts on the tracks it contains. In this example, the folder track is minimized, hiding the details of these tracks. You can click the plus sign at the bottom-left corner of the folder track's Track List area to view these tracks once again. You can also rename folder tracks as you would any other tracks through the Inspector area.

Figure 6.25
Folder parts appear in the folder track.

How To

To rename a track by using the Inspector area:

1. Click in the name box at the top part of the Inspector area.
2. Type in a new name for your track.

Group Channel

A group channel assigns the output of different audio channels to this group channel. By adding automation or effects to this group, you affect all the audio channels assigned to this group. For example, if you don't have a multiple output sound card, you could assign different tracks to group tracks and use the groups as submixes. Typically, you could send all the drum and percussion tracks to one group, all the back vocals to another group, and the strings (if you have violins, altos, cellos, and contrabasses, for example) to another group. Then, if you want to increase the string section, all you have to do is raise the group channel fader rather than raise the audio channel faders for each string instrument.

Group tracks do not contain any recorded or imported events (audio or MIDI). Since MIDI tracks sending events to an external device don't actually create any sounds, just data, you can't send them to group channels either. This is because the audio aspect of these tracks is not handled by Cubase, but rather by the sound module itself. On the other hand, you can control MIDI automation through the Mixer panel. This said, if you have assigned a VSTi to your MIDI track, at least two channels are created in your Mixer panel: one representing MIDI control and another for audio control. In some cases, a VSTi might even generate more than two such channels as they offer multiple outputs for greater routing flexibility. For example, this is the case of the HALion sampler. Since all VSTi use your computer's sound card to generate their sound and Cubase's audio engine controls your sound card, the audio channels of VSTi can be assigned to a group track.

The Inspector area of a group track offers the same controls as an audio track with a few exceptions:

▶ You can't record on a group track so there are no Record or Monitor buttons.

▶ Group tracks take their input from other channels you may assign to them, so you won't find any input selection field. You can, however, assign the output of the group to a desired bus (or even another group) for output.

We take a closer look at how to use group tracks later in Chapter 12.

Marker Track

We've already discussed Marker tracks in Chapter 4, so you should already be familiar with this track class. However, let's take a closer look at the fields found in the Marker track's Track List area: the Zoom, Locate, and Cycle fields. These three fields hold drop-down menus that display the Markers, locators, and cycle markers currently present in your project.

▶ The Zoom field fills the Event Display area with the content found between the selected Markers (cycle markers always hold a left and right or start and end Marker position). You can use this field to change the focus of your work quickly from one region to another in your project.

▶ The Locate field moves your play line to the location of the Marker you select in this field. If you select a Marker during playback, the play line jumps to that location and continues playing from that point forward. If your project is not playing, the play line simply jumps to this point and waits for your next action.

▶ The Cycle field moves your left and right locators to the location of the cycle marker you select in this field. Moving your left and right locators does not move your play line to the left locator's position, however. This said, you can use the number one key on the numeric keypad as a keyboard shortcut to move your play line quickly to the new location.

Ruler Track

Cubase users (SX only) have the ability to add a second ruler track in their project in order to view time displayed in more than one format at a time. When working on a musical project, you can have one ruler display time as bars and beats while the second ruler displays seconds. When working on a video project, one ruler can display bars and beats while the second ruler displays timecode information.

Ruler tracks do not have any controls available in the Inspector area.

You can add a ruler track the same way you added in other tracks in your project.

How To

To change the format displayed in a ruler track:

1. Click on the time format icon in the Track List area (see Figure 6.26).
2. Select the desired time format from the drop down menu.

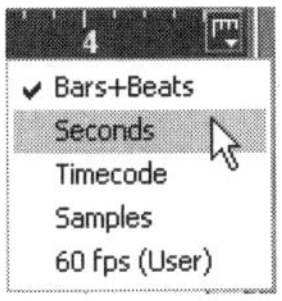

Figure 6.26
Changing the time format on the ruler track.

Video Tracks

When you are working with video projects, chances are you might have a copy of the project in a digital video format. Cubase loads a compatible video file into a project and creates a video track where you can place this video file as a visual reference for your work. You can place more than one video file on one, but can't have more than one video track per project.

Video editing options are fairly limited inside Cubase, as this is not a video editing software. This said, you can cut, copy, paste, and resize audio files on a video track. PC users will probably find that using QuickTime offers the best performance and flexibility as their video engine since DirectShow might not play video files properly if you edit video events or place more than one video file on a video track.

Now You Try It

For information about using the instructions found in this section and to find out where you can get the working files, please consult the section called *About the Exercise Files* in the Introduction section.

7

MIDI and Audio Recording

Now, it's time to start getting some MIDI and audio into your project. This chapter looks at the two known ways of getting content into a project: by recording it and by importing it. We'll look at how you can set up different parameters to ensure that what you record sounds right. For example, using the Auto-Quantize feature, you can automatically adjust recorded MIDI events so that they match up with a rhythmic grid. We'll also take a look at how to set up a metronome click so that you can use this as a reference guide when recording MIDI or even audio events into a project.

You'll also see how easy it is to move around in a project and see either a small section of your project or move out and get the bigger picture. Mastering the zoom tools and options will save you lots of grief and scrolling time because there's nothing more annoying than having to scroll up and down or left and right all the time to see what you want or where you are.

After these events are recorded, we'll look at how you can apply different functions to these events to correct errors before we start editing them in a MIDI editor. And, finally, recording is not the only way you can get media into a Cubase project. You can also import audio, MIDI, and video in different formats using the import features included in Cubase.

Here's a summary of what you will learn in this chapter:

▶ Set up for MIDI recording.

▶ Adjust MIDI filters to record only the MIDI messages you want.

▶ Configure a metronome.

▶ What the different quantize methods are and how to apply them to recorded events.

▶ Set up Cubase to record digital audio.

▶ Use Cycle modes when recording audio and MIDI.

▶ Import files into a project and how Cubase handles the different formats

MIDI Recording Preparations

In Chapter 4, we looked at the different recording modes available in the Transport panel. In Chapter 6, we looked at the different settings available in a MIDI track to record and play back events that were recorded on that track. Now, it's time to put it all together and look at different MIDI recording situations. For example, do you want to do the following:

▶ Record only one MIDI source?

▶ Record multiple MIDI sources simultaneously?

▶ Record over something you previously recorded?

▶ Tell Cubase to start recording automatically at a certain point and stop recording after it crosses another location in your project?

MIDI Recording Preferences

MIDI recording preferences play a role in Cubase's behavior during the recording process. These preferences are found in several sections of the Preferences option found in the File (PC)/Cubase (Mac) menu. After you set up these preferences, you won't have to change them again as they will remain there until you change the settings again and apply these changes.

Under the Editing section you should look at the following MIDI-related recording preferences:

▶ **Enable Record on Selected Track.** This check box will automatically arm a track for recording as soon as you select it. When you select another track, it becomes unarmed for recording once again, while arming the next track. This is a convenient option when you want to record ideas quickly on a track without having to remember to arm it each time. Only record-enabled tracks will record events when you press the Record button on the Transport panel.

Under the MIDI section you should look at the following MIDI-related recording preferences:

▶ **Reset On Record End, Part End, and/or Stop.** When either of these options is selected, Cubase sends a Reset message to all connected MIDI devices. This message sends an All Note Off message and a Reset All Controllers message. You can also send a Reset message to all your MIDI devices if ever an error occurs that causes a MIDI device to sound off a stuck note by using the Reset option found in the MIDI menu.

▶ **Length Adjustment.** When this option is set to a value other than zero, Cubase adjusts the length of two consecutive notes playing on the same pitch and on the same channel to make sure there is a small space between these two MIDI events. The value you enter is the number of ticks found between these two similar notes.

▶ **Chase Events.** The check boxes found in this section of the MIDI preferences refer to how Cubase deals with MIDI controller events that have been recorded. Will it look back to see if there has been a patch change since you've stopped, or will it simply play the notes, leaving the current patch on your MIDI device playing? If you check the box, it will not look or chase events that occurred before the project's current location. If the box is left unchecked, it will look back to see if such a change occurred and will send a patch change (for example) to set the patch value appropriately. Here's another example—you stop playback while the pitch bend value is not at zero. Then you decide to move a few bars back. If the chase events for the pitch bend are checked, the MIDI device will still be set at that pitch bend value and the note will sound out of tune. If the pitch bend is chased (the check box not selected), Cubase will look back to find the last value of pitch bend, which will probably be a zero, reset this value in the MIDI device, and play the pitch bend accurately.

Under the Record section you should look at the following MIDI-related recording preferences:

▶ **Snap Record Parts to Bars.** When this option is selected, Cubase automatically extends a part to the closest bar before the part begins and after the part ends when you record on-the-fly from a location other than a bar's beginning. This makes it easier to move parts later on when you want to edit MIDI events on your track.

▶ **Solo Record in Editors.** When you want to make sure the events you record go into the part you are editing (when a MIDI editor window is opened), you can enable this option. This Record option enables the edited track while preventing any other tracks from also recording new events for as long as the MIDI editor is opened.

▶ **MIDI Record Catch Range in ms.** When you start recording from a specific point, sometimes you might play a note just a little too early for Cubase to include it in the recording. This results in a missing note at the beginning of a part. To avoid this, you can tell Cubase to catch events that are played slightly before the actual recording begins. The value represents the number of milliseconds Cubase uses as a catch range when a recording is activated.

▶ **Retrospective Record.** Have you ever played a great MIDI part, only to realize that you forgot to play the Record button, or got inspired by something you were playing while Cubase was stopped? With the retrospective record feature, you can tell Cubase to remember MIDI events you play even if you are not recording them. As long as the Record Enable button is active for the MIDI track in question, the Retrospective Record option checked, and a sufficient buffer size in which Cubase stores these events is set (the default value should be fine for most cases), all the MIDI events you played can be restored to this track just as if you had pressed record in the first place.

Under the Record section you should look at the following MIDI-related recording preferences:

▶ **Return to Start Position on Stop.** Returns the play line to the location from which it started when you click Play or Record rather than having it stay at its current stop location.

▶ **Deactivate Punch-in on Stop.** Disables the otherwise enabled Punch-in button whenever you click the Stop button or press the spacebar on your keyboard.

▶ **Stop after Automatic Punch-out.** Stops playing automatically right after it hits the punch-out location, or when the postroll time is played if this setting is also enabled. A preroll and postroll setting is enabled when you've entered a value for either of these fields in the Transport panel and when the Use Pre-/Post-Roll option is checked in the Transport menu.

MIDI Filtering

When recording MIDI events, you are recording many different types of MIDI messages. The most obvious type of MIDI message are the channel voice messages, which include Note On, Note Off, Program Change, and so on. You can decide to record all MIDI messages, or only specific MIDI messages, filtering any other messages from the recording. In other words, you can choose which MIDI events you want to record. This can be useful when you want to avoid recording lots of useless data that can bog down your MIDI output port when passing these events through an already crowded port. Also, some MIDI devices send events that might not be essential to your performance. Cubase allows you to filter out these messages.

How To

To filter MIDI events during recording or playback:

1. Select Preferences > MIDI Filter from the File(PC)/Cubase(Mac) menu (Figure 7.1).

2. In the Record section of the MIDI Filter area, check all the types of events you do not want Cubase to record. Events that are already recorded will continue to play.

3. If you want to filter out events while you are playing as well, check the appropriate types of events in the Thru section. Once again, recorded events will play back, but checked event types in this section will be filtered out from the MIDI input.

4. In the Channels section, click the MIDI channels from which you do not want to record. In Figure 7.1, messages coming on Channels 11 through 16 will not be recorded.

5. Finally, if you want to add additional controller messages to the filtered list, use the Controller Selection field in the Controller section to scroll through the types of controller messages and click the Add button to add them to your filtered list.

6. Click Apply and then click OK when done.

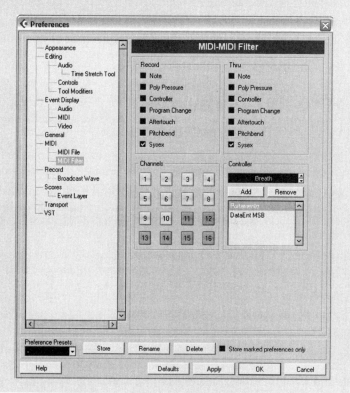

Figure 7.1
The MIDI Filter area in Cubase's Preferences dialog box.

As you've noticed in the previous steps, these settings are optional and in most cases, filtering the System Exclusive (SysEx) messages is all you need to do (which, by default is already filtered). On the other hand, you can deselect the SysEx filter if you want to save your external MIDI device's system exclusive information into a project.

System Exclusive messages are used to transmit parameter settings from and to a MIDI device that are not supported by any other type of MIDI message. In most cases, System Exclusive messages are device specific and are used to recall or store settings that are used by a device to produce a sound or program, such as a reverb type or cutoff frequency setting.

What you just did through the MIDI Filter area influences the general behavior of Cubase. In other words, it applies these settings on all MIDI tracks until you change these settings once again. You can, however, decide to filter out, or even convert, certain MIDI events into other MIDI events in a track as you are recording it. This is done through Cubase's Transformer.

The Transformer comes in two flavors: as a MIDI effect called *MIDI Transformer* and as a track input called *Input Transformer*. When used as an effect, it transforms events that are already recorded on a track. When it is used as an Input Transformer, it transforms the events before it records them. You can access the Input Transformer's panel through its appropriate button (described in Chapter 6) found in the MIDI settings section of the Inspector area.

USING THE INPUT TRANSFORMER

One very useful application of the input transformer consists of applying a filter to each MIDI track in order to transform the current Omni On Input mode of Cubase into an Omni Off Input mode.

Currently, you can choose the MIDI input port as the source of incoming MIDI events, but you can't select which MIDI channel triggers events on a specified MIDI track. In other words, it doesn't matter what channel your MIDI keyboard is set at, it will send MIDI into Cubase and Cubase will play any MIDI messages sent to all record enabled tracks at the same time. As long as a MIDI track's input and output ports are set up properly, you can't control the channel to which a MIDI track responds, only the port.

Although this is fine in most cases, you might need to have control over which MIDI track plays back MIDI events on specific channels, for example, if you are using another computer to record a MIDI sequence and use Cubase simply as a rack of VST instruments. Without the possibility of selecting the input's MIDI channel, you'd have to use one MIDI port per MIDI track in order to get Cubase to play more than one VSTi at a time.

By using the input transformer on each MIDI track, you can force a MIDI track to only respond to MIDI events with a specific MIDI channel, allowing you to control up to 16 VSTi per MIDI port instead of only one. You can find out more on the input transformer's control in Appendix C, which discusses the Logical Editor. Both the Logical Editor and Input Transformer use similar controls. You can also download a template file from the Wavedesigners download page (http://www.wavedesigners.com).

Setting Up Your Metronome

To help you keep the beat while you are recording, you can activate the Click button on the Transport panel. This enables the metronome. You can use either a MIDI device to generate the click produced by the metronome or your computer's speaker, or both, if you want.

How To

To configure your metronome settings:

1. Ctrl(PC)/⌘(Mac)-click the Click button on the Transport panel, or from the Transport menu, select the Metronome Setup option.

   The Metronome Setup dialog box appears as shown in Figure 7.2.

2. Check the MIDI Click and/or the Audio Click check boxes, depending on which type of click you want to hear.

   The MIDI click will send a MIDI Note On event through a MIDI port to get a MIDI device to play the click track, while an audio click is simply a click sound playing through your sound card.

3. If you've selected the MIDI Click check box, make sure to select a proper MIDI port connected to the device that will play the MIDI click and the proper MIDI channel (by default, this is set to Channel 10 because this channel is usually reserved for drum sounds and is appropriate for clicks). You may also change the MIDI note value of the high and low notes. High notes are played typically on the first beat of a bar, whereas low notes are played on the other beats. Finally, you can adjust the velocity of these notes in the same area.

4. For the audio click, it's a little simpler because you can only adjust the volume of the click produced by the computer's speaker. Note that you can enable both MIDI and audio clicks simultaneously if you'd like.

5. In the Click during area, the two first options determine if the metronome plays automatically only when you are in Record mode or Play mode, or both.

6. If you want your metronome clicks on a different value than your signature setting, such as every eighth note rather than every quarter note in a 4/4 bar, you can check the Use Count Base option and set the value using the up and down arrows to the right of this check box in order to adjust the beat subdivision for your metronome's click.

   The Precount options allow you to set up how the metronome will react when the Precount/Click button is enabled on the Transport panel. Typically, a precount will sound off a user-defined number of bars before starting playback. This is useful when you are not using the preroll value in the Transport bar.

7. In the Precount Bars field, enter the appropriate number of bars you want Cubase to sound off before it actually starts playing or recording. This will have no influence on the metronome if the Precount button is disabled in the Transport panel.

TIP

When the Tempo track is not active, tempo changes will not be heard during playback of the project. If the From Tempo Track option is checked while the Tempo track is not active, the tempo of the metronome will not match the tempo of the project. It is therefore recommended that you uncheck this option when you want to work with a disabled Tempo track.

8. Check the Use Signature option if you want to use a signature that is different from the project's tempo track signature. You can play your project at a different tempo setting when the Tempo track is disabled, but the signature setting is always active. For example, if your project switches from a 4/4 bar to a 3/4 bar, you want the metronome to correspond to this change as well. On the other hand, if you don't want to use the signature values found in the Tempo track, check this box.

9. When you have completed setting these options, click OK.

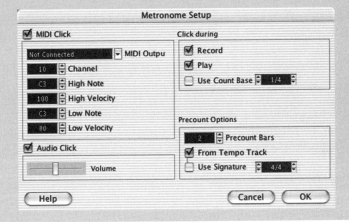

Figure 7.2
The Metronome Setup dialog box.

Recording MIDI

Before you start recording MIDI, it's a good thing to make sure your MIDI Thru Active option is selected in the Files (PC)/Cubase (Mac) > Preferences > MIDI dialog box. This will send the MIDI information Cubase receives through the MIDI output port you assign on the desired MIDI tracks.

How To

To record MIDI events on one or multiple tracks:

1. Activate the Record Enable button on the MIDI track you want to use to record incoming MIDI events.

2. Select the MIDI input port from which the MIDI events arrive.

3. Select the MIDI output port to the device or VSTi of your choice. This is where you determine what you will hear during the recording process.

continued

4. Configure the Bank and/or Program fields in the MIDI Settings section of the Inspector area or in the Track List area.

5. Select the appropriate MIDI channel for the track's MIDI output.

6. In the Transport panel, set the appropriate Record mode (Normal, Merge, or Replace).

7. In the Transport panel, set the appropriate Cycle mode if you want to record in cycles (Mix, Overwrite, Stacked or Keep Last).

8. Set the location of your left and right locators appropriately. For example, if you want to record from Bar 5 Beat 1 to Bar 9 Beat 1, set the left and right locators to Bar 5 and 9, respectively.

9. If you want Cubase to start recording at a specific bar and stop recording at a specific bar without recording in Cycle mode, you can enable the Punch-in and Punch-out buttons on the Transport panel.

10. Activate the metronome click on the Transport panel if you want to hear a click while recording. You can Ctrl (PC)/⌘(Mac)-click to access the Metronome settings (see the appropriate section discussing this dialog box earlier in this chapter).

11. Press Record and start playing. If you've enabled the metronome click, the precount value you've entered in the Metronome Setting dialog box determines how many bars Cubase counts before it starts recording.

12. Press the Stop button on the Transport panel (or spacebar on the keyboard) when done. If the Punch-out button was enabled, Cubase should stop automatically when it reaches that location.

RECORDING MULTIPLE MIDI CHANNELS AT ONCE

When transferring a MIDI sequence from one sequencer to Cubase, or when several musicians playing on MIDI instruments need to be recorded simultaneously, you will need to take additional measures in order to record MIDI events.

If you want for all the MIDI events to be recorded onto the same track and split up (dissolve) all the events depending on the MIDI input channel later, you'll need to set up your MIDI output channel to ANY rather than to a specific channel. This will allow the incoming events to be redistributed to external devices according to their MIDI channel settings. This works well when you transfer a sequence. You'll find out more about dissolving MIDI parts later on in this chapter.

If you want to record onto separate tracks from the beginning, you will need at least one MIDI input port per part you need to record. Each MIDI input will then be recorded onto its own track.

Finally, if you only have one MIDI port and want to record and monitor MIDI events coming on multiple MIDI channels simultaneously, refer yourself to the previous tip under the MIDI Filter section above.

Now that you've just recorded events on a track or multiple enabled tracks, you might want to record over a portion of this recording to correct errors that would be too long to edit in the editor or simply because you feel like it. In the previous steps, you were using the left and right locators as a point of reference to both begin playback and recording, as well as to stop recording. You may also use the preroll value in the Transport panel to begin playback before you start recording and the postroll value to have Cubase continue playing after you've stopped recording. The instructions on using the preroll and postroll functions were described earlier in Chapter 4's "Locators" section.

Quantizing Your Events

Quantizing information means that you set a virtual grid to which notes or events cling. When you are recording MIDI information, your notes might be recorded a little bit before, or a little bit after, a beat. This is done because humans are not as steady and consistent as the timing in Cubase. Sometimes, this is a good thing, and sometimes it isn't. So, when you want to make sure that everything falls into place, or falls exactly on the beat, you can use the Quantize function to nudge MIDI events to their closest quantize value. For example, if you set your quantize value to a quarter note (1/4), every note you record when playing on your keyboard clings to the closest quarter note in the bar where you recorded your MIDI information. Setting your quantizing value higher splits the grid into more subdivisions for each bar in your arrangement.

Quantizing MIDI events affects the way MIDI events are played back, but it does not affect your recorded material; thus, it is not changed permanently, and the original position values are kept with the project regardless of the undo history list. At times, however, you might want to requantize a series of events, using the quantized position as a reference. Because quantizing always refers to the original position of the events, you can use the Freeze Quantize function. When you freeze the quantization, you basically tell Cubase that you want to use the new quantized position as a point of reference to requantize your events rather than their original position. Remember, however, that after you use the Freeze Quantize function, you can no longer go back to the original position of the recorded events.

Quantize Methods

As mentioned earlier, the basic quantize method consists of moving the start of an event to the closest quantize grid value. This is referred to as overquantizing. Cubase offers different quantize methods, which handle events in different ways, giving you more control over how notes are affected when applying a quantization.

As displayed in Figure 7.3, the same original content (found in the upper-left corner) has been treated to different quantization methods. All of these examples use the same eight-note quantize grid.

> ▶ **Over quantize method.** Moves the start position of the event to the closest quantize grid setting.

> ▶ **End quantize method.** Moves the end position of the event to the closest quantize grid setting.

> ▶ **Length quantize method.** Does not affect the start position, but adjusts the length of each event to fit the value found in the quantize grid setting. In this example (Figure 7.3, second row, second column to the right), each note is one eighth-note in length.

▶ **Iterative quantize method.** Is a looser version of the overquantize method because it moves the start position of an event in proportion with an iterative strength value, which is found in the Quantize Setup panel. Another difference with the overquantize method is that it uses the current location (this could be the quantized location) of the event rather than its original location (unquantized location). This implies that you can quantize an event and then requantize it differently using the iterative quantize method.

Figure 7.3
Quantize method
examples.

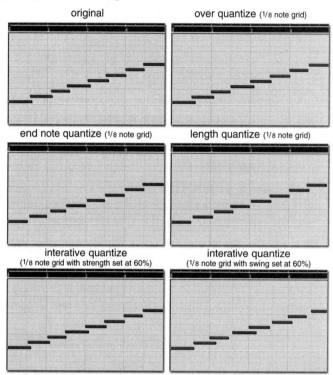

The Quantize Setup panel offers a beefed-up version of the overquantize method, giving you control over a number of different parameters, allowing you to be more creative with the quantization of events. This panel gives you the opportunity to move an otherwise pretty square and static grid around, changing its reference points by different increments. Here are the controls you have over the grid in the Quantize Setup panel (see Figure 7.4):

▶ The Grid drop-down menu allows you to set the quantize reference value for its grid. These represent note subdivisions, as seen earlier in Chapter 4.

▶ The Type drop-down menu offers three options: straight, dotted, and tuplet, which also corresponds to how the grid is separated. This was also discussed in Chapter 4. So, for example, selecting the one-eighth-note value for the grid and the tuplet type creates a gridline every 1/8 tuplet.

▶ The Swing slider allows you to shift the position of a straight grid type, producing a swing or a shuffle feeling. This also works best when the Tuplet field is set to Off. As you can see in Figure 7.4, the swing slider is set at 54%. If you look at the display in the middle of the panel, the actual $1/8$ grid is shown in pale thin lines above, whereas the swing grid is indicated by the bold lines at the bottom of this same display box.

▶ The Tuplet field allows you divide the grid to accommodate more complex rhythmic patterns, such as triplets or quintuplets. An eighth note quintuplet is as long as an eighth note, but is divided in five. In other words, you could play five notes within an eighth-note value.

▶ The Magnetic Area slider allows you to set the area around which events are affected. In other words, it creates a magnetic field around the grid; any events within that area are pulled towards that gridline, whereas events beyond the magnetic area are not affected. Again, if you look in the middle display, this is represented by the thick pale area around the swing grid mentioned previously (this is displayed as a pale blue color on your screen).

Figure 7.4
The Quantize Setup panel.

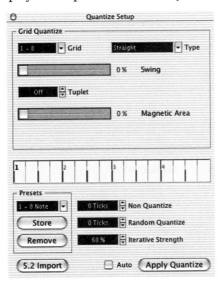

▶ The Grid Display area found in the center of the Quantize Setup panel shows you the result of your settings in the Grid Quantize area above. The entire display area represents a single $4/4$ bar.

▶ The Presets area allows you to select different quantize presets that are stored on your computer and enables you to create new ones or remove presets you don't use. You will also see later when we discuss hitpoints, that you can create a quantize preset using an audio drum loop, for example.

▶ The Non Quantize field allows you to set an area around the center of the grid's position where events are not affected. Each tick value represents $1/120$th of a sixteenth-note. In other words, any note found within this range is left unquantized, creating a more human-like (read "looser") feel to the quantization.

▶ The Random Quantize field, as with the Non Quantize field, enables you to humanize the quantize grid by adding or removing small amounts to a quantized note's position. In Figure 7.4, the Random Quantize field adds or subtracts up to six ticks from every note that is affected by the quantization.

▶ The Iterative Strength field allows you to set the strength level of an iterative quantize method. With higher percentage values, events are moved closer to the grid setting. With lower percentage values, events are not moved as close to the grid setting, allowing for more variations.

Setting Up Your Quantize

Because the quantize setting influences how events are quantized, no matter which method you use, it's a good idea to start by setting up how you want Cubase to quantize these events before applying a method. This is especially true with the auto-quantize method.

How To

To set up quantize parameters:

1. Select Quantize Setup in the MIDI menu to open the Quantize Setup panel (as shown in Figure 7.4).

2. If you already have a preset saved, select it from the Presets drop-down menu. Otherwise, complete the following steps.

3. From the Grid drop-down menu, select the appropriate grid value for your setting.

4. From the Type drop-down menu, select the appropriate type for your setting.

5. If you want to use tuplets, use the up or down arrow to the right of the Tuplet field to select the appropriate tuplet type. Otherwise, leave this field displaying the Off selection.

6. If you want to create a Swing or Shuffle field, click and drag the Swing slider to the right. Higher percentages result in more pronounced swing or shuffle feels.

MONITORING QUANTIZE SETUP CHANGES BEFORE APPLYING THEM

At this point, you might want to listen to the result before you complete the settings. To do this, you can double-click on a MIDI part to open it in a MIDI Editor, enable the cycle playback mode, set your left and right locators around the content found in this part, and finally check the Auto check box in the Quantize Setup panel. When you click Play, you will hear the effect of the quantize settings as you change them in the panel without committing to them. This dynamic preview, however, is only available with MIDI events. You can apply a quantize setting to audio events or audio slices inside a part, but changing the quantize setup only affects the audio when you click the Apply button in the Quantize Setup panel.

7. Set the Non Quantize value appropriately by using the up or down arrows. Remember that events within this range are not affected by the quantization.

8. Set the Random Quantize value appropriately by using the up or down arrows.

9. If you want to use the iterative quantize method, set the strength value by using the appropriate field in the Quantize Setup panel. The higher the value, the more it acts as an overquantize method.

Now that you have set up your quantization properties, let's save this as a preset so that you can use it later without having to redo all these steps. You will notice that there are already default presets available. You can use those next time, or save a customized setting for later use. Remember that a song's feeling is greatly influenced by its rhythmic definition. This implies that all parts follow the same "groove" or "feel." This feel is often the result of consistency throughout the instruments, parts, and song. Saving presets of quantize settings and reusing these presets throughout your song can help in creating this consistency.

How To

To save a quantize setting to a preset:

1. After you set up the appropriate parameters in the Quantize Setup panel as shown previously, click the Store button in the Quantize Setup panel to create a new preset.

2. Double-click the new preset to rename it. The Type In Preset Name dialog box appears (see Figure 7.5) with the default name given to your preset.

3. Type in the new name and click OK to close the dialog box.

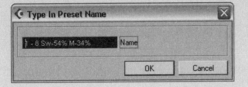

Figure 7.5
The Type In Preset Name dialog box.

How To

To remove a quantize setting from the preset list:

1. From the Quantize Setup panel's Presets drop-down menu, select the preset you want to remove.

2. Click the Remove button.

Applying Quantize

There are several ways you can quantize events, and you can use any combination of methods to accomplish the task at hand.

▶ You can apply a standard overquantize method to already recorded events. This method simply shifts the start position of selected events to the closest grid line as set in your project window or editing window (depending on which window is opened when you apply this quantize method).

▶ You can apply an automatic quantize value during the recording process. This records the events as you play them, but places them automatically according to the quantize setting of your project. In other words, you can still unquantize events that were recorded with the automatic quantize (the AUTO Q button in the Transport panel) feature enabled.

▶ You can also use the Quantize Setup panel, which gives you more control over the effect quantization has on your events. For example, using the different parameters available in this panel, you can adjust the strength of the quantization, the swing factor, and the magnetic area of the grid, as well as create a grid for more complex rhythmic values, such as tuplets.

▶ Finally, you can use quantization as a MIDI effect on a track's insert or send effect.

How To

To apply an automatic quantize value during the recording process:

1. Choose the appropriate quantize setup or quantize grid setting.
2. Enable the Auto-Quantize (AUTO Q) button on the Transport panel.
3. Start the recording process.

How To

To apply an automatic quantize value during the editing process:

1. Open the MIDI part you want to edit in the MIDI Editor.
2. Open the Quantize Setup panel and choose the appropriate quantize setup.
3. Check the Auto option in the Quantize Setup panel. Any changes you make in the quantize setting from this point forward affect the events in the MIDI Editor.

How To

To apply a quantize method to selected events:

1. Choose the appropriate quantize setup or quantize grid setting.
2. Select the events or parts you want to quantize.
3. Press the Q key on your keyboard, or select the appropriate method you want to use from the MIDI menu: Over Quantize (Q), Iterative, or (in the Advanced Quantize options) Quantize Ends or Quantize Lengths.

When you want to quantize the length of MIDI events, you can use the Length Quantize drop-down menu from the MIDI editor's toolbar to determine an appropriate length value for your events. You can't, however, set the length value outside of the MIDI editor.

If you want to apply a quantization on a single track as a track effect, your best bet is probably to use a MIDI insert effect (or a send effect) and select the Quantizer MIDI effect. This MIDI effect is basically a quantize effect with four parameters: a quantize grid selection and a swing factor slider, both of which are identical in function to the Quantize Setup panel's parameter. The following two parameters play similar roles as well. The strength slider determines a percentage of strength, where 100% causes all the events to move to the closest grid line, offering a very tight rhythm. Lower percentages loosen up this rhythm, moving events toward the grid lines, but at a lesser degree. The delay slider inserts with positive values, or removes with negative values, a number of milliseconds to the event's position. This either creates a delayed or anticipated effect, depending on the slider's setting, and unlike the delay parameter in the track's Setting section in the Inspector area, this parameter can be automated through time. The advantage of using the Quantizer effect rather than quantizing events allows you to change the quantizing itself in time through automation, creating a more dynamic feel.

How To

To apply a quantize effect as a MIDI track insert (or send):

1. Select the MIDI track you want to use.
2. Make the Track Inserts section in the Inspector area visible.
3. From one of the insert slots available, select the Quantizer effect from the drop-down menu.
4. Adjust the four parameters in the panel or Alt-click(PC)/Option-click(Mac) the Edit button to open the effect in a floating window and edit the parameters from there.

Because a quantized note can always be unquantized, its original position is always stored in the project's memory. When you want to start quantizing from the current position of the quantized events rather than using the original position of these events, you can reset the original position to the current, quantized position by using the Freeze Quantize command.

How To

To freeze quantized events:

1. Select the events you want to freeze (replace the original position with the quantized position).
2. From the MIDI menu, select Advanced Quantize > Freeze Quantize.

How To

To undo a quantize on selected events:

1. Select the events or parts you want to unquantize.
2. From the MIDI menu, select Advanced Quantize > Undo Quantize.

Creating Groove Quantize Presets

Cubase also offers the possibility to create a customized quantize setting, which is extracted from the rhythmic content of previously recorded MIDI events. For example, you record a drum part and get just the groove you are looking for. Since the rhythmic "groove" of the percussions and drum parts are usually something you would want to apply to other musical parts, you can convert the MIDI groove you played in a reusable groove template that you apply to other MIDI parts.

How To

To create a groove quantize from MIDI events:

1. Select the MIDI part containing the groove you want to save in the project window. Note that the groove quantize preset will not contain the actual MIDI note events, only its related rhythmic and velocity information.
2. Select from the menu bar MIDI > Advanced Quantize > Part to Groove.

When you create a Groove quantize, it will appear in the Quantize Setup preset drop-down menu. Once a Groove quantize is selected, the Quantize Setup dialog box will offer a different set of controls as described above.

▶ **Position.** You can think of the position parameter like the iterative strength where the position percentage represents the strength of the quantization from the groove's source. The difference between the normal iterative value and the position is that the latter influences the groove after the possible prequantize setting (see below).

▶ **Velocity.** Indicates that a percentage of the preset's velocity level is applied to the selected event's recorded velocity. With higher values, the velocity is closer to the groove preset than it is to the original. With lower values, velocities are not changed as much, with no change if the value is set at zero.

▶ **Length.** Indicates that a percentage of the preset's length level is applied to the selected event's recorded length. With higher values, the length is closer to the groove preset's length than it is to the original. With lower values, lengths are not changed as much, with no change if the value is set at zero.

▶ **Prequantize.** This prequantizes the groove quantize preset in order to increase the accuracy of the quantize process. If the MIDI you recorded and the quantize type do not match appropriately, you might get unexpected results. It's also a good way to get the velocity information from a MIDI part you play and apply it to another set of events.

▶ **Maximum Move in Ticks.** Ticks are the smallest time increments inside a Cubase project. This parameter will determine the maximum distance a MIDI event will be allowed to move from its original recorded position.

▶ **5.2 Import.** Allows you to import Cubase VST 5.2 version Groove Quantize presets. You apply a groove quantize preset as you would apply any another quantize type—by selecting the events and then selecting the groove quantize as a quantize type.

Quantizing Audio

Selected audio events in the project window can also be quantized and snapped to a grid, depending on the Snap mode currently active. However, audio events use the snap point marker as a quantize reference instead of the start point of the event. This and other audio quantizing features will be discussed further in Chapter 11 of this book.

Recording Audio

At this point, let's assume that you have already configured your studio for audio recording and that you understand how audio goes into your computer through the sound card and comes out of it into an external audio monitoring system (self-powered studio monitors or headphones, for example). If you have not configured your audio connections already, you should do so before proceeding because you might want to test things out as you read the information found below.

Before you begin recording audio, you should configure the project's sample rate and format through the Project Setup dialog box (the default key command is Shift+S) if you haven't done so already. After you start recording in one sampling rate, you can't change it. All audio files in a project have to be recorded (or imported) at the same sampling rate. You should also make sure that the digital clock of the audio card is set up correctly if you are using a digital input to record your audio. The digital clock defines the exact sampling frequency of the sound card. If your sound card is receiving its digital clock information from an external digital audio device, your sound card should be set to follow this device's sampling frequency.

How To

To configure the digital clock on your sound card:

1. Select the Device Setup option in the Devices menu.
2. In the Device Setup dialog box, select the VST Multitrack option.
3. In the VST Multitrack option, click the Control Panel button to access your sound card's configuration panel.

continued

4. In your sound card's configuration panel, set the master clock (digital clock) appropriately. If your external device is set as master (or internal), you should set your sound card to follow the external device's digital clock by using the appropriate option for your card (you might have to consult your sound card's documentation if you are unsure how to do this). Remember that it is better to have your sound card's digital clock control other devices rather than have other devices control your sound card. In this case, make sure that the external digital audio devices follow your sound card's digital audio clock by setting them appropriately. You will find more information in Chapter 14.

5. When done, close your sound card's configuration panel.

6. Back in Cubase, click Apply.

7. Click OK to close the Device Setup dialog box.

Note that if you don't have any digital connections with other devices in your studio setup, you probably don't have to worry about the digital clock of your sound card because it is probably set appropriately to follow its internal clock.

How To

To record a single track of audio in Cubase:

1. Right-click(PC)/Ctrl-click(Mac) in the Track List area and choose Add Audio Track from the context menu. If you already have audio tracks in your project, you don't need to create a new one; just select an existing empty audio track.

2. Select the appropriate audio track configuration to determine the channel format of audio files that will be recorded onto that track.

3. Click OK to close the Add Audio Track dialog box.

4. In the Name field for the new track, or the existing track if you didn't create one, name your track appropriately.

TIP

When audio is recorded, Cubase names the audio file according to the name of the track. This makes it easier to manage audio clips later on.

5. Click on the Enable Record button in the audio track. You can do this either through the Track Setting section in the Inspector or in the Track List area.

6. Select the Input Bus from the track's In field. This tells Cubase where the audio for this track comes from.

7. Select the Output Bus from the track's Out field. This tells Cubase which audio outputs will be used to monitor the recorded signal.

8. In the Inspector area of the selected track, open the audio channel section.

9. Enable the Monitor button to monitor the input level of the audio signal (see Figure 7.6).

10. Start playing as you would during recording to adjust the input level of the audio. Remember that the fader in the audio channel does not influence the input level, only the output (monitored) level. If you need to adjust the input level, you need to use one of the following alternatives: Adjust the level coming out of your instrument, adjust the level coming out of the mixer (if your signal passes through a mixer before heading to Cubase), or adjust the input level from your sound card's control panel applet if it allows it. Cubase SX users may want to adjust the input channel first as it offers phase reverse and up to 48.2 dB of gain or cut within the mixer.

TIP

The longer an audio chain is, the more likely it will pick up noise along the way. Increasing the audio's amplitude level later in the audio chain will also increase the noise that has been added before in this chain. As a rule of thumb, it's always better to increase a signal's amplitude at the source than it is at the input bus level (once it has already been converted) or passed through electronic components.

Figure 7.6
When the Monitor button is active, the level meters next to the fader become input level monitors.

11. In the Transport panel, select the appropriate recording mode. When recording audio, Normal is usually the appropriate choice.

12. If you want to start a recording at a specific point in time and stop recording at another specific point in time, adjust the left and right locators appropriately and enable the Punch-in and Punch-out buttons on the Transport panel.

13. If you want to hear a metronome click while you are recording (but not in the recording signal), make sure that the metronome click is not routed into the recorded signal. You can configure your metronome click through the Metronome Setup dialog box. After your settings are made, close the dialog box and enable or disable the metronome click from the Transport panel (the default key command is C).

14. Place your play line at the position where you want your recording to begin.

15. Click the Record button and begin recording the audio.

16. Click the Stop button to manually stop the recording if you haven't enabled the Punch-out button.

Recording Audio in Cycle Mode

Working in Cycle mode allows you to run a section of your song over and over again. While this section plays, you can try different things out and record them. When you're done, you can try either to reproduce the best ideas you had while practicing, or simply use portions of the different takes you've just made if you were recording what you just did. That's the whole point behind cycle recording.

In Cubase, when you are recording in Cycle mode, you are looping a portion of the project found between the left and right locators. When you record audio in this mode, Cubase records a long audio file, but can define events and/or regions associated with each lap that was recorded during the cycle mode recording process. What it actually defines depends on the current setting found in Cubase's preferences (see Figure 7.7).

Figure 7.7
The Cycle Record Mode options found in the Cubase Preferences dialog box.

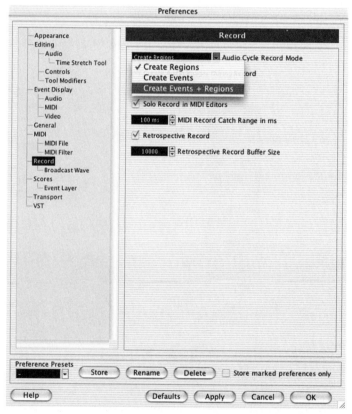

Cubase can identify each recorded lap in two different ways when you record in Cycle mode: events or regions (or both).

▶ When you record in Cycle mode and create events, Cubase creates a single, long audio clip, but each time a lap (a cycle) is completed, an event is inserted on the track. The event that appears when you stop recording is the one recorded during the last lap (or cycle). All the other events are still on the track but under this last event. Because you can only hear one event at a time on a track, you need the To Front option found in the project window's context menu as shown in Figure 7.8.

This option appears when you right-click(PC)/Ctrl-click(Mac) over the overlapping events. You should create and work with events when you want to split the events up to create an edited version using parts of each take.

Figure 7.8
Selecting which take you want to bring to the front after a cycle recording.

▶ When you record in Cycle mode and create regions, Cubase creates a single, long audio clip where a region defines each lap (cycle). The difference here is that there is only one event on your track, but using the Set To Region option (also displayed below the To Front option in Figure 7.8), you can choose which region you want to display in this event. Because regions are created, you can also see the defined regions in the Pool (see Figure 7.9) and in the Sample Editor. You should create and work with regions when you want to select an entire region as the desired take for the event.

Figure 7.9
The Regions created during cycle recording are named Take *, where the asterisk represents the number of the lap/take.

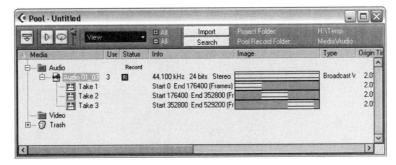

▶ Finally, you can set Cubase to create both events and regions. This places a number of overlapping events on your track and creates identical regions in the Media Pool. By doing this, if you decide to go back to a take and modify it, you can place the region from the Pool onto a track. However, beware of mixing both methods of editing (events and regions) when working on a track. When using the Scissors tool to split an event, you split all the overlapping events. Selecting an event in one portion and a region in another might not give you the result you were going for.

How To

To change your Cycle Recording Mode Preferences:

1. Select Preferences in the File (PC)/Cubase(Mac) menu.
2. Select Audio in the Preferences dialog box.
3. Select the desired option in the Cycle Record Mode drop-down menu (see Figure 7.7).
4. Click Apply and then OK to close the dialog box.

How To

To choose which event you want to hear when editing a track:

1. Start by listening to each take one after the other, identifying the segments you want to keep in each take. To bring a different take to the front, right-click(PC)/Ctrl-click(Mac) over the track and select the appropriate take from the list as shown in Figure 7.8.
2. Adjust your Grid setting in the project toolbar to the desired value, especially if you don't want to be restricted to splitting at bar intervals.
3. Select the Scissors tool and split the event where you want to switch from one event to another (see the top part of Figure 7.10).
4. Select the Object Selection tool from the toolbar or the project window's context menu.
5. Right-click(PC)/Ctrl-click(Mac) on each new event to select the appropriate take to bring to front (see the bottom part of Figure 7.10).

Before: all events play Take 5

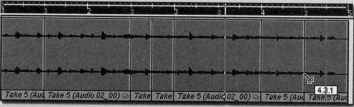

After: every event plays the desired Take

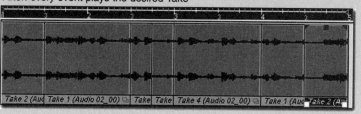

Figure 7.10
Using the Scissors tool splits all overlapping events on a track, allowing you to create a new version using different takes.

Importing Files

When working on a project, you can record events, but you can also import events that are already on your hard disk or use content from another source. All the import functions of Cubase can be found in the File menu under the Import submenu.

As an alternative to using the Import submenu, it is now possible to drag MIDI and audio files from your file management system directly into a project. Note that when importing an audio file, Cubase will prompt you to copy the file into the active project folder. It is recommended that you keep all your audio files inside this project folder and that you accept that a copy of the audio file be created there. You can always work with audio files from different locations on your hard disk, but keep in mind that backing up a Project with all the files will be easier if you keep all content in one folder.

About Audio CD Track Imports

Cubase allows you to grab audio tracks directly from an audio CD by using the Import Audio CD option.

There are two ways you can perform this task and which one you choose depends on what you want to do with these imported tracks. In both ways, the Audio CD Import window is the same; however, if you use the submenu option in the File > Import menu, the imported tracks automatically appear in your project window starting at the current play line's location and on the selected audio track. If you don't have an audio track present, one is automatically created for you. The other option is to import from the Media Pool using this window's right-click (Ctrl-click on a Mac with only one button) and choosing the Import Audio CD option. In this case, the audio track is imported in the pool only and no events appear in the project's Event Display area. This might be the method of choice if you want to import several audio tracks at a time.

How To

To import an audio track or tracks from an audio CD:

1. If you want to place the content of the audio track directly in your project, follow these steps; otherwise, skip to Step 4.

2. Create an empty audio track (for safety) and select it in the Track List area.

3. Position your play line at the location where you want the start of the track to occur.

4. Select the Import Audio CD from the File > Import menu or right-click (Ctrl-click on Mac) in the Media Pool and select the Import Audio CD option found at the top of the context menu.

5. The Import from Audio CD dialog box appears as displayed in Figure 7.11. Choose the appropriate drive containing the audio CD from which you want to import. This field is found in the upper-left corner of the dialog box.

6. Select the transfer speed you want to use to import these files. Note that faster speeds result in a faster transfer, but slower speeds limit the potential for errors that can occur during the transfer. *continued*

PREVIEWING CD TRACKS
You can preview a track before importing it by using the Play button found in the lower-right portion of the dialog box.

7. If you don't want to grab the entire track, you can move the Grab Start and Grab End arrows found in the Track Display area below the Play button. This changes the value in the Grab Start and End columns in the Track Display above, allowing you to import only sections of the audio.

8. In the Grab column, select the tracks you want to import. If you want to select more than one track, hold the Ctrl(PC)/⌘(Mac) key while you click on nonsequential tracks or select the first track you want to import, hold down the Shift key, and click the last track you want to import to select all the tracks in-between.

9. If you want to give a different name to your tracks (the default name being "Track XX," where XX corresponds to the track number), type in a new name in the File Name field.

10. If you want to change the folder destination, click the Change Folder button, browse your computer's hard drive, and select a new destination folder. The folder to which the files will be imported is displayed just under the File Name field.

11. When you are ready, click the Grab button at the bottom of the dialog box. This begins the extraction process. The files appear in the Grabbed Files section when the extraction is completed.

12. When this process is complete, click the OK button.

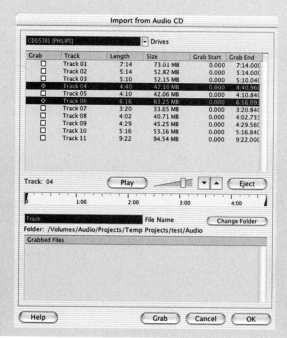

Figure 7.11
The Import from Audio CD dialog box.

Importing Audio from Video Files

Sometimes, all you need from a video file is its audio track, not the video track itself. If that's what you want, the Import Audio from Video File option will create a separate audio file from the selected video and place it in your project. The format of the audio file will be converted to the project's settings, and a copy of this audio track can be found in the project's folder. In other words, the original video file will not be used once you've imported the audio file from it.

About OMF

New to Cubase users (SX version only) is the possibility to import (and export as well) files saved in OMF format. OMF stands for *Open Media Framework*, and it is a platform-independent file format intended for transfer of digital media between different applications. Because this format is adopted by most professional video editing applications (such as AVID and Final Cut Pro, for example) and also allows sessions that were edited in ProTools to be compatible with Cubase SX (or Nuendo), using the OMF format when you save projects makes sense if you expect you'll have to work with one of these applications.

OMF files can be saved using one of two formats: 1.0 or 2.0. OMF files do not contain video media files, but references to video files, so if you are working on a video project and an OMF file is sent to you, you will need to import video files into your project separately. The OMF file will include markers telling Cubase where the video file goes.

About Cubase Documents Imports

You can import documents created in earlier versions of Cubase, such as song, arrangement, or part documents. In each case, there are some limitations to what will be imported into your new Cubase SX/SL project. Because none of the previous formats contained any actual audio files, you must reassociate audio events with their audio files on the hard disk if you've moved them since the last time they were saved.

Here's a list of what will be imported when you import a song or arrangement file into Cubase SX/SL:

▶ MIDI events and parts with their MIDI port output settings are imported. If the MIDI output doesn't exist anymore, Cubase displays a "pending output" message in those tracks, allowing you to remap them to a new MIDI output.

▶ The volume and transpose settings found in the MIDI track parameters remains in the new project—any other MIDI track parameter is ignored (such as delay, compression, or shadow tracks).

▶ All the MIDI part parameter settings are included, with the exception of the transpose settings.

▶ MIDI drum tracks are converted to regular drum tracks with a drum map associated. However, MIDI output settings for individual drum sounds are ignored.

▶ The volume, pan, and EQ automation data found in the VST Channel Mixer are imported; however, any plug-in or DSP factory settings are also ignored.

▶   Where multiple audio tracks were routed to the same audio channel, new separate
     audio tracks are created because Cubase SX/SL always uses one channel per track.
     A series of separate audio channels are also created in the mixer.

Any other setting is either ignored or removed. Also note that because song files could contain
multiple arrangements, you are prompted to choose which arrangement you want to use when
importing such a song file. To import all the arrangements in a song, you need to repeat the import
process for as many times as there are arrangements in the song. When you import a song or an
arrangement, a new project is created. When you import a part, a new track is created in the
project window.

How To

To import a Cubase VST song, arrangement, or part:

1. Select Import and the appropriate Cubase file type (Cubase Song, Cubase
   Arrangement, or Cubase Part) you want to import from the File menu.
2. Browse the content of your hard disk to locate the song, arrangement, or part.
3. Select the file and click Open.
4. If a Pending Output dialog box appears, assign the missing MIDI outputs to
   corresponding outputs or temporary ones until the file is imported. You can change
   these settings after that.

About MIDI File Imports

You can import Standard MIDI files of Type 0 and 1 in a project or create a new project with the
imported MIDI files. The difference between a MIDI file of Type 0 and 1 is that in Type 0, all the
MIDI events are found in one single track. After importing such a file, you need to make sure the
MIDI track hosting this imported track is set to play over *any* MIDI channels. A Type 1 file
contains as many MIDI tracks as there are MIDI channels used in the file. Cubase creates as many
MIDI tracks as it needs to host the newly imported MIDI file. When importing a MIDI file, it is
imported at the beginning of the project.

How To

To import a MIDI file:

1. Select File > Import > Import MIDI File.
2. Browse to the location of the file you want to import.
3. Select the file and click the Open button.

Note that you can also drag and drop a MIDI file from any location in your computer
(Explorer, Desktop, etc) into a Cubase Project.

About Audio File Imports

Because sometimes you might want to use prerecorded material in your project, Cubase allows you to import this material in two different ways. The first way is to simply drag WAV, AIFF, WMA (Windows Media Audio), or MP3 files from Windows Explorer (or the Mac's Launcher) onto a track, or below the last track in Cubase to create a new track. The second way is to click the File menu's Import option and then the Audio File option from the submenu. Note that when importing WMA or MP3 files, Cubase creates a WAV or AIFF copy of this file on your hard disk, rather than using the WMA or MP3 file directly. Just remember that WAV and AIFF files can be much larger than their WMA or MP3 counterparts.

You can also import Recycle files. Recycle files are generated by the software called Recycle, which is developed by Propellerhead. The purpose of Recycle is to cut drum loops into smaller parts, allowing you to reuse these samples at different tempos without changing the pitch. This process is similar to the process used in the Sample Editor.

How To

To import audio files:

▶ From the Windows Explorer window or the Mac Launcher window, drag the compatible files into your project or into the Media Pool.

Or:

1. Select File > Import > Import Audio File.
2. Browse to the location of the file you want to import.
3. Select the file and click the Open button.

NOTE
You can also perform an Import Audio File function from the Media Pool by selecting the Import button or by right-clicking(PC)/Ctrl-clicking(Mac) in the pool and selecting the Import Audio File option.

Now You Try It

For information about using the instructions found in this section and to find out where you can get the working files, please consult the section called *About the Exercise Files* in the Introduction section.

8

MIDI Editing Windows

The main advantage of MIDI over audio can be summed up in one word: flexibility. MIDI's flexibility comes from the fact that you can modify the harmonic, rhythmic, melodic, as well as sonic content of any musical part at will when your performance is recorded as MIDI events. Once the editing is completed, setting things down as audio for the final mixdown is usually desired. Using MIDI devices such as samplers, musicians can also recreate a wide variety of musical instruments. Now that MIDI triggered VSTi can benefit from processing, typically reserved for audio, the creative power for musicians is even greater. The MIDI editors in Cubase reflect these facts very well and give you full control over every aspect of MIDI editing. This is, after all, where Cubase earned its first stripes as professional software, and it continues to do so by offering different editing environments to reflect the versatility MIDI offers when it comes to its editable parameters.

Here's a summary of what you will learn in this chapter:

▶ Explore the different areas of the Key, Drum, and List Editors.

▶ Work with the MIDI editing tools available in the MIDI editors.

▶ Understand the differences between each editor and the purpose behind them.

▶ Learn how to edit MIDI note events and control change events.

▶ Discover how to use step recording to enter MIDI events into a project.

▶ Learn how to use and create drum maps.

CHAPTER 8

MIDI Editor

Each track class has its own associated editing window. Different types of events are associated with an editor by default. You can change this in some cases; in other cases, there is no way to get around it. The associated editor displays events that are appropriate to the track's class, so it is optimized for the events recorded in its window. Using another editor does not allow you to manipulate the information as easily. However, you can edit events in a nonassociated editor by selecting the part(s) in the project window and selecting the desired editor from the MIDI menu.

There are six MIDI related editors to choose from in Cubase:

▶ **Key.** Uses the piano roll analogy, in which events appear along a strip moving from left to right as you play the events. The pitch is determined by the vertical position of the scrolling events, and the position in time is determined by the horizontal position of these events. The longer an event is, the longer the box in the scroll is, as in a piano roll. The first events in a part being edited appear at the left of the piano roll, and the last events in that part appear at the right of the piano roll. This editor also allows you to edit Control Change messages on separate lanes below the piano roll view. It is the default editing environment for MIDI tracks that are not associated with drum maps.

▶ **Drum.** Uses the piano roll analogy like the Edit window, but with a small difference: There are no lengths to events—only trigger times (Note On positions) are displayed. Also, instead of a piano layout on the left side representing pitch values, you will find a list of percussion names associated with pitch values. It is the default editing environment for MIDI tracks that are associated with drum maps.

▶ **List.** Uses a table representation where it displays the raw MIDI data for any edited parts (more on that can be found in subsequent sections).

▶ **Score.** Uses a traditional music staff display to edit your MIDI parts. Note that Cubase SL offers a limited number of scoring tools compared to the editing power of SX.

▶ **Tempo Track.** Allows you to see and edit a graphical representation of tempo and time signature changes. Because this editor does not contain any other types of MIDI events, it is associated with the Tempo button found on the Transport panel.

▶ **Browser.** Displays not only MIDI events (similar to the List editor), but also displays audio, video, tempo changes, and time signature changes found in the project's tracks.

Editor Toolbar

There are many ways to edit MIDI events to get what you want. Using the tools available in the Key or Drum Editor's toolbar will most likely always be part of the solution because it holds the tools that you need to select, move, remove, or add events from the editor. To help you out in your editing tasks, the editors always contain a context menu available through the right-click(PC)/Ctrl-click(Mac), which holds a copy of the tools available in the toolbar. Finally, you can always use key commands to switch from one tool to another (see Appendix G for a complete list).

Solo Editor and Acoustic Feedback

The first two buttons on the left of the toolbar are the Solo Editor and Acoustic Feedback buttons (see Figure 8.1). The Solo button allows you to edit a MIDI part without hearing the other parts played in the background, "soloing" the events found in the MIDI Editor only. The Acoustic Feedback button allows you to hear MIDI notes corresponding to the notes selected with the Selection tool or when moving a note in time or on different pitch values. This is basically the MIDI equivalent of the audio Scrub tool. When selecting a group of notes, you will be able to hear the note in the group you choose to click on when dragging the selected notes to another location or pitch.

Figure 8.1
The Solo Editor and Acoustic Feedback buttons in the Key and Drum Editor's toolbar.

Show Info Line

The following button toggles the information bar on/off. This bar reveals information on the selected event or events and also allows you to modify this information by clicking in the field corresponding to the information and changing the values manually. For example, you could select an event and change its length numerically by clicking in the Length field as seen in Figure 8.2. You could also quickly transpose a series of selected events by changing the pitch value, which corresponds to the pitch of the first selected event in time. Every other selected event would be transposed to its relative pitch. (You can change the pitch value by clicking in the Pitch field and changing the value.)

USING THE SCROLL WHEEL
Once a value is selected in the Info line, you can use the scroll wheel on the mouse to increment or decrement values.

Figure 8.2
The Information bar in the Key or Drum Editor.

Tool Buttons

Next, you will find a series of nine tools that are used to apply different editing operations on MIDI events found in your editor (see Figure 8.3). These tools are not unlike the ones found in the project window, but also offer editor-specific characteristics.

Figure 8.3
The Key Editor tools, from left to right: the Object Selection, Draw, Line, Eraser, Zoom, Mute, Scissors, Glue, and Time Warp tools.

▶ **Object Selection tool.** Serves as a selection tool and a resizing tool. Use this tool when you want to move, copy, and select a range of events or when you want to change the start or end position of existing events in your editor.

▶ **Draw tool.** Adds events by drawing them one-by-one inside the editor or to modify controller information in a freehand style.

▶ **Line tool.** Performs as a multifunction tool. As you can see by the Figure 8.3 small arrow in the lower-right corner of the button, there are additional functions available to this tool. In fact, this tool operates in two modes. The Line mode allows you to either draw a series of events in the shape of the tool (you can switch between line, parable, sine, triangle, and square) or to shape controller information in one of these shapes as well. Finally, the Paint mode inserts multiple notes by dragging your cursor across the editor in a freehand style.

▶ **Eraser tool.** Erases events by clicking on the event while this tool is active or by dragging your eraser over the events.

▶ **Zoom tool.** Drags a box over a range so that your current view corresponds to the box's content. In other words, it zooms in on the content you want to view. You can also elect to simply click on a note to zoom into that note.

▶ **Mute tool.** Is an alternative to the Eraser tool because it allows you to mute a note so that you don't hear it, but without erasing it. This provides a way to mute certain events that you're not sure you want to get rid of, but that you don't want to hear right now. You can also drag the Mute tool across a number of events to mute them all.

▶ **Scissors tool.** Splits selected events at a specific grid line when the quantize grid is active.

▶ **Glue tool.** Glues notes together. More specifically, when playing at the same pitch value, it glues the event that follows the event you click on.

▶ **Time Warp tool.** Creates tempo changes in the Tempo track to match recorded musical events. Note that the Time Warp tool available in the project window, the Sample editor, and the Audio Part editor will play similar roles: a tool that helps composers in the task of matching linear time (seconds, frames, and samples) with musical time (bars and beats). However, time warp is applied differently to MIDI than it is to audio. Since this type of tool is most useful when working in sync with video projects, you will find more on this tool in Chapter 14.

Autoscroll

Continuing our trip along the default toolbar, the next button allows you to toggle the Autoscroll function on or off (see Figure 8.4). This only affects the scrolling in the editor because there is also an Autoscroll button in the project window. The Autoscroll function basically follows the project cursor in your window. When the line hits the right edge, the page moves to the right, scrolling the content from right to left as the cursor moves forward in time. When the Autoscroll function is off, you can play the events in the editor without worrying if the content in your window will start moving as you're editing events and the project cursor passes the right side of your window.

Figure 8.4
The Autoscroll button
and the Part list selection
field.

Part List

The next two buttons and the following drop-down menu offer different editing options related to multipart editing inside the MIDI editor. In fact, you can select several MIDI parts in the project window and edit them simultaneously. If you want to view a part's border limits inside the editor, you can enable this button. When enabled, you will see a MIDI part start and end handle. Clicking and dragging either one of these handles will modify the part's borders. Any changes that you make here will be visible in the project window as well. The Edit Active Part Only button next to it works well when you have several MIDI parts opened in the editor at once. By enabling this button and selecting the Active MIDI part from the drop-down menu next to it, Cubase will apply changes or edits to the selected events in this active part. For example, if you do a Select All function followed by a Delete function with the Edit Active Part Only disabled, all events in all the MIDI parts currently opened would be deleted. If the Edit Active Part Only is enabled and that MIDI 01, for example, is selected in the part list, then only the events found in that part will be deleted.

Insert Velocity

The Insert Velocity field modifies the velocity value associated with notes that you enter in the MIDI editor by using the Pencil, Draw, or Line tools. Whenever you enter MIDI events using one of these tools, the velocity that appears in this field will be given to the MIDI event. You can change this value in one of three ways:

1. Click in the field and type in the desired value.
2. Click on the up and down arrows next to the current value to increase or decrease the value.
3. Select one of the preset values available in the Ins. Vel. drop-down menu above the value itself.

You may use the Setup option at the bottom of this menu to change the values it holds. You may also configure key commands to change the values through them.

Snap and Quantize

The Quantize fields in the MIDI editor are similar to the ones found in the project window. You can activate the Snap button (first button on the left in Figure 8.5) to make the fields to the right of this button active. The Quantize field lets you choose the distance between each grid and influences many operations inside the editor. For example, setting your grid to 1/32 note allows you to move, cut, and insert events at thirty-second note intervals. In other words, the grid quantize setting prevents you from moving, cutting, or inserting events at positions other than the one defined by the field.

The Length Quantize field influences the length of events you add into the editor. For example, when using the step recording technique (covered in detail later in this chapter), if you add notes with a quantize value of 1/4 Note and a length quantize value set to the Linked to Quantize Value, all notes are at quarter note intervals and are of quarter note length. The Insert Velocity field, on the other hand, allows you to determine the velocity of Note On events when adding them with the Draw tools.

Figure 8.5
The editor's quantize settings.

Step MIDI Input

Step MIDI input is meant for the rhythmically challenged—those less-than-proficient keyboard players who have great ideas but just need some help entering them into a sequencer. It's also great to create rhythmically complex patterns such as machine-like drum fills using sixty-fourth notes at 120 BPM. It is also useful for musicians who can't enter MIDI events in their computers using VSTi because their sound card's latency is too high. No matter what the reason, step recording means that you can enter notes or chords one by one without worrying about timing.

Figure 8.6
The Step Recording tools.

Table 8.1 describes the function associated with each one of these buttons:

Table 8.1
The Step Recording buttons found on the editor's toolbar (from left to right in Figure 8.6 and from top to bottom in this table)

Button Name	Button's Function
Step Input	Enables or disables the step input recording options. Note that when this button is activated, the Autoscroll function is disabled.
MIDI Input	Changes the selected note in your editor to the note played on your keyboard when this button is active.
Move Insert Point	Adds the event you play on your controller keyboard at the position corresponding to the next quantize value following the playback line, pushing the events currently present to the next quantize value (when this option is enabled). When this option is disabled, events added using the step recording insert point are added to the current position of the insertion line, leaving the previous recording content in place. See Figure 8.7 for an example of how this works.
Record Pitch	Works with the MIDI controller. When enabled, it gives the pitch value of the note you play to a selected event in the Edit window, effectively replacing the current selected pitch with the new pitch from your keyboard controller.
Record Note On Velocity	Works with the MIDI controller. When enabled, it assigns the Note On velocity parameter of the note you play to the selected event in the Edit window. When disabled, the velocity assigned to the note you record comes from the Velocity field in the toolbar. Pressing lightly on your keyboard adds notes with low velocity values, whereas pressing harder adds a higher velocity value to the notes recorded through the step recording method.
Record Note Off Velocity	Assigns the Note Off velocity—otherwise identical to the Note On velocity.

Mouse Position

Because the Key and Drum editors are based on a matrix divided in pitch (vertical axis) and meter or time (horizontal axis), moving your mouse around in this matrix might become difficult, especially when you want to add an event at the far right of the screen where the keyboard reference is far from your mouse's position. That's when the following field becomes useful. On the top, you can see the current location of your mouse in the vertical or pitch axis, whereas the bottom field represents the meter or time position of your cursor. Using these fields when adding events helps you find the exact position to place your mouse, in order to add, select, or modify an event.

Figure 8.7
An example of the Insert button's effect on events recorded in Step Record mode.

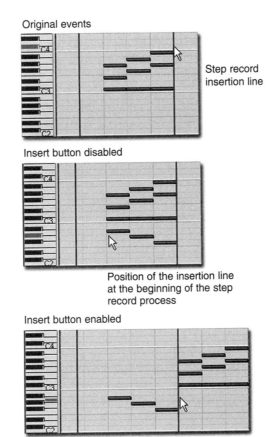

Original events

Step record insertion line

Insert button disabled

Position of the insertion line at the beginning of the step record process

Insert button enabled

Previous events are pushed further in time

Independent Track Loop

The Independent Track Loop controls that follow consist of an on/off toggle button and a start and end point setting for the loop itself. This allows you to create a loop with the MIDI events found in your MIDI editor between the start and end location that you set in these fields. When you enable the Independent Track Loop button, pressing the Play button on the Transport panel will cause the project to play normally, but the events inside the MIDI editor that are defined in the loop will cycle independently. For example, set this function so that the events playing a drum rhythm in the editor loop from bar 1 to bar 3. This will allow you to modify your rhythm for these two bars while hearing the rest of the project playing through time normally. In other words, this independent track loop creates a minicycle within the editor just as the left and right locators create a cycle in the project window. Both are independent from one another. The only dependency is that when the cycle in the project window is turned on and reaches the end, both cycles will go back to the beginning together.

Colors Scheme Selector

The Colors Scheme Selector field is a visual help option that does not affect anything in the editor other than the colors that are displayed in it. You can choose to give a different color to the different velocities (shown in Figure 8.8), pitches, MIDI channels, or parts. How you choose to use this coloring tool depends on what you are editing. For example, if you are editing events from different channels in a single window, you might want to select the Color by Channel option. On the other hand, if you have selected several parts and opened them in the editor, selecting the Color by Part option might make it easier to locate which events belong to which part.

Figure 8.8
The Colors Scheme
Selector field and the
Chord/Note display.

Chord Symbol and Note Display

The Chord Symbol and Note Display provides a convenient way of displaying information about the chords or notes that are under the project's cursor. You can update the display by moving the project cursor over a chord you want to see or look at the display area as the project plays to monitor the chord names as they are refreshed when the cursor passes by. You can change the format of the chord symbol displayed by clicking on the chord name in the display.

There are two additional sets of tools available in the MIDI editors that are not displayed by default: the Nudge Palette and the Edit VSTi Panel button. To learn more about customizing toolbars, please consult Appendix D.

Nudge Palette

This tool palette offers a convenient way of nudging the position (in time) of selected events. From left to right (see Figure 8.9):

▶ **Trim Start Left.** Moves the start position one quantize value to the left. Changing the quantize value field will influence how much each increment will be.

▶ **Trim Start Right.** Same as above, except it moves the start to the right instead.

▶ **Move Left.** Moves the entire selected event(s) to the left (earlier in time) without affecting the event's length.

▶ **Move Right.** Moves the entire selected event(s) to the right (later in time) without affecting the event's length.

▶ **Trim End Left.** Moves the end position one length quantize value to the left. Changing the quantize length value field (Length Q) will influence the size of each increment.

▶ **Trim End Right.** Same as above, except it moves the end to the right instead.

Figure 8.9
The Nudge Palette and
the Edit VSTi Panel.

Edit VSTi Panel

When a MIDI track is assigned to a VSTi, events recorded on this track will play through the sounds generated by this VSTi. The Edit VSTi panel opens the VSTi panel to make changes in this instrument's parameters (see Figure 8.9). If a MIDI track opened in the editor is not going through a VSTi, the button will not be active.

Key Editor Display Areas

The MIDI editor offers two main display areas—one for the MIDI note events and another for the Control Change messages. In the Note Display area, you will find a keyboard lying sideways. The ruler spanning from left to right represents the time at which events occur. You can change how time is displayed by right-clicking in the ruler and selecting one of the many display formats available or by selecting the desired format from the ruler format selection menu found at the right of the ruler itself.

USING THE RULER TO CONTROL ZOOM

In the MIDI Editor (as well as in all the other windows), when you click in the lower half of the ruler and drag your mouse up or down, you zoom out and in, respectively, centering your display on the position where you clicked to start the zoom. Holding down your mouse and moving it left or right moves the window and the project cursor in time. When you release your mouse, the project cursor snaps to the closest quantize value (if the Snap is active).

The Controller Display area is a customizable portion of the window that displays one or more controller types, such as volume, pan, expression, pedal, pitch bends, and so on. Using additional controller lanes gives you a better view of the MIDI messages associated with the part you are editing (see Figure 8.10).

How To

To add a controller lane to the MIDI Editor:

1. Right-click(PC)/Ctrl-click(Mac) anywhere in the editor.
2. From the context menu, select the Create New Controller Lane option at the bottom of the menu.
3. From the newly created lane, select the controller name you want to display from the drop-down menu found on the left margin of the lane. Note that controllers that contain events are indicated by an asterisk (*) at the end of the name.

If the controller you want to view is not displayed in this list, select the Setup option at the bottom of the drop-down menu. The Controller Menu Setup dialog box appears. In this dialog box, you will find two areas: the In Menu area and Hidden area.

▶ **To add a controller to the menu:** Select it from the Hidden area and click the double arrow button below the area.

▶ **To remove a controller from the menu:** Select it from the In Menu area and click the double arrow button below the area. Click OK when you are finished adding or removing controllers to the menu and then select the new controller to add its corresponding lane.

▶ **To remove a controller lane:** Select the Remove This Lane option at the bottom of the same context menu you used to add one.

Control Change messages found in the Controller Display area are represented by blocks, whereas note velocity values are represented by lines that are aligned with each note. Moving a note moves the velocity value with it, but doesn't move the Control Change messages. The field below the controller's name represents the value of the controller if you were to add this value at the current cursor position. Note that the frequency at which you can add Control Change messages depends on your current quantize value. So, if your quantize grid is set to 1/2 Note, you can only add controllers at half-note distances from each other. To enter a greater number of control change messages, disable the Snap mode or set the quantize value to a smaller fraction of a beat. This has the advantage of creating smoother changes, but also the disadvantage of creating a much greater number of MIDI events that can bog down the MIDI at the port's output. This is especially true when you are using lots of MIDI in your project.

Figure 8.10
The Key Editor with note display on top and two controller lanes below.

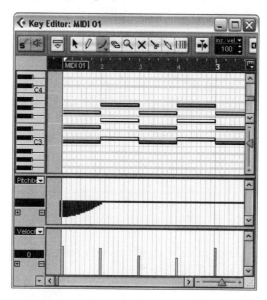

Editing MIDI Events

The main purpose of the MIDI Editor is to edit the MIDI events found in the part or parts you've opened in it. This is done by using a combination of tools and functions available to you in the editor. The main tools are available in the toolbar of the editor, but many of the functions you can apply are found in the context menu of the editor (see Figure 8.11). These are available by right-clicking(PC)/Ctrl-clicking(Mac).

In the upper portion of this menu, you will find all the tools available in the toolbar, and in the lower portion you will find a shortcut to the same operations available in Cubase's menu bar.

Editing MIDI events is not unlike editing text in a word processor. For example, if you want to copy, cut, or move a group of events, you need to select these events first and apply the desired operation on these selected events. That's when you use the Object Selection or Arrow tool.

Figure 8.11
The MIDI Editor's context
menu.

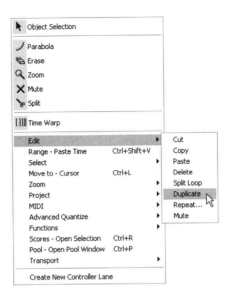

How To

To select events:

▶ To select a single event, just point and click on it.

▶ To select a group of events, click and drag a selection box around these events.

▶ To select multiple specific events, but not necessarily continuous, hold the Shift key down as you select the events you want.

▶ To select all the notes on the same pitch in a part, hold the Ctrl(PC)/⌘(Mac) key down and click on the corresponding pitch in the Keyboard Display area to the left of the Event Display area.

After events are selected, you can apply different functions. For example, you might want to move a group of notes to somewhere else in the part. If you want to keep these events in line with the current quantize grid, or to another quantize grid, you should make sure the Snap to Grid button is enabled and that your quantize grid setting is set to the appropriate value. To move one event, you simply need to click and drag it to its new location. To move several events, you select them as mentioned previously and then click and drag one of the selected events to the new destination. You can move both notes and control change values this way, provided that the appropriate controller lane is visible. If you move the velocity value of a note, you will also move the note. This is a good way to move notes in time while making sure your mouse doesn't go up or down, causing the notes to be transposed as you move them. Note that you can also achieve this by holding the Ctrl(PC)/⌘(Mac) key down as you move the notes. This limits your movement to the horizontal axis. You can also move selected notes by using the up and down keys on your keyboard.

Again, as with text in a word processor application, when you want to paste, repeat, or duplicate events, you need to select them, bring these events into the clipboard, decide where you want the clipboard to put them by placing your insertion point (in Cubase this is the project cursor), and then apply the Paste, Repeat, or Duplicate function. As with the project window, it is possible to hold the Alt(PC)/Option(Mac) key down as you move selected events to copy these events rather than move them. You will see a small plus sign (+) appear next to your arrow as you move the mouse. If you hold down the same key (Alt or Option) and click on the bottom right corner of the part of event in the project window, and then drag it across time while the cursor displays a pencil, copies of the events will also be created.

Cubase offers additional functions that make editing MIDI easier. For example, you can use the Select options in the editor's context menu or in the Edit > Select submenu to define what you want to select. Using this method, you can position your left and right locators across two bars, click in the Note Display area, use the Select in Loop option, and all the MIDI events found between the locators are selected; now click on a controller event and repeat these steps. This includes both the Notes and the Control Change messages within this range. You can copy these events, position your project cursor at another location, and then paste the events.

 EDITING MIDI NOTE EVENTS AND CONTROLLERS SIMULTANEOUSLY
You can also select both note events and controllers to cut or copy them by selecting one type of event at a time and holding the Shift key down as you select the next type (for example, drawing a box over the note events, then holding Shift and drawing a box over the pitch bend information in the Controller lane). This might be a practical alternative when you don't want to cut or copy all the control change events found inside the left/right locator range.

Muting Events

As an alternative to muting an entire track, you may also mute selected events (Notes and Control Change messages) inside the MIDI Editor.

How To

To mute one or several events:

▶ Select the events you want to mute with the Arrow tool and press the Shift+M keys on your keyboard or select the Mute option from the Edit menu.

▶ Or select the Mute tool and click the note you want to mute.

▶ Or select the Mute tool and drag a selection box around the events you want to mute and click on any of the selected notes with the mute tool. All events within the box's range are muted.

How To

To unmute muted events:

▶ Select the muted events you want to unmute with the Arrow tool and press the Shift+U keys on your keyboard or select the Unmute option from the Edit menu.

▶ Or select the Mute tool and click the muted events you want to unmute.

▶ Or select the Mute tool and drag a selection box around the muted events you want to unmute and click on any of the selected notes with the mute tool. All events within the box's range are unmuted. If there are events that weren't muted, they are now muted, so make sure you don't include any unmuted events in your range.

Splitting and Resizing Note Events

Besides moving, cutting, and copying events, you can also split or resize events. These operations can also be applied to a single event, a group of selected events, or a range of events.

How To

To resize a note or a group of notes:

1. To resize a group of notes, start by selecting the events with the Arrow or Object Selection tool.

2. Bring your cursor over the start or end of the events you want to resize. The arrow turns into a double-headed arrow (see Figure 8.12).

3. Click and drag the edge to the desired length. Note that if the snap grid is active, your movement is restricted to the quantize grid setting. If you want to resize the events without turning the Snap to Grid off, you can hold the Ctrl(PC)/⌘(Mac) key down as you move your mouse.

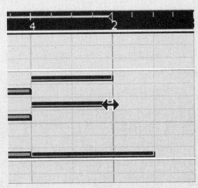

Figure 8.12
When resizing events, the Arrow tool becomes a double-headed arrow when you cross a resizable zone on the event displayed.

USING THE NUDGE PALETTE

As you saw earlier in this chapter, you can also use the Nudge palette tools to resize selected events.

If you want to split notes rather than resize them, you can use one of three methods: Use the Scissors tool at the desired location on the note or selected note; use the Split Loop function in the Edit menu or context menu (this splits the notes at the current left and right locator positions); or use the cursor's position to split all note events that cross it. This is also done through the Split at Cursor option found in the Edit menu or Context menu. No matter which method you use, the quantize grid setting influences where the split occurs.

QUICK SPLIT

Clicking on a note event using the selection tool while holding the Alt(PC)/Option(Mac) key will split the event where you clicked. If more than one event is selected, all events will be split.

Merging Note Events

The Glue tool is the Scissors tool's counterpart. It allows you to glue the following event of the same pitch or merge the selected event with the next one in time.

How To

To merge note events:

1. Select the Glue tool from the toolbar or in the context menu.
2. Click the first note you want to glue.
3. Clicking again glues the current note to the next note of the same pitch. For example, in the bottom part of Figure 8.13, the note to the right would be joined with the note on the left.

Figure 8.13
A before and after look at the Glue tool in action.

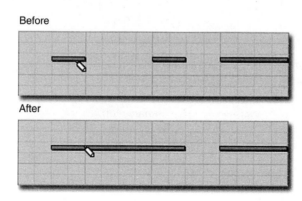

Using the Draw Tool

The Draw tool in the Key Editor window and the Drumstick tool in the Drum Editor window offer similar functions. The difference with the Draw tool is that you can drag a note to determine the length of that note, whereas the Drumstick tool repeats the event using the quantize value to determine the spacing and the insert length value to determine the length of each event in the Drum Editor window. Another difference is that the Line, Parabola, Sine, Triangle, Square and Paint tools in the Key Editor can be used to add note events in the Event Display area, whereas these tools are only available to modify control change values in the controller lanes of the Drum Editor.

How To

To create notes using the Draw tool in the Key Editor:

1. Set the quantize grid and length values you want them. The length determines how long each note is, and the quantize grid determines the spacing between the notes.

2. Select the Draw tool from the toolbar, or right-click(PC)/Ctrl-click(Mac) in the editor to select the Draw tool or use the key command (by default, this is the number 8 in the Key Editor and 0 in the Drum Editor).

3. Adjust the velocity setting in the toolbar to the desired value.

4. Click where you want to add your note. This adds a note with a length corresponding to the length value in the quantize length setting. However, if you click and drag, you can draw longer notes that increase by length quantize value increments. If you are adding notes using the Drumstick tool (in the Drum Editor) and you drag your drumstick to the right, additional Note On events are added at intervals set by the quantize grid.

In Figure 8.14, the quantize grid is set at sixteenth note intervals, the length for each note inserted is linked to the quantize value. This means that when you click to insert a note, it is one sixteenth note in length. Each inserted note has a Note On velocity of 89 as defined in the Insert Velocity field. In the upper two parts of this figure, you can see how these settings influence how notes are added when either clicking near the quantize grid lines or clicking and dragging over several grid lines. In the lower two parts, you can see the same operation but with the Drum Editor equivalent of the Draw tool, which is the Drumstick tool.

Events are always created with the same MIDI channel as the part you are editing. After you have inserted notes using the Draw tool, you can modify their length by clicking on the existing note and dragging it farther to the right to lengthen the note or dragging it to the left to shorten that note. Remember that note lengths always snap to the next quantize grid value as long as the Snap to Grid button is enabled in the editor's toolbar.

The Draw tool has some limitations—you can change only the end of an event or events using this tool. If you want to modify the beginning, you should use the Selection tool as described in earlier sections of this chapter. You can also modify controllers with the Draw tool, described later in this chapter.

Figure 8.14

Adding note events in the
Key and Drum Editor by
using the Draw or
Drumstick tool.

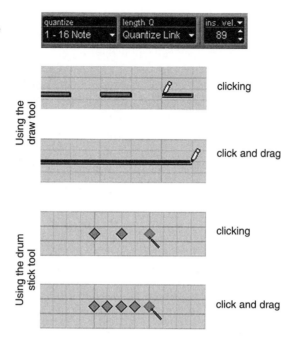

Using The Line Tool

The Line tool, like the Draw tool, inserts both note and controller events. However, each type of line has its own characteristics, in the sense that you can create different shapes using the different tools under the Line tool. The best use for these tools is to edit control change information, creating MIDI ramps, such as pan effects or fade outs. Here's a look at these tools and their capabilities.

The Paint tool (only available in the Key Editor) enters notes pretty much anywhere you want. Moving the mouse up and down adds notes on different pitches, whereas moving the mouse left and right adds them at different points in time. When drawing note events, the Paint tool is different from the Draw tool because it adds a note each time your cursor crosses a grid line. Both tools work the same where you are inserting control change events.

The Line tool draws a line across the Note Display or the Controller Display area to create events along the line at interval, length, and velocity in the case of notes, determined by the quantize setting. Figure 8.15 displays such lines: in the left half, note events are added and in the right half, controller (Control Change) messages are added. In the case of controller events, you can also use the Line tool to edit existing controller messages to create a linear ramp.

Figure 8.15
Adding note and
controller events using
the Line tool.

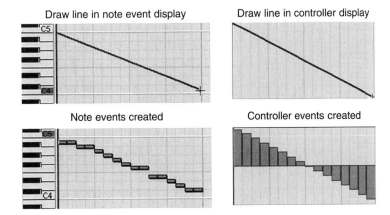

Draw line in note event display

Draw line in controller display

Note events created

Controller events created

How To

To insert events using the Line tool:

1. Set the quantize values appropriately. You can also leave the snap to quantize grid off; however, this generates a greater number of events, which, combined with other dense MIDI tracks, can create a bottleneck in your MIDI stream, causing poor performance.
2. Select the Line tool from the toolbar or the context menu.
3. Click where you want your line to begin. If you want to move this point after clicking, you may hold the Alt+Ctrl (PC)/Option+⌘(Mac) down to move the start point to a new location.
4. Position the mouse where you want the line to end.
5. When you are satisfied, click again to add the events.

The Parabola tool is similar to the Line tool with the exception that it draws a parabolic ramp rather than the linear ramp found with the Line tool (see Figure 8.16). Inserting events or modifying existing events using this tool is done in the same way as with the Line tool, with the following additional options:

▶ Press the Ctrl(PC)/⌘(Mac) key to change the type of curve created.
▶ Hold the Alt+Ctrl(PC)/Option+⌘(Mac) keys down after you clicked to insert your start point to move this point to a new location.

The sine, triangle, and square ramps have similar options. However, the farther away from the center point you move your mouse (from where you clicked), the greater the amplitude of the shape will be. A small movement upwards, for example, will create a small variation. Dragging your mouse downward from the start point inverts the shape of the ramp.

Figure 8.16
The different parabolic ramps available when using the Parabola tool.

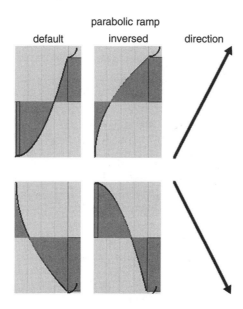

parabolic ramp

default   inversed   direction

How To

To create a ramp using the Sine, Triangle, or Square tools:

1. Select the appropriate tool from the toolbar.
2. Set the quantize grid if you want to use this setting to control how many and where the events will be created. For a smooth curve or change, disable the Snap to Grid option.
3. Click where you want to start inserting the events and drag your mouse to the right.

    ▶ To adjust the frequency of the shape, hold the Shift key down as you move your mouse to the left or right to adjust the period of the frequency to the desired length. After you are satisfied with this period, release the Shift key and drag your mouse to the location where you want the shape to stop inserting events.

    ▶ Hold the Alt(PC)/Option(Mac) key down while dragging the mouse to anchor the position and direction of the curve or shape at the start point.

    ▶ Hold the Ctrl(PC)/⌘(Mac) key down while dragging the mouse to anchor the position and direction of the curve or shape at the end point.

    ▶ Hold both Alt+Ctrl(PC)/Option+⌘(Mac) keys down after having inserted the start point to allow you to move the start point to a new location.

4. Release the mouse button at the desired end point location to insert events corresponding to the current shape setting.

Using Step Recording

As mentioned earlier in this chapter, the step recording functions are available in the toolbar of the Key and Drum Editors. When enabling the step recording functions, a new insert point bar (blue) appears in the Note Display area. You need to keep an eye on the location of this line because events that are inserted appear at the grid line immediately to the right of this insertion point. You can move this line by clicking inside the Note Display area at the location where you want to insert events.

How To

To record MIDI in Step Recording mode:

1. Select or create a MIDI track.

2. Create an empty part in that track by using the Pencil tool or by clicking on an existing part to select it.

3. Double-click on this part to open it in the MIDI Editor. If this track is associated with a drum map, the Drum Editor opens. Otherwise, the default editor for MIDI events is the Key Editor.

4. Enable the Step Recording button in the editing window's toolbar. All the step recording buttons should automatically be activated with the exception of the MIDI Connector.

5. Activate the Snap to Grid button.

6. Set the quantize grid and the length quantize value. This influences how far apart each event will be and how long the events will be as well.

7. Position your insertion point where you want to begin your recording by clicking inside the Note Display area of the editor.

8. If you do not want to use the Note On velocity to record the events, turn this option off and set the Insert Velocity field to the desired velocity.

9. Play a note or a chord on your controller keyboard.

    The notes will be recorded as you play them, at intervals set by the quantize grid and the length set in the Length Quantize field. Cubase records the velocity at which you are playing the notes or chords (unless you turned this option off), so try to enter the notes at the approximate velocity at which you want them to play back.

10. If you want to move forward or backward in time, use the left and right arrows on your keyboard. The insertion point where the notes will be added is displayed in the editor's Meter Display Position field in the toolbar.

11. If you want to insert an event between two other events, activate the Insert button in the editor's toolbar, position your insert point (blue line) where you want to insert a note or a chord, and simply play the note or chord. If you want to insert a note without moving the content found to the right of this location, disable the Insert button on the toolbar.

12. When done, don't forget to turn the Step Recording button off; otherwise, Cubase continues to insert events that you play on the keyboard in this part.

Zooming

In MIDI editors (Key, Drum, and List), the zooming functions are similar to the ones found in the project window with the exception that you do not have a Presets menu next to the horizontal or vertical scroll bar. However, you do have access to the Zoom submenu options found in the context menu [right-click(PC)/Ctrl-click(Mac)] or in the Edit menu.

You can also use the Magnifying Glass tool on the toolbar to draw a selection box around the range you want to zoom into. Clicking inside the editor with the Magnifying Glass tool zooms in one step at a time and Ctrl(PC)/⌘(Mac)-clicking zooms out one step at a time. Note that the data can be zoomed vertically and horizontally at the same time by holding down the Ctrl(PC)/⌘(Mac) key while using the zoom tool.

Editing Multiple Tracks

You can edit more than one track of the same class at a time in the Edit window. When selecting parts on different tracks in the project window and opening them in the MIDI Editor, you can edit the parts for all the selected tracks at once. This becomes useful when you want to compare events on different tracks in a single editing window. If you select a MIDI track associated with a drum map, the MIDI events for this track are displayed as normal MIDI events without the drum mapping information. In other words, if you want to edit multiple drum mapped events, select only tracks that contain a drum map association.

If you have assigned different colors to different parts in the project window, you can also see the parts' colors in the MIDI Editor.

How To

To edit more than one track at a time:

1. Click the first part you want to edit in a track.
2. Shift-click the next part you want to edit in another track or with the Selection tool and drag a selection box over the range of parts you want to edit simultaneously.
3. Press Ctrl(PC)/⌘(Mac)+E or select Open Key (or Drum) Editor from the MIDI menu, or double-click on one of the selected parts.

The editing window appears with multiple tracks displayed, as shown in Figure 8.17. The active part is displayed with its part color and black borders around each event in the window. The title of the editor also reflects which part is active. The other parts are visible but inactive and displayed as gray events.

Figure 8.17
The MIDI Editor can display more than one part at a time.

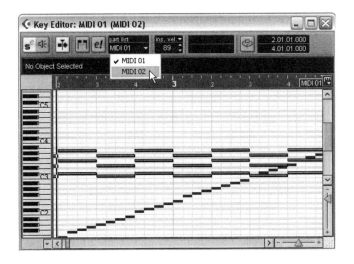

The Information Bar

If you need to determine the start position or the velocity value of an event, the Information bar is your greatest ally. You can modify any parameters of a selected event or events directly from the Information bar by clicking in the Value field below the parameter's name and using the scroll wheel of your mouse (if you have one) to change the value, or entering a new value using your keyboard. When more than one event is selected, the parameter values are displayed in yellow rather than white. You can change parameters of multiple selected events in one of two ways: either relative or absolute. By default, parameters change relatively; however, holding the Ctrl(PC)/⌘(Mac) key down causes the parameter value to become absolute. For example, if you have a G4 with a velocity of 64 and a C5 with a velocity of 84 selected, the Information bar pitch displays the C5's parameters. Table 8.2 shows how this works.

Table 8.2
How relative editing of multiple selected events works in the Information bar compared with absolute editing

Original Parameters (Pitch/Velocity)	Value Entered	Change when Relative (Default)	Change when Absolute (with Ctrl key/⌘ pressed)
C5/64	D5/84	D5/84	D5/84
G4/104	See above	A4/124	D5/84

MIDI Controllers

Editing MIDI control messages as they appear in the controller lanes is no different than editing note events. The tools that allow you to select or enter new events work the same way here as they did with note events. However, because the quantize grid setting influences the frequency at which these events are inserted when creating new control messages, it is important to make sure that this quantize configuration is set appropriately for the task at hand.

CHAPTER 8

When you are editing Control Change messages, it is important to understand the following principle. When you delete a Control Change message, the value preceding the deleted message replaces the deleted information. For example, if you have three sustain pedal values of 127, 0, 127 and decide to delete the second value, then you only have two values of 127 in your lane (see Figure 8.18).

Figure 8.18
A before and after look at what happens when you remove intermediate values in controller lanes.

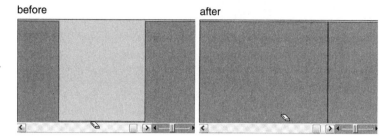

before   after

Drum Track Editor

What you have just read about the Key Editor applies for the most part to the Drum Editor as well. The Drum Editor window treats every single drum or percussion instrument with its own parameters. One of these parameters is the quantize value associated with each instrument. The Drum Editor can either treat them separately or apply a general quantize value to all of them, depending on the state of the General Quantize button found in the title bar. For example, you can set a different quantize value for the kick drum and the hi-hat, which can be useful when using the step recording method. The quantize value determines the spacing between each entered event. When the General Quantize option is disabled, the individual quantize settings take over. When the General Quantize option is enabled, the quantize value set in the toolbar dictates the quantize grid for each instrument in the part. Changing the quantize value for an instrument does not affect the general quantize value you set in the Drum Editor, but does affect the frequency at which events are added when using the Drumstick tool (same as the Draw tool in the Key Editor). You will notice that the Drumstick tool has also replaced the Draw tool, but they play a similar role in both editing windows.

Try this out by creating a drum track. Set the quantize value for the kick drum at quarter notes and the hi-hat's quantize value at sixteenth notes. Disable the General Quantize button in the toolbar. Now, use the Drumstick tool to draw events on these instruments by simply dragging it from left to right, holding the mouse button down. You will see that a kick is added on every beat and a hi-hat on every sixteenth note.

Another small difference is that when you add an event with the Drumstick tool, clicking it a second time removes it, unlike the Draw tool, which usually edits the note by dragging the event to make it longer or shorter. Because you can set an individual length for each instrument in a drum track, you can't extend the length in the Event Display area. There is a very simple reason for this treatment: Most percussive sounds are, by nature, quite short or without any sustained material, and they also are not looped. So, it really doesn't matter if you extend the event, because most instruments play the sound until the end, and the MIDI Note Off event's position has little or no effect on this note, no matter how long you hold it. Unlike a guitar or keyboard note, the position of the attack, or Note On event, is more relevant in this case than the actual end of the event. As a direct result of this, there are no Scissors or Glue tools in the Drum Editor.

Drum Editor Display Areas

As with the Key Editor, the Drum Editor is divided into task-specific areas. In this case, it is divided into five basic areas. The toolbar and Information bar as mentioned earlier in this chapter are quite similar and offer minor differences. Most of these differences have already been addressed; however, there is also an additional Solo Drum button in the toolbar, which lets you solo a specific instrument within the Drum Editor. The drum sound list and its columns replace the keyboard display of the Key Editor. The number of columns displayed here (see Figure 8.19) depends on the drum map associated with the track. This represents individual parameters for instruments that are defined in your drum map.

Below the drum sound list, in the left corner are the Map and Names field. The Map field selects a map from the drum map list or sets up a new drum map if you haven't already done that. The Name field selects from a drop-down menu, the names of instruments associated with different pitches when you don't want to use a drum map. So this field is grayed out when a drum map is selected.

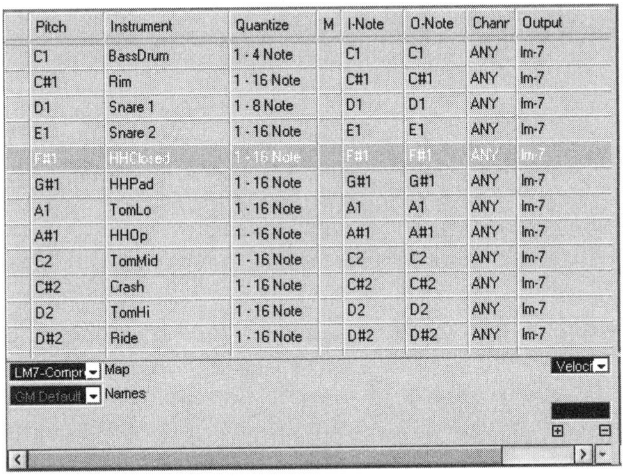

Figure 8.19
The drum sound list and the active Map and Name fields (at the bottom-left corner).

Pitch	Instrument	Quantize	M	I-Note	O-Note	Chanr	Output
C1	BassDrum	1 - 4 Note		C1	C1	ANY	lm-7
C#1	Rim	1 - 16 Note		C#1	C#1	ANY	lm-7
D1	Snare 1	1 - 8 Note		D1	D1	ANY	lm-7
E1	Snare 2	1 - 16 Note		E1	E1	ANY	lm-7
F#1	HHClosed	1 - 16 Note		F#1	F#1	ANY	lm-7
G#1	HHPad	1 - 16 Note		G#1	G#1	ANY	lm-7
A1	TomLo	1 - 16 Note		A1	A1	ANY	lm-7
A#1	HHOp	1 - 16 Note		A#1	A#1	ANY	lm-7
C2	TomMid	1 - 16 Note		C2	C2	ANY	lm-7
C#2	Crash	1 - 16 Note		C#2	C#2	ANY	lm-7
D2	TomHi	1 - 16 Note		D2	D2	ANY	lm-7
D#2	Ride	1 - 16 Note		D#2	D#2	ANY	lm-7

LM7-Compr ▼ Map   Veloci ▼
GM Default ▼ Names

If you drag the divider line between the Note Display area and the Drum List area to the right, you will see some of the columns that might be hidden. The drum list can have up to nine columns, each representing a control over an instrument.

▶ The first unnamed column allows you to select the instrument and hear the instrument associated with this pitch. By selecting an instrument, you can also view the velocity values associated with Note On events for this instrument in the controller lane.

▶ The Pitch column represents the pitch associated with a particular instrument. This cannot be changed because most instruments are already preprogrammed to play a certain instrument on an assigned pitch value.

▶ The Instrument column represents the name of the sound associated with this row's pitch. The name that appears in this column depends on the drum map you have associated with this part or the name list you have selected in the Name field below the Map field if no drum maps have been associated with the track.

CHAPTER 8

▶ The Quantize column represents the quantize value setting for each instrument. You can change this setting by clicking on the current value and selecting a new one. You can also change all the instruments' quantize value settings by holding the Ctrl(PC)/⌘(Mac) key down as you make your selection. The list that appears offers the same options as the editor's Quantize Grid drop-down menu.

▶ The M column controls whether an instrument is muted or not. To mute an instrument, click in the instrument row in the M column. To unmute that instrument, click for that instrument once again.

▶ The I-Note column stands for the Input Note value, or the note as recorded from the controller keyboard or drum machine, which is important to understand when we discuss the Drum Map feature in the next section. You can use the scroll wheel on your mouse to change this value, or click in the field and enter a new value. Note that this and following parameters only become visible after the track is assigned to a drum map.

▶ The O-Note column stands for Output Note Value, or the note that plays back the sound you want to map. By default, the O-Note is the same as the I-Note, but you can remap the input to another output when using drum maps. Again, this is discussed in the next section. You can change the value of this column the same way as in the I-Note column.

▶ The Channel column selects the MIDI channel you want to assign to the instrument in a particular row. Each row can be played through a different MIDI channel. Again, for this to work, your drum track has to be set to play the Any setting in the project window. You can use the scroll wheel on your mouse to change this value, or click in the field and enter a new value.

▶ The Output column assigns an instrument to a different MIDI output port. Each row or instrument in the drum part can be assigned to a different MIDI output if desired. To change the output, click the appropriate row in the Output column and select a new MIDI output from the pop-up menu. Each note in a drum track can be assigned to a different instrument. For example, you could have the kick drum played by a GM device, the snare played by the VSTi LM-9, and so on. For this to work, you need to set your track's MIDI channel in the Track List area of the project window to the Any setting; otherwise, all the sounds in the track are played by the same instrument.

To the right of the drum sound list is the Note Display area (see Figure 8.20). The horizontal axis represents different instruments or pitches, according to the information found in the drum sound list on the left and the time line divided by the quantize setting. Rectangles are replaced by diamonds, each of which represents a Note On event. Notes are in line with the quantize grid when the grid line crosses the diamond in its center.

Below the Note Display area are the controller lanes. Whereas the Key Editor displays the velocity of every note, the Drum Editor only displays the velocity of the selected instrument. In Figure 8.20, the current selected instrument is the HHClosed. Therefore, the velocity values you see represent the velocities associated with the Note On events of this instrument. For every other Control Change message, the editor behaves the same way as in the Key Editor described earlier.

Figure 8.20
The Note and Controller
Display areas of the Drum
Editor.

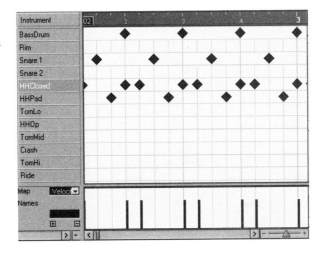

CHAPTER 8

Working with Drum Maps

Because not all instruments are created equal, they all operate differently, assigning different sounds to different keys. For example, one instrument's drum setup could use all the notes in a C scale to map its drum sounds, whereas another instrument might use every chromatic note to map its drum set. This is fine when you know which note is playing which sound. But what if you want to try a different drum set or drum machine? Do you need to rerecord all your beats because C1 is not the bass drum anymore? Well, not really. That's where drum mapping becomes very handy.

As you read in the previous section, in the Drum Editor, you have two columns that display Input notes and Output notes. This is used to remap what was recorded on one note but now will play as if it were recorded on another note, remapping the event to correspond to a new drum instrument map. To do this, you can either create your own drum map or load one that has already been programmed. Cubase comes with ready-made drum maps on its CD; before you start creating your own drum map, check your CD or your Drum maps folder if you've installed them on your computer.

Drum maps are essentially a list of 128 sound names associated with a pitch, Note In, and Note Out event. You can assign one drum map per track. For obvious reasons, if you use two tracks with the same MIDI output and MIDI channel, you can have only one drum map assigned to that instrument. Finally, you can assign only one Note In instrument per note name or note number, but you can have more than one Note In assigned to the same Note Out.

Because your drum map is a way of reassigning the keys you play to other keys at the output, remember that each note in a drum map corresponds to a pitch value. Each pitch value (note number) can be associated with an instrument name, such as Kick Drum 1, Snare, Hi-hat, and so forth. You can then assign the played note to that named instrument, which in turn is associated to a pitch, such as C1 (or note number 36). For example, you could create your perfect drum kit layout in which you position the instruments the way you want them on the keyboard (or other MIDI interface). Take, for example, the left portion of Figure 8.21. This could be your permanent drum layout setup that you use as a template for all drum parts. You could base this on your favorite drum layout if you wanted. From this point forward, you want all your drum sounds to map to the notes that are associated with the sounds on this layout. In the drum map on the right, you can see that the bottom half does not need remapping because the sounds in this setup are similarly positioned to play the same notes. Things change when you get into the cymbal sounds. Where you want the Ride 1 sound, the current drum setup plays a Crash 1 and your Ride Cymbal 1 sound is associated with another pitch. The solution: You remap the I-note in the drum map of the currently loaded instrument to C#4 and the O-note to D4. This way, you can play the C#4 and hear the Ride Cymbal. Because the C#4 is associated with the D4 pitch value, a D4 is actually recorded onto your MIDI track. Now, if you have a D4 recorded on your track, which in this drum map is a Ride Cymbal 1, what happens when you load another drum kit where D4 is a cowbell? Let's say that your ride is now on E5—all you need to do is set the O-note of the pitch D4 to E5, and you will hear the ride sound once again.

Figure 8.21
Example of a drum map
in action.

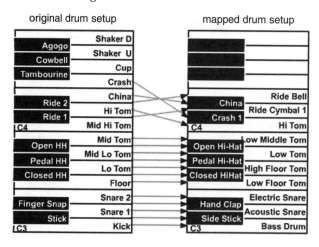

Assigning a Drum Map to a Track

How To

To load a drum map and assign it to a drum track:

1. In the MIDI Setup section of the Inspector area, in the Map field, select the Drum Map setup option. The Drum Map Setup dialog box opens (see Figure 8.22).

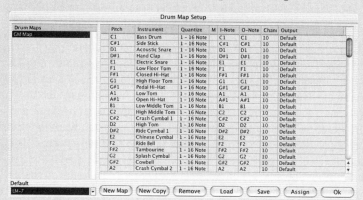

Figure 8.22
The Drum Map Setup
dialog box.

2. In the Drum Map Setup dialog box, click the Load button.

3. Browse to the folder containing your drum map files (*.drm), select it, and click the Open button.

4. Select your newly loaded drum map from the drum map list.

5. In the Default field below the drum map list, select the default MIDI port associated with this drum map.

6. Click the Assign button to assign this drum map to the current track.

Or:

1. Assign the generic GM Map to the MIDI track containing the drum parts.

2. Double-click on a part in the Event Display area for this track to open it in the Drum Editor.

3. From the Drum Editor, below the drum list, select the Drum Map setup option.

4. From this point forward, follow Steps 2–6 from the previous list.

Creating a Drum Map

As mentioned earlier, you can create your own drum maps or start from existing ones and edit them. The editing process takes place inside the Drum Map Setup dialog box.

How To

To create a drum map:

1. Click the New Map button.

2. Select the new map in the Drum Map field to rename it.

3. Next to each pitch in the list of instruments, enter an appropriate instrument name. It is a good idea to have the drum kit loaded so that you can hear the sounds as you are entering instrument names.

4. Adjust the Quantize, the I-note, the O-note, the Channel, and the Output fields if needed.

5. Repeat these steps for all the sounds available in your drum kit.

6. Click the Save button when you are satisfied with your current settings.

7. Name the file and browse to the location where you want to save the file; then click Save once again.

Later on, if you feel you have loaded drum maps that you don't want to use anymore, you can select the unnecessary drum map and then click the Remove button from the Drum Map Setup dialog box.

CHAPTER 8

List Editor

The List Editor, like the Key and Drum Editors, modifies your MIDI and audio events. The difference with the List Editor is that all the events are "listed" in rows of information and sorted by the order in which they were recorded. This is different than the Key or Drum Editors in the sense that you can have three notes displayed at the same place in a piano or drum roll, but in the list they all have their own row. This makes it a good place to look for glitches like note doubling (two notes playing the same channel and the same key at the same time), or consecutive patch changes that you've entered by mistake and that make your sound module behave erratically. When you want to edit notes and change velocity levels or edit controllers, the Key and Drum Editors are better suited for these tasks.

List Editor Display Areas

Before we take a look at the values in the columns and what they mean, let's look at the different parts of the List Editor (see Figure 8.23). The toolbar offers some similarities with the other MIDI editors. You will find, however, some new elements. The Insert menu allows you to select the type of event you want to insert, for example.

Figure 8.23
The List Editor, from left to right: the List area, the Event Display area, and the Value area.

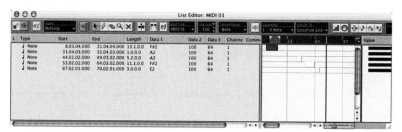

The other difference in the List Editor's toolbar is the Filter button, represented by the letter F. This is different from the Information button in the Key Editor, but displays or hides a bar beneath the toolbar. This bar represents elements that you can filter from the display areas below. They are hidden from your view, but any modification you make can affect these events as well, unlike the Mask. But not to worry, usually, if you can see it, it's hard to erase it. The Mask field, contrary to the Filter toolbar, allows you to view only the type of event or controller selected. It filters events as well, but events that do not correspond to the selection you make in this field. Both filter and mask options are there to help you isolate and manage the events displayed in the areas below, making it easier to focus your editing on the events you want to edit in this window.

How To

To filter a type of event in the List Editor:

1. Make the Filter bar visible.
2. Click in the check box next to the event type name in the Filter bar.

Below the toolbar, there are three areas giving information: the List area, the Event Display area, and the Value area (see Figure 8.23).

The Value area shows the Data 1 value from the List area. This value can be edited by using the Draw tool. In fact, as soon as you enter the area, your tool changes to the Draw tool automatically. When you make a modification to the value in this area, the change is reflected in the column titled Data 1.

The start, end, and length columns in the List area appropriately display the start time of the event, the end time of an event when this event has one, and the length of the event, again when the event has a length. Where it becomes a little bit less obvious is when you look at the Value columns. Table 8.3 describes what each column represents depending on the event's type.

Table 8.3
Description of information present in the List area

Type	Data 1	Data 2	Comment
Note	Pitch of the note	Note On velocity	
Poly Pressure	Note number	Pressure amount	
Control Change	Controller type	Change amount	
Program Change	Patch number		
Aftertouch	Pressure amount		
Pitch bend	Fine value of bend	Coarse value of bend	
System Exclusive			The SysEx message

The Event Display area shows events as they occur in time, like the Key or Drum Editors. The difference is that the vertical axis of the display shows the order in which these events occur rather than the pitch itself. If you move an event to the left, before another event occurs, it also moves up in the list as Cubase refreshes its display after you release the mouse button.

To modify events in the Event Display area, select the events you want to move and drag them to the left or right to move them in time where you want the event or events to occur.

Creating And Editing Events

To insert an event in the List Editor window:

1. Select the type of event you want to insert from the Insert Type menu.
2. Right-click(PC)/Ctrl-click(Mac) in the right area of the List Editor window where the events appear and select the Pencil tool from the toolbox.
3. Click where you want to insert the event. The horizontal ruler on top represents the time and each row represents an event at that time.
4. If you want to move your event in time, use your Selection tool and move the event left or right by dragging it. The Column view reflects that change.

CHAPTER 8

To edit several events at once:

1. Select the first event you want to edit in the Column Display area.

2. Ctrl(PC)/⌘(Mac)-click the last event in the list you want to edit, thus selecting all the events between the two. If you want to edit nonsequential events, Shift-click each event.

3. Press and hold the Alt key down before you make your modifications to all the selected events. If you want to modify a series of events proportionally, hold the Ctrl+Alt(PC)/⌘+Option(Mac) keys down before making the changes.

Now You Try It

For information about using the instructions found in this section and to find out where you can get the working files, please consult the section called *About the Exercise Files* in the Introduction section.

9

Audio Editing

As with MIDI, audio has its own editing environment. Actually, audio has three different editing environments: the Media Pool, the Sample Editor, and the Audio Part Editor. The Media pool allows you to manage your audio events and regions and doubles as a resource center for media content that have been recorded or imported into Cubase. The Sample Editor lets you manipulate recorded or imported audio and create regions and slices using the hitpoint calculation tool. Finally, the Audio Part Editor lets you edit and position a group of events and regions inside an audio part.

The Browser window, on the other hand, allows you to manage the content found in your project window, where tracks in Cubase become like folders inside your computer—containers that can hold objects and other folders. In Cubase, tracks are containers that hold events, parts (which are themselves containers that hold events), parameters, and automation. Every time you add an event or change automation, this information is added to the Browser window.

Here's a summary of what you will learn in this chapter:

> ▶ Look at the Media Pool and how it operates.
> ▶ Find out how you can optimize the audio content in your project.
> ▶ Create a backup copy of your audio content and project files.
> ▶ Use offline processes in different audio editing environments.
> ▶ Create, edit, and manage regions.
> ▶ Create and use hitpoints.

The Pool

The Pool is the audio and video file managing window, and it is similar to Windows Explorer or Apple Launcher (see Figure 9.1). All references to audio clips that were recorded or imported into a project are represented in the pool. Each project has its own pool, which can be saved separately and have its contents imported into another project. You may also open more than one pool in a single project, allowing you to share pool resources between projects. The pool also allows you to view your audio clip references (called *events*) and corresponding regions. You can use the pool to monitor, update, and manage these references.

You will find three default folders in the pool: the Audio, Video, and Trash folders. You can create any number of additional subfolders within these folders, but you can't rename or delete them.

There are many ways to access the Pool window as seen in Chapter 2. The simplest method is to use the Open Pool button on the project window's toolbar.

Figure 9.1
The Pool window.

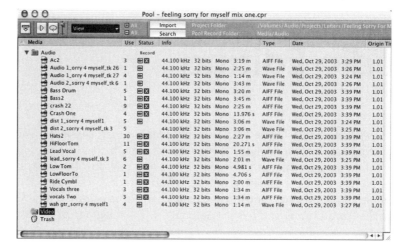

The Pool Areas

The pool is divided into two main areas: the toolbar and the main display area. A third, less obvious but very important, area of the pool is its menu options, found under the Pool menu and through a right-click (PC)/Ctrl-click (Mac). Most of the operations other than monitoring audio objects are done through this menu.

To the left of the toolbar is the Information bar button. Enabling this button reveals the Information bar at the bottom of the pool where you will find the current status information of your pool.

The two buttons to the right of the Information bar button can be used to hear a selected event or region found in the Media column below. The Play button starts playing the file and the Loop button (next to it) loops the playback. To stop the playback, you can click the Play button again.

The View field allows you to select which column is displayed in the pool below. There are a total of nine information columns available. Adding a check next to a name (by selecting it in the View drop-down menu) adds this row to the columns displayed in the pool. Selecting the Hide All option hides every column to the right of the Media column.

Next to the View field are two little buttons displaying plus (+) All or minus (-) All. As in Windows Explorer or Apple Launcher, this allows you to expand the tree found under the Media column. When a plus sign appears to the left of an object, it means that there are other objects inside this one. This could be regions inside an event, events inside a folder, or objects inside one of the three default folders if you've minimized the displayed content using the minus all button.

The Import button allows you to import media files from your hard disk into the pool. You can use this button to import any media format supported by Cubase.

How To

To import media files into the pool:

1. Click the Import button in the pool.

2. Browse the hard disk to find the location of the file you want to import. After a file is selected, you can preview it by using the Play button found below the File Display area in the Import Options dialog box.

3. Select the file and click the Open button to import it to the current pool.

4. If the file you want to import is not currently in the Audio folder of your project, Cubase prompts you to select different import options (see Figure 9.2). If the file you want to import does not correspond to the current project sample rate and bit depth, you are asked if you want to convert these files. Remember that in order to use a file in your project, it has to have the same sample rate as this project. On the other hand, you can have different word lengths (number of bits used by each sample).

5. Click OK when you have finished making your selections. This adds the current file or files to your pool.

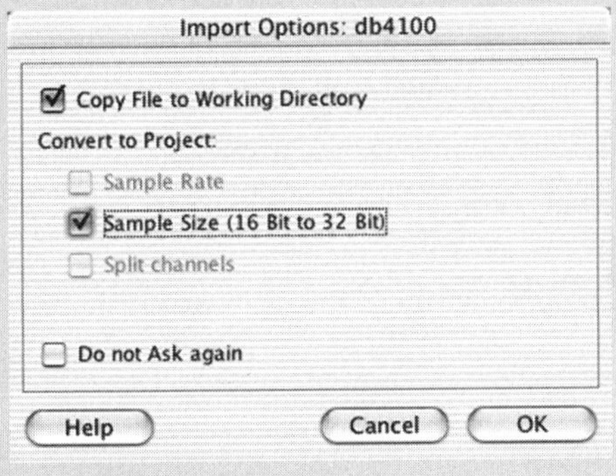

Figure 9.2
The Import Options
dialog box.

Import Options: db4100

☑ Copy File to Working Directory
Convert to Project:
☐ Sample Rate
☑ Sample Size (16 Bit to 32 Bit)
☐ Split channels

☐ Do not Ask again

(Help)   (Cancel)   (OK)

The Search button, found below the Import button, allows you to search the content of hard disks to find files you might want to import in your project. Clicking this button opens the Search panel at the bottom of the pool. This interface is similar to any search tool on your computer. It allows you to enter a name of a file you want to search for or use wildcard characters to find multiple files containing specific strings of characters (see the example in Figure 9.3).

How To

To search for files you want to import:

1. Click the Search button in the Pool's toolbar.

2. In the Name field of the Search panel, type in the name of the file you want to find. You can use wildcard characters to widen your search criteria.

3. In the Folder field, select the drive or drives you want to look in or select a specific path to look in at the bottom of the drop-down menu.

4. Click the Search button. The search results appear in the list to the right.

5. Check the Auto Play check box if you want to automatically preview the files found by the search. To preview a file, select it in the list. If the Auto Play option is not activated, you can click the Play button below the Search button in this panel. You can also adjust the level of the preview by using the preview level fader.

6. To import the selected file or files, click the Import button.

7. Cubase brings up the same Import Options dialog box as when you use the Import button in the toolbar. Make the necessary selections and click OK to import the files to your pool.

Figure 9.3
The Search panel found in the pool when the Search function is activated.

To the right of the Import and Search buttons, you can see the project folder's path and its associated Pool Record folder. By default, the Pool Record folder is found inside the project folder and is called *Audio*. This allows you to easily create a backup file of your project, including the media files associated with it.

Directly below the toolbar, above the columns, you will find column headers for each column in the pool. You can use the column headers to sort the information the column holds by clicking on the header. This adds a little arrow pointing up or down depending on the sorting order, next to the column's header, indicating that this column is used for sorting purposes. You can also use the column headers to change the columns' order by dragging the header horizontally to a new location. The header is inserted to the right of the column found on the left edge of the header's border when you drag it.

Understanding the Information

The Media column displays the names and types of media used in the project, as well as folders that you might have created inside the pool to organize your media files. You will find three types of icons displayed next to the name (see Figure 9.4); these represent an event object, a region object, and a sliced event object. Region objects are positioned under the event object it refers to. You can click on the plus sign to expand an event object to reveal its defined regions.

Figure 9.4
Icons associated with different objects in the Pool window.

folder   Record folder   event object   region object   sliced event
                                                                            object

---

How To

To rename objects in the pool:

1. Select the object you want to rename. A light blue box appears around it.
2. Click again to make the blue box change into a frame as shown in Figure 9.5.
3. Type in the new name for the object.

Figure 9.5
Renaming an object in the Pool window.

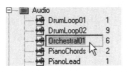

The Used column displays the number of times the object in the row appears in the project. In other words, how many times you've used it. Objects that aren't used in the project have no value in this column. You will notice that used sliced objects are incremented by the number of slices found in the object every time you repeat, copy, or duplicate the corresponding part in the project window. For example, if your drum loop is divided into eight slices, the Used column displays sixteen if you used this object twice in the project (thus creating two parts), even if these are shared copies of the same object.

The Status column offers information on the status of the objects inside your pool. The following table describes each icon's meaning in this column.

Table 9.1
Understanding the Status column's icons

Icon	Its Meaning
Record	Represents the content found in the pool's record folder; found next to the Audio folder. If you create a folder in the pool, you can click in the Status column next to this folder to make this the new record folder. Subsequent recordings appear under this folder. This does not create a new folder on your hard disk, but helps you manage the appearance of your files in the pool. For example, you could create a folder for a vocal session called "Vocals." By clicking in the Status column next to this folder, the record moves next to it, and all recordings made from this point on appear in this pool folder.
	Represents events that have been recorded since the last time you opened the project, making it easy to find newly recorded material.
	Represents events that are not located in the pool record folder. These events have been imported from another location on your hard disk. This occurs when you have not selected the Copy to Project Folder option when importing them. In other words, if you were to save your project's folders, these files would not be included, unless you use the Prepare Archive function described later.
	Represents events that have been processed offline. In other words, there are references made to both the original clip and the portions that have been processed and saved in the Fades or Edits subfolders found in your project's folder.
	Represents files that have not been found when loading the project. You can use the Find Missing File function to scan these missing files. This is explained later in this chapter.
reconstructible	Represents files that have been processed in some way by using offline processes or effects and for which some of the processed portions have been lost or misplaced. Cubase displays this indication in the Status column when it can reconstruct the missing portions.

How To

To create a folder in the pool:

1. In the Pool window, select the Audio or Video folder or another existing folder, depending on where you want your new folder to appear.
2. Right-click (PC)/Ctrl-click (Mac) and select the Create Folder option. You can also find the same option in the Pool menu.
3. Name your folder appropriately.

The Info column displays one of two things: either the file format and length details or a region's start and end locations.

The Image column displays a graphical representation of the event or the region within the event's boundaries. You will notice that all the events have the same length; however, Regions are represented as a proportion of this length. You can quickly preview the content of an object by clicking on its image representation.

How To

To preview an audio object using the Image column in the Pool window:

▶ To begin playback, click anywhere in the image. Playback occurs from the point you clicked until the end of the object or until you stop the playback.

▶ To skip to another portion of the same object, click approximately where you want to hear in the display before the preview ends.

▶ To stop the playback, click beside the Image column next to the image, or click the Play Preview button in the toolbar.

▶ To loop the playback, click the Loop button in the toolbar. The object loops from the point where you click in the image to the end or until you stop the playback.

The Path column displays the path to the original clips (audio files) on your hard disk. Note that processed files refer to a different file, but this is not displayed in the path. This measure is taken to ensure that you don't even have to think about the fact that additional files are created when you process a portion of the audio by using an offline process (not real time).

The Date column tells you when the clip was originally created.

The Origin Time column corresponds to the original position in time where this object was placed or recorded in the project. You can change this time directly in the column. Doing so may become useful because you can use the origin time or the locator time as a point of insertion when using the Insert Into Project option found in the Pool menu (or context menu). This function allows you to insert a selected object at the origin or cursor location.

How To

To insert an object at its origin time or cursor location in the project:

1. Select the Audio track in which you want to insert the object in the project window. If you want to insert the object by using the cursor location, position the play cursor at the desired location.

2. In the Pool window, adjust the origin time value appropriately by typing the new value in the object's row or by using your mouse's scroll wheel to adjust the values for the time. You don't need to adjust the origin time if you are using the cursor location option.

3. Select the Insert Into Project > At Origin or At Cursor option in the Pool menu.

CHAPTER 9

The Reel Name column represents the physical name given to a reel or tape from which the media was originally captured when you are working with imported OMF files, as this information may be included as part of the file format. If you are not using imported OMF files, you will not need to concern yourself with the Reel Name column.

Pool Functions

Generally speaking, the pool is not something you worry about or use the most at the beginning of a project. When your project is taking shape, you will probably also want your pool to take shape by organizing it and using it as an effective "pool" of audio/video source material.

We've already discussed certain managing functions related to the pool through the creation of folders in which to put additional media objects, or renaming existing objects. Let's take a look at other typical pool functions.

Dealing with Missing Files

When you save your project and reload it later, Cubase may not be able to find files it used in this project. You might have deleted them by mistake, or intentionally deleted them because you didn't need them anymore, but forgot to update your pool before saving it, so the reference to a missing file still exists. This section discusses different situations that can occur and how to deal with them.

When references to files are found, but the files themselves are not found in the specified folder (as might occur if you moved the files since you last saved your project, or if you renamed the files outside Cubase), you can use the Find Missing Files option from the Pool menu. Missing files are identified with a question mark in the Status column.

How To

To find missing files in the pool:

1. From the Pool menu, select Find Missing Files. The Resolve Missing Files dialog box appears (see Figure 9.6).

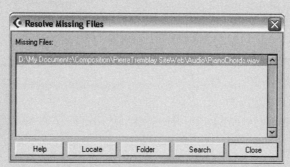

Figure 9.6
The Resolve Missing Files dialog box

2. If you want to locate the files yourself, click the Locate button. If, on the other hand, you want Cubase to attempt to find them, click the Search button. If you want Cubase to look for them in a specific folder, click the Folder button and choose the desired folder.

3. Depending on the option selected in Step 2, you are offered different solutions or results. However, if you have chosen the Search option, a new dialog box appears, allowing you to change the name of the file you are looking for. This might be helpful if you remember renaming the file after saving it with the project. Simply enter the new name in the appropriate field and then click the Start button to begin the search process.

4. If the search successfully found the missing files, you need to select the file you want from the list displayed and accept it by clicking the Accept button. This updates the link to the file in your pool.

In the event that a file is missing, even after a search (or you don't want Cubase to keep referring to a file because you've erased it anyway), you can use the Remove Missing Files option from the Pool menu. This affects any object in the pool with a question mark in the Status column.

In some cases, a portion of a file that has been processed might become corrupt or missing, just like any other file. But because this represents a portion of an audio clip that's been processed, the actual settings or processing history is saved with the project file and available through the Offline Process History dialog box. Because this processing history is saved, you can reconstruct the missing portion of the processed audio clip by using the Reconstruct option in the Pool menu (see Figure 9.7). Cubase tries to reconstruct the processed portion using the original clip and the settings available in the Offline Process History dialog box. For this option to be enabled, the Status column of the object needs to display the word "reconstructible."

Figure 9.7
Cubase indicates clips for which portions of processed events are missing by displaying the word "reconstructible" in the Status column.

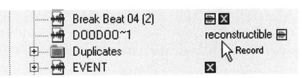

Optimizing the Pool

Many of the pool-related functions allow you to optimize the content of the clips it holds. When you are working on a big project, the pool can quickly get crowded and overwhelming. When you are editing, you don't want to worry about how the pool looks and how much space is used by your pool, until you start running short on space or get tired of looking for sounds in a pool that contains many useless audio clips at this point in the project.

We've already discussed how you can create folders to organize your clips. You can also drag and drop objects inside a folder to organize your files. When you delete events or Regions from the pool, they often end up in the Trash folder. This means that the files are still using space on your computer. You can use the Empty Trash option in the Pool menu to free up some of that hard disk real estate. When using this function, Cubase prompts you once again to make sure you really want to erase the files from the hard disk or only remove them from the pool (see Figure 9.8). If you choose to erase the files, you cannot get them back because this function can't be undone. This is one of the only ways from within Cubase that you can erase audio clips from your disk.

CHAPTER 9

Figure 9.8
Cubase offers you a last chance to keep the files on the computer or completely erase them from your hard disk.

Besides the trash you've collected, there might be some files that were used at the beginning, but aren't being used any longer. If you don't need them, you can use the Remove Unused Media option in the Pool menu. This time, you are prompted to choose if you want to remove these files from the pool completely (the files are still on your hard disk) or just send them to the Trash folder. Note that if you remove them from the pool and don't need them, these files still take up space on your computer. It is, therefore, recommended that you always use the Trash folder as a transitional stage when optimizing your pool. When you are finished, empty the trash.

When you record a long segment that includes useless audio, you can create Regions, resize, or split the events in the project window to hide unneeded portions. However, this does not remove them from your hard disk. The Minimize File option in the Pool menu looks at your current project and produces new files (audio clips) for the audio portions of the selected object that are used in the project. This effectively removes unused portions from the original file on the hard disk and initializes the offline process history for this file. Before using this option, it might be advisable to consider another option available in Cubase that allows you to minimize the file sizes of all audio clips for your project. This can be achieved by using the Save Project To New Folder option in the File menu. This option allows you to save all the files referenced in a project, as well as the project file itself, to a new folder, minimizing the space used by the project. However, by doing this, you still have the original content in the original folder where you began the project. If you want to revert to this project at a later date, the files will still be there.

How To

To minimize file sizes in your project:

1. Select the files you want to minimize in the Pool window.
2. Choose the Minimize File option from the Pool menu.
3. When completed, Cubase prompts you to save the project so that the new file references take effect. Click the Save button.

Archiving and Exporting a Pool

When you want to save a backup of your project or use it in another studio, it is important that you have access to all the files that are used in the project. Saving the project using the Save command updates the project file, but chances are, you might have files that are in different folders or on hard disks inside your computer. When using the Prepare Archive option in the Pool menu or in the Pool's context menu, Cubase makes a copy of all the audio clips used in your project to the audio project folder, and it allows you to freeze all offline processes you might have applied to an audio file, which prevents you from having to copy the content of the Edit folder onto a backup disk. After this operation is completed, you can simply copy the project file, its Audio folder, and any video file referenced in the project to a backup CD, for example.

How To

To prepare a project for backup:

1. Select the Remove Unused Media option from the Pool menu.
2. Click the Trash button when prompted to choose between trashing and removing from the pool.
3. Select the Empty Trash option from the Pool menu.
4. Click the Erase button when prompted once again. This removes whatever files are not used in your project and erases them from your drive.
5. Select the Prepare Archive option from the Pool menu.
6. Because this is a backup, you can either opt to freeze the edits or not. If you choose not to, make sure to include the Edit folder on your backup media inside the project's folder.
7. Save the project file.
8. When you are ready to back up your files, be sure to include the project file, its Audio subfolder, and the video files you might have used with the project on the backup medium.

If you are in the final stages of a project and want to save a final version of the project files, you can do so by repeating the previous steps with the addition of a couple more steps to save only the necessary material. Before heading on to Step 3 from the previous list, you can use the Conform Files option from the Pool menu to change all audio files in your project. This converts all of your files to the current sample rate and word length set for your project. You can use the Minimize Files option, as described earlier, to reduce each file to the size it's actually used for in the project. Then proceed until Step 7 and use the Save Project To New Folder option in the File menu instead.

When working between projects, you might want to use the pool from one project in another project. This is possible through the use of the Export and Import Pool options, allowing you to save the status of objects in the pool and retrieve them from another project. Note that the pool itself does not contain the audio files because these are located in the Audio folder. But you can save the references, Regions, slices, and other pool-specific settings. Exporting a pool offers a great way to store drum loops and sound effects that have been edited. Whenever you want to use these sounds later on, all you need to do is import the pool into your current project.

How To

To export or import a pool:

1. Prepare your pool by making sure all your files conform to the project's format, removing or searching for missing links, and emptying the trash.

2. From the Pool menu, select the Export Pool option.

3. Type a name for your pool.

4. Click the Save button.

5. To import the saved pool inside another project, select Import Pool from the Pool menu.

Pool Interaction

Beyond the inner pool functions, you can also use the pool to drag events from it into the project window as shown in Figure 9.9. When you drag an object from the pool into the project window, the location of this object depends on two variables:

▶ The snap and quantize grid settings

▶ The position of the snap point inside the audio event or Region; because the snap point can be anywhere in the event, the event snaps the snap point to the closest grid line in the project window

The location displayed above the cursor as you move the selected object over a track indicates the position at which the snap point or start point of this object will be placed (depending on the variables mentioned). When the blue line next to the cursor and location display the desired location, simply drop the object into place.

Figure 9.9
Dragging a region from the pool into an Audio track in the project.

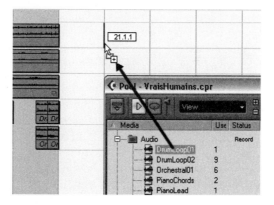

When you drag an object from the pool to the project window's event display area, below the last track, an Audio track corresponding to the event's configuration will be automatically created. For example, dragging a mono event will create a mono track while a stereo event will create a stereo track. However, if an existing event already exists on a track, make sure it has the same configuration as the event you are inserting. Although you will still hear a mono event on a stereo track and vice versa, controlling the amplitude and pan of this event might produce unexpected results.

You can also create a new audio file from a region in the Pool window by highlighting this region and then selecting the Bounce Selection option in the Audio menu. This prompts you to choose an appropriate folder for the new file. After you save, it is added to your pool as a new event.

Offline Processes in the Pool

When you apply any type of offline process (from the process, VST, or DirectX plug-ins) to an object inside the pool, this processing affects the entire object. For example, if you apply a delay effect to a region, the whole region is affected. If you want to apply a process to a portion of a region, use the Sample Editor instead. Offline processes in the Pool window can be viewed in the Offline Process History panel found in the Audio menu, as is the case with processes applied in the project window or Sample Editor.

How To

To apply an offline process to an object from the Pool window:

1. Select the object in the Media column.
2. From the Audio menu, select the desired process you want to apply.
3. Make the appropriate setting in the process' dialog box.
4. Click the process button.

Sample Editor

The Sample Editor is the default editor associated with audio events and regions. It allows you to perform many types of editing tasks in a nondestructive environment. It is in this editor that you can create regions within an event or process an event by using offline processes and effects. You also use the Sample Editor to work with hitpoints.

Hitpoints are special markers that you can add to an audio event, which allow you to create audio slices representing individual beats in the event. After you have created slices from hitpoints, you can use the event in the project and change the tempo of this project without affecting its pitch, or use the timing of the audio event to determine the tempo of a project. You can also use this timing to create a groove map that can be applied to other audio or MIDI events through the Quantize Setup panel.

Sample Editor Areas

The Sample Editor is divided into two areas (see Figure 9.10): the Sample Display area (on the left in the figure) and the Region Display area (on the right in the same figure). It also displays a number of bars similar to the other editors: the toolbar, the Sample Overview bar, the Status bar, the ruler, and the Level Scale bar.

CHAPTER 9

Figure 9.10
The Sample Editor
window.

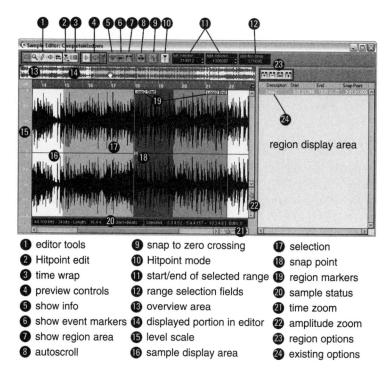

① editor tools   ⑨ snap to zero crossing   ⑰ selection
② Hitpoint edit   ⑩ Hitpoint mode   ⑱ snap point
③ time wrap   ⑪ start/end of selected range   ⑲ region markers
④ preview controls   ⑫ range selection fields   ⑳ sample status
⑤ show info   ⑬ overview area   ㉑ time zoom
⑥ show event markers   ⑭ displayed portion in editor   ㉒ amplitude zoom
⑦ show region area   ⑮ level scale   ㉓ region options
⑧ autoscroll   ⑯ sample display area   ㉔ existing options

The first five buttons in the toolbar are used to perform different operations in the editor, such as selecting a range, zooming in or out, editing the waveform, performing audio playback, or scrubbing. We'll discuss these tools later on as we talk about the operations available in this window. Following the sample editing tools is the Hitpoint Editing tool, which is a multifunction tool button allowing you to edit hitpoints when you are in Hitpoint mode.

The Play and Loop buttons have the same properties as in the Pool window. The small fader next to the Loop tool allows you to control the preview level when playing an event inside the sample editor. Note that this level does not affect the level of an event in the project window.

The Show Info button will display information below the waveform display area about the clip or event being edited. You can change the ruler format affecting the type of values represented in this bar by selecting a different format in the Ruler Format menu or where the current format is displayed in the info bar itself. The button to the right of the Show Info button allows you to show or hide the audio event's boundaries if this event is used in the project window. Clips found in the Pool that have not been used in the project window (therefore, no actual event has been created) will cause the Sample Editor to not display this button. When you open an event by double-clicking on it in the project window, this Show Event Borders button will appear in the toolbar. If, on the other hand, you load an event by double-clicking on it from the Pool window, this button will not be visible. When visible, you can use the special event border markers to alter the start and end points of an event inside the Audio Part Editor. The last button in this trio allows you to show or hide the regions' management portion of the Sample Editor window. This area will display information on regions currently associated with an audio clip or event, as well as allow you to create, remove, rename, select, edit, or preview regions.

How To

To edit the start and end of an event in the Sample Editor:

1. In the toolbar, activate the event border display.
2. Select the Range Selection tool in the toolbar.
3. Click the start or end event point marker and drag it in the desired direction. For example, moving the start point to the right shortens the event and moving it to the left lengthens it. Note that you can't extend these markers beyond the limit of the audio clip the event refers to.

Changing these markers also affects the event as it appears in the project window.

Using the Show Regions button reveals the region area as shown in Figure 9.10 and also displays region markers if there are any. This area allows you to create a region from a selection in the Sample Display area, remove an existing region, select the highlighted region in the Sample Display area, and play the highlighted region. If the Region Display area is not visible, you can use the Show Region Display Area button in the toolbar of this window. Unless you have recorded audio in Cycle mode with the Create Region option, events do not normally contain any regions when recorded or imported. It is through editing options or preference settings that regions are created, or, as we see later in this chapter, through the Sample Editor's Region Display option buttons.

The Autoscroll button, located by default to the right of the Show Regions button, has the same property as it does in the project window.

The Snap to Zero Crossing button will force any selection you make to move to the nearest zero crossing. Enabling this function is a useful way of making sure that regions you create or process will not begin or end with a portion of the audio not crossing at zero percent amplitude (silence). This helps in preventing clicks, pops, and other audio glitches from occurring due to jumps in audio amplitudes at the beginning or end of a region. You will find more on this later in this chapter.

The next button and the subsequent fields in the toolbar are related to hitpoints, which are described later in this chapter.

The Overview area displays a thumbnail view of the current event loaded in the Sample Editor. You can have only one event loaded in this editor at a time, so this overview displays only one event or several regions defined in this event.

The Sample Display area displays one or two channels of audio, depending on the event's configuration (mono or stereo). With Cubase SX, the Sample Editor will also display surround formats with up to six channels. The waveforms are displayed around a zero axis at the center of each waveform and displayed in the level scale on the left of this area. Each lane splits the waveform in two halfway lines above and below the zero axis line. You can customize the elements displayed in this area by right-clicking (PC)/Ctrl-clicking (Mac) in the Sample Editor, selecting the Elements option at the bottom of the context menu, and checking or deselecting elements found in this submenu. You can also change the level scale representation from

CHAPTER 9

percentage to dB display, or decide to hide the level scale altogether by right-clicking (PC)/Ctrl-clicking (Mac) in the level scale area itself (at the top, to the left of the ruler bar) and choosing the appropriate option in this context menu.

Basic Editing Functions

It goes without saying that the Sample Editor allows you to cut, copy, and paste audio data inside the Sample Editor. These basic editing functions are similar to any other type of application. For example, cutting and pasting audio can be summed up in four basic steps:

1. Select what you want using the Range Selection tool.
2. Apply the desired function, such as Cut or Copy, from the Edit menu.
3. Position the cursor to place the content of the clipboard if you want to paste what you have just cut or copied.
4. Paste the content using the paste command in the Edit menu [Ctrl+V (PC)/⌘+V (Mac) are the default key commands].

You can also insert silence within an existing audio clip. This might be useful when you want to add pauses between specific audio content.

How To

To add silence in an audio event:

1. With the Range Selection tool selected, drag a selection box over the area where you want to add silence.
2. Adjust the start and end point if needed by dragging the edge of the selection.
3. Select Edit > Range > Insert Silence [this is also available in the editor's context menu or by pressing Ctrl+Shift+E(PC)/⌘+Shift+E(Mac)].

Working with Regions

Regions allow you to define portions within an audio event that you can reuse several times in a project. For example, you could create regions from a 16-bar groove played by a drummer, naming each region appropriately: intro, beat, break, fill, ending. Then you can drag the region from the Region Display area in the Sample Editor into the project window, just as you did when dragging objects from the pool into the project window.

How To

To create a new region:

1. With the Range Selection tool, click and drag over the area in the Sample Editor that you want to include in the new region. At this point, you don't need to be precise.

2. When you have a good idea of the range, right-click(PC)/Ctrl-click (Mac) and select Zoom > Zoom to Selection. This allows you to view your selection close up. Note that the selection appears in a light teal color, whereas a selected region appears as a darker shade of teal because a region is usually displayed in a darker shade of gray.

3. You can edit the start or end of your selection to fine-tune the region by clicking and dragging the edges of your selection. When our cursor becomes a double-headed arrow (occurs when the cursor crosses one of the selection's edges), you can modify the selection without losing the selection (see Figure 9.11).

4. Enable the Loop button and click the Play Preview button in the toolbar to hear the selection. Make any necessary modifications to your selection.

5. When you are satisfied with the selection, enable the Region Display area if you haven't done so already.

6. Click the Add button.

7. Type in a name in the Name field for your new selection.

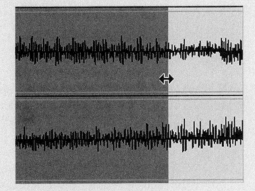

Figure 9.11
Fine-tune your selection by dragging the edges when the Range Selection tool displays a double-headed arrow.

USING THE SNAP TO ZERO OPTION

When you are making a selection, it is a good practice to keep the Snap to Zero Crossing button enabled. This option makes sure the amplitude of the audio signal is at its lowest possible value (zero percent or minus infinity when displayed in dB), reducing the chances that glitches might occur during playback due to an abrupt change in amplitude. When this option is enabled, you will notice that your selection might skip over areas in the Sample Display area because Cubase cannot find a proper zero crossing in that portion of the audio.

How To

To modify an existing region:

1. Click in the column to the left of the region you want to edit in the Region Display area. This column does not have a name, but allows you to move the Sample Display area to the area of this region.
2. Click the Select button. The region's start and end markers appear.
3. Right-click(PC)/Ctrl-click(Mac) and select Zoom > Zoom Selection to center the selection in the display area.
4. With the Range Selection tool, drag the region's start or end point to the new desired location.

You can also change the start and end location numerically by changing the values manually in the Start and End columns in the Region Display area.

How To

To add a region to a project from the Sample Editor:

▶ Click in the empty column to the left of the Description column in the Region Display area and drag the region to the desired location in the project window.

About the Snap Point

The snap point is to audio what the Note On time is to quantizing. Because audio events or regions don't necessarily begin at a specific quantize value, you can change the location of the sensitive area that is used to snap to the current quantize grid. This is called the *snap point* and is displayed as a blue line with an S in a box found in its center. In Figure 9.12, you can see that the event begins earlier, but the actual audio occurs later in time. If this corresponds to a strong rhythmic division, you can move the snap point to this location. When moving the event on the track in the project window or in the Audio Part Editor, the object snaps to the grid using this location rather than the event start position. If you don't change this, by default, the snap point is placed at the event start point.

How To

To edit the snap point's position:

1. Open the event or region in the Sample Editor.
2. Make sure the audio event elements are visible in the window. If not, select Elements > Audio Events from the editor's context menu.
3. Zoom to view the current snap point and the place where you want to place it.
4. For more precision, you can use the Scrub tool or the Play tool to find the exact place where the snap point should go.
5. Click and drag the S (in the box on the snap point line) and move it to the appropriate location.

Figure 9.12
Example of an audio event's snap point.

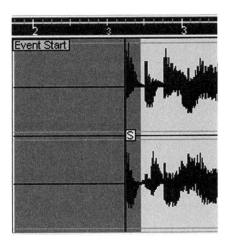

Working with Hitpoints

In Cubase, the main purpose of hitpoints is to define individual beats in a rhythmic part and use the location of these special markers to slice up this part into separate beats, replacing a single audio event by a series of audio slices in an audio part.

Let's take a look at Figure 9.13 as an example. Here, we have the same drum beat played in three different ways. Although there are four representations of this beat in the figure, the original beat never changes speed when played at different project tempo values. It stays constant and the number of bars it covers at different tempo values varies because the number of bars passing when the tempo is higher also increases. The upper portion of both pairs represents the sliced version of the same beat. As you can see, in both cases, the part ends at the beginning of Bar 2, whereas in the original version, it ends after Bar 2 when played slower and before when played faster.

The same drum beat has been placed on two tracks: in the upper track, a sliced version of the beat and on the lower track, the original version. A screenshot was taken while the project was set at 120 BPM (upper couple of tracks) and another at 90 BPM (lower couple of tracks). Notice how the sliced version in both tempos ends at the beginning of Bar 2, whereas the original content spreads across Bar 2 when the tempo is at 120 BPM and doesn't reach Bar 2 when the tempo is set at 90 BPM. That's because slicing up the beats creates a snap point at the beginning of each, which follows the beat position in the bar/beat grid.

Figure 9.13
Using sliced parts instead of original audio at various project speeds.

project tempo=120 BPM

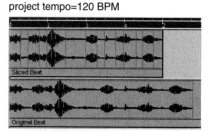

project tempo=90 BPM

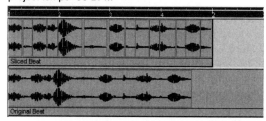

Another useful way of using hitpoints is when you have an audio segment for which you want to determine the exact speed. Because hitpoints allow you to identify beats within an audio sample, it also calculates the tempo value automatically after you tell Cubase how many bars and beats are included in the selection.

Using hitpoints works best with audio content with strong attacks. You can still get tempo values out of sustained material, but the result this produces when you change the pitch can be disappointing.

Creating Hitpoints

The best way and main purpose of working with hitpoints is to load a drum beat or rhythmic content in the Sample Editor. Hitpoints are created in Cubase by detecting attack transients that are characteristics of beats in an audio file. Thankfully, you don't need to do all of the calculations alone. This said, to get the best results, you will need to fine-tune the results you get from Cubase and also make sure that your audio content is appropriate for hitpoints. For example, audio with well-defined drum beats with high peaks and low valleys works better than sustained material. Also, drum beats that have lots of effects, such as reverb or delay, will be harder to slice accurately.

How To

To create hitpoints:

1. Open the audio event to which you want to add hitpoints in the Sample Editor. You can open an event from the pool or the project window. If the event is inside a part, this opens the Audio Part Editor; double-click on the event from the Audio Part Editor to open it in the Sample Editor.

2. If the area in which you want to create hitpoints for is shorter than the event itself, start by selecting a range that defines a clear, loop-friendly beat, such as a one, two, or more bar segment.

3. Preview the selection by enabling the Loop option and clicking Play in the Sample Editor.

4. Adjust the start and end position of the selection if you have created one; otherwise, you don't need to adjust any selection.

FIGURING OUT THE LENGTH OF A LOOP

Try counting how many bars and beats are in your selected looped segment, if you can feel the beat subdivision; for example, the HiHat might play sixteenth notes. You can use this as your hitpoint quantize value later. It will also be helpful in telling Cubase how many bars and beats are in the loop.

5. Enable the Hitpoint mode from the window's Toolbar button. If this is the first time you enable this button with the current audio event inside the Sample Editor, Cubase will ask you a few questions on the audio content.

6. Check the Use level scan (detect normalized) because this will improve the chances of getting an accurate slicing of your audio loop.

7. Check the Adjust Loop if you can help Cubase find the appropriate hitpoints by entering the information in the fields below. If you are not sure about the values that need to be entered in these fields, skip to Step 11.

8. Set the Maximum number of bars value. The Maximum bars represents the number of bars you counted in the loop selected. If, on the other hand, you want to use only the first bar in a four-bar loop, for example, setting a maximum bars to "1" will tell Cubase you want to create slices only for the first bar.

CREATING GROOVE QUANTIZE TEMPLATES

You can create Groove Quantize templates from the timing information Cubase extracts from a sliced audio loop. You can then apply this Groove Quantize template to other audio or MIDI events. This said, to create a Groove, you can use only 1-bar drum patterns. If your audio content is longer than one bar, you should enter 1 in the maximum bar number, making sure that the groove you are trying to capture as a template is in that first bar. If not, you should select the bar you are targeting for the Groove Quantize.

9. Set the beats value from the drop-down menu. This does not affect the bar count, but rather which beat subdivision will remain as hitpoint slices. You can change this value later on if you are not sure, but chances are, the 1/16 value will work in most cases. With smaller beat subdivisions, you will get more slices, and vice versa.

10. The Minimum and Maximum BPM fields will help Cubase determine the right tempo. The smaller the range, the more precise this approximation will be.

continued

11. Click on the Process button. Cubase will calculate the hitpoints for your audio segment, adding them along with the waveform display. The spacing between each hitpoint depends on the settings you included earlier, the sound itself as well as the beat subdivision value. The ruler also displays a special selection corresponding to the maximum bar length you set in Step 8 (see Figure 9.14).

12. If there are too few hitpoints for the number of beats in your looped segment, increase the hitpoint sensitivity slider value by sliding it to the right. Move this slider slowly until you've reached a satisfactory number of hitpoints. On the other hand, if you have too many hitpoints, move the slider to the left to reduce the number of hitpoints.

Figure 9.14
The hitpoint fields on the Sample Editor toolbar appear when the Hitpoint mode is enabled.

At this point, it is possible that each portion found between hitpoints represents a beat perfectly. Clicking on the Speaker button will allow you to hear the sound between two hitpoints individually by clicking anywhere between these two hitpoints. If each portion sounds like a beat without clicks or noticeable glitches at the beginning or the end, you are ready to create audio slices or a Groove Quantize template from the hitpoint's locations. However, in most cases, you will need to fine-tune the hitpoints before you do so.

Editing Hitpoints

You can move, erase, or create new hitpoints manually when in Hitpoint mode. The best way to move a hitpoint to an appropriate location or to create a new one is to zoom into the audio display area in order to properly position your hitpoint. When you preview a slice, it is important that each slice (space between two hitpoints) contains only one "hit," such as a kick, snare, or combination of instruments on the same beat subdivision. It is also important that the end of the slice does not end in a glitch. This is usually the case when the next hitpoint arrives just after the next sound has started, picking up that sound's attack transients at the end of the slice.

If you look at the example in Figure 9.15, you will notice that the hitpoint occurs directly on the beat. The instrument will probably sound like it does also because its peak is heard around this area as well, but as you can also notice, the attack begins before the hitpoint location. This causes the previous slice to play the beginning of the attack for the next slice, resulting in a glitch-like sound at the end of the slice. Moving the hitpoint a bit to the left, in this case, prevents this glitch from happening even if it means placing the hitpoint slightly before the quantize value. This only adds to the feel of the beat itself. We see how you can create a groove map later on, using the hitpoint locations as the template for this groove.

Figure 9.15
The hitpoint is placed at a quantize value, but the sound begins before the quantize value.

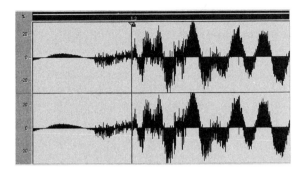

How To

To move a hitpoint:

1. Enable the Snap to Zero Crossing button on the toolbar. This will restrain your movement to areas in the audio where the audio is silenced, reducing the risk of clicks and glitches at slice edges.

2. Zoom into the area you want to edit.

3. Select the Move Snap button from the Hitpoint tool. This button has three functions: Disable, Lock, and Move. Note that you can also move the hitpoint by using any other tool, except the Draw tool, by clicking and dragging inside the little triangular-shaped handle at the top of each hitpoint.

4. Click the hitpoint's handle and drag it to the desired location.

5. After you are satisfied with the location of this hitpoint, you can lock it.

6. Repeat this operation for other hitpoints, if necessary.

Locked hitpoints can be moved, but they remain visible if you choose to change the sensitivity slider later.

In some cases the current hitpoint sensitivity slider works well, but it skips specific points where an attack hit can be heard. When this is the case, you can add hitpoints manually.

How To

To insert a hitpoint manually:

1. Enable the Snap to Zero Crossing button on the toolbar.

2. Zoom into the area you want to edit.

3. Select the Draw tool from the toolbar.

4. Click at the location at which you want to add a hitpoint. If you hold your mouse button down as you add the hitpoint, you can position it exactly where you want it if the original location isn't exact.

On the other hand, sometimes there are too many hitpoints around a certain area. That's when you need to manually remove a hitpoint. Here's how you do this.

How To

To remove hitpoints:

1. In the Hitpoints tool, select the Disable Hitpoints option.
2. Click the hitpoints you want to remove (disable).

Now that you have created hitpoints and fine-tuned their locations, as well as made sure all the hitpoints correspond to actual attack hits, you need to create either slices or a groove quantize template. Hitpoints by themselves only mark where the slices or quantize values should be. They also help in telling you what the original tempo of the selected segment is in the Sample Editor's toolbar. Besides that, hitpoints will have no effect on the audio file later on if you decide to change the tempo of the project.

Creating and Using Audio Slices

After you've created hitpoints and are satisfied that each hit in your drum loop or rhythmic content is identified correctly with a hitpoint, you need to create the audio slices that will be used in the project window. Slices are similar to small regions, but are not handled as regions by Cubase in the sense that a sliced event does not display a number of corresponding regions in the pool as does an event with regions, as described earlier in the "Working with Regions" section.

How To

To create audio slices:

1. This requires that you have previously created hitpoints and have properly positioned your hitpoints in the selected audio event.
2. While the Hitpoint mode is still active, select Advanced > Create Audio Slices from the Audio menu (or the editor's context menu).

To use the sliced loop, you can drag a sliced object from the Pool window to an Audio track in the project window. When you place a sliced event on an Audio track, an audio part is automatically created with the corresponding slices inside this part. From this point on, when you want to edit the slices in the part, the Audio Part Editor opens. This allows you to move the slices around in the part, apply a different quantize setting, or reorganize your loop to create variations of it.

After you've placed a sliced event on a track, you might notice that changing the tempo to a value lower than the original tempo of the loop might create audible gaps between each slice. You can solve this problem by using the Close Gaps function available in the Advanced submenu of the Audio menu. This function can also be used in other instances; however, this is probably the best use for it. As Figure 9.16 displays, the small gaps that occur between each slice are removed after

Cubase time stretches each slice to compensate for the missing audio content. Note that extensive use of this over large gaps alters the sound quality of your audio content, so you should use this function on small gaps only.

How To

To close gaps between slices in a part:

1. Select the audio part(s) in the Audio Part editor.
2. From the Audio menu, select the Advanced > Close Gaps option.

Figure 9.16
A before and after look at how the Close Gap function affects slices.

before (the close gap function is applied)

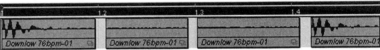

after (the close gap function is applied)

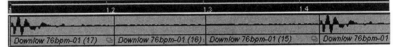

Creating and Using Groove Maps

When creating hitpoints in a drum loop, you are placing markers where important beats and beat subdivisions occur in this loop. By doing so, you are, in essence, creating a rhythmic blueprint that holds the rhythmic feel of your loop and this can be applied to other audio or MIDI events through the Quantize Setup panel. This rhythmic extraction is called a *Groove Map* or *Groove Quantize*.

How To

To convert hitpoints into a groove map:

1. Create hitpoints in an audio loop as described earlier in this chapter.
2. When satisfied with the result, from the Advanced submenu found in the Audio menu, select the Create Groove Quantize option.

Note that this works better if you use at least one slice per eighth-note; otherwise, your map will be very coarse and will only affect events on beats.

How To

To apply a groove map to events:

1. Select the events you want to quantize. This can be in the project window, the MIDI Editor, or the Audio Part Editor.

2. Press the default Shift+Q key command to bring up the Quantize Setup panel, or select Quantize Setup from the MIDI menu.

3. Click the Presets drop-down menu and select the corresponding quantize groove. By default, the groove map is given the name of the event used to create it. You can, however, rename it by selecting the preset, double-clicking on the name in the Preset field, and typing a new name for it.

You see how the events will be quantized by looking at the quantize preview display in the center of the Quantize Setup panel.

Now You Try It

For information about using the instructions found in this section and to find out where you can get the working files, please consult the section called *About the Exercise Files* in the Introduction section.

10

Browsing and Processing Options

The Browser window provides a complete list of all the events used in a project, making it a perfect environment to troubleshoot all kinds of objects as well as a tool that lets you quickly edit details within a project. For example, you can rename a number of events directly from the Browser window. Any changes you make here are reflected in all other windows.

In this chapter, we also look at offline (not in real time) processes inside Cubase and the advantages they may provide over online processes (processed in real time) when you need more processes than your computer can handle. Because Cubase offers a nondestructive editing environment, making changes to processes applied directly to audio objects has never been easier.

In this chapter, you will:

> ▶ Understand and use the Browser window.
> ▶ Use the Offline Process History panel.
> ▶ Use the Edit History panel.
> ▶ Use offline audio processes to control different aspects of your sound.
> ▶ Use VST and DirectX plug-in (PC versions only) effects without taxing your computer's CPU.

The Browser Window

When you want to see every type of event used in your project in a track hierarchy format, the Browser window is the one for you (see Figure 10.1). This window is similar to the List Editor described earlier in the sense that events are displayed in lists, but this is where the similarities end. Because the Browser window displays all types of events in hierarchal lists, it also implies that you can modify them by using the different fields it displays for each type of data.

Browser Window Areas

The Browser window is divided into two areas and a toolbar. In the left area called the *Project Structure*, you will find a tree with the file name for the current project as its root. Linked to the file are all the tracks available in the current project. In other words, each type of track currently present in your project is displayed here. If the track contains data (this could represent events, regions, parts, or automation parameters), it is displayed under the track's name. The details for the events or data found on a track are visible in the List area found on the right side. The behavior of the browser is similar to that of Windows Explorer or Apple Finder—in which selecting a folder on the left reveals its content on the right.

The toolbar offers a few options:

▶ The Time Format field selects how time values in related columns are displayed. Changing the format in this field changes all values in columns below.

▶ The next drop-down menu works with the Add button that follows it. You can use this field to select the type of event or object you want to add and then click the Add button to add it to the list. What you can add depends on what is selected in the Project Structure area. For example, when a MIDI track is selected, you can add a MIDI part; when a marker track is selected; you can add a marker or cycle marker.

▶ The Filter drop-down menu actually works like the Mask function in the List Editor. You can use this to select the type of MIDI events you want to see. For example, selecting the Controller option from this menu displays only the Controller messages found in the track. Besides MIDI, you can only use this filter with marker tracks. You have the option to view the cycle markers, regular markers, or both.

▶ The Sync Selection check box is a very convenient option that allows you to select in the Project window, the event you select in the Browser window, and vice versa. If you want to troubleshoot an object in your project, you can open the Browser window and check this option. Next time you select an object in your project, when you open the Browser window, this object is displayed in the List area.

Figure 10.1
The Browser window.

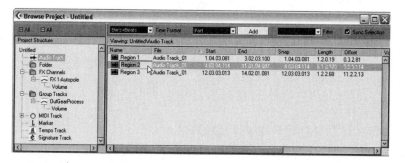

The List area on the right of the Browser adapts its content to the selected objects in the hierarchy structure on the left. For example, if you select an audio track on the left, its events are displayed on the right. If you select one of those events in the Project Structure area, the details for this event appear in the list on the right.

After you can see an event's details, you can make any modifications you want in the appropriate column. At the top of each column are the column headers. You can click and drag a column header to move it to another location to change the order in which these columns appear. You can also click in the column header to change the sorting order. The column used for sorting displays an arrow pointing up or down, depending on the type of sort used.

To expand the entire project structure or to hide the details in each track, you can use the +All/-All buttons found in the upper-left corner of the window.

Understanding the Information

Although it is possible to add events in the Browser, because of its list nature, its environment is more appropriate when editing existing events. When you want to make changes to events in the Browser, it's important to understand what each column represents. In most cases, the column header describes well what its content represents. However, some columns might appear ambiguous. To clear that up, the following list describes the columns that aren't so obvious.

▶ **Snap column.** Represents the absolute position of the snap point for this object (audio event). This can be different from the start point because the snap point is used to adjust the position of an event with the grid setting of the project or editor. Changing this value does not change the position of the snap point in relation to the event's start, but rather moves the snap point (and its event) to the location entered in this field.

▶ **Length column.** Represents the length of the event. Editing the value affects the length of the event, moving its end position, not its start position.

▶ **Offset column.** Represents the location in the audio clip that corresponds to the start of the event. This offset location value is found in the audio event or region and in the MIDI and audio part. When you change this value, the part or event stays in place on the audio track, but the content inside the part or event slides forward or backward in time.

As for the other columns, you can change the values by entering data directly in the appropriate row and column juncture.

Audio Menu Options

After an audio clip is recorded and its event displayed on the audio track, most of the operations you can apply to this event can be found in one of two places: the Audio menu in the Project window or in the context menu [through right-click(PC)/Ctrl-click(Mac)] of the same window.

The Audio Editing options are found in the Audio menu in the Project window and under the Audio submenu option in the context menu of the Project window when an audio object is selected in the window. These options relate to editing functions of audio objects on a track and display the currently available options depending on the object selected.

Spectrum Analyzer and Statistics

The two first options in this category are the Spectrum Analyzer and Statistics functions, which are available only in Cubase SX. These functions allow you to look at and analyze an audio object to find problem areas, such as identifying a noise frequency or determining if there is any DC offset in an audio file. A DC offset can occur when a sound card adds DC current to a recorded audio signal. This current results in a recorded waveform that is not centered on the baseline (-infinity). Glitches and other unexpected results can occur when sound effects are applied to files that contain DC offsets. The Statistics dialog box in Figure 10.2, for example, reveals that this value is set at -75.69 dB on the left and -74.74 dB on the right; in other words, not at minus infinity. From the information the Statistics dialog box provides, you can correct the situation by applying the Remove DC Offset process to the audio object, increasing the dynamic range of your digital audio file.

Figure 10.2
The Statistics dialog box.

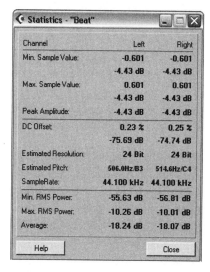

Channel	Left	Right
Min. Sample Value:	-0.601	-0.601
	-4.43 dB	-4.43 dB
Max. Sample Value:	0.601	0.601
	-4.43 dB	-4.43 dB
Peak Amplitude:	-4.43 dB	-4.43 dB
DC Offset:	0.23 %	0.25 %
	-75.69 dB	-74.74 dB
Estimated Resolution:	24 Bit	24 Bit
Estimated Pitch:	506.0Hz/B3	514.6Hz/C4
SampleRate:	44.100 kHz	44.100 kHz
Min. RMS Power:	-55.63 dB	-56.81 dB
Max. RMS Power:	-10.26 dB	-10.01 dB
Average:	-18.24 dB	-18.07 dB

How To

To use the Spectrum Analyzer (Cubase SX only):

1. Select the audio object you want to analyze. If you select a part with multiple events or regions inside, Cubase opens an analysis window for each object inside the part.

2. The Spectrum Analyzer's Analysis Options dialog box appears. Because the default settings give the best results in most cases, leave these settings as is and click the Process button.

3. The various options inside the Spectrum Analyzer result window allow you to view the content of the analysis in different ways. Clicking the Active check box analyzes another audio object and replaces the current analysis window with the new analysis. Otherwise, a new window opens, and this window remains open until you close it.

How To

To use the Statistics function (Cubase SX only):

1. Select the audio object you want to analyze. If you select a part with multiple events or regions inside, Cubase opens an analysis window for each object inside the part.

2. The Statistics dialog box opens showing you the results of the statistics (see Figure 10.2). Close the dialog box when you are finished reviewing the information.

Detect Silence

The main purpose of the Detect Silence function (see Figure 10.3) is to create different regions from a long audio event that may contain silent parts. For example, if you record a vocal track, the singer might sing in certain parts and be silent in others. If you chose to record the performance from beginning to end, you end up with a recording that contains both usable and useless content. To automate the region creation process, the Detect Silence function allows you to set an audio level threshold below which events are considered as silent. Then, in the same dialog box, you can determine how long this silence has to be before considering it a silent part. After you have set up your preferences appropriately and are satisfied with the result displayed in the preview area, you can create sequentially numbered regions that appear in both your Media Pool and in the Project window, replacing the current object with the newly created regions. This operation does not remove any audio content from the original audio clip; it merely creates regions that hide the unwanted portions of your audio. This said, by default the *Strip Silence* option found in the Detect Silence dialog box is selected. This will cause Cubase to hide (strip) any silent sections to disappear from the current Project.

Figure 10.3
The Detect Silence dialog box.

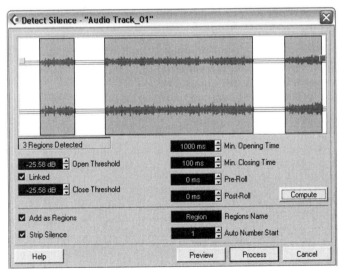

How To

To create regions using the Detect Silence function:

1. Select the audio event or region (this doesn't work on parts) for which you want to create regions.

2. Select the Audio > Detect Silence option from the context menu [right-click(PC)/Ctrl-click(Mac)] or select Detect Silence from the Audio menu.

3. The Detect Silence dialog box appears (Figure 10.3). Start by setting the Open Threshold level by clicking and dragging the green box found to the left of the display area. You should set this low enough to make sure that the content you want to keep becomes part of the region, but high enough that the noise or silence is left out of the region.

4. Set the Minimum Opening Time to an appropriate value in milliseconds. Remember that 1000 milliseconds is equal to one second. How you set this up will depend on the actual content you are trying to process.

5. Repeat the same operation for the Minimum Closing Time field.

6. Click the Compute button to preview where the regions will appear and click the Preview button to hear the result.

7. If you are not satisfied with the result after previewing, continue tweaking the settings in this dialog box until you are satisfied with the preview's results.

8. Make sure the Add as Regions and the Strip Silence check boxes are selected. This creates the regions and removes the silence from the regions it creates.

9. If you want to give a specific name and number to the regions this function creates, you can use the Regions Name field to enter a new name and the Auto Number Start field to adjust the number of the first region Cubase creates.

10. Click the Process button to create the new regions and hide the silent (unwanted) portions of the audio clip.

Converting Audio Objects

As discussed earlier, it is possible to convert one object type to another in the Project window. For example, changing an event into a part, changing a part into several events, or creating a part with several selected events in order to move them as a unit. You might also want to have the flexibility of using event envelopes over portions of audio found in an audio part; since audio parts don't have envelopes associated with the part itself, converting the part to separate events might offer the flexibility you are looking for. This said, there's nothing stopping you from using event envelopes on events inside the Audio Part editor, but it's just one window away, and sometimes, that's too far.

How To

To convert one audio object type into another:

▶ **Convert an event into a region.** Select the event or events. In the Project window's context menu under the Audio submenu, select the Event as Region option.

▶ **Convert an event into a part.** Select the event or events. In the Project window's context menu under the Audio submenu, select the Event to Part option.

▶ **Convert a region into a part.** Select the region or regions. In the Project window's context menu under the Audio submenu, select the Event to Part option.

▶ **Convert a part into independent objects (regions or events).** Select the part or parts. In the Project window's context menu under the Audio submenu, select the Dissolve Part option.

Bounce Selection

Let's say you've just used the Detect Silence function, and you've created a region that excludes the silent parts of the original content. You might want to create a new audio file with only the content of this new region. In this case, use the Bounce Selection function to create a new file or audio clip from the selected object on your track. You can also create a new audio file from a part containing several objects inside. We discussed the possibility of creating the perfect take out of portions of different takes using the Set to Region and To Front options with events and regions. After you are satisfied with this final take, it is possible to select the resulting events or regions, glue the objects together, creating a part with multiple objects inside, and then bounce all the events to a new file. You can also use the Bounce Selection option to bounce the audio and its effect to a new track.

How To

To bounce audio objects to a new file:

1. Select the objects you want to bounce to a new file.

2. You may adjust the fade handles (see the next section for more details) if you want to include these fades in the new file.

3. From the context menu or the Audio menu, select the Bounce Selection option.

4. Cubase asks you if you want to replace the current selection in the Project window with the newly created file. Select Yes if you want to do so, or No if you simply want the file to appear in your pool.

Working with Fade Envelopes

In Cubase, you can create two types of fades and crossfades. You can opt to have Cubase process fades in real time using the fade envelopes, or you can process these fades, creating small fade segments that are seamlessly integrated into your project. Either way, you get the same result. However, using realtime fades means your computer calculates these fade curves every time you play the project. If you are short on computer resources, you might want to opt for the processed version (more details later in this chapter). This section describes how to use realtime fade envelopes found on region and event objects.

When selecting a region or an event on an audio track, you will notice the appearance of little boxes and triangles. Those found at the bottom of an object are resize handles that can be used to resize an audio region, event, or part. However, the ones found on the top corners of the event and region objects are meant to control the fade-in or -out properties of this object, and the handle found in the middle is used to control the overall sustain level (amplitude) of the object between the fade-in and -out. In Figure 10.4, this handle is shown at its maximum value (default). Clicking this blue box with the Selection tool controls the overall output level of this object. This offers a different form of automation because this envelope (similar to an Attack-Sustain-Release envelope) moves along with the event, whereas track automation is not associated with the object on the track.

You can control the fade curve for both the fade-in and fade-out on region and event objects.

Figure 10.4
Control handles found on region and event objects in the Project window and Audio Part Editor.

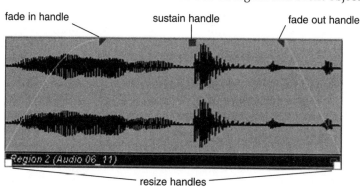

fade in handle   sustain handle   fade out handle

resize handles

How To

To change the fade curve type of an audio object:

1. Select the event or region you want to edit.

2. Adjust the fade-in or fade-out by using the appropriate handles.

3. To modify the fade type, select Open Fade Editors in the Audio menu or Audio submenu of the context menu, or double-click on the fade-in part itself. This brings up both Fade-in and Fade-out dialog boxes (see Figure 10.5).

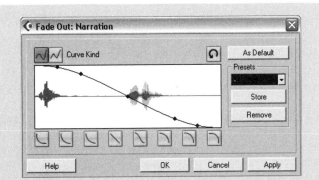

Figure 10.5
The Fade-out dialog box

4. Select the spline (logarithmic curve) or linear curve type you want to use with your object.

5. You can choose from different curve types below the display or use these as a starting point, editing the curve by clicking and dragging the handles inside the display.

6. If you want to store this curve for later use, click the Store button, type in a name, and then click OK.

7. Click the Apply button to accept your changes and then click OK.

8. Repeat this operation for the other fade curve if necessary.

If you want to apply a default type of curve to all the objects in your project, you can use the Auto Crossfade Settings button found besides the track's name in the Inspector area. After you've changed the default crossfade setting, all new fades will use this curve setting unless you change it on an object.

How To

To change the default crossfade (fade) settings:

1. Click the Auto Crossfade Settings button to the left of any track's name in the Inspector area.

2. The Auto Fades dialog box appears. Click the Fades tab.

3. Select the appropriate settings on this tab. These settings are applied by default afterward.

4. Click the Crossfades tab.

5. Select the appropriate settings on this tab as well.

6. Selecting the Auto Fade-in, Auto Fade-out, and Auto Crossfade options applies the same settings to all subsequent fades in your project from this point forward.

7. Clicking the As Default button saves your settings as the default value for subsequent projects. *continued*

CHAPTER 10

8. If you do not want your fade settings to be the same on every track, deselect the Use Project Settings check box. However, if you do want all the tracks to use these settings, keep the check in the box.

9. Click OK.

You can also apply a fade to objects on several tracks at once using the Range Selection tool. When your range crosses the start point of an object, a fade-in is created over that range (see the lower-right region in Figure 10.6). When your range crosses the end point of an object, a fade-out is created over that range (see the lower-left region in Figure 10.6). When your range doesn't cross either the start or end position, a fade-in and -out will respectively begin and end at the borders defined by the Range Selection tool (see the upper region in Figure 10.6). Notice that all the curve types for the fade-ins and -outs are identical. This is because the project uses a default auto fade setting.

Figure 10.6
Using the Fade to Range function.

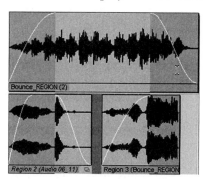

How To

To apply a fade over selected objects in a range:

1. Click the Range Selection tool in the toolbar or in the Project window's context menu.

2. Drag a selection box over the desired range.

3. Select the Adjust Fades To Range function from the Audio menu, or press A (default key command), or select the same function in the context menu's Audio submenu.

If, after all this, you decide you don't want a fade on this event or region, you can either move the handles back to their default position (no fades) or select the events and then choose the Audio > Remove Fades function.

Finding Your Objects

As your project starts to grow, you will want an easy way to find events in the pool. When the pool gets crowded, it can be time-consuming to look for this object's name in the pool. That's why you can use the Find Selected in Pool function, which does just that: finds the selected event from the Project window in the Pool.

How To

To find a selected object in the pool:

1. Select the object you want to find.
2. Then select the Audio > Find Selected in Pool function.

This brings up what you were looking for, highlighted in the pool.

Audio Processing Options

Audio processing, as with audio fades, can be applied to audio in two different ways: You can apply effects that are processed in realtime, or you can apply processing while Cubase is not playing the project. In the former case, to automate the effects, you can change the parameters or change the effects altogether. In the latter case effects are not applied while the file is being played, but calculated beforehand, and then playing the rendered processed file (or portion of the file) each time you play the project. Processing audio in non-realtime offers a CPU-intensive friendly method of processing audio since the CPU doesn't have to process the audio every time you press play. When adding a realtime effect or process, the audio passes through an insert, send, or master effect that is processed by your computer. The effect itself is not saved to an audio file, although the effect's parameters are saved as part of your project. Every time you play the project, the computer starts processing once again. This is why you can change parameters easily. On the other hand, it can add a serious load on your computer that can slow it down to a grind when your realtime processing needs exceed the computer's capabilities.

Processing files offline, changing the portion of the audio and saving this processing with the file, allows you to create the effects without changing the original file's content and does not require any processing time during playback because the files are simply read from the hard disk. The disadvantage is that you cannot automate this processing by using automation in real time. There are many instances, however, where automation is not needed. When you want to optimize a file or add an effect to a portion of an audio clip, event, region, or slice, processing this portion and writing the effect to a file might be more effective than using realtime effects, not to mention reducing the load imposed on your computer. Pitch shifting and time stretching operations are notoriously known to be heavy computer resource consumers, so using them in offline processes is highly recommended.

You can apply realtime effects and processes through the insert effects and FX channels (which are insert effects on a special audio track). You can apply processes and plug-in effects through the Plug-ins or Process submenus found in the Audio menu, or through the same submenus in the Project window's context menu.

Using Audio Processes

In audio terminology, any effect applied to an audio signal is referred to as an *audio processing*. However, in Cubase, processes refer to a specific type of processing. In fact, all processes found under the Process function in Cubase are meant to change audio without adding effects to it, such as reverbs, chorus, and delays.

You can apply processing to an entire selected audio event or region in the Project window, or apply it to a portion selected by using the Range Selection tool. You can also apply processing to the same elements that are found inside a part after you open them in the Audio Part Editor. Selecting an event or region in the pool applies the processing to the entire selected object. Finally, you can apply a process to a selected portion of an event or region in the Sample Editor. All processes in any of these situations are found in the Process's submenu in the Audio menu or in each window's Process submenu options.

Because some objects may be shared (used more than one time in the project's time line) when applying a process to one of them, Cubase asks if you want to create a new version or change all the instances of this object across the project's time line. If you opt to create a new version, the selected object is the only one affected by this process, and the processed version of the object replaces the original content in the Project window (not on your hard disk). If you want all the shared instances of this object (event or region) to change, then you can select the Continue button (see Figure 10.7). This replaces the currently selected object rather than creating a new version, which causes all shared occurrences to change as well in the project.

Figure 10.7
Cubase can replace the selected object or create a new one.

About Pre- and Post-CrossFade Options

In some processes, you will find a Pre-CrossFade and Post-CrossFade option under the More button in the Process's dialog box. These options allow you to apply the process gradually over time (pre-crossfade) and end the process also gradually over time (post-crossfade). As displayed in Figure 10.8, this process would take 410 milliseconds before completely implemented, and it would start reverting from processed signal to nonprocessed signal over the last 217 milliseconds of the object. So, if this were applied to the Gain process, for example, it would take 410 ms to reach the Gain setting in the Process window and would go back to the original gain over the last 217 ms of the object being processed.

To access these options, you can click the More button found in the Process' dialog box and check the options you want to apply after setting the parameters to the desired value. If you don't want to see these options (but still apply them if the options are selected), click the Less button.

Figure 10.8
The Pre- and Post-
CrossFade options.

Envelopes

The Envelope process (see Figure 10.9) creates a volume level envelope by using a fade-like display to control the amplitude of the signal.

How To

To apply an envelope process to a selected object:

1. Select the desired object.
2. Select the Envelope process from the Process option in the Audio menu.
3. Select the type of curve you want to use for the envelope.
4. To add handles, click along the envelope line where you want to insert the handle and drag it to the desired position.
5. To remove handles, drag the handle outside the display area.
6. To store or remove a preset, click the Store or Remove buttons.
7. To preview the result, click the Preview button. You can make changes to the envelope as you are previewing. To stop the preview, click the Stop button.
8. When satisfied with the settings, click the Process button. Click Cancel if you want to cancel the process.

Figure 10.9
The Envelope process
dialog box.

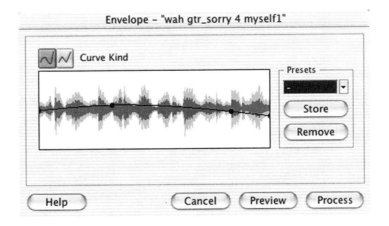

Fade-in and Fade-out Processes

The controls in the fade-in and fade-out processes are identical to the auto fade controls described earlier. The only difference is that fade processes are saved with the audio in a new file. You can apply this process using the Fade options available in the Process menu, rather than using the fade envelopes on events and regions in the Project window.

Gain Process

The Gain process adds or removes gain from the currently selected object or objects. Moving the slider to the right adds gain, whereas moving the slider to the left reduces it. You can also enter the desired amount of gain in the Gain field by typing in the appropriate value. When clicking the Preview button, Cubase indicates if this gain change causes the object to clip (digital distortion), as displayed in Figure 10.10. If this occurs, reduce the gain until Cubase displays "No Clip Detected."

How To

To apply a Gain process to a selected object:

1. Select the desired object.
2. Select the Gain process from the Process option in the Audio menu.
3. Make the appropriate adjustments in the dialog box.
4. To store or remove a preset, click the Store or Remove buttons.
5. To preview the result, click the Preview button. You can make changes to the envelope as you are previewing. To stop the preview, click the Stop button.
6. When satisfied with the settings, click the Process button. Click Cancel if you want to cancel the process.

Figure 10.10
The Gain process dialog box.

Merge Clipboard Process

This process merges the audio content that has been previously copied to the clipboard with the currently selected object. Besides the Pre- and Post-CrossFade options available under the More button of this dialog box, the Merge Clipboard process (see Figure 10.11) specifies a mix ratio between the audio selected for processing and the audio on the clipboard through a percentage slider. On the left side, you can see the proportion of the original (selected) object and on the right side, the proportion of the audio previously copied in the clipboard.

How To

To merge the content of the clipboard with a selected object:

1. Select the desired object.
2. Select the Merge Clipboard process from the Process option in the Audio menu. This implies that you have previously selected audio in the Sample Editor and have copied this content to the clipboard.
3. Make the appropriate adjustments in the dialog box. To preview the result, click the Preview button.
4. When satisfied with the settings, click the Process button.

CHAPTER 10

Figure 10.11
The Merge Clipboard process dialog box.

Noise Gate Process

The Noise Gate process (see Figure 10.12) removes sound from an audio signal that is below a threshold level by muting it. Imagine a gate that opens when a signal is strong enough (above threshold) and closes when the signal is not strong enough (below threshold). You can use this to silence portions of an audio signal during silent passage. For example, you can use a noise gate to remove a guitar amplifier's humming noise from a recording during passages where the guitar player is not playing. A noise gate does not remove the noise when the guitarist is playing because the signal will most likely be loud enough to pass the threshold, but the noise at that point should be less noticeable because it blends in with the guitar sound. If the noise level is too loud even when the guitarist is playing, you should consider using a noise reduction plug-in or rerecording this part.

The attack time represents the time it takes for the gate to open, letting the sound through, and the release time represents the time it takes for the gate to close after the signal goes below the threshold level. The minimum opening time defines the minimum amount of time the signal has to be over the threshold before the gate can close again.

How To

To apply a Noise Gate process to a selected object:

1. Select the desired object.
2. Select the Noise Gate process from the Process option in the Audio menu.
3. Make the appropriate adjustments in the dialog box. To preview the result, click the Preview button. If the signal you are processing is stereo, you can select the Linked Channels check box to determine how the Noise Gate process will treat the signal.
4. When satisfied with the settings, click the Process button.

Figure 10.12

The Noise Gate process dialog box.

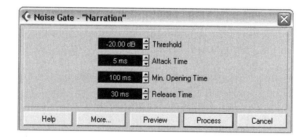

Normalize Process

Normalizing an audio signal affects its overall amplitude level by adjusting its highest peak to the value set in the Normalize process dialog box. It is similar to the Gain process in the sense that it acts on the level of the signal, but instead of calculating the level generally, it brings these levels up in proportion to the highest peak found in the signal, making sure that there is no clipping in the signal as a result of the level change. You can set the level value you want to assign to the highest peak level in this object by adjusting the slider or entering a value in the Maximum field.

How To

To apply a Normalize process to a selected object:

1. Select the desired object.
2. Select the Normalize process from the Process option in the Audio menu.
3. Make the appropriate adjustments in the dialog box (see Figure 10.13). To preview the result, click the Preview button.
4. When satisfied with the settings, click the Process button.

Figure 10.13
The Normalize process
dialog box.

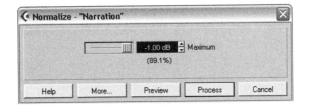

Phase Reverse Process

Reversing a phase does not change the shape of a sound file, but it changes the direction this shape takes. For example, the slopes going up will now go down and vice versa. When you mix different sound files, phase cancellation can occur. This produces a hollow sound. Inverting the waveform on one of the files can prevent this phase cancellation from occurring. In other words, if the phase of the current audio file does not sound correct, changing the direction of the phase might fix the problem. A good way to detect this problem is to occasionally monitor the audio in mono. If you can barely hear the signal, then you might have phase cancellation occurring. In Cubase, you can reverse the phase of both channels in a stereo file, or only one or the other. You should preview the result before applying this process.

How To

To apply a Phase Reverse process to a selected object:

1. Select the desired object.
2. Select the Phase Reverse process from the Process option in the Audio menu.
3. Make the appropriate adjustments in the dialog box (see Figure 10.14). To preview the result, click the Preview button. Note that this dialog box will not appear if you are processing a mono audio file.
4. When satisfied with the settings, click the Process button.

Figure 10.14
The Phase Reverse
process dialog box.

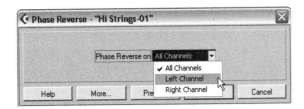

Pitch Shift Process

The Pitch Shift process changes the pitch of a selected object throughout the duration of this object or applies a change of pitch that varies through time by using an envelope to determine when the pitch is shifted upwards or downwards.

At the top of the Transpose tab (see Figure 10.15), you will find a keyboard layout that can help you set the relationship between the pitch of the original audio content and the pitch-shifted one. In this example, the original content played a pitch equivalent to D3, so the pitch shift base area is set to D3, making this note appear red on the keyboard display. Clicking another note changes the pitch shift settings automatically to match the value needed to get this pitch. In this case, B2 is pressed and displayed in blue on the keyboard. If you want to create a multivoice effect, creating several pitch shifts simultaneously, you can enable the Multi Shift option, which adds other notes to the process. Remember that the base note, unless selected as a shifted note as well, will not be part of the multishifted signal. You can use the Listen Key or Listen Chord button to hear the notes you selected.

The Pitch Shift Mode area sets accuracy values. For example, moving the accuracy slider toward the left favors sound quality over rhythmic accuracy. Moving it toward the right does the opposite. In other words, the content being shifted determines how this setting should be applied. If you are shifting vocal content, you should check the Formant Mode option, which helps to keep the qualities associated with voice when shifting it. The Algorithm drop-down menu offers three types of algorithms in Cubase SL and a fourth type in Cubase SX (MPEX Algorithm). When you want to preview the result, you should use the Mode 1 algorithm and avoid the MPEX algorithm because it is not designed to preview pitch shifting in real time. However, when processing to file, you should always use the best quality possible (better quality algorithms only take longer to process).

The Time Correction option changes the pitch without changing the time it takes to play the shifted content. If this option is not selected, events shifted upwards play faster and events shifted downwards play slower.

Figure 10.15
The Pitch Shift process'
Transpose tab.

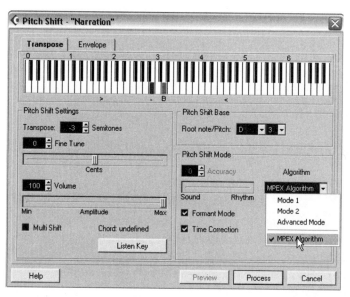

Clicking the Envelope tab at the top of the dialog box reveals the envelope settings for this process (see Figure 10.16). Using an envelope rather than a keyboard changes how the audio is shifted through time. In this example, the Pitch Shift Setting's Range field is set to two semitones, which means that at the top of the display area, events are shifted upward by this amount and downward at the bottom. The Transpose value setting represents the currently selected handle's value. In this case, the area found under the cursor, and from that point forward is transposed upwards by two semitones. So, using these settings, the pitch shift transposes the first portion of the audio two semitones below the current note at the beginning of the object, and halfway through pitch shifts two semitones above the current note played by the original file. The Pitch Shift Mode options are identical to the Transpose tab. Notice, however, that the accuracy settings are not available in both tabs when the MPEX Algorithm is selected.

Figure 10.16
The Pitch Shift process'
Envelope tab.

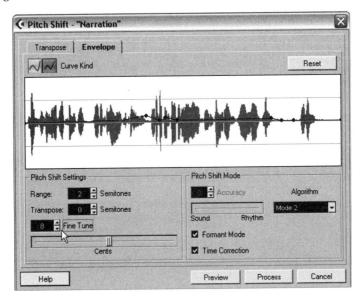

How To

To apply a Pitch Shift process to a selected object:

1. Select the desired object.
2. Select the Pitch Shift process from the Process option in the Audio menu.
3. Make the appropriate adjustments in the dialog box. To preview the result, click the Preview button.
4. When satisfied with the settings, click the Process button.

DC Offset, Reverse, and Silence Processes

These three processes offer very different results; however, they do not offer any settings. The purpose of the DC Offset process was explained earlier in this chapter in the "Spectrum Analyzer and Statistics" section. This process removes any offset that might be present in your audio signal. If you have SX, it might be a good idea to look at the statistics of a file. If you need to remove a DC offset, run the process on the file. The Reverse process simply reverses the data horizontally, making it sound as if it is playing backwards. The Silence process brings all the samples in a selection to a zero value, creating an absolute digital silence.

Stereo Flip Process

The Stereo Flip process (see Figure 10.17) can be applied on stereo objects only because it manipulates the stereo channels of the selected object. You have four modes available in this process, which are available in the Mode field. For example, you can merge both channels together to create a mono sounding file, or subtract the left channel from the right channel to get a karaoke-like effect.

How To

To apply a Stereo Flip process to a selected object:

1. Select the desired object.
2. Select the Stereo Flip process from the Process option in the Audio menu.
3. Make the appropriate adjustments in the dialog box. To preview the result, click the Preview button.
4. When satisfied with the settings, click the Process button.

Figure 10.17
The Stereo Flip process dialog box.

Time Stretch Process

Time stretching changes the duration of a selected object without changing the pitch or rhythmic integrity. In the Time Stretch process dialog box (shown in Figure 10.18), there are several ways you can attain that goal.

In the Input area, you will see information on the selected object, such as the Length in Samples field, Length in Seconds field, and a field where you can enter the tempo in BPM if you know it. You can also enter the number of bars and time signature. So, if you want to know the BPM (beats per minute), you can listen to the segment, count how many bars and beats pass, and enter the time signature of the event. Cubase calculates the tempo automatically. You can then use the Output area to determine the result of the Time Stretch process.

Let's look at some practical examples. If you want to change the tempo of a drum loop by using this process, you need to find out how many bars are in the loop as well as the loop's time signature of the selected audio content. Then enter the new BPM in the Output area's BPM field. This also determines the correct amount of samples, seconds, and range this new processed file will cover. If you are preparing a TV jingle and your spot has to be exactly 29.5 seconds, you can enter this amount in the Output area's Seconds field. Now, let's say your current object is just short of a five-bar area, between Bars 12 and 17. If you want it to cover this range, set the locators to Bars

12 and 17, select the object, and apply the Time Stretch process. When this dialog box opens, click the Set to Locators Range button to enter this value as the output length (five bars in this case).

This process changes the quality of the audio to a certain degree. The more time stretching you apply, the worse your result is. Optimally, you should stick within a plus or minus ten percent range; otherwise, you might hear some undesirable artifacts in the sound. In fact, if you don't select the Effect check box found to the right of the Time Stretch percentage, you can only apply a plus or minus 25 percent change. If, on the other hand, you want to create an effect, check this option to change the factor anywhere between 10 and 1,000 percent.

As with the pitch shifting process, you can adjust the focus of the accuracy toward the sound quality or the rhythmic accuracy. The algorithms used also influence the end result. Higher algorithms take more time to process but yield better results. You will also find an algorithm specifically designed for drum tracks.

On the other hand, if you are trying to adjust the tempo of an audio drum loop to match your project's tempo, you might want to consider using hitpoints to create slices in the Sample Editor. You will find more about this in the next chapter.

Figure 10.18
The Time Stretch process
dialog box.

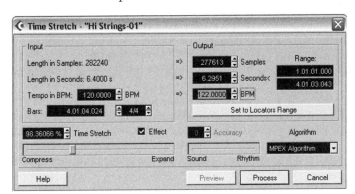

How To

To apply a Time Stretch process to a selected object:

1. Select the desired object.
2. Select the Time Stretch process from the Process option in the Audio menu.
3. Make the appropriate adjustments in the dialog box. To preview the result, click the Preview button.
4. When satisfied with the settings, click the Process button.

Using VST and DirectX Plug-Ins

VST or DirectX (PC version only) plug-in effects, as you saw earlier in this book, can be added as an insert, or used as a send effect through an FX Channel track. When doing so, you are processing the audio in real time, as described at the beginning of the section discussing audio processing options. You can also apply VST or DirectX plug-in effects available on your computer to a file directly if you want to affect only a portion of a track or if you don't want to add an additional load on your computer's processor.

Remember that when you apply one of these effects to a selected object, the processed result is saved in a special file, leaving your original file intact. This new file is seamlessly integrated into your project. In other words, you won't even feel or see it's a different file, besides the fact that this portion is processed.

Because VST and DirectX plug-in effects vary from one computer to another, we will not discuss the specific settings of these plug-ins, but understand that you can use these effects in an offline process (non-realtime) the same way as you would use them in an online process (realtime). The only difference is that you can't automate changes in the effect during the offline processing time.

How To

To add a plug-in effect to a selected object:

1. Select the desired object.
2. Select the desired plug-in from the Plug-ins submenu in the Audio menu (see Figure 10.19). DirectX effects are available under the DirectX submenu.
3. Make the appropriate adjustments in the dialog box. To preview the result, click the Preview button.
4. When satisfied with the settings, click the Process button.

Figure 10.19
The Plug-ins submenu options; the More Plug-ins submenu holds additional plug-ins when the current submenu can't display them all.

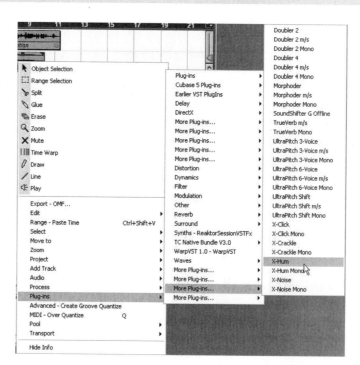

Optimizing Projects After Processing

When you process several files using offline processes, a number of additional files are created on your hard disk in the Edit folder. These files are necessary to preserve the original audio clip intact while providing the option to change an applied process. For example, as described earlier in this chapter, you can change the settings of a process, or with Cubase SX, you can also change the parameters or replace a process with another process. For each offline process line created in the Offline Process History dialog box of a selected object, there exists an equal number of processed files representing the portion of this object that has been processed on your hard disk. This makes it very convenient, but you should also realize that asking Cubase to move back and forth from one file to another and managing several tracks with multiple edited portions costs you in overall performance.

If you start noticing that your performance meter for the CPU or the hard disk starts to creep up, causing Cubase to feel slow or unresponsive, you should consider performing the following steps to help get things back to a more fluid working environment:

▶ Use the Save Project to New Folder option in the File menu. When Cubase prompts you to enter a name for the new project's version, make sure to check all the options in the Save to Folder Options dialog box (see Figure 10.20). The *Minimize Audio Files* option will copy only the used portions of audio files used from the Pool in the Project to the new folder. For example, if you've only used 30 seconds of a 2-minute recording, only this 30 seconds will be copied over. The Freeze Edits renders a new version of the audio events with all the edits currently found in the Offline Process History dialog box for each event that has been processed up until now, while the Remove Unused Files option will not save events that are not used in the Project, even if they are found in the Pool.

Figure 10.20
The Save to Folder
Options dialog box.

▶ If you don't want to save your entire project to a new folder, you can select audio events that contain the most editing done through offline processes and choose the Freeze Edits from the Audio menu. Cubase asks you if you want to create a new file or replace the existing one. Choose the appropriate option. Either way, this improves the performance because Cubase doesn't have to skip from one file to another.

▶ Make sure that your disk is defragmented regularly to avoid slowing down your computer because of inefficient disk reading caused by fragmented files.

Freezing VSTi

While we are on the subject of project optimization, new to Cubase is the Instrument Freeze function, which you might have noticed in the VST Instrument panel (F11). If you like trying different things while you are composing, chances are you might also load up your memory with VSTi instances, which play small parts here and there in your project. This is what makes using Cubase such a great experience. What's not so great is when you run out of resources and your computer starts its, "I've had enough" routine, crackling the sound, jerking playback and other related computer behaviors.

The Instrument Freeze will create a temporary audio render of the VSTi for all MIDI events routed through the selected VSTi you chose to freeze. As a result, the MIDI track becomes locked from editing and muted, the VSTi unloads from memory, and Cubase creates a special audio rendering corresponding to the result of the MIDI events going through the VSTi. This offers the advantage of hearing what you heard before: MIDI events playing through a VSTi without the resource real estate required by VSTi. The frozen audio will not appear in the project as a separate audio channel, but will continue to be controlled in the Mixer panel through its VSTi channel. So, any volume, EQ, or routing will continue to have an effect on the sound. If you want to change something in the MIDI track, you can unfreeze the VSTi, change the MIDI, and refreeze again.

This is by no means the most efficient way to work, but it does offer a solution for those of us trying to get the most out of our computers before purchasing a new one with more horsepower. Once a VSTi is unfrozen, the freeze file is removed from its special Freeze folder, which can be found inside the project's main folder. Note that parts that are muted will not be frozen. In other words, the result of a freeze, in terms of what you hear, is identical to the VSTi generating the sounds in real time.

How To

To freeze a VSTi:

1. Bring up the VSTi panel (F11).
2. Click on the Freeze button next to the desired VSTi in the list (see Figure 10.21). Cubase will create the audio render. This might take anywhere from a few seconds to a few minutes, depending on the complexity of the process and computer resources available.

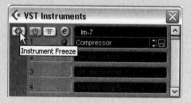

Figure 10.21
The Freeze button in the VST Instrument panel.

To unfreeze a VSTi, press on the Freeze button once more.

When a VSTi is frozen, the Freeze button will appear orange, and you won't be able to make any changes to the MIDI tracks being sent to this VSTi.

The Offline Process History Panel

When you apply a process to an audio object or a portion of an object through offline processing, an entry is made in this event's Offline Process History panel. Remember that offline processes mean that the effect is not calculated during playback (online), but when the project is stopped (offline). Each process is displayed on its own row. You can decide to modify the settings of a process if it's available.

For example, you can select the Normalize process and change the amount of normalizing within this process. If a process does not have any parameters to modify, such as the Reverse process, for example, clicking the Modify button simply displays a warning telling you this process cannot be modified. You can also replace one process with another. For instance, you can select the Reverse process and select another process in the drop-down menu below the Replace by button. This brings up the new process' dialog box. Once replaced, the old process is removed from the list, and the new process takes its place. Before letting you replace a process, Cubase asks you if this is what you really want to do. Finally, you can remove a process from the list by selecting it and clicking the Remove button, no matter where it is in this list, as long as you haven't applied resampling or time stretching processes which affect the overall number of samples (and ultimately this event's position in the Project). For example, in a list of four offline processes, you can select the third one and change it without affecting the first or second one. The forth will be updated accordingly.

If you have the SX version, you can also use the Offline Process History panel with any plug-in effect (VST or DirectX). This means that you can apply any kind of offline process from the plug-ins installed on your computer and cancel or modify the parameters inside that plug-in.

There is only one instance in which it is not possible to remove a process: If you change the length of an audio clip through time stretching, cutting, deleting, or copy/pasting, you can only remove or modify this process if it is the last one in the list. In this case, this is indicated in the Status column (see the Delete action in Figure 10.22).

Figure 10.22
The Offline Process
History panel.

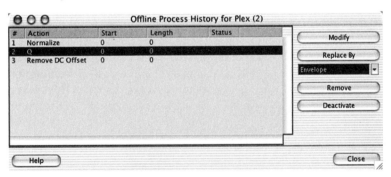

How To

> **To modify, replace, or remove an action from the Offline Process History panel:**
>
> 1. Select the event containing offline processes you want to modify.
> 2. From the Audio menu, select the Offline Process History option.
> 3. Select the process you want to modify (A), replace (B), or remove (C).
> 4a. Click the Modify button and edit the parameters inside the Process' dialog box and then click the Process button to update the Offline Process History panel.
> 4b. Select the new process you want to use instead of the currently selected one in the drop-down menu below the Replace by button, click the Replace by button, make the necessary adjustments in the Process' dialog box, and click Process to update the Offline Process History panel.
> 4c. Click the Remove button to remove this process from the list.
> 5. When you have completed modifying, replacing, or removing the processes, click the Close button.

Because the history of each offline process is saved with the object affected, you still have access to this history after you close Cubase and reload the project into memory. This is not the case for the Edit History panel described in the next section.

The Edit History Panel

When you apply a transformation, such as deleting an object, moving, and so on, each action is saved in a list, allowing you to undo several actions. You can do this by using the Undo function in the Edit menu if you only have a few steps to undo; however, if you want to look at all the steps and undo a whole bunch in one go, you can use the Edit History panel, which is also found under the Edit menu (see Figure 10.23).

This panel displays the actions on the left and the target object for this action on the right. The latest actions appear at the top of the list, whereas the earliest actions appear at the bottom. The panel is separated by a blue line. Clicking on this line and dragging it down creates a selection. All the actions that are included in this selection will be undone. This means that you can undo from the last edit to the first one, unlike in the Offline Process History panel, in which you can edit any action in the list.

You should know that when you save and close your project, the Edit History panel is reset and is not available until you start editing again. However, only saving your document without closing it keeps this list available.

Figure 10.23
The Edit History panel.

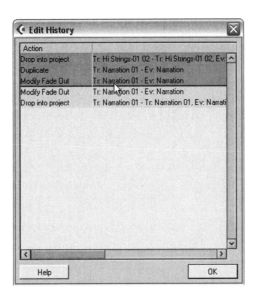

Now You Try It

For information about using the instructions found in this section and to find out where you can get the working files, please consult the section called *About the Exercise Files* in the Introduction section.

11

Project Editing

The Project window is your main working area. This area is where you record audio and MIDI events and edit different track parameters through the Inspector or Track List area. However, the Event Display area is where you will do most of your editing tasks. When you can't do it in there, that's when you open an editor to fine-tune these editing decisions.

Because the editing capabilities of Cubase are quite extensive, you need to understand that the options available at any given time depend on the context itself. In most cases, this context is determined by the selection or the window in which you are working. For example, if you select a part, the Dissolve Part option is available but the Events to Part option is not. When you select an event, the Dissolve Part option is not available, but the Events to Part option is.

There are different ways to select what you want in the Project window. When you want to select objects, you can use the Object Selection tool; when you want to select a range, you can use the Range Selection tool. In some cases, you can use items found in the Select submenu options (Edit > Select). For example, you can use the Select from Cursor to End option, which selects all objects crossing the cursor's location or appearing after it in the Project window.

Here's a summary of what you will learn in this chapter:

▶ What are the differences between destructive and nondestructive editing?

▶ How to work with the different zooming functions, menus, and tools.

▶ What are the differences between MIDI functions and MIDI parameters?

▶ What are the differences between audio events, regions, and parts?

▶ How to work with fade envelopes attached to objects in the Project window.

▶ What can you do with the audio objects in your Project window?

▶ How to edit events and parts inside the Event Display area of the Project window.

▶ How the Audio Part Editor works and what is its relation to the Project window?

CHAPTER 11

Destructive and Nondestructive Editing

Sometimes, we get musical ideas that require us to take risks or try things out, and listen to them see how they sound. If you don't like it, it's nice to be able to put things back the way they were. If only life could be so easy! Most of us have used the Undo command time and time again. When you are typing an e-mail to a friend, you can undo operations many times over until you get it right. However, if you save the e-mail, open it later to change things, and save it once more, you are replacing the original e-mail with the new one unless you saved the new version under another name.

Working with audio files is quite similar in the sense that a Cubase project offers you a way to reorganize the information inside the application without affecting the saved data on the disk. Furthermore, Cubase, unlike an e-mail text file, doesn't even change the content of the files it refers to unless you specifically tell it to. If you applied the same philosophy to editing e-mails, you'd have a document with text that doesn't change, but you could place this text anywhere you wanted inside the actual e-mail and then save the layout of the e-mail separately. In Cubase, the media files are called *clips*. These clips are on the hard disk inside a project subfolder appropriately called *Audio*. When you save a project file, the project itself does not contain the audio, but merely a link to the original audio clip. When you split an audio event and place it somewhere else, you are changing the reference points found in the project file to the audio clip, but you are still not editing or transforming the original clip in any way. The same applies for effects or volume changes you might add to a project; all of these transformations do not affect the original audio file. This type of editing is referred to as *nondestructive editing*.

If we push the editing further and decide to apply a time stretch, a normalize, or fade out to a portion of an audio clip, Cubase still does not touch the original content of the file because it creates additional files in another folder inside your project folder. If this is not enough to convince you that Cubase is a completely nondestructive environment, you can also use multiple undo levels through the History option in the Edit menu. In addition, the Offline Process History in the Edit menu allows you to select processing you applied to an audio file—let's say seven steps ago—and edit the parameters of that processing without affecting the other six steps you did after that.

Destructive editing, on the other hand, has one advantage: It requires less space. Whenever you are working on large files, every processed audio bit in your project remains unless you decide to clean up the audio through another function called *Remove Unused Media*, which is discussed later. Keep in mind that a project can grow quickly, and you should prepare sufficient hard disk space when working with a digital audio multitrack project using high resolution recordings. If space is not an issue, then enjoy the benefits of working in an environment that allows you to undo steps that led your music in the wrong direction and to take creative risks with the audio files you record.

Working with Events, Regions, and Parts

As mentioned earlier in this chapter and in Chapter 6, Cubase uses different levels of audio references. The basic recording is saved as an audio file, which is referred to as an *audio clip* inside Cubase. An audio event is automatically created in your Project window once the recording is completed. Cubase can also create regions, which are portions of an audio clip that you can reuse somewhere else in a project. You can also convert audio events into a region or a part. Because regions can be reused elsewhere and parts can contain more than one region or event, making it easy to move a number of events at a time, you might find it easier in certain instances to convert your events into regions or parts. All three types of audio objects offer different editing properties when placed on a track. Table 11.1 takes a look at how different these objects are.

Table 11.1
Differences between events, regions, and part objects on an audio track

Events	Regions	Parts
You can modify the length of an event on a track, but you can't extend the event beyond the limit of the file it refers to.	You can modify the length of a region on a track and can extend it beyond the limits of the region itself but not beyond the limit of the clip the region refers to.	You can extend the boundaries of a part as much as you want because a part does not refer to a particular audio clip, event, or region.
Audio events have envelopes (fade in, sustain level, fade out). You can use these envelopes to control the level of the event. The envelope is locked with the event, so when you move the event, the envelope follows.	Audio regions also have envelopes (fade in, sustain level, fade out). You can use these envelopes to control the level of the event (see Figure 11.1). The envelope is locked with the region, so when you move it, the envelope follows.	Audio parts do not have envelopes associated with them, but the events and regions they contain have individual envelopes that can be edited inside the Audio Part Editor.
The default editing window for events is the Sample Editor.	The default editing window for events is the Sample Editor.	The default editing window for events is the Audio Part Editor.
On an audio track, you can convert an event into a region or a part using the Events to Part option found in the Audio menu.	On an audio track, you can convert a region into a part using the Events to Part option found in the Audio menu. Also, if you have resized an object beyond the original region's boundaries, you can bring back the object to its original region's size using the Events From Region option found in the Audio menu.	You can dissolve an audio part containing several events and regions to create independent objects on a track using the Dissolve Part option found in the Audio menu.

Figure 11.1
Comparing audio events
(top), audio parts
(middle), and audio
regions (bottom).

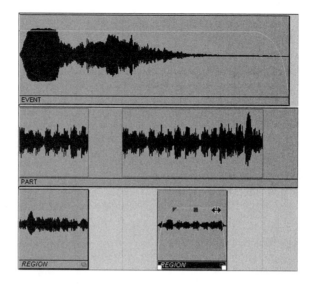

Changing Your Focus

Moving around in a project, finding what you want to edit, focusing on the task at hand, and then looking at the project in a more global perspective is as much a part of your work as editing MIDI and audio events themselves. Changing your display and opening and closing windows is unfortunately part of the computer-based musician's reality. Having two monitors side by side, displaying different parts of your desktop helps, but this is not always a feasible solution. That's why it's important when you work on a project, to know, understand, and use shortcuts that can quickly change your visual perspective to fit the task at hand inside a project.

Fortunately, Cubase offers many options in this respect, allowing you to get to what you need in different ways. The idea is not necessarily to use all these techniques, but to find out what is possible and to use a working method that makes it easy for you to quickly perform necessary tasks.

Using the Overview Panel

While the event display area in the Project window allows you to view your project from start to finish, most of the time, you will need to zoom in closer to have greater accuracy over the editing process. The Overview panel gives you a way to always keep an eye on the entire project and the relation of the current event display within the project, and this works, no matter what your Project window's zoom level. When you click the Overview button in the Project window's toolbar, a white bar spanning the entire length of the Project window appears. The total amount of time displayed in this overview depends on the Project's length value, which you can change in the Project Setup dialog box. This bar contains, from left to right, the "mini me" version of your project, tracks, events, or parts on these tracks. Besides displaying the content of your project, a blue box indicates the portion of the project currently visible in the Event Display area of the Project window. You can use this box to navigate throughout your project.

How To

To navigate using the overview rectangle:

1. To draw a rectangle anywhere in the Overview panel, click and drag your mouse in the upper half of the display as illustrated by the number 1 in Figure 11.2. Your cursor should represent an arrow when trying to do this. The size of the rectangle determines the content displayed in the Event Display area.

2. To move the position of the rectangle without changing its size, click and drag inside the lower half of the blue rectangle as illustrated by the number 2 in Figure 11.2. The zoom level remains the same; however, you can use this technique to scroll in time throughout your project.

3. To resize the left or right border of the rectangle, causing the content to zoom in (when you reduce the box) or zoom out (when you enlarge the box), click and drag in the lower half of the left or right edge of the rectangle, as illustrated by the number 3 in Figure 11.2.

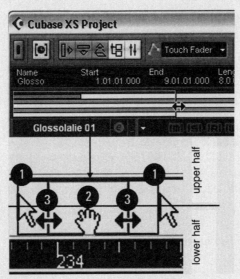

Figure 11.2
The Overview panel functions explained.

Using Cycle Markers

In Chapter 4, you saw that it was possible to navigate through a project by using markers and cycle markers. You also saw how you could use cycle markers in the drop-down menu found on the left of the horizontal zoom bar to fit the content found within a cycle marker inside the Event Display area. This is one way of traveling from one end of your project to another quickly, while at the same time focusing on the content you want to edit.

CHAPTER 11

Using the Zoom Tools

When it comes to zooming options, Cubase does not leave you out in the cold. There are a number of ways you can control the content displayed on your screen by using the different tools at your disposal. Here's a look at these options. Note that each number in the list corresponds to the number in Figure 11.3.

How To

To zoom into your work using the appropriate tool:

1. The Zoom tool. Allows you to zoom into the area found within the rectangle you draw on the screen using this tool. Begin by selecting this tool from the Project window's toolbar and then click and drag a rectangle around the area you want to zoom into. Holding down the Ctrl(PC)/⌘(Mac) key while using the Zoom tool can zoom vertically and horizontally at the same time.

2. The Event and Content Vertical Zoom bar. Allows you to adjust the vertical axis of the content found inside the events or parts. Drag the handle up to make the events spread out within the event or part's vertical boundary, or drag the handle down to reduce the vertical space these events take within the event or part's vertical boundary.

3. The Zoom context menu. Displays a variety of zooming options. (The Zoom submenu is found by right-clicking in the Event Display area and pointing to the Zoom option.)

4. The Vertical Zoom menu. Enables you to set your zoom level to a number of tracks or rows. Selecting the Zoom Tracks N Rows or Zoom N Tracks brings up a dialog box in which you can type in the number of tracks you want to fit in your Event Display area. This menu is available by clicking on the downward pointing arrow found between the vertical scrollbar and the vertical Zoom bar.

5. The Vertical Zoom bar. Allows you to zoom in or out vertically, affecting the height of tracks in your Event Display area. You can either drag the handle in the Zoom bar to get the desired height for each track or click on the arrows above and below to increase or decrease by one row at a time.

6. The Horizontal Zoom bar. Allows you to zoom in or out horizontally (in time). You can either drag the handle in the Zoom bar to get the desired time frame inside the Event Display area or click the left or right arrows to increase or decrease by the time frame one step at a time.

7. The Horizontal Zoom menu. Enables you to select a cycle marker and zoom into it or save a zoom level as a preset that you can recall later. For example, you can create two states, one for a larger perspective and another for a more detailed look at events or parts on your timeline. Then you can use this menu to toggle between the two (or more) zoom settings. Use the Add option to save the current zoom state to memory and the Organize option to manage the items available in this menu. This menu is available by clicking on the downward pointing arrow found between the horizontal scrollbar and the horizontal Zoom bar.

8. The Ruler bar. Allows you to zoom in or out by clicking and dragging your mouse. Click in the lower half of the Ruler bar and drag your mouse down to zoom in or drag your mouse up to zoom out, drag your mouse to the left to move back in time or right to move forward in time. Your zoom always centers on the position of your mouse in the ruler.

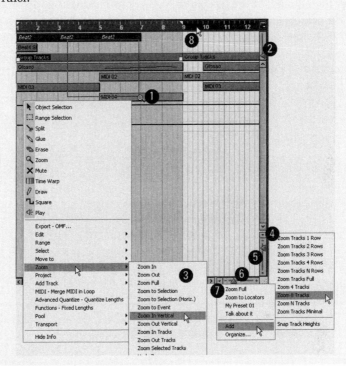

Figure 11.3
The various zoom controls.

CHAPTER 11

MIDI Menu Options

The MIDI menu is divided into five sections. The first one allows you to open different types of editing windows. The second one was discussed previously in this chapter and relates to quantizing. The fourth section relates mostly to the logical editor functions which are described in Appendix C. The last section is basically a MIDI reset function, which acts as a panic button on a MIDI patch bay, sending out *All Notes Off* and *Reset Controllers* messages on all MIDI output ports and channels. You can use this when you experience stuck notes after recording, playing, or editing a track. This leaves us with the central section, which relates to MIDI-specific functions.

Transpose

The Transpose option in the MIDI menu allows you to transpose selected MIDI events. Unlike the Transpose field in the Inspector area, this option changes the MIDI note numbers. In other words, after you transpose MIDI events using this option, you actually see the transposition in the different MIDI Editors. You can also use this option when you want to transpose only a certain number of events in a part or on a track rather than transposing an entire track using the track parameter setting or a MIDI effect.

Another difference between the Transpose option found in the MIDI menu and the one found in the Track Parameter section in the Inspector area is that you can define a lower and upper barrier for your transposition. When doing so, you tell Cubase that notes above or below a certain value are outside of the desired transposed range possibility, so Cubase transposes the notes that are outside this range in a way that makes them fit inside the range. This is done by octave-shifting these notes. If you look at the example in Figure 11.4, you will notice that a two-semitone transposition will occur and that the Keep Notes in Range option is checked. This makes it possible to set a note value in the upper and lower barrier fields. If the events you want to transpose contain a G6, for example, this note is transposed one octave down, then two semitones up, resulting in an A5 rather than an A6.

Figure 11.4
The MIDI menu
Transpose dialog box.

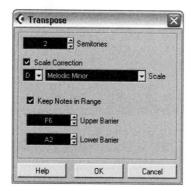

How To

To transpose selected events using the MIDI Transpose option:

1. Select the MIDI part, parts, or events inside a MIDI part you want to transpose.

2. From the MIDI menu, select the Transpose option.

3. In the Transpose dialog box (see Figure 11.4), set the number of semitones you want to transpose by using the up or down arrows on the right of the field. If you have a mouse with a scroll wheel, you can click on the number in the field and scroll your wheel up to increase or scroll your wheel down to decrease the value of semitones.

4. If you want to keep the notes within a specific range, check the appropriate check box option, and then set the lower and higher barrier range. Note that if your range is too narrow, some notes will not be transposed with the correct pitch.

5. Click OK to apply your changes.

MIDI Merge In Loop

Now let's say you've applied different MIDI effects to a track as inserts or sends; you've also assigned different track parameter values to a MIDI part. When trying to edit certain details, you realize that the details you want to edit are played in real time by the various settings you have assigned to this track. If you want to merge these effects with the MIDI track and create a new version of the MIDI events that contains an editable set of MIDI parameters based on the result of the MIDI effects and parameters you've assigned, you can use the Merge In Loop option found in the MIDI menu. Here's an example: You've recorded a piano accompaniment and played certain chords. After recording these chords, you've applied the Track FX MIDI effect using a different scale. When listening back to your new chord coloring, you like the result, but you'd like to change a note in one of the chords so that it fits better with the rest of the arrangement. But because this is a real-time effect, you can't really change a note that you didn't play to begin with. That's when the merge MIDI In Loop option comes in handy. You will probably also want to merge the realtime MIDI effects with the recorded events before exporting MIDI parts to MIDI files so that you can use them in another application.

How To

To use the merge MIDI In Loop option:

1. Start by identifying the MIDI events you want to merge. This can be a MIDI part on one track or several MIDI parts on several tracks over several channels.

2. After you've identified what you want to merge (or freeze), set the left and right locators to include this content.

3. Mute any other MIDI track you don't want to include in this process.

4. If you want to keep the original content intact, create a new MIDI track.

5. If you have chosen to create a new MIDI track for the merged destination, select it in the Track List area; otherwise, select the desired destination track (this might be the same track as the original content).

6. From the MIDI menu, select the Merge MIDI In Loop option. The MIDI Merge Options dialog box appears as displayed in Figure 11.5.

Figure 11.5
The MIDI Merge Options dialog box.

7. You have three options to enable or disable. The Include Inserts and Include Sends options convert any MIDI messages generated by effects into editable MIDI messages in the new merged part. If you have selected a track that already contains MIDI events as a destination track, you can choose to erase this content by checking the Erase Destination option. If you do not check this option and there is already a part on the destination track, a new part appears on top of it.

8. Click OK after setting your options.

Dissolve Parts

Let's say you have a MIDI file that you want to import into Cubase. You do so by using the Import MIDI File option (described later in this chapter), only to realize that it contains only one track with all the different channel information and events on this single track. If you look at the example in Figure 11.6, the first track named "Original" contains MIDI events on three distinct channels. After applying the Dissolve function, three additional tracks appear below with the appropriate MIDI channel, program change, and corresponding MIDI events for each channel.

Figure 11.6
The first track has been dissolved into three tracks.

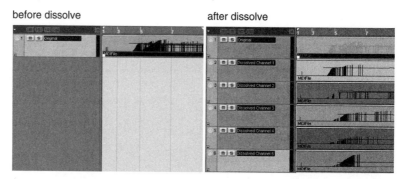

before dissolve   after dissolve

Similarly, you might record a drum pattern in cycle mode using the LM-7 VSTi drum, adding instruments to your pattern every time the cycle begins to get a full pattern. This is probably the simplest way of doing a drum pattern. But after all your instruments are recorded, they are all contained in the same part. If you want to assign a different MIDI effect on the snare drum, this could only be done if each instrument was played on a different channel. Because your drum is already recorded, you can use the Dissolve Part and select the Separate Pitches option instead of the Separate Channels option. In Figure 11.7, the first track corresponds to the original drum loop. The following tracks represent each pitch (in this case, an instrument of the drum kit). By assigning each instrument on a different channel, you can assign different MIDI effects to each piece of the drum kit while still using only one instance of the VSTi. This also allows you to render each MIDI track as a separate audio track so that each drum instrument can be treated independently.

Figure 11.7
An example of a dissolve by separating pitches.

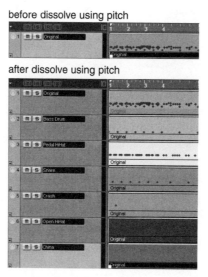

before dissolve using pitch

after dissolve using pitch

How To

To dissolve a MIDI part:

1. Select the MIDI part you want to dissolve.

2. In the MIDI menu, select the Dissolve Part option.

3. If you have more than one MIDI channel embedded in the selected part, Cubase offers you two choices: Separate Channels or Separate Pitches (see Figure 11.8). Select the appropriate option. On the other hand, if there is only one MIDI channel in the selected part, you can only separate pitches.

4. Click OK to continue.

Note that the original track is automatically muted after being dissolved.

Figure 11.8
The Dissolve Part dialog box.

O-Note Conversion

The concept of O-Note is directly related to drum maps; this function only becomes active when a MIDI part associated with a drum-mapped MIDI track is selected. Drum maps use three specific note names to identify a drum instrument: the pitch, the I-note (input note), and the O-note (output note). The pitch is associated with a drum instrument and cannot be modified. So a C1 can be associated with a kick drum, for example. The I-note is the note you play on your MIDI keyboard interface to trigger a specific instrument. In practice, playing a C1 note should trigger a kick drum because that's what is loaded. The O-note is the note sent out by the drum map. In theory, the I-note and the O-note are usually the same.

Why all these note names? Well, sometimes, you might want to reorganize which note triggers which instrument in order to lay out the drum kit more efficiently on your keyboard. This can make it easier, for example, to play a drum part on notes you are accustomed to using. That's when you start playing with the drum mapping, changing the I-note and O-note values. As long as your MIDI part plays this drum, you are fine, but if you want to convert this to a *non* drum-mapped track in order to export your file as a MIDI file, you need to convert the drum map appropriately so that the sound you hear corresponds to the output note played by the drum map. And that's when you need to use the O-note Conversion tool. This basically converts the MIDI note number values into whatever O-note mapping you have made, allowing you to play the part as a regular MIDI track while still hearing the appropriate sounds played by the drum kit it was meant for.

CHAPTER 11

How To

To perform an O-note conversion:

1. Select the MIDI part(s) associated with your drum map that you want to convert.
2. From the MIDI menu, select the O-Note Conversion option.
3. A warning message might appear; click Yes if you want to proceed anyway or Cancel if you are not sure this is what you want to do.

About MIDI Functions

The MIDI functions in the MIDI menu play a similar role to the MIDI track parameters. However, there are different reasons that would motivate you to use a MIDI function rather than a setting in the track parameters. For example, track parameters affect all events (parts) on a given track, whereas MIDI functions can be applied to selected parts in the Project window or selected events in a MIDI Editor window. Another example is that parameter settings do not show up in the MIDI Editor, whereas MIDI functions actually change the appropriate value in the MIDI message, making it visible in the MIDI Editor. In other words, if you want to try things out before committing to them, you can use the track parameters, but when you want to affect or change the MIDI events permanently, you are better off using the MIDI functions found in the MIDI menu.

In the MIDI Functions option found in the MIDI menu, you will find a submenu containing various functions. Most of these functions are self explanatory. For example, Delete Doubles deletes any MIDI events that are doubled (two notes playing at the same time and at the same pitch). Some of these functions display a dialog box, whereas others perform their task without needing additional input.

How To

To use a MIDI function:

1. In the Project window, select the parts you want to edit using the MIDI function, or double-click the MIDI part and select the events you want to edit if you don't want to affect all the events in the part.
2. From the MIDI menu, select the MIDI Functions option and then the appropriate MIDI function you want to apply.
3. Change the values needed in the dialog box if one shows up and click OK to complete; otherwise, the function is automatically applied.

Edit Menu Options

The editing options inside the Project window are available in one of two places: in the Edit menu or through the Project window's context menu in the Edit submenu. This is where you will find the basic Cut, Copy, and Paste options, which work the same way as in any other application. In addition, you will find other options specifically designed to give you more control over project editing tasks.

Splitting

When you want to divide objects in the Project window, you have several options at your disposal.

Using the Scissors tool, you can click on an existing event. The position of the split is determined by the Snap to Grid settings if it is active or by the location of your click. You can also use the cursor's position to determine where the split will occur.

How To

To split objects at the cursor's location:

1. Position the cursor at the desired location.
2. Select all the objects crossing the cursor at this location that you want to split. All nonselected objects will not be split.
3. From the Edit menu, select the Split at Cursor option.

If you want to quickly create a loop section with the objects (parts or events) between the locators, you can use the locators' position to determine where a split will occur. After these objects are split, for example, at Bar 5 and Bar 9, you can select only the objects that occur in this range and copy them elsewhere.

How To

To split objects at the locators' position:

1. Position the left and right locators at the desired position.
2. Select the objects you want to split.
3. From the Edit menu, select the Split Loop option. Selected objects crossing the left or right locators are split as displayed in Figure 11.9.

Figure 11.9
Using the Split Loop
option.

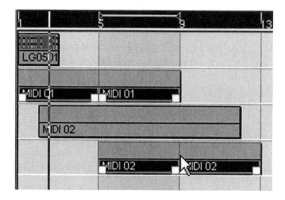

Another quick way to split objects is to use the Range Crop option. This option allows you to select a series of objects and remove the area that is outside of the selected objects in the range (see Figure 11.10).

Figure 11.10
A before and after look at
the Range Crop function
applied on a selected
range.

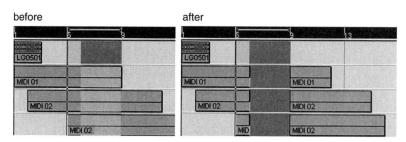

How To

To set the Range Crop function to a desired range:

1. Select the Range Selection tool.
2. Click in the upper-left corner where you want your range to begin and drag over the range and tracks you want to include in this range.
3. In the Edit menu, select the Range > Crop option.

Using the Range tool with the Split option, you can also achieve an effect similar to the Split Loop option. In this case, however, all the objects within the selected range would be split at the start and end position of this range.

How To

To split a range of selected objects:

1. Select the Range Selection tool.
2. Click in the upper-left corner where you want your range to begin and drag over the range and tracks you want to include in this range.
3. In the Edit menu, select the Range > Split option.

In other instances, you might want to insert an amount of time in the middle of recorded events, but don't want to have to select all the events and split them, and then move all the events after the split to a new location. This operation can be done in one easy step by using the Insert Silence option in the Edit > Range submenu. All the events in the selected range are split, and the objects crossing the start point of the range are split and then moved at the end point of this range (see Figure 11.11).

Figure 11.11
A before and after look at the Insert Silence option applied on a selected range.

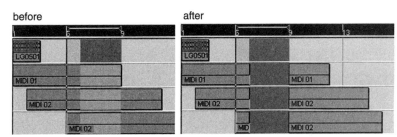

Inversely, if you want to remove the time, including events recorded within this range, you can use the Delete Range option from the Edit > Range submenu. This deletes events within a selected range and deletes the time, moving all events following the range to the start point of this range.

Still using the Range tool, you can copy the content found inside a range and paste it back into the project using the Paste Time or Paste Time at Origin. This is different than the regular Paste function because the Paste Time option pushes existing events forward, effectively adding the contents of the clipboard at the cursor's location, whereas the regular Paste function pastes the contents of the clipboard over any existing events. The Paste Time at Origin function works like the Paste Time, but pastes the contents of the clipboard at the original time it was copied from.

Duplicate

When you want to make a single copy of selected events or parts, you can use the Duplicate function from the Edit menu. This function works with the Object Selection or the Range Selection tools. The result varies depending on the objects you select or the range you select.

When using the Object Selection tool, duplicated events appear after the end point of the latest object selected. For example, looking at Figure 11.12, you can see that three parts were selected, ranging from Bar 1 to Bar 9. The duplicated events start at the closest snap grid location (if this option is active) after Bar 9.

CHAPTER 11

Figure 11.12
A before and after look at the Duplicate function while using the Object Selection tool to determine the duplicated content.

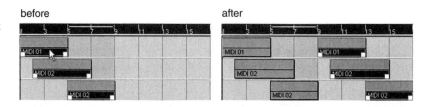

When using the Range Selection tool, only the portion found within the range is duplicated. This means that new events are created to conform to the selected range. In Figure 11.13, the events in the first and second track before the selection are not duplicated. Duplicate events from the selected range appear after the end point of the current range. In both cases (using a range or objects), if there are objects where the duplicated objects are suppose to be pasted, these events are left in place but overlap with the new content. So, you should make sure that there is no content where duplicated events will appear.

Figure 11.13
A before and after look at the Duplicate function while using the Range Selection tool to determine the duplicated content.

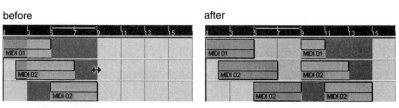

How To

To duplicate objects using the Object Selection or Range Selection tool:

1. Select the appropriate tool (Object Selection or Range Selection).
2. Select the objects or range you want to duplicate.
3. From the Edit menu, select the Duplicate option.

Repeat

If you want to make more than one duplicate copy of selected objects or a selected range of objects, you should use the Repeat option from the Edit menu. This is a great way to repeat looped material several times instead of copying it several times over. In this case, Cubase asks you how many copies you want to make of the selected objects or range. If you are repeating objects, you will also be asked if you want to create shared or real copies. Remember that when you edit one instance of a shared copy, all the subsequent instances share this editing. If you want to edit only one copy of the repeated material, you should either choose to create real copies or select the shared copy you want to edit and transform it into a real copy using the Edit > Convert To Real Copy option.

The Repeat option follows the same behavior as described in the Duplicate option. As you can see in Figure 11.14, selected events appear after the last end point of the selected objects. In Figure 11.15, the portion outside of the range is not repeated. Also, Cubase assumes you want to create real copies when you are using the Range tool to repeat this content.

Figure 11.14
A before and after look at the Repeat function while using the Object Selection tool to determine the repeated content.

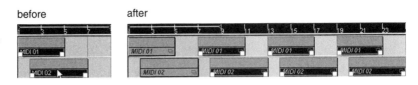

When using the Repeat function, you will also notice that the position of the left and right locators have no effect on the placement of the repeated material. On the other hand, the Snap Grid settings play a role on where your repeated objects appear if you have selected objects that do not start or end on bars.

Figure 11.15
A before and after look at the Repeat function while using the Range Selection tool to determine the repeated content.

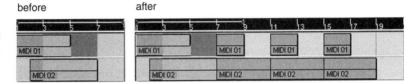

How To

To repeat selected objects or range over time:

1. Select the appropriate tool (Object Selection or Range Selection).
2. Select the objects or range you want to repeat.
3. From the Edit menu, select the Repeat option.
4. Enter the number of times you want this selection to be repeated.
5. If you have selected objects rather than a range, check the Shared Copies option if you want to do so.
6. Click OK.

Fill Loop

Another variation on copying events is offered through the Fill Loop option also found in the Edit menu. This option allows you to determine a cycle region between the left and right locators in which events will be repeated. If events cannot fit completely inside this area, the last copy is split (see example in Figure 11.16).

Figure 11.16
A before and after look at the Fill Loop function while using the Object Selection tool to determine the content that is repeated until the right locator's position.

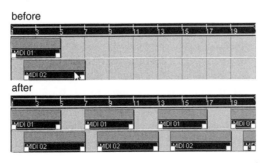

As with the Duplicate and Repeat options, you can also use the Range Selection tool to determine which range will be used to fill a loop section (see example in Figure 11.17). This is a great way of creating a section structure inside a project where all selected objects are repeated until they arrive at the right locator position.

Figure 11.17
A before and after look at the Fill Loop function while using the Range Selection tool to determine the content that is repeated until the right locator's position.

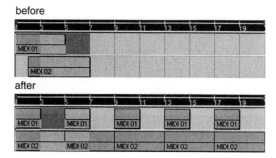

How To

To fill an area with selected objects using the Fill Loop option:

1. Select the appropriate tool (Object Selection or Range Selection).
2. Position your left and right locators to the desired locations where you want the fill to begin and end.
3. Select the objects or range you want to use in the fill.

ALTERNATE FILL OPTION
You can also copy a looping content in the Project window by dragging the lower-right corner handle of a part while holding down the Alt(PC)/Option(Mac) key. Each copy will snap to the end of the previous event/part. While holding down the Alt/Option key, the selection tool will turn into a pencil, indicating that the Fill option is active.

Normal Sizing

Different objects have different sizing restrictions. For example, you can resize an audio event, but not beyond the extremities to which the original audio clip refers. The same restriction goes for audio regions: You can expand the audio region's event in the Project window beyond this region's boundaries, but not beyond the original clip's boundaries. In terms of audio or MIDI parts, you have no restrictions because a part does not actually refer to any content; it only acts as a container for this content. This being said, you might want these objects to react differently to the sizing you apply. Normally, when you change an event by moving its start or end point, the content within the event stays in place and only the start or end points move, as illustrated in Figure 11.18. Moving the end of the MIDI part in this case (middle segment) moves the end point back in time, whereas moving the start point inward causes the events occurring before the new start point to be ignored during playback. But the events playing during Bar 3 in the original version are still playing at Bar 3 in the resized version.

Figure 11.18
Resizing an event using the Normal Sizing tool (which doubles as the Object Selection tool).

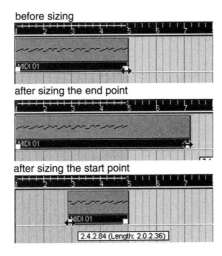

before sizing

after sizing the end point

after sizing the start point

2.4.2.84 (Length: 2.0.2.36)

How To

To resize objects (events or parts):

1. In the Project window's toolbar, select the Object Selection tool (a.k.a. Normal Sizing tool).
2. Select an object to view its resizing handles.
3. Move the handles in the desired direction.

CHAPTER 11

Sizing Moves Contents

In other instances, you may also want to move the content inside of the object (event or part) when resizing it. Looking at the top of Figure 11.19, you can see the original content. In the middle segment, the start point has been moved forward in time, but as you can see, the MIDI events displayed are the same at the beginning as the original event. Similarly, in the bottom segment, the end point is moved back in time, adding extra time at the beginning of the event. This is done when the Sizing Moves Contents option is selected from the Object Selection tool's pop-up menu.

Figure 11.19
Resizing an event using the Normal Sizing tool (which doubles as the Object Selection tool).

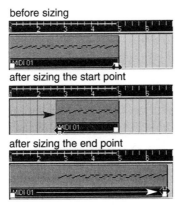

before sizing

after sizing the start point

after sizing the end point

How To

To resize objects while moving its contents:

1. In the Project window's toolbar, select the Sizing Moves Contents option from the Object Selection's pop-up menu.

2. Select an object to view its resizing handles.

3. Move the handles in the desired direction.

Sizing Applies Time Stretch

The last option available in the Object Selection's pop-up menu allows you to time-stretch objects so that the events inside fit in the new object's size. This stretching can be applied to both audio and MIDI events. Figure 11.20 displays both types of events being stretched. In the top portion, MIDI events' note length values are adjusted to fit within the new proportion. If you stretch in a proportion that changes the quantizing of events, you might have to do a bit of editing inside the MIDI Editor to get the MIDI events to work with the quantize grid. In other words, if you don't want too much hassle with this, try stretching in a proportion that is suitable to the time subdivision currently used in your project. Using this option on audio is a great way to make a drum loop, for example, fit inside a specific number of bars—especially when the tempo difference is minimal. If you look at the audio example in Figure 11.20, you can see that the original content is less than one bar long. Stretching it allows you to loop it properly using the Fill Loop or Repeat options described earlier in this chapter. You may select the quality applied to audio through the File(PC)/Cubase(Mac) > Preferences > Audio > Time Stretch Tool panel. The option you select in this dialog box is applied to all audio events that are being stretched using this tool.

Figure 11.20
Resizing an event using the Sizing Applies Time Stretch option.

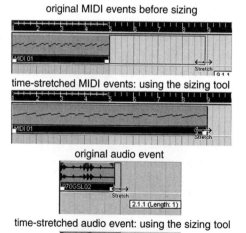

original MIDI events before sizing

time-stretched MIDI events: using the sizing tool

original audio event

time-stretched audio event: using the sizing tool

To stretch the content of an object while resizing it:

1. In the Project window's toolbar, select the Sizing Applies Time Stretch option from the Object Selection's pop-up menu.
2. Select an object to view its resizing handles.
3. Move the handles in the desired direction.

You should know that applying time stretching on an audio file in a large proportion will probably create some major artifacts in the sound itself. You should avoid using time stretch in a proportion greater or less than twenty-five percent of the original content's length. As for MIDI events, because the only thing that changes when time stretching an event is a value in a field, there are absolutely no restrictions in this respect.

Shifting Events Inside an Object

Cubase also offers you the possibility of shifting events inside an object without moving the object's position. This is done by offsetting the position of the audio clip inside the object's start and end points, as illustrated in Figure 11.21. You can also shift MIDI events inside a MIDI part. In both cases, there is only one condition that applies: The object in which the events are found has to be smaller than the events themselves. For example, if you have MIDI events at Bar 1, Beat 1 and Bar 3, Beat 4 within a MIDI part that spans from Bar 1 to Bar 4, you cannot shift these events inside because the container covers the same area as the events inside the container.

Figure 11.21
Shifting event's position within an object.

original audio event

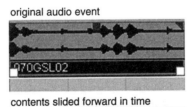

contents slided forward in time

How To

To shift events inside an object:

1. In the Project window's toolbar, select the Object Selection tool.
2. Select the object you want to shift.
3. Hold down the Ctrl+Alt(PC)/⌘+Option(Mac) keys and drag the content to the left or right.

You can use this technique creatively by shifting a drum loop, for example, trying out different beat combinations when playing a shifted event along with other events in the same time line.

If you want to fine-tune or edit the shift offset values, you can access these parameters inside the Browser, which is covered in Chapter 10.

Muting Objects

When trying out things inside the Project window, you might want to mute a track by using the Mute button found in the Inspector and Track List area. However, if you only want to mute a number of events, you can do so by selecting these events followed by the Mute option found in the Edit menu. The default key command to mute events is Shift+M. After an object is muted, you can unmute it with the Shift+U key command or by selecting the Unmute option—also found in the Edit menu.

Lock

If you've worked hard at positioning events in the time line, you can lock them in place to prevent time-consuming mistakes. When an object is locked, a tiny lock icon appears in the bottom-right corner of the object next to the end point handle. You can lock selected events by using the Lock option in the Edit menu [Ctrl+Shift+L(PC)/⌘+Shift+L(Mac)]. After objects are locked, you cannot move or edit them from the Project window. To unlock objects, select the corresponding option in the Edit menu or press [Ctrl+Shift+U(PC)/⌘+Shift+U(Mac)].

Disabling Audio Tracks

After you start recording audio inside a project, you will gather many more audio files than you'll probably use in the final project because you will most likely have different takes from which to choose and different versions of the same audio content. You might also create several working tracks along the way that are not used anymore. Simply muting these tracks only mutes the output level, but the information on these tracks is still read, causing your hard disk to look for them and load them anyway. After a while, these muted tracks might start dragging your project down. To avoid this kind of situation, you can disable tracks that are not currently being used in your project, which offers the advantage of shutting down all disk activity related to the audio content found on these tracks, while still remaining in your project in case you need them later on.

How To

To disable audio tracks:

1. Right-click(PC)/Option-click(Mac) in the Track List area.
2. From the context menu, select Disable Track.

You can enable a track after it has been disabled by repeating this operation. The option in the context menu is replaced by Enable Track instead.

Audio Part Editor

This editor is the audio equivalent of the MIDI Editor and many of the functions you can apply in it can also be applied in the Project window. The main purpose for this editor is to edit events inside an audio part the way you would edit them in the Project window. You can look at the Audio Part Editor as a mini version of the Project window, where all edits are made for a single part found in the Project window.

How To

To create an empty audio part in the Project window:

▶ Double-click between the left and right locators on an audio track.
▶ Or, with the Pencil tool selected, click and drag a range on an audio track.

How To

To create an audio part from existing events in the Project window:

▶ With the Glue tool selected, glue two or more events together on the same track.
▶ Or, select an event on a track, and then select the Audio > Events to Part option.

Because this is the default editor for audio parts, double-clicking on an audio part in the Project window opens the Audio Part Editor. If you have created shared copies of a part you open in the editor, any editing you do is applied to all copies. If you don't want this to happen, you should convert your shared copy into a real copy beforehand. Shared copies display the name at the bottom of the part in italics and real copies display the name in regular font style.

HIDING OR SHOWING THE EVENTS NAME

You can change how events appear by selecting the appropriate options in the File(PC)/Cubase(Mac) > Preferences > Event Display options. You will find different options, one of them called *Show Events Name*. If this option is not selected, you will not see the difference between shared and real copies.

How To

To convert a shared copy into a real copy in the Project window:

1. Select the part you want to convert in the Project window.
2. From the Edit menu, select the Convert to Real Copy option.

Shared copies are usually created when you hold the Alt+Shift(PC)/Option+Shift(Mac) keys down when dragging an event to copy.

Audio Part Editor Areas

The Audio Part Editor's toolbar offers much of the same options found in the Project window. The tools used to edit events in a part are the same and work the same way here as they do in the Project window. The Play Preview and Loop Preview buttons enable you to hear the content of a part in a loop or play the content of a selected event in a part in a loop when this button is active. The Information bar and ruler also offer the same options as in the Project window.

The Audio Part Editor offers the possibility of using lanes to place and organize audio events on a track. In Figure 11.22, you can see events placed in different rows. These rows are called *lanes*, and although they appear similar to tracks in the Project window, they behave differently. You can have as many lanes as you want in an Audio Part Editor, but only one audio event can be heard at any time. This means that when events overlap on the same track, the one on top is heard, cutting off the one below. When events overlap across different lanes, the event on the lowest lane gets priority. You can bring an event to the front when they overlap on the same lane in much the same way as you do in the Project window—by using the To Front option in the context menu [right-click(PC)/Ctrl-click)(Mac)].

11.22
The Audio Part Editor.

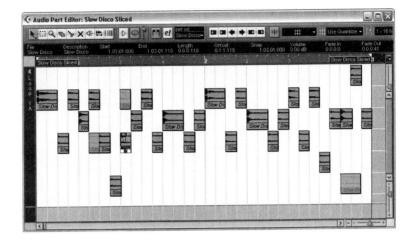

CHAPTER 11

How To

To hear the content of an event in the Audio Part Editor:

▶ Activate the Solo button and start playback normally. The Project window's locators and play line's position determines what is heard.

▶ Or click the Play Preview button in the editor's toolbar. Activating the Loop button plays the content in a loop.

▶ Or select an event and click the Play Preview button to hear only the selected event.

▶ Or choose the Speaker tool and click where you want to start the playback. Cubase plays from the location where you click until the end of this event in the editor.

▶ Or choose the Scrub tool and click and drag the mouse to the left or right. The playback plays in the direction and at the speed you move your mouse.

Audio Operations

Because the operations in this editor are identical to the ones available in the Project window, please refer to that section for details on these operations. However, here is an alternative to editing events as separate objects in the Project window. As mentioned earlier, it is possible to record multiple takes in a single audio clip, creating several regions or events within this clip. By creating a part on a track and placing several takes inside this part, you can edit them inside the Audio Part Editor by using the different lanes to create your perfect take.

As you can see in Figure 11.23, the "take 3" was edited inside the Audio Part editor to get a better version out of the take. Using different lanes at the beginning to place your events, the Scissors tool to split the events where you want (the snap and grid settings influence where you can split), the Mute tool to mute the portions you don't want to hear, and snap points to reposition your events along an appropriate grid, reorganizing musical ideas becomes very easy. When you move events on lower lanes to hear them, you can hold down the Ctrl(PC)/⌘(Mac) key to restrict your movement to the vertical axis. This is useful when you don't want to move an event in time. You can also apply auto fade, crossfade, and offline processes to events inside the Audio Part Editor.

Figure 11.23
Assembling takes in the Audio Part Editor.

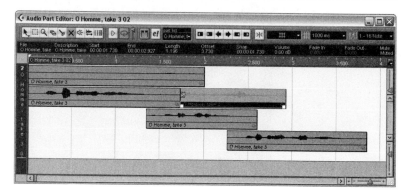

You can import audio events or regions into the Audio Part Editor just as you would do when dragging events or regions from the Sample Editor or Pool window.

Now You Try It

For information about using the instructions found in this section and to find out where you can get the working files, please consult the section called *About the Exercise Files* in the Introduction section.

12

Mixer and Channel Settings

Up until now, we have explored both the project window and the editing environments provided for MIDI and audio tracks. This chapter discusses the mixing environment inside Cubase and ways you can edit settings applied to a channel. The Mixer in Cubase offers an interface that resembles a typical mixing console. In this Mixer, you will find a replica of settings that have been described in Chapter 6, as well as functions described in Chapter 7 when discussing MIDI and audio recording.

So, why this fancy mixing window? Instead of having to select tracks in the Track List area, then expanding the Channel section of the Inspector area for each channel you want to view, and then switching to the Inserts section or Send Effects section, everything is available to you in a single window. This not only makes it easier to see the settings applied to all your tracks, but it also makes it easy to automate the mix for an entire project, as you will see later. A mixing environment is all about flexibility, accessibility, and your personal aesthetics when it comes to how music or sound appeals to your ears. The last part is yours to develop; fortunately, however, Cubase offers both flexibility and accessibility.

Here's a summary of what you will learn in this chapter:

▶ Explore the different areas of the Mixer window.

▶ Learn how to save channel settings and apply them to other channels inside the Mixer window.

▶ Find out how to customize your Mixer window to fit the tasks at hand.

▶ Learn how to use additional audio outputs by activating buses.

▶ Understand what channel EQs are and how to use them.

▶ Understand what dynamic control is and how to use it.

▶ Learn how to use groups to create submixes and monitor mixes.

Mixer Areas

The Mixer window offers a common window for all types of channels present in your project (see Figure 12.1). A channel for each audio, MIDI, and group track is represented in the Mixer window, offering controls, such as volume, pan, mute, solo, and read and write automation. To help you with this process, a panel on the left of the Mixer window controls common elements found in the mixer. Cubase SX users can extend the Mixer window to display insert and send effect settings, EQ settings for audio and group channels, output levels, or an overview of settings applied to a channel.

CHAPTER 12

Figure 12.1

The Mixer window.

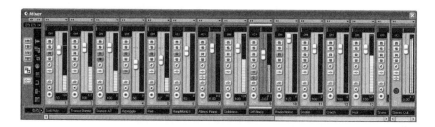

Common Panel

The Common panel found on the left of the Mixer (see Figure 12.2) controls global settings for this Mixer window, as well as its appearance and behavior. Here's a look at each item in the panel from top to bottom.

Figure 12.2

The Common panel found on the left of the Mixer window.

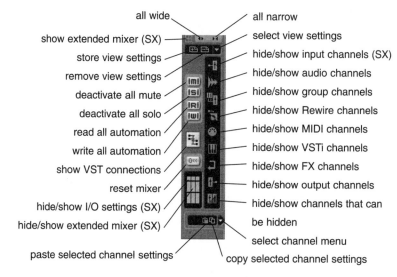

Show Extended Mixer (SX only) button offers a way to reveal the extended portion of the Mixer in SX. When the extended portion of the Mixer is visible, a minus sign button will appear above this button. You can use this minus sign to hide the extended portion of the Mixer.

All Wide/All Narrow buttons make all channels in the current Mixer wide or narrow respectively. The same settings appear individually on each channel, allowing you to set one channel narrow or wide independently. But when you click here, all the channels change to wide or narrow at the touch of a button. When a channel is displayed in Narrow mode, all its functions remain active; however, some of the controls are hidden away, allowing more channels to fit on your desktop. This becomes convenient when working with a project that has more channels than can fit in your current desktop resolution.

Store View and Remove View buttons let you save a set of mixer display options as a preset and retrieve them later from the Select Channel View Set menu (see Figure 12.3). Creating your own presets allow you to customize the mixer to display the information you need to see for specific tasks, as audio recording, mixing, or other common tasks you need to perform in this window.

Figure 12.3

Selecting a channel view
set in the Mixer.

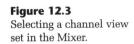

Preset 1
AudioRecording
MixRegular
✓ MixExtended

How To

To store a channel view set:

1. Set up the mixer view options appropriately so that they display the information to which you want to have quick access.

2. Click on the Store View button.

3. Enter a name for your preset, for example "Audio EQ" if you selected to display only audio channels with their EQ settings in the Extended panel.

4. Click the OK button.

You can remove view sets by first selecting a view set and then clicking on the Remove View button. You can use up to three different Mixer window configurations with Cubase SX. You can take advantage of this feature to organize your mixing environment in a way that suits you best. For example, you can choose to display all MIDI channels in one mixer and display audio channels in another. You can access the additional mixers through the Devices menu.

The following four buttons are also found on each channel. In the Common panel, they serve as a master control and monitoring of the current status of channels available in the Mixer window. When one or more tracks in the Mixer window are muted, the Mute button is lit. Clicking this button cancels all current mute settings, unmuting all channels in the project. The Solo button plays a similar role in the sense that it appears lit when one or more tracks are in Solo mode. Clicking this button deactivates the solo monitoring for all channels in the project. The Read and Write buttons activate or deactivate the read or write automation on all channels by changing the state of the button in the Common panel. If one or more channels are already in Read or Write mode, the Mixer window is lit as well to indicate that a channel is currently actively reading or ready to write automation.

The Show VST Connections button does the same thing as the "VST Connections" option found under the Devices menu; it will bring the VST connections window up, allowing you to make modifications to the current input and output bus configurations.

The Reset Mixer button resets all the channels or only the selected channels in the Mixer. When you reset a channel, you deactivate all Solo, Mute, EQ, insert, and send effect settings. The volume fader will also be set to 0 dB and pan to center position.

Below the Reset Mixer button is a 3-part toggle zone (SX only) where the three rows represent the Input/Output (I/O) settings area of the mixer, the Extended panel, and the Channel portion of the mixer (which can't be hidden). Revealing or hiding a portion of the mixer does not change anything in your mixer's setting; it only hides certain parts from view. The corresponding portion of the Mixer window is visible when the area is highlighted in this small representation. Clicking on one of these areas will either reveal or hide it.

If you want to copy the settings of a selected track to another, you can use the buttons and menu found at the bottom of the Common panel. For example, if you want to have the same EQ, inserts, and sends settings on several vocal tracks, you can make the settings on a first channel and when you are satisfied with these settings, copy and paste them to one or more channels. Subsequently, all the channels to which you copied these settings will be the same.

How To

To copy a channel's settings to another channel:

1. Adjust the settings of the channel you want to copy.

2. Make sure this channel is selected in the Mixer. If not, click the bar over the channel's name below or above the fader to select it (see Figure 12.4), or select it from the Channel Selection drop-down menu in the Common panel.

Figure 12.4
A selected channel (left) compared to a nonselected channel (right).

3. Click the Copy Channel button. The Paste button becomes active.

4. Select the channel to which you want to paste the copied settings.

5. Click the Paste Settings button in the Common panel.

6. You can repeat this paste operation to any number of channels by selecting it and clicking the Paste button again.

The following nine buttons (eight in Cubase SL) hide or show the channel types associated with each button. These are, from top to bottom: Input channels (SX only), Audio channels (disk-based digital audio recording), Group channels, Rewire channels, MIDI channels, VSTi channels, FX channels and Output channels (previously known as *Master Output channels*). The last option allows you to show/hide "Can Hide" channels. You can set a channel's display property to hideable (explained later). When selecting the Hide channels set to "Can Hide" option in the

Common panel, all channels that can be hidden from view will be hidden. This can be useful when working with ghost tracks, or tracks that you use to place events temporarily, but that are not part of your mixing process. Hiding them from view makes it easier to focus on the tasks at hand.

Extended Common Panel

The Extended panel is visible to Cubase SX users when clicking on the Show Extended Mixer button in the Common panel's area as seen above. When the Mixer is in Extended mode, the Common panel area now reveals an additional set of options (see Figure 12.5). As with the options found in the non-extended Common panel, the options found here are also available for each channel in the Mixer. The difference once again is that when you select an option in the Common panel, all channels in the current Mixer will display the same type of information. For example, clicking on the Show All Inserts button in the Common panel will change the information displayed in the extended portion of the Mixer for all channels to the insert settings. You can, however, change the displayed extended panel for a specific channel by selecting a different display option for this channel. Note that changing the displayed information does not in any way change the settings made to a channel, only the information displayed changes.

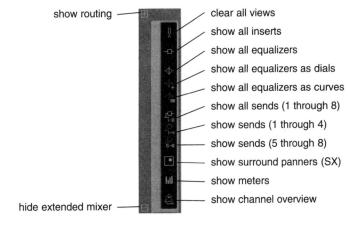

Figure 12.5
The extended portion of the common panel in the Mixer window.

show routing — clear all views
show all inserts
show all equalizers
show all equalizers as dials
show all equalizers as curves
show all sends (1 through 8)
show sends (1 through 4)
show sends (5 through 8)
show surround panners (SX)
show meters
show channel overview
hide extended mixer —

Depending on which option you choose to view in the extended Mixer area, different panels will appear, as shown in Figure 12.5. What you will find depends mostly on the type of channel; for example, the Clear View panel appears when you select a type of panel that is not available for the type of channel (see Figure 12.5).

You will notice that there are no MIDI EQ settings in the Extended panel. When you choose to display the EQ for other channels, the MIDI channel's Extended area keeps displaying whatever was there before you chose the extended EQ display.

The MIDI insert's Extended panel displays the four Inserts settings. Each insert has the following functions:

▶ Enable/disable the Insert
▶ Open the Insert's edit window
▶ Select the MIDI Insert effect

Figure 12.6
The Common panel's extended functions in Cubase SX.

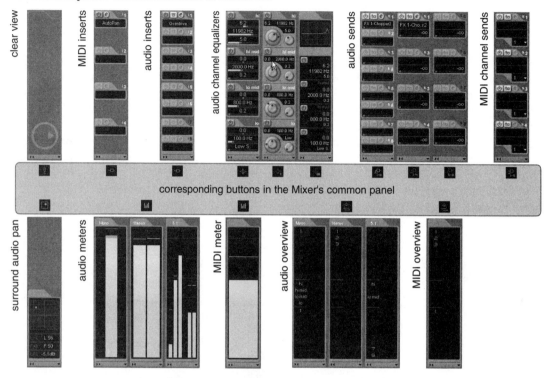

Audio inserts have the same controls as the MIDI inserts; however, the list displayed in the Insert Selection menu is different.

Both extended EQ display options offer the same controls in different display options.

▶ An On/Off button to enable or disable the EQ band

▶ A gain control (top slider in Slider mode and inner knob in Dial mode)

▶ A frequency control (second slider in Slider mode and outer knob in Dial mode)

▶ A Q setting (third slider in Slider mode and lower small knob in Dial mode)

The MIDI sends in the Extended panel display the following settings for each of the eight (in Cubase SX) or five (in Cubase SL) send effects:

▶ An On/Off button to enable or disable the MIDI sends

▶ An open effect's editing panel button

▶ A pre- or post-fader selection button

▶ An effect selection menu

▶ A MIDI output port selection menu for the output of the effect

▶ A channel setting for the output of the effect

The audio sends offer the following controls:

▶ An On/Off button to enable or disable the MIDI sends

▶ An open effect's editing panel button (only in Slider mode)

▶ A pre- or post-fader selection button (only in Slider mode)

▶ An effect selection menu

▶ A send to effect level (represented by a slider in Slider mode and dial in Dial mode)

The settings displayed in the Extended panels are the same settings that are available in the Inspector area of each track, so if you don't have Cubase SX, you can still modify these settings in the Inspector area of the channel, or you can click on the "e" button (Edit Channel Settings) next to the channel's level fader to open that channel's additional settings panel.

Routing Panel

The Routing panel is found at the very top of Cubase SX's Mixer. You won't find this feature in the Cubase SL version. In here, you can choose the input and output buses for audio channels and input and output MIDI ports for MIDI channels. The content of each field in this panel is discussed later in this chapter since each channel type (MIDI or audio) holds its own controls.

If you don't see the Routing panel in SX, click on the top plus sign found in the upper-left corner of the Mixer (see Figure 12.7). To hide the panel once again, click again on this button (now showing a minus sign). In SX, this is a great panel to set up multiple track inputs when recording bands instead of going through the Inspector area. In the end, it's basically a question of working preference or type of project you do that will determine if this tool is for you. Knowing it's there when you need it is still a good thing.

Figure 12.7
The Routing panel found
in SX's Mixer window.

Audio Channels

In the Mixer window, audio tracks, VSTi, and group channels offer similar settings and are considered as audio channels. This said, they do offer some minor differences both in features and options. So let's take a closer look at each class of audio channel.

Disk Channels (Audio Tracks)

In the Mixer, an audio track in which you record digital audio content such as a voice, guitar, or bass is referred to as the *disk channel* to distinguish it from other channels that are handled as audio channels, such as the VSTi and group channels. The function of each control found in Figure 12.8 is described in the following list:

▶ **Audio Input selection field (SX only).** Selects the input bus when preparing your channel to record or monitor audio through it. Remember that the bus connects the channel to the input of your sound card as defined in the VST Connections panel.

▶ **Audio Output selection field (SX only).** Selects the output of a channel to monitor it through speakers or sending the channel through groups instead.

CHAPTER 12

▶ **Inverse Phase button (SX only).** Inverses the input phase of an audio signal. This can be handy when you notice that a signal's phase cancels another signal when preparing for a recording session. Recording with two microphones that are not positioned optimally will often be responsible for this type of problem. Other times, this can be caused by grounding problems in the studio wires.

▶ **Input Gain control and display (SX only).** Controls the gain of a signal as it enters the channel during the recording process. The display tells you the amount of change in dB. This can be a positive value when you increase the gain or a negative value when you reduce it. You can adjust the gain by holding down the Alt(PC)/Option(Mac) key down while dragging the gain knob up or down. A fader will appear as you start the dragging motion; this should make it easier to adjust the gain appropriately.

▶ **Wide/Narrow Toggle.** View each channel in a wide (default) or narrow width format. Setting channels to narrow makes it easy to view more channels inside the window without having to scroll horizontally inside the Mixer when your project contains several tracks. However, the number of visible parameters is reduced, making it harder to edit them. In other words, setting a channel to narrow makes sense when you are satisfied with the current setup for this channel or when you don't need to see all the parameters for this channel.

▶ **Channel View Options menu.** In SX this allows you to change the panel visible in the extended area of the Mixer and make a track "hideable." In SL, you can only make a track hideable or not. Checking the Can Hide option makes the track hideable. When you select Hide Channels and set it to the Can Hide option in the Mixer's Common panel, any channel with the Can Hide check mark will be hidden from view (see Figure 12.2).

▶ **Pan control and display.** The Pan control displays a numeric and graphic representation of the pan setting for this channel. Ctrl(PC)/⌘(Mac)-clicking brings the pan back to its center position, which is represented by a C in the numeric display.

▶ **Channel Setting Option buttons.** These are the same buttons found in the audio channel section in the track's Inspector area. Whatever settings you made in the Inspector are displayed here and vice versa. These functions are Mute, Solo, Read, Write, Open Channel Editor panel, Insert Bypass, EQ Bypass, Send Effect Bypass, Monitor Input Level, and Record Enabled. Remember that when the Monitor button is active, the level indicator to the right of the channel fader becomes an input level monitor; changing the level of this fader will not have any effect on the input level. Below the Record Enabled button is the audio channel icon. This corresponds to the same icon found on the show/hide audio channels in the Common panel of the Mixer. When you enable this button in the Common panel, all channels with this icon will be hidden from view.

▶ **Channel Fader and Level indicator.** The channel fader controls the output level of this channel (except when you are in Input Level Monitor mode). To bring the fader to its default 0 dB position, hold the Ctrl(PC)/⌘(Mac) key down as you click on it. If you want to move the fader by smaller, more precise increments, hold the Shift key down as you move the fader. This is very useful when you want to create slow and precise fade effects with automation. The numeric display below the fader tells gives you the position value (in dB) of this channel's fader. If you have a scroll wheel on your mouse, you can adjust the selected channel's fader level by moving the wheel up or down.

▶ **Peak Margin indicator.** Directly below the output level for the channel, the peak margin indicator represents the distance between the highest audio peak in this track and the maximum digital audio level. This value resets itself if you move the channel's fader or if you click inside the field. It's important to keep an eye on this margin because you don't want the audio on this track to go above zero dB, but you don't want it to always stay very low when recording either. Ultimately, the peak margin indicator should remain between -12 dB and 0 dB when recording.

▶ **Channel Name.** You will find the name of the channel below the fader. You can use the area above this one to select the channel or change the name by double-clicking on it. When a channel is selected, the area above the name will appear colored. You can select more than one channel at a time by holding down the Shift key as you make your selection.

Figure 12.8
The audio channel in the Mixer window.

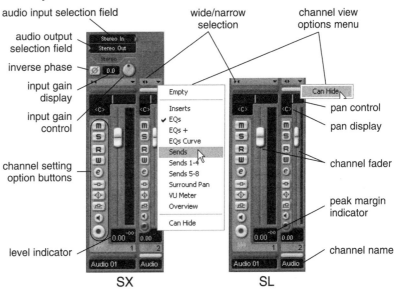

wide (left) and narrow (right) views

Rewire

Rewire is a software-based technology that lets you share application resources inside your computer—more specifically, Rewire-compatible ones. Developed by Propellerhead and Steinberg, most products sold by either company are compatible with this technology, but now more and more third-party application developers have joined in by making their applications Rewire-compatible.

What Rewire does is quite nice, and it's simple to use. It patches the outputs of one software application into the inputs of another software application and synchronizes them. This has the same effect as a VSTi, except that Rewire instruments or Rewire software applications are not running inside Cubase, as a VSTi is. Active Rewire channels appear as additional channels in

Cubase's Mixer. This allows all Rewire-compatible applications to share the same sound card, assigning each Rewire instrument a different output if you want, and also providing a common transport control and timing base; you can control playback for all applications from Cubase.

How To

To use Rewire:

1. Launch Cubase first. It is important that your other Rewire applications are launched after Cubase; otherwise, both applications run independently, and conflicts, when attempting to access the sound card, might prevent you from using either applications.

2. Make sure the Release ASIO Driver in Background option is not selected in Devices > Device Setup > VST Multitrack.

3. In the Devices menu or the Devices panel, select the Installed Rewire Application option. If you don't have any Rewire applications installed, you will not have this option. The Rewire panel appears, as shown in Figure 12.9. What appears in this panel depends on the Rewire-compatible applications installed on your computer. In this example, Ableton Live is installed.

Figure 12.9
The Rewire panel; active channels appear lit.

4. Click the Activate button on the left of the channels you want to create inside Cubase's Mixer.

5. If you want to rename a channel, click in the Display As column and type in the label you want to use.

6. Launch your Rewire application.

At this point, the Transport bars in both applications are linked together. This means that you can start and stop your playback within any application, and the others will follow. If you record events, this is recorded in the application that is active, or, in other words, the recording takes place in the application in which you clicked the Record button. So, recording is independent, but playback follows and if you use cycle playback or recording, all applications follow this loop. When you have a loop playing in Ableton Live, for example, this loop stays looped. Cubase always sets the tempo setting when the Tempo track is active. If you change the tempo in Cubase's Tempo track, the other applications follow the lead. If you are not using the Tempo track, you can change the tempo setting in either application and the playback reflects it. In other words, if you start playback at 100 BPM in Live and Cubase is not set to play the tempo from the Tempo track, it plays at 100 BPM.

All Rewire channels containing recorded events that are not muted when you export your mixdown from the File > Export > Audio mixdown option are included in this output file.

One thing to look for is the sample playback rate. Make sure both applications are set to a compatible sampling rate. If your Rewire application is not set to the same sampling rate as Cubase, the Rewire application might not play the right pitch.

If your Rewire application uses MIDI to trigger sounds like VSTi, you will need to create a MIDI track and select the Rewire-compatible MIDI output port to send the MIDI events to the Rewire application in order for it to generate the sounds that will appear in the audio channel inside Cubase. If, on the other hand, the Rewire-compatible application is audio-based, using audio loops or events on tracks of its own, then simply activating the bus to which the audio is routed inside Cubase will do. For example, if you have audio tracks in a Rewire application that are coming out through a Main Mix bus, activating this bus inside Cubase (as is the case in the example found in Figure 12.9) will cause the audio routed to the Main Mix of that application to be sent (rerouted) into the Cubase Mixer's Rewire channel (see Figure 12.10).

Figure 12.10
The Audio of Rewire channels from the third-party application (left) is routed into a Rewire channel inside Cubase (right).

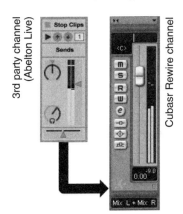

VSTi and Rewire Channels

MIDI tracks that are assigned to a VSTi (see Figure 12.11) or Rewire MIDI output port are represented by two channels in the Mixer window: one MIDI channel to control MIDI-related settings associated with the Rewire or VSTi and one audio channel that can be processed just as the disk audio channel described previously. There are, however, some differences in an audio VSTi or Rewire and a disk audio channel:

▶ You can't assign an audio input bus to a VSTi or Rewire audio channel.

▶ There are no Record Enable buttons on this audio channel because the events are recorded through the MIDI channel instead (see the "MIDI Channels" section for details on this).

▶ There is no Monitor button because there are no audio inputs to monitor.

▶ Below the Bypass Send Effect button, you will find a VSTi Edit button that opens the VSTi interface and changes settings in the instrument. Because the Rewire instrument is not inside Cubase, you need to access that application to make changes to the instrument's settings.

▶ The icons for VSTi or Rewire channels are associated with VSTi or Rewire types respectively. When you choose to hide these types of channels (VSTi or Rewire) from the Common panel on the left of the Mixer, all channels with these icons are hidden from view.

▶ The color behind the fader is different from the audio disk channel.

The MIDI channel of the VSTi and Rewire (when applicable) offers the same settings as the MIDI channels described later in the "MIDI Channels" section. It is the audio from a VSTi or Rewire channel that can be exported as an audio file without having to use the Record function in the Transport panel. Instead of recording the audio output, Cubase actually renders the audio output of a VSTi or Rewire channel to an audio file. This audio file can then be imported back into the project to play as any other audio channel in your project.

Figure 12.11
The MIDI routed through the VSTi (left) and audio output of VSTi (right) channels.

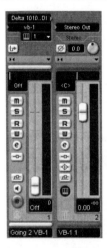

As you will probably notice, some VSTi have multiple output support. As a result, Cubase creates multiple VSTi channels in the Mixer. The HALion sampler VSTi, for example, offers up to 18 audio channels (one surround, four stereo, and four mono outputs).

Group Channels

When a group track is created in a Project, a group channel is also created in the Mixer. Groups are used as outputs only, where you can assign other channels to play through a group channel and then process all the channels sent to that group as one entity in the group's channel settings. For example, if you have several tracks for your drum kit, you can assign all the individual tracks to play through the group channel, and assign a reverb to this channel. This applies the same reverb level to all the parts of the drum kit instead of applying an individual reverb level on each track. Moreover, when you want to change the overall level of the drum, you only need to adjust the group's level instead of individual volume levels for each instrument if they are all on separate tracks. Here are some differences between the audio disk channel and the group channel:

▶ You can't assign an audio input to a group channel because it only serves as an output.

▶ There is no Record Enable button on this audio channel because there are no inputs.

▶ There is no Monitor button because there are no audio inputs to monitor.

▶ The icon for group channels is associated with this channel type (see Figure 12.12). When you choose to hide this type of channel (group) from the Common panel on the left of the Mixer window, all channels with this icon are hidden from view.

▶ The color behind the fader is different from the audio disk channel.

Figure 12.12
A group channel in the Mixer window.

MIDI Channels

A MIDI channel is added to the Mixer window each time you create a MIDI track in the project window. As you saw in the "VSTi and Rewire Channels" section, even if these instruments are considered as audio plug-in effects, you still need MIDI to record events that will be played by these audio effects, and as such, they are also MIDI-triggered instruments needing a MIDI channel. The MIDI channel in the Mixer window displays an exact replica of the MIDI Channel section in the Inspector area with the exception of the View Options menu. The function of each control found in Figure 12.13 is described in the following list:

▶ **MIDI Input and Output port selection fields (SX only).**Chooses the source and destination of MIDI events for this channel.

▶ **MIDI Channel selection field (SX only).** Chooses the destination channel for your MIDI events.

▶ **VST Instrument Edit button (SX only).** Opens the VSTi interface panel and makes parameter changes to the instrument or loads and changes presets into the VSTi.

▶ **Input Transformer button (SX only).** Accesses the Input Transformer panel for the selected track.

▶ **Wide/Narrow Toggle.** Serves same function as with audio channels described earlier in this chapter.

▶ **Channel View Options menu.** Serves same function as with audio channels described earlier in this chapter.

▶ **Pan control and display.** Displays a numeric and graphic representation of the pan setting for this channel. Ctrl(PC)/⌘(Mac)-clicking brings the pan back to its center position, which is represented by a C in the numeric display. The pan control actually corresponds to the MIDI Controller #10.

▶ **Channel Setting Option buttons.** Same buttons found in the MIDI Channel section in the track's Inspector area. Whatever settings you made in the Inspector are displayed here and vice versa. These functions are Mute, Solo, Read, Write, Open Channel Editor panel, Insert Bypass, Send Effect Bypass, Monitor Input, and Record Enabled. Below the Record Enabled button is the MIDI channel icon. This corresponds to the same icon found on the show/hide audio channels in the Common panel of the Mixer. When you enable this button in the Common panel, all MIDI channels will be hidden from view.

▶ **Channel Fader.** Controls the MIDI Controller #7 (Volume), which can only be an integer value between 0 and 127. You should also be aware that the fader's default position is set at 100; holding down the Ctrl(PC)/⌘(Mac) key as you click on the fader's handle will bring it back to this value. You can also hold the Shift key down while moving your fader to get a greater level of precision. The level display on the right of the fader, unlike the audio channels, does not represent the output level of the instrument. This level cannot be monitored because the sound of the MIDI instrument is not monitored through the MIDI channel itself. In fact, this represents the velocity value of Note On and Note Off messages. Changing the volume level with the fader to the right does not, therefore, affect the level displayed in this bar, and no digital clipping can occur because of high velocities being monitored by this display.

▶ **Current MIDI value and Peak Margin Indicator.** Both fields display MIDI values. The first represents the current position of the MIDI fader, and the second represents the highest MIDI note on velocity value.

Figure 12.13
The MIDI channel in the Mixer window.

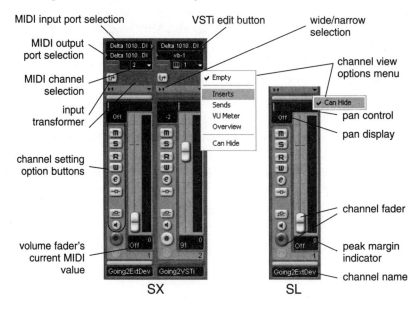

Output Bus Channels

The output bus channels represent each output you have created in the VST Connections panel. How you use the output buses you create depends on the project at hand and the number of available outputs on your sound card. Depending on how you set up your system or how many outputs your sound card has, you will generally use the two main outputs of your sound card to monitor your Cubase project. If you have more than two outputs (and probably inputs), you can use these additional outputs for additional buses. These additional buses can serve to feed an external effect processor, a headphone amplifier, another recording device, or a multispeaker monitoring system typical in surround systems.

Each output bus you create in the VST connections will appear when you make the output bus channels visible in the Mixer. You can also change or create bus output configurations through the VST Connections panel (F4 is the default key command to access the panel). If your sound card only offers a pair of stereo outputs, then creating a single stereo output bus and perhaps two mono output buses should be enough since you can't separate the signal on its way out anyway (besides the two mono signals). If you want to group a series of channels together and control their settings as one group, you should use a group channel rather than a bus.

Output buses, like other audio channels, can also have up to eight (five in SL) different assignable insert and send effects. Assigning effects to output buses can be useful when you want to optimize the overall level of a project, want to down-sample your project from 32-bit (or 24) to 16-bit by using dithering, or simply want to add a subtle reverb on the entire mix. Then again, output buses don't have to be used only for mixing purposes as mentioned earlier. The last two insert effects on SX—inserts 7 and 8—are post-fader, contrary to the typical pre-fader insert configuration. In the SL version, only the insert 5 is post fader.

When a project's sample record format is set to 32-bit floating point, you don't need to worry about digital clipping on audio channels after the channels are recorded and there was no clipping at the input. That's because the processing inside Cubase is done using this 32-bit (floating point) format which makes it very difficult to actually get digital clipping. However, after the signal is sent to the output, it is converted to the sound card's format; in many cases, this is 16-, 20-, or 24-bit. Because of this binary downsizing, digital clipping becomes a very real possibility if the clip indicator lights up above one of the output (or input) bus channels (see Figure 12.14). You should try to avoid any clipping, especially when you are preparing a final mix from your output buses. The clip indicator is located below the Bypass EQ button in each bus output. You will also notice that there are no sends on output buses. The remaining controls in the output bus channels are the same as in any other audio channel.

If you are using SL and would like to use inserts to prepare a final mix using an overall dynamic maximizer or dithering plug-in, you can create a group channel that will act as the main outputs for your project, include the automation on this channel if you wish, and then send the output of this group to the main output bus where you add the desired inserts, making sure you don't record any automation or add any EQ on this output bus. By doing so, you are tricking Cubase into thinking you are applying effects as post-fader since the fader of the group where the desired mix lies is before the inserts you just added to the main output bus.

Figure 12.14
Output bus channels in
stereo (left), mono
(center), or Surround
(right) configuration (SX
only).

PREPARING A 16-BIT MIXDOWN

If you are preparing your project for a final CD mixdown and want to convert the
files from 32- or 24-bit to 16-bit, you should apply the UV22 dithering plug-in
effect as your last insert effect for the bus containing the audio content.

Input Channels

Available in SX only, the input channels (input buses) are the entry point equivalent of their exit
point counterpart: the output buses. As such, they also offer the same controls inside the mixer
with one difference—you can't solo an input bus

You can use input channels (input buses) in SX to monitor the signal as it enters the input and
adjust its level accordingly. SL users will need to access their sound card's input level control as
an alternative to input buses controls.

How To

To change the physical input or output assigned to a bus:

▶ In the VST Connections panel, select the desired output from the available
outputs next to the appropriate bus.

After an input or output bus is active, it becomes available at the top of the audio channels in the
SX Mixer. You can send any audio channel (disk audio, VSTi, Rewire, and group channels) to any
active bus (see Figure 12.15).

Figure 12.15
Selecting a bus in the
Mixer window's audio
channel, fielding Cubase
SX.

input bus

output bus

RENAMING BUSES

You can also rename buses inside the Mixer by clicking where the current bus
name exists and entering a new name for this bus.

Working with Mixer Settings

Besides saving mixer channel views, described earlier in the Common panel's section, there are a
few other mixer settings you can save. After a setting is saved, you can load it later, applying these
saved settings elsewhere in the Mixer. Saving mixer settings applies only to audio-related
channels: disk, VSTi, Rewire, and groups. These options are available by right-(PC)/Ctrl-
(Mac)clicking over any audio channel in the Mixer (see Figure 12.16). The setting you save will be
those of the currently selected channel. Similarly, once you have saved a setting, it will be loaded
in the selected channel. Remember that selected channels display a lit area above and below the
channel's fader. These options include:

▶ **Save/Load Selected Channels.** Saves all the selected channel settings, including
bus routing so that you can load saved settings onto another channel.

▶ **Save/Load All Mixer Settings.** Saves all the current audio channel settings so that
you can retrieve them later by using the Load All Mixer Settings.

To load saved Mixer settings, you simply need to select the appropriate channel, select the load
setting option desired, look for the file on your hard disk, and load it in the Mixer window.

In the same menu (see Figure 12.6), you also have the option to link or unlink channels. When
channels are linked, the volume, EQ and send effect settings, the bypass insert, and the bypass
send effect settings you apply to one channel also affect all the other channels linked to this
channel.

CHAPTER 12

Figure 12.16
The context menu
options available in the
Mixer.

Always on Top	
Link Channels	Ctrl+G
Unlink Channels	Ctrl+U
Add Track	▶
Save Selected Channels	
Load Selected Channels	
Save All Mixer Settings	
Load All Mixer Settings	
VU-Meter Settings	▶
Reset VU-Meters	

How To

To link or unlink channels in the Mixer window:

1. Select the first channel you want to link. To select a channel, click above its name or above the pan display on the selection button area (see Figure 12.17).

2. Shift-click on the other channels you want to link with this first channel.

3. Right(PC)/Ctrl(Mac)-click over one of the selected channels.

4. Select the Link Channels option from the context menu.

5. To unlink them, select one of the linked channels and select Unlink Channels from the same context menu.

Figure 12.17
Selecting a channel in the
Mixer by using the
selection buttons.

You can also customize the behavior of VU-Meter found on audio channels:

▶ **Hold Peaks:**Causes the VU-Meter to hold the highest peak detected in the channel for a defined amount of time. How long this time represents depends on your preferences. To change these preferences, select File(PC)/Cubase(Mac) > Preferences > VST and then change the value in milliseconds found in the Change VU-Meter Peak's Hold Time field. This can be any value between 500 and 30,000 milliseconds (0.5 to 30 seconds).

▶ **Hold Forever.** Causes the peak levels to remain until meters are reset. Clicking on the Peak Margin Indicator below the meter will reset this parameter.

▶ **Fast Release.** Causes the VU-meter to respond very quickly to peaks in the signal rather than as a standard VU-meter.

USING HOLD PEAK

You can enable/disable the hold peak option simply by clicking inside the VU meter of any channel inside the Mixer.

The Reset VU-Meters option in the same menu offers a quick and easy way to reset all peaks, both in the graphic display as well as in the numeric display, and this is for all channels in the Mixer.

ADDING TRACKS INSIDE THE MIXER

You can add tracks to your project from within the Mixer by selecting Add Track option in the Mixer's context menu. The track will be added to the right of the currently selected track.

Working with Effects

Chapter 6 discusses how you can apply insert effects, send effects, and EQ to a channel through its Inspector area. Working with effects in the Mixer is no different. The only difference is that all the channels are side-by-side (in SX), making it easier to adjust the different settings of several tracks. SL users can use the Channel Setting panel described in the following section. This won't allow you to see all the effect settings side-by-side in the same window, but you'll get a bird's eye view of all the effects (inserts, EQ, and sends) in the same window.

When working on a mix, it is important to understand that the more effects you have running simultaneously in real time (online as opposed to offline), the more processing power it requires from your computer. With this in mind, it is highly recommended that you use the send effects (through FX channels) whenever possible, rather than using the inserts, if you're going to apply the same effect more than once while using the same settings. By doing so, you will use fewer computer resources, which will allow you to save these resources for when you really need them.

Channel Settings Panel

The Channel Settings panel offers a convenient way of editing all channel settings in a single window. You can access a Channel Settings panel through the Edit Channel Settings button in the Inspector's Channel section, the Track List area, or in the Mixer window (see Figure 12.18).

CHAPTER 12

Figure 12.18
The Edit button opens the Channel Settings panel.

inspector

track list

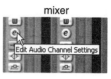

mixer

Audio Channel Settings

The audio Channel Settings panel for every audio channel offers the same five areas (see Figure 12.19). Here they are from left to right:

▶ The Common panel displays a Mute and Solo button that allows you to see if there are any other tracks that are muted or soloed. If one of these buttons is lit, clicking on it unmutes or removes the Solo mode for all channels. Below these two buttons is the channel Reset button, which brings all channel settings to their default position and removes any active inserts or send effect assignments for this channel. Following are the paste channel settings, copy channel settings, and Channel Selection menu. You can use this menu to open another existing channel from the drop-down list. This replaces the current channel settings with the newly selected channel settings.

▶ The audio channel display offers identical settings to the ones found in the Mixer or Channel section of the Inspector area in the project window. Any changes you make here or anywhere else are reflected in all parts of the project. The options available in this area will vary, depending on the type of audio channel displayed.

▶ The audio inserts display the current inserts settings for this channel. As with the audio channel settings, any changes you make here or in any other window in the project update the channel's settings in all windows.

▶ The EQ settings offer a graphical display of the four-band parametric EQ available for each audio channel. See the following section for more information on this area.

▶ The Send Effects Setting panel, as with the inserts, displays the current settings for this channel.

Figure 12.19
The audio Channel Settings panel.

Inserts Settings

In the upper portion of this area are a few controls. The first one on the left selects whether or not you want to see a normal insert selection panel as you have already seen in the Mixer window, or a routing panel, which allows you to route a mono or stereo effect in a surround channel (SX only). The third option will display the insert's preset selection menu so that you can choose from the list of presets how the insert will affect this channel. By default, this menu is set to Normal because being able to select the insert is your first step anyway. When a selection is made, the rest of the area below will change to reflect this selection. Cubase SX users will find more about surround mixing options and handling effects in a surround project in the Appendix E.

To the right of this drop-down menu is the Reset Inserts button, which removes any insert settings and brings back all parameters related to the inserts to a default setting. The Bypass button next to the Reset button, allows you to bypass all the inserts at once. Remember that bypassing inserts does not affect the current insert setup and offers a way to compare the sound of a track with and without the inserts. Finally, the last button in this area of the Audio Channel Settings panel is the Edit Inserts button, which opens all the assigned inserts for the currently edited window.

EQ Settings

"EQing" (pronounced "ee-cueing") is part of the recording and mixing process in probably 99 percent of recordings today, and at some point in your creation process, you will find it to be a very useful tool. This said, it can be used correctively or creatively. Too much equalization, and you might lose the purity of the well-recorded original sound... then again, maybe this is what you were going for. You can use an EQ to increase or decrease specific frequencies to help the general quality of the sound, to correct certain flaws in the recording due to poor microphone performance, to remove noise generated by fluorescent lighting or air conditioning, and in more ways than this chapter allows us to mention. In Cubase, you have four bands of parametric EQ per channel. Note that MIDI channels do not have EQ controls.

Each EQ band gives you control over gain, frequency, and Q.

▶ The Gain control is the amount of gain or reduction that you apply to a frequency. You can add or reduce from + or -24 dB.

▶ The Frequency control determines what frequency is affected by your gain or cut. You can set each band to any frequency between 20 Hz and 20,000 Hz. Each channel offers four bands that can be independently enabled or disabled.

▶ The Q is the control you have over the width of the range of frequencies surrounding the center frequency of a band. The lower the numeric values for this field, the greater the width; the higher the numeric values for this field, the narrower the width. A narrow Q is useful for isolating a problematic frequency, such as a 60 Hz cycle, that is often associated with electrical equipment. A wide Q is useful to enhance or reduce a large area of the harmonic structure of a sound, such as boosting the high end of the sound.

How To

To adjust the EQ settings for an audio channel:

1. From the Track List area, the Channel section in the Inspector area, or the Mixer window, click the Edit Channel button.

   This launches the Channel Settings panel. Note that Cubase SX users can also adjust EQ settings directly in the Mixer window by displaying the Extended panel of the Mixer window and selecting the EQ panel for the desired channel. The following steps describe the procedure within the Channel Settings panel.

2. Activate the desired band by clicking on its Activation button (see Figure 12.20). If you don't activate the band, the changes you make have no effect on the sound.

Figure 12.20
An EQ band is active when the On button is lit.

band is not active      band is active

3. To select a frequency, click and drag the outer ring above the frequency display window for the active band. You can also click in the frequency display to type your frequency or click on the graph above the bands, moving the square handle next to the number corresponding to your band. If you have a scroll wheel on your mouse, you can also use it to change the values inside the numeric field after it is selected.

NOTE

Moving the band's control (in the graphic display area) using the left or right handle changes the frequency; moving it up or down adds or removes gain from that band. If no band control handles appear, it's because you haven't activated any bands. You can kill two birds with one stone by clicking on the green line to activate the band corresponding to the area where you click and moving the control handle that appears to where you want it.

4. Adjust the gain by clicking and dragging the inner ring above the frequency display or by using either the box in the graph or by clicking in the gain area and typing your value. You can enter a maximum value of - or +24. This corresponds to a cut or a boost of 24 dB.

5. To change the Q for the band, you need to use the Q dial found over the Q display. Drag it up to increase or down to decrease the value. You can also click in the Q display area to type your Q value. You can enter any number between 0 and 12. The lo (low) and hi (high) bands have additional settings that were described earlier in Chapter 6.

To hear the sound without the EQ active, and to make sure that the settings you are applying actually help your sound, you can use the EQ Bypass button in the Channel section of this panel.

After you are happy with the result, you can store your settings for later use.

How To

To store an EQ as a preset:

▶ Click the Store EQ button at the top of the EQ section. This button displays a folded page with a plus sign inside.

You can recall a preset by clicking the Presets drop-down menu and selecting the desired preset from the list.

How To

To rename a stored EQ preset:

1. Select the preset from the list found in the top portion of the EQ area.
2. Double-click on its name.
3. Type the new name and click OK.

If you want to remove a preset from the list, select it and click the Remove button. This button displays a folded page with a minus sign inside and is to the right of the Store button.

MIDI Channel Settings

The MIDI Channel Settings panel offers a convenient way to edit all MIDI channel settings for a selected MIDI channel in a single window. You can access a Channel Settings panel through the Edit button in the Inspector's Channel section, the Track List area, or in the Mixer window (see Figure 12.18).

The MIDI Channel Settings panel offers four areas (see Figure 12.21). Here they are from left to right:

▶ The Common panel displays the same options as the audio Channel Settings panel. Please refer to that section for more details.

▶ The MIDI channel display offers settings identical to the ones found in the Mixer or Channel section of the Inspector area in the project window. Any changes you make here or anywhere else are reflected in all parts of the project.

▶ The MIDI inserts display the current inserts settings for this channel. As with the MIDI channel settings, any changes you make here or in any other window in the project update the channel's settings in all windows.

▶ The Send Effects Setting panel, as with the inserts, displays the current settings for this channel.

Note that you can change the channel currently displayed in the MIDI (or audio) Channel Settings panel by accessing the drop-down menu found in the lower left corner of the panel. This makes it easy to navigate or change the settings for different channels without changing your view.

Figure 12.21
The MIDI Channel
Settings panel.

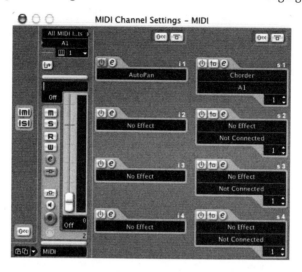

Using Groups

The benefits of using groups were described earlier in this chapter. This section describes how to use a group in a mix situation.

A group channel appears in the Mixer whenever a group track is created. After a group track is created, you can assign the output of other tracks to a group channel in the Mixer window. Group channels can be useful to create submixes, in which a series of related tracks are mixed and sent to a group. You can then use the group's fader as a general level control for all tracks routed to this group.

How To

To use a group as a submix group fader:

1. Start by creating a group channel track in the project window.
2. Name this group appropriately. In Figure 12.22, the group is called *DrumKit.*

Figure 12.22
Naming your group helps
to identify it later when
assigning channels.

3. In the Output Bus selection field found in the Inspector, in the Channel Settings panel, or in the Mixer (SX users only), select the group's name from the channel's Output Selection field. For example, in Figure 12.23, the channel is sent to the group channel named "DrumKit."

4. Repeat Step 3 for all the channels you want to send to this group or any other group channel.

Figure 12.23
Selecting a group as the output for a channel.

in the inspector

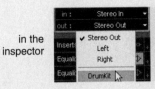

in the Mixer or Channel Settings panel

Now that you have assigned different channels to a group, you can adjust their relative level and use the group's channel fader to adjust the overall level being sent to the master fader.

You can also create a monitor mix that can be sent to any external devices, such as headphones amplifier, effects or another recording device by using one of the send effects. Instead of sending the signal of this channel to an FX channel, you can route the signal to a group channel and then assign the output of this group channel to another available bus. Using this method allows you to send each channel to two sets of outputs (see Figure 12.24), giving you an independent control on levels being sent to each output. Note that you need at least two sets of outputs on your sound card to use this effectively.

Figure 12.24
Using the group channels as an output bus (left) or as a send destination (right).

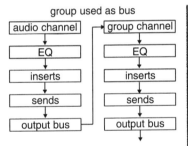
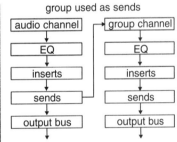

How To

To use a group as a monitor mix (for headphones or external effect processing):

1. Start by creating a group channel; name it and choose an output bus for this Group.

2. Select the channel you want to send to the group channel using the send effects.

3. Click the Channel Settings Edit button. Cubase SX users can also use the Extended panel in the Mixer window and display the Send Effects panel for each channel.

4. In the Channel Settings panel, Activate an empty send effect slot.

5. In this empty effect slot, select the appropriate group as the send effect destination. In Figure 12.25, the group is named *DrumKit*.

continued

Figure 12.25
Assigning a group
channel as a send effect.

5. Adjust the level being sent to the send effect (in this case, the group output channel).

6. If you want to send another channel to a send effect assigned to a group, use the Select Channel menu in the Channel Settings' Common panel. If you are in the Extended panel (SX users), simply select another channel.

7. Repeat Steps 3 through 6 for each additional channel you want to send to this subgroup mix.

8. Adjust the group's level being sent to its output. You can also adjust the output level of output bus.

TIP

If you don't want to have to assign individual channels to a group through send effects in each channel, you can create a submix group. Let's take our previous example of the DrumKit group; you assign all channels to this group. Then you create a second group that you call something like "Headphone Mix." All you need to do is assign the send effect for the DrumKit group to the Headphone Mix output, and then you assign the Headphone Mix output to another bus and voilà! (See Figure 12.26 for a diagram of this example.)

Figure 12.26
Example displaying how
the signal travels when
using a group as a
headphone submix.

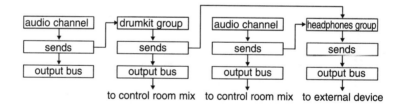

Now You Try It

For information about using the instructions found in this section and to find out where you can get the working files, please consult the section called *About the Exercise Files* in the Introduction section.

13
Working with Automation

Mixing a recording is an art form unto itself—the art of listening. Being a great musician doesn't mean you're going to be a great mixing engineer, and being a great mixing engineer doesn't mean you will be a great musician. No matter what your speciality is, the goal is to get everything in perfect balance. The mixing process inside Cubase is not unlike the traditional mixing process in the sense that external mixer desks have many of the same features that Cubase offers. Where Cubase shines is through its integration of traditional mixing techniques and the addition of real-time effect processing and automation inside a single application.

Here's a summary of what you will learn in this chapter:

▶ Use the Mixer window to record mix automation events.

▶ Use the automation subtracks to record mix automation events.

▶ How to create and edit plug-in parameter automation.

▶ How to edit recorded automation.

▶ How to use SysEx to automate external MIDI devices.

▶ How to use external MIDI remote controllers with Cubase in a mix automation setting.

Cubase provides support for VST effects that come with the program or those bought as plug-ins, and it also provides support for third-party DirectX effects (under the Windows environment). These can produce the same result as VST effects, but are a little more CPU intensive than their VST counterparts because they were written using different standards. Since VST plug-ins have been written for Cubase, this type of plug-in is more effective inside Cubase than DirectX. On this note, be aware that to use DirectX effects, you need to have a DirectX-compatible computer and the latest DirectX support available. You also need to install those third-party DirectX effects on your computer.

ABOUT DIRECTX

Be sure to consult Steinberg's Web site to find out which DirectX version you need and to verify that your other plug-ins support the same DirectX drivers. DirectX technology applies only if you have the PC version of Cubase.

Automation in the Mixer

Automation affects the way audio events are played, and the computer is responsible for this processing, whereas MIDI automation is processed by the MIDI instrument. There are two sets of automation that you can apply: MIDI channel automation and audio channel automation (which includes all types of audio channels as described in Chapter 12). Table 13.1 displays a list of what you can automate in the Mixer window:

Table 13.1
Parameters available for automation in the Mixer window

MIDI Channel Settings VSTi	Audio Channel Settings (including Rewire, Groups and FX channels)
Volume	Volume
Pan	Pan and Surround Panner (SX only)
Mute	Mute
Track parameter on/off switches	EQ Bypass button
Transpose	The settings for up to 4 EQ modules
Velocity shift	Effect send activation switch
Random settings	Effect send levels
Range settings	Effect send pre/post switch
Insert effects bypass switches and parameters	Effect send bypass switch
Send effects bypass switches and parameters	Insert effect program selection

ABOUT AUTOMATING VSTI AND REWIRE CHANNELS

Cubase is a multitrack recorder and a MIDI sequencer that integrates both types of channels inside the same mixing environment, as described in Chapter 12. Because some MIDI tracks might be assigned to VSTi or Rewire compatible applications, this creates additional channels inside your Mixer window: one for the MIDI volume level and another for audio related controls, which also includes a volume level fader. To avoid confusion when mixing levels for these specific channels, you should only use the audio channel to control pan and volume levels when mixing VSTi and Rewire instruments. Otherwise, it is difficult to pinpoint exactly where to change things if you start automating both MIDI and audio volume levels.

We have discussed the Mixer window before, so its options should be familiar to you by now. Although we have looked at how to move faders or pans and how to add effects, we have not learned how to automate these movements. Unlike traditional mixers, Cubase allows you to record most of the manipulations you make inside the mixing environment, including effect automation.

Automation Subtracks

Automating inside Cubase is not limited to the Mixer window. You can also add automation to the automation tracks available in each track in the project window (see Figure 13.1). Automation parameters can be displayed in several ways:

How To

To view automation subtracks:

▶ Click the plus sign in the lower-left corner of the desired track in the Track List area of the project window (see Figure 13.2).

▶ Or, right-(PC)/Ctrl-(Mac) click over the track in the Track List area and select the Show Automation, Show Used Automation, or Show Used Automation for All Tracks options from the context menu.

Figure 13.1
Automation subtracks.

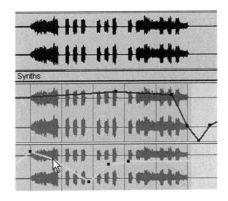

Figure 13.2
The show/hide automation subtracks button.

Automation recorded in these subtracks is no different than the automation recorded in the Mixer window. Automation is always displayed under the track it is associated with; an automation line is displayed over a background representation of the content currently playing in the track. The only difference is the way you record these events. When automation is recorded or edited in one location, it is updated in the other location as well.

Cubase offers two automation methods: by recording the automation using the Read/Write buttons on mixer channels, or by actually drawing automation points on the automation subtracks. Both methods offer similar results, and actions you do using one method will update the results in the other. For example, you can record automation in the Mixer and then later decide to edit this automation using the Pencil tool inside the project window.

All track classes have their own sets of subtracks, depending on what can be automated on them. For example, VSTi tracks can hold as many subtracks as there are parameters and channels available for that particular VSTi. Similarly, a Rewire folder track will appear as soon as you enable a Rewire channel in your project. If you record automation for this channel, the automation is stored in additional subtracks, corresponding to the parameter you edited. Even MIDI tracks have automation subtracks for mixer-related settings, inserts, or send parameter automation. Normally, MIDI will use Control Change messages along with System Exclusive messages to automate MIDI devices, but since some of the parameters you can automate inside Cubase are not supported by MIDI, MIDI automation subtracks pick up where MIDI left off. The more parameters you automate in a single channel, the more automation subtracks you will create for this track.

When automating FX channels, each parameter you move during the automation process will generate a subtrack associated with this channel. So you can, for example, progressively make a room bigger by changing (over time) the room size, reverb time, and predelay parameters on a reverb just as easily as you can create a fade out or pan movement on an audio track.

Recording Automation

Because you can record automation in the Mixer window, as well as by using automation subtracks, we will look at these two methods separately. If you are using an external control surface to control specific parameters inside Cubase, you will probably find that recording automation is easier when done through the control surface, rather than adding events in the automation tracks associated with each channel in the project window. On the other hand, editing previously recorded automation might be easier if done through the project window.

Before heading into the automation section, remember that you can set the levels and pans of audio channels in the Mixer without using automation, just as you would on a normal mixer desk. This allows you to monitor your tracks appropriately without adding automation to them. As long as the Write or Read Automation buttons (found in the Common panel on the left of the Channel Mixer window) are not activated (not lit), the faders, pan, and any other effect settings stay at the same position. If the Read Automation button is not activated in the Common panel, Cubase will not read any automation. However, disabling automation doesn't mean that you lose the automation you have previously recorded.

Using Read and Write Buttons

To record your mix automation using the Mixer window, the Channel Settings panel, or the Channel section found in the Inspector area, you need to use both Read and Write Automation buttons to achieve your goal: the Write button to record the automation and the Read button to read whatever you record afterwards or during a previous pass. To activate the automation writing process, click the Write Automation button of the desired channel. Clicking this button in any of the mentioned areas activates the same function in all subsequent windows where the channel is represented (the Inspector area, the Track List area, the Channel Settings panel, and the Mixer window). By clicking the Write Automation button directly in the channel, you activate the writing automation functions for this channel only. If you want to activate the write channel automation for all channels at once, you can use the Write Automation button found in the Common panel of the Mixer window, as demonstrated in Figure 13.3. Which one you use depends on what you want to achieve.

When you activate the Write button on a channel or in the Common panel of the Mixer, Cubase is ready to record any change in parameter settings. If you don't move a parameter, Cubase will not record any data for this parameter.

Figure 13.3
Writing automation by using channel and common write functions.

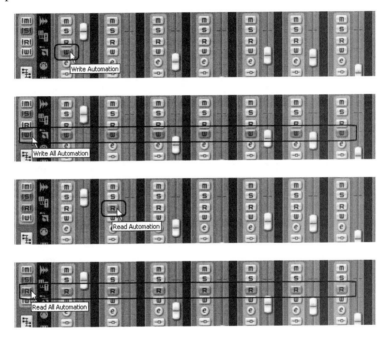

After you have recorded automation, you need to activate or enable the Read Automation button for Cubase to read whatever automation you have recorded. Otherwise, the information is present, but your automation is not read. As with the Write Automation button, the Read Automation button is found in several windows inside your project and enabling it on a channel in one window enables it in all the other windows as well. The Global Read Automation button found in the Common panel of the Mixer window also activates the Read option for all channels in the Mixer at once.

Recording Channel Track Automation

This section describes how to record channel track automation, which any channel settings mentioned earlier in this chapter, as well as MIDI and audio channel settings. The actual settings you can record are determined by the track class itself.

How To

To record channel automation:

1. Open the Mixer window (F3 is the default key command).
2. Activate the channel's Write Automation button. This button is lit when active.
3. Position your playback cursor and click the Play button on the Transport panel (or press the spacebar).
4. Move the appropriate faders, knobs, switches, and so on (this includes any settings mentioned in Table 13.1).
5. Stop the playback when done.

After automation has been recorded, you can listen to it by activating the Read Automation button and bringing the play cursor to the same location you started recording automation. Click the Play button to see (and hear) your recorded automation.

After your automation is recorded, you can use the channel's automation subtracks to view each setting that was automated. We'll get into this a little later in this chapter.

Recording Parameter Automation

Recording parameter changes in a plug-in effect, such as a VSTi or send effect, is quite similar to recording channel settings in track automation. However, these automation events are recorded in separate tracks and subtracks, created automatically as soon as you move one of the controls of an effect or VSTi when the Write Automation button is activated inside the plug-in (this can be a VSTi or VST effect plug-in; PC users cannot automate DirectX effect plug-in parameters). This type of automation is normally used to change the parameters of effects or a VSTi, creating dynamic changes in the plug-in through time during playback. For example, you can automate the Cutoff frequency by moving this parameter in the VSTi panel (provided there is such a parameter on the instrument itself).

How To

To record plug-in parameter automation:

1. Open the desired effect's panel.
2. Activate the Write Automation button found inside the panel. This button is lit when active.
3. Position your playback cursor and click the Play button on the Transport bar (or press the spacebar).
4. Move the appropriate faders, knobs, switches, and so on. You might need to consult the documentation provided with the effect to find out which parameters are

automatable as this varies from one effect to the next (see an example in Figure 13.4, featuring the a1 synthesizer VSTi plug-in).

5. Stop the playback when done.

Once automation has been recorded, you can listen to it by activating the Read Automation button as mentioned earlier in this chapter.

Figure 13.4
Moving the Attack parameter in this example, while the Write Automation button is active and the project is playing, records the changes through time to this parameter.

About Automation Modes

In Cubase SL, there is only one automation mode available. This is called *Touch Fader mode.* In this mode, the program starts writing automation as soon as you click a control or parameter, such as the volume fader, and stops writing when you release the mouse button.

In Cubase SX, there are four additional automation modes: Autolatch, X-Over, Overwrite Mode, and Trim:

▶ With Autolatch, the program starts writing the automation as soon as you click a control, such as the volume fader, and stops writing when you deactivate the Write Automation button. In other words, the last automation value is continuously written until you turn off the Write Automation button within the channel mixer found in the Inspector area or in the Mixer window. This mode is useful if you want to write over a long section that contains previously recorded automation that you want to replace. It is also useful when using an external control surface to control your mix. Because Cubase has no way of knowing which control you want to rewrite, it starts writing as soon as you move a control and keeps the value sent by this control until you stop playback or you switch the Write Automation button off. Make sure, however, that you don't touch any other controls when doing this; otherwise, you might end up replacing automation by mistake. Note that this also applies for some VSTi and VST plug-in effects parameters.

▶ X-Over works much like the Autolatch mode, with one exception: When you cross a previously recorded automation curve, the write process is automatically turned off.

▶ Overwrite Mode is also similar to Autolatch mode with the exception that it only affects volume automation. Use this mode when you want to redo any previously recorded volume automation.

▶ Trim, like the Overwrite mode, works only on the volume automation. What makes it different, however, is that it does not erase previously recorded automation, but rather offsets the previously recorded automation. For example, let's say you recorded a volume automation, starting your automation at -10 dB.

While you listen to the result, you realize that the automation is good, but the whole thing is too soft. Using the Trim mode, you can place the play cursor a bit before your previous automation, enable the Write Automation button, and raise the fader slightly after pressing play. As a result, all the following automation will be raised proportionally by this amount. So, if you start your automation at -7 dB instead, the rest of the automation will have shifted proportionally.

How To

To change the automation mode (in Cubase SX only):

1. In the project window, click the Automation Mode Selection field in the toolbar (see Figure 13.5).

Figure 13.5
The Automation Mode Selection field in the SX project window's toolbar.

2. Select the desired automation mode from the drop-down menu.

Drawing Automation

This section describes how to add automation to any channel automation.

How To

To draw channel settings automation values in an automation track:

1. In the project window's Track List area, select the track for which you want to create automation events.
2. In the bottom-left corner of the selected track, click the Show/Hide Automation button (plus sign) to reveal the first automation subtrack.
3. Select the desired parameter you want to automate from the Parameter field (see Figure 13.6). If the parameter you want to automate doesn't appear in this list, click the More option to display a dialog box revealing additional automatable parameters available for this track, select the one you want and click OK to return to the subtrack. At this point, the Parameter field should display the selected parameter.

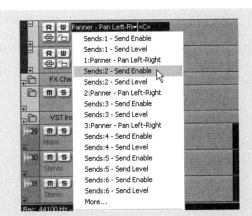

Figure 13.6
Selecting an automation parameter.

4. If there are currently no automation values that have been added to this parameter, a blue (or black, if the Read Automation button is not enabled) horizontal line appears next to this subtrack in the Event Display area. Click the Draw tool to select it.

5. To add a handle, click near the location inside this lane where you want to add an automation value. The line automatically becomes blue if it wasn't before, because adding automation will automatically enable Read Automation. If you want to create a ramp between two points, release the mouse. However, if you want to create a curve, drag your mouse to the next desired location and value (see Figure 13.7).

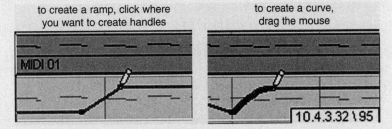

Figure 13.7
Creating a ramp between two separate points (left) and a curve by dragging your mouse (right).

6. Repeat Step 5 to add more automation handles along this parameter's subtrack.

Note that an automation handle is added at the location where you click, as long as you are using the Pencil or Draw tools and stay inside the subtrack's boundaries.

If you want to create automation events to another parameter for the same channel, you can either select another parameter from the Parameter field to display a new parameter in the same subtrack or click the Append Automation Track button as displayed in Figure 13.8. When the new subtrack is visible, repeat Steps 3–6 from the previous list.

Figure 13.8
Appending automation subtracks.

Note that choosing a different parameter in a subtrack that already contains automation does not remove or cancel the automation it holds. When a parameter contains recorded automation events, an asterisk appears after this parameter's name in the Parameter field of the automation subtrack (see Figure 13.9). Using asterisks, you can spot quickly which parameters contain automation already. This makes editing and troubleshooting much more efficient.

Figure 13.9
Parameters with recorded automation events appear with an asterisk in the Parameter field.

After you've recorded automation on a track, you can select the Show Used Automation option available in the Track List's context menu [right-click (PC)/Ctrl-click (Mac)]. You can add automation to several parameters by using a single subtrack, changing the parameter's name to view, or adding new automation, and after you are done, reveal all automation subtracks containing events. Remember that each parameter has its own subtrack.

Under the Line tool are several shapes of line tools: the Line, Parabola, Sine, Triangle, and Square tools. As described in Chapter 8, these tools can be used to create automation values, such as pan effects. However, using the Parabola and Line tool, you can create consistent automation curves instead of drawing handles freely.

Figure 13.10
Using the Parabola to create consistent automation curves.

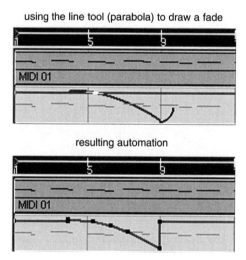

Similar to drawing individual automation handles using the Draw tool, adding handles with the Line tool will automatically activate the Read Automation button and activate the automation.

How To

To add automation using the Line tools:

1. Select the desired line shape you want to use.
2. Select the desired track and expand its automation subtracks.
3. From the Parameter selection field, select the desired parameter for which you want to create some automation handles. You may also append the automation subtracks if you want.
4. If the parameter you want to automate doesn't appear in this list, click the More option to display a dialog box revealing additional automatable parameters available for this track (see Figure 13.11), select the one you want, and click OK to return to the subtrack. At this point, the Parameter field should display the selected parameter.

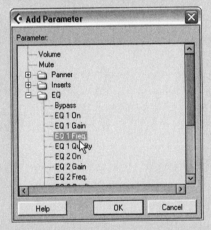

Figure 13.11
The Add Parameter dialog box.

4. Click and drag the cursor in the automation track to add automation points. The options pertaining to the shapes, frequency, amplitude, and starting point of the Line tool are the same as the ones described in Chapter 8.

Hiding and Removing Automation Subtracks

When working with automation, you can hide automation tracks that you don't need to see in order to clear up your working area. Hiding automation subtracks does not prevent automation from being read. If you don't want to hear the changes made by automation, simply turn the Read Automation button off. At any time, you can also mute a specific type of automation by clicking the Mute Automation button in the subtrack's Track List area. For example, Figure 13.12 displays the Pan parameter automation as muted, whereas the Volume parameter automation is not muted. This means that the track plays the volume automation, but not the pan automation.

Figure 13.12
The subtrack's Mute
Automation button.

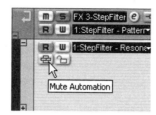

How To

To hide automation subtracks:

▶ To hide all automation subtracks, select the Hide All Automation option from the context menu [appears after right-click(PC)/Ctrl-click(Mac) over the Track List area].

▶ To hide all automation for one track, click the Show/Hide Automation button for this track (the minus sign in the lower-left corner of the track containing the automation subtracks).

▶ To hide only one automation subtrack, click the Show/Hide Automation button of the subtrack above it (the minus sign in the lower-left corner of the subtrack containing the automation you want to hide).

How To

To remove automation subtracks:

▶ To erase all automation events for a subtrack's parameter, select the Remove Parameter option from the Parameter field of this subtrack. This will remove the automation subtrack, as well as all the automation handles on the selected subtrack.

▶ To erase some of the automation events on a subtrack, select them by using the Selection tool or Range Selection tool and delete them by using the Delete or Backspace key. You can also click on the selected automation events (handles) using the Eraser tool.

▶ To remove unused subtracks that might have been left behind after editing, select the Remove Unused Parameters option from the Parameter field in one of the subtracks.

Editing Automation

After you've recorded automation, editing it is not very different. You can use the Mixer window to edit this automation through the Write/Read Automation buttons or by editing the recorded automation parameters in their respective automation subtracks. As mentioned earlier when describing the automation modes, SX users can switch between these modes to use the mode that best suits their editing needs.

How To

To view the automation previously recorded:

1. In the project window, right-click(PC)/Ctrl-click(Mac) in the Track List area.
2. Select the Show Used Automation option from the context menu. If you want to see all automation recorded on all tracks, select the Show Used Automation for All Tracks instead.

You will probably notice that some parameters do not allow intermediate values. This is the case for switch type parameters, such as a Mute, Bypass, or Foot Pedal MIDI message. Because these parameters are either on or off, there are only two acceptable values: 0 or 127. When editing their automation, you can only enter these values, and the automation handle will automatically jump to one position or the other.

Using Write Automation

To edit already recorded automation using the Write Automation button on a channel, you just need to write over the automation again. As soon as you touch the control (by clicking on it and holding it or moving it to a new location), the old automation is replaced by the new one, until you release the mouse. At that point, if the Read Automation button is also active, Cubase continues reading the automation as it appears on the parameter's automation subtrack.

Using Automation Subtracks

When you open a parameter subtrack containing recorded automation, you will notice that points appear along the automation line. Here's a look at how you can edit the points on this line:

How To

To edit recorded automation subtrack:

▶ **To move an existing point.** In the project window, select the Object Selection tool and move the point to a new location by clicking and dragging this point to the new desired location. Note that the quantize grid settings, if the Snap is active, influence where in time you can move this automation.

▶ **To move several automation points simultaneously.** With the Object Selection tool, drag a selection box over the points you want to move. The selected points become red. Click and drag one of the selected points to the new location. You can also Shift-click on several points if you want to edit noncontinuous points instead.

continued

▶ **To draw over an existing automation.** In the project window, select the Draw, Line, Parabola, Sine, Triangle, or Square tool from the toolbar and click where you want to start drawing over the existing automation and drag your tool until the point where you want to stop replacing the existing automation. The first and last point where you draw this automation automatically creates a connection to the existing automation line. You can use the different options associated with each tool to create different shapes; for example, use the Ctrl(PC)/⌘(Mac) key to invert the parabola curve.

▶ **To erase existing automation points.** Click on the point or drag a range over several points using the Object Selection tool. After the desired points are red, press Delete, Backspace on your keyboard or use the Eraser tool to erase them.

▶ **To move or erase all automation points on a subtrack.** Right-click(PC)/Ctrl-click(Mac) over the desired subtrack's Track List area and select the Select All Events option from the context menu. After it is selected, you can move or erase these points. Note that if you want to remove all automation for a parameter, you can also use the Remove Parameter option from the subtrack's Parameter field.

You can also use the Browser window to edit automation, as you would edit any other events in your project (see Figure 13.13). Simply expand the track to reveal the automation events and then select the automation parameter in the Project Structure panel to reveal the list of events it holds in the right panel. Then you can select a value and change it in the list. If the Sync Selection option is checked in the Browser window's toolbar, Cubase displays the event you are editing in the project window.

Figure 13.13
Editing automation in the
Browser window.

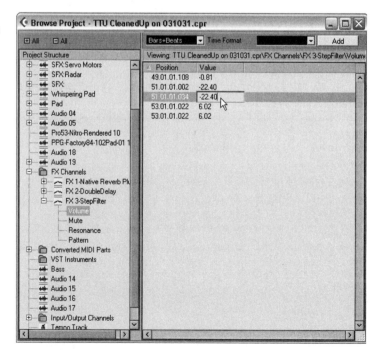

MOVING EVENTS ALONG WITH THEIR AUTOMATION
Quite often, we start working on a project, record events, and add automation to subtracks below these events. But if you need to move these events, it would be nice if the automation could move along with it. The "Automation follows Events" option does exactly that: keeps the automation attached to the event; when you move the event, the automation moves with it. Check this option in the Edit menu or in File(PC)/Cubase(Mac) > Preferences > Editing page

Using SysEx

SysEx (System Exclusive) is used to send data that is specific to a MIDI device, such as a dump of its patch memory, sequencer data, waveform data, or information that is particular to a device. In other words, SysEx is used to change MIDI device parameters that no other MIDI message can, because it is the only way MIDI can retrieve or send parameter data from and to a device.

When working with Cubase, SysEx can serve two main purposes:

▶ You can save all the parameters of a MIDI device used in a project using a bulk dump procedure.

▶ Because you can't automate the parameters of an external MIDI device using automation tracks, you can use SysEx to record parameter changes on your device's front panel into Cubase and then have Cubase play back these parameter changes through MIDI.

You could say that SysEx controls *how* sounds are produced, whereas other MIDI events control when sounds are produced. You do have some control over how a note is played with MIDI events, such as the control provided by Control Change messages; however, this does not affect how the sound is produced by your MIDI device in most commonly used situations.

It is important that a direct MIDI connection between the sender and the receiver be made. You can work with SysEx messages even with devices in a daisy chain; however, this requires extra precautions, such as assigning a different device ID number for each device in the chain, making sure that the base MIDI channel in your external MIDI device is also different from one device to the next in this chain. These precautions help make sure that the MIDI device you meant to communicate with only processes the SysEx messages.

Recording SysEx

There are two reasons you should record SysEx. The first reason is to save all the values that make up one program, or all programs, in the instrument or device, so that when you play a project, it remembers the external device's setup. This includes how the device's parameters are configured, especially when you've made changes to the original sounds provided by the manufacturer. This allows you to recall the device's parameters as they were when you saved the song. The next time you load your project, you won't have to change anything on your device when you load the project because the parameters were stored with the project file using SysEx. This is called a *bulk dump*.

The second reason is to store codes that instruct the instrument to change one of its settings, such as the cutoff frequency of a filter, or the decay of a reverb during playback or at the beginning of the project. System Exclusive can be used as a last resort for things that can't be done with regular MIDI messages. This is done through SysEx parameter changes.

Recording a Bulk Dump

Usually, you will find a function or utility button on the front panel of your MIDI device, which allows you to send a bulk dump. This means that you will be sending SysEx messages. From that point, you can choose what kind of information you want to send. For example, you might send user patches, performances, or system settings. If there are no such buttons on your device, there are two workaround solutions:

▶ Get an editor/librarian software that identifies your device and initiates a SysEx bulk dump request from this application. This allows your software to receive the appropriate SysEx information from your external MIDI device.

▶ Find out what message to send to the device to make it dump its settings via a MIDI output. Use the List Editor in Cubase to insert that message in a MIDI track. Writing such a SysEx string is fairly complicated, and requires an extensive study of the fine print in the operation manual; so if in doubt, stick with the first method and get an editor/librarian—it'll save you lots of headaches.

Because your MIDI device stores values for its parameters in its memory, changing these values results in changing the parameters' settings. Usually, your MIDI device can send all or some of these parameters to Cubase using a bulk dump. This action is performed using SysEx messages.

After your device's SysEx has been dumped into Cubase, you can send it back to the device later to reset all the parameters to the way they were when you saved them. Most hardware MIDI devices have specific functions that allow you to send a bulk dump of all or some of your device's parameters. To find out which function or where this function is, you need to consult your device's documentation.

How To

To record a SysEx bulk dump from an external MIDI device into Cubase:

1. Make sure the MIDI Out of your device is connected to the MIDI In of your computer or Cubase.

2. Inside Cubase, select in the File(PC)/Cubase(Mac) menu > Preferences > MIDI > MIDI Filter. This brings up the MIDI-MIDI Filter preferences (see Figure 13.14).

3. Deselect the SysEx check box under the Record section and leave it checked (default) under the Thru section. This allows you to record it from the MIDI input port, but does not echo the SysEx events through the MIDI output port. Echoing these events back would create a SysEx MIDI loop that could corrupt the transport.

4. Click Apply and then click OK to close the dialog box.

CHAPTER 13

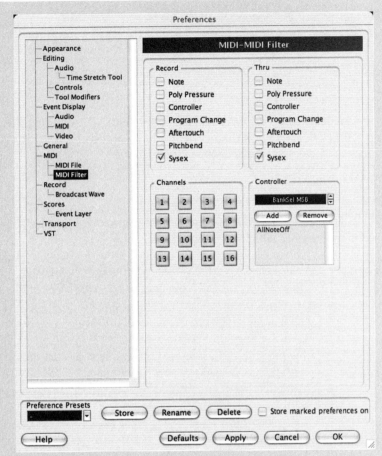

Figure 13.14
The MIDI Filtering option
in Cubase.

5. Create a new MIDI track in your project. This track should be used only for the SysEx events.

6. Assign the MIDI input port appropriately. This should be the port used by the MIDI device to send SysEx to Cubase.

7. Position your cursor at the beginning of your project. Make sure the Metronome click and Cycle Recording mode are disabled.

8. If you already have events recorded in this project, mute all the tracks. When recording a bulk dump of your device's parameters, the SysEx messages require a large portion of your MIDI bandwidth.

9. Click the Record button on the Transport panel.

10. Press the appropriate buttons on your MIDI device to initiate the bulk dump. You might notice during the transmission that your device displays a special message on its LCD screen telling you it's currently transmitting SysEx. When the device is finished with its transmission, you should see a message, such as "Done" or "Completed."

continued

11. When the external MIDI device has completed the bulk dump, you can stop the recording. Depending on the information you transmitted in this bulk dump (if it's just a few parameters or the entire set of parameters in your device), this process might take a few seconds or a few minutes. This creates a single MIDI part, which contains all the SysEx messages.

12. Save the project.

13. Mute this track to avoid having the SysEx retransmitted every time you click Play, or select the Not Connected option from the MIDI output port selection field in the Inspector or Track List area for this track.

Here are some tips when recording SysEx bulk dumps:

▶ Just record the parameters you need to record. Usually, you can tell your MIDI device what type of bulk dump you want to perform. This saves space in your sequencer and speeds up the SysEx transfer back to your MIDI device. In a live performance, you don't want to wait too long between projects for SysEx to be uploaded to your MIDI devices, so keeping things to a minimum is useful.

▶ If you only want Cubase to send parameter information and patch information to your external MIDI device before a song starts to play, put the SysEx information before the first bar if possible, or before the occurrence of MIDI events in your song. This prevents you from having lags in MIDI sent to your devices caused by a long SysEx message being sent simultaneously with other MIDI events.

▶ If all you want to do is change the sound settings (program) during playback, you might be better off creating two different programs and using a program change during playback rather than using a SysEx message. Program changes are more efficient in this case and take less time to update your external MIDI device.

▶ Avoid sending SysEx bulk dump from Cubase to several external MIDI devices simultaneously.

▶ Make sure when you record a bulk dump, that you are using the same device ID number as you will use when sending this bulk dump back to the MIDI device. Otherwise, the device might not accept the SysEx bulk dump.

▶ Certain sequencers allow you to send a SysEx bulk dump automatically whenever you load a MIDI file. Use this feature to configure your devices appropriately for each song, however, keep the previous tips in mind.

Recording Parameter Automation Through SysEx

If you only want to record certain parameter changes, you can proceed in a similar way. This is useful if you want to change a parameter during playback. Remember that MIDI is transmitted over a serial cable, which implies that information is sent one after the other, not side-by-side. In the case of SysEx, the entire SysEx message has to be transmitted before the rest of the MIDI messages can resume their course. So, if you want to record SysEx parameter changes as you are playing notes, the more SysEx messages you are sending, the longer it takes for the other events to be transmitted. Keep your SysEx events as short as possible, or if you can, make sure not to overload your MIDI port with this type of message.

How To

To record parameter changes into Cubase during playback by using SysEx messages:

1. Make sure the MIDI Out of your device is connected to the MIDI In of your computer or sequencer.

2. You might need to disable any SysEx filters from your sequencer's MIDI filter options, as mentioned in the bulk dump procedure described earlier.

3. Create a new MIDI track in your project where you want to record the SysEx. You can record SysEx parameter changes in the same track as the rest of your MIDI messages being sent to this device, but it is not recommended.

4. Chances are, if you want to update parameters during playback, you probably already have a MIDI track with recorded events. At this point, you'll want to hear this track if you want to update the parameters for the sound used in this track, so make sure this track is not muted.

5. Position your cursor at the appropriate location and click the Record button on the Transport panel.

6. Make the changes to your external MIDI device's parameters when it is appropriate in the project.

7. Stop the recording process when done.

8. Rewind and start playback to hear the result.

Because you recorded the SysEx events on another track, if you are not satisfied with the result, you can always erase these events and start over without affecting the other types of events recorded for this part. For example, let's say you have a synth line playing on MIDI port A, channel 1, and you want to change the cutoff frequency of the sound used to play this line as it evolves in the song. You will have one track that contains the notes played by the synth and another track that performs the change in the cutoff frequency using SysEx. Erasing the SysEx events does not affect the notes because they are on separate tracks.

Transmitting Bulk Dumps

After your bulk dump is recorded in your project, you will probably want to send it back to your MIDI device when the time comes to restore the saved information. This is fairly easy to do because you already know how to do a bulk dump in one direction. The following list describes the steps you should take when transmitting the information back to your external MIDI device.

How To

To transmit recorded SysEx bulk dumps to your external MIDI device:

1. Assign the appropriate MIDI output port for the track containing the SysEx bulk dump events. This should be the output port connected to the MIDI input of your external device.

2. If your MIDI device can deactivate its SysEx reception, make sure this option is disabled. In other words, you want your MIDI device to respond to incoming SysEx information.

3. Solo the track that contains the SysEx data. This might not always be necessary, but it's a good precaution to take, because you might have more than one SysEx data track or might have other events that will cause the transfer to interrupt abruptly.

4. Click Play on the Transport panel to begin transmitting a SysEx part to the external MIDI device. You should see some information on the front panel of your external MIDI device to the effect that it is receiving SysEx.

As when your project is receiving SysEx, you should take the same precautions when sending SysEx to your MIDI device. For example, try not to send more data than required. If all you need to recall is a single program's parameters, avoid sending full bulk dumps to your machine. If the bulk dump serves to set up your device for a project, try putting your SysEx in the count-in bars before the actual song starts.

Using a Remote Control Mixer

It is possible to use a MIDI remote control device to record and edit automation inside a Cubase project. Recording automation using such a device is no different than using the controls inside the Mixer window in Cubase. However, editing recorded automation events is a little different. If your remote control MIDI device does not have touch sensitive controls, Cubase does not have any way of knowing if a control is sending information or not once you moved it. As a result, when you activate the Write Automation button in the Mixer window and move a control on your MIDI controller, all following automation is replaced until the moment you stopped playback or disabled the Write Automation button once again. To avoid recording over automation by mistake, you should only enable the Write Automation button on the channels you want to overwrite automation, or avoid moving controllers associated with automation that you want to keep.

To use a controller device with Cubase, you have to install it in the Device Setup panel.

How To

To install a MIDI remote control device:

1. Select the Device Setup option from the Devices menu.
2. Click the Add/Remove tab on the right side of the dialog box (see Figure 13.15).
3. Select the appropriate device from the supported devices list. If your device is not in this list, select the Generic Remote device.
4. Click the Add button in the bottom-right corner of the dialog box. This adds the selected device to your list on the left.
5. Click the Setup tab on the right side of the dialog box.
6. Select the appropriate MIDI input and output ports connecting the controller to Cubase.

CHAPTER 13

Figure 13.15
Adding a MIDI device controller to your device setup.

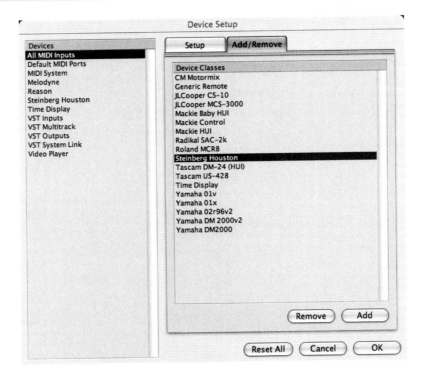

You can now use your controller with Cubase. How this controller interacts with Cubase depends greatly on the controller itself. You need to refer to this controller's documentation for further details.

Most remote control devices can control both MIDI and audio channel automation in Cubase SX even if their parameter setups are different; however, when audio specific parameters are associated with MIDI tracks, such as EQ parameters, they are then ignored by Cubase.

Now You Try It

For information about using the instructions found in this section and to find out where you can get the working files, please consult the section called *About the Exercise Files* in the Introduction section.

14

Working in Sync

Synchronizing Cubase to other devices is one of the most important, yet underused, tasks in a typical recording environment. Synchronization is often something we have to deal with, but resist because it can lead to all kinds of problems. On the other hand, when done properly, it can save you lots of time (which usually converts itself into money) and allow you to accept new and interesting projects, such as film and video sound tracks or sound design and editing. More and more, working in sync implies making two computers work hand-in-hand, where one computer is running the main project and a second computer is running a rack of effects and VSTi, all working in perfect sample-accurate sync, as if they were only one computer. Sharing the workload between computers like this is becoming increasingly popular since the more computers you have, the more processing you can apply, making the workflow a lot smoother. Not to mention the fact that it may also extend the life of your older computer as well, or help to push the upgrade cost a bit further down the road.

In this chapter, you will discover the VST System Link; a networking system provided with Cubase that can transform your second computer into an impressive VSTi rack and a third computer into a processing power house, all linked together, mixing everything inside your first computer. This technology was developed by Steinberg and allows different host computers to share resources by using the digital audio hardware you already have in place, as long as you have a VST System Link compatible application running in every computer.

Here's a summary of what you will learn in this chapter:

▶ Understand the difference between a Word Clock, a timecode, and a MIDI Clock.

▶ Learn how and when to use a specific timecode.

▶ Learn how and when to use a MIDI Clock.

▶ Understand what MIDI Machine Control is and how you can use it.

▶ Determine why digital clocks are important when using digital audio devices.

▶ Find out what VST System Link is and how you can use it.

▶ Learn how to synchronize devices together by using different synchronization methods.

▶ Determine how you can deal with events that need to stay synchronized to time, whereas others are synchronized to bars and beats.

▶ Find out how to work with online video files.

About Word Clock, SMPTE, and MIDI Clock

Before we start looking at how Cubase handles synchronization, it is important to understand the different types of synchronization, its terminology, and the basic concepts behind these terms. The idea behind synchronization is that there will always be a sender/receiver relation between the source of the synchronization and the recipient of this source. There can only be one sender, but there can be many receivers to this sender. There are three basic concepts here: timecode, MIDI Clock, and Word Clock.

Timecode

The concept behind timecode is simple: It is an electronic signal used to identify a precise location on time-based media, such as audio, videotape, or in digital systems that support timecode. This electronic signal then accompanies the media that needs to be in sync with others. Imagine that a postal worker delivering mail is the locking mechanism, the houses on the street are location addresses on the timecode, and the letter has matching addresses. The postal worker reads the letter and makes sure it gets to the correct address, the same way a synchronizing device compares the timecode from a source and a destination, making sure they are all happening at the same time. This timecode is also known as SMPTE (*Society of Motion Picture and Television Engineers*), and it comes in three flavors:

▶ **MTC (MIDI Timecode).** Normally used to synchronize audio or video devices to MIDI devices such as sequencers. MTC messages are an alternative to using MIDI Clocks (a tempo-based synchronization system) and Song Position Pointer messages (telling a device where it is in relation to a song). MTC is essentially SMPTE (time-based) mutated for transmission over MIDI. On the other hand, MIDI Clocks and Song Position Pointers are based upon musical beats from the start of a song, played at a specific tempo (meter-based). For many nonmusical cues, such as sound elements that are not part of a musical arrangement but rather sound elements found on movie sound tracks (for example, Foley, dialogue, ADR, room tones, and sound effects), it's easier for humans to reference time in some absolute way (time-based) rather than musical beats at a certain tempo (music-based). This is because these events are regulated by images that depict time passing, whereas music is regulated by bars and beats in most cases.

▶ **VITC (Vertical Interval Timecode).** Normally used by video machines to send or receive synchronization information from and to any type of VITC-compatible device. This type of timecode is best suited for working with a Betacam or VTR device. You will rarely use this type of timecode when transferring audio-only data back and forth. VITC may be recorded as part of the video signal in an unused line, which is part of the vertical interval. It has the advantage of being readable when the playback video deck is paused.

▶ **LTC (Longitudinal Timecode).** Also used to synchronize video machines, but contrary to VITC, it is also used to synchronize audio-only information, such as a transfer between a tape recorder and Cubase. LTC usually takes the form of an audio signal that is recorded on one of the tracks of the tape. Because LTC is an audio signal, it is silent if the tape is not moving.

Each one of these timecodes uses an hours: minutes: seconds: frames format.

ABOUT MOVIE SOUND TRACKS

The sound track of a visual production is usually made up of different sounds mixed together. These sounds are divided into six categories: Dialogue, ADR, Foley, Ambiances, Sound Effects, and Music.

The dialogue is usually the part played by the actors or narrated off-screen.

The ADR (*Automatic Dialogue Replacement*) refers to the process of rerecording portions of dialogue that could not be properly recorded during the production stage for different reasons. For example, if a dialogue occurs while there is a lot of noise happening on location, the dialogue is not usable in the final sound track, so the actor rerecords each line from a scene in a studio. Another example of ADR is when a scene is shot in a restaurant where the atmosphere seems lively. Because it is easier to add the crowd ambiance later, the extras in the shot are asked to appear as if they are talking, but, in fact, they might be whispering to allow the audio boom operator to get a good clean recording of the principal actors' dialogue. Then, later in a studio environment, additional recordings are made to recreate the background chatter of people in this restaurant.

The Foley (from the name of the first person who used this technique in motion pictures) consists of replacing or enhancing human-related sounds, such as footsteps, body motions (for example, noises made by leather jackets, or a cup being placed on a desk, and so on), or water sounds (such as ducks swimming in a pond, a person taking a shower, or drowning in a lake).

Ambiances, also called *room tones*, are placed throughout a scene requiring a constant ambiance. This is used to replace the current ambiance that was recorded with the dialogue, but due to the editing process, placement of camera, and other details that affect the continuity of the sound, it cannot be used in the final sound track. Take, for example, the rumbling and humming caused by a spaceship's engines. Did you think that these were actually engines running on a real spaceship?

The sound effects in a motion picture sound track are usually not associated with Foley sounds (body motion simulation sounds). In other words, "sound effects" are the sounds that enhance a scene in terms of sonic content. A few examples are explosions, gun shots, the "swooshing" sound of a punch, an engine revving, a knife slashing, etc. Sound effects aren't meant to mimic but to enhance.

And last but not least, the music, which comes in different flavors, adds the emotional backdrop to the story being told by the images.

CHAPTER 14

Frame Rates

As the name implies, a frame rate is the amount of frames a film or video signal has within a second. It is also used to identify different timecode uses. The acronym for frame rate is "fps" for Frames Per Second. There are different frame rates, depending on what you are working with:

▶ **24 fps.** This is used by motion picture films and in most cases, working with this medium will not apply to you because you likely do not have a film projector hooked up to your computer running Cubase to synchronize sound.

▶ **25 fps.** This refers to the PAL (*Phase Alternation Line*) video standard used mostly in Asia and SECAM/EBU (*Sequential Color And Memory/European Broadcast Union*) video standard used mostly in Europe. If you live in those areas, this is the format your VCR uses. A single frame in this format is made of 625 horizontal lines.

▶ **29.97 fps.** Also known as 29.97 nondrop and may also be seen as 30 fps in some older two-digit timecode machines (but not to be mistaken with the actual 30 fps timecode; if you can't see the 29.97 format, chances are the 30 format is its equivalent). This refers to the NTSC (*National Television Standards Committee*) video standard used mostly in North America. If you live in this area, this is the format your VCR uses. A single frame in this format is made of 525 horizontal lines.

▶ **29.97 fps DF.** Also known as 29.97 drop frame (hence the DF at the end). This can also be referred to as 30 DF on older video timecode machines. This is probably the trickiest timecode to understand because there is a lot of confusion about the drop frame. To accommodate the extra information needed for color when this format was first introduced, the black-and-white's 30 fps was slowed to 29.97 fps for color. Though not an issue for most of you, in broadcast, the small difference between real time (also known as the wall or house clock) and the time registered on the video can be problematic. Over a period of one SMPTE hour, the video is 3.6 seconds or 108 extra frames longer in relation to the wall clock. To overcome this discrepancy, drop frames are used. This is calculated as follows: Every frame 00 and 01 are dropped for each minute change, except for minutes with 0's (such as 00, 10, 20, 30, 40, and 50). Therefore, two frames skipped every minute represents 120 frames per hour, except for the minutes ending with zero, so 120×12 = 108 frames. Setting your frame rate to 29.97 DF when it's not—in other words, if it's 29.97 (Non-Drop)—causes your synchronization to be off by 3.6 seconds per hour.

▶ **30 fps.** This format was used with the first black-and-white NTSC standard. It is still used sometimes in music or sound applications in which no video reference is required.

▶ **30 fps DF.** This is not a standard timecode protocol and usually refers to older timecode devices that were unable to display the decimal points when the 29.97 drop frame timecode was used. Try to avoid this timecode frame rate setting when synchronizing to video because it might introduce errors in your synchronization. SMPTE does not support this timecode.

Using the SMPTE Generator Plug-in

The SMPTE Generator (SX Only) is a plug-in that generates SMPTE timecode in one of two ways:

▶ It uses an audio bus output to send a generated timecode signal to an external device. Typically, you can use this mode to adjust the level of SMPTE going to other devices and to make sure that there is a proper connection between the outputs of the sound card associated with Cubase and the input of the device for which the SMPTE was intended.

▶ It uses an audio bus output to send a timecode signal that is linked with the play position of the project currently loaded. Typically, this tells another device the exact SMPTE location of Cubase at any time, allowing it to lock to Cubase through this synchronization signal.

Because this plug-in is not really an effect, using it on a two-output system is useless because timecode is not what you could call "a pleasant sound." Because it uses an audio output to carry its signal, you need to use an audio output on your sound card that you don't use for anything else, or at least one channel (left or right) that you can spare for this signal. Placing the SMPTE Generator on an empty audio track is also necessary because you do not want to process this signal in any way, or the information the signal contains will be compromised.

How To

To use the SMPTE Generator plug-in:

1. Create a new audio track.
2. Open the Track Inserts section in the Inspector area.
3. From the Plug-ins Selection drop-down menu, select the SMPTE Generator.
4. Expand the audio channel section in the Inspector area.
5. Assign the plug-in to a bus that doesn't contain any other audio signal. If you don't have an unused bus, see if you can use one side in a left/right setup and then pan the plug-in on one side and whatever was assigned to that bus to the other side. For example, use a bass on the left and the SMPTE Generator on the right.
6. Click the Edit button to access its panel (see Figure 14.1).

Figure 14.1
The SMPTE Generator panel.

7. Make sure the Framerate field displays the same frame rate as your project. You can access your Project Setup dialog box by pressing the Shift+S keys to verify if this is the case. Otherwise, set the Framerate field to the appropriate setting.
8. Make the connections between the output to which the plug-in is assigned and the receiving device.
9. Click the Generate button to start sending timecode. This step verifies if the signal is connected properly to the receiving device.

continued

CHAPTER 14

10. Adjust the level in either the audio channel containing the plug-in or on the receiving device's end. This receiving device should not receive a distorted signal to lock properly.

11. After you've made these adjustments, click the Link button in the Plug-in Information panel.

12. Start the playback of your project to lock the SMPTE Generator, the project, and the receiving device together.

MIDI Clock

MIDI Clock is a tempo-based synchronization signal used to synchronize two or more MIDI devices together with a beats-per-minute (BPM) guide track. As you can see, this is different than a timecode because it does not refer to a real-time address (hours: minutes: seconds: frames). In this case, it sends 24 evenly spaced MIDI Clocks per quarter note. So, at a speed of 60 BPM, it sends 1,440 MIDI Clocks per minute (one every 41.67 milliseconds), whereas at a speed of 120 BPM, it sends double that amount (one every 20.83 milliseconds). Because it is tempo-based, the MIDI Clock rate changes to follow the tempo of the master tempo source.

When a sender sends a MIDI Clock signal, it sends a MIDI Start message to tell its receiver(s) to start playing a sequence at the speed or tempo set in the sender's sequence. When the sender sends a MIDI End message, the receiver stops playing a sequence. Up until this point, all the receiver can do is start and stop playing MIDI when it receives these messages. If you want to tell the receiver sequence where to start, the MIDI Clock has to send what is called a *Song Position Pointer message*, telling the receiver the location of the sender's song position. It uses the MIDI data to count the position where the MIDI Start message is at in relation to the sender.

Using MIDI Clock should be reserved for use between MIDI devices only, not for audio. As soon as you add digital audio or video, you should avoid using MIDI Clock because it is not well-suited for these purposes. Although it keeps a good synchronization between similar MIDI devices, the audio requires much greater precision. Video, on the other hand, works with time-based events, which do not translate well in BPM.

MIDI Machine Control

Another type of MIDI-related synchronization is the MIDI Machine Control (MMC). The MMC protocol uses System Exclusive messages over a MIDI cable to remotely control hard disk recording systems and other machines used for recording or playback. Many MIDI-enabled devices support this protocol.

MMC sends MIDI to a device, giving it commands such as play, stop, rewind, go to a specific location, punch-in, and punch-out on a specific track.

To make use of MMC in a setup in which you are using a multitrack tape recorder and a sequencer, you need to have a timecode (SMPTE) track sending timecode to a SMPTE/MTC converter. Then you send the converted MTC to Cubase so that it can stay in sync with the multitrack recorder. Both devices are also connected through MIDI cables. It is the multitrack that controls Cubase's timing, not vice versa. Cubase, in return, can transmit MMC messages through its MIDI connection with the multitrack, which is equipped with a MIDI interface. These MMC messages tell the multitrack to rewind, fast forward, and so on. When you click Play in Cubase, it tells the multitrack to go to the position at which playback in Cubase's project begins. When the multitrack reaches this position, it starts playing the tape back. After it starts playing, it then sends timecode to Cubase, to which it then syncs.

Digital Clock

The digital clock is another way to synchronize two or more devices together by using the sampling frequency of the sender device as a reference. This type of synchronization is often used with MTC in a music application such as Cubase to lock both audio sound card and MIDI devices with video devices. In this case, the sender device is the sound card. This is by far the most precise synchronization mechanism discussed here. Because it uses the sampling frequency of your sound card, it is precise to 1/44,100th of a second when you are using a 44.1 kH sampling frequency (or 0.02 milliseconds). Compare this with the precision of SMPTE timecode (around 33 milliseconds at 30 fps) and MIDI Clock (41.67 milliseconds at 120 BPM), and you quickly realize that this synchronization is very accurate.

When you make a digital transfer between two digital devices, the digital clock of the sender device is sent to the receiver device, making sure that every bit of the digital audio from the sender device fits with the receiver device. Failure to do so results in signal errors and will lead to signal degradation. When a receiver device receives a Word Clock (a type of digital clock) from its sender, it replaces its own clock with the one provided by this sender.

A digital clock can be transmitted on one of these cables:

▶ **S/PDIF (Sony/Phillips Digital InterFace).** This format is probably the most common way to connect two digital devices together. Although this type of connection transmits digital clock information, it is usually referred to by its name rather than Word Clock. S/PDIF connectors have RCA connectors at each end and carry digital audio information with embedded digital audio clock information. You can transmit mono or stereo audio information on a single S/PDIF connection.

▶ **AES/EBU (Audio Engineering Society/European Broadcast Union).** This is another very common, yet not as popular type of digital connector used to transfer digital information from one device to another. AES/EBU uses an XLR connector at each end of the cable; like the S/PDIF format, it carries the digital audio clock embedded in its data stream. You can also transmit mono or stereo audio information on this type of connection. Because this type of connection uses XLR connectors, it is less susceptible to creating clicks and pops when you connect them, but because they are more expensive, you won't find them on low-cost equipment.

▶ **ADAT (Alesis Digital Audio Technology).** This is a proprietary format developed by Alesis that carries up to eight separate digital audio signals and Word Clock information over a single-wire, fiber-optic cable. Most sound cards do not provide ADAT connectors on them, but if yours does, use it to send and receive digital clock information from and to an ADAT compatible device.

▶ **TDIF (Tascam Digital InterFace).** This is a proprietary format develop by Tascam that also provides eight channels of digital audio in both directions, with up to 24-bit resolution. It also carries clocking signals that are used for synchronizing the transmission and reception of the audio; however, it does not contain Word Clock information, so you typically need to connect TDIF cables along with Word Clock cables (see below) if you want to lock two digital audio devices using this type of connection.

▶ **Word Clock.** A digital clock is called *Word Clock* when it is sent over its own cable. Because Word Clock signals contain high frequencies, they are usually transmitted on 75-ohm coaxial cables for reliability. Usually, a coaxial BNC connector is used for Word Clock transfers.

To be able to transfer digital audio information in sync from one digital device to another, all devices have to support the sender's sampling rate. This is particularly important when using sampling frequencies other than 44.1 or 48 kH, since those are pretty standard on most digital audio devices.

When synchronizing two digital audio devices together, the digital clock might not be the only synchronization clock needed. If you are working with another digital hard disk recorder or multitrack analog tape recorder, you need to send transport controls to and from these devices along with the timing position generated by this digital clock. This is when you have to lock both the digital clock and timecode together. Avoid using MIDI Clock at all costs when synchronizing with digital audio. The next section discusses different possibilities and how to set up Cubase to act as a sender or a receiver in the situations described previously.

When doing digital transfers between a digital multitrack tape and Cubase, it is important that both the Word Clock (digital clock) information and the timecode information be correlated to ensure a no-loss transfer and that for every bit on one end, there's a corresponding bit on the other. This high-precision task can be performed through ASIO Position Protocol (APP).

APP uses the ASIO driver provided for your sound card and a compatible APP digital device, such as Alesis' ADAT. In this type of setup, the ADAT provides the master (sender) Word Clock and the timecode information to Cubase. The ASIO 2.0 compatible driver of your sound card simply follows this information and stays accurate to the last sample.

VST System Link

It seems that we never have enough power in one computer to do all that we want to do. Well, Steinberg understands this and developed a protocol called *VST System Link*, which connects two or more computers together using a digital audio connection as the link between these two computers. After your computers are hooked up together, the VST System Link, makes it possible to run two or more VST System Link compatible host applications in perfect digital audio sync with each other. It does this without any network cards, hubs, or other type of connection.

After the computers are linked, you can activate the system link and use VSTi in one computer and control them using a keyboard hooked up to the second computer. You can also have audio tracks in two different projects on two different computers playing in complete sync. This means that you can split the tracks of your song into two projects, processing some tracks here, other tracks there, sharing the workload between two computers even if the computers are not in the same room as you are. If you don't want to split up your audio tracks, you can still run all your effects on one computer and monitor the result in the other. Using this system, you could run Cubase with Nuendo or V-Stack, or on a Mac and a PC, for example. V-Stack is a System Link host, but without the Cubase or Nuendo tracks. In other words, you can load VSTi, but you can't record any events in it. You can visit Steinberg's Web site for more information.

About System Link

VST System Link uses a single bit of the digital audio stream as a carrier for transport and synchronization information. It can also use other bits of the digital audio stream for MIDI information. Several computers can be linked in a daisy-chain configuration—each one passing on the accumulated information to the next via standard digital audio cables, with routing to the various systems controlled by a master (sender) software running on the first computer in the chain.

To run a VST System Link, you need the following items:

▶ Two or more computers. All computers must have an ASIO 2.0 compatible sound card.

▶ A host application (such as Cubase SX, SL, SE, V-Stack, Nuendo, or Cubase VST 5.2 System Link version) running on each computer.

▶ All sound cards must have one of the following digital audio connectors: SPDIF, ADAT, TDIF or AES/EBU. This said, your sound card might have an ADAT connector, but it might not work with System Link. If you are investigating potential sound cards, make sure to find out if your sound card has been tested successfully with System Link before purchasing it for this purpose. You can find information on the sound card's manufacturer Web site or at the Steinberg Web site or forums (http://forum.cubase.net).

▶ At least one digital cable for each computer in your VST System Link network.

Linking Computers

In its simplest form, you can connect two computers by using a simple S/PDIF or AES/EBU digital connection, as shown in Figure 14.2. In this scenario, Computer A's digital Out goes into Computer B's digital In and vice versa. If you don't have a digital mixer or even an analog mixer, you can simply send the analog output of Computer A to your monitoring system. Because the system link only uses one bit in your digital connection, you can still use the other 15 bits (19 or 23, depending on the digital word length available in your sound card) to transmit digital audio from Computer B to Computer A. Therefore, you would be mixing both the content of Computer A & B inside Computer A, sending the final mix to a pair of control room monitors.

It is important, as in any digital linkup, that one of the two computers be the digital clock sender (master clock) and the other, the digital clock receiver (slaved clock).

In Figure 14.3, we've replaced the analog mixer with a digital one, allowing us to connect digitally to the mixer and use this mixer to forward any instruments you might want to record. As with the previous setup, Computer A is the digital clock sender and the two other devices are receivers.

Figure 14.2
Setting up a system link
between two computers
using S/PDIF or EBU.

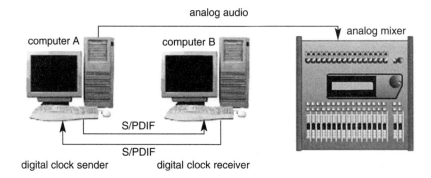

However, you could set the digital mixer as a digital clock sender and have the two computers receiving. It all depends on how your studio is set up. The figure displays an ADAT connection between each component in the linked network. This is probably the most convenient way of doing it, giving you eight digital channels that you can patch anywhere you want, but you could also do this with a S/PDIF or an AES/EBU connection.

This type of setup is pretty simple as well, but it also has some limitations. Because the ADAT carries the audio information from A to B, you will be using Computer B to monitor or mix. Computer A, on the other hand, is receiving the digital mixer's outputs through its ADAT connection. You, therefore, have to configure your setup to properly monitor and record events from Computer B, or use Computer A as your main station, using the digital mixer's ADAT outputs to monitor Computer B.

Figure 14.3
Setting up a system link
between two computers
and a digital mixer using
any digital connection.

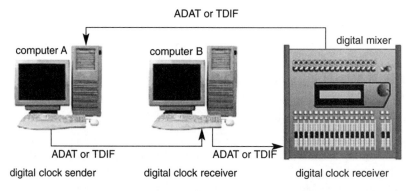

Figure 14.4's setup is similar to the one provided in the previous figure; however, in this case, an S/PDIF (this could be another format as well) feeds the digital input of the digital mixer, allowing you to monitor or control from Computer A, and then to the digital mixer to monitor the output in speakers. You could also draw an S/PDIF connection from the mixer's digital output to Computer A's digital input. As you can see, connecting hardware using System Link is quite easy. Now, let's look at how it all works inside Cubase.

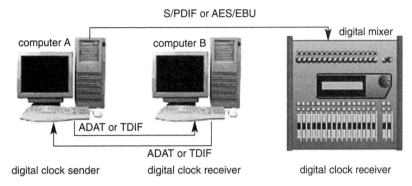

Figure 14.4
Setting up a system link between two computers and a digital mixer by using two digital connections.

Latency Issues with System Link

As you saw earlier in this book, latency is the delay that happens between the processing stage and the monitoring stage—for example, the delay between the moment you press a note on your keyboard and the time it takes for a VSTi to play that note. With ASIO driver sound cards and Cubase, this can be kept to a minimum, hopefully below 10 or 12 milliseconds. However, when linking computers together, the latency is the total amount of latency caused by all computers. So, if you have 10 milliseconds of latency on both, your total latency when linking computers is approximately 20 milliseconds. Note that latency does not affect the synchronization of events with the rest of your events because Cubase's technology compensates for this latency. Because the more latency you have, the more delay you hear between the action and the result, the harder it is for you to focus on the task at hand when recording events through a linked system with a high latency time.

You can generally adjust the latency time of a sound card by changing its DMA buffer size, as mentioned earlier in this book. If you are not sure how to change these values, consult the driver documentation for your hardware device (sound card).

Setting Up System Link Inside Cubase

To configure your system link properly, you should start by setting up one computer and then the next, establishing a successful link. If this setup works, you can proceed with a third or fourth computer, adding one when you've established a working link.

All projects in all linked computers must be set at the same sampling frequency and should also be at the same tempo setting to work properly.

The following setup procedure assumes that you have properly connected the digital audio cables between the two computers, as illustrated in the previous section.

How To

To set up two computers using the VST System Link:

1. On Computer 1, access the sound card's Control panel in order to set it as digital clock master. You can usually access this panel by clicking Devices > Device Setup > VST Multitrack > Control Panel. From that point on, where you need to click depends on the sound card you are using. Make sure the digital clock source of your sound card is set to internal. This will be the digital clock sender (or master).

2. On Computer 2, repeat what you just did for Computer 1, but in this case, set the digital clock to receive its digital clock from the appropriate external source. For example, if you have an S/PDIF connection between both computers and a project running at a sample rate of 44.1 KHz, set Computer 2's digital clock to "External 44.1 KHz".

3. On both computers, set the sampling rate for the project. It is important that all sampling rates match the source's sampling rate.

4. Make sure all additional digital format settings, such as Emphasis on S/PDIF, for example, are turned off in all computers. These settings are usually associated with the sound card's Control panel. S/PDIF emphasis may cause the System Link not to work properly. Also make sure that there is no volume gain or reduction, pan, or processing at the sound card's Control panel stage.

5. In both computers, create input and output buses. The buses will connect the outputs of Computer 2 to the inputs of Computer 1. The number of buses you create and how you configure them will depend on your computer's hardware connections and your needs.

6. Associate these input and output buses to your sound card's digital audio ports on both computers. This may be S/PDIF, ADAT, TDIF or AES/EBU. If you only have an S/PDIF digital connection, you will be limited to a stereo bus going from Computer 2 to Computer 1 and vice versa. We assume at this point that you are using Computer 1 to monitor what comes from Computer 2.

7. On Computer 2, create an audio track or select the existing audio channel you want to monitor in Computer 1's mixer.

8. Set the output bus for that channel to the digital audio output you will be using for System Link. For example, this could be the ADAT outputs 1-2 on Computer 2.

9. On Computer 1, create an audio track or select the existing audio channel you wish to monitor from Computer 2's System Link channel.

10. Set the input bus for that channel to the corresponding digital audio input you will be using for System Link. Following the example above, this would be the ADAT inputs 1-2 on Computer 1. In other words, the ADAT outputs 1-2 of Computer 2 are feeding the ADAT inputs 1-2 on Computer 1.

11. Enable the Monitor Input button in the audio channel if you want to monitor audio coming into Computer 1 from Computer 2.

At this point, you have established that whatever is assigned to an output in Computer 2 can be monitored through a corresponding channel in Computer 1, providing that you choose the corresponding input setting in this computer. But there's still no locking happening between the two computers, just monitoring. So, let's activate the system link.

How To

To activate the VST System Link:

1. On Computer 1, select the Device Setup option from the Devices menu.
2. Select the VST System Link option in this dialog box and make sure that the Setup tab in the right portion of the window is active (see Figure 14.5).

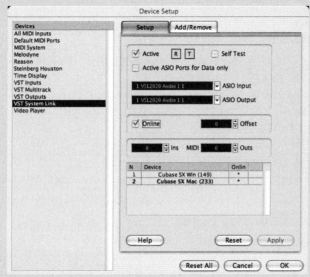

Figure 14.5
The Device Setup VST System Link options.

3. Next to the ASIO Input field, select the digital input from which you want to receive system link information.
4. Next to the ASIO Output field, select the digital output to which you want to send system link information.
5. Click the Active check box to activate the system link.
6. Repeat Steps 1 to 5 on Computer 2.
7. After the setting is completed on Computer 2, click the Online check box to activate it.
8. Repeat this operation (enabling the Online check box) on Computer 1.

You should note that the ASIO Input and Output ports you will be using for System Link can be the same ones you use to carry digital audio information from one computer to the other. If you only have an S/PDIF connection between both computers, this connection can serve to monitor the audio and to synchronize the transport functions that the system link provides. The only difference is that if you are using a 24-bit resolution, one of the S/PDIF channels will have 24-bits for the audio where the one assigned to carry the system link information will have 23-bits of audio and 1 bit for the system link. This should not cause any noticeable effect in the signal.

After you have completed this setup on the second computer, you should see the R (Receive) and T (Transmit) indicators next to the Active check box in the device setup start flashing to indicate that the computers are linked together and receiving or transmitting information when you begin playback on Computer 1 (or 2). You should also see the name and number of the computer appear in the box found in the lower half of the Device Setup dialog box. In Figure 14.5, Computer 1 is running Cubase SX on Windows while Computer 2 is running Cubase on Macintosh.

Next to the computer name, you can see the Online column. When a computer is online, you can remote control its transport operations. For example, you can start Computer 2 from the Transport panel of Computer 1. However, if you want to set a computer offline so that it stays linked, but independent, deselect the Online option in the Device Setup dialog box.

You are now ready to put your VST System Link setup to the test. If for some reason you find yourself unable to communicate between your computers using System Link, try these tests:

▶ Try to connect using another digital connection on your sound card. For example, if ADAT doesn't work, try S/PDIF.

▶ Look on the sound card manufacturer's Web site to find out if you have the latest drivers.

▶ Look on the sound card manufacturer's Web site to find out if your sound card supports VST System Link or if there is any support for it. Some sound cards are known not to work with VST System Link. This is the case with the popular Delta 1010 sound card from M-Audio at the time of writing this book. Checking the Web site, as mentioned, is a good habit since new drivers can often solve such issues.

▶ Look on Steinberg's Web site for additional information on tested sound cards.

Using System Link MIDI Ports

Besides the fact that system linking your computers together controls transport functions from one computer to another and monitors the outputs of one computer on another, it also provides 16 additional MIDI ports. As you probably know, a MIDI port can carry up to 16 channels of MIDI. In other words, VST System Link provides you with an additional 256 MIDI channels. These MIDI ports can, however, only be used to control VSTi. As you might recall, Cubase does not have a MIDI input channel selection field. This will make using MIDI channels useless unless you add an input transformer filter as was mentioned earlier in Chapter 7.

How To

To use a system link MIDI port between two computers:

1. On Computer 1, create a MIDI track.
2. From the Track List area or the Track Setting section in the Inspector area, select the VST System Link MIDI output port of your choice.
3. Enable the Record Ready button for this MIDI track.
4. On Computer 2, open the VST Instruments panel and load an appropriate VSTi in an available slot.

5. Create a MIDI track or select an existing MIDI track.

6. Enable the MIDI Monitoring button for that track.

7. In the MIDI input port, select the VST System Link port number corresponding to the one you chose on Computer 1 (in Step 2).

8. In the MIDI output port, select the VSTi you have just activated.

9. Bring up the Mixer window (for SX users) or open the Channel Settings panel (for SL or SX users).

10. Select the appropriate output bus for the VSTi channel. This is the output bus you created earlier that routes the output of the VSTi to the digital output of Computer 2 to the digital input of Computer 1.

11. Back in Computer 1, create an audio channel.

12. Route the input of this channel to the corresponding input bus (this is the bus that will receive the digital audio from Computer 2).

13. Enable the Monitor Input button on this channel.

Now when you play the keyboard, the MIDI is recorded into Computer 1 because that's where the track is set as Record Enabled, but it is the VSTi on Computer 2 that generates the sound. This sound is monitored through an audio channel on Computer 1. On Computer 2, the MIDI track is only set to monitor whatever MIDI events are coming in and send those events to the appropriate MIDI output port (in this case, a VSTi).

You could also elect to proceed differently. For example, you could record on Computer 1 using a VSTi as your output or another external device and then after recording, simply assign the output of that track to the VST System Link and follow the same earlier steps. Another option is to play the events on your keyboard through Computer 1 and record on Computer 2 instead. In this case, you enable the Record Ready button for this track on Computer 2 rather than using the Monitor button. All this depends on how you want to proceed, depending on the task and the resources at hand and where you want to place your events. A good rule of thumb to follow is always to keep all the recorded content in one place. This will make it easier to back up your information later on.

Using both techniques mentioned above, you can also send audio from Computer 1 to be processed by an FX channel in Computer 2 and then send the resulting audio back into an audio channel in Computer 1. In this case, you route the audio you want to process on Computer 2 to the output bus created for this purpose in Computer 1. In Computer 2, you create two tracks: one for the FX you want to use and another for the audio. This audio channel takes its input from the System Link bus, as described earlier, and then, sends its audio through the Sends FX. It is the output of the FX channel that is routed to the System Link bus and monitored in Computer 1.

Resolving Differences

Synchronizing Cubase implies that you are resolving the differences between different machines to follow a single sender clock, which guides other clocks and tells them where they should be at all times. The next section discusses how to resolve these differences and set your software and hardware preferences accordingly, depending on the situation at hand.

Cubase offers solutions for most synchronization situations. If you have an ASIO 2.0 compatible driver for your sound card and an ASIO 2.0 compatible external device, it allows you to have not only a sample accurate synchronization, but also provides a Positioning Protocol that calculates the relation between the Word Clock position and the timecode position to offer stable synchronicity. If your external hardware does not support ASIO 2.0, use MIDI Timecode options instead. You might want to consult your manufacturer's documentation in regards to ASIO 2.0 implementation to find out more about the possibilities it has to offer.

There are three different methods used by Cubase to synchronize to other devices: Resolving, Continuously Resynchronizing, and Referencing. These are not settings you can adjust in Cubase, but rather ways that Cubase uses to stay in sync.

▶ **Resolving.** Implies that all devices are synchronized to a single digital and timecode reference, resolving their clock to the sender's. This is the best synchronization method, but not always practical in a small home studio because it often requires an external module, called a *House Sync*, which connects all devices and locks them together using a very stable clock.

▶ **Continuous Resynchronization.** Implies that a timecode is sent to a digital audio device, which in turn, uses this timecode as a reference to make sure its digital clock is always in sync, thus continually resynchronizing itself to this timecode.

▶ **Referencing.** Implies that you create a SMPTE audio track by selecting the SMPTE Generator plug-in (as mentioned earlier in this chapter) whenever you don't have a timecode available but need to lock two devices together. This creates a timecode reference (sender), such as a timecode track found on an analog multitrack recorder. Generating such a file guarantees that the timing in this file coincides with the timing (clock) of your sound card because it is this sound card's clock that is being used to generate the file in the first place.

Internal and External References

First, you need to determine where your synchronizing reference is coming from. Because Cubase offers very stable synchronization, you might want to consider using this as your source, making it the sender for other devices. But in the real world, this is not always possible.

Cubase can be the receiver, sender, or both simultaneously. It can receive a sync signal from a sender sync device and send this sync signal to another receiver device, regenerating the sync information for a stable synchronization.

You need to keep two important factors in mind when working out synchronization between devices, especially when you connect multiple devices using digital connections, such as the ones mentioned earlier in this chapter:

▶ What device is responsible for the digital clock information? In other words, who will be sending its Word Clock information to others? If you don't have any digital connections in your studio, chances are your sound card is the sender. If this sound card is connected to any other device through a digital connection, you need to look at how it is connected and how it is set up. How devices are interconnected digitally influences how digital audio flows between these devices (see Figure 14.6).

▶ Where does the time-related (such as timecode and positioning) information come from? If you are working with an SMPTE video, multitrack tape recorder with a timecode on it, chances are, you need to slave (set as the receiver) Cubase to these devices. How devices are interconnected with a timecode reference influences who controls the transport and location functions.

Figure 14.6
Top: the computer is master (sending) while the other device is slaved (receiving); Bottom: the computer is slaved to the other device.

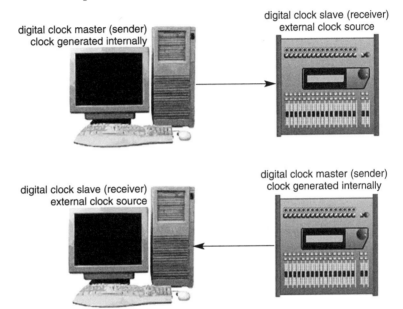

digital clock master (sender)
clock generated internally

digital clock slave (receiver)
external clock source

digital clock slave (receiver)
external clock source

digital clock master (sender)
clock generated internally

These are two synchronization issues that are often misunderstood, but essential in today's digital studio. So, let's first determine if you need to worry about digital synchronization, and then we'll look at timecode synchronization.

1. Does your sound card provide a digital connection of some sort (S/PDIF, ADAT, Word Clock, TDIF, or AES/EBU)?

   ▶ *No, it doesn't.* Then your computer's sound card is the digital clock reference (sender).

   ▶ *Yes, it does provide a digital connection.* Read the following question:

2. Is your sound card set to follow its internal Word Clock or is it set to follow an external Word Clock (or digital connection that carries Word Clock information)?

   ▶ *My sound card's digital clock is set to internal.* Then your sound card is the digital clock reference (sender). You should make sure other devices are set to follow (receive) this digital clock. This is done through your sound card's Control panel. Figure 14.7 shows an example of a sound card Control panel; however, yours might differ, depending on your sound card model, manufacturer, and driver version.

▶ *My sound card's digital clock is set to follow an external clock.* Then your sound card is receiving an external digital clock, and you should make sure that it is locked to this digital clock. This is done through your sound card's Control panel, as well as in the digital clock control settings on the sending device. It is important that the digital clock sender is connected with the digital clock receiver at all times.

Figure 14.7
Setting up your sound card's Word Clock source in the sound card's Control panel.

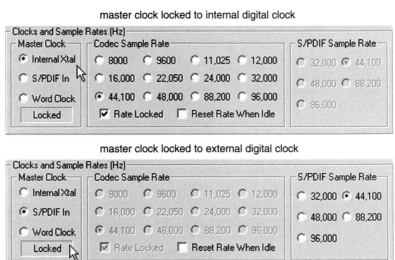

After you've established that the proper digital connections are made and that the sender/receiver relation has been established, you can configure the second step in the synchronization setup: Who controls the timecode? Let's look at some potential setups.

Setting Up Synchronizations

Let's take a closer look at the Synchronization dialog box (see Figure 14.8).

Figure 14.8
The Synchronization Setup dialog box.

Synchronization Setup

Timecode Source
- ⦿ None
- ◯ MIDI Timecode
- ◯ ASIO Positioning Protocol
- ◯ VST System Link

Machine Control
- ⦿ None
- ◯ MIDI Machine Control

Options
- 6 ⬍ Drop Out Time
- 3 ⬍ Lock Time

MIDI Machine Control Settings
- Not Connected ▼ MIDI Input
- Not Connected ▼ MIDI Output

MIDI Timecode Settings
- Not Connected ▼ MIDI Input

Send MIDI Timecode
Port
☐ US–224 MIDI
☐ US–224 Control Port
☐ Port 1

Send MIDI Clock
Port
☐ US–224 MIDI
☐ US–224 Control Port
☐ Port 1

(Help)   (Cancel) (OK)

▶ **Timecode Source.** Selects the source of your timecode. If Cubase is not receiving a timecode from any other devices or if Cubase is the source of timecode, this option, by default, is set at None. Otherwise, you can select the appropriate timecode source. In the event that you are slaving Cubase's time to a MIDI Timecode, you need to select the MIDI input on which the MTC arrives.

▶ **Machine Control.** Lets you select whether Cubase receives and transmits MMC, as described earlier. In the event that you have connected Cubase to a MMC-compatible device, you need to select both the MIDI input and output ports that communicate the MMC information to and from this device in the appropriate fields in the upper-right portion of this dialog box (see Figure 14.8).

▶ **Options fields.** Sets both the Drop Out Time and Lock Time options. The dropout time is a frame value. When you are receiving timecode from a tape recorder, degradation of the timecode signal might occur, leaving the timecode unreadable for a number of frames. If this is the case, Cubase stops playing and then starts playing again when it can understand the timecode again. To avoid this problem, you can raise the amount of dropout time tolerated by Cubase before it stops playing. If your timecode is really bad, you might want to consider rerecording the timecode track rather than setting this option high because the shift in timecode between the estimated timecode (the one Cubase estimates it's at when the signal is dropped) and the real timecode (the one on the Sync reference) might create undesired effects. The Lock Time option represents the amount of frames Cubase needs to receive before it starts playing after it locks to that timecode. If you have many events to chase, such as program changes and mix automation parameters, you might want to set this to a higher value in order for all the data to load and play properly when Cubase starts playing. On the other hand, if you don't have that many events to chase, you can set this to a lower setting. Finally, the Ignore Hours check box allows you to ignore the hour value in the timecode. This has no effect on the position of the timecode itself unless you run projects that are longer than one hour. However, if you work on projects for which each section of a film starts with a different hour setting, ignoring the hour helps you in establishing an adequate offset time, if needed.

▶ **Send MIDI Timecode and Send MIDI Clock.** Selects the MIDI outputs Cubase uses to send these types of signals. If you have a drum machine that needs to receive a MIDI Clock, for example, you need to select the MIDI output connected to this drum machine.

How To

To set up synchronization properties:

1. To open the Synchronization dialog box, Ctrl(PC)/⌘(Mac)-click on the Sync button in the Transport panel or select Sync Setup from the Transport menu.
2. Select the appropriate timecode source for your project.
3. If you have selected MIDI Timecode as your timecode source, select the appropriate MIDI input port on which the MTC arrives.
4. If your project requires that you connect with a MIDI Machine Control compatible device, select this option and set the appropriate MIDI output port to send and receive the MMC.
5. If you have other devices connected to your computer that require Cubase to retransmit synchronization signals to them, such as MTC or MIDI Clock, select the appropriate MIDI output ports.
6. You should leave the options (dropout time and lock time) in the Synchronization Setup dialog box at their default values. In the event that you need to change these values due to a bad timecode coming from a tape recorder or other source, you may access this dialog box and adjust the values until the timecode locks properly.
7. Close the Synchronization Setup dialog box.
8. Activate the Sync button on the Transport panel. Cubase now waits for an incoming sync signal.

To achieve better results when synchronizing Cubase to MTC, it is recommended that the sync box converting LTC timecode to MTC also sends out Word Clock information as well. This provides a more stable synchronization for both MIDI and audio. This option requires that:

▶ You have a sync box generating Word Clock information.

▶ Your sound card's Word Clock options are set to follow an incoming clock signal.

Most SMPTE to MTC converters work fine until you start using audio in your project. If there is no audio clock information, the audio might shift during the project to adjust itself to a less accurate MTC signal.

When you configure Cubase to lock to an external timecode source, you might have to change the current start time setting. The start time setting found in the Project Setup dialog box (Shift+S) tells Cubase the timecode reference of Bar 1, Beat 1—in other words, the time at the beginning of the project. When working with video, for example, chances are that the timecode does not start at 00:00:00:00. It is a common practice to start the timecode at a different hour for each reel of film. For example, a 90-minute movie might be divided on nine reels and then transferred on the same videotape or separate videotapes. To make sure that cues on reel four are not mistaken for cues on reel seven, the timecode for reel four starts at four hours (04:00:00:00) and reel seven at seven hours (07:00:00:00). Furthermore, a lead-in time might be added before the reel to allow for video and audio calibration, setting the timecode to begin at least thirty seconds before the hour (in reel four, this is 03:59:30:00). If you want your song to begin at Bar 1, Beat 1, you need to offset the start time in Cubase to correspond to the timecode accordingly. In this example, you can set the start time for reel four to 04:00:00:00, which tells Cubase that Bar 1, Beat 1 (1.1.000) corresponds to this value.

The Display Offset field in the Project Setup then brings back the time displayed in the ruler to a 00:00:00:00 time. The fact that your song starts at the timecode address of 04:00:00:00 doesn't mean that you want to calculate the time starting at four hours. Changing the time in this field sets your start position (1.1.000) at something other than a time equivalent to 00:00:00:00 (see Figure 14.9).

Figure 14.9
Adjusting the Start and
Display Offset settings to
match incoming
timecode.

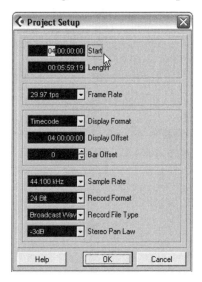

Getting Cubase to Sync with Others

Figure 14.10 displays a simple setup where a video player sends SMPTE information (most likely LTC, in this case) to a MIDI interface. The MIDI interface (or patch bay) acts as a SMPTE to MTC converter, relaying the MTC to Cubase. In this setup, you should set the digital clock of your sound card to Internal and set the timecode source to MTC, making sure to select the MIDI input port on which the MTC arrives.

Figure 14.10
Simple synchronization
diagram.

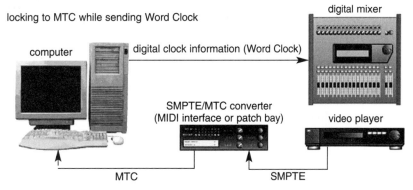

CHAPTER 14

If, for some reason, the digital mixer or other digital device connected to your computer has to be the sender Word Clock, make sure your sound card follows the incoming clock by setting its digital clock source to External (this might be an S/PDIF, ADAT, AES/EBU, or Word Clock connection—see Figure 14.11). Consult your sound card's documentation to configure it appropriately.

In Figure 14.11, the setup is different in the sense that Cubase locks to an incoming MTC source; however, in this case, this MTC and the Word Clock information comes from a synchronizer. The synchronizer's role is to correlate both timecode and Word Clock together, making it the unique source feeding Cubase. This type of setup helps in keeping a simple, yet stable synchronization between devices. It also allows you to hook up other digital devices to the synchronizer in an effort to ensure that the source of the Word Clock information and MTC all come from one source. In this case, as in the previous example, Cubase's synchronization option should be set to follow an MTC source, and your sound card should be set to follow an external digital clock (in effect, slaving to it).

Figure 14.11
Another simple
synchronization diagram.

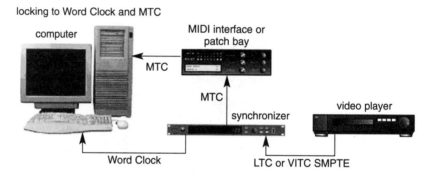

In Figure 14.12, things might look complicated, but you can break this down one item at a time. In fact, this type of setup displays different ways that devices can be interconnected, transmitting, and receiving various synchronization protocols at once.

Let's start with the drum machine. In this setup, Cubase is connected through its MIDI interface to a drum machine, sending a MIDI Clock synchronization signal to it. For the drum machine to lock with Cubase, you need to check the appropriate MIDI output port to send MIDI Clock in the Synchronization Setup dialog box. You also need to set your drum machine to receive an incoming MIDI Clock; otherwise, it does not respond to this signal.

Below the drum machine is a multitrack tape recorder with a compatible MIDI Machine Control (MMC) interface. By connecting both the MIDI input and output to your computer's MIDI interface, you create the necessary MIDI bridge between Cubase and the tape recorder, as described earlier in the MMC section. But for MMC to work, the tape recorder has to send out timecode information to the computer. This is done through the LTC (SMPTE) signal being sent to the synchronizer. The synchronizer converts the LTC into MTC, sending it to the computer. Note here that if all you have is a tape recorder and a computer, you don't need the synchronizer in between, but you still need an SMPTE to MTC converter. In either case, for the timecode source in Cubase to read the incoming MTC signal, the MMC option needs to be selected, and the appropriate MIDI input and output ports receiving and transmitting the MMC information also need to be selected.

So, in this setup, Cubase's timecode source is external, yet it still generates a MIDI Clock to slave the drum machine to the project's location and tempo setting.

Figure 14.12
A more complex studio setup involving different types of simultaneous synchronization.

complex synchronization setup

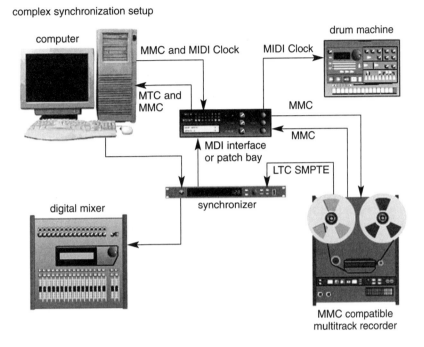

Now, let's try a little quiz to see if you understand these connections. In this setup:

1. Which device is responsible for the timecode information?
2. Which device is responsible for the transport commands?
3. Which device is responsible for the Word Clock information?
4. Which device is responsible for the MIDI clocking information that controls the drum machine?

Answers: In this setup:

▶ The tape recorder provides the timecode source.

▶ The MMC provides the transport controls, but it is Cubase that controls the MMC.

▶ The computer's sound card provides the Word Clock along with the MIDI Clock.

▶ Cubase converts the timecode from the tape recorder into MIDI Clock, which then controls the drum machine.

Linear Time and Musical Time

When working with video, you might want to place some sound effects, ambiances, or Foley where and when these events occur onscreen. These are timing-sensitive events, not bar-and-beat sensitive events. Changing the tempo of a song might not only change where a song starts in relation to the video, but it also shifts all these time-sensitive events with it as well. Changing the timebase of a track from musical to linear keeps events on this track from shifting in time when the tempo of the project changes. Furthermore, if you want to lock all events on this track from being edited or moved by mistake, you can lock the track.

Looking at Figure 14.13, you can see the same two audio events on the same two tracks. Even though all audio events are the same in both examples, the tempo setting is different in the upper portion than it is in the lower one. The track 2 (Narration 03) is set as a linear timebase track, whereas the track 1 (Audio 01) is set as a musical timebase. Track 2 contains a narration and track 1 a beat. In the top portion, you can see in the Transport panel that the tempo is set at 75 BPM and the display shows that the play line is at Bar 3, Beat 1, which at 75 BPM occurs 06 seconds and 11 frames after the beginning of the project.

In the lower portion, things have changed; the events were not moved, but the Tempo track has been deactivated, bringing the tempo up to 120 BPM from its previous 75 BPM. As you can see, the track 2 (Narration 03) did not move in time and neither did the play line, but both are now at Bar 4, Beat 1, past the fourth 16th-note. That's because in the time needed to play three bars at 75 BPM, you can play more bars at 120 BPM. Looking at the Transport panel, which displays both Bars & Beats (on the left) and Timecode (on the right), you can see that the time in frames remains the same, while the time in bars and beats changes. Also, the linear tracks remain unchanged, while musical tracks are adjusted according to fit the new tempo setting.

Figure 14.13
Comparing linear timebase events with musical timebase events at different tempo settings.

Time Warping

The Time Warp tool provides a way to match musical (tempo based) references to linear (time based) references. Time Warp also provides a way to find out the tempo of a MIDI or audio recording that was made without a metronome. Once you have determined the starting point of this recording, you can then create tempo changes that will make the bars match up to the events you recorded. This is different from the Beat Calculator since Time Warping works with previously recorded material, and tempo changes are added to align this recorded material with the project's bars and beats, whereas the Beat Calculator provides a way to enter a tempo value at a specific location inside the project by tapping the desired tempo.

When you use the Time Warp tool, the tempo value of the last tempo event (before the click position) is adjusted. If there are other tempo events later on the Tempo track, a new tempo event will be created where you clicked with the Warp tool to adjust the tempo, preventing these later tempo changes from moving from their original positions. By holding down the Shift key as you are inserting a new tempo event, you can also create a new tempo event between two existing ones, without affecting the position of these two previous tempo change events. You will also notice that the Ruler bar will turn burgundy when the Warp tool is selected and inserted tempo changes appear as markers along this bar (see Figure 14.14).

Figure 14.14
The Ruler displays tempo changes when the Warp tool is active.

You can select a range of events using the Selection Range tool in the project window or in other editors and use the Time Warp option on this selection. Tempo changes will then be confined to the selection within the range. Tempo events will be inserted at the start and end of the selection range, which makes this technique useful if you need to adjust the tempo within a certain area but want all material outside that range to stay in place.

When you use the Time Warp tool in an editor, a tempo event will be added at the start of the edited part or event.

How To

To add a Tempo change using the Warp tool:

1. Enable the tempo track; the Warp tool will be disabled if the Tempo track is not active.

2. Enable the Snap function and set your Snap mode appropriately. This will help in making sure a tempo change occur on bars, at the cursor's location or at an event's start point.

3. Select the Warp tool from the toolbar. At this point, you probably have an event that you want to match up with a marker (this might represent a specific visual cue) or a bar's first beat.

continued

4. Click in the window (Project or editing) at a musical position and drag it so that it matches a position in the material you are editing (see Figure 14.15). This could be the start of an event, a certain cue within a video event, or a downbeat in an audio loop. When you drag the mouse, the events inside the project (or editor) are temporarily converted to linear time, locking them in place while the bar/beat grid becomes elastic, with an anchor at the beginning of the project, or if you already have tempo changes, the elastic portion will be limited to the area found between tempo changes.

5. When you are satisfied with the location of the tempo change, release the mouse. You will see a tempo change marker appear in the ruler bar with the BPM value rounded off to the closest integer value next to it.

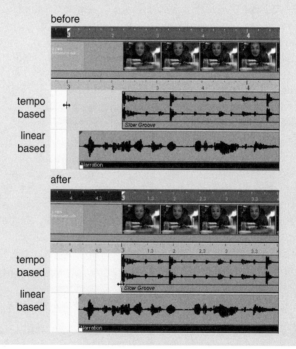

Figure 14.15
Using the Time Warp tool to add tempo changes.

How To

To Erase a tempo change using the Warp tool:

▶ While the Warp tool is selected, hold down the Shift key while clicking on an existing tempo change in the ruler bar.

▶ Open the Tempo editor, select the tempo change, and delete it or click on it with the Eraser tool.

After the Warp tool is selected, you can see the tempo changes in the Ruler bar and move these tempo changes by dragging their marker to a new location. You will notice that the cursor changes to a pointing hand when you hover over the tempo change marker.

Using Musical Events Follow Mode

By default, the Warp tool will be set to Warp Grid and this is what we have discussed up until this point. When you click the Warp tool, there is a drop-down menu that reveals a second Warp mode: Warp Grid (Musical Events Follow). With this option, contrary to the default Warp Grid mode where all tracks are temporarily switched to Linear mode, which keeps their location in time intact and moves the grid around, here none of the events are locked in place. Instead, you can adjust the length of events to match the tempo change, which allows you to also match musical or audio cues with visual cues.

How To

To match musical cues to video cues by using Warp tool:

1. Enable the Tempo track; the Warp tool will be disabled if the Tempo track is not active.

2. Enable the Snap function and set your Snap mode appropriately. This will help in making sure tempo changes occur on bars, at the cursor's location or at an event's start point. Which mode you choose depends on what you are trying to achieve.

3. Select the Warp Grid (musical events follow) mode from the Warp tool drop-down menu.

4. Switch the tracks that you don't want to move to linear time. This can be the audio guide track that accompanies the video, for example, or any time-sensitive sound or musical event, such as a sound effect that occurs at a specific time. All events found on tracks set to Linear Time mode will not be affected by the changes in tempo created by the Warp tool in this mode (musical events follow).

5. Insert a marker where the musical cue should occur (this corresponds to the visual cue). Adding a marker will make it easier to snap the tempo change to this cue, especially if the Snap to Events mode is selected. Also, you can position the marker with frame accuracy, making for a tight tempo change as well. To make this task easier, SX users can add a second ruler track and display both tempo and timecode information (each ruler track displaying its own format). This will allow you to see with accuracy where the frame changes occur.

6. Click and drag the start point of the musical event (tempo-based) to the location of the marker to make the start point match the marker or referenced time-based event (a video event in Figure 14.16). This assumes that there are no other tempo changes later in the Tempo track. However, if you already have tempo changes and simply want to add a new one, hold the default Shift modifier key, which will add a new tempo change between the existing ones instead of moving the previous tempo changes.

continued

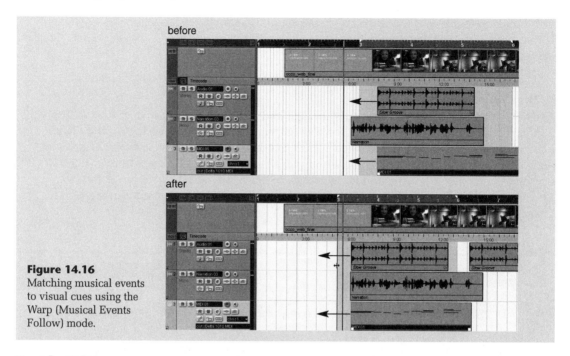

Figure 14.16
Matching musical events
to visual cues using the
Warp (Musical Events
Follow) mode.

Inside Editors

Working with the Warp tool inside an editor (Audio Part, Sample, or MIDI) is fairly similar to working with the Warp tool in the project window. However, when you add a tempo change inside one of these editors, an additional tempo change is added before and after the event or part in the project in order to keep previous events or parts in place. Also, the Musical Events Follow mode is not available in the Sample Editor, and the events on the track where the event being edited is located are temporarily switched to linear time.

Using the Warp tool inside the MIDI Editor is also similar to the Sample Editor. When working with Warp inside the editor, Cubase will add a tempo change before and after the event in the project window to prevent events occurring after this event from being moved from their current location. There are two Warp modes available in the MIDI Editor.

Tempo Mapping Freely Recorded Events

The Warp tool offers a great way of creating a tempo map of freely recorded MIDI or audio events. Freely recorded refers to musical performances that were recorded without the use of a metronome, which implies that there will be slight changes in the tempo throughout the entire project. Recording performances without the metronome gives more expressive freedom to the musician being recorded, but makes it harder to add other musical events and match everything together within a bar and beat grid. That's why using the Warp tool to create tempo changes and align musical down beats with the project's grid comes in very handy.

Typically, you can start by aligning the beginning of the event to the beginning of the project (bar 1, beat 1). Once the start point is established, you can zoom in as close as you can to see some detail. This can be done in any of the editing windows that support the warp tool. By shift-clicking along the events inside a part or inside the project window to add tempo changes, you can map out the entire performance, making it easy to build an arrangement around this performance.

Working with Video Files

With the arrival of DV cameras on the market, more and more video enthusiasts are using their computers to edit movies. Cubase allows you to take these video files and add sound to them to create original soundtracks or musical scores.

There are two basic methods of viewing a video inside Cubase: using your computer monitor to display the video, which implies your computer's CPU is processing the video codec in real time, or by using a special video card that connects to an external monitor. In the latter case, the video card handles the video codec and frees up the computer resources, giving you a better quality image and a bigger image all together while working on the sound.

The PC version of Cubase supports three playback engines: Microsoft DirectShow, Video for Windows, and Apple's QuickTime format. The Mac version supports the QuickTime format. In either platform, this implies that you can open AVI, QuickTime, or MPEG files in the following codecs: Cinepak, Indeo, DV, MPEG, or M-JPEG. To use the QuickTime playback method on a PC, you need to install QuickTime on your computer. If you haven't done so already and want to use the multipurpose method, a QuickTime installer is available on the Cubase SX/SL CD.

How To

To set up for online video files in a Cubase project:

1. In the Devices menu, select the Device Setup option.
2. In the Device Setup dialog box, highlight the Video Player option to view the corresponding settings in the right side of the dialog box, as shown in Figure 14.17.
3. In the Playback Method drop-down menu, select the desired playback method.
4. Under Video Window, select the size of the window you want to use. Note that the larger the Video window is, the more processing is required by your computer.
5. Click the Apply button and then click OK.

continued

CHAPTER 14

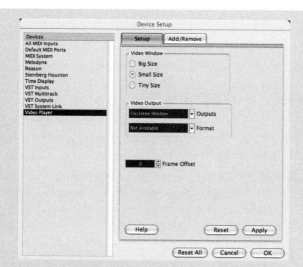

Figure 14.17
The Video Player settings
in the Device Setup
dialog box.

6. In the File menu, select Preferences.

7. Under Event Display, select Video. This page offers two options.

8. Click the Show Video Thumbnails to see a thumbnail preview of the video in the video track.

9. The video cache size represents the cache memory reserved to display thumbnails in the video track. If you are using a long video file or want to stretch the video track to see bigger frames, you need to increase the cache size for the thumbnails to display properly. Otherwise, leave this setting at the default value.

10. Click OK to close the window.

How To

To import an online video file into a Cubase project:

1. Back in the File menu, select Import and then Video File.

2. Browse to the location of your file, select it, and then click Open. This adds the video file to the Media Pool.

3. Right-click(PC)/Ctrl-click(Mac) in the Track List area and select Add Video Track from the context menu.

4. From this point, you can use one of two methods to add your video to the video track. First, you can right-click the video in the pool and select the Insert Into Project option in the context menu. Then you can choose if you want to insert it at the current cursor position or at the video's original time. Second, you can drag the video, as you would for an audio event, in the video track at the desired location.

Note that when the Video window is active, you can Right-click(PC)/Ctrl-click(Mac) on it to expand the window to full screen.

15
Mixdown and Mastering

After you have finished the recording, editing, mixing, automation, and tweaking stages, comes the final mixdown stage. If you are not familiar with creating a final mixdown, make a CD and have your friends listen to what you have done and ask them if they have any comments on the sonic content of your music. When you have collected enough comments to safely assume that everything you have done up until now is how you want it, you can start distributing the music you call your own. On the other hand, if you don't feel you need comments from others to know whether what you did sounds great, you can go straight from mixdown to mastering within Cubase.

This chapter describes different possibilities involved in mixing down these arrangements into a stereo mix. Let's take a look at the last steps after you have finished working on the arrangements. For now, just remember the following steps as you read how to do them later in the chapter.

Here's a summary of what you will learn in this chapter:

▶ Create an audio version of your external MIDI instrument.

▶ Touch up your mix to include the newly converted MIDI tracks into audio tracks.

▶ Export a mixdown of this in a format to create a first draft CD.

▶ Listen to this CD in different environments, collect comments, and go back to your project to make changes.

▶ Generate a new audio mixdown of your material.

▶ Export files in a format compatible with your audio mastering tool.

▶ Create a second draft CD and listen to it again in different environments.

▶ Burn the master copy of your CD.

▶ Distribute your project.

Including Your MIDI in the Mixdown

MIDI is a great way to lay down ideas and record music using synthesizers (external or sound card-based), samplers, and drum machines, among other things. However, distributing your work on a CD or through the Internet using MIDI is probably not the greatest solution. This is because, even with the General MIDI standard, the sounds they produce are not necessarily what you had in mind, and CDs just don't support MIDI. VST Instruments and Rewire instruments are also MIDI-based, so they won't work well outside the VST environment. So you need to convert your MIDI events into audio events when you are satisfied that the tracks are what you want them to be. In the next couple of sections, you will see how to do this. Note that if you are using sounds generated by a synthesizer, wave table, or any other sound-generating device found on your sound card, or if you are using any software-based sampler that is not VSTi or Rewire compatible, you need to convert them into audio files to include them in your final audio mix.

Converting Your MIDI Tracks

There are a few ways you can approach this task: the simple way, the multitrack way, and the sample-based way.

The simple way involves mixing all your MIDI events using the Mixer and then recording a stereo mix of all MIDI events as a stereo audio file that you place on an audio track in Cubase.

The multitrack method involves recording each MIDI instrument as a separate audio file, mono or stereo, depending on the instrument itself. Later, you can treat these instruments the same way as you do any other audio track in Cubase, using the Mixer windows to adjust the effects and levels. With both methods, the recording starts where the MIDI events start on a track, recording them as you record any instrument.

In the sample-based method, you proceed in the same way, but for space efficiency purposes, you record only the parts that are different and then copy these parts on the tracks, as you would do for a drum. For example, if the bass line of a verse remains the same for the first eight bars and then changes for the second eight bars of each verse, you record the first eight bars, copy it across the track, and then record the second eight bars for the remainder of the verses. Which method you use is entirely up to you and involves the same procedure with different levels of manipulations.

How To

To convert MIDI tracks playing external MIDI devices into audio tracks:

1. Start by turning the MIDI metronome off, especially if the same device you are using to record generates this.

2. Mute all your audio tracks and create an empty stereo (or mono) audio track. If you have a multi-input sound card *and* a mixer with multiple output buses, you can record more than one track at a time, if you are recording your MIDI tracks on separate audio tracks. Just make sure to read Step 4 carefully to avoid having feedback loops.

3. Set up your MIDI tracks to play only the events (tracks) that send MIDI information to external devices, muting all other tracks and unmuting the tracks you want to record. You can use the Solo button to quickly isolate a specific track for recording.

4. Connect the outputs of your MIDI devices to the inputs of your sound card. If you have an external mixer, send the output of your mixer into the inputs of your sound card, making sure not to include the output of your sound card in the mix. This can be done in different ways, depending on your mixer capabilities. For example, if you have buses, assign all your MIDI devices to the bus or buses you are sending to the input bus that you will be using to record the audio. Make sure that the output

buses associated with your sound card outputs are only sending audio to your monitoring system, not back into the mixer's bus that is assigned to your computer. If your mixer does not have a busing system, mute the inputs of your mixer, corresponding to the outputs of your sound card. This way you won't have a feedback loop. You may want to consult your sound card's manual to find out how to route the output of the soundcard back into the input internally, using the sound card's mixer application if you are using the audio outputs as sound generators for your VSTi and Rewire instruments.

5. Create an audio track and select the desired configuration for it.

6. Select the appropriate input bus for this track.

7. Activate the Record Enable button.

8. Activate the Monitor button on the audio channel you are using to record the MIDI.

9. Press Play to begin playback and adjust the input level of your audio channel. Remember that the Mixer's channel faders only control the output level, not the input level. SX users may adjust the input level from the Input Bus channels. SL users can adjust the input level using an external mixer, the sound card's Control panel, or volume control on the MIDI device itself.

10. After you are satisfied with the input levels, position the play cursor before the MIDI events you want to record.

11. You can set the punch-in and punch-out to automatically engage and disengage the recording at the left and right locator respectively.

12. Start the recording of your MIDI events as audio events.

13. If you need to repeat the recording process, repeat Steps 2 through 12 before every recording and mute the previously recorded MIDI and audio tracks, creating a new track for every recording.

14. If you choose to use the sample-based technique, you need to place the newly recorded events at their proper location on each track.

After you have completed the MIDI to audio conversion, you can move all your MIDI tracks into a folder track and mute it while listening to the newly created audio tracks. Because there might be volume changes between the original MIDI tracks and the audio tracks, you will probably want to adjust their levels by using the automation in the Mixer. You may also assign inserts, send effects, or adjust the EQ for these tracks before moving on to the final mixdown of all audio tracks.

About VSTi and Rewire Channels

Since VSTi and Rewire channels exist as audio channels within Cubase's Mixer, they will be included in the audio mixdown when the Audio Mixdown function is used. Remember to unmute these tracks if you want to include them in the mixdown file; otherwise, they will not be included in your exported audio file.

About Dithering

Using 24-bit resolution and above during the production process helps enhance the dynamic qualities of your project, while reducing the possibility of audible noise levels. It also increases the signal-to-noise ratio, which is the level of the noise with no signal applied expressed in dB below a maximum level. As you saw earlier in this book, this ratio (in theory) is around 146 dB in a 24-bit recording and 194 dB in a 32-bit recording. Such a ratio suggests that when you record a sound using 32-bit resolution, your noise floor is at −194 dB, which is inaudible and negligible by any standards. Of course, in practice, you rarely get such impressive signal-to-noise ratios due to many noise-generating elements before and after the sound card's converters, but the ratios are consistently more impressive when using higher bit rates. Unfortunately, when you mix down to transfer to a 16-bit DAT recorder, or want to record it on a CD for compact disc players, you need to bring this precision down to 16-bit.

There are two methods used to accomplish this: truncating and dithering. Truncating simply cuts the lower part of the digital word that exceeds the 16-bit word length. Here's an example—if you have a sample that would be stored in 24-bit, it looks like this:

> ▶ 1110 0111 1100 0111 0011 1100

Now, if this sample were truncated to 16-bit, it would look like this:

> ▶ 1110 0111 1100 0111

What happened is that the last eight digits were cut off. These last eight digits are often reverb trails dying in the noise, or harmonics of instruments at low-level intensities. Cutting them off usually adds what is known as *quantizing errors*. This quantizing error sounds unnatural to human ears.

The solution is to add a special kind of random noise to the sound when you need to bring down the resolution. This random noise is dither noise. What it does is to change the last bit in a 16-bit word randomly, creating a noise at −98 dB, which is pretty low. But, in reality, this noise is low enough to perceive sounds at -115 dB. Dithering is not needed when you are working in a 24-bit or 32-bit environment. So keep this for the end.

How To

To set up dithering on your final mixdown:

1. Open the Mixer window (F3 is the default key command).

2. Because dithering is and should be the last step in your mixdown process, it should only be added when you are preparing the final mixdown to a 16-bit sound file. Because of this, load the UV22 dither plug-in (in Cubase SL) or UV22HR (in Cubase SX) in the last Insert (Number 5 in SL or Number 8 in SX). The UV22 and UV22HR plug-ins are located by default in the Other VST effect's submenu (see Figure 15.1).

3. Make sure the effect is enabled.

4. In the effect's Edit panel, select the Normal Auto preset. This will suit most of your dithering needs.

Figure 15.1
The UV22 dither processor above and its UV22HR counterpart (available in Cubase SX only) below.

With this final option set, you are now ready to export your mix to an audio file.

Broadcast Wave Properties

Now that your project is ready to be exported, it might be a good time to add information about who created the files. This is done through the Broadcast Wave properties. The information you enter here will be embedded in all the digital audio recordings/renderings you do, until you decide otherwise. Think of it as a way to protect your property by letting everyone who uses a file you created know you are the actual owner. Broadcast wave information contains three basic fields: a description, an author, and a timestamped reference.

How To

To enter information that will be embedded in broadcast wave files:

1. Select File(PC)/Cubase(Mac) > Preferences from the menu bar.
2. Under Record, select Broadcast Wave. The Record-Broadcast Wave panel will appear in the right portion of the dialog box (see Figure 15.2).
3. Enter any information you want in these fields. Remember that this information will be embedded in the audio files.
4. Check the options below when you want to include the information you entered in the type of file identified next to the option.
5. Click Apply then OK.

Figure 5.2
The Broadcast Wave
information panel.

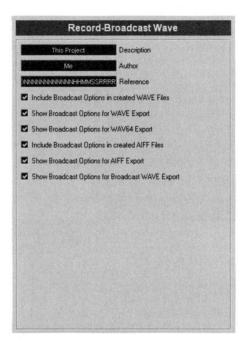

Exporting Your Final Mix

After you are satisfied with your mix and want to render a final mixdown, you can use the Export Audio Mixdown function found in the File > Export > Audio Mixdown. This function does not export MIDI tracks, as mentioned earlier, but does export VSTi and Rewire channels, so the following steps assume that you have already converted your MIDI tracks into audio tracks. You can also use the Export Audio Mixdown function to render a selection, a track containing effects or a VSTi.

How To

To export your final mix as an audio file:

1. Mute the tracks you don't want to include in your audio mix and unmute those you want to include.

2. Position your left locator where you want to begin the audio mix and the right locator where you want to end the audio mixdown.

3. If you want to export the automation when rendering a mixdown, make sure all the appropriate Read Automation buttons are enabled.

SUBZERO!

It is important to make sure that the output bus used for the rendering of any audio mixdown does not clip at any time during playback, because this clipping will cause distortion in your final mixdown. So, make sure that your levels stay below zero at all times and that the clip indicator in this bus does not light up.

4. Select Export > Audio Mixdown from the File menu. The Export Audio Mixdown dialog box appears, as shown in Figure 15.3.

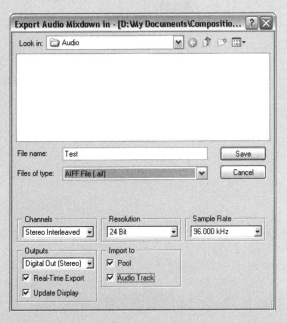

Figure 15.3
The Export Audio
Mixdown dialog box.

5. In the Export Audio Mixdown In dialog box, choose the proper folder in which to save the file. By default, Cubase will display the project's folder.

6. In the File name field, enter a name for the file you want to export.

7. Choose the number of Channels, word length Resolution, and Sample Rate you want to use for your exported file. SX users can also select a multichannel mixdown if the output bus is multichannel. For example, you can select the N. Channel Interleave option if you want to create a single file containing all the channels assigned to a surround bus. If your bus is configured as a 5.1 surround setup, the N. will stand for 6 channels interleaved. Also, the N. Channel options are available only if you select a file type (see below) that does not compress the audio content.

SPLITTING STEREO FILES

Note that the Stereo Split (or N. Channel Split in SX), found in the Channels area of the dialog box, creates a left and a right mono file rather than a single stereo interleaved file. This might be useful if you need to use this file in another audio application that does not support stereo interleave files, such as older Pro Tools versions.

8. Select the appropriate settings in the Files of type and Coding fields that you want to use for this file. If you are preparing an audio mixdown to burn on a CD, for example, chances are you will need to select a WAV or AIFF format. For Web distribution, MP3, Ogg Vorbis, RM, or WMA will be more appropriate. The Wave64

continued

CHAPTER 15

format (SX only) should be selected when you expect the resulting file will be upwards of 2 GB.

9. Under the Outputs section, select the appropriate bus you want to mix down. SX users can also mix down specific channels, such as VSTi or audio channels.

10. Check the Real-Time Export option when one of your VST plug-ins requires this to have time to update correctly during the mixdown process or if you are using a third party Rewire-compatible application which is not loaded inside Cubase, but as an external application. This is not always required, but if your audio mixdown doesn't sound after rendering to file, redo the mixdown and check this option.

11. Check the Update Display option if you want to monitor the levels during mixdown. If a clip occurs, you will be able to see it and adjust the levels appropriately to avoid the problem.

12. If you want to import this file into your Media Pool or add it as a new track in your project, check the appropriate options in the Import To section.

13. Click Save when done. Cubase will display the ID3 Tag Options dialog box, which enters embedded information (such as the ones discussed in the Broadcast Wave options earlier).

14. Enter the appropriate information in each field.

15. Check the Insert options if you want to include the information in the file.

If you have checked the Import to Audio Track option, Cubase creates a new audio track and names it *Mixdown*. After the newly created track is in place, make sure to mute the source tracks for this new track (containing the audio mixdown). If you have chosen not to import the audio rendering of your mix back into your project, you can proceed with your work as usual, continuing whatever work needs to be done, or save and close your project and start working on the mastering of your album, as discussed later in this chapter.

File Format Options

You can export your final mix in two different lossless formats: WAV and AIFF. Both are standard formats and compatible with Mac and PC computers. You need to have your files in either of these formats to create an audio CD. But you need to leave the WAV format at its default "PCM/uncompressed Waves" format if you want to be able to import it back into your project. SX users can also use the Wave64 or .W64 file format, which supports file sizes above 2 GB.

The Internet and the Web have been quite helpful to musicians in allowing them to publish their material online and use it as an effective distribution medium and a way to promote their skills. This is one of the reasons why other Web-related exporting formats are now available and also considered standards in the industry. Among those, Cubase supports RealNetworks RealMedia format, Microsoft Windows Media format, MP3 format (from MPEG Layer 3), and Ogg Vorbis compression format. There are obviously a few other formats available, but they were not supported by Cubase at the time this book was written.

WHAT IS OGG VORBIS?

Ogg Vorbis is an audio compression format that is roughly comparable to other formats used to store and play digital music, such as MP3 and other digital audio formats. It is different from these other formats because it is completely free, open, and unpatented.

Although not all artists realize it, MP3 is what is known as a "lossy" format. Thus, much of the sound data is removed when MP3 files are created. This results in a file with sound quality inferior to that of a CD. Vorbis is also a "lossy" format, but uses superior acoustic models to reduce the damage. Thus, music released in Vorbis sounds better than a comparably sized MP3 file.

Also, artists should be concerned about licensing terms for formats. If you decide to sell your music in MP3 format, you are responsible for paying Fraunhofer a percentage of each sale because you are using their patents. Vorbis is patent and license-free, so you never need to pay anyone in order to sell, give away, or stream your own music.

To find out more about this format, you can visit http://www.vorbis.com.

Because these formats were developed with the Web in mind, they make it easy to stream or distribute content over a low-bandwidth system. As a result, a certain amount of data compression is applied to these file formats. The more you compress the files, the smaller they are, and this is also directly related to sound quality—the smaller the file, the worse the sound quality. All these compression algorithms are lossy, meaning that they remove data from the original file when saving it into this new format and by doing so, they reduce sound quality as well.

There is a big difference between data compression, which is used to compress the size of a file, and dynamic compression, which is used to control the dynamics of the audio signal. The dynamic compression does not influence the size of the file. You will have a chance to experiment with this and will have to find a compromise that you need to be comfortable with in the end. Keeping this in mind, remember that there are more people using 56 Kb modems to download and listen to music than there are people with high-speed access. This is changing rapidly; however, until the time comes when everyone has high-speed access to the Internet, make sure your potential customers will not be discouraged by the size of your file.

The next two sections describe particularities related to RealMedia, Windows Media, and MP3 format conversion when exporting your files for Web distribution.

RealMedia and Windows Media

RealNetworks was one of the first companies to develop an algorithm to compress and deliver audio and video files over the Internet by using a streaming technology. Today, Microsoft has joined RealNetworks in the leadership race to establish the most popular streaming standard for distribution of audio and video content over the World Wide Web. Microsoft's version of streaming media technology is called *Windows Media format.*

CHAPTER 15

The principle behind streaming technology is the same, no matter which format you use. The idea is to make available to Internet users a compressed file that varies in quality and size, depending on the settings you choose when compressing this file. The streaming client (a compatible player) resides on the end user's computer. When you click on a link, the reference file associated with this link tells the client's computer to load the player into memory and start streaming the content from the server to the workstation. The player starts playing the content as it arrives rather than waiting for it to be completely downloaded, thus reducing the waiting period before a user can listen to the content of this file.

For this to work properly, a reference (or go-between) file is often created (see Figure 15.4). This reference file is known as a *metafile*, and it contains a simple piece of information: the location of the media file itself. Because a metafile is so small since it only contains a link to a content file, it is downloaded quickly into your computer. After the metafile is downloaded, the computer loads the player associated with this type of file and then reads the address, telling the server to start sending packets of data. The packets of data are stored into a buffer memory until the buffer memory is filled up. Once filled up, the player begins to play the actual content. The time it takes to fill up the buffer memory depends on the connection speed a user has, the connection speed of the server, the traffic over the Internet at that moment, and the size of the media file itself. For example, filling the buffer for a 100 Kb file is quicker than if the file is 100 Mb. But after this buffer is loaded, the file begins to play while your Internet connection stays active, continuing the transfer of the rest of the information for this file.

Figure 15.4
How information flows as streaming media over the Internet.

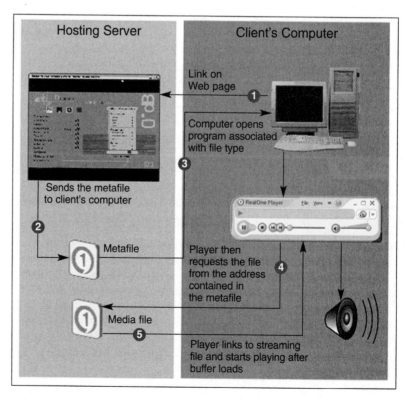

Now that you understand the basics of how streaming works, choosing the Attributes or Coding options to use when exporting an audio mixdown will be easier. You will notice that when the File of Type field displays Real Media or Windows Media formats, options appear below that let you select the type of streaming content you want to create. As a rule of thumb, whenever higher quality settings are chosen, you can bet it will take more time to compress and will end up generating larger files. With RealAudio files, for example, choosing a 56K Modem Coding option means that the stream created will be suitable for Internet users navigating with a standard 56K Modem. The resulting file will therefore be optimized for a 34 kilobits-per-second stream of data. You should know that this will definitely not offer the best sounding audio quality, but it will give you the possibility of reaching a larger audience than if you choose a higher quality coding.

How To

To export a file for RealPlayer or Windows Media Player compatibility:

1. Proceed in the same way as you would for any other type of file (as described earlier in this chapter), up until you reach the format of the file you want to export. From there, you proceed as follows.

2. Next to the File of Type field, select RealAudio File G2 (.rm) or Windows Media Audio File (.wma) as your file type.

3. Next to the Coding field (RealAudio) or Attributes (Windows Media), select the appropriate format for your content.

REALAUDIO SPECIFIC OPTIONS

Remember that the compression you apply here influences both the file size and the quality of the end result. If you are targeting the general public, then using a 34 kBit/s (Kilobits per second) format is more suitable. On the other hand, if you are targeting people who have high bandwidth access, such as businesses or other users you know are using a faster connection, you can select a higher bit rate.

Make sure to select the bit rate and the appropriate type of codec compression: If you have music, you should use the Mono or Stereo Music presets. If you have mostly voice content with no music, use the Voice presets.

The RealNetworks codec treats those two types of audio information in a very different way, so making the right selection here is paramount. If your content contains both musical and vocal content, go for the music presets.

Choosing mono music over stereo music adds definition, as it uses the additional space to allow a wider range of frequencies, whereas the stereo music is encoded in stereo and offers a stereo image with less high frequencies, as those are reduced to allow for the stereo information to fit in the same amount of bits per second.

Finally, below the Coding field, an information box tells you what this RealPlayer preset is most appropriate for, such as the example in Figure 15.5 in which the "56K Modem (34 kBit/s) Music (Stereo)" preset has been chosen.

continued

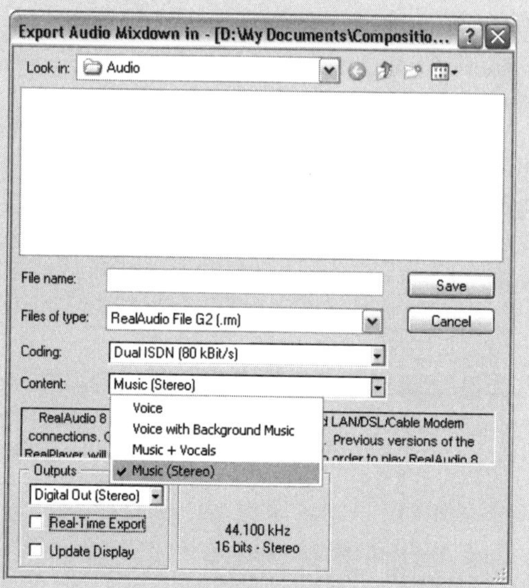

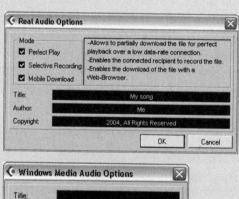

Figure 15.5
The RealAudio options in
the Export Audio
Mixdown In dialog box.

4. Click on the Save button. This brings up either the RealAudio Options dialog box, as shown in Figure 15.6, or the Windows Media Audio Options dialog box, as shown in Figure 15.7.

Figure 15.6
The Real Audio Options
dialog box.

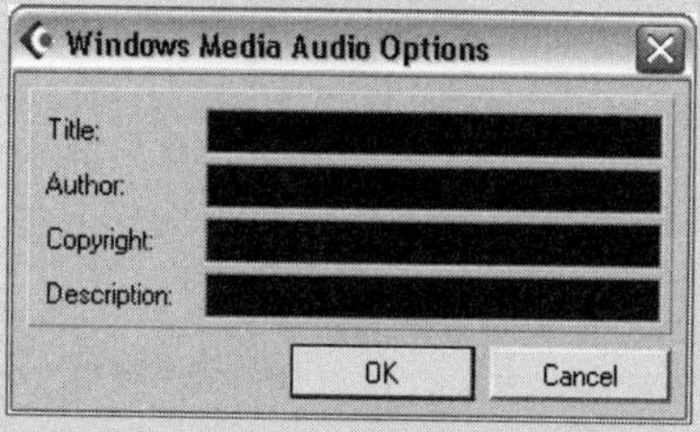

Figure 15.7
The Windows Media
Audio Options dialog
box.

5. Enter the appropriate Title, Author, and Copyright information for your song. This information appears in the user's Player window when a file is being played. If you are using the RealAudio format (this does not apply for Windows Media), check the appropriate Mode options. When you add a check to an option, a short description of what this feature does appears to the right of the option.

6. Click OK. This can take several minutes if your project is long or your computer is slow.

While the file is being rendered in the selected format, a progression dialog box appears (see Figure 15.8), as with any other exporting feature. To avoid errors during the mixdown process, do not use your computer to do other tasks until the process is completed.

Figure 15.8
The Export Audio progression dialog box monitors the progression or aborts the process.

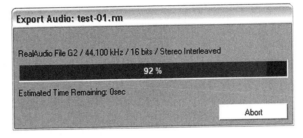

ABOUT WINDOWS MEDIA PRO

An extension of the Windows Media Audio format developed by Microsoft, WMA Pro files can be decreased in size with no loss of audio quality, depending on the advanced audio codecs and lossless compression used. WMA Pro features the possibility of mixing down to 5.1 surround sound. Note that PC users with Windows XP will be the only ones able to hear this type of format in surround since other Windows OS do not support surround files. They will simply hear a stereo version of the file instead. For specific information on settings found in the corresponding dialog box, start the HTML Help in Cubase, select the Index tab, and look for the *WMA Pro files* topic.

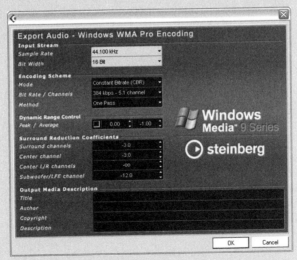

Figure 15.9
The Windows Media Pro dialog box.

MP3

Exporting a mixdown to MP3 format is similar to RealAudio (RA) or Windows Media (WMA) format in that they are meant to be sent over the Internet and then played on a computer. This format has literally changed the face of audio distribution, allowing for high-compression algorithms that reduce file sizes without compromising audio quality too much when using higher bit rates.

Cubase SX allows you to save a mixdown in MP3 format (available as an upgrade for Cubase SL users). As with RA and WMA, the smaller the files, the lower the quality. Compare this as an example: The compact disc standard of 44.1 kHz, 16-bit, Stereo in Wav format uses a bandwidth of 172.3 kilobytes per second, whereas an MP3 file compressed at 320 kbps (the highest quality available with the MP3 codec from Steinberg) uses only 39 kilobytes per second of bandwidth. This is because a one-minute file in WAV or AIFF CD compatible (44.1 kHz, 16-bit, Stereo) format uses 10.09 megabytes of disc space, whereas the MP3 file at 320 kbps uses only 2.29 megabytes, making it easier to transfer over the Internet or store on limited storage mediums, such as memory sticks or MP3 players. The MP3 standard relies heavily on algorithms that compress the information and then on the computer's processor to decompress this information as it plays back, as does any other file compression algorithm (ZIP, ARJ, Stuff It, and so on). The difference being that MP3 algorithms are specifically designed for audio content.

How To

To export a file for MP3 compatibility:

1. As with RA and WMA, proceed with the export process as was demonstrated earlier in this chapter until you reach the format of the file you want to export. Then proceed as follows:

2. Next to the Files of type field, select MPEG Layer 3 (.mp3) as your file type.

3. Next to the Attributes field, select the appropriate format for your content as shown in Figure 15.10.

Figure 15.10
Selecting the attributes for your MP3 files in the Export Audio Mixdown In dialog box.

4. In the Quality field, select the Highest option, which takes more time to compress but yields better results.

5. Click the Save button. The ID3 Tag Options dialog box appears (see Figure 15.11). If you've entered information in the Broadcast Wave preferences, this information appears here automatically.

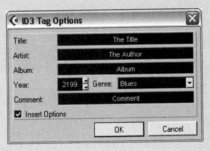

Figure 15.11
The ID3 Tag Options
dialog box.

6. Make the necessary changes and click OK to start generating the file.

More on OMF

As you already saw in Chapter 7, the OMF Exporting option (available in SX only) allows you to save in a platform and application friendly format. It's friendly in the sense that this is a standard supported by more applications than the current .CPR or Cubase Project file might be. In other words, if you stay within Cubase, you won't need to use the OMF export format, but if your project needs to be added to another application, such as Final Cut Pro, or AVID, and so on, exporting to OMF format will save everyone lots of time since most of the project settings will be available in the OMF version of your project. This implies that you won't have to reimport and position all the audio content in another application. However, if the other user does not own the same plug-ins as you do, the FX won't be accurate.

Exported OMF file will keep references to all audio files that are played in the project (including fade and edit files) and will not include unused audio files referenced in the Pool. It won't contain any MIDI data either, so it's important that you convert all your MIDI parts into audio events before exporting to OMF. If your project contains a video file, the only thing that will be included in the OMF file is the start positions of Video Events. You will need to manually import video files later in the other OMF application.

How To

To export a project to an OMF format:

1. Select Export > OMF from the File(PC)/Cubase(Mac) menu. The OMF Export Setup dialog box appears.

continued

Figure 15.12
The OMF Export Setup
dialog box.

2. Select the desired OMF File version, depending on which OMF version is supported by the application in which you plan to import the file later on. You might want to check with the studio where you need to bring this file before you make a selection here.

3. Select whether you want to include all audio data used in the project inside the OMF file (Export All to One File) or use references to external files only (Export Media File References). If you choose the latter option, make sure to include all media files along with the OMF file on the backup copy that you bring to the other studio. If you know that you can save everything in an OMF file that will fit onto a CD or DVD-R (or DVD-RAM), you might be better off creating a self-contained, all-in-one OMF file to avoid any missing files later on.

4. If you are exporting to a 2.0 compatible OMF file, you can choose to include the fades and volume settings for each event. To do so, check the Export Clip Based Volume option.

5. By default, the current project sample size and sample rate are selected for the OMF export, but you can specify another resolution and sample rate for the exported files.

6. Click OK and specify a name and location in the file dialog that appears.

About Mastering

Mastering is the art of subtlety and involves adjusting your final mixes so that they all sound coherent and cohesive when played one after the other. This means that the first mix you did two months ago when you started working on your album sounds as good as the one you created last night at 4:00 a.m. after consuming large amounts of caffeine.

When preparing an album, mastering is a must before pressing your master copy. The mastering process is used to reduce the aforementioned differences between various mixes by patching together every song in a one-to-two day span—listening to the songs in the order they will appear on your album and correcting the overall harmonic colors and dynamic range of your songs.

It is also a good idea not to master your album with the same listening reference as you used for the recording and mixing process because your ears have probably grown accustomed to this sound and may no longer be as critical to some aspects or coloring of the music. Furthermore, if your monitoring system is adequate at best, you will probably benefit from a professional mastering facility rather than a home studio mixing environment, because the better ones provide the best all-around listening and processing equipment to truly isolate problems in the consistency between your songs, not to mention a fresh pair of ears listening to your project. This can add a whole new untapped dimension to your project, which is especially true if you want to use this as a commercially distributed album. Finally, there will always be, no matter what the critics of pricey studios might say, a difference in quality between a home studio filled with inexpensive equipment with low-quality components and a quarter million dollar mastering facility in which every piece of equipment in the room is meant to optimize your sound.

If you don't have the financial resources or don't feel the need for a professional mastering because your project is for small and local distribution only, there are no recipes here and no settings that can apply to every situation, but rather pointers that should help you get the most out of a mastering session. If you are unsure as to how your mix sounds, try listening to music that you find is similar in style to what you have done and sounds like what you want your music to sound like. Then see if you can emulate these qualities. Another way of evaluating your mix is by listening to it in different environments, such as a car stereo, the room next door, or at a friend's place. Remember that the fresher your mind and ears are, the better it is for the mastering process. So, avoid starting a mastering session after a long day of work, or after mixing the last song on your album.

▶ Mastering is not where you mix your songs. If you are not satisfied with a mix, you should remix it rather than trying to fix it at the mastering stage.

▶ This might be very obvious to most people, but just in case: NEVER master an album using your headphones as a reference. The proximity of headphones will give you false information about depth of field and presence of certain musical events, and most people do not listen to music through headphones; they listen to it through loud speakers.

▶ When exporting your audio mixes in Cubase for the mastering process, use the highest quality available. If you have worked in 96 kHz, 32-bit stereo format and have a reliable system that can reproduce these specifications, go for it. You can always convert your final result after the mastering process to 44.1 kHz, 16-bit stereo format.

▶ Before you start your mastering session, sit down and listen to all the songs in order with your notepad and a pencil at hand. Take notes on inconsistencies between one song and another.

▶ Generally, there are two important things that you want to adjust in a mastering session, and this should be kept in mind throughout the entire mastering process of a single album: EQ and dynamics. Both should be consistent from song to song.

▶ When tweaking the EQ, you are not trying to reinvent the mix, just tweaking it. Give the bass more definition, add presence to the vocals and crispness to the high-end, and most of all, make sure that all songs have the same equalization qualities.

▶ Dynamics give punch and life to a mix. Make sure all your tracks come into play at the same level—this doesn't mean they should all be loud or soft, but consistent with the intensity of the song. If a song is mellow, it can come in softer, but the soft intensity in one song has to be consistent in relation to the soft intensity of another song. As with EQ, consistency is the key.

▶ There are more and more software packages out there that do a pretty good job at EQing and compressing audio. Steinberg's Wavelab, Clean and Mastering Edition, and IK Multimedia's T-Racks are just a few tools you can use to help you get the most out of your home mastering session.

Creating an Audio Compact Disc

Creating your CD is often one of the last things you do before having people outside of your studio environment listen to your music. After you create an audio mixdown of your MIDI and audio tracks as a premaster file (in whatever format you used to do so), master one or more tracks as discussed earlier, save your files and convert them into a compact disc compatible format, you are ready to create a compact disc.

Cubase does not offer any tools to actually burn (record) a CD. But Steinberg offers one solution through Wavelab. This is by no means the only tool available. If you purchased a CD recorder, it might have come with a CD recording application. One thing is certain: You need software capable of creating a CD-DA compatible disc (Compact Disc Digital Audio). This brings us to formats. When creating CDs, the two most common types of CDs are CD-ROM and CD-DA. CD-ROMs contain data suitable for your computer. CD-DA contains audio that is suitable for both your computer and CD player. There are two variations of this: the Enhanced CD and the Mixed Mode CD, which are available in some software and some CD recorders. The Enhanced CD is a multisession CD, containing a series of CD-DA compatible tracks in the first session, making it compatible with your home CD player, and a second session containing data, which is read by computers only. In Mixed Mode, it's the reverse: The data tracks are at the beginning and the audio tracks follow. This usually means that your CD player will not read it. This type of CD is used for multimedia content, such as games, or educational, or multimedia sales presentations. In light of this, understand that you need to select the proper type of CD when creating a CD within the software application. There are a few rules to follow if you want your CD to play back in any CD player.

When recording a CD, there are three aspects that come into play: the format of the CD (CD-ROM, CD-DA, Enhanced CD, Mixed Mode, and so on), the session, and the disc. A session is an instance in which you decide to write something on a CD. For example, today you decide to record a wave file onto a CD. You write a session and to complete the process, you close the session for the disc to be understood by the CD-ROM drive. A disc is closed when you can't record anything else on it and opened when you can add other sessions to it. In our previous example, if you close the session but leave the disc open, you can record another session on it, making it a multisession disc, each time closing the session but leaving the disc opened for another recording. When you want to close the disc because the disc is full, you can do so after the last session you record, disabling it from being recorded anymore. This is called a multisession CD, which is common in

CD-ROMs, Enhanced CDs, and Mixed Mode CDs, but this method of recording the CD is not compatible with audio CDs.

For an audio CD to play in a consumer CD player, you can only have one closed session and one closed disc in CD-DA format unless you are using the Enhanced CD format. When creating an audio CD, you may use two methods of writing the information onto disc: TAO short for *Track-At-Once* or DAO short for *Disc-At-Once*. You will probably want to consult your software and hardware documentation to see if these features are supported, but for now, understand that TAO records the audio CD one track at a time, leaving a two-second gap between each song that you added to the CD recording session. The DAO, on the other hand, does not record this two-second gap between each song you added to the CD recording session (see Figure 15.13).

Figure 15.13
Creating a music CD in the Nero Express.

With these basic principles in hand, you can create audio CDs in your own home by using the audio CD creation software of your choice. It is also a good idea to create intermediate audio CDs to listen to your music on other sound systems and see if you are pleased with what you hear before you produce the final master. Most new domestic CD players accept an audio disk on rewritable media (CD-RW). Rewritable CDs are outside the specifications, but can be, if your player is compatible, a good way to create test mixes. But remember that for your CD to play, it has to be in audio CD format (CD-DA) and not in data CD format (CD-ROM).

Backing Up Your Work

Making backup copies of your work as you go is paramount. Not only does it prevent you from having to rerecord your material if you make mistakes and erase files, but it is also a good way to keep source material from being lost because of hard drive crashes. Another good reason to back up files as you are working with them is that you can always go back and change things later in an arrangement or create a new arrangement altogether by using the source material rather than the master two-track recording. If these are not good enough reasons for you, consider this last piece of advice: When you are working on a project for someone else and charging studio time, I doubt that your client will be impressed by your work if you lose recordings!

There are many ways to do backups inside and out of Cubase:

▶ Create an Archive folder containing all the audio present in the Audio Pool of your project by using the Prepare Archive function in the Pool menu as shown in Figure 15.14. This prompts you to select a destination folder where a copy of all the audio files used in the pool are copied, making it easy to save this folder on a backup media, such as a CD-R (Compact Disc-Recordable), CD-RW (Compact Disc ReWritable), tape backup, or removable media drive. After you've saved the audio files, you can also copy the .CPR and video files as you might also need to include them in the backup.

▶ Use the Save Project to New Folder command in the File menu and copy the content of this folder to your backup media. This is probably the quickest way, but only once your project is nearly completed, especially if you check the Freeze Edits and remove unused audio options from the command's dialog box.

Figure 15.14
Using the Prepare Archive function in the Pool window's context menu or in the Pool menu to save all audio files in a single folder for backup.

▶ Use your CD creation software to create a data disc that contains all the source material (audio, arrangements, song, preset, and setting files) used for this project, making sure to label your CD accordingly.

▶ Use a backup software or disk imaging software to create a backup image of your files.

Keeping in mind that computer crashes occur unfortunately quite unexpectedly, and that disc failures are not as infrequent as we would wish, making backup copies of your work makes sense—even after each working session. This way, you reduce the amount of time lost if ever something bad happens...

Reading the documentation provided with your CD burning software to understand how it works and how you can retrieve information from backup disks might prove useful, so take a little bit of time to familiarize yourself with these options.

16

Score Editing

Creating a score with Cubase offers a way of turning your MIDI sequence into sheet music that musicians can read. To accomplish this task, you take what you recorded into your MIDI sequencer and convert it into musical notation. When you create and edit a song in Cubase, you create different tracks of MIDI events. Each one of those tracks can become a sheet of music. You can combine different tracks to create a more complex conductor score or create a lead sheet to give chord and rhythm indications to a group of studio musicians.

We will only scratch the surface of scoring possibilities offered in Cubase, as this could be a subject of an entire book. This chapter is meant to give you a quick look at the scoring possibilities found in Cubase. For a more in-depth look at the scoring capabilities of Cubase functions, you should read the online documentation provided with the software. We cover the basics and some of the more advanced techniques involved in scoring with Cubase. Finally, this chapter assumes that you know how to enter notes in a MIDI sequencer and focuses on laying out the information in a proper way.

Score editing functions are available in both SX and SL versions; however, the SL version does not support the Page mode display discussed in this chapter. In other words, whenever references are made to this mode, it applies only to SX users.

Here's a summary of what you will learn in this chapter:

▶ About the score function and inherent differences with other editors in Cubase.

▶ How to prepare a project to get the best scoring results out of MIDI events.

▶ How the score function uses layers to place different types of symbols.

▶ What Layout settings are and why you should use them when preparing music sheets for musicians.

▶ How you can adjust Staff settings for each staff in your score.

▶ How to understand and work in different score modes.

▶ What you can do with the extended toolbar functions to change the appearance of notes on staves.

▶ How to use the Symbol Palette to insert additional markings in your score in order to make it easier for musicians to read.

▶ How to work with different types of text in a score.

▶ How to print and export a score to paper or graphic files.

About Score Editing

Scoring can be just as complex as the music it attempts to represent. To understand and make the best of Cubase's scoring capabilities, it is useful to know music and music notation. What is important in score editing is that the result is legible to other musicians. In many ways, the score approximates the basic MIDI information in a sequence. A musician, in turn, interprets this score by playing the notes or symbols that appear on the sheet music, and you can play back this performance as an audio or MIDI interpretation, depending on the instrument the musician plays. When transforming MIDI into a score, using the MIDI already present in your project offers a good starting point. But often, the performance irregularities that make the music sound great might not be appropriate for the conversion to scored events on a music sheet. If this is the case, you might have to rerecord some MIDI parts. In other words, a good sounding MIDI recording might not necessarily translate very well into a good-looking score. Cubase offers ways to help you optimize the MIDI data so that it looks good on paper, but sometimes you will be better off copying the MIDI events and editing them a bit to make these events look good as a musical sheet. For example, you could quantize the MIDI copy so that it corresponds to clean lengths and end points, which translates better on paper.

Since you can only transform MIDI events into a music sheet, if you are recording a project that contains mostly audio content, you have to create additional MIDI tracks to create a score out of it. One thing to remember about MIDI recording is that the length and precision of your MIDI events greatly influences how the information is displayed in the score itself. You can tell Cubase how to interpret the information for an optimized layout; however, to avoid manipulating the events extensively, you should quantize everything before you start editing your score. Figure 16.1 shows a simple melodic line that was played without quantization.

On the top part, you can see how Cubase interpreted the information, creating a complex series of ties between the notes to reproduce what was played. On the lower part, you can see the same melodic line, but quantized and enharmonically corrected. This means that the "accidents," or notes that are outside the regular scale, have been adjusted to better reflect a correct way of scoring musical notes. This is possible because Cubase takes the MIDI events and compares them with the score settings to display the score layout and matches both sets of information with standard scoring practices. So, depending on your score settings and how you recorded your MIDI events, your results will vary.

Figure 16.1
How MIDI events appear in the score; a before (top) and after (bottom) look at a simple melodic line taken from the MIDI events.

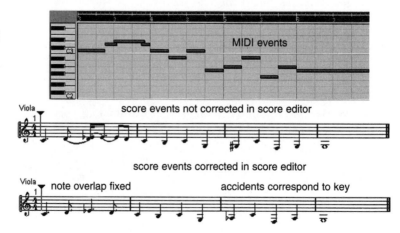

Score Editor Window

The Score Editor window, like the Key, Drum, List, and Audio editing windows, is available from the MIDI menu.

How To

To launch the Score Editor:

▶ Select a MIDI part or track and press Ctrl(PC)/⌘(Mac)+R on your keyboard or select Score Edit from the MIDI menu.

In the Score Editor, you have two basic display modes: Page mode (SX only) and Edit mode.

You can switch from Page mode to Edit mode by selecting the option in the Score menu. This is a toggle option, meaning that if you are in Edit mode, the option displays Page mode to switch to that mode, and, inversely, if you are in Page mode, the option displays Edit mode. By default, Cubase opens the editor in Edit mode. The main difference between the two is that Page mode is like the Page Display mode on a word processor: It lets you see the page as it will appear once printed and includes the elements that are part of the page layout. Therefore, you can position your title, add printing elements, and so on. Both editing modes display similar toolbars, so let's look at the functions of these tools.

Whenever you make a staff active by clicking in the area to the left of a staff, the content found in another opened editing window reflects the content of that activated staff. An active staff displays a thick border at the beginning of each staff line, and the Score Editor's title bar shows the name of the active staff. In Figure 16.2, the Cello staff is the active one.

Figure 16.2
The active staff indicator—in this case, the Cello is active; any other opened editing window also displays this staff.

There are five separate rows of tools inside the Score Editor. Which ones are visible is determined by the first toolbar's Show/Hide buttons (see Figure 16.3).

Let's look at each of these rows to understand its purpose:

▶ **Toolbar.** The first section below the Title bar, this represents most of the tools found in other editing windows.

▶ **Info Line.** The black row displays information on a selected event. When one event is selected, the information for this event is displayed in white. When more

Figure 16.3
From left to right:
Show/Hide Info, Tool
Strip, Filter view.

than one event is selected, the information appears in yellow. To reveal or hide this row, you can click the Info button found in the toolbar.

▶ **Tool Strip.** This displays many of the tools you need to insert and edit notes, rests, and symbols in your score (see Figure 16.4). You will find more information regarding this toolbar later in this chapter. To reveal or hide this row, you can click the Tool Strip button found in the toolbar.

▶ **Filter bar.** This displays a series of check boxes. Each check box is an invisible item that you can choose to see by checking the appropriate box. Filtered items do not appear on printed paper. To reveal or hide this row, you can click the Show Filter View button found in the toolbar (see Figure 16.3).

▶ **Ruler bar.** Shown in points in Figure 16.4, and visible in Page mode, the Ruler bars aligns text elements from your score with a horizontal and vertical ruler, found on the top and left part of the editing window. You can change the units displayed in this Ruler bar by right-(PC)/Ctrl-(Mac)clicking in the Ruler. A context menu displays the available options. To hide the rulers, select the Off option from this context menu.

Figure 16.4
The Score Window
toolbars.

Score Preferences

The Score Preferences window offers different behavior options that can be set on or off. One of the options that you will find here makes your cursor change to the Arrow tool after a symbol has been inserted. This is useful when you don't insert the same symbol very often and want to position your symbol precisely after you've inserted it. Most of the options are self-explanatory and are well documented, but if you don't know what an option does, click the Help button at the bottom of the page to get context-sensitive help.

How To

To change your score behavior preferences:

1. Select Preferences from the File (PC)/Cubase(Mac) menu.
2. Select the Scores option on the left side of the dialog box (see Figure 16.5).
3. To toggle an option, click the option to add a check mark in the State column.
4. Click Apply to accept your changes and then click OK to close the dialog box.

Figure 16.5
The Score Preferences
dialog box.

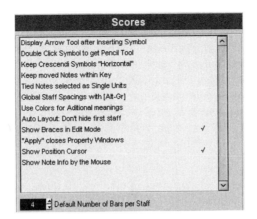

You will find most of the global preferences relating to the score in the Global Settings submenu found in the Score menu. These options offer a wide range of options you can set to make your score look and react the way you want.

Understanding Score Layers

When working on a score, you are placing and editing symbols on three different layers: the note layer, the layout layer, and the global layer.

The note layer represents MIDI events that you may open from a MIDI track. These MIDI events become note symbols on the note layer. On this same layer, you also find other note dependant information that is represented by symbols, such as tempo changes, dynamic indications, or special symbols that represent how notes should be interpreted graphically, such as a trill or an arpeggio. These symbols are all present as long as the note symbols associated with them are present. When you move a note or a bar containing a note, the associated symbols follow. On the other hand, Cubase allows you to lock certain elements on note layers, or create your own set of note layer events that can't be edited by assigning these elements to a layer and activating it. For example, in Figure 16.6, the note layers 1 and 3 are active (editable) and layer 3, when active, lets you edit stem lengths and keys. In other words, when layer 3 is disabled, you can't edit stems and keys. When working on a dense musical project, controlling the aspects that can or cannot be modified makes editing easier.

Figure 16.6
Layer control options.

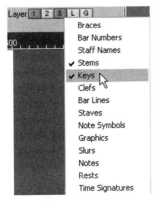

The layout layer represents elements that quite often define a group of instruments on a score and define how an instrument appears on a page. For example, a bracket across a brass section is considered as a layout item. You might decide that each brass part contains six staves per sheet by defining a layout called *brass* and then applying this same layout to all the instruments in that section. However, symbol elements that are in one layout do not appear in another layout, so when you want to have certain indications repeated on all the parts, use a symbol that is part of the global layer. Think of the layout layer as a preset setting for a group of instruments, where you can save the number of bars per staff, staves per page, and layout symbols for this particular layout. To lock the layout layer from editing, you can deactivate it from the layer control options (see Figure 16.6).

The global layer represents symbols that are not associated with notes but give indications to the musician on how to play a part and are part of the greater picture (global) of the score. For example, coda indications or rehearsal markings are considered layout symbols. To better understand the layout layer, let's look at an example. When preparing a big band arrangement, you need to create individual parts for each musician and a score for the conductor. Starting with the conductor's score, open all the tracks corresponding to the instruments in the arrangement, and then move notes, quantize note symbols so that they look good on paper, and add certain indications. Chances are, when you create the individual music sheets, you'll want to see the same indications on each sheet. Take, for example, rehearsal marks such as letters identifying different sections of a song. These indications are placed and saved in the layout layer. To lock the global layer from editing, you can deactivate it from the layer control options (see Figure 16.6).

Global Settings

These settings influence the properties of global symbols, as described earlier, as well as settings that relate to how Cubase handles specific representation of symbols (see Figure 16.7), such as accidentals in the current score or text sets, which are style templates that you can assign to different types of text in your score.

Figure 16.7
The Global Settings options.

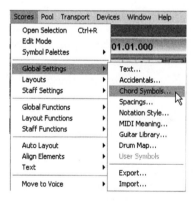

Text Settings

The Text Settings in the Global Settings submenu offer two tabs of options: the global text and text attribute sets. The Global Text tab sets font attributes for different parts of your score, including bar numbers, track names, time signatures, and so on (see Figure 16.8). The Attribute Sets tab lets you create template text sets that you can use throughout your score.

Figure 16.8
The Text Settings dialog
box.

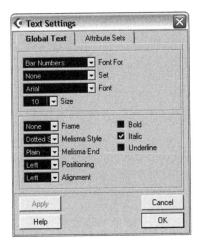

How To

To create a text attribute set:

1. Select Global Settings > Text from the Score menu.
2. Click the Attribute Sets tab in the Text Settings dialog box.
3. In the Set field, type a name for your set. For example, if you want to create a set for lyrics, call your set "Lyrics." When you add lyrics, you can apply that set (similar to styles in Word for all you Word experts) to them without having to set your font, size, and attributes each time.
4. Change the font, its size, and its attributes (Bold, Italic, or Underline).
5. Select a frame type if you want to see a frame around your text.
6. Select a proper Melisma style setting. A melisma is a line that appears after a syllable when you are adding lyrics to indicate that the syllable is stretched over many notes. Figure 16.9 illustrates this. The melisma style represents the line itself, and the melisma end is how the line should end. In Figure 16.9, the melisma style is solid, the end is plain, and the text's attribute is italic. You learn how to use melisma when looking at how to use text later in this chapter.

Figure 16.9
Example of a text set
using a melisma.

7. Adjust the Positioning field to the left or right. This influences which side of the text is used to align this text with notes when the notes are moved around.
8. Adjust the Alignment field as appropriate (left, center, or right). This only makes a difference when you have more than one line of text. It is similar to a paragraph alignment setting, aligning the text to the left, to the center, or to the right.

continued

9. Press the Store button to store this set.

10. Press Apply to accept your changes and then click OK.

The set you have just created is accessible in the Score > Text > Font Setting option or in the Text Settings dialog box found under Global Settings > Text as well.

Accidentals Settings

The Accidentals dialog box, as shown in Figure 16.10, lets you determine how accidental notes should appear in your score. An accidental is an altered note that doesn't belong to the key signature. The rule for accidentals is that when one appears in a bar, each time the same note appears in this bar, it keeps the accident active until the next bar. If you want to add precision to this setting by repeating the accident each time the same note appears in the same bar, you can tell Cubase to repeat the accident. The right part of this page offers you a choice of most common tensions used and a sharp or flat setting for each one. The paramount rule is to go for clarity. Repeat an accidental in the same bar wherever there is a potential for confusion. Even though an accidental is cancelled by a bar line, a cautionary (bracketed) accidental in the next bar is often helpful.

For example, if you have a Cm with a flat ninth note, you can decide to show this as either a D flat or as a C minor chord with an augmented octave (C sharp). As a rule of thumb, keep flat tensions as flat notes and sharp tensions as sharp notes. Therefore, in our example, a musician would prefer reading a D flat rather than a C sharp.

Figure 16.10
The Accidentals dialog box.

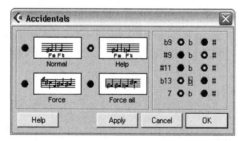

How To

To set the accidentals preferences in a score:

1. Select Global Settings > Accidentals in the Scores menu.

2. Select the options you want to apply to your score. The dialog box is divided into two sections. On the left, you can choose how the accidental notes are handled and on the right, you can select how you want specific tensions in a chord to be represented.

3. Click Apply and then click OK.

Chord Symbols

The Chord Symbols in the Global Settings submenu offer two tabs of options: the chord types and chord font settings.

The Chord Types tab displays different ways of showing chord symbols. How to set up this page depends on how you prefer seeing chords displayed and from which scoring school you are. Different schools of thought exist on this subject, so the choice is up to you.

The Chord Font tab offers you three styles of music chords: English, with the A to G scale; DoReMi (which is French for C, D, E), with the Do to Si (C to B) scale; and German, which is similar to the English style except that the B key letter is replaced by the H key letter and B flats become B.

You can select the font type and a font size for each part of the chord. Look at the sample in Figure 16.11 to see how the change affects the layout of the chord.

Figure 16.11
The Chord Settings dialog box.

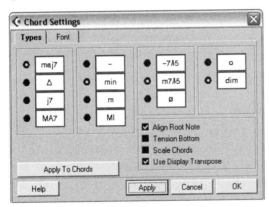

Other Global Settings

The Spacing option found in the Global Settings submenu is where you can tell Cubase how much space you want between elements on your score layout. You can set each element to a default value, or you can change it to customize the display of your score. To change a value, you select the field and enter the value manually.

The Notation Style option offers three tabs of options: switches, beam and bars, and options. All of these options define how you want certain elements to be displayed in a score. For example, the Beams and Bars tab displays properties for bar numbering and layout in your score and beam properties, such as angles of beams when tied beams are slanted.

MIDI Meaning (Figure 16.12) offers a way to tell Cubase how you want it to interpret through MIDI velocity and length values the musical notation markings you added to the current score. For example, if you inserted a dynamics value of "ff" or fortissimo (very loud), when Cubase plays back the passage, it will send out MIDI notes with a velocity 50 percent louder than what it currently is. So if you've entered all notes step-by-step, using the pencil tool, or your keyboard, at a default velocity value (lets say 64), then Cubase will play that note at a velocity of 96 (50 percent louder than the default value). Another example, if you set up a staccato accent symbol (.) to mean Length=25%, Velocity=110%, notes with this accent would be played back with a quarter their actual length and 1.1 times their actual velocity.

Figure 16.12
MIDI Meaning dialog
box.

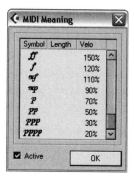

When working with chord intensive songs and creating guitar parts at the same time, you will find it useful to use the Guitar Library. This tool allows you to create and collect different guitar chord symbols along with their chord names (see Figure 16.13). In this dialog box, you can create new chords, remove them, and save them to a file.

Figure 16.13
The Guitar Library dialog
box.

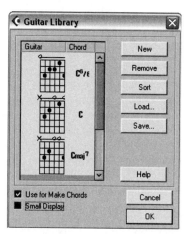

How To

To create chords for your guitar library:

1. Select Global Settings > Guitar Library from the Scores menu.
2. Click the New button to create a new chord. A blank fretboard appears.
3. Double-click the fretboard to open the Guitar Symbol editor (see Figure 16.14). This dialog box is divided into two parts. On the left, you will find the fretboard. Clicking a fret adds a finger position on the fret. Clicking it again removes it. You can also click above the fretboard to add open string or an indication not to play this string (an X is inserted). Consecutive clicks change the symbol from one to the next. Clicking the top-left corner outside of the fretboard adds position numbers. In the right section, you can enable the large symbol display or the horizontal symbol display by checking the Large or Horizontal check boxes. The Frets field changes

the number of frets displayed in the symbol, whereas the Capo fields creates Capodaster symbols across the strings.

4. Create your chord by adding the appropriate finger symbols in the fretboard on the left.

5. When done, click OK. This chord creates a new guitar symbol in your library.

Figure 16.14
The Guitar Symbol dialog box.

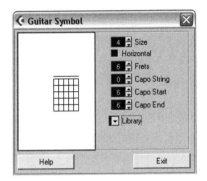

How To

To add a guitar symbol in your score:

1. Select Symbol Palettes > Others from the Scores menu.

2. Click the Guitar Chord symbol in the Tool palette.

3. Click in the score where you want to add a guitar symbol. The Guitar Symbol dialog box appears.

4. Either select a chord that you have created earlier from the Library drop-down menu, or create the chord as was described earlier. This dialog box differs slightly from the one you used when creating a guitar chord for the library because it has an Apply button rather than an Exit button.

5. Click the Apply button to insert the symbol in your score. You can also insert the notes associated with your chord by clicking the Insert Notes button.

6. Continue adding guitar chord symbols and then close the dialog box when you are done.

You can easily save your guitar chord library for later use with another project by clicking the Save button in the Guitar Library dialog box. To load a previously saved library, simply click the Load button instead and browse your hard disk for the file. Finally, to remove a guitar chord from your library, simply select it and click the Remove button.

It is also possible to create drum parts by using an existing drum map associated with a MIDI drum track through the Score Drum Map Settings dialog box (see Figure 16.15). This dialog box associates a drum instrument to a different pitch for the score layout and changes the head of the note in this score to represent an instrument, making it easier for a drummer to read. You can also change the voice that is assigned to each drum instrument when working with polyphonic voice layouts.

Figure 16.15
The Score Drum Map
Settings dialog box.

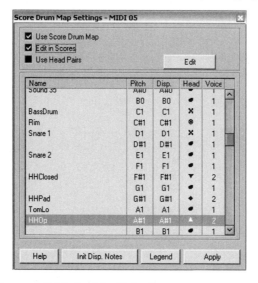

Here's a look at the options available in this dialog box:

▶ **Use Score Drum Map check box.** Associates the drum map used for the selected drum track and associates the name of each instrument in the drum map. When you click the Legend button, Cubase adds a note in the score for each instrument defined at the pitch used in the score to help the drummer understand how you've laid out the drum part.

▶ **Edit in Scores check box.** Makes changes directly in the score's window, updating any changes you make there in this dialog box. For example, if you move the Bass Drum from an E3 to a D#3, the change appears here as well.

▶ **Use Head Pairs check box.** Associates a note length value to the symbol displayed in the score. When an instrument plays a note that is long (longer than a quarter note), the head in the left column is used. If the instrument plays a shorter note (shorter than or equal to a quarter note), the head in the right column is used. Note that this option is not selected in Figure 16.15, so you only see one column of note heads. The Edit button edits the pairing of note heads.

▶ **Drum map display.** Is a series of rows in which each row represents an instrument and its properties. The columns show the instrument's name, the pitch associated with this instrument according to the drum map (which you can't change), the pitch displayed in the score, the note head associated with the instrument, and the voice assignment. The displayed note has no effect on the I-note, O-note setting for the drum map. The purpose of this option is to make it easy to lay out your drum part in a staff without having notes appearing far below a staff. Assigning instruments to voices allows you to control the direction of the note stems by using the polyphonic staff settings covered later in this chapter.

▶ **Initial Display Notes button.** Resets the displayed note value to the original pitch note value in the score.

▶ **Legend button.** Adds a series of notes at the current quantize value interval (also using the quantize length value setting for the note lengths). This serves as a guide to the drummer so that he/she can understand which note value is associated with the drum's instrument (see the bottom part of Figure 16.16).

Figure 16.16 shows a MIDI drum part opened in the Score Editor on top. Notice that the notes appear low on the treble clef staff. You can also see that the stems are all going in the same direction; accidents appear because some notes are associated with black note pitches and the spacing between each note is limited. All of this makes it very difficult for a drummer to understand what exactly needs to be played. On the lower half, the MIDI events have been formatted for the score layout of a drum part. A legend appears at the beginning, showing the drummer which note plays what. Also, the HiHat has been assigned to a second voice, allowing for stems to be sent up while the kick and snare have stems pointing down, making it easier for the drummer to interpret.

Figure 16.16

A before and after look at a MIDI drum part being edited in the Score Editor.

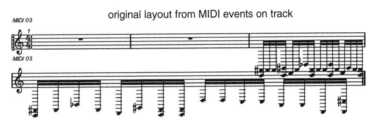

The last two options in the Global Settings submenu export all of your settings to a file for use in another project or in another studio and import setting files that you have previously saved.

Layout Settings

The Layout Settings submenu in the Scores menu manages layouts that are available in your project and switches from one layout to another. Usually, a layout is created when you open the Score Editor with a certain number of tracks or a single track selected. For example, if you open the Score Editor after selecting all the brass tracks, piano, bass, and drum tracks, and start editing the layout for these tracks, a layout is created.

The Layout Settings dialog box (see Figure 16.17) edits this layout. This dialog box is divided into two parts. On the left, you will find the tracks that are currently part of this layout. The first and second columns are used to add braces or brackets.

How To

To add braces or brackets in a layout:

1. From the Scores > Layout Settings, select the layout you want to edit from the available layouts in your project.

2. Once selected, go back to the Scores > Layout Settings and select the Setup option. The Layout Settings dialog box appears (shown in Figure 16.17).

3. Click and hold in the braces or brackets column next to the first track where you want to begin joining the braces or brackets. With your mouse button still depressed, drag it down over the tracks you want to join together.

4. Click OK when done.

Notice in Figure 16.17 that the braces span over all the tracks in this layout, whereas the brackets divide the four first tracks from the rhythm section.

Figure 16.17
The Layout Settings dialog box.

▶ The T column displays the time signature above the staff rather than inside the staff itself. Clicking in the track row in this column adds a check mark, indicating that this track will be displayed this way.

▶ The check in the N column determines if the track's name appears at the beginning of each track. Notice also that there is a check box in the lower-right corner of the other section of this window. The Show Staff Names option supersedes the N column in the sense that it determines if the names appear or not. Then you can add a check in the track's row to display a name for this track. You may also check the From Tracks option if you want Cubase to take the names from your tracks in the project window.

▶ The L column determines if the layout symbols that you have inserted are visible next to this track. In other words, you can decide if a rehearsal mark, for example, is repeated over each track in this layout.

Looking at Figure 16.18, you can see in the top half that the L and N columns for the Piano part are checked. Consequently, the rehearsal mark and the name "Piano" appear above the piano staves. In the lower half, the N and L columns are not checked; therefore, the rehearsal mark and the name above the piano staves do not appear in the score's layout.

Figure 16.18
How the layout settings affect the appearance of the score.

How To

To rename a layout:

1. Select the layout you want to edit from the Layout Settings submenu in the Scores menu.

2. Then select Layout Settings > Setup from the Scores menu to open the Layout Settings dialog box.

3. In the upper-right corner, in the Name field, type the new name you want to give to your layout. In Figure 16.17, the layout has been renamed "Conductor Layout."

In the right portion of the Layout Settings dialog box, you will find the following items:

▶ **The layout's Name field.** This field changes the name of the current layout.

▶ **The Size option.** By default, a layout is set at 100% size. However, if you want to fit more tracks into one page, you might reduce the size until all the staves from the instruments in your orchestra fit in a single page. This can be very useful when creating an orchestral score.

▶ **The Multirests option.** By default, this option is set to Off. However, if you want to display several complete bars of silence as a multirest symbol, showing the number of bars that the musician has to count instead, you can set the minimum number of bars you can have before the layout will tie the rests in a multirest symbol (see Figure 16.19).

Figure 16.19
Example of a multirest symbol; this tells the musician that he/she has to count thirteen bars of silence.

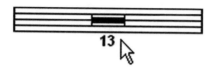

▶ **The Real Book check box.** When this option is selected, the clefs for the instruments in this layout are displayed in the first staff only rather than at the beginning of each stave.

▶ **The Staff Separators check box.** When this option is selected, a special symbol appears between each stave to separate them from the preceding stave. This option is handy when you are working on a multi-instrument layout and your score displays more than one set of staves (called a system) per page.

▶ **The Modern Time Signature check box.** This option changes how the time signature appears in the score's layout. Figure 16.20 shows how the time signature is displayed when this option is not selected (above) and when it is selected (below).

Figure 16.20
The Modern Time Signature not selected above and selected below.

The second option in the Layout Settings submenu found in the Scores menu manages the list of layouts available. Appropriately named *Show List*, this option brings up a dialog box displaying a list of existing layouts for your current project. You can use the Show List dialog box to do the following:

▶ **Rename a layout.** By double-clicking the name of a layout and renaming it.

▶ **Delete a layout.** By selecting it and clicking the Remove button.

▶ **Import the layout symbols from another layout into the current loaded layout.** By selecting the layout containing the symbols you want to import and clicking the Form button.

▶ **Switch to another layout.** By selecting a layout in the list and clicking the Show button.

▶ **Remove layouts for which there are no longer track combinations.** By clicking the Clean Up button.

Staff Settings

The Staff Settings menu offers various options related to how a selected staff is displayed and how MIDI events on this staff are handled throughout the score. In other words, what relates specifically to a staff's appearance can be controlled through the parameters available in the Staff Settings dialog box (see Figure 16.21).

These settings affect everything from the way a staff name is displayed, to the way beams are displayed, and also how many voices are available for polyphonic voice splitting. You can even set up a staff to handle guitar-specific tablatures.

Figure 16.21

The Staff Settings dialog box displaying the Main tab.

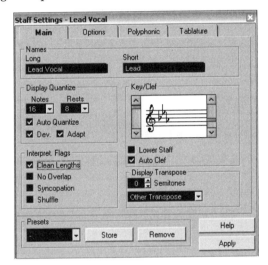

CHAPTER 16

How To

To configure the staff settings:

1. In the Score window, select the staff you want to configure.

2. In the Score menu, select Staff Settings > Setup. Note that you can also open the Staff Settings dialog box by double-clicking to the left of a part.

3. Make the necessary adjustments throughout the four tabs (Main, Options, Polyphonic, and Tablature) and then click Apply.

4. If you want to configure another track, simply select the other track. The Staff Settings dialog box updates its content to reflect the currently selected track.

After you are satisfied with the settings of a track and want to keep these settings for later use on another track, you may save these settings in a preset by clicking the Store button in the Staff Settings dialog box. You can also start with the existing presets by selecting it from the Presets drop-down menu.

For a full description of each item found in this dialog box, you may click the Help button. Cubase displays an online help file for each tab in the dialog box. Understanding each option saves you time and lots of headaches when addressing issues you are having with the staff's layout properties in your score.

Working Modes

There are two modes available in the Score editor for SX: Page mode and Edit mode. In Cubase SL, you will only have access to the Edit mode. You can do most functions in Edit mode, which is the standard mode for editing. As mentioned earlier, you can toggle between Page and Edit through the Score menu's top option. The advantage of working in Page mode is that you can see how your page is laid out and add layout graphics, text, and annotations. Figure 16.22 shows the Page mode display with the title and copyright information properly displayed, and Figure 16.23 shows the Edit mode display. Notice the difference in the placement of text such as title and copyright information.

Figure 16.22
The Page mode display (SX only).

Figure 16.23
The Edit mode display.

Tool Strip Functions

The main function of the score's Tool Strip is to select the note value you want to add to a score. However, it holds many more little tools to help you lay out your page. You can show or hide this toolbar by using the appropriate button in the toolbar of the Score Editor.

Insert Buttons

For starters, the first button on the left is called the *Voice Selector Insert button*. If a track contains more than one voice, you can select in which voice within this polyphony you want to add your note. In Figure 16.24, you can see the active staff has two voices because next to the word Insert, you have two numbers: 1 and 2. These represent the number of voices currently available in this staff. In this example, this represents the soprano and alto voices in a choir score. Stems going up are assigned to the soprano voice and stems going down to the alto voice. When you insert a note on a staff with more than one voice, you can choose to which voice the note will be inserted by selecting it through the Insert buttons.

How To

To add notes to a specific voice in a polyphonic staff:

1. Select the polyphonic staff for which you need to add notes.

2. Select the voice number in the tool strip corresponding to the voice number to which you want to add notes. In Figure 16.24, notes would be added to the second voice since the number "2" is selected.

If you see only one number next to the word *Insert*, this means that all your notes on this staff are assigned to one voice. Simply click on the number corresponding to the desired voice. To see more than one voice, set your staff to Polyphony mode in the Staff Settings dialog box found under the Score menu.

Figure 16.24
The voice selector in the tool strip displays how many voices are available in the active staff.

Next on the tool strip, you find the L button. When activated, this Lock button prevents you from moving objects and notes from one staff to another. Most of the time, you will want to leave this off. However, if you need to transpose selected notes very high or very low, so that they appear below or above the current staff, enable it so that Cubase does not think you want to move the notes to another staff.

Following the L button, you will find note values. These are used to select the note values you want to add to your score. When you select a note value, the quantize length value in the toolbar switches automatically to correspond to the value of the note you selected. For example, if you select a whole note, the quantize length displays "1/1 Note" value. When you switch to a quarter note, quantize length displays a "1/4 Note" value. Note, however, that the quantize grid setting remains the same.

Enharmonic Shift Buttons

The Enharmonic Shift buttons provide a way to change the enharmonic notes in your score. Enharmonic notes are different ways to represent the same pitch. For example, E flat or Eb could be represented by D sharp or D# or even F double-flat (Fbb). The Off button turns the enharmonic shift to off, and the No button hides the accidentals. If you use many accidental notes, you might want to add additional markings. For example, if you have many voices on a staff and each one plays an accidental C sharp (C#), you can select subsequent C sharp notes in the bar and click the Question Mark button (?). This adds a helping accident. The notation rules don't require you to add this accident, but because you want to help the musicians who are reading the score, this provides them with additional information. Clicking the Parentheses button [( )] adds this accidental in parentheses.

Function Buttons

The I button, short for *Information*, shows you information on a selected element in your score. What appears after you select the I button depends on what you select. For example, if you select a clef and click this button, the Clef window appears and allows you to change it. On the other hand, if you select a note and click this button, the Set Note Info dialog box appears, allowing you to modify different parameters for note representation.

By default, notes above the third line in the staff have stems going down, and notes below this same line have stems going up. The Flip Stems button manually flips the stems of selected notes in the other direction.

The Group button adds a beam across a series of selected notes. Figure 16.25 shows notes that were grouped together in the first bar.

How To

To group a series of notes:

1. Select the notes in a staff you want to group together.
2. Then click the Group button on the Extended toolbar.

How To

To ungroup notes:

1. Select the notes that are in a grouped beam.
2. Then click the Group button on the Extended toolbar.

Figure 16.25
The Group button
function.

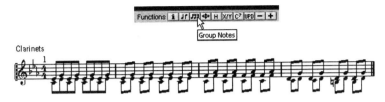

The Auto Layout button is a shortcut button for the Auto Layout function found in the Score menu. If you select an entire staff, it performs like the Move Bars. You can use this function to optimize the layout of bars on a staff.

The H, or Hide button, hides the selected elements from view. Use this function to hide elements from the score, such as rests or bar lines. This can be useful when you want to hide certain symbols from view while you are working on other aspects of your score layout. After you are done, you can unhide these symbols to view them again, or keep them hidden if you want your score to look this way.

How To

To hide symbols using the Hide function in a score:

1. Select the symbols (bars, notes, rests, layout text, or anything else) you want to hide from view.
2. Click the Hide button in the Extended toolbar or select Staff Functions > Hide from the Scores menu.

Chances are, if you have decided to hide symbols rather than delete them, you will at some point want to see them again or at least see what has been previously hidden.

How To

To reveal hidden symbols from your score

1. Make the Filter View bar visible by clicking the appropriate button in the score's toolbar (see Figure 16.3).
2. Check the Hidden Notes option to reveal the hidden notes and the Hide Filter option to reveal the other hidden symbols.

The Reveal function, however, does not remove the hide property from these hidden elements. As soon as you uncheck the Hidden Notes and Hide options, what is set as hidden returns to its hidden state. You can, however, remove this property from the hidden symbols. However, this is done differently for notes and other symbols.

How To

To remove the hidden property associated with a symbol:

1. Make the Filter View bar visible by clicking the appropriate button in the score's toolbar (see Figure 16.3).

2. Check the Hidden Notes option to reveal the hidden notes and the Hide Filter option to reveal the other hidden symbols.

3a. To remove the hidden note property for notes, select the hidden notes you want to unhide by dragging a box over these notes, double-click on one of them to bring the Set Note Info dialog box (or click the "I" button in the Extended toolbar), and uncheck the Hide Note option in this dialog box.

3b. To remove the hidden property from a symbol, select the hide symbol you want to remove and press Delete or Backspace on your keyboard.

As you can see in Figure 16.26, the top part shows the Hide filter as disabled. Therefore, the hidden symbols do not appear in the staff. The middle part of the figure shows the enabled state for the hidden symbols, revealing where hidden symbols are. You can then select them and remove them from your staff. In the bottom part, you can see that the meter and bar that was hidden previously now reappear on the staff as it was before you hid them from view.

Figure 16.26
The Hide function: With the Hide filter active, you can see the the location of hidden symbols.

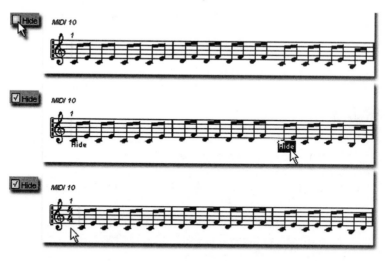

The X/Y Position button reveals the graphical position of your cursor in a horizontal (X/vertical; Y horizontal) display. When you click on a non-note event—the title, for example—you will see the Delta X (dX) and Y (dY) coordinates of the selected object changing as you move it around the screen. Use this to fine-tune the positioning of your graphic elements on the score. The X/Y Position window also allows you to toggle between the different ruler formats: inches, centimeters, points, and millimeters.

How To

To change the format of the ruler:

▶ In the Position Info window, click the upper-left corner of the window where it says "Measure in..."

▶ Or right-click(PC)/Ctrl-click(Mac) in the ruler and select another measurement format.

▶ Or click the menu arrow above the top of the horizontal scroll bar and select the appropriate measurement system you want to use.

In the last column (see Figure 16.27), you have the "To Prev Staff" and "To Next Staff" values. These values represent the space between the current selected staff and the previous and following staff in the score. Double-clicking either of these values allows you to type in a new spacing value.

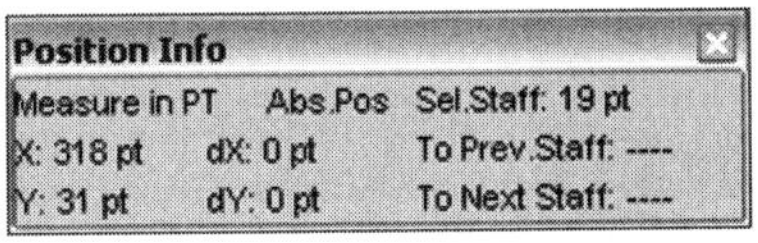

Figure 16.27
The Position Info window.

The C7 button is "Make Chords," which creates a chord out of the selected notes in your score. To make chords, you need to have a three-note polyphony (minimum) to get accurate results from the Make Chords button. After your chords are created, they appear above the selected staff. You will find more information on chords in the following sections of this chapter.

After you have completed your editing, you may need to refresh your layout. If your layout is not refreshed properly, you can force an update by clicking on the UPD button or Update button. You can also do this through the Force Update option found in the Global Functions submenu in the Scores menu.

Symbol Palettes

In the Score menu, you will discover the Symbol Palettes option. In this option, you will find many palettes available to add graphical elements to your score. None of these symbols actually affects how the music is played back, but they are used to add interpretation indications for the musicians. There are 10 palettes from which to choose, and they all work pretty much the same way.

How To

To add a symbol from a symbol palette on your score:

1. Choose the appropriate symbol palette (the one that contains the type of symbol you want to use).

2. Click on a symbol; then click on the score where you want to add it. If the symbol needs more information, a dialog box appears to let you enter additional fields or text as required.

After you have a palette displayed, you can switch from one palette to another by right-clicking(PC)/Ctrl-clicking(Mac) anywhere in the button area of the symbol palette, as shown in Figure 16.28. This reveals the list of palettes from which you can choose. Selecting another palette replaces the displayed palette with the new one. Holding down the Ctrl(PC)/⌘(Mac) key as you make your selection does not replace the existing palette, but rather opens a new, additional one.

Figure 16.28
Changing the displayed symbol palette from the context menu.

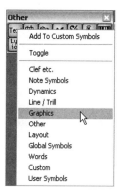

The last palette available is the Custom palette. This palette stores symbols you use most often from other palettes into your own customized symbol palette.

How To

To add symbols to the Custom palette:

1. Right-click(PC)/Ctrl-click(Mac) over the symbol you want to add to the custom palette.

2. From the context menu, select the Add To Custom Symbols option.

3. Repeat this operation for every symbol you want to add to the Custom palette.

Symbols appearing on the custom palette can be removed by selecting the Remove From Custom Symbols option once you are viewing the custom symbol palette.

The first option on the Palette's context menu is the toggle option. Use this to switch from a vertical palette layout to a horizontal layout.

Some of the symbols in these palettes might be grayed out if you are in Edit mode. To activate these disabled symbols, switch to Page mode (SX only). That's because the symbols contained in the Layout and Global palette are only added to the layout and global layer respectively. In the Edit mode display, you can see these layers, but it is better to edit them in Page mode instead.

Working with Chords

You might have a harmony happening in your staff. You might also have a piano or guitar part with chords played as a harmonic rhythm track. In both cases, you can choose to add a chord symbol over the track by selecting the track and then clicking on the Make Chords button in the tool strip, as discussed in the previous sections of this chapter. After your chords are created, chances are you will want to tweak them, because Cubase might not interpret them properly all the time.

Before you start creating chords, it is a good thing to set your chord display preferences in the Scores > Global Settings > Chord Symbols dialog box, as discussed earlier. What you set in this dialog box determines how the chords are displayed on the score and in the Chord Edit dialog box. For example, if you set the Major chord type to display MA7 rather than maj7 or simply j7, the MA7 appears in the Chords dialog box when you edit the chord. The chords you create after setting your preferences follow the rules you set here.

The next step is to actually create the chords by using the Make Chords button on the tool strip or by using the Chords button found in the symbol palette called Other (Scores > Symbol Palette > Other).

How To

To create a chord from selected note symbols on your score:

1. Select the note symbols on the staff over which you want to create chord symbols. Note that you need at least three notes per chord selected in order for the automatic chord function to work.

2. Select the staff over which you want the chords to appear by using the up or down arrows.

3. Click the Make Chords button or select this option in the Scores > Staff functions submenu.

Sometimes, you might not have a complete chord structure, but want to have one. Instead, you might simply have a melody and want to add some chord indication. In this case, you need to create your chords by using the Edit Chord Symbol dialog box.

How To

To create custom chords:

1. Select the Symbol Palettes > Other from the Score menu.
2. Click the Make Chords button (C7).
3. Then click over the staff to which you want to add a chord. The Edit Chord Symbol dialog box appears, as shown in Figure 16.29.

Figure 16.29
The Edit Chord Symbol dialog box.

4. Enter the note that corresponds to the root of your chord. For example, if you played F, A, and D, this could be a D minor chord, with a root of D, or an F6 chord, with a root of F. Which chord it is depends on many things, so you have to know a bit about harmony to make that kind of decision.

5. Next, enter the chord type. This tells the player if the chord is a major, minor, diminished, half-diminished, augmented, or a sustained fourth degree chord. If you are not familiar with these terms, you might want to use automatic chord construction, found in the Score toolbar, instead. In the example in Step 4, the chord was a minor chord, so in this case, you would select minor.

6. Next, add the highest tension found in your chord. For example, if you have a minor seventh and a minor ninth, add the minor ninth tension, because it is understood in scoring theory that the minor ninth also contains a minor seventh (unless otherwise noted). On the other hand, if you have a tension on the fifth, such as a sharp fifth or flat fifth added to your flat ninth, you can type in the values manually. Figure 16.30 displays a D minor with a sharp fifth and a major seventh chord on the left. The center column displays different ways you can add the tension by clicking in the Tension field, and the right column displays the result, depending on the way you typed in the tension. Note that the syntax used here is useful when you have complex tensions. Normally, you don't have to type anything if you have a simple tension.

7. The last field in your Edit Chord Symbol dialog box is for the bass note. If you want the bass to play a note different from the ones found in the chord, select that note in the pop-up menu. If your bass plays a note that is part of the chord structure but not the root, you usually don't have to write it in. However, in the example in Figure 16.30, if you want the bass to play an E, which is not part of the chord structure as it appears, you would add this in the bass note.

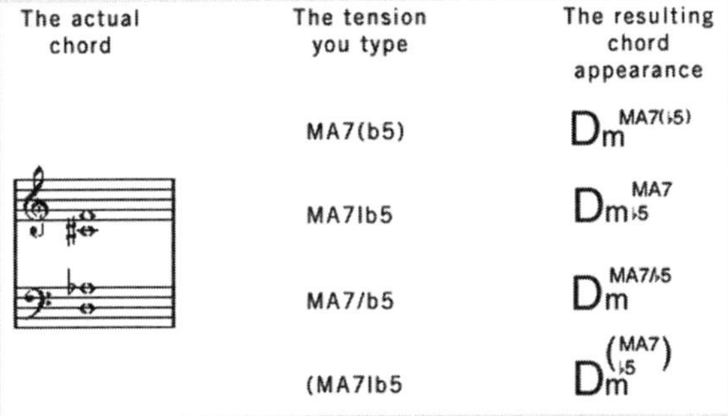

Figure 16.30
Adding text in the Tension field allows you to customize the tension's layout in the chord structure.

8. If your chord needs to be an enharmonic chord, like D sharp instead of E flat, check the Enharmonic Shift check box.

9. If you want to keep this chord structure for later use in your score, click the Store button. This saves the structure in the library of your song file after you save this file. You will notice that the root of the structure does not appear in the library. This is because you might want to use the same structure with another key later on. To use it later on, just select the root note and then select the structure from the drop-down menu.

When creating chords using the Make Chords function, Cubase uses the Quantize value set in the Score window to determine the maximum number of chords it will add. If you don't want to have too many chords, reduce the Quantize value to represent a realistic number of chords per bar. There are no fixed number of chords in a bar, but usually, this should not be more than four chords per bar; in most cases, it is one to two chords per bar. The best way to create chord tracks is to play a MIDI track containing the chord structure played as simply as possible.

Cubase uses all the vertical notes in your layout to analyze and create these chords. If you have melodic lines or musical lines with many transitional notes, the software might interpret those notes as chords, giving you a superfluous amount of tensions and chords. So, when you create chords, select only the tracks that contain the basic harmonic structure of your song and set your Quantize value to the desired amount beforehand.

Cubase also assumes that chords are in their root positions. This means that if you play a first or second inversion of a chord—let's say a C chord played E-G-C or a second inversion G-C-E—it interprets this as a C chord on an E bass or a C chord on a G bass. To avoid this, simply hold the Ctrl key down as you click the Make Chords button in the Score toolbar. If you find that the chords produced automatically by Cubase do not match the correct harmonic structure of your song, you can double-click on a chord and change its structure in the Edit Chord Symbol dialog box. Again, Cubase only tries to interpret the chord, but because this is often a question of interpretation and context, some chords will be wrong, and you will need to edit them.

Adding Text

In a score, you usually want to add comments and indications, as well as lyrics and song information. In Cubase, there are five types of text that you can add in a score:

▶ **Normal text.** This type of text can be used to enter comments or indications to the musician on how to play a particular passage. If you move a bar or staff, normal text moves with it as it is tied to these elements.

▶ **Lyrics.** This type of text is used to enter lyrics to a song. This type is specifically designed to add text under or over a staff, adjusting its position as you adjust the spacing of notes, bars, and staves. Lyrics are tied to the note position under or over which it is positioned. If you move the notes, the lyrics follow.

▶ **Layout text.** Think of this type of text as normal text you want to see for a group of instruments, rather than a single instance of this text somewhere. For example, if you are editing a brass quintet piece, you might add a comment in the conductor's part that appears at the top of the page when you print out this particular layout. When you open the trumpet part on its own, this comment does not appear because it is part of a different layout. The same applies for the four other individual parts that you create for this quintet.

▶ **Global text.** This type of text appears, unlike the layout text, on each individual layout or music sheet you create. Let's take the previous example of the brass quintet—adding a comment using the global text, you would find the text appearing on the conductor's score and on each individual part of the brass quintet. Global text is not tied to any notes, bars, or staves. This implies that if you move any of these elements around, the global text stays in place.

▶ **Staff Name text.** Staff text is linked to the staff setting and the layout setting. Usually, this represents the name of the track or of the instrument playing on that track in long and short format. For example, if you're laying out a violin staff in an orchestral score, the first staff could be named "Violin" and the following staves could be named "Vln." Staff name text usually appears at the beginning of each staff, depending on your staff and layout settings.

If you want to add lyrics to a song, you should always use the Lyrics Symbol found in the Other symbol palette (Scores > Symbol Palettes > Other).

How To

To add lyrics:

1. Start by selecting the staff under which you want to insert the lyrics.
2. Select Symbol Palettes > Other from the Score menu.
3. Click the Lyrics button in the palette. Your cursor changes to the Pencil tool.
4. Click under or over the note where you want to add the lyric and enter the first syllable for your word or enter a word.

5. Press the Tab key to move to the next note. If you have a word or a syllable that stretches over many notes, press the Tab key to move under or over the next note in order to add the next syllable or word.

6. Repeat until there are no more lyrics to add. When done, click outside of the box.

After you've completed inserting the lyrics, you can adjust the melisma lines to stretch a syllable or a word over a series of notes. A melisma, as discussed earlier in this chapter, is a line that carries through several notes.

How To

To stretch a word or syllable across several notes:

1. Click the word or syllable you want to stretch by using the Selection tool.

2. Drag the handle of the selected syllable to the right of where you want the melisma to end, as shown in Figure 16.31.

Figure 16.31
The selected word appears in reverse highlight, and the handle appears as a square in the lower-right corner of the highlighted word or syllable.

You can move lyrics up or down by using the Selection tool, but you can't move lyrics to the left or right. You can also copy words or syllables by selecting them and keeping the Alt(PC)/Option(Mac) key held down as you move the selection to a new area in your score. If you want to move all the lyrics you just entered at once, hold the Shift key down and double-click the first word or syllable in the lyrics. All elements from that set of lyrics are highlighted and ready to move.

Your lyrics might be crammed into a small space the first time you look at them on the score. To arrange the spacing so that the lyrics don't appear too squeezed, select Auto Layout > Move All Bars from the Score menu.

If you have created text attribute sets, you can select the lyrics, right-click(PC)/Ctrl-click(Mac) and select the desired set from the context menu. If there are no sets available, you need to create one before using this method.

Printing and Page Setup

The ultimate goal in using the Score functions is to print the result on a page so that musicians can read it. When you are in Page mode, you will see a gray border appearing around your page in

Page mode display (shown previously in Figure 16.23). The default settings for your printer determine where this border appears.

How To

To change the page size and margin settings:

1. From the File menu, select Page Setup. The default printer setup window appears.
2. Set the paper size and page orientation to the desired values.
3. Adjust the margin values for Top, Bottom, Left, and Right.
4. Click the Printer button at the bottom of the Page Setup dialog box.
5. Choose the printer you want to work with and click OK, or edit the printer's properties and then click OK twice.

It is also possible to export a score or a portion of the score to a graphic file for editing in a graphic editing or desktop publishing software.

How To

To export a score to a graphic file:

1. Make sure you are in Page mode editing.
2. Select in the Scores menu, Global Functions > Select Range.
3. In the Score window, drag a box over the range you want to export to a graphic file. You can adjust the handles of the selected range by using the Arrow tool, if needed.
4. Select in the Scores menu, Global Functions > Export Score.
5. Adjust the Resolution field to get the desired resolution for your graphic file.
6. Select the desired file format for your graphic file.
7. Type in a name for your file and select an appropriate folder in which to save the file.
8. Click the Save button.

If you want to export an entire page of the score, only execute Steps 4–8 from the previous list. You need to repeat this operation for each score page in your layout.

Now You Try It

For information about using the instructions found in this section and to find out where you can get the working files, please consult the section called *About the Exercise Files* in the Introduction section.

Appendix A
The How To Do It Reference Guide

This appendix refers to every "How To" section in this book, offering you a quick guide to finding out how an operation can be done. Each "How To" section has been divided into a category and placed in a corresponding table in this appendix. There are 10 tables (categories) in all. Here's a look at what you can find in each category:

▶ **Setup Operations.** This holds operations that relate to configuration procedures, setting up a project or your environment inside a project.

▶ **Display Information.** This holds operations that explain how to display windows, panels, and certain dialog boxes within Cubase or zooming specific operations.

▶ **Project and Transport Specific Operations.** These operations relate to project tasks that are not related to audio or MIDI, such as Marker and Folder tracks and transport operations.

▶ **Non Object-Specific Operations.** These are editing procedures within a project that are not specifically related to MIDI or audio alone, such as quantizing functions and options that might be found in the Edit menu that don't relate to a specific type of object (event or part) in a project.

▶ **Recording Operations.** This holds operations that directly affect the recording process and the recording operations themselves.

▶ **Audio Editing Operations.** This holds all audio specific editing operations.

▶ MIDI Editing Operations. This holds all MIDI specific editing operations.

▶ **Mixing Operations.** This holds operations that directly affect the mixing process and the mixing operations themselves.

▶ **Automation Operations.** This holds operations that directly affect the automation process and the automation operations themselves.

▶ **Score Operations.** This holds operations that directly affect the score process and the score layout operations themselves.

Each header contains a table with columns corresponding to the following information:

▶ **How To column.** Represents the actual task, function, or option title as it appears in the book.

▶ **Chapter Number column.** Tells you in which chapter this can be found.

▶ **Heading Title column.** Tells you in which section of the chapter this can be found.

▶ **Page Number column.** Tells you the page number on which you will find the corresponding "How To" steps.

Table A.1
Setup operations

How To:	Chapter Number	Heading Title	Page Number
Activate the VST System Link	14	Setting Up System Link Inside Cubase	357
Add a bank to your device's setup	5	Managing a MIDI Device	119
Add a MIDI device	5	Adding a MIDI Device	117
Add a preset or a folder to your device's setup	5	Managing a MIDI device	121
Add multiple presets to your device's setup	5	Managing a MIDI Device	119
Change the physical input/output assigned to a bus	12	Input Channels	314
Configure the digital clock on your sound card	7	Recording Audio	177
Configure your DirectSound drivers	3	DirectX Drivers	56
Configure your metronome settings	7	Setting Up Your Metronome	166
Create a child input/output bus (SX only)	E	Surround Bus	471
Create customized track controls for the track list area	D	Customizing Track Controls	469
Create your own custom colors and associated color names	4	Project Editing Setup Buttons	82
Enable and configure a Snap to grid	4	Setting Up a Quantize Grid	86
Enable direct monitoring mode	3	Direct Monitoring	64
Enter information that will be embedded in broadcast wave files	15	Broadcast Wave Properties	381
Export a MIDI device setup file	5	Managing a MIDI Device	119
Import a MIDI device setup file	5	Managing a MIDI Device	119
Install a MIDI remote control device	13	Using a Remote Control Mixer	344
Load a bank or instruments in a VSTi	5	Setting Up a VSTi	113

Table A.2
Displaying information

continued

APPENDIX A

Table A.3
Project and Transport specific operations

How To:	Chapter Number	Heading Title	Page Number
Add an audio track to a project	6	Audio Track	141
Add an FX channel track to a project	6	FX Track	154
Add a tempo change	5	About the Tempo Track	124
Add a Tempo change using the Warp tool	14	Time Warping	371
Add a time signature change	5	About the Tempo Track	124
Add commands to a macro	D	Macros	464
Add cycle markers in a project	4	Adding Markers	89
Add markers in a project	4	Adding Markers	89
Assign a color to parts and events	4	Project Editing Setup Buttons	82
Change the order of a track in the Track List Area	5	The Track List	109
Change your Cycle mode on the Transport panel	4	Record Modes	94
Change your Cycle Recording mode preferences	7	Recording Audio in Cycle Mode	180
Change your locator's position in the Transport panel	4	Locators	96
Create a macro	D	Macros	464
Create a marker track	4	Working with Markers	87
Create a new project	3	Creating a New Project	71
Create a template project	D	Creating Templates	462
Create a window layout	D	Window Layout	461
Erase a tempo change using the Warp tool	14	Time Warping	371
Find missing files in the pool	9	Dealing with Missing Files	226
Import a Cubase VST song, arrangement, or part	7	About Cubase Documents Imports	185
Import an online video file into a Cubase project	14	Working with Video Files	375

continued

Match musical cues to video cues using Warp tool	14	Using Musical Events Follow Mode	373
Move the left and right locators to the position of a cycle marker	4	Navigating Using Markers	90
Move tracks into a folder track	6	Folder Track	156
Move your play cursor to the position of a Marker	4	Navigating Using Markers	90
Organize your window layouts	D	Window Layout	461
Position your project cursor at the locator's position	4	Locators	96
Rename a track using the Inspector area	6	Folder Track	156
Set up for online video files in a Cubase project	14	Working with Video Files	375
Use a macro in a project	D	Macros	464
Use Rewire	12	Rewire	308
Zoom into the location of a cycle marker	4	Navigating Using Markers	90

Table A.4
Non object-specific editing operations

How To:	**Chapter Number**	**Heading Title**	**Page Number**
Add a track to your project	6	Adding Tracks	130
Apply a groove map to events	9	Creating and Using Groove Maps	244
Apply a quantize method to selected events	7	Applying Quantize	173
Apply an automatic quantize during the editing process	7	Applying Quantize	173
Apply an envelope process to a selected object	10	Envelopes	257
Change the order of overlapping parts or events	6	Audio Track	141

APPENDIX A

continued

Table A.5
Recording operations

Table A.6
Audio editing operations

How To:	Chapter Number	Heading Title	Page Number
Add a plug-in effect to a selected object	10	Using VST and DirectX Plug-ins	265
Add a region to a project from the Sample Editor	9	Working with Regions	234
Add silence in an audio event	9	Basic Editing Functions	234
Apply a fade over selected objects in a range	10	Working with Fade Envelopes	255
Apply a Gain Change process to a selected object	10	Gain Process	258
Apply a Noise Gate process to a selected object	10	Noise Gate Process	259
Apply a Normalize process to a selected object	10	Normalize Process	260
Apply a Phase Reverse process to a selected object	10	Phase Reverse Process	261
Apply a Pitch Shift process to a selected object	10	Pitch Shift Process	261
Apply a Stereo Flip process to a selected object	10	Stereo Flip Process	264
Apply a Time Stretch process to a selected object	10	Time Stretch Process	264
Apply an offline process to an object from the Pool window	9	Offline Processes in the Pool	231
Bounce audio objects to a new file	10	Bounce Selection	251
Change the default crossfade (fade) settings	10	Working with Fade Envelopes	252
Change the fade curve type of an audio object	10	Working with Fade Envelopes	252
Close gaps between slices in a part	9	Creating and Using Audio Slices	242
Convert hitpoints into a groove map	9	Creating and Using Groove Maps	243
Create a folder in the pool	9	Understanding the Information	223
Create a new region	9	Working with Regions	234
Create an audio part from existing events in the project window	11	Audio Part Editor	295
Create an empty audio part in the project window	11	Audio Part Editor	295
Create audio slices	9	Creating and Using Audio Slices	242
Create hitpoints	9	Creating Hitpoints	238
Create regions using the Detect Silence function	10	Detect Silence	249

continued

APPENDIX A

Table A.7
MIDI editing operations

How To:	Chapter Number	Heading Title	Page Number
Add a controller lane to the MIDI Editor	8	Key Editor Display Areas	197
Apply a quantize effect as a MIDI track insert (or send)	7	Applying Quantize	173
Assign a program to a MIDI track	5	Using Installed Devices in the Inspector	123
Create a drum map	8	Creating a Drum Map	215
Create a ramp using the Sine, Triangle, or Square tools	8	Using the Line Tool	204
Create chords in the Chorder MIDI effect	B	Chorder	444
Create notes using the Draw tool in the Key Editor	8	Using the Draw Tool	203
Create patterns in the Step Designer MIDI effect	B	Step Designer	447
Dissolve a MIDI part	11	Dissolve Parts	282
Edit a MIDI insert effect's parameters	6	MIDI Track Inserts	138
Filter a type of event in the List Editor	8	List Editor Display Areas	216
Import a MIDI file	7	About MIDI File Imports	186
Insert events using the Line tool	8	Using the Line Tool	204
Load a drum map and assign it to a drum track	8	Assigning a Drum Map to a Track	214
Merge note events	8	Merging Note Events	202
Resize a note or a group of notes	8	Splitting and Resizing Note Events	201
Save a MIDI effect preset	B	Saving Your Presets	441
Set your MIDI input port	6	Setting Up a MIDI Track	131
Transmit recorded SysEx bulk dumps to your external MIDI device	13	Transmitting Bulk Dumps	343
Transpose selected events using the MIDI Transpose option	11	Transpose	279
Use a MIDI function	11	About MIDI Functions	284
Use the Compress MIDI effect	B	Compress	450
Use the MIDI Merge In Loop option	11	MIDI Merge In Loop	280
Use Zones in the Chorder MIDI effect	B	Chorder	444

APPENDIX A

Table A.8
Mixing operations

How To:	Chapter Number	Heading Title	Page Number
Add a MIDI insert effect	6	MIDI Track Inserts	138
Adjust an EQ band from the audio track equalizer section	6	Audio Track Equalizer	148
Adjust the EQ settings for an audio channel	12	EQ Settings	319
Adjust the EQ settings using the Equalizer Curve	6	Equalizer Curve	149
Assign a MIDI track send	6	MIDI Track Sends	139
Bypass all the tracks sent to the same effect	6	Audio Track Sends	150
Bypass one or all MIDI inserts from playback	6	MIDI Track Inserts	138
Bypass/activate the signal sent to all send effects in a track	6	Audio Track Sends	150
Bypass/activate the signal sent to one send effect in a track	6	Audio Track Sends	150
Change the automation parameter displayed in a subtrack	5	The Track List	109
Convert MIDI tracks playing external MIDI devices into audio tracks	15	Converting your MIDI Tracks	378
Store a channel view set	12	Common Panel	300
Edit the routing of an insert effect in a surround output bus configuration	E	Routing Effects in Surround Outputs	
Export a file for MP3 compatibility	15	MP3	389
Export a file for RealPlayer or Windows Media Player compatibility	15	RealMedia and Windows Media	385
Export a project to an OMF format	15	More on OMF	391
Export your final mix as an audio file	15	Exporting Your Final Mix	382
Link or unlink channels in the Mixer window	12	Working with Mixer Settings	315
Mute speakers in the surround panner	E	Surround Panner	474
Rename a stored EQ preset	12	EQ Settings	319
Reveal or hide a track's automation subtracks	5	The Track List	109

Table A.9
Automation operations

APPENDIX A

Table A.10
Score operations

How To:	Chapter Number	Heading Title	Page Number
Add a guitar symbol in your score	16	Other Global Settings	405
Add a symbol from a symbol palette on your score	16	Symbol Palettes	419
Add braces or brackets in a layout	16	Layout Settings	409
Add lyrics	16	Adding Text	424
Add notes to a specific voice in a polyphonic staff	16	Insert Buttons	415
Add symbols to the Custom palette	16	Symbol Palettes	419
Change the format of the ruler	16	Function Buttons	416
Change the page size and margin settings	16	Printing and Page Setup	425
Change your score behavior preferences	16	Score Preferences	400
Configure the staff settings	16	Staff Settings	413
Create a chord from selected note symbols on your score	16	Working with Chords	421
Create a text attribute set	16	Text Settings	402
Create chords for your Guitar Library	16	Other Global Settings	405
Create custom chords	16	Working with Chords	421
Export a score to a graphic file	16	Printing and Page Setup	425
Group a series of notes	16	Function Buttons	416
Hide symbols using the Hide function in a score	16	Function Buttons	416
Launch the Score Editor	16	Score Editor Window	399
Remove the hidden property associated with a symbol	16	Function Buttons	416
Rename a layout	16	Layout Settings	409
Reveal hidden symbols from your score	16	Function Buttons	416
Set the accidentals preferences in a score	16	Accidentals Settings	404
Stretch a word or syllable across several notes	16	Adding Text	424
Ungroup notes	16	Function Buttons	416

Appendix B
Using MIDI Effects

MIDI effects control how MIDI is played and can also be used creatively, depending on the MIDI effect you apply to a MIDI track. When used as an insert, MIDI events pass through the MIDI effect, which transforms the events played at the MIDI output port of the track in which it's inserted. When used as a send effect, MIDI events still pass through the MIDI effect, but you can also send the output of the MIDI effect to another MIDI output port and/or MIDI channel. This gives you a great tool to create new MIDI events that can add interesting effects to your original content.

All the steps in the following sections describing how to use an effect assume that you have already assigned the effect to a MIDI track's insert or send effect and have configured the MIDI output appropriately (if using a send effect).

These effects have been grouped into two categories: the event creation effects and the event modifying effects.

Saving Your Presets

As with many other windows, panels, and dialog boxes in Cubase, you can save settings made to MIDI effects as a preset for later use. You will find a Presets menu (see Figure B.1) whenever it is possible to save a pattern or setting. When you save a preset, you can later retrieve it and use it on another track or in another project.

How To

To add a plug-in effect to a selected object:

1. Click the Save button next to the Presets menu (it's the button representing the folded page with a plus sign inside).
2. A Preset Name dialog box appears. Enter a name for your preset and click OK.

To remove a saved preset, select it and click the Remove button next to the Save button (the button with a minus sign inside).

Figure B.1

Managing your MIDI effects presets by using the preset functions in each MIDI effect.

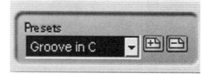

Event Creation Effects

These effects generate MIDI events when passing a track through them. This implies that new MIDI messages are produced as a result of these effects.

Arpache 5

The Arpache 5 is an arpeggio and note pattern generator (see Figure B.2). There are three main areas in this effect that control how the effect generates its arpeggios. The Playmode area with its six buttons determines the direction of the arpeggiated notes. An arrow pointing up means that the notes generated move upwards along the chord or note you play and an arrow pointing down means that the notes move downwards. The question mark generates a random direction based on the note or notes you played. The Order button activates the Play Order section, which creates a specific order in which notes are played in your arpeggio. If you look at the last staff in Figure B.3, you will notice that the Play Order used was 1-2-1. Because the chord played was C-E-G, the lowest note is considered as Note 1 and the highest as Note 3. In this case, the arpeggio plays a 1-2-1 pattern before going up one level; then it repeats this pattern, creating a more complex arpeggio.

The Quantize field determines the distance between each note in the arpeggio. In this case (Figure B.2 and B.3), this is set to sixteenth notes. The Length field determines the length for each note. The Semi-Range determines the range in semitones covered by the arpeggio. This defines how high or how low the arpeggio will go from the lowest note played. In this example, the range is set to 24 semitones, or two octaves.

Because the Arpache can be played in real time or assigned to a track, you can decide if you want to include the chords or notes you play to trigger the effect by using the Thru button. When this button is active, you hear the chords as you play them. When this button is deactivated, you only hear the notes generated by the Arpache, unless of course you already have notes recorded on a track. In this case, you can set the MIDI output port for this track to Not Connected. This allows you to hear the events generated by the events recorded on the track without hearing these actual events. In our Figure B.3 example, this would prevent us from hearing the original C chord while we hear the resulting arpeggio.

Figure B.2

The Arpache 5 MIDI effect panel.

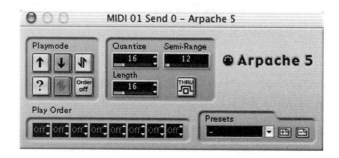

Figure B.3
Different results generated by the different Playmode settings; the name above each staff indicates which play mode was used when generating these events.

Autopan

The Autopan generates Control Change messages over a period of time. Its best use, however, is to create an autopan effect, creating pan values that change over time. In the example provided in Figure B.4, you can see that a square wave has been selected. The different wave buttons choose how the events are created. The frequency of each wave, or its period, is determined by the Period field. In this example, it is set to quarter notes. This means that the pattern of the wave repeats every quarter note. The Density field determines how often a value is added. Again, in this example, the density is set to sixteenth notes. As you can see, there is a value added every sixteenth note in the controller lane of the Key Editor. The Controller field chooses which Control Change message is added to the MIDI track. In other words, this example uses the AutoPan with the Pan Control Change message, but you can use any other Control Change message if you want. The Min and Max fields set a minimum and maximum value for generated Control Change messages. Because this example uses a square wave, each value that is added is either 0 or 127. But if you were to use a sine or random wave, for example, you could have intermediate values as well.

You should also know that when you want to use a smoother transition between pan value changes, you will achieve a better result with a higher density value. However, the shorter both your period and density are, the more MIDI events you generate, and this might cause your MIDI port to choke if it is overwhelmed by such MIDI events.

The two last waveforms on the right can be used with the AmpMod field, which controls the amplitude modulation variations of the controller messages. This works much like a low-frequency oscillator, adding a variable waveform into the equation, thus creating a more complex change in the waveform appearance of the generated messages.

APPENDIX B

Figure B.4
The Autopan MIDI effect
panel over the MIDI
result (in the Key Editor)
provided by this effect.

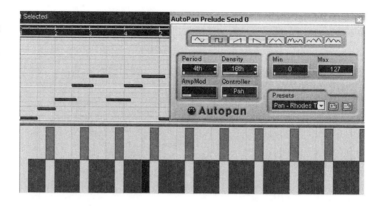

Chorder

The Chorder effect generates chords when you play a single note. It offers three basic modes: Normal, Octave, and Global.

In Normal mode, you can assign a chord to each note of your keyboard, up to 128 different chords. You create chords using the upper keyboard, clicking on notes you want to include in your chord, and you define the key that triggers this chord by selecting it on the lower keyboard. In Figure B.5, playing the C3 note generates the chord found in the upper keyboard.

The Octave mode is similar; however, you can have up to 12 chords, or one per semitone in an octave. This means that no matter which C key you press, it plays the same chord at the corresponding octave.

In Global mode, the entire keyboard plays the same chord, so the Trigger Note keyboard shown in Figure B.5 is not visible. The chord plays the corresponding chord at the pitch determined by the key you play.

In all three modes, you can also assign zones. Zones create different chords for the same note and are triggered in one of two ways: either by velocity or by note combination.

When chords are triggered by velocity, the velocity scale is divided equally among the number of zone splits you create. For example, if you have two zones, playing a note at a velocity range of 0 to 63 plays one chord (the one you assigned to Zone 1), and playing a note with a velocity between 64 and 127 plays the second zone chord (the one assigned to Zone 2). If you use notes to determine which zone is played, you can only play one chord, or one note at a time. The lowest note you play determines the pitch of the chord, and the second simultaneous note you play determines which other note is played. The interval between the two determines which zone is played. For example, if you play the notes G3 and G#3, the interval is one semitone; therefore, the chord played is the one assigned to this zone. If you play G3 and A3, the interval is two semitones; so, the Zone 2 chord plays, and so on, for a maximum of eight different chords for eight different zones.

Figure B.6 displays an example of chords changing, depending on the method used. The upper staff shows the notes played to trigger the different zones when notes are used to switch between zones. As you can see, the interval between the two notes in this staff is a semitone. This tells the Chorder you want to hear the chord assigned to that zone. In the third bar, the pitch is now different, but the relation between the two notes in the first staff is the same, so the Zone 1 chord

Figure B.5
The Chorder MIDI effect panel in Normal mode.

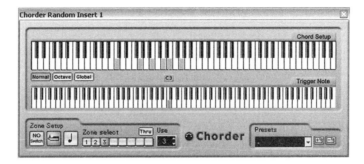

is played starting on the lower note's pitch. The second staff from the top shows the notes played to trigger the different zones (each note is played at a different velocity). The lower two staves show the chords generated, which are a C Major 9th chord, C Major 7#11 chord, and a C 13 added.

Figure B.6
Using different chords associated with different zones to create harmonic structures in the Chorder MIDI effect.

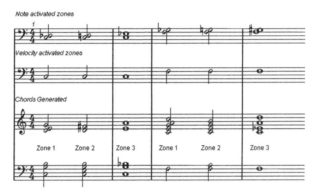

Because the three modes are similar, we take a look at how to create chords and zones in the Octave mode. Remember that in Normal mode, you can have up to 128 different chords. The note that plays them does not affect the pitch, but serves as a trigger. In Octave mode, the same applies, with the exception that you hear a different octave, depending on the octave you play the trigger note in, and in Global mode, the played pitch determines the chord's pitch. The example in Figure B.6 was generated by using the Global mode using three separate zones.

How To

To create chords in the Chorder MIDI effect:

1. Select the desired mode. The following steps assume you selected Octave mode.
2. In the trigger keyboard, click the note you want to use to trigger the chord. The note becomes red.
3. In the Chord Setup keyboard, click the notes you want to include in the chord. Clicking the note turns it blue, meaning it will be part of the chord. Clicking it again removes it from the chord.
4. Play that note on your keyboard controller to hear the result.
5. Repeat Steps 2–4 for each additional chord you want to create in your octave.

APPENDIX B

How To

To use zones in the Chorder MIDI effect:

1. Click the up or down arrow in the Use field to add the desired number of zones for each note. You can have up to eight zones.

2. Select the first trigger note on the Trigger Note keyboard (only available in Normal or Octave modes).

3. Select the desired zone number button to make the chord for that zone.

4. Add notes to the Chord Setup keyboard by clicking on the notes you want to add to the chord.

5. Select the next zone number button to add a new chord to the same trigger note, but different zone.

6. Repeat Steps 2–4 for all the zones.

7. Select another trigger note from the Trigger Note keyboard and repeat Steps 3–6 for as many trigger notes as you want (this is also determined by the mode you have selected).

8. Select the Velocity Zone Split button (second button to the right in the Zone Setup area) or the Note Zone Split button (third button to the right in the Zone Setup area).

Density

The Density MIDI effect panel (see Figure B.7) creates random notes to simulate a denser MIDI track or mute notes to simulate a sparser track. Which one it does depends on the percentage you assign to the slider bar in the control panel. When a value of 100 is displayed, this means 100% density and no changes are made to the MIDI events. A larger value causes the effect to generate progressively more random notes, and smaller values cause it to start muting progressively more and more notes. You can use this to create MIDI effects by using a MIDI loop that varies through time, for example.

Figure B.7
The Density MIDI effect panel.

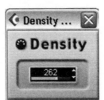

MIDIEcho

The MIDIEcho (see Figure B.8) is similar to an audio delay but creates MIDI events to simulate this echo rather than changing the actual sound coming from the MIDI instrument. It does this through a number of parameters that you can adjust to get the desired echo effect and also offers the possibility to change the pitch of echoed notes. Here's a look at these parameters:

▶ **Quantize.** Determines how close the echo is to a quantize value. The values can be adjusted using the slider bar or the up and down arrows on the right side of the field. When using the slider bar, each value corresponds to 1/480 tick of a quarter note.

▶ **Length and Length Decay.** Determines the length value of each note. It can be adjusted the same way as the Quantize parameter. As for the Length Decay, this determines if each repeated note is the same length or not.

▶ **Repeat.** Determines how many echoes are generated from the input note. You can have up to 12 repeated notes.

▶ **Echo-Quantize.** Determines the time between the input note and its first echo.

▶ **Velocity Decay.** Increases or decreases the velocity of repeated events by a certain velocity amount. You can set this parameter to values between plus or minus 36.

▶ **Pitch Decay.** Changes the pitch of each repeating echo by the amount of semitone you assign to this parameter, where each value corresponds to a semitone. So, a value of seven makes each echo repeat a perfect fifth above the preceding echo. You can use this to create arpeggios by adding or subtracting notes to repeated notes.

▶ **Echo Decay.** Increases or decreases a value corresponding to the time added or removed between each echoed event. If you set this to a positive value, echoes repeat with more and more time being added between each repetition, or with less and less time if you set this parameter's value to a negative number.

You can start with presets and change the parameters to find the desired effect.

Figure B.8
The MIDIEcho MIDI
effect panel.

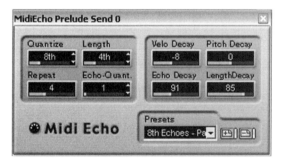

Step Designer

The Step Designer MIDI effect is a step sequencer that allows you to create up to 100 patterns using up to 32 steps per pattern. Each step is defined by the quantize setting in the Step Designer's panel. The Step Designer does not use or need incoming MIDI events. You create these patterns inside the interface itself. Let's take a look at the pattern creation process inside the Step Designer. Each number in the following steps corresponds to the numbers in Figure B.9.

How To

To create patterns in the Step Designer MIDI effect:

1. Select the Pattern number from the Pattern field.

   You can copy a pattern from one to another by clicking Copy, selecting the next pattern, and then clicking Paste. The Random button creates a random pattern, and the Reset button resets all steps.

2. Adjust the length in steps, quantize value, and swing value for the steps inside the grid below.

   For example, a Length of 16 means that there are 16 steps in the sequence. A Quantize of 16 means that each step is a sixteenth note. You can add a Swing amount to create a shuffle or swing feel to your pattern.

3. Select the range you want to see.

   There is an octave range displayed on the left. Clicking and dragging this bar moves the range up or down. This does not affect steps placed inside the grid, but only affects the events that you see. Events that are in the grid, but outside of view are displayed as red events with their note number, and they are in the upper row when found above the current view or in the lower row when below the current view.

4. If you want to shift an entire octave up or down, use the Shift Octave buttons. This, unlike dragging the range described in Step 3, affects the notes found in the grid on the right.

5. Add the events in the grid. The steps falling on beats are displayed in black numbers below the grid, and the steps falling between beats are displayed in a cyan (or turquoise) color. To add a step on the second beat at D1, align your cursor at the crossroad of the appropriate column and row and click inside the grid. Clicking again on an inserted note removes it. You can also drag your mouse across the grid to add several events.

6. If you want to tie two or more notes together, click the Tie button corresponding to the step or steps following the first step number where you want the tie to begin. For example, in Figure B.9, if you want to tie the second step to the first, you click in the tie line on the Tie button number 2.

7. You can adjust different control change parameters. To choose which controller is displayed below the step grid, click the Controller drop-down menu and select the controller of choice. The default controllers displayed are Velocity, Gate (which allows you to shorten the notes), Harmonics, and Brightness (how the last two controllers change the sound depends on the instrument playing back the steps found in the Step Designer). If you want to adjust other controllers not found in this list, click the Setup button and choose the appropriate controllers from the dialog box.

8. Adjust the selected controller corresponding to each previous step by dragging the vertical bar up or down to get the desired effect.

9. If you want to shift all the steps one step forward or backward in time, use the Shift Time buttons. This can create interesting variations to a beat or rhythmic pattern.

10. If you want to reverse all the steps in your grid (the last step becomes the first and vice versa), click the Reverse button. This option can also be used to create interesting beats or rhythmic variations.

11. When you are satisfied with the patterns that you have created, you can save them as a preset. Each preset can hold up to 100 patterns. So, before you save a preset, you can choose another pattern and edit it by repeating the previous steps. When all the patterns have been created, you can proceed to saving them in a preset.

After your patterns are created, you can automate the changes by recording MIDI events using note events on the MIDI track. The notes you record as MIDI events in the part are not played back by your VSTi or other external MIDI device. Pattern 1 corresponds to C1 on your keyboard, subsequent patterns follow on C#1, and so on. In other words, recording a MIDI note playing on C1 at bar 1.1.000 and then a C#1 on bar 5.1.000 causes the Step Designer to play the Pattern 1 from Bar 1 to Bar 5 and then change to Pattern 2 from Bar 5 until you enter the next MIDI note corresponding to a new pattern.

How To

To automate the pattern changes in a MIDI track using the Step Designer MIDI effect:

1. Create your patterns in the Step Designer as previously described.

2. In the Event Display area, position the left and right locators so that they cover the range of bars where you want to create automation events for the Step Designer.

3. Double-click the MIDI track to create a new part that corresponds to the length found between the left and right locators.

4. Double-click this part to open its associated editor (Key or Drum).

5. Set up your quantize grid appropriately and activate it.

6. Select the Draw tool from the toolbar.

7. Enter notes at the location in the part corresponding to desired pattern change locations. Remember, C1 is Pattern 1, C#1 is Pattern 2, and so on.

Figure B.9
The Step Designer MIDI
effect panel.

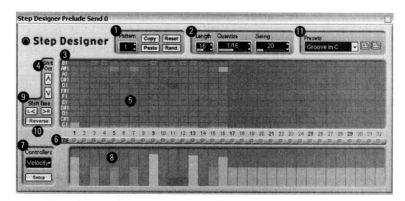

Event Modifying Effects

MIDI effects in this category do not create any new MIDI events, but modify them in some way.

Compress

The Compress MIDI effect (shown in Figure B.10) compresses or expands the velocity values of events on a MIDI track by adding or reducing the Note On velocity of these events. The Compress effect has three controls: the Threshold level, the Ratio, and the Gain control. The Threshold level determines the velocity value needed to trigger the compress effect. The Ratio can act as an expander or a compressor depending on the value set in this field. A one-to-one ratio means there is no change in the velocity values. A ratio greater than one-to-one compresses the velocity values by that proportion, and a ratio that is less than one-to-one expands the velocity value by that same ratio. For example, if you have a ratio of 2:1, for every two values passing the threshold, only one is added to the final velocity. So, if you have a threshold of 80 and play a velocity of 100 with a ratio of 2:1, the end velocity result is 90. On the other hand, if you have a ratio of 1:2, playing a note with a velocity of 90 using the same threshold causes the velocity to move up to 100.

The Gain control determines a value that is added or removed to the velocity of MIDI events passing through this effect.

Unlike the previous MIDI effects described in this appendix, this effect does not generate new MIDI events, but simply modifies the events going through it.

How To

To use the Compress MIDI effect:

1. Adjust the Threshold value to the desired velocity value. Velocities below this threshold are not affected.

2. Adjust the ratio appropriately to expand or compress the velocity of events passing through the effect.

3. Adjust the Gain level to add or remove velocity values to all the events in this MIDI track.

Figure B.10
The Compress MIDI
effect panel.

Control

The Control MIDI effect controls up to eight MIDI control change parameters. As you can see in Figure B.11, the left column is used to set the value for a controller that is defined in the right column. You can select any available controller from the drop-down menu in this (right) column. You can use this to automate different control change parameters using MIDI automation as described in Chapter 13.

Figure B.11
The Control MIDI effect
panel.

MicroTuner

This effect simulates different types of tuning. It does so by giving you control over fine-tuning between each semitone in a chromatic scale and then applies these tuning modifications over the range of the keyboard. The best way to use this is to use one of the many available presets. Changing the tuning for one MIDI instrument playing strings, for example, might help make the overall sound a bit richer if this instrument were doubled by another string pad that is not microtuned.

The Micro Tuner panel (shown in Figure B.12) features 12 sliders, one for each semitone. Each one can be adjusted separately. You can also select the Convert method, which adjusts the microtuning method, depending if this is applied to a VSTi or external MIDI device using SysEx to alter the tuning of the device in question.

Figure B.12
The Micro Tuner MIDI
effect panel.

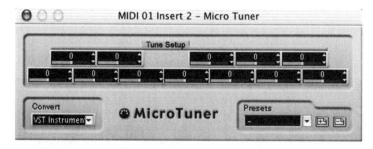

Note to Control Change Converter

This MIDI effect (see Figure B.13) converts a MIDI note number into a value that you can assign to a MIDI Control Change message. For example, you can create a MIDI track, play notes, and then assign this MIDI effect to affect the pan. Whenever a note is played high in the keyboard range, the pan goes on one side and when a note is played low, the pan goes on the other side. All you need to do is select which MIDI Control Change message you want to use with the converted note number values.

Figure B.13
The Note2CC MIDI effect
panel.

Quantizer

The Quantizer (shown in Figure B.14) offers the same effect as the main over quantize functions that were described in Chapter 7. In this case, you can assign to a track and change the quantize values dynamically by using automation. It offers the same parameters as the quantize setup; however, it does add a delay parameter that lets you assign a delay in milliseconds that can be added to each quantized note.

Figure B.14
The Quantizer MIDI
effect panel.

Track Control

The Track Control controls additional parameters provided by GS and XG compatible MIDI devices. Roland GS and Yamaha XG MIDI devices extend on the General MIDI (GM) standard by offering more sounds and better control over them. The Track Control effect provides a ready-made interface to control these devices when using such a device as your MIDI track output. If you don't have a GS or XG compatible device, this effect does not serve any purpose.

The panel itself (see Figure B.15) offers different controls of specific parameters displayed below the control. You can choose from the top drop-down menu which type of controls you want to see, depending on the GS or XG instrument you want to control.

Figure B.15
The Track Control MIDI
effect panel.

Track Effects

The Track Effects (see Figure B.16) offers essentially the same parameters as the Track Parameters section, with one addition: the Scale Transpose module. You can use this if you need to add random values to MIDI events and the two random generators in the Track Parameter are already used for something else, or when you want to use the Scale Transpose module.

Figure B.16
The Track FX panel.

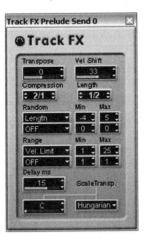

This module sets a scale and assigns a mode to your track, converting any recorded or played notes to notes found in the transpose scale and mode. If you take a look at Figure B.17, you will notice that a C major scale was recorded in the first staff. Using the Track Effect MIDI effect with the Scale Transpose set to an Oriental mode preset from the drop-down menu with a scale based on C, the notes in the original major scale are transformed to fit this new mode (lower staff in Figure B.17). In other words, you can quickly change the colors of harmonic and melodic content by using this feature in the Track Effects. Here's an example: If you use the default C scale and play in this scale as well, you can change the mode so that a C major scale becomes a C minor or C pentatonic scale instead. You can also change the scale itself to any other note in a 12-tone scale and all other notes will be changed appropriately.

Figure B.17
Using the Track Effects effect to modify the scale mode of melodic or harmonic content.

Input Transformer

The Input Transformer offers a way to transform MIDI events going in using the same tools and menus described in the Logical Editor, which is described in Appendix C. The main difference is that the transformer acts as a MIDI effect assigned to a track, modifying events in real time, whereas the Logical Editor edits selected events as a process applied to MIDI events, changing these MIDI events rather than transforming them as they are being played. Please refer to Appendix C for more details. Note that you can use the Merge MIDI function as described earlier in Chapter 11 to convert the realtime processing applied by the Input Transformer into editable MIDI events inside the MIDI editing windows.

Appendix C
Logical Editing

Logical editing is another way of editing MIDI data. Using this method, you create specific parameters for Cubase to look for and then decide to change them, delete them, or move them. This is for the MIDI-savvy user, because you need to know how MIDI messages work to fully understand how logical editing works.

The Logical Editor affects events differently, depending on the location from which you launch it, but it always performs the tasks in the same way. For example, if you are in the Project window and have not selected any MIDI parts, it performs edits on all the parts for the selected tracks. On the other hand, if you have a part selected, it looks for and edits only events in that part. Finally, if you are in MIDI Editor, the Logical Editor performs its modifications on the events selected in this part or all events if none are selected.

You may use already created logical edit presets included with Cubase, or you may create your own and save them. Logical edits are stored as separate files on your hard disk and are common to any project.

Let's take a look at an example to begin describing how this interface works. You may refer to Figure C.1 to see what the following example is describing.

Figure C.1
The Logical Editor used to transpose notes between C2 and G4 up a fifth.

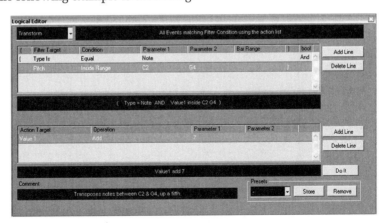

Suppose you want to transpose notes that are between C2 and G4, up a perfect fifth. You can start by defining a function. Functions are what you want to do with the events you edit logically. In this case, you want to transform notes. So, in the upper-left corner of the interface, you select Transform from the drop-down menu (functions in this list are described later in this appendix).

What do you want to transform? In this case, once again, you want to transform notes. In Logical Editor terms, this is the target. To correctly target what you want to transform, you have to define it by using a filter, which tells Cubase what to look for, a condition that needs to be met, and parameters within the filter that should be applied. In our example, the target for your filter is a type that is equal to notes. That's why you see "Type is" under the Filter Target, "Equal" under the Condition, and "Note" under the Parameter column.

Now, do you want to transform all notes? In our example, we only want to transform the notes between C2 and G4. This is a second "target" you want to apply to the Logical Editor, so you add a second line using the Add Line button. If, at the end of the first line, you have a Boolean expression with the word "And," this tells Cubase to look for the target set in the first line *and* the second line. Events must then match both targeted conditions for the logical editing to occur. We then apply a filter to our second target, saying we want notes, but the pitch is important in our editing. So, Cubase filters certain pitch values. Because we want only pitch values between C2 and G4, the condition that needs to be met is set to "Inside Range." By selecting this type of condition, you can enter a note value in the Parameter 1 and Parameter 2 columns. These parameters correspond to the Pitch Inside Range values, which in this case are C2 and G4.

At this point, we've told Cubase to target a type of event that is equal to notes and the pitch value must be inside the C2 and G4 range. From this point forward, you tell Cubase what to do with these targeted events. This part occurs in the lower portion of the window.

Changing the pitch of these notes corresponds to the value 1 in the MIDI message because the pitch is the first value passed by the Note On message. You can, therefore, select this as the target for your action in the Action Target column. Now, what you want to do is transpose these notes up a perfect fifth. In other words, you want to add seven to each value passed on. This refers to MIDI note numbers. For example, a C2 note is equal to the MIDI note number 48. If you add 7 to this value, you get the note value 55, which is G3—a perfect fifth above C2. The operation you want to apply in our example is "Add" and the Parameter 1 value is 7.

All that you need to do from this point is click the Do It button to apply this logical edit to the selected events or parts. What the Logical Editor affects depends on the location from which you launched the editor and if any events were selected. The Logical Editor edits a selected track, a selected part, or a selected range of events in a part, depending on the point at which you launch the Logical Editor.

Remember that using the Logical Editor allows you to modify events in a way that normally takes much more time if done manually in one of the editors. The previous example is just one of many ways you can transform MIDI events quickly and effectively, not to mention the creative aspects of the Logical Editor. For example, creating a textured melody using a copy of the MIDI events, transposed a third above but using a velocity level set at 25 percent of the original version, simply adds color to this melody without having it stand out. The following sections allow you to get an understanding of these principles, and you can decide how you want to apply them.

Logical Editor Parameters

Let's take a closer look at the parameters found in the Logical Editor. The following paragraph contains the logic established by the Logical Editor. If you don't understand what this means right away, don't panic, just read on as each of these terms is described in the following sections. By the end of this appendix, you'll probably get it.

A *function* is applied to a *target*. This *target* is defined by meeting certain *conditions*, which serve as a *filter* mechanism to achieve this desired *target*. After a target is identified, you can apply an *action* to a *parameter* through an *operation*.

About Functions

The function determines what you want to do inside the Logical Editor. When selecting certain functions, you need to define an action in the bottom half of the editor, whereas other functions only need to have a target, for example, the Delete function. The functions available in the upper-left corner of the Logical Editor include:

▶ **Delete.** Deletes the targeted notes that pass through the filters.

▶ **Transform.** Transforms the targeted events that pass through the filters. The transformation is set by the values set in the Action section (or processing stage found in the lower half of the window). This doesn't add any new events; it just changes the existing ones.

▶ **Insert.** Adds the targeted events that pass through the filters. The transformation is set by the values set in the Action section. This adds new events to the part(s).

▶ **Insert Exclusive.** Adds the targeted events that pass through the filters, while deleting the events that do not pass through the filter.

▶ **Copy.** If you launch the Logical Editor from the Project window, it copies the events that pass through the filters out of the part or parts and then creates a new part or parts with the extracted events only. You cannot use this function if you are not launching the Logical Editor from the Project window.

▶ **Extract.** If you launch the Logical Editor from the Project window, it cuts the events that pass through the filters out of the part or parts and then creates a new part or parts with the extracted events only. You cannot use this function if you are not launching the Logical Editor from the Project window.

▶ **Select.** If you launch the Logical Editor from the MIDI Editors, it simply selects the events that pass through the filters for future processing directly in the editor, after you have exited the Logical Editor. You cannot use this function if you are not launching the Logical Editor from the Editor windows.

The best way to understand all of this is to look at some of the presets. Load them and look at how they change the values in different parts of the window. Because the preset names are pretty descriptive, you'll get a good sense of what's happening.

About Filter Target

This field tells the Logical Editor what to look for.

▶ **Position.** Requires you to enter a position in the Parameter 1 (and Parameter 2 field if you choose a range in the Condition column). For example, you might want to select notes between Bar 3 and Bar 4.

▶ **Length.** Requires you to enter a length value in the Parameter 1 (and Parameter 2 field if you choose a range in the Condition column). For example, you might want to select only quarter notes.

▶ **Value 1, 2, and 3.** Usually added as a second line in the targeted filter area because the value they represent depends on their type. For example, if you add a first line that reads, Type is Equal to Note, then on the second line, Value 1 automatically represents the pitch. If you select Value 2 instead, this automatically represents the velocity of the note, and Value 3 represents the Note Off velocity. In other words, the type selected determines what the value represents.

▶ **Channel.** Specifies a specific channel for your transformation. You enter the channel number in the Parameter field. If you set the condition to a range, you then add this range to both Parameter fields. For example, to select all events between Channel 4 and 7, the line should read as follows: Channel Inside Range 4 and 7.

▶ **Type (from the Filter Target column).** Chooses what type of MIDI message you want to target. Parameter 1 offers you the following choices: note, polyphonic pressure, control change, program change, aftertouch, and pitch bend messages.

▶ **Property.** Chooses events for which a specific property is either set or not set. These properties include the following options: an event can be muted, selected, or locked. For example, you can target all events that are not muted in a part by entering the following information: Property is not set to muted.

About Conditions

As you have just seen in the Filter Targets, the condition column varies depending on the targeted events. For example, choosing the Type target offers different conditions than if you select the Property target. Generally speaking, the conditions are similar to mathematical conditions.

As a practical example, suppose you want to find events that are not between Bars 5 and 9 of a project. You would choose the Filter Target Position, with a condition that reads Outside Range. You would then proceed to the Parameter fields and enter 0005.01.01.000 in Parameter 1 and 0009.01.01.000 in Parameter 2. You could even specify a range within a bar using the Inside or Outside Bar Range condition. In this case, a bar range display appears, allowing you to drag a range within a bar to determine this range. The values corresponding to this range are added to the Parameter 1 and 2 columns.

About Boolean Expressions

The Boolean expression column is used when more than one line is present in the target area for the Logical Editor. If you want Cubase to include events targeted in one line *and* the other, use the "And" Boolean. If you are trying to achieve one or the other, select the "Or" Boolean.

Figure C.2 displays an example of Boolean expressions in use. In this case, notes with a velocity ranging from 0 to 64 "Or" 100 to 127 will be targeted. Notice the Boolean expression between the first and second line is "And." This tells Cubase that you are looking for Note events, but wait, there's more, you also want it to look for notes with specific velocity values.

You will also notice the braces at the beginning of line two and at the end of line three. These allow you to set boundaries, as in a mathematical formula. For example, $2 + 3 \times 4$ is not the same as $2 + (3 \times 4)$. If you were to have these braces, defining that the velocity needed is one of the conditions; the other condition is the length. In the same way here, we want to find notes that have a velocity of 0 to 64 or 100 to 127, and then we could add a fourth line stating that the length has to equal 1.000. The end of the third line would have the "And" Boolean expression.

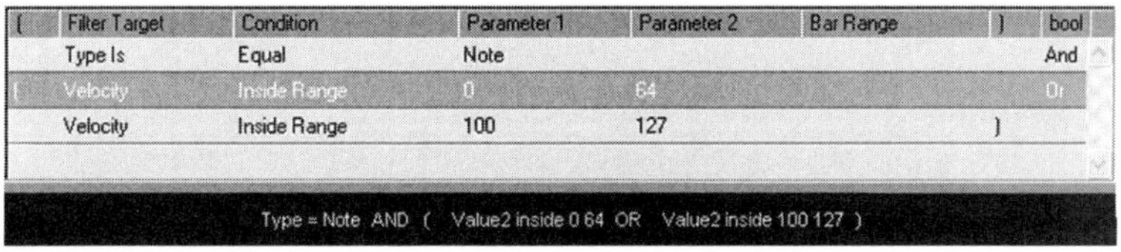

Figure C.2
Example of a setting
using a Boolean value.

[	Filter Target	Condition	Parameter 1	Parameter 2	Bar Range	]	bool
	Type Is	Equal	Note				And
[	Velocity	Inside Range	0	64			Or
	Velocity	Inside Range	100	127		]	

Type = Note AND (Value2 inside 0 64 OR Value2 inside 100 127)

Specifying an Action

After you've determined what the target is, you can specify the type of action you want the Logical Editor to apply to those targeted events. This is done in the second (lower part of the window) section of the Logical Editor.

The Action Target column holds the same options as the Filter Target. That's because you can apply an action to the same types of events that you can target. However, it doesn't mean that if you targeted the note events with a certain velocity, that you will necessarily apply an action to the velocity of those events. You could change the position of those events, for example. How the action is applied is determined by the Operation column. As with the Condition column in the previous section, the Operation column holds different options, depending on the Action Target column's selection.

If we take the target specified in Figure C.2, for example, we could select notes with a specific velocity and apply the actions specified in Figure C.3. As we can see, the position of the notes is changed by adding 200 ticks to these notes. Furthermore, their length is modified by setting a random length value between 600 ticks and 1000 ticks (there are 480 ticks in each quarter note).

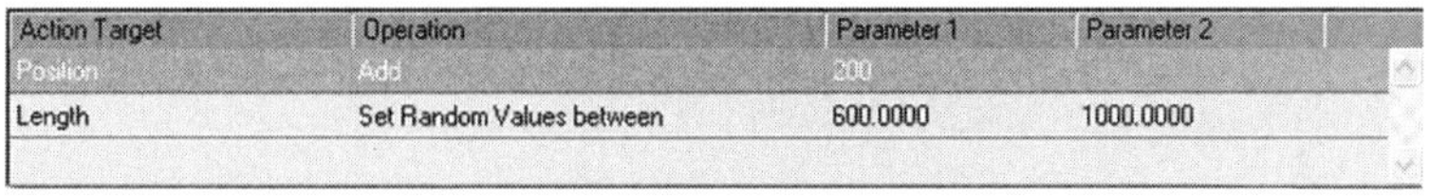

Figure C.3
An example of actions
taken on targeted events.

Action Target	Operation	Parameter 1	Parameter 2	
Position	Add	200		
Length	Set Random Values between	600.0000	1000.0000	

APPENDIX C

Appendix D
Optimizing Through Customizing

This appendix discusses ways that you can customize settings and create reusable documents to suit your working preferences.

Window Layouts

If you find yourself constantly opening the same sets of windows every time you create a new project or open an existing one, you should create custom window layouts. Window layouts are saved separately and are common to all projects inside Cubase. Window layouts save the current position and state of windows inside your project. You can create several layouts and recall them through a set of default key commands. By doing so, you can create a layout for your editing tasks, another one for your audio record tasks, and another layout for your mixing tasks.

How To

To create a window layout:

1. Open the windows you want to display on your desktop. For example, if you always place your Project window in the upper-right corner and VST Instruments panel on the bottom of your desktop, place these windows there.

2. After you are satisfied with the window layout, select Window Layouts > New from the Window menu or press the default key command Ctrl(PC)/⌘(Mac)+0 (from the numeric keypad).

3. Name your layout appropriately.

4. Repeat these steps to create an additional window layout.

How To

To organize your window layouts:

1. Select Window Layouts > Organize from the Window menu or press the default key command W.
2. Click the Remove button if you want to remove a layout from the list. Click the New button if you want to save the current layout or Activate if you want Cubase to display the selected layout in the Window Layouts panel.

Creating Templates

When we work, we often start with basic settings. For example, if you have a favorite VSTi that you load for drums, a favorite window layout, a typical bus routing, or a number of tracks that you always name the same way, you might consider creating a template. Templates are Cubase project documents that are saved in a Templates folder found inside your Cubase program folder. Saving a project as a template before you start recording events into it allows you to save all these settings, including preferences, output and input settings, and all of the previously mentioned settings. To use a template, you simply select Create New Project from the File menu. This displays the New Project dialog box (see Figure D.1). The options available in the New Project dialog box are the template files found in the Template folder.

Figure D.1
Templates appear in the New Project dialog box when you create a new project.

How To

To create a template:

1. Organize your project as you normally do. For example, create the tracks you normally use, activate the outputs/inputs, assign send effects, and so on.

2. When you are satisfied that this is a worthy template, select the Save As Template from the File menu.

3. Enter a name for your template. The name you enter in this dialog box is the name that will appear in the New Project dialog box, as shown in Figure D.1. This is also the name given to the file.

Because templates are just like regular files, you can rename or delete the files from your hard disk to rename or remove a file from the template list. It also implies that you can save events within a template file.

Another way you can customize your environment at startup is by saving your default preferences as the Default.cpr file in the Cubase program folder. To edit the default file, simply open it, make the desired changes, and save it. Once a Default.cpr file is saved, you need to select the Open Default Project option in the File(PC)/Cubase(Mac) > Preferences > General > On Startup field. The On Startup field determines what actually occurs when launching Cubase, so any selection you make here will affect Cubase's behavior at every startup.

Customizing Key Commands

Throughout this book, references are made to key commands (keyboard shortcut keys). Although Cubase provides a default set of key commands, which are associated with a number of functions and operations, you can change these default settings to better reflect your working habits.

The commands that can be associated with keyboard shortcuts are found under File > Key Commands. This will bring up the Key Commands dialog box. At the top of this page, you will find a Search field and to the right of this field, a magnifying glass icon. All the commands are grouped by category in the area below the Search field. The easiest way to find a command is still to type in its name in the Search field and then click on the magnifying glass to display the first match Cubase finds in the Category area below. After a command is found, you can see if a keyboard shortcut is associated with this command by looking at the Keys column in the same area.

APPENDIX D

How To

To customize a key command:

1. Inside the Key Commands dialog box, select the command to which you want to assign a keyboard shortcut.
2. Click inside the field called *Type in Key* to make this field active. If the selected command already has a keyboard shortcut associated to it, the field titled Keys (above) will display the associated key or key combination.
3. Press the key or key combination (for example Alt+G) you want to associate with the currently selected command. If the key or key combination is already assigned to another command, Cubase will display the name of this command in the area below called *Assigned to*.
4. Press the Assign button to associate the keys you entered to the selected command. The keys should appear in the Keys area above. If a previous keyboard shortcut was already assigned to this command, it will be replaced by the new one you have just created.

The Recycle bin icon below the Keys area will remove the keyboard shortcut associated with a selected command, while the Presets field below manages the previously saved presets or allows you to save a preset to memory. Note that there are already presets available for Cubase 5 or other applications users. Using the same shortcuts to do the same tasks from one software to the next can make sense, so if you're used to working with a specific set of keyboard shortcuts, this dialog box customizes the key command associations to better meet your needs.

Macros

Using Cubase macros is a way to save a number of tasks that you perform regularly one after the other. For example, you can quickly create four audio tracks, a Marker track, select a window layout, and select a zoom level. Performing these tasks can take many steps, or one single step when programmed as a macro command.

How To

To create a macro:

1. From the File menu, select the Key Commands option.
2. In the Key Commands dialog box, click the Show Macro button. This reveals the Macro section at the bottom of the dialog box (see Figure D.2).
3. Click the New Macro button to add a new macro in the Macros area.
4. Double-click the new macro's name and type in a new name for the macro.

Figure D.2
Creating Macro
commands in the Key
Commands dialog box.

Now your new macro is created, but it won't do anything. Let's add commands to it.

How To

To add commands to a macro:

1. In the Key Commands dialog box, click on the category of command you want in the Commands area. Categories are represented by little folders. You may also click on the plus sign to their left to reveal the actual commands found in the desired category.

2. From the displayed commands, select the command you want to add to your macro.

3. Click the Add Command button in the Macro section to add the selected command in the Commands area of the Macro section.

4. Repeat the previous steps for each command you want to add to your macro.

5. When you've completed adding commands to your macro, click OK to close this dialog box.

When you launch your new macro, the commands you have just entered will be executed in the order in which you entered them in the macro.

How To

To use a macro in a project:

1. From the Edit menu, select the Macro option at the bottom of the menu. The applicable macro commands appear in the submenu of the Macro option (see Figure D.3).

2. Select the macro command you want to apply to start the list of commands it holds.

Figure D.3
Selecting a macro command.

Customizing Toolbars

You can now change the tools that are displayed in a window's toolbar and save these layouts for further use. This can come in handy when you need certain tools during one part of your creative process, but not during another and don't have enough space onscreen to display all the tools at once.

How To

To change the appearance of a toolbar:

1. Right-click anywhere in the toolbar. A context menu will display all the options that are available for this toolbar. The options with checkmarks next to them are currently visible, while the ones without checks are not.

2. Select an option with a checkmark to hide it from the toolbar or select an option without a checkmark to show it in the toolbar.

You can also save these customizations and select them later from the same context menu as shown in Figure D.4.

Figure D.4
Selecting a macro
command.

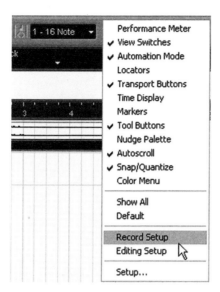

How To

To save a toolbar customization:

1. Right-click anywhere in the toolbar.
2. Select the Setup option at the bottom of the context menu. Items that appear under the Visible Items columns (see Figure D.5) are currently visible, while the items in the Hidden Items column are not.
3. By using the arrow buttons in the center, you can move items from one column to the next. You can also use the Move Up and Move Down buttons to change the order of appearance of the visible items.
4. Once you are satisfied with your changes, click on the diskette icon at the bottom of this dialog box to save the changes into a preset. Note that clicking on the Recycle bin will delete the currently displayed preset.
5. Another dialog box will appear, prompting you to enter a name for your preset. Enter a descriptive name for your preset. The name you enter here will appear next to the selection arrow (see Figure D.4).
6. Click OK twice to return to the previous window.
7. You can now select the newly created preset in the toolbar's customization context menu.

If you want to return the toolbar to its default state, you can do so by selecting the Default option in the same context menu, or also choose to display all the available toolbar items by selecting the Show All option instead.

Figure D.5
The Toolbar Setup dialog
box.

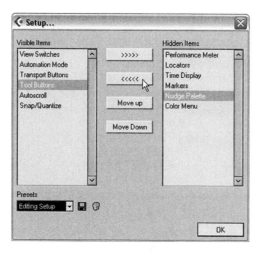

Customizing Your Transport Panel

You can choose to hide certain portions of the Transport panel if you don't need to use them or if you want to free up some valuable desktop space. Also, most of the time, we use certain tools more during certain types of projects or during certain steps in a project. For example, after you've completed the recording session, the Punch-in/Punch-out buttons won't be of much use.

How To

To show/hide Transport panel sections:

1. Right-click anywhere on your Transport panel (except where values can be changed with your cursor).

2. From the pop-up menu, check the sections you want to see and uncheck the sections you don't want to see, as shown in Figure D.6.

Figure D.6
Customizing your
Transport panel.

Customizing Track Controls

While working with controls in the track list area is convenient, sometimes dealing with all the controls available might become cumbersome and confusing. Certain controls are used only during the recording process, while others are used only during the editing process. Furthermore, some might never use a particular control on the track list, using the Mixer panel instead, while others never use the Mixer panel and only use the track list.

You can customize the controls that are present in the track list area, save these settings for each track class and recall them later on when you need them.

How To

To create customized track controls for the track list area:

1. Right-click(PC)/Control-click(Mac) in the track list area and select the Track Controls Settings option, or you can select the same option from the Track Controls drop-down menu found at the top of the track list area.

   The Tracks Controls Settings dialog box will appear (see Figure D.7).

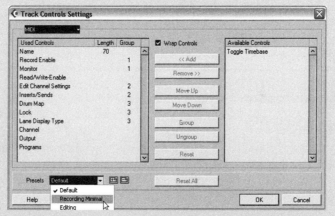

Figure D.7
The Track Controls Settings dialog box.

2. Select the track type from the Track Type drop-down menu found in the upper-left corner of the dialog box. The control elements in the left area are those currently visible in the track list area. The control elements found in the right area are those available, but not currently visible. Before creating a preset, let's look at an existing one to see if there's not already a preset that would suit your needs.

3. From the Preset menu in this dialog box, select the appropriate preset to see its current track control settings.

4. To Add a control to the current preset, select the control under the Available Controls column on the right and then click on the Add button between the two areas.

continued

5. To Remove a control from the current preset, select the control under the Used Controls column on the left and then click on the Remove button between the two areas. As you probably noticed, the selected control moves from one side to the other. You can also change the order in which they appear in the track list area.

6. Select the control in the Used Controls area that you want to modify and click on the Move Up or Move Down buttons to move this control where you want it in the list. To make sure two or more controls always stay together on the same line when you resize the track list area, you can group them.

7. Select the first control you want to group; then Ctrl(PC)/⌘(Mac)-click on the other controls you would like to group together. Note that if a control is already in a group, you'll need to ungroup it first before you can group it with another control.

8. Click on the Group button to group the controls together.

9. Repeat Steps 4 through 8 until you are satisfied with the result.

10. Click on the Add Preset button to create a new preset.

11. Enter the desired name in the field and click OK.

12. Click OK once again to return to the Project window.

Remember that you can always remove unwanted presets by selecting them and clicking on the Remove Preset button.

How To

To select a customized track control setting:

▶ Select the appropriate preset from the Track Controls drop-down menu found at the top of the track list area.

Appendix E
Surround Mixing in SX

Cubase SX offers the possibility of mixing in several surround modes, as well as in stereo mode. Mixing in surround, however, requires a multiple output sound card to monitor the signal sent to these additional outputs. It also requires an external monitoring system that supports surround sound. Surround refers to a multichannel positioning system rather than a standard stereo (left/right) positioning. The advantage of mixing in surround is that beyond the left/right field available in stereo mixes, you can literally place your sound anywhere in space around the listener by using various surround configurations. For example, an LCRS multichannel configuration offers a 4-channel setup, and a Surround 5.1 configuration on the other hand offers a 6-channel configuration. How you position the speakers depends on the standard you wish to use and the room for which you are mixing. For example, movie theaters often place the left and right channels behind the screen, close to the left and right walls, while the center channel is also behind the screen, but in the center of it. The LFE channel (for bass effect) will also be behind the screen, while the left and right surround channels will be along the three other surfaces of the theater itself.

To use surround mixing in Cubase, you need to create a surround output bus that is connected to a multioutput sound card. You may also create a surround input bus, but an audio channel does not have to be surround in order to be sent to a surround output bus. When you do send an audio channel to a surround output bus, the Surround Panner appears at the top of the channel in the panning area, offering you control over more than the typical left and right channels. You may also choose to route an audio channel (disk-based, VSTi, Rewire or FX channel) to a specific set of outputs within the surround bus channels. In that case, the pan control would remain the same as if you were routing the signal through a mono or stereo output bus. Figure E.1 shows how an audio channel displays the pan control when it is assigned to a surround output bus.

Surround Bus

In order to work with surround configurations, you need to create surround buses beforehand. Creating surround buses is done the same way you create other types of output or input buses, with the exception being that you choose a surround configuration instead of a mono or stereo bus configuration in the VST Connections panel.

After you have created a surround bus (input or output), you can associate each channel in the bus with an ASIO device port. How many ASIO device ports you need depends on the surround configuration you choose. For example, a 5.1 configuration will create a 6-channel configuration while an LCRS configuration uses only four (Left, Center, Right, and Surround).

Figure E.1
An audio channel using
surround pan control.

When you want to assign an audio channel to a surround bus, you can decide to route the output through one of the multichannel surround buses or to all of the channels at once. Figure E.2 displays a channel that is being routed to the center channel of the surround bus. As you can see, the pan area of the channel does not offer a surround panning option since the signal is sent to only one output channel within the surround bus.

Figure E.2
An audio channel routed
through a single channel
of a surround output bus.

After a surround bus is created, you can also create child buses. A child bus offers a convenient way of routing an audio channel through a set of outputs within a surround bus. For example, you can create a stereo child bus within a 5.1 surround configuration where the left and right channels are grouped within the surround bus. Routing an audio channel through a child bus allows you to control where the sound will occur in that child bus, so you will have a stereo pan control rather than a surround pan control. In other words, creating a child bus can make it easier to route audio through a surround bus, yet keep a stereo control (affecting both channels) when adjusting the pan and volume for this channel. For example, if you are creating a surround input bus to capture a multichannel performance or surround atmosphere, you can create child buses to represent the left/right pair and then a left surround/right surround pair,. When adjusting the level of the inputs, changing the volume for the left side will also affect the right side as they are being grouped inside the surround bus configuration.

How To

To create a child input/output bus (SX only):

1. Select the surround bus in which you want to create a child bus. This is done inside the VST Connections window (F4 being the default key command).

2. Right-click(PC)/Ctrl-click(Mac) on the selected surround bus and choose Add Child Bus and the appropriate Child Bus suboption that you want to create. In Figure E.3, selecting Stereo would create a child bus for the left and right channels within this surround bus.

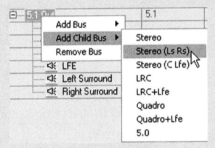

Figure E.3
Creating a child bus
within a surround bus.

You will notice that the ASIO device ports assigned to the newly created child bus will be the same as those assigned to the surround bus. Changing these ports in the child bus will also change them in the surround parent bus.

Surround Routing Options

When working with surround buses, both as input and output, many routing options are available. Depending on which routing option you choose, several pan control options will be available. Table E.1 offers a quick look at the surround signal routing options and the types of pan control each routing option offers.

Table E.1
Surround signal routing options

Source	Destination	Pan Control
Mono	To single channel inside the surround bus	None, the output channel is mono and will be heard in the associated ASIO device port.
Mono	To child bus inside the surround bus	Will be handled as a standard stereo or multichannel, depending on the child bus configuration. The pan might affect the surround position or any other location, depending on the current parent bus configuration. For example, if the bus is in 5.1 (6-channels) and the child bus set as an LCR subset (3-channels), the channel will display the Surround Panner to control the location. On the other hand, if your child bus is Stereo (Left/Right), the mono channel will be panned within the left/right spectrum (not surround panned, but part of the surround configuration).
Mono	To surround bus	The Surround Panner positions the signal anywhere within the current surround bus configuration.
Stereo	To stereo child bus inside the surround bus	Same as with mono signal sent to a stereo child bus (see above).
Stereo	To surround bus	The Surround Panner positions the signal anywhere within the current surround bus configuration.
Surround	Surround	No pan control; all channels will play in the same channel as they came in from. You should avoid sending a multichannel input signal configuration into another multiinput signal configuration or into a mono or stereo output bus. For example, avoid sending a 5.1 multichannel input signal into an LCRS output bus. Doing so will result in loss of sound positioning precision.

Surround Panner

The Surround Panner will automatically become available in a channel's pan control area when mono or stereo audio channels are routed through a surround output bus or a multichannel child bus (but not a stereo child bus). You can position and automate the position of the sound within the surround configuration by clicking on the small dot inside the surround pan display. Double-clicking on the Surround Panner display will open the Surround Panner Control, which offers greater control over the setup and behavior of the panner. The Surround Panner offers three different modes: standard, position, and angle (see Figure E.4).

Figure E.4
Surround Panner modes
(from left to right):
standard, position, and
angle.

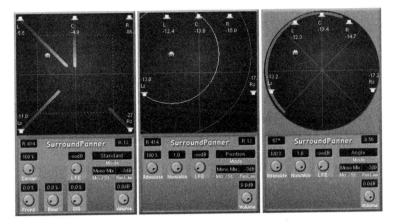

In the upper part, all three modes offer a representation of the speaker position and the position of the sound in relation to the speakers. The lower part offers a variety of controls over the behavior of the panner itself. To switch from one mode to the next, you select the desired option in the Mode drop-down menu found in the panner. Note that the actual number of speakers and how they appear in the upper part depends on the current surround bus configuration. Here's a look at the differences between each mode.

▶ In Standard mode, speakers are aligned to the front and back, similar to a typical movie theater setup. The space between each front speaker in this mode may not be the same in every room since the width of the left/right speakers will depend on the size of the room. This is the default mode and is most appropriate for moving sounds from one channel (position) to the next without attenuating the level of this signal while it travels between both positions.

▶ In Position mode, speakers are also aligned to the front, but not necessarily to the back. Instead, the surround speakers (in a 5.1 or 5.0 setup) are located on the side. Furthermore, the front speakers should be equally spaced from the center as well as the sides. In other words, if you were to divide the front by five, each line would be equally spaced, with lines 1 and 5 representing the left and right walls respectively, while lines 2 and 4 would represent the left and right speakers. This mode is also similar to movie theaters. The display is also different, as it shows circles around the position (or location) of the sound rather than the intensity of the sound emanating from the speakers. Each circle corresponds to a -3 dB decrease in amplitude from the current position of the sound to the first circle, another 3 dB to the next, and so on.

▶ In Angle mode, all speakers are considered at equal distance from the center point (the ultimate sweet listening spot). This is probably the most common configuration for 5.1 surround sound, but not a typical movie theater representation. This said, the angle mode will work well in most surround configurations. In this mode, a red arc helps you determine the perceived range of a source, and the sound will be at its loudest in the middle of the arc and the weakest towards the ends.

Figure E.5
The Surround Panner in
Angle and Y-Mirror
modes.

In any mode, the speakers represent an optimal speaker setup and the lines, especially in standard mode, give you an indication of how loud or soft a sound will be in any given speaker. You may decide, however, to mute a speaker, forcing Cubase to redistribute the sound through the remaining audio channels (hooked to the corresponding speakers) and effectively muting any signal going to that speaker.

How To

To mute speakers in the Surround Panner:

▶   Alt(PC)/Option(Mac)+click on the speaker you want to mute.

▶   Repeat the operation on the same speaker to unmute the speaker.

In the same display where you found the speakers, you will find either one or two control handles, depending on the mix mode set (see the following list). The control handles allow you to place the source of the sound appropriately in the surround sound mixing field. Lines emerge from the speakers, indicating the level being sent to each output. In the example provided in Figure E.4 (standard mode), you can see the single control placed in the upper-left portion of the display. Consequently, the front-right speaker's level is set to -86 dB, the center speaker to -4.9, and the left speaker to -5.5, while the left surround and right surround output levels are set to -11 and -27. These are the levels required to position your sound in the current configuration. Consequently, the level of this channel is distributed to each output by using these levels. The only speaker that is not represented in this display is the low frequency subbass speaker, which has its own control in the lower part of the panner.

You can move the source of a signal by dragging the control handle where you want in this display (and in any mode). If the source is stereo and if you are not using the Mono Mix mode (found in the lower part of the panner), you will find two control handles labeled L and R. When positioning a stereo sound within the Surround Panner, you will always move the right control handle (labeled R). The direction the left control handle takes depends on the surround mixer mode set. You have four basic mix modes to choose from:

▶ **Mono Mix.** When used on a stereo source, both sources are mixed into a mono channel and you control where this channel is positioned in the surround field (see Figure E.4).

▶ **Y-Mirror.** This causes stereo sources to become mirrored vertically. Moving the right control handle's position to the left or right causes the left field to move in the opposite direction. Moving this control to the front or back causes the left control to move in the same direction. In other words, the position of the right control is reflected vertically (the Y-axis).

▶ **X-Mirror.** This causes stereo sources to become mirrored horizontally. When you move the right control handle's position to the left or right, the left field moves in the same direction. When you move this control to the front or back, the left control moves in the opposite direction. In other words, the position of the right control is reflected horizontally (the X-axis).

▶ **X/Y-Mirror.** This causes stereo sources to become mirrored both vertically and horizontally. In other words, the left control always moves in the opposite direction of the right control.

In the Standard mode, the Center Level control determines the percentage assigned to the center speaker. When this slider is set to zero percent, the signal that would be positioned in the center speaker is shadowed by the left and right speakers instead, creating a virtual center speaker without using this source. By default, this value is set to 100 percent.

Still in the Standard mode, the following three rings are called Divergence controls, and they determine the attenuation curves used when positioning sound sources, for X-axis front (the first ring to the left), X-axis back (the center ring), and Y-axis (the ring on the right). By default, these values are set at zero percent. Raising these values changes the shape of the dotted line square representation inside the graphic display and causes the signal to start appearing in other speakers even when you place the source on a single speaker. This occurs because you change the attenuation curve and set the room to react unnaturally, attenuating the sound coming from one source more than the sound coming from another source. As a result, the speakers generate a different level to compensate for this attenuation.

In Position or Angle modes, the Center and Divergence controls are replaced by the Attenuation and Normalize controls. The Attenuation control increases the volume of the source in its current surround position, while the Normalize increases the overall level of all speakers so that the sum of the amplitude from all speakers is at 0 dBFS when the Normalize control is set at 1. Note that you should not use the normalize parameter to replace a dynamic control over the surround channels because normalizing doesn't prevent peaks from occurring in the signal. Such peaks could cause one of the surround channels to clip and cause distortion. You should use the Attenuation control when a sound, once positioned appropriately, still sounds too loud in the surround mix.

The subbass (LFE) speaker control in all modes will adjust the level being sent from this source in the subbass channel if such a channel exists in your surround configuration. For example, there are no LFE channel in an LCRS configuration, so this control would not be available in such a case. You can also adjust the level of the LFE channel by using the slider next to the Surround Panner display in the mixer channel or by entering a value in the extended portion of the mixer (see Figure E.6).

Figure E.6
Adjusting the amount of
signal sent to the LFE
channel.

You can automate the Surround Panner as you would any other channel automation described in Chapter 13.

Routing Effects in Surround Outputs

As you might have anticipated, using effects in Surround mode might become an issue because most effects are designed to work on two channels rather than four, five, or six channels. Cubase offers some surround plug-ins and support for third-party surround plug-ins through a special signal path diagram, which is accessible in the Channel Settings panel for the Surround Output Bus (see Figure E.7). This routing is also available in stereo or mono channels; however, the surround configuration only shows up when you are editing the surround output bus. By default, the section found in Figure E.7, which displays the surround routing, usually displays the inserts for this output. To change the view to edit the routing instead, select the routing option from the drop-down menu above this area.

Each vertical line in this display corresponds to a channel (ASIO device port) in the surround output bus. By assigning multiple instances of the same effect to different channels in the bus, you can effectively affect all channels in the bus. Lines that are interrupted by handles before and after the insert effect indicates that the signal will be processed by this effect on this channel inside the bus. In this example (Figure E.7), the Surround Dither effect is the only truly surround effect since it affects all channels at once. On the other hand, there are three instances of the Multiband Compressor. The first is partly hidden by the drop-down menu, but the compressor affects the first two channels (left and right), the second affects the left and right surround channels, and the third (found in the Insert 6 slot) affects the center and LFE channels. This allows you to apply the same or different settings to each pair, or each channel within the bus.

Figure E.7
Routing insert effects in a surround output bus.

Figure E.8
The Routing Editor: In this example, the left and right channels are processed by the effect.

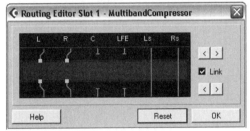

The Routing Editor (Figure E.8) displays three types of paths: broken lines with boxes, broken lines without boxes, and passing lines. The connector at the top represents the input of the insert, and the connector at the bottom represents its output. If a line is broken with a box on each side of the connector, it means that the signal is routed through the effect. In other words, the channel will be routed through that effect. In Figure E.8, this is the case for the first two lines on the left. If a line is broken without boxes, the signal is muted from this point on in the signal path. In the same figure, this is the case for the two center lines (channels). If the line passes through without breaking, it means that the signal bypasses the effect altogether (see the last two lines in the figure). You may decide to process a channel, yet send the output of this process to another channel. For example, you could process the left and right surround channels with a reverb and send the output of this reverb effect into the left and right channels instead, as is the case in the example found in Figure E.9. In this example, the left and right channels will contain both the source signal bypassing the reverb and the reverb's processed output, which contains the signal originally found on the left and right surround channels.

The set of arrows separated by the link check box moves the input channels or the output channels sideways to modify the routing. When the Link check box is active, both input and output channels will move together.

Figure E.9
Routing the output of an effect into another channel within the surround bus.

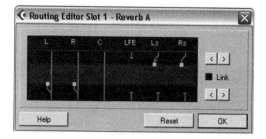

How To

To edit the routing of an insert effect in a surround output bus configuration:

1. Open the VST Output Channel Settings for the Surround bus.
2. Assign the desired effect to the insert effect's slot.
3. Double-click the routing diagram. The Routing Editor dialog box will appear.
4. Check or uncheck the Link option, according to your needs (see description above).
5. Click on the input arrows (top pair) to move the connections to the desired channels.
6. Click on the output arrows (lower pair) to move the connections to the desired channels.
7. Click OK when done.

Exporting a Surround Mix

After you have completed your surround mix, you can export it as you would normally export a final stereo mix. The only difference with surround mix is that you can choose an additional number of output file formats in the File > Export > Audio Mixdown dialog box, as shown in Figure E.10. The Output field needs to be set at the appropriate multichannel bus output in order for Cubase to render a surround mix properly. The Channels field determines how many files will be rendered. For example, if you have a 5.1 surround mix, you can choose to render a mixdown as a single 6-channel interleaved file or 6 separate channels.

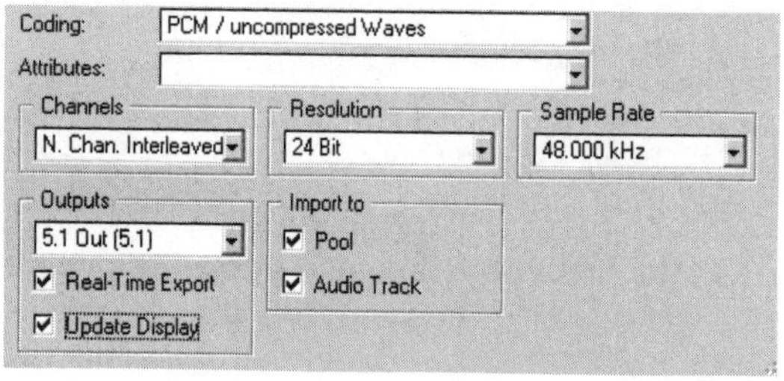

Figure E.10
Exporting audio files for a surround sound mix.

Appendix F
Cubase Resources on the Web

This appendix gives you some of the best-known resources for information on the World Wide Web. These links have been separated into two sections for your convenience: "Finding Help" and "Plug-In Resources and VST instruments."

For a more extensive and up-to-date list of resources on the Web, please visit www.wavedesigners.com. This site offers all the files needed for this book's exercises (Now You Try It sections) as well as links to resources, forums, and tutorials on other applications.

Finding Help

Cubase is pretty well-documented and now that you have a book that simplifies the most common functions and operations, you might still want to learn more about specific issues. The resources listed here offer some relief and insight by sharing their knowledge base with you. They can also provide updates on available upgrades, fixes, and patches, and the most valuable of all—discussion forums where thousands of users like you join to discuss many topics.

If you want to subscribe to a Cubase newsgroup, you should look for alt.steinberg.cubase. There are also a number of online mailing lists for Cubase users. To subscribe to the main mailing list of Cubase users, send an e-mail to cubase@yahoogroups.com. You should also look for upgrades directly on Steinberg's FTP site at the following address: ftp.steinberg.net.

Cubase Forums

If you are looking for news, tips, and tricks, or discussion forums on Cubase and other Steinberg products, this is the place to go. This site provides the information you can't find on Steinberg's site, but it has close ties with that company.

http://forum.cubase.net/

Steinberg's Information Center

This is ground zero for Cubase users. Steinberg provides additional tutorials, information on newly released software, plug-ins, and VST instruments. It is also a good place to look for special events, such as trade shows or master classes.

http://www.steinberg.net/

K-v-R VST

This site is dedicated to VST instrument resources, such as up-to-the-minute news, resources, beta testing results of software applications, ASIO and latency issues related to sound cards, VST instrument patches, and much more. This is a very nice and well-thought-out site. A must if you want to get quick information.

http://www.kvr-vst.com/

Plug-In Resources and VST Instruments

Cubase as a stand-alone software is quite nice, but adding VST or DirectX compatible plug-ins or VST instruments transforms it into an unusually versatile creative instrument. In this section, you will find some of the manufacturers that develop third-party software that can be integrated into Cubase. For a complete list of all VST plug-ins and instrument manufacturers, you can visit Steinberg's site (www.steinberg.net). Once there, select the Professional section in the portal page. Once in the main Professional section, select World of VST under the Share menu on the right of the page. Once inside the World of VST, click on the VST instrument Details link to access all the information available on VSTi.

Arboretum

This is another top-notch plug-in maker. Arboretum has developed tools that will transform your sound in many different ways. Countless recording artists, including Nine Inch Nails, White Zombie, and Public Enemy, have used its Hyperprism plug-in series. The effect the plug-ins produce is as amazing as the names for these plug-ins: HyperVerb, New Granulator, Hyperphaser, Formant Pitch Shifter, Harmonic Exciter, Bass Maximizer, and so on.

http://www.arboretum.com

Native Instruments

You can't talk about VST instruments without talking about Native instruments. This company has created some of the best "virtual synthesizers" on the market. The legendary B3 organ has been perfectly reproduced (sometimes surpassing the original) by their B4 software version, for example.

http://www.native-instruments.net/

Propellerhead

This company seems to have worked closely with Steinberg throughout the years because some of their applications work very well in conjunction with Steinberg's Cubase products. This is the case for Reason, which can be controlled from Cubase and adds a rack full of instruments to your Cubase production system.

http://www.propellerheads.se

Prosoniq

Have you ever wondered what an Orange Vocoder was? To find out, you can head out to Prosoniq's Web site. Again, this company has turned out some very cool VST-compatible plug-ins. With Orange Vocoder, Prosoniq offers you an all-digital simulation of a realistic analog vocoder effect that is fully customizable and comes with an 8-voice virtual analog synthesizer unit, Freeform EQ, and Filterbank Reverb, all in one plug-in.

http://www.prosoniq.com

Spectral Design

This company develops software that is distributed by Steinberg, so it's safe to say that its products integrate very well in Steinberg's suite of software. The deNoiser, deClicker, Clean, and Freefilter applications are probably their best-known products. The deNoiser plug-in works especially well with constant noises in your recording, such as hums and tape hiss.

http://www.spectral-design.com

TC Electronics

TC Electronics (Formerly TC Works) have been at the forefront of the high-end plug-in industry with their TC Native Bundle. All tools are heavily performance optimized, so they really work in your multitrack environment without bringing the computer to its knees. The intuitive user interfaces make these plug-ins invaluable tools you'll be able to use instantly. They also produce a very nice VST instrument called *Mercury-1*, which nicely emulates old analog monophonic synthesis.

http://www.tcelectronic.com

Waves

Waves has been developing plug-ins originally for Pro Tools as TDM software. With the arrival of VST and the potential power this format provided, they proceeded in developing their VST version of their popular plug-in packages. The Native Power Pack is the package that started it all for Native users. This package includes a De-Esser and a special two-tap version of SuperTap that rounds out the essential collection for everyday music and production work. They also provide support for 88.2/96 kHz for many native components. A one-stop shop for all your professional processing needs.

http://www.waves.com

Index

INDEX

THOMSON
COURSE TECHNOLOGY

Professional ■ Trade ■ Reference

Push Cubase SX/SL 2 to its limits!

You've already mastered the major features of Cubase SX/SL. Why not put your new skills to use as you find out what Cubase is really capable of? *Get Creative with Cubase SX/SL* is your hands-on guide to completing amazing music projects using Cubase. You'll start with the creative process of conceiving and developing your idea. From there, you'll move on to the actual production process of capturing, shaping, and manipulating your idea using Cubase SX/SL. Whether you want to use Cubase to compose your next hot song or to create soundtracks, jingles, or multimedia presentations, the information that you need to complete your project efficiently and with professional-sounding results can be found in the pages of *Get Creative with Cubase SX/SL*.

Get Creative with Cubase SX/SL
ISBN: 1-59200-134-3
$29.99

Check out our Cool School Interactus interactive CD-ROMs for additional Cubase SX/SL training! Get all the details online at www.courseptr.com.

THOMSON
COURSE TECHNOLOGY
Professional ■ Trade ■ Reference

Call **1.800.842.3636** to order
Order online at **www.courseptr.com**

THOMSON
————✦————
COURSE TECHNOLOGY ™

Professional ■ **Trade** ■ **Reference**

PUT SOME POWER
BEHIND YOUR MUSIC!

You already know the
basics. Now you're
ready to take your
music to the next level.
With the *Power!* series,
you can master the
advanced features of
cutting-edge software
like SONAR, Cubase,
Logic, and more! Each
book is full of in-depth
tips and techniques
designed to help you
complete your projects
efficiently and with
awesome results.

SONAR 3 Power!
ISBN: 1-59200-339-7

Reason 2.5 Power!
ISBN: 1-59200-138-6

Logic 6 Power!
ISBN: 1-59200-128-9

**Avid Xpress Pro
Power!**
ISBN: 1-59200-151-3

**Ableton Live 2
Power!**
ISBN: 1-59200-088-6

**Home
Recording Power!,
2nd Edition**
ISBN: 1-59200-127-0

THOMSON
————✦————
COURSE TECHNOLOGY ™

Professional ■ Trade ■ Reference

Call **1.800.842.3636** to order
Order online at **www.courseptr.com**

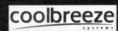

THOMSON
COURSE TECHNOLOGY

Professional ■ Trade ■ Reference

GET INTERACTIVE WITH CUBASE SX 2!

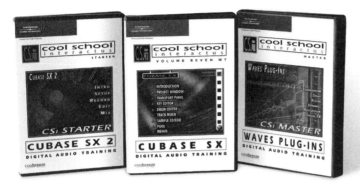

You're well on your way to mastering Cubase SX 2. Don't stop now! Check out the bonus **Cubase SX 2 CSi LE CD** for an interactive learning experience. It includes more than 60 minutes of Cubase SX 2 movie tutorials that you can view again and again.

To check out the tutorials, double click the appropriate "Cubase SX 2 CSi LE" icon (Mac OS9, OSX or Win). You will need QuickTime 6.0 (www.Apple.com) to view the movie tutorials.

Cubase SX 2 CSi LE provides just a taste of the detailed information covered in *Cubase SX 2 CSi Starter, CSi Volume 7–Cubase SX,* and *CSi Waves Plug-Ins CSi Master.* You'll get a sneak peek at these CSi tutorials:

CSi vol.7 Cubase SX–Colin MacQueen
1. What's new in Cubase SX 2 part 1
2. What's new in Cubase SX 2 part 2

Cubase SX 2 CSi Starter–Colin MacQueen
3. Importing Audio
4. Mixer Setup

CSi vol.7 Cubase SX–Colin MacQueen
5. Pool Window Tips
6. QuadraFuzz

Waves Plug-Ins CSi Master–John Hughes
7. Waves SuperTap

Music Loops–Jeff Ciampa

It's sure to get you hooked on the CSi experience! For more information on the full product versions or additional interactive CD-ROM products, go to www.CoursePTR.com. Check out our online courses and Movie Libraries at www.CoolSchoolOnline.com.

Minimum System Requirements:

Windows:
Pentium III 400 MHz or faster
Windows ME or XP
64 MB RAM minimum
24X CD-ROM drive or faster
800x600 display, 1000s of colors
QuickTime 6.0 or greater
(available at www.quicktime.com)
16-bit sound card

Mac:
PPC G3 300 MHz or faster
System OS 9, OS X 10.2, or higher
32 MB RAM minimum
24X CD-ROM drive or faster
800x600 display, 1000s of colors
QuickTime 6.0 or greater
(available at www.quicktime.com)

If you experience difficulties, you can request help by sending an e-mail to **Tech.support@thomson.com** or by calling **800.648.7450**.

Waves Plug-Ins CSi Master
ISBN: 1-59200-231-5 ■ $79.99

CSi Volume 7—Cubase SX
ISBN: 1-59200-164-5 ■ $79.95

Coming March 2004!

Cubase SX 2 CSi Starter
ISBN: 1-59200-368-0 ■ $49.99

THOMSON
COURSE TECHNOLOGY

Professional ■ Trade ■ Reference

coolbreeze
systems

Call **1.800.842.3636** to order!
Order online at **www.courseptr.com**

License Agreement/Notice of Limited Warranty

By opening the sealed disc container in this book, you agree to the following terms and conditions. If, upon reading the following license agreement and notice of limited warranty, you cannot agree to the terms and conditions set forth, return the unused book with unopened disc to the place where you purchased it for a refund.

License:

The enclosed software is copyrighted by the copyright holder(s) indicated on the software disc. You are licensed to copy the software onto a single computer for use by a single user and to a backup disc. You may not reproduce, make copies, or distribute copies or rent or lease the software in whole or in part, except with written permission of the copyright holder(s). You may transfer the enclosed disc only together with this license, and only if you destroy all other copies of the software and the transferee agrees to the terms of the license. You may not decompile, reverse assemble, or reverse engineer the software.

Notice of Limited Warranty:

The enclosed disc is warranted by Muska & Lipman to be free of physical defects in materials and workmanship for a period of sixty (60) days from end user's purchase of the book/disc combination. During the sixty-day term of the limited warranty, Muska & Lipman will provide a replacement disc upon the return of a defective disc.

Limited Liability:

THE SOLE REMEDY FOR BREACH OF THIS LIMITED WARRANTY SHALL CONSIST ENTIRELY OF REPLACEMENT OF THE DEFECTIVE DISC. IN NO EVENT SHALL MUSKA & LIPMAN OR THE AUTHORS BE LIABLE FOR ANY OTHER DAMAGES, INCLUDING LOSS OR CORRUPTION OF DATA, CHANGES IN THE FUNCTIONAL CHARACTERISTICS OF THE HARDWARE OR OPERATING SYSTEM, DELETERIOUS INTERACTION WITH OTHER SOFTWARE, OR ANY OTHER SPECIAL, INCIDENTAL, OR CONSEQUENTIAL DAMAGES THAT MAY ARISE, EVEN IF MUSKA & LIPMAN AND/OR THE AUTHORS HAVE PREVIOUSLY BEEN NOTIFIED THAT THE POSSIBILITY OF SUCH DAMAGES EXISTS.

Disclaimer of Warranties:

MUSKA & LIPMAN AND THE AUTHORS SPECIFICALLY DISCLAIM ANY AND ALL OTHER WARRANTIES, EITHER EXPRESS OR IMPLIED, INCLUDING WARRANTIES OF MERCHANTABILITY, SUITABILITY TO A PARTICULAR TASK OR PURPOSE, OR FREEDOM FROM ERRORS. SOME STATES DO NOT ALLOW FOR EXCLUSION OF IMPLIED WARRANTIES OR LIMITATION OF INCIDENTAL OR CONSEQUENTIAL DAMAGES, SO THESE LIMITATIONS MIGHT NOT APPLY TO YOU.

Other:

This Agreement is governed by the laws of the State of Massachusetts without regard to choice of law principles. The United Convention of Contracts for the International Sale of Goods is specifically disclaimed. This Agreement constitutes the entire agreement between you and Muska & Lipman regarding use of the software.